Essays on Marx's *Capital*

Historical Materialism Book Series

The Historical Materialism Book Series is a major publishing initiative of the radical left. The capitalist crisis of the twenty-first century has been met by a resurgence of interest in critical Marxist theory. At the same time, the publishing institutions committed to Marxism have contracted markedly since the high point of the 1970s. The Historical Materialism Book Series is dedicated to addressing this situation by making available important works of Marxist theory. The aim of the series is to publish important theoretical contributions as the basis for vigorous intellectual debate and exchange on the left.

The peer-reviewed series publishes original monographs, translated texts, and reprints of classics across the bounds of academic disciplinary agendas and across the divisions of the left. The series is particularly concerned to encourage the internationalization of Marxist debate and aims to translate significant studies from beyond the English-speaking world.

For a full list of titles in the Historical Materialism Book Series available in paperback from Haymarket Books, visit: www.haymarketbooks.org/series_collections/1-historical-materialism.

Essays on Marx's *Capital*

Summaries, Appreciations and Reconstructions

Geert Reuten

Haymarket Books
Chicago, IL

First published in 2024 by Brill Academic Publishers, The Netherlands
© 2024 Koninklijke Brill NV, Leiden, The Netherlands

Published in paperback in 2025 by
Haymarket Books
P.O. Box 180165
Chicago, IL 60618
773-583-7884
www.haymarketbooks.org

ISBN: 979-8-88890-357-5

Distributed to the trade in the US through Consortium Book Sales and Distribution (www.cbsd.com) and internationally through Ingram Publisher Services International (www.ingramcontent.com).

This book was published with the generous support of Lannan Foundation, Wallace Action Fund, and the Marguerite Casey Foundation.

Special discounts are available for bulk purchases by organizations and institutions. Please call 773-583-7884 or email info@haymarketbooks.org for more information.

Cover art and design by David Mabb. Cover art is a detail from *Painting 16, Rhythm 69, (William Morris Block Printed Pattern Book, with Hans Richter Storyboard, developed from Richter's Rhythmus 25 and Kazimir Malevich's film script Artistic and Scientific Film – Painting and Architectural Concerns – Approaching the New Plastic Architectural System)*. Paint and wallpaper on canvas (2007).

Printed in the United States.

Library of Congress Cataloging-in-Publication data is available.

Contents

Preface IX
About the Author XI

Abstracts of all chapters 1

PART A
General outlines of, and comments on, the three volumes of Marx's Capital

1 Karl Marx: his work and the major changes in its interpretation (2003) 15

2 Marx's conceptualisation of value in *Capital* (2019) 37

3 Dialectical method (1998) 63

4 Marx's method (1998) 69

5 The interconnection of Systematic Dialectics and Historical Materialism (2000) 76

PART B
Capital I – outlines and comments

6 The difficult labour of a theory of social value; metaphors and systematic dialectics at the beginning of Marx's 'Capital' (1993) 107

7 Money as constituent of value; the ideal introversive substance and the ideal extroversive form of value in Marx's *Capital* (2005) 135

8 Productive force and the degree of intensity of labour; Marx's concepts and formalisations in the middle part of *Capital I* (2004) 153

9   The inner mechanism of the accumulation of capital: the acceleration triple; a methodological appraisal of 'Part Seven' of Marx's *Capital I* (2004)   181

PART C
Capital II – outlines and comments

10   Marx's *Capital II*, The circulation of capital – general introduction (1998; with Christopher Arthur)   207

11   The status of Marx's reproduction schemes; conventional or dialectical logic? (1998)   219

12   Some notes on Marx's macroeconomics *avant la lettre* (2023/2014)   261

PART D
Capital III – outlines and comments

13   Marx's *Capital III*, the culmination of capital; Introduction (2002)   269

14   Marx's rate of profit transformation: methodological, theoretical and philological obstacles – an appraisal based on the text of *Capital III* and manuscripts of 1864–65, 1875 and 1878 (2009)   282

15   The productive powers of labour and the redundant transformation to prices of production; a Marx-immanent critique and reconstruction (2017)   305

16   The notion of tendency in Marx's 1894 law of profit (1997)   337

17   'Zirkel vicieux' or trend fall? – the course of the profit rate in Marx's '*Capital III*' (2004)   365

18   Accumulation of capital and the foundation of the tendency of the rate of profit to fall (1991)   390

19 From the 'fall of the rate of profit' in the *Grundrisse* to the cyclical development of the profit rate in *Capital* (2011; with Peter Thomas)   413

20 Destructive creativity; institutional arrangements of banking and the logic of capitalist technical change (1998)   431

21 The rate of profit cycle and the opposition between Managerial and Finance Capital; a discussion of *Capital III* Parts Three to Five (2002)   448

   Appendix A: List of the author's academic publications on Marx's *Capital*   489
   Appendix B: List of the author's academic publications on, or within, the post-Marx marxian paradigm   492
   Appendix C: Authored and edited books   495
   Index of names   497
   Index of subjects   502

Preface

This book covers a selection of the articles that I wrote on Marx's *Capital* dating from 1991 to 2019.[1] The articles are organised in the systematic order of the three volumes of Marx's *Capital*, rather than in the historical order of their writing. Each single volume of *Capital* is treated in Parts B–D of the book. Part A covers articles that regard all or several volumes.

My own appreciation of Marx's *Capital* has been influenced by at least two factors. First, the publication of Marx's manuscripts in the *Marx-Engels-Gesamtausgabe* (MEGA).[2] These reveal especially for Volumes II and III (edited by Engels) to what extent Engels had a mark on their initial publication (1885 and 1894). The MEGA is an enormously rich source for the student of *Capital*, and I have also learned a lot from the MEGA editors' thorough comments on the editing.

Second, over the years my appreciation of Marx's writings has increased enormously. This has to do with the distinct research phases of 'investigation' (*Forschung*) and 'systematic exposition' (*Darstellung*) and the problems thereof for a grand work such as *Capital*. I have experienced some of these problems for my own (relatively minor) endeavours in systematic exposition.[3]

For many of the current book's chapters dated 1993–2014, I benefitted a lot from the contributors to the annual meetings of the 'International symposium on Marxian theory' each of which used to be devoted to a particular volume or a specific aspect of Marx's *Capital*.[4]

Given that the articles included in the book have previously been published separately, they can be read in any preferred order. For that purpose, the next but one section includes the abstracts of all chapters of the book.

---

[1] Articles not collected here are listed in Appendix A.

[2] https://mega.bbaw.de/de/struktur/ii-abteilung. The second division of the MEGA covers Marx's manuscripts of and in preparation for *Das Kapital* from 1857 to 1882 (MEGA publications from 1976 to 2003 – extending to 2012 for the final editions prepared by Engels until 1894).

[3] My first endeavour was *Value-form and the state: the tendencies of accumulation and the determination of economic policy in capitalist society* (1989, 325 pages, with Michael Williams). The second was *The unity of the capitalist economy and state: a systematic-dialectical exposition of the capitalist system* (2019, 635 pages). My endeavours are, in comparison with Marx, minor because of the size of the works, but foremost because Marx founded a major paradigmatic shift that I could build on.

[4] In those years the group published 11 books on Marx's *Capital* – for these, and their contributors, see https://chrisarthur.net/international-symposium-on-marxian-theory-ismt/.

Format matters. References: a superscript after a year of publication refers to the edition of a work (e.g. Marx 1867^1; Marx 1890^4). Quotation marks: double quotation marks refer to citations, including cited phrases; phrases in single inverted commas are mine and are used to emphasise some concept. Cross-references to sections within a chapter are as, e.g., §3. References to a section of *Capital* are written in full, e.g. Section 3.

Acknowledgements. I have expressed my gratitude to the respective commentators on each chapter of the book.[5] I also thank the editors of the Historical Materialism Book Series (see p. ii) for including the book in the series. Those acknowledgements relate to the academic content of the book. English not being my native language, Simon Mussell has for the last decade been my standing copy-editor and I am very grateful to him for polishing my English, which applies to various original articles from which some of the following chapters derive, as well as to the current book overall. For the material production and publication of the book, I thank Danny Hayward (manager of the Historical Materialism book series) and the for Brill working staff members Bart Nijsten (production editor) and Debbie de Wit (associate editor). Finally, I thank the (for me) anonymous production workers for materialising the book.

Geert Reuten
July 2023

---

5 Summed up, in alphabetical order, these commentators are: Alexander van Altena (1×); Christopher J. Arthur (10×); Riccardo Bellofiore (6×); Jurriaan Bendien (1×); Mark Blaug (3×); Marcel Boumans (1×); Andrew Brown (1×); Suzanne de Brunhoff (1×); Sebastian Budgen (1×); Martha Campbell (6×); Guglielmo Carchedi (2×); John B. Davis (1×); Ben Fine (1×); Roberto Finelli (1×); Roberto Fineschi (1×); Duncan Foley (1×); Claus Germer (1×); Jörg Glombowski (1×); Rolf Hecker (1×); Michael Heinrich (1×); Makoto Itoh (1×); Costas Lapavitsas (1×); Gerald Levy (1×); Pichit Likitkijsomboon (1×); Francisco Louçã (1×); Paul Mattick Jr. (6×); Mary Morgan (4×); Margaret Morrison (1×); Fred Moseley (8×); Patrick Murray (10×); Anitra Nelson (1×); Regina Roth (1×); Warren Samuels (1×); Tony Smith (10×); Nicola Taylor (2×); Boe Thio (1×); Massimiliano Tomba (1×); Michael Williams (3×).

About the Author

Geert Reuten taught economics for 35 years at the School of Economics of the University of Amsterdam, where he is currently a guest research associate. From 2007–2015 and 2018–2019 he was a member of the Senate of the Netherlands for the Socialist Party and spokesperson for financial, monetary and economic affairs.

He has authored four academic books, edited six books, and published 80 articles in academic journals and collections (the articles can be accessed at http://reuten.eu). He has also written 75 assessments of Dutch law proposals and published 65 articles in non-academic journals and newspapers.

Books in English by the same author
- *Design of a worker cooperatives society; an alternative beyond capitalism and socialism, and the transition towards it* (Brill, 2023).
- *The unity of the capitalist economy and state – a systematic-dialectical exposition of the capitalist system* (Brill, 2019).
- *The culmination of capital: Essays on volume III of Marx's 'Capital'*; editor, with Martha Campbell (Palgrave Macmillan, 2002).
- *The circulation of capital: Essays on volume II of Marx's 'Capital'*; editor, with Christopher Arthur (Macmillan, 1998).
- *Value-form and the State; the tendencies of accumulation and the determination of economic policy in capitalist society*; with Michael Williams (Routledge, 1989).
- *The value-form determination of economic policy: A dialectical theory of economy, society and state in the capitalist epoch*; with Michael Williams (Grüner, 1988).

Abstracts of all chapters

Below the number of pages of each chapter refer to those of the current book.

Part A. General outlines of, and comments on, the three volumes of Marx's Capital

1. **Karl Marx: his work and the major changes in its interpretation** (2003, 22 pages). From *Companion to the history of economic thought*, edited by Warren Samuels, Jeff Biddle and John Davis, Oxford: Blackwell, pp. 148–66.

    Abstract: Marx's magnum opus, *Capital*, is an analysis of the capitalist system. The changing appreciation of this work throughout the twentieth century has been influenced by both the degree to which other works of Marx were, or could be, taken into account (§2) and, relatedly, developing methodological views; five methodological aspects are briefly reviewed – historical materialism, critique, naturalistic versus socio-historical concepts, value-form theory, systematic dialectics (§3). The article provides a synopsis of the general structure of Marx's *Capital*, outlining for each volume of *Capital* what 'capital' is, how it works and its resulting process (§4).

2. **Marx's conceptualisation of value in *Capital*** (2019, 26 pages). From *The Oxford handbook of Karl Marx*, edited by Matthew Vidal, Tony Smith, Tomás Rotta and Paul Prew, New York: Oxford University Press, pp. 129–50.

    Abstract: This chapter reviews the three conceptual stages of the determinants of the commodities' value in Marx's *Capital*. It concludes that the dynamic second stage (designed in 1866–67) overrules the third stage – of prices of production (designed 1864–65). The first stage (*Capital I*, Part One) is an important though static averages account, positing that the commodities' value is determined by average socially necessary labour-time. The second stage (*Capital I*, Part Four) is a dynamic account of the 'intensity of labour' and the mainly technology-determined 'productive power of labour', each one implying, first, that clock-time of labour is an insufficient measure and, second, that rates of surplus-value diverge between sectors of production. Whereas intensity-determined inter-sector rates of surplus-value might equalise due to intra-labour competition, Marx posits no mechanism for such equalisation regarding the technology-determined productive power. The third stage posits the transformation of values into prices of production (*Capital III*, Part Two – its text being based on a manuscript from 1864–65). The article's main finding is that the determinant of the 'technology-associated productive power' was a novel result of Marx's 1866–67 final version of *Capital I* (1867). It makes Marx's earlier third stage redundant.

3. **Dialectical method** (1998, 6 pages). From *The handbook of economic methodology*, edited by John B. Davis, D. Wade Hands and Uskali Mäki, Cheltenham: Edward Elgar, pp. 103–7.

    Abstract: After a brief outline of the distinction between historical dialectics and systematic-dialectics, the entry focuses on the latter. It does so by bringing out main elements of this method in so far as they relate to some of the problems that face the mainstream philosophy of economics.

4. **Marx's method** (1998, 7 pages). From *The handbook of economic methodology*, edited by John B. Davis, D. Wade Hands and Uskali Mäki, Cheltenham: Edward Elgar, pp. 283–7.

    Abstract: This article distinguishes Marx's method for the study of sequences of social formations (or modes of production), that is, his 'historical materialist' method, from his method of studying the systematic interconnections of a single social formation such as the capitalist one. All commentators agree that in *Capital* Marx applies a particular systematic method for outlining these interconnections, by way of moving in stages from abstract to concrete categories. There is, however, disagreement on the status of each of the stages, as well as on the mode of progression from one stage to the other. Accordingly, Marx's method in *Capital* is termed differently. For a long time the method has been looked upon as a logical-historical approach (an interpretation propagated by Engels), or as a method of successive approximation where one starts with simplifying assumptions that are gradually dropped (propagated by Sweezy 1942). Other interpretations have focused on the particular dialectic adopted by Marx. The second part of the article expands on the latter.

5. **The interconnection of Systematic Dialectics and Historical Materialism** (2000, 28 pages). From *Historical Materialism*, 7, pp. 137–65.

    Abstract: Within the Marxian paradigm – and far more so than in other paradigms – the work of its founder, Marx, has been a continuous inspiration for new theoretical developments. This is fine. However, in much twentieth-century Marxian theory, this has gone along with an inclination to present new theoretical developments as new interpretations of (especially) Marx's *Capital* instead of as reconstructions. This article illustrates this for two main building blocks of the paradigm, namely its method and its theory of value, focusing for the former on 'historical materialism' and 'systematic dialectics' and for the latter on the concepts of 'social form' and 'abstract labour'. More specifically, this illustration is articulated in an engagement with work of Patrick Murray on these issues. One main conclusion is that, as with all founders of new paradigms, Marx is bound to express his break with the old ideas to a large extent in the traditional language – in his case that of Hegel and of classical political economy – which inevitably opens up enormous problems of interpretation. Rather than focusing on (perhaps dubious) re-interpretations, clarity would be served if Marxian scholars were to present their new theoretical findings as reconstructions.

Part B. Capital 1 – outlines and comments

6. **The difficult labour of a theory of social value; metaphors and systematic dialectics at the beginning of Marx's *Capital*** (1993, 28 pages). From *Marx's method in Capital: a re-examination*, edited by Fred Moseley, Atlantic Highlands, NJ: Humanities Press, pp. 89–113.

    Abstract: This essay scrutinises Marx's theory of value as presented in the first chapter of Volume 1 of *Capital*, focusing on Marx's method. It is indicated that interpreting the type of abstractions that Marx uses is crucial to the examination of his value theory (§2). Regarding the content of Marx's value theory, the article focuses on the concepts of concrete labour and abstract labour. It is concluded that Marx presents an 'abstract-labour-embodied theory of value' (§3). Section 4 discusses contemporary rival interpretations and developments of Marx's value theory, classified as 'labour-embodied' (in two variants) and 'abstract-labour' theories of value. Although Marx provided the rudiments of a theory of social value (which nobody after him took any further) he was much enmeshed in the physical substance–embodiment metaphor inherited from Hegel (substance) and classical political economy (embodiment). The Marxian tradition, rather than taking off from the core rudiments of Marx's theory of social value, seems to have 'fetishised' the metaphors. As a result, much Marxian theory has tended to theorise the economy in one-sided physical terms. Section 5 provides some elements of a methodological outline of how a social labour theory of value may be derived from Marx's theory by way of reconstructing that theory. The reconstruction is one along the lines of a systematic dialectic as briefly introduced in section 1.

7. **Money as constituent of value; the ideal introversive substance and the ideal extroversive form of value in Marx's *Capital*** (2005, 18 pages). From *Marx's theory of money: modern appraisals*, edited by Fred Moseley, London/New York: Palgrave Macmillan, pp. 78–92.

    Abstract: This essay discusses Marx's views on money as set out in *Capital I*, Part One (Chapter 3), in relation to his analysis of the commodity in the same part of that work (Chapter 1). For Marx the ideal immanent (or introversive) substance of the value of commodities is 'abstract labour' (*sic*). Marx posits 'time' of abstract labour as the 'immanent measure' of value; however, this is a notion at a high level of abstraction. It does not provide a measure in the usual sense of measuring. (We could measure time of heterogeneous concrete labour, but this is not what Marx is getting at.) The notion of value thus posited is what I call the simple-abstract notion of value (of Chapter 1). This simple notion is complemented by the ideal extroversive form of the value of commodities: money (Chapter 3). It is only henceforth that 'value' has been fully constituted. Consequently 'abstract labour' disappears from Marx's vocabulary. Money establishes the actual commensuration – the homogeneity – of commodities and it is the only one actual ideal measure of value (adopting a particular standard). The introversive substance and the extroversive form of value are inseparable – value cannot be concretely measured without money.
    This interpretation relies on a dialectical interpretation of Marx's frequent use in Chapter 3 of the German text of the term *Veräußerung* (and other terms with the same root of *äußer*), which I translate by extroversive as opposed to the introversive or immanent of Chapter 1. In the English text of Chapter 3, the continuity of the term disappears due to a variety of substitutes.

8. **Productive force and the degree of intensity of labour; Marx's concepts and formalisations in the middle part of *Capital I*** (2004, 28 pages). From *The constitution of capital: essays on Volume I of Marx's 'Capital'*, edited by Riccardo Bellofiore and Nicola Taylor, London/New York: Palgrave Macmillan, pp. 117–45.

    Abstract: Marx's account in *Capital* of the production of surplus-value is examined (Volume I, Parts Three to Five), especially his formalisations in relation to the conceptual progress in the book. It is indicated that his formulas convey theoretical results rather than explanatory processes/mechanisms. This becomes an obstacle particularly when Marx introduces the key concepts of 'productive force' (in modern jargon: technique of production) and intensity of labour', leaving behind any simple explanation of value in terms of labour-time. In face of this, the essay sets out an elementary and immanent reconstruction of Marx's formalisation, in which the rate of surplus-value is cast in terms of all of Marx's main explanatory variables: extensity of labour, wages, productive force and intensity of labour.

9. **The inner mechanism of the accumulation of capital: the acceleration triple; a methodological appraisal of Part Seven of Marx's *Capital I*** (2004, 24 pages). From *The constitution of capital: essays on volume I of Marx's 'Capital'*, edited by Riccardo Bellofiore and Nicola Taylor, London/New York: Palgrave Macmillan, pp. 274–98.

    Abstract: It is argued that for an appraisal of Marx's 'general law of capitalist accumulation' in Volume I of *Capital*, it is crucial to take account of its level of abstraction. Here Marx considers accumulation merely as a moment of the 'immediate process of production' and so restricts it to what he calls 'the inner mechanism' of capital accumulation ('inner' determinations are not more important than 'outer' determinations – the former have no existence without the latter; and the outer determinations may modify the actualisation of the inner). Marx's warnings about this have been de-emphasised in the English translations of the work. The terrain of 'the general law' is the impact of capital accumulation on the working class. Its core is an acceleration triple of growing capital accumulation, increasing productive forces of labour and an increasing 'technical composition' of capital – presented in three phases of complication. In unfolding the dynamic interaction of this triple, Marx introduces the cyclical development of accumulation, though merely as an empirical reference. It is shown that, in this volume, Marx does not – and methodologically could not – develop a theory of the cycle, and a fortiori no labour-shortage theory of the cycle. 'Centralisation' of capital is equally introduced by way of empirical reference.

Part C. Capital II – outlines and comments

10. **Marx's *Capital II*: the circulation of capital – general introduction** (with Christopher Arthur; 1998, 12 pages). From *The circulation of capital: essays on volume II of Marx's 'Capital'*, edited by Christopher Arthur and Geert Reuten, London/New York: Macmillan, pp. 1–16 (a section introducing that book's essays has been omitted).

Abstract: The second volume of Marx's *Capital*, entitled *The circulation process of capital*, was posthumously published by Engels on the basis of Marx's manuscripts. The book covers the circuits of capital, its turnover, and its reproduction on a social scale. This brief introductory article treats four subjects: (1) The interconnection of Volumes I and II of Marx's *Capital*; (2) A schematic outline of *Capital II*; (3) German and English editions; (4) The manuscripts and Engels's editorial work.

11. **The status of Marx's reproduction schemes; conventional or dialectical logic?** (1998, 42 pages). From *The circulation of capital: essays on volume II of Marx's 'Capital'*, edited by Christopher Arthur and Geert Reuten, London/New York: Macmillan, pp. 187–229.

    Abstract: In Part Three of the second volume of Capital (Engels's edition 1885), Marx presents the macroeconomic circulation of capital in terms of what he calls 'reproduction schemes'. The main part of the article outlines Marx's fascinating design of the schemes. Next, this design is examined from the perspective of his method: is it akin to a modelling approach as we find it in modern orthodox economics, or does it rather fit into a systematic dialectics methodology? More so than any other part of Marx's work, his theory of reproduction influenced orthodox economics: it laid important foundations for its later macroeconomics and theory of the business cycle. Why particularly this text? In answering this question, the article examines the systematic character of the exposition of Marx's reproduction theory, focusing on its procedure in laying out assumptions. It is concluded that, while the text may not be incompatible with a systematic-dialectical methodology, it is defective in that respect; rather the textual evidence favours the view that Marx, in this part, takes a particular modelling approach.

12. **Some notes on Marx's macroeconomics *avant la lettre*** (2023/2014, 5 pages). Notes written for the current book, though they mainly derive from a 2014 Netherlandic publication in *Tijdschrift voor Politieke Economie* 8(3), pp. 97–114.

    Abstract: Whereas the term 'macroeconomics' dates from 1933, macroeconomic reasoning emerged gradually. According to Lawrence Klein, Marx's theory is "probably the origin of macro-economics". Some of the previous chapters alluded to the parts of Marx's *Capital* where he adopts macrosocial and macroeconomic analysis and exposition of the capitalist mode of production. The current notes expand on some aspects.

Part D. Capital III – outlines and comments

13. Marx's *Capital III*: the culmination of capital; Introduction (2002, 13 pages). From *The culmination of capital: essays on volume III of Marx's 'Capital'*, edited by Martha Campbell and Geert Reuten, London/New York: Palgrave Macmillan, pp. 1–15 (a section introducing that book's essays has been omitted).

Abstract: This introductory chapter starts with a brief discussion of why writing about Marx's *Capital III* is not only interpretative – this is true for any work – but is also bound to be reconstructive. The next section outlines a general overview of *Capital III*'s seven parts in the light of the earlier two volumes.

14. Marx's rate of profit transformation: methodological, theoretical and philological obstacles – an appraisal based on the text of *Capital III* and manuscripts of 1864–65, 1875 and 1878 (2009, 23 pages). From *Re-reading Marx: new perspectives after the critical edition*, edited by Riccardo Bellofiore and Roberto Fineschi, London/New York: Palgrave Macmillan, pp. 211–30.

Abstract: The third volume of Marx's *Capital* was posthumously published in 1894 as edited by Friedrich Engels. Part Two of *Capital III* sets out the transformation of the rate of surplus-value into the general rate of profit. This essay discusses this text in confrontation with Marx's manuscripts of 1864–65, from which Engels edited *Capital III*, as well as with some of the manuscripts of the 1870s, first published in 2003. A first finding, not related directly to the manuscripts, is that confusion among different levels of abstraction is the methodological obstacle for this transformation. Second, a theoretical obstacle is Marx's assumption of equalised rates of surplus-value maintained throughout most of Part Two of the 1864–65 manuscript. Third, the 1864–65 manuscript is a research manuscript far removed from resolutions fit for a final exposition. Fourth, Marx himself was disappointed with what he had reached (in the 1864–65 manuscript) – so much so that it is unlikely that he intended to maintain the 1864–65 transformation procedure when he wrote, in 1866–67, the final version for the first edition of *Capital I*. It is therefore misleading to interpret the *Capital I* text in the 'light' of Engels's edited *Capital III* text – at least as far as Marx is concerned.

15. **The productive powers of labour and the redundant transformation to prices of production: a Marx-immanent critique and reconstruction** (2017, 32 pages). From *Historical Materialism*, 25(3), pp. 3–35.

    Abstract: The famous Marxian 'transformation problem' originated from a research manuscript written by Marx in 1864–65, from which Engels assembled *Capital III* (1894). Unequal capital compositions, equal rates of surplus-value and equal rates of profit among different sectors are posited and reconciled using the problematic concept of 'prices of production'. Yet the assumption of equal rates of surplus-value is at odds with the subsequent text of *Capital I* (1867), where Marx presents various determinants of the rate of surplus-value and connects productive powers of labour diverging between sectors with divergent *value-generating potencies* of labour. Given the other determinants, diverging rates of surplus-value then result. Marx disregarded these productive power differentials when he originally formulated his transformation. In a reconstruction, building on *Capital I*, this omission is rectified. It makes prices of production and hence the dual account systems redundant. The transformation problem then evaporates.

16. **The notion of tendency in Marx's 1894 law of profit** (1997, 28 pages). From *New investigations of Marx's method*, edited by Fred Moseley and Martha Campbell, Atlantic Highlands, NJ: Humanities Press, pp. 150–75.

    Abstract: This essay examines the concept of 'tendency' in economic theory in general, and especially in Marx's theory of the tendency of the rate of profit to fall in *Capital*, Volume III (Engels's edition 1894). The main question addressed is whether Marx's concept of tendency refers to a 'power' or 'force' which may not be directly observable or to an 'expression' or 'result' which is directly observable. Section 1 reviews related notions of tendency in the works of Roy Bhaskar and J.S. Mill. Section 2 examines all the editions of Volume III of *Capital*, including a recently published German edition of Marx's 1864–65 manuscript without Engels's editing. In section 3.1 it is concluded that Marx's texts are ultimately ambiguous. One can interpret the texts as supporting either the 'power' notion of tendency or the 'expression' notion of tendency. Section 3.2 briefly sketches the implications of the 'power' notion of tendency for empirical research and argues that the cross-fertilisation of methodological, theoretical, and empirical research is the most promising way to reclaim a 'real-world political economy' whose aim is to provide theoretically informed explanations of important empirical phenomena.

17. **'Zirkel vicieux' or trend fall? – the course of the profit rate in Marx's *Capital III*** (2004, 25 pages). From *History of Political Economy*, 36(1): 163–86.

    Abstract: Of Marx's theory of 'the tendency of the rate of profit to fall' – set out in *Capital III*, edited by Engels (1894) – there are two main interpretations. The first says that the profit rate will vary (cyclically) around a *falling trend*; the second, that the profit rate will vary *cyclically* but not necessarily around a falling trend. Both interpretations, however, are countered with inconsistencies in the 1894 text. This article shows that Marx's manuscript (1863–65) is less ambiguous, leaning more towards the interpretation of cyclical development, and that the first interpretation more likely expresses Engels's (1894) view on the matter. The above regards the main text of the article (±11 pages). Its Appendix 1 compares some key texts in *Capital III*, Part Three with the manuscript. Appendix 2 briefly compares the *Capital III* text with that of manuscripts from 1857–58 and 1861–63; it is concluded that we see in Marx's views a movement from a law about the *historical destination* of the capitalist system to a theory about the *functioning* of the system.

18. **Accumulation of capital and the foundation of the tendency of the rate of profit to fall** (1991, 23 pages). From *Cambridge Journal of Economics*, 15(1), pp. 79–93.

    Abstract: Especially since Okishio (1961) the theory of the tendency of the rate of profit to fall (TRPF) is controversial in marxist economics, because microeconomic foundations for it seem inadequate. The 'Okishian' argument is based on a comparative static equilibrium approach. It is indicated how within a dynamic disequilibrium framework of capital stratification these foundations may well be provided; the rate of profit for innovating capitals may then rise, whilst that for the economy as a whole may fall. Nevertheless, tendencies are not trends; the TRPF seems to be manifest cyclically, interconnected with other tendencies of accumulation.

19. **From the 'fall of the rate of profit' in the *Grundrisse* to the cyclical development of the profit rate in *Capital*** (with Peter Thomas; 2011, 18 pages). From *Science & Society*, 75(1), pp. 74–90.

    Abstract: Marx's views on the "law" or "tendency" of the rate of profit to fall developed throughout his life from a law about the historical destination of the capitalist system as tending towards breakdown (the *Grundrisse* text of 1857–58), into a theory about the functioning of the capitalist mode of production as a (potentially) reproductive system (the 1864–65 manuscript of *Capital III*). The first view is compatible with a "naturalistic" and teleological philosophy of history; it presupposes a unilinear conception of time and implicitly posits a diachronic "exhaustion" of an originary rate of profit. The second view opens the way towards a type of "conjunctural analysis", founded upon a cyclical notion of time as a synchronic intensification of contradictory articulations in a synchronically given system.

20. **Destructive creativity; institutional arrangements of banking and the logic of capitalist technical change** (1998, 17 pages). From *Marxian economics: a reappraisal* (vol. 2), edited by Riccardo Bellofiore, London/New York: Macmillan, pp. 177–93.

    Abstract: Marx's theory of 'the tendency for the rate of profit to fall' is presented in Part Three of the third volume of *Capital* (Engels's edition 1894). This theory of profit is the apotheosis of Marx's exposition of the internal logic of the capitalist system: the valorisation-devalorisation contradiction. This essay takes this theory of profit as the starting point from which to articulate its exposition at a less abstract level, taking into account the technological stratification of capital in various branches of production (Part Two of Volume III) as well as finance capital (Part Five of Volume III). Because of accounting practices, devalorisation is expressed either by a fall in the profit rate or by the devaluation of capital. Two important manifestations of this are the cyclical destruction of means of production and the unemployment of labour. While the development of profit is manifest in cycles, its actual exhibition – via economic crises or continued inflationary reproduction – is determined by the institutional make-up of the banking system.

21. **The rate of profit cycle and the opposition between Managerial and Finance Capital; a discussion of *Capital III* Parts Three to Five** (2002, 40 pages). From *The culmination of capital: essays on volume III of Marx's 'Capital'*, edited by Martha Campbell and Geert Reuten, London/New York: Palgrave Macmillan, pp. 174–211.

    Abstract: This essay discusses Parts Three through Five of Marx's *Capital III* (Engels's edition of this book is from 1894). On the basis of the texts of Marx's manuscript (1863–65), it is argued that *Part Three* presents a theory of the rate of profit 'cycle'. Its name, the 'tendency for the rate of profit to fall', is, therefore, rather misleading (§1). In *Parts Four and Five* Marx aptly conceives of joint stock capital or share capital (JSC) as a form of interest-bearing capital. He also envisioned the appearance of JSCs as pointing to a complete separation of capital ownership and capital in process, or between capital ownership and labour as including managerial labour. Finally then, for Marx, Finance Capital is the dominant capital (§2). It is argued that this view neglects the difference between legal ownership and economic ownership. In fact, managers of JSCs command their company's capital and have economic ownership of what I call managerial capital, as grown out of retained profits and especially also out of revaluation of capital. So management has, at least potentially, a firm stake in capital generally. In this way the developed form of capital is, contrary to Marx, posited as an 'internal opposition-in-unity', where factions of capital are in conflict over the distribution of profit. Further it is argued that a potential conflict between Managerial and Finance Capital modifies the way the profit rate cycle gets expressed, namely in the revaluation and devaluation of capital (§3).

PART A

General outlines of, and comments on, the three volumes of Marx's Capital

∴

Contents
1. Karl Marx: his work and the major changes in its interpretation (2003) p. 15.
2. Marx's conceptualisation of value in *Capital* (2019) p. 37.
3. Dialectical method (1998 handbook entry) p. 63.
4. Marx's method (1998 handbook entry) p. 69.
5. The interconnection of Systematic Dialectics and Historical Materialism (2000) p. 76.

CHAPTER 1

Karl Marx: his work and the major changes in its interpretation

2003 article, originally published in *Companion to the history of economic thought*, edited by Warren Samuels, Jeff Biddle and John Davis, Oxford: Blackwell, pp. 148–66.
(For its abstract see the Abstracts of all chapters, p. 1.)

Contents

Introduction 15
1   On Marx and his *Capital*   16
2   The many Marxes, the many *Capitals*   17
3   Interpretations of Marx's method in *Capital*   19
    3.1   Historical Materialism   19
    3.2   Critique   20
    3.3   Naturalistic versus socio-historical concepts   21
    3.4   Value-form theory   21
    3.5   Systematic Dialectics   23
    3.6   Conclusions   25
4   A synopsis of the systematic structure of *Capital*   25
    Capital I: Production   26
    Capital II: Circulation   29
    Capital III: Destination   30
    Summary   31
5   Marx's theory and Marxian theory as a strand   31
References   32

Introduction[1]

Karl Marx is known for a 30-page political pamphlet, *The Communist Manifesto*, written in 1848 together with Friedrich Engels, and for a 2,200-page socio-

---

[1] I am grateful for comments by Chris Arthur, Mark Blaug, Gerald Levy, Paul Mattick, Patrick

economic work, *Capital*, published in three volumes in 1867, 1885 and 1894, the last two edited by Engels. The collected works of Marx and Engels extend to over 50 thick volumes.

Marx's magnum opus, *Capital*, is an analysis of the capitalist system (the term 'communism' is mentioned some five times in notes; perhaps five out of 2,200 pages refer in passing to some future society). Marx wrote the work between 1857 and 1878 while living in London. British capitalism provided his main empirical material.

The changing appreciation of *Capital* throughout the twentieth century has been influenced by both the degree to which other works of Marx were, or could be, taken into account (§2) and, relatedly, developing methodological views (§3). A reading of the work (§4) is bound to take methodological sides.

1   **On Marx and his *Capital***

Marx was born in 1818 in Trier and died in 1883 in London. He studied law and philosophy and received a PhD in 1841. Trained to pursue the positions of either a state official or university professor, both his studies and the repressive political climate in Prussia induced a different course. During his student years he helped fight for democratic rights, opposing the vested political regime. His subsequent writings and editorship of a liberal journal brought him into conflict with Prussian censorship. He sought refuge in Paris (1843–45), Brussels (1845–47), Cologne (1848–49), and finally, in 1849, settled in London.

In the hectic 1842–49 period, Marx studied and wrote on philosophical, political, and economic issues, and developed his materialist conception of history (§3.1). He also made contact with radical socialist groups, and met Friedrich Engels, his lifelong personal, political, and intellectual friend. In 1848, aged 30, he and Engels wrote the *Manifest der Kommunistischen Partei*.

From 1849 to about 1865 Marx reduced his political activities and concentrated on serious analysis of the capitalist system, combining research with journalistic work to earn his living. Many thousands of pages were drafted for his magnum opus in a creative and highly productive period. At the same time, he and his family lived in poverty. Income from Marx's journalistic work was scarce; to survive, they relied on gifts from relatives and friends, especially Engels.

Murray, Tony Smith, Nicola Taylor and the editors of this book, especially Warren Samuels and John Davis.

Marx's research plans were extremely ambitious. He aimed to write a complete systematic analysis of society: economic, social, political, and historical. By 1858 he planned to write six books. The first of these came to completely occupy his mind and energies. It grew to the three volumes of *Capital* that we now have, together with a sequel account of political economic theories (another three volumes). Marx brought to press himself only the first volume of *Capital* (1867).

After its 1867 publication, Marx continually revised Volume I, especially its key value-theoretical Part One (the volumes are organised into parts). A second German edition dates from 1873 and a French edition, in instalments, from 1872–75. This process of revision should be kept in mind for those who seek consistency between Volume I and the manuscripts for Volume III, composed in 1864–65.

In the years 1865–70 and 1877–78 Marx wrote much of Volume II of *Capital*, without completing it. He had gotten re-involved in political activities, but his health also seriously deteriorated. As we will see below, Marx's *Capital* project employs a demanding systematic methodology. Towards the end of his life, the requirements for the organisation of the work grew beyond his fading energy.

After Marx's death, the two remaining volumes of *Capital* were edited from Marx's drafts and notebooks by Engels (1885, 1894) and the sequel by Kautsky (1905–10). The drafts are in varied states of completion – the second half of both Volumes II and III consists of reorganised notebooks – and the editors inevitably had their impact on the result. In fact, Marx had considered them unfit for publication.

2   The many Marxes, the many *Capitals*

Developing historiographic views, as well as developing Marx scholarship, have affected the interpretation of Marx's *Capital* (§3). This is not different from other authors. However, in the case of Marx especially, an additional factor is important: the time lags between the posthumous publications of his writings – as well as their translations into (for example) English. *Table 1* provides examples.

A 27-year lag between the publication of Volumes I and III meant that *Capital I* had a life of its own. In 1932 (1938 and 1963 in English), two works of Marx were published that shed new light on his views on money and the capitalist labour process. In 1953 (1973 in English) the *Grundrisse*, an early 800-page draft of *Capital* in dialectical style, was published, shedding new light on both the method and content of *Capital*. Even in the 1990s important new manuscripts were published, and others are still forthcoming. The result is that throughout the twentieth century, and continuing to the present day, there have been many Marxes and many *Capital*s.

TABLE 1   'Many Marxes': dates of publication of some major works

(1) First publication in German		(2) Years 1–3	(3) First English translation		(4) Date of manuscript	(5) Years 1–4 Ms– German	(6) Years 3–4 Ms– English
1867	*Das Kapital I*	19	1886	*Capital I*	1861, 1863, 1865–67[a]	0	19
1885	*Das Kapital II*	22	1907	*Capital II*	1865–70, 1877–78	7	29
1894	*Das Kapital III*	15	1909	*Capital III*	1864–65	29	44
1905–10	*Theorien über den Mehrwert* (3 vols)	48–61	1952–71	*Theories of Surplus Value*[b]	1862–63	47	108
1932	*Pariser Manuskripte*	31	1963	*Economic-philosophical manuscripts*	1844	88	119
1932	*Die deutsche Ideologie*[c]	6	1938	*The German Ideology* (Parts I & III)	1845–46	86	92
1953	*Grundrisse*[d]	20	1973	*Grundrisse*[e]	1857–58	95	115
1992	*Ökonomische Manuskripte 1863–67* [including the *Capital III* manuscripts]	–	–	–	1863–67	125–29	–

a   Work on second German edition, 1867–72; and on French edition 1872–75.
b   First Volume 1952, *A history of economic theories*; extracts 1951.
c   Extracts 1902–03, 1921 and 1927.
d   Earlier scarcely available edition 1939–41; its Introduction was published in 1903.
e   Extracts 1964 and 1971.

It is illusory to think that new textual 'evidence' changes views overnight, especially for path-breaking publications. The 1953/1973 publication of the *Grundrisse* has only had a major impact since the mid-1980s. Keynes, himself author of the path-breaking publication *The General Theory*, explained the reason in its Preface: "The difficulty lies, not in the new ideas, but in escaping from the old ones …".

The early appreciation of the 1894 (English, 1909) *Capital* Volume III, or even the 1867 (1886) Volume I of *Capital*, has shaped the interpretation of Marx in all standard histories of thought, in both the first half of the twentieth century and since. As difficult as it is to write a history, it is much harder to revise a history that has become part of the received view. Whatever textual 'evidence' arises, a range of interpretations – perhaps a moving range – will likely ensue.

Table 1 requires a general historiographic note. Columns 1–3, ordered according to dates of publication, are its core. The order of publications – impact – is relevant for a general history of thought. A history of the intellectual development of Karl Marx, or of the 'making' of *Capital*, requires an historical ordering by manuscripts dates (column 4). These are very different historiographic perspectives. (For the latter perspective, the making of *Capital*, Oakley's succinct 1983 book is very informative, even if at the time he lacked full information about Engels's editorial work.)

3   Interpretations of Marx's method in *Capital*

Interpretations of Marx's *Capital* are intimately related to interpretations of his method, of which five major aspects are examined below. Some version of the first, historical materialism (§3.1), was shared by most commentators until around 1970. The interpretation of Marx's method in the following period is more complex. Subsequent subsections – roughly in historical order – add in these further complications, in each case building on the methodological aspect of the previous subsection.

3.1   *Historical Materialism*

Marx embraced, and was the originator of, a materialist conception of history (often called 'historical materialism' – the label is not Marx's). Analytically and institutionally, any society can be seen as a number of domains: political and legal, cultural including education, and economic. For Marx, the development of the economic domain (the "relations of production") is key to the development of a society at large (a 'social formation', such as a feudal or a bourgeois/capitalist society). What happens in the "superstructure" – the juridico-political and cultural domains – is understood in terms of the "base structure" – the economic relations and their requirements. Two aspects are fundamental to the economic relations themselves: first, the relationship between (a) the social layer or class that does the actual work, and (b) the layer or class that has the power to live off the surplus produced by the former, and that usually also possesses the means of production that the former works upon; and second, the "forces of production", the amalgamation of the labour process in relation to technology (the latter understood in grand, epochal terms).

This schema is especially significant in analysing *changes* in structures and their aspects, particularly their dynamic interaction during uneven development. 'Grand' history can be seen in terms of revolutionary transitions – 're-structuring' into more fitting aspects. (Note that especially in the first half of the twentieth century this schema has often been interpreted mono-causally, running from the forces of production, instead of as a dialectic between all structures and aspects.)

Marx developed these ideas when he was 25–30 years of age. They can be seen clearly in the *Manifesto*. One plausible reading of *Capital*, or one dimension of it, is as an analysis of the economic base structure of capitalism. Note, though, that the work does not contain an explicit analysis of social class (except for a just over one page unfinished 'chapter' on classes at the end of Volume III of *Capital*, the term class is hardly ever used in *Capital*). Furthermore, even if there are a few – very few – mostly speculative references to transitional elements within capitalism, transition is not what the work is about.

3.2 *Critique*

Especially important in reading *Capital* is the methodology Marx developed alongside his materialist conception of history, namely his method of "critique" – largely acquired from Hegel (post Kant – cf. Benhabib 1986). Almost all Marx's works carry the term *"Critique"* [*Kritik*], which is distinguishable from 'criticism'. The latter adopts a normative *external* criterion (ethical, aesthetic or methodological) to evaluate society or such social products as artistic and scientific endeavours. The method of *critique* evaluates society and social products on the basis of the norms and standards of the object of inquiry itself. An object of inquiry is analysed *from within itself*. Its norms and standards are taken to their logical conclusions, detecting possible inconsistencies and contradictions – as when capitalist business both lauds 'market competition' and seeks to eliminate competitors and achieve monopolistic positions.

In *Capital* Marx addresses both a material ontological constellation and ideas about it. When the original title, *Das Kapital; Kritik der politischen Ökonomie*, is translated as: *Capital; A Critique of Political Economy* (Penguin editions), the double meaning of the German is lost. The English translation correctly indicates that the work is a critique of a science but omits that the work is as much – in my view, in the first place – an internal critique of "the political economy", an ontological constellation.

Marx scholars today accept 'internal critique' as a major aspect of Marx's method in *Capital*. However, controversies remain over the method and content of *Capital*, since other aspects are not necessarily ruled out. For example, is 'Marx's' 'labour theory of value' (he never used the expression) still an external norm, or is the concept of value adopted from the object of inquiry? (See further §3.4.)

3.3 Naturalistic versus socio-historical concepts

Marx simultaneously historicises social and economic concepts – the critique is an historicised critique. Social self-understanding usually takes the current social constellation and its concepts for granted, as 'natural', or as the norm ('ethnocentrism'). They are then used to evaluate history or other contemporary societies. (For example, some Americans deploy *their* notions of 'market', 'competition', 'economic freedom', 'political democracy' to evaluate other societies.) Marx identified the 'mainstream' political economy of his time as that body of self-understanding in Great Britain and France of 1850 set in ahistorical or *naturalistic* terms (cf. Mattick 1986).

From this perspective, Marx sometimes distinguished a trans-historical, or general-material, denotation of concepts – 'goods' and 'work' – from their historical, in this case capitalist, counterpart – 'commodities' and 'labour' (Arthur 1986; Murray 1988). His aim was not to construct a second language, but to show that in the social domain naturalistic entities do not exist. No trans-historical 'human needs', 'utility', 'wealth', 'goods', 'work', or 'technology' exist; they are always 'defined' and subsumed' within a socio-historical constellation (on human needs, see Campbell 1993; and on wealth and on subsumption generally, Murray 2000, 2002). Whereas J.S. Mill historicises 'the laws of distribution' – still eternalising/naturalising 'the laws of production' – Marx is a complete de-naturaliser. Anything human is set in an historically specific *social form*.

3.4 Value-form theory

The view that Marx's *critique* is an historicised critique, and that everything human takes on an historically specific *social form* (§3.3), is highlighted in the recent 'form theoretic' interpretation for which *Capital* is an exposition of the capitalist social form 'value' [early proponents are Eldred and Hanlon 1981 and Eldred, Hanlon, Kleiber and Roth 1982–85 who build on work by Backhaus 1969; Rubin 1972 [1923] is an important rediscovered precursor].

The general methodological idea of 'form theory' (springing from Aristotle and Hegel – cf. Murray 1997) is that 'content' and 'form' necessarily go together (for both natural-physical objects and anything created by human beings). 'Form' is of the essence of content, just as much as form cannot exist without content. Any actual social formation requires an historically specific form of production and distribution (e.g. tradition, power, democratic decision-making), the capitalist form being *value as expressed in monetary dimension*. But isn't it the case that things – sugar, cigar or car – already have a content and form? True. In fact, it is 'truer' than the question purports. They surely have a physical form, but from Marx's point they necessarily also have a social form that can be *distinguished* but not *separated* from their physical being. In capitalist economies things are not merely exchanged in markets in terms of value, but are *produced as* values, which affects how things are qualitatively.

In a traditional interpretation of *Capital*, Marx introduces in its first chapters a 'labour theory of value' – building on the Classical Political Economy of Smith and especially Ricardo – 'value' being a naturalistic concept, reckoned in a labour-time dimension. In this interpretation, Marx presents a *'positive'* theory of value. Hence the *materialist internal critique* aspect of Marx's method must, for this part of *Capital* at least, be de-emphasised (note that the 'labour-time theory' interpretation antedates the *critique* interpretation). For this traditional interpretation, later parts of *Capital* set out how concrete market phenomena can be 'reconciled' with this 'positive' theory.

For *value-form theory*, this first part of *Capital* is a key *materialist critique* text. When commodities are *produced* for sale – a specific characteristic of capitalism – the concrete, utility-producing character of labour is completely secondary to the producer; labour matters to the extent that it is value-producing 'abstract labour', a mere expenditure of time. This same text also shows how value (the abstract time facet of labour) is necessarily expressed in abstract monetary terms – and in monetary terms *only*. Later parts of *Capital* set out even more complex forms, culminating in the *profit form* of value, in which things are not merely produced as values, but specifically according to the measure and success-norm of capital: profit and the rate of profit.

How can we appraise these two opposing interpretations? To any reader of *Capital* it will be obvious that for Marx value is not simply determined by labour-time. The discussions of changing productivity and intensity of labour throughout Volume I problematise such a notion. Nevertheless, Marx often uses the simplified notion as an analytic reference point. Thus, whereas Marx's value-form theory is a fundamental break from Classical Political Economy, he maintains remnants of a Ricardian labour-time theory of value (Backhaus 1969).

I think that the 'labour-time theory of value' interpretation cannot be maintained because too many texts are inconsistent with it. The same applies, however, to a comprehensive monetary value-form interpretation. There are two lines of reasoning within *Capital*. Marx shares the fate of those who made a fundamental break (a *césure*), or a paradigm shift, from past conceptions. New conceptions must be formulated in the inherited language. Initial breaks must be partial, inconsistent, or flawed, and need to be completed by researchers following up the break. This, however, does not make the partial break less of an accomplishment (Reuten 1993; for a different view, see Murray 2000).

3.5 Systematic Dialectics

Also controversial is a final methodological interpretation, arising in the middle of the 1980s, which views *Capital* as Systematic Dialectics. Historical Dialectics describes the evolution and succession of distinct social formations; Systematic Dialectics theorises about one particular social formation, such as the capitalist system, setting out the whole of its object of inquiry as a completely *endogenous* system, or at least its necessary components and processes.

A major impetus for this interpretation was the 1953/1973 publication of Marx's *Grundrisse*, a rough draft of *Capital* that was, as mentioned in §2, more so than *Capital* written in a dialectical style. As indicated, a publication, such as the *Grundrisse* in this case, will not change inherited interpretations overnight. A second impetus was the dedication by a number of scholars (some stimulated by the *Grundrisse* reading) to the study of the Hegel–Marx connection (cf. Burns and Fraser 2000). As the studies of Marx's *Grundrisse* and Hegel's Systematic-Dialectical works converged, the new interpretation of *Capital* gradually emerged. [For beginnings, see Banaji 1979, Arthur 1986, and Murray 1988. A comprehensive Systematic-Dialectical interpretation is Smith 1990; cf. his 1993a, 1993b. See Mattick 1993 for critique of the interpretation. For general accounts of the methodology of Systematic Dialectics, not necessarily related to *Capital*, see Reuten and Williams 1989, pp. 3–36, Arthur 1998, and Reuten 2000.]

A Systematic Dialectic operates on several conceptual levels, from abstract and simple to concrete and complex. Its starting point is also an entry into its whole object of inquiry, formulating that whole both abstractly and simply. Gradual concretion and increasing complexity are achieved at subsequent levels of abstraction; at a final level of 'abstraction', the complexity of concrete empirical reality should be attained.

An un-theorised, or naive, empirical reality is the beginning of research. From that, after a complex and creative investigation, the initial highest level of abstraction is reached – the starting point of the systematic presentation (indicated in the previous paragraph). Thus, empirical reality (at first naive, in the end systematically theorised) is both the beginning and the end of the research. A rough outline of this process from the empirical to the abstract to the concrete is found in one of Marx's few methodological texts (Marx 1903).

Marx identifies neither these levels of abstraction in *Capital* nor how to get from one level to the next. So this must all be inferred in this interpretation of *Capital*.

The grand systematic of *Capital* is in terms of its three volumes: (1) 'The production of capital' (from the commodity to money to capital, and from the production of capital through surplus-value to the accumulation of capital);

(II) 'The circulation, or, the organic interconnections of capital'; and (III) 'The destination and concrete shapes of capital' (profit and the rate of profit, and competition and the distribution of the fruits of capital into profits of enterprise, interest and rent). The three volumes are each made up of parts, which provide more detailed levels of abstraction.

Levels of abstraction are conceptual terrains. In dialectics, concepts are not fixed – as in conventional 'linear logic' (cf. Arthur 1997) – but manifest ongoing *conceptual progress* from one level of abstraction to another. An axiomatic translation of one level into another is inconsistent with the methodology. In general, when a level of abstraction insufficiently captures the whole, the process is driven forward. Capturing the whole means formulating 'a system' that can, in principle, reproduce itself endogenously. At each operating level of abstraction, the 'discovery' of its endogeneity limits pushes the process to a new, richer, more complex level. Such a level is institutionally more complex and requires new categories and concepts. With it come both a reconceptualisation and the concretion of the conclusions of earlier levels of abstraction.

To *some* extent the method may be envisioned as one of successive approximation (Sweezy 1968 [1942]) – but only with the *major* proviso precluding fixed definitions (they only apply at their own level of abstraction). Indeed, a *recurrent reconceptualisation* occurs. A succinct example comes from Marx's *Results* (1933, p. 969), when he contemplates Volume I of *Capital*:

> Originally, we considered the *individual commodity in isolation*, as the direct product of a specific quantity of labour. Now, as the *result*, the *product of capital*, the commodity changes in form (and later on, in the price of production, it will be changed in *substance* too).

Earlier he had written (p. 954):

> The commodity may *now* be *further* defined as follows: ... The labour expended on each commodity can no longer be calculated except as an average, i.e., an ideal estimate. ... When determining the price of an individual article it appears as a merely ideal fraction of the total product in which the capital reproduces itself.

The manuscripts for the final versions of the three volumes of *Capital* that we have are dated in 'odd' order (Table 1). Inasmuch as Marx reworked and reconceptualised his manuscripts for Volume I, this would have affected the re-study of the levels of abstraction in Volumes II and III. The three volumes of *Cap-*

ital are not only in different states of draft (ranging from mere notes to final versions), but, more important for a Systematic Dialectic, in different states of conception. It is thus especially important to remember, for a Systematic-Dialectical interpretation of *Capital*, that its last two volumes cannot be seen as conceptually final.

3.6 Conclusions

By 2000 Marx scholars have largely agreed that *Capital* analyses its object of enquiry from within, aiming to drive *the object's* (capital's) own standards and processes to their logical conclusions. Marx's method of critique is largely an historicised critique. Whether it is a totally historicised critique – as highlighted in the value-form interpretation – is disputed. While most Marx scholars also agree that some type of conceptual development, or at least 'successive approximation', exists in *Capital*, whether it is as rigorous as the Systematic-Dialectical interpretation claims is disputed.

All of these different overall interpretations of *Capital* can find confirmations in Marx's texts. However, there is increasing evidence, from §3.1 to §3.5, falsifying each successive position. We might thus say that *Capital* is a rich heuristic source of a variety of different reconstructive theoretical approaches.

4 A synopsis of the systematic structure of *Capital*

A synopsis of the general structure of Marx's *Capital* must be informed by some methodological interpretation. The present synopsis relies on the most recent Systematic-Dialectical interpretation, not pushed too far, and with dialectical jargon avoided. Most Marx scholars will recognise the general outline of this structure – if perhaps not all details. The general scheme of the structure – see *Table 2* on p. 26 – has some affinity with a sophisticated schema of Arthur (2002a).

The *Table 2* scheme implies that, for example, the answer to the question 'What is it?' at the first level (I-A) is insufficient. Subsequent levels (II-A, III-A) provide reconceptualisation and concretion. The same applies to the question of 'How it works' (I-B to III-B) and 'The resulting process' (I-C to III-C). This involves a 'vertical' conceptual progress; we also have a 'horizontal' conceptual progress (from I-A to I-B etc.). Below, each entry is considered in turn, with extra space devoted to the first (I-A).

References to *Capital* are by volume number and page number. References to the secondary literature are provided for the most controversial issues only. For various methodological aspects of *Capital* see Moseley (ed.) 1993 and Moseley

TABLE 2   The systematic of *Capital*

Capital	A *What it is*	B *How it works*	C *The resulting process*
Volume I Its production *How it arises*	Parts 1 and 2 From commodity to money; from money to capital	Parts 3–6 Production process of capital	Part 7 Accumulation of capital (Annex, Part 8)
Volume II Its circulation *How it operates*	Part 1 Capital as circuit	Part 2 Turnover of capital	Part 3 Extended social reproduction of capital
Volume III Its destination *How it culminates*	Part 1 Measure of capital – profit-form and profit rate	Part 2 Competition and movement of capital; formation of general profit rate	Part 3 Cyclical evolution of the profit rate Parts 4–6 Industry, commerce, finance, landed property (Reflection, Part 7)

and Campbell (eds) 1997; recent articles with further references on the three volumes can be found in Bellofiore and Taylor (eds) 2003, Arthur and Reuten (eds) 1998, Campbell and Reuten (eds) 2002, and Bellofiore (ed.) 1998.

Capital I: Production

I-A   *What is capital? – How it arises*
'Capital' might be a sum of money, a quantity of means of production, or an investment in commodities. All such 'shapes' of capital have in common that they are value forms. For Marx 'the commodity' is the elementary shape of the value-form. Therefore he starts with its analysis (*Capital I*, Part One), turning in succession to money and capital.

There are two aspects to Part One. First, Marx seeks in 'value' a reference point for all his Volume I analysis. The problem of a suitable reference point has troubled all great economists, from Petty through Smith, Ricardo and onward to Keynes and later. A main problem in understanding Marx's text is that he seeks (cf., §3.2) an endogenous reference point, one *internal to his object of enquiry*.

(In contradistinction to external constructs, such as – later on in history – index numbers, or Sraffa's standard commodity.)

Secondly, Marx seeks *not* a naturalistic, but an historically specific social reference point (cf., §3.3); one that applies to a society in which commodities are systematically *produced* with a view to sale (I, pp. 138–9, 153–4, 174). The two aspects appear to combine into one problematic, posing an even greater difficulty for the text.

The reference point for value is "abstract labour" measured by labour-time (I, p. 129). (Therefore Marx's theory has often been interpreted as a 'labour theory of value'.) Simultaneously, Marx posits, first, that value exists only in a "value-relation or an exchange relation" and, secondly, that it is manifested in the value form *par excellence*, the money form (I, 138–9, 152, cf., 255). Indeed, throughout *Capital*, Marx always expresses value and value entities in monetary terms (£'s). (Thus it seems that Marx adopts a monetary measure of value.) I think, then, that we must accept that there is an ambiguity here, which can only be resolved in a reconstructive way (see, e.g., Backhaus 1969; Bellofiore 1989; Reuten 1993; Smith 1998; Bellofiore and Finelli 1998; Arthur 2002b).

Note that, like the concept of capital, the concept of money – as introduced in Part One, is developed throughout Volumes II–III. Marx starts from a notion of commodity money; this is procedural within a 'successive approximation' approach (cf. Campbell 1997, 1998, 2002; Williams 2000).

Marx develops the (level 1) concept of capital in sequence from an analysis of the commodity and money. Part Two of *Capital I* introduces capital proper. Marx's answer to the question 'What is capital?', towards the end of this Part, is abstract and formal: it is inherent to capital that it expands 'in movement': "The movement of capital is ... the unceasing movement of profit-making" (I, pp. 253–4). It is a movement from money (M) into more money: $M \ldots M + \Delta M$. However, "unless it takes the form of some commodity, it does not become capital" (I, p. 256). Marx uses the formula M–C–M′ (where C is the value of a commodity, or of commodities, and $M' = M + \Delta M$). This is a formula of exchange, derived from the simpler M – C – M. The latter is a strange buying (M – C) in order to sell (C – M). It is an "inversion" of C_i–M–C_j; that is, selling C_i in order to buy a qualitatively different C_j (I, p. 258). Here, money is merely a facilitator – it does not really matter. In the strange, inverted form M – C – M, however, money is all that matters; by making sense only as M – C – M′, when the end result is an increment (ΔM), a "surplus-value" as Marx calls it. In M – C – M′ value is:

> the subject of a process in which, while constantly assuming the form in turn of money and commodities, it changes its own magnitude, throws

off surplus-value from itself considered as original value, and thus valorises itself independently. For the movement in the course of which it adds surplus-value is its own movement, its valorisation is therefore self-valorisation. (I, p. 255)

So capital is a movement of self-valorisation, of throwing off surplus-value. (Note that Marx has 'bracketed' the notion of 'profit' and replaced it by the more abstract notion of 'surplus-value'. Later on (III-A) we will see "surplus-value" transformed into "profit" and the latter again in the sum of "profit of enterprise", interest and rent. Before examining the processes of that distribution – in Volume III – Marx's concern is to explain the abstract total. In Volume I (and II) he proceeds from the temporary assumption that each capitalist owns means of production and requires no hiring or borrowing of land, dwellings, or external finance (I, p. 710).)

Part Two closes by formally introducing a particular commodity and commodity market, that of labour-power, the existence of which is predicated on workers' lack of means of production. It includes a brief introduction to the value of labour-power; that is, the wage that in principle should be sufficient to reproduce the labour-power – 'sufficient' depending on physical, historical, and moral elements (I, pp. 272–5).

1-B   *How capital works – how it arises*

Capital, we saw, is a movement of self-valorisation, of throwing off surplus-value. The middle part of Volume I considers "not only how capital produces, but how capital is itself produced" (I, p. 280). How can surplus-value be explained? Recall $M - C - M'$. "The change in value of the money ... cannot take place in the money itself ... The change must therefore take place in the commodity ..." (I, p. 270). Hence the key to $M - C - M'$ lies in C. Marx next shows that the production process is the site where the value of C is turned into C'.

In the exchange $M - C$, capital in money-form is turned into capital in commodity form: means of production and labour-power. Labour-power is exchanged against the wage, and labourers sell their labour potential. During production, labour is 'subordinated' to capital: "the worker works under the control of the capitalist ... the product is the property of the capitalist and not that of the worker" (I, pp. 291–2). Because the means of production are static elements, a change in C can only be engendered by the *active* living element: labour. Labour alone can generate a surplus-value beyond the wage. In labour resides the potential to produce a surplus-product, or, in value-terms, surplus-value. Marx calls the ratio between the amount of surplus-value and the capital laid out in wages the "rate of surplus-value" or the "degree of exploitation of labour-power by capital" (I, pp. 320–7).

The body of the middle part of *Capital I*, which is more than 400 pages long, consists of a detailed analysis of methods and (organisational) techniques for increasing the rate of exploitation. Throughout, Marx uses the labour-time reference point. Nevertheless, as previously indicated, all of his value entities are expressed in monetary terms (£'s); the same applies to all his numerical examples (cf. Elson 1979a).

I-C   *Capital's resulting process – how it arises*
"Earlier we considered how surplus-value arises from capital; now we have to see how capital arises from surplus-value. The employment of surplus-value as capital, or its reconversion into capital, is called accumulation of capital" (I, p. 725). In Part Seven, Marx shows how capital's growth results in three simultaneous dynamic processes: (1) the propagation of a reserve army of unemployed labour, especially by way of the introduction of labour-expelling techniques of production pressing down the wage rate; (2) cyclical growth of capital; and (3) centralisation of capital.

The final Part Eight provides an historical account of the conditions of the buying and sale of labour-power: ownership of the means of production by capitalists. This is the precondition for the I-A starting point, and so rounds off this level of analysis as a circle.

Capital II: Circulation

II-A   *What is capital? – How it operates*
In I-A, Marx treats capital as 'movement'. Indeed, all of Volume I describes movement, resulting in expanded movement (valorisation and accumulation). In Part One of Volume II this is made explicit. Capital is shown to be a continuous movement through four manifestations/shapes, together constituting the circuit of capital:

$$\to M \longrightarrow_E\longrightarrow C\,[\text{MP; LP}] \cdots P \cdots C' \longrightarrow_E\longrightarrow M' \to$$

Capital in the shape of "money capital" (M) is transformed in the exchange process (–E–) into the shape of "production capital" (C); specifically, means of production (MP) and labour-power (LP). The latter work up the former in the process of production (···) where we have the shape of "capital in process" (P); this constitutes a metamorphosis into valorised "commodity capital" (C'), with C′ different qualitatively from C, as well as quantitatively in value terms (C′ > C). Finally, another exchange transforms the expanded commodity value C′ into a monetary value equivalent M′, the shape of expanded "money capital". The process can now resume on an expanded scale – wherein capital is accumulated.

II-B   *How capital works – How it operates*
Until Part Two, capital has been implicitly treated as an expanding flow (fixed capital as introduced in Volume I was set to zero). Now Marx explicitly distinguishes circulating from fixed capital. It is shown how capital as movement works in production in terms of length of production periods and turnover-times of capital. 'Time' is key to capital. Speeding up any of the phases of the circuit means that a given quantity of capital can turn around more production.

II-C   *Capital's resulting process – how it operates*
Part Three presents the circulation of capital in the context of the economy as a whole. Using a two-sector 'model', Marx specifies dynamic interconnections pertinent to economic growth and conditions for balanced growth. These conditions are very severe and the implication is that balanced growth is possible, though unlikely.

Capital III: Destination

III-A   *What is capital? – How it culminates*
Part One of Volume III considers surplus-value (flow) in relation to total capital invested (stock) and introduces the key capitalist *profit form*: "A sum of value is ... capital if it is invested in order to produce a profit ..." (III, p. 126). This involves a conceptual transformation of both "surplus-value" and "capital" such that the rate of profit measures the valorisation of capital. Profit and the rate of profit are capital's continuity measures.

III-B   *How capital works – how it culminates*
The profit-form brings a new dynamic (III, pp. 263, 267, 275); Part Two shows how the profit rate measure works. Since for capital its particular physical content does not matter (bread, spirits or bibles), another aspect of capital's movement is its flow to branches where it attains the highest profit rate. Thus competition between capitals produces an averaging of the profit rate. Concomitantly we have a further commodification of workers who must move "from one sphere to another and from one local point of production to another" (III, p. 298).

With the profit-form, the concept of price developed in Volume I is modified. After this, however, Marx surprisingly tries to make quantitative translations between the conceptual levels, comparing the transformed profit-form entities with a calculation prior to the profit form. In this Marx underscores the dynamic introduced at this level. The literature on the interpretation and reconstruction of this 'transformation' is enormous; for references, see Moseley 1993, Mohun 1994, Foley 2000, Bellofiore 2002, Laibman 2002, and various articles in Bellofiore (ed.) 1998, Vol. 1.

III-C *Capital's resulting process – how it culminates*
Part Three presents the resulting dynamic of diachronic change in the average rate of profit through the profit-enforced introduction of cost-reducing techniques of production. These generate cyclical rate-of-profit increases to the *initiating* capital and a simultaneous cyclical *average* rate-of-profit decrease, as reversed in cyclical restructuring of capital (for this interpretation, see Reuten 2002a, 2004 – cf. Lebowitz 1976; Fine and Harris 1979; Groll and Orzech 1987).

No longer restricted to undifferentiated "industrial capital", Parts Four to Six show capital separated into functionally different and *conflicting* factions: industrial, commercial, financial, and real estate. Profit now separates and is distributed as profit of enterprise, interest and rent (Moseley 2002). The final Part Seven is a draft for further concrete manifestations of the whole. It also emphasises Marx's fundamental point that capitalism is an historically specific and mutable mode of production that conceals its class structure (Mattick 2002; Murray 2002).

Summary
In *Capital* the one-dimensionality of the capitalist social form – the value-form as expressed monetary terms – is the basis for capital as a "movement of self-valorisation". Volume I treats the aspect of self-valorisation as movement and Volume II movement in macrosocial context. In Volume III these aspects are articulated in the working of the profit-form and the 'concrete abstraction' of a dimensionless rate of profit – money over money. That non-dimensionality, indifferent to content, drives the base structure of a capitalist society.

5   Marx's theory and Marxian theory as a strand

The main interpretations of Marx's work should be distinguished from the twentieth century growth of 'Marxian theory' as one strand alongside, in economics, the institutionalist, neoclassical, post-Keynesian, and others (for a historiography, see Howard and King 1989; 1992). Marxian theory and institutionalism share an interdisciplinary emphasis, although Marxian theory is a multidisciplinary project conducted by philosophers, economists, political scientists, sociologists, social geographers, and historians.

Current Marxian theory includes three types of research. A *first* type, nearest to Marx's work, is empirical research based on Marx's theory (such as the long run development of the macroeconomic profit rate – e.g., Moseley 1991; Duménil and Lévy 1993; Wolff 2001). Even more complicated than in mainstream economics, the concepts behind the statistical data differ from the theoretical concepts. Of course, such empirical studies involve interpretation of Marx's theory.

If one finds Marx's work to be inconsistent or unsatisfactory, a *second* type is theory reconstruction. Reconstructive work ranges across all fields of Marx's writings (particularly all components of Table 2). Methodological work is a facet of this type (see, e.g., the contributions in Albritton and Simoulidis (ed.) 2002).

A *third* type is non-reconstructive theory development. For example, elements of business cycle theory – corresponding to their level of analysis (column 3 of Table 2) – are found in all three volumes of *Capital*. Building on those elements, contemporary Marxian business cycle researchers may seek for an empirically testable theory of the cycle; this has requirements other than those intended, or at least reached, by Marx (for references, see Reuten 2002b). Other examples are economic policy research (not reached in *Capital*) or, more generally, the study of the institutional conditions surrounding the accumulation of capital in different historical periods of capitalism ('phases', or 'social structures', or 'regimes' of accumulation; see the contributions in Albritton et al. 2001).

Although much of this work has drifted away from *Capital*, or at least beyond it, we nevertheless see in the former considerable reference to the latter (critically or complimentarily). This is an interesting aspect of Marx's status within the history of thought. It is also a fascinating aspect of the study of the history of thought generally, namely that it can serve as a rich heuristic source of inspiration for current ideas.

References

Albritton, Robert, and John Simoulidis (eds) 2002, *New dialectics and political economy*, Basingstoke: Palgrave.

Albritton, Robert, Makato Itoh, Richard Westra, and Alan Zuege (eds) 2001, *Phases of capitalist development: booms, crises and globalizations*, Basingstoke: Palgrave.

Arthur, Christopher J. 1986, *Dialectics of labour: Marx and his relation to Hegel*, New York: Blackwell.
Arthur, Christopher J. 1997, 'Against the logical-historical method: dialectical derivation versus linear logic', in Moseley and Campbell (eds) 1997, pp. 9–37.
Arthur, Christopher J. 1998, 'Systematic dialectic', *Science & Society*, 62(3): 447–59.
Arthur, Christopher J. 2002a, 'Capital in general and Marx's *Capital*', in Campbell and Reuten (eds) 2002, pp. 42–64.
Arthur, Christopher J. 2002b, 'The spectral ontology of value', in Andrew Brown, Steve Fleetwood, and J.M. Roberts (eds), *Critical realism and Marxism*, London: Routledge, pp. 215–33.
Arthur, Christopher J., and Geert Reuten (eds) 1998, *The circulation of capital: essays on volume II of Marx's 'Capital'*, London/New York: Macmillan/St. Martin's Press.
Backhaus, Hans-Georg 1969, 'Zur Dialektik der Wertform', in A. Schmidt (ed.), *Beiträge zur Marxistischen Erkenntnistheorie*, Frankfurt am Main: Suhrkamp. English translation: M. Eldred and M. Roth 1980, 'On the dialectics of the value-form', *Thesis Eleven*, 1: 99–120.
Banaji, Jairus 1979, 'From the commodity to capital: Hegel's dialectic in Marx's *Capital*', in Elson (ed.) 1979, pp. 14–45.
Bellofiore, Riccardo 1989, 'A monetary labor theory of value', *Review of Radical Political Economics*, 21(1–2): 1–25.
Bellofiore, Riccardo (ed.) 1998, *Marxian economics: a reappraisal*, 2 vols., London: Macmillan.
Bellofiore, Riccardo 2002, '"Transformation" and the monetary circuit: Marx as a monetary theorist of production', in Campbell and Reuten (eds) 2002, pp. 102–27.
Bellofiore, Riccardo, and Roberto Finelli 1998, 'Capital, labour and time: the Marxian monetary labour theory of value as a theory of exploitation', in Bellofiore (ed.) 1998, pp. 48–74.
Bellofiore, Riccardo, and Nicola Taylor (eds) 2003, *The constitution of capital: essays on volume I of Marx's 'Capital'*, Basingstoke: Palgrave.
Benhabib, Seyla 1986, *Critique, norm, and utopia*, New York: Columbia University Press.
Burns, Tony, and Ian Fraser (eds) 2000, *The Hegel–Marx connection*, London: Macmillan.
Campbell, Martha 1993, 'The commodity as necessary form of product', in R. Blackwell, J. Chatha, and E.J. Nell (eds), *Economics as worldly philosophy; essays in political and historical economics in honour of Robert L. Heilbroner*, New York: St. Martin's Press, pp. 269–302.
Campbell, Martha 1997, 'Marx's theory of money: a defense', in Moseley and Campbell (eds) 1997, pp. 89–120.
Campbell, Martha 1998, 'Money in the circulation of capital', in Arthur and Reuten (eds) 1998, pp. 129–58.

Campbell, Martha 2002, 'The credit system', in Campbell and Reuten (eds) 2002, pp. 212–27.

Campbell, Martha, and Geert Reuten (eds) 2002, *The culmination of capital: essays on volume III of Marx's 'Capital'*, London: Palgrave Macmillan.

Duménil, Gérard, and Dominique Lévy 1993, *The economics of the profit rate: competition, crises and historical tendencies in capitalism*, Aldershot: Edward Elgar.

Eldred, Michael, and Marnie Hanlon 1981, 'Reconstructing value-form analysis', *Capital & Class*, 13: 24–60.

Eldred, Michael, Marnie Hanlon, Lucia Kleiber, and Mike Roth 1982–85, 'Reconstructing value-form analysis 1–4', *Thesis Eleven*, 1982/4, 1983/7, 1984/9, 1985/11. Modified as 'A Value-form Analytic Reconstruction of *Capital*', in appendix to M. Eldred, *Critique of competitive freedom and the bourgeois-democratic state*, København: Kurasje, pp. 350–487.

Elson, Diane 1979a, 'The value theory of labour', in Elson (ed.) 1979b, pp. 115–80.

Elson, Diane (ed.) 1979b, *Value: the representation of labour in capitalism*, London: CSE Books.

Fine, Ben, and Laurence Harris 1979, *Rereading Capital*, London: Macmillan.

Foley, Duncan 2000, 'Recent developments in the labor theory of value', *Review of Radical Political Economics*, 32(1): 1–39.

Groll, Shalom, and Ze'ev B. Orzech 1987, 'Technical progress and values in Marx's theory of the decline in the rate of profit: an exegetical approach', *History of Political Economy*, 19(4): 591–613.

Howard, Michael C., and Jesse E. King 1989/1992, *A history of Marxian economics: volume I, 1883–1929; volume II 1929–1990*, London: Macmillan.

Laibman, David 2002, 'Value and the quest for the core of capitalism', *Review of Radical Political Economics*, 34(2): 159–78.

Lebowitz, Michael A. 1976, 'Marx's falling rate of profit: a dialectical view', *Canadian Journal of Economics*, 9(2): 232–54.

Marx, Karl 1867, 4th edn. 1890, *Das Kapital, Kritik der Politischen Ökonomie, Band I, Der Produktionsprozeß des Kapitals*, MEW 23 [cited English translation by Ben Fowkes, *Capital, a critique of political economy, volume I*, 1976, Harmondsworth: Penguin].

Marx, Karl 1885; 2nd edn. 1893, ed. F. Engels, *Das Kapital, Kritik der Politischen Ökonomie, Band II, Der Zirkulationsprozeß des Kapitals*, MEW 24 [cited English translation by David Fernbach, *Capital: a critique of political economy, volume II*, 1978, Harmondsworth: Penguin].

Marx, Karl 1894, ed. F. Engels, *Das Kapital, Kritik der Politischen Ökonomie, Band III, Der Gesamtprozesz der kapitalistischen Produktion*, MEW 25 [cited English translation by David Fernbach, *Capital: a critique of political economy, volume III*, 1981, Harmondsworth: Penguin].

Marx, Karl 1903, 'Einleitung' (zu Grundrisse der Kritik der Politischen Ökonomie), ed.

Karl Kautsky, *Die Neue Zeit* [cited English translation by M. Nicolaus, 1973, see Marx 1953, pp. 81–111].

Marx, Karl 1933, *Resultate des Unmittelbaren Produktionsprozeßes*, Frankfurt: Verlag Neue Kritik. First English translation by R. Livingstone 1976, 'Results of the immediate process of production', in *Capital: a critique of political economy, volume I*, trans. B. Fowkes, Harmondsworth: Penguin, pp. 948–1084.

Marx, Karl 1953 [1939–41], *Grundrisse der Kritik der Politischen Ökonomie (Rohentwurf)*, first English edition 1973, *Grundrisse*, trans. M. Nicolaus, Harmondsworth: Penguin.

Marx, Karl n.d. *Capital, volumes I–III* [disc version of Lawrence & Wishart/International Publishers edition], Marx and Engels, Classics in Politics, London: The Electronic Book Company (ElecBook).

Marx, Karl, and Friedrich Engels, *Collected works* (CW), London/New York/Moscow: Lawrence & Wishart/International Publishers/Progress Publishers.

Marx, Karl, and Friedrich Engels, *Gesamtausgabe* (MEGA), Berlin and Amsterdam: Akademie Verlag/Dietz Verlag/Internationales Institut für Sozialgeschichte Amsterdam.

Marx, Karl, and Friedrich Engels, *Marx Engels Werke*, Berlin: Dietz Verlag.

Mattick Jr., Paul 1986, *Social knowledge: an essay on the nature and limits of social science*, London: Hutchinson.

Mattick Jr., Paul 1993, 'Marx's dialectic', in Moseley (ed.) 1993, pp. 115–34.

Mattick Jr., Paul 2002, 'Class, capital, and crisis', in Campbell and Reuten (eds) 2002, pp. 16–41.

Mohun, Simon 1994, 'A re(in)statement of the labour theory of value', *Cambridge Journal of Economics*, 18: 391–412.

Moseley, Fred 1991, *The falling rate of profit in the postwar United States economy*, London: Macmillan.

Moseley, Fred (ed.) 1993, *Marx's method in 'Capital': a re-examination*, Atlantic Highlands, NJ: Humanities Press.

Moseley, Fred 1993, 'Marx's logical method and the "transformation problem"', in Moseley (ed.) 1993, pp. 157–84.

Moseley, Fred 2002, 'Hostile brothers: Marx's theory of the distribution of surplus-value in volume III of *Capital*', in Campbell and Reuten (eds) 2002, pp. 65–101.

Moseley, Fred, and Martha Campbell (eds) 1997, *New investigations of Marx's method*, Atlantic Highlands, NJ: Humanities Press.

Murray, Patrick 1988/1990, *Marx's theory of scientific knowledge*, Atlantic Highlands, NJ: Humanities Press.

Murray, Patrick 1997, 'Redoubled empiricism: the place of social form and formal causality in Marxian theory', in Moseley and Campbell (eds) 1997, pp. 38–65.

Murray, Patrick 2000, 'Marx's "truly social" labour theory of value: abstract labour in Marxian value theory', *Historical Materialism*, 6: 27–66 (Part 1) and 7: 99–136 (Part 2).

Murray, Patrick 2002, 'The illusion of the economic: the trinity formula and "the religion of everyday life"', in Campbell and Reuten (eds) 2002, pp. 246–73.

Oakley, Allen 1983, *The making of Marx's critical theory: a bibliographical analysis*, London: Routledge and Kegan Paul.

Reuten, Geert 1993, 'The difficult labour of a theory of social value: metaphors and systematic dialectics at the beginning of Marx's *Capital*', in Moseley (ed.) 1993, pp. 89–113.

Reuten, Geert 2000, 'The interconnection of systematic dialectics and historical materialism', *Historical Materialism*, 7: 137–66.

Reuten, Geert 2002a, 'The rate of profit cycle and the opposition between managerial and finance capital: a discussion of *Capital III* parts 3–5', in Campbell and Reuten (eds) 2002, pp. 174–211.

Reuten, Geert 2002b, 'Business cycles: Marxian approach', in Brian Snowdon and Howard Vane (eds), *Encyclopedia of macroeconomics*, Aldershot: Edward Elgar, pp. 73–80.

Reuten, Geert 2004, '"Zirkel vicieux" or trend fall? – the course of the profit rate in Marx's *Capital III*', *History of Political Economy*, 36(1): 163–86.

Reuten, Geert, and Michael Williams 1989, *Value-form and the state; the tendencies of accumulation and the determination of economic policy in capitalist society*, London: Routledge.

Rubin, Isaak Illich 1972 [1923], *Ocherki po teorii stoimosti Marksa*, 3rd edn, Moscow 1928, Engl. transl. Miloš Samardžija and Fredy Perlman, *Essays on Marx's theory of value*, Detroit: Black & Red.

Smith, Tony 1990, *The logic of Marx's Capital: replies to Hegelian criticisms*, Albany, NY: State University of New York Press.

Smith, Tony 1993a, 'Marx's *Capital* and Hegelian dialectical logic', in Moseley (ed.) 1993, pp. 15–36.

Smith, Tony 1993b, *Dialectical social theory and its critics*, Albany, NY: State University of New York Press.

Smith, Tony 1998, 'Value theory and dialectics', *Science & Society*, 62(3): 460–70.

Sweezy, Paul M. 1942/1968, *The theory of capitalist development*, New York: Modern Reader Paperbacks.

Williams, Michael 2000, 'Why Marx neither has nor needs a commodity theory of money', *Review of Political Economy*, 12(4): 435–51.

Wolff, Edward 2001, 'The recent rise of profits in the United States', *Review of Radical Political Economics*, 33: 315–24.

CHAPTER 2

Marx's conceptualisation of value in *Capital*

2019 article, originally published in *The Oxford handbook of Karl Marx*, edited by Matthew Vidal, Tony Smith, Tomás Rotta and Paul Prew, Oxford: Oxford University Press, pp. 129–50. (In the printed handbook version, the internal cross-references are mixed up, because the copy-editor numbered the Introduction without changing the cross references accordingly – the digital version is OK.)
(For its abstract see the Abstracts of all chapters, p. 1.)

Contents

Introduction 38
1   The background 39
    1.1   The aim of capital and Capital 39
    1.2   Marx's paradigmatic break from classical political economy 40
    1.3   Method: conceptual progress 40
    1.4   The historical order of Marx's writings of and for Capital 40
    1.5   Marx as continuous critic of Marx 41
    1.6   Marx's 'averages' account in *Capital I* 41
2   The static conceptualisation of value: averages (*Capital I*, Part One) 42
    2.1   Elements of the initial static or average account of value: Chapter 1 42
        (a)   The value of commodities and the concept of abstract labour 42
        (b)   Socially necessary labour-time and the intensity of labour 43
        (c)   The productive power of labour 44
        (d)   Complex potentiated labour and the reduction to simple labour 45
        (e)   Labour creates purely social value in the form of commodities (labour is not itself value) 46
    2.2   Money as the measure of value in practice: Chapters 2–3 47
    2.3   Some concluding remarks on the social dimensions adopted by Marx 48
3   The dynamic conceptualisation of value: deviation from averages (*Capital I*, Part Four) 48
    3.1   The dynamics as presented in *Capital I*, Part Four 48
        (a)   The intensity of labour 48
        (b)   The empowerment of labour 49

    3.2   The new matter about technique related empowerment of labour: comparison with 1861–63 and 1864 manuscripts   51
    3.3   *Capital I*, Part Four: return to averages   51
4   Manifestation of value in prices of production (the *Capital III* manuscript for its Part Two)   52
    4.1   Marx's 1864–65 manuscript for *Capital III*: prices of production   52
5   Incompatibilities: interpretation versus reconstruction   54
    5.1   Incompatibilities   54
    5.2   A reconstruction   54
    5.3   Philological puzzles   56
Summary   58
References   59

Introduction[1]

Marx in *Capital* never uses the term 'labour theory of value' as a denotation for his own work, and with two exceptions he does not even use the term 'theory of value'.[2] Nevertheless the concept of 'value' is a key one throughout this work. One of Marx's main concerns is to trace the 'why' and 'how' of 'the accumulation of capital' that dominates capitalist society, and he sees the value-form of commodities as its "cell-form".

This essay sets out the three main stages of Marx's conceptualisation of the value of commodities in *Capital*. After a preliminary section, I begin with what I call the 'static averages' account of *Capital I*, Part One (§2). We then move to what I call Marx's 'dynamic account' of the commodities' value in *Capital I*, Part Four. We will see that the two main factors of this dynamics are the "intensity of labour" and the "empowerment of labour", each changing and diverging within and between branches of production – the empowerment of labour along with the changing and diverging "productive powers of labour". Although Marx introduces each of these concepts already in Part One, he keeps them as constant on average until Part Four. One upshot of the dynamic account is that clock-time is an insufficient measure for labour-time. I will indicate that whereas the intensity of labour already figured in Marx's manuscripts of 1861–65, the "empowerment of labour" related to technique was a new insight of Marx during the 1866–67 composition of the first edition of *Capital I* (§3).

---

1   I am most grateful to Tony Smith for his comments on an earlier version of this article.
2   One exception is a single phrase in the Postface to the 2nd edition of *Capital I*, and the other a single phrase in *Capital III*, Ch. 8.

Section 4 moves to the third stage, that of Marx's transformation of the value to the price of production of commodities, as we find it in *Capital III*, Part Two (written in 1864–65, published as edited by Engels in 1894). Section 5 shows how this manuscript is incompatible with Marx's new insights from 1866–67, and also how it is fairly easy to account for the incompatibility by way of a reconstruction; easy, but with rather far-reaching consequences in face of the history of Marxian theory.[3]|[4] (Footnote 4 sets out the way of referencing.)

In Sections 1 to 4 I try to give a fair interpretation of Marx's conceptualisation of value throughout *Capital*, leaving out any ideas stemming from my own contributions to Marxian theory.

[Annotation. Throughout this essay I translate Marx's German 'potenzierte Arbeit' as 'empowered labour', whereas in my 2017 (Chapter 15 below) I used the term 'potentiated labour'.]

1 The background

In this section I briefly introduce six items that are relevant for the rest of the essay, including the conclusions drawn.

1.1 *The aim of capital and Capital*

Marx's *Capital* sets out an exposition of the capitalist mode of production. The ultimate aim of capitalists (enterprises and their financiers) is the accumulation of capital. In *Capital* Marx shows how, via the production of surplus-value, capital is produced by labour. The value-form of commodities is the elementary

---

[3] Throughout the essay I make a distinction between Marx's and Marxian works indicating with the latter the work of those working in Marx's tradition or paradigm.

[4] Because each of the exact translations and the exact dating of Marx's manuscripts is quite important, I adopt the following conventions here. In all QUOTATIONS emphasis by Marx is in *italics*; my own emphasis is <u>underlined</u>. In all quotations, insertions in [square brackets] are either by the translator or editor as in the edition quoted from, or by me to complete an ellipsis. Insertions in {curly brackets} are mine, usually regarding the German to English translation; the German terms in this case are in italics. Ellipses within one, or at the end of, a sentence are indicated by three dots ... Ellipses indicated by three dots within brackets (...) regard those of one or several sentences. My REFERENCES to Marx include mostly an English and a German version. For these I use the following convention: (a) for texts published by Marx or Engels, as 'Marx 1890^4 [1867^1] MEW', where the dates with superscripts denote the edition and the addition MEW the edition quoted from (in this case *Marx-Engels Werke*) or the addition EDF (in this case English transl. David Fernbach); (b) for manuscripts (ms) not published literally by Marx or Engels, as 'Marx {1864–65 ms}1993 MEGA', where

form of the production and accumulation of capital. Core to Marx's exposition is the dual character of commodities (as useful entities and as values) and the dual character of labour along with it. This is why the concept of value and especially labour's production of value is a core one.

1.2 Marx's paradigmatic break from classical political economy

Marx, the founder of the political economy paradigm that bears his name, accomplished a paradigmatic break from both Hegelian philosophy and classical political economy. Marx shares the fate of all founders of paradigms: the break to a large extent has to be formulated in the language of the former paradigm. This brings with it inevitable ambiguities. These ambiguities and problems of interpretation are in one way or the other resolved or accommodated by those working in the new paradigmatic language (this is what Kuhn, in *The structure of scientific revolutions*, called "puzzle solving"), which may take the shape of 'reconstructions' of the originator's work.

1.3 Method: conceptual progress

Related to the previous point there has always been controversy over Marx's method among Marxian authors, mainly as relating to the character of his break from Hegel. However, few dispute that Marx in *Capital* adopts a method of layered *conceptual progress*, starting with general and relatively uncomplicated concepts, to particular and complex concepts (this method might be denoted as a type of systematic dialectics, or as what Sweezy (1968 [1942]) called "successive approximation"). This applies to all of Marx's main concepts, and especially also to his concept of value.

1.4 The historical order of Marx's writings of and for Capital

We see this conceptual layering also in the design of the three volumes of *Capital*. As is well known, Marx completed only its first volume, the other two were edited by Engels on the basis of Marx's manuscripts. For all of Marx's main concepts, and especially also for that of value, it is most relevant that the manuscript for 'Capital III' and much of that for II, was written before *Capital I* (see *Table 1*, rows 1–3).

---

the date in braces indicates the (probable) year of the manuscript, the year following it is the first year of publication, and the addition the edition quoted from (in this case *Marx-Engels-Gesamtausgabe*) or the addition EBF (in this case the English transl. by Ben Fowkes). I refer to the MEW for those texts not digitally available in the MEGA at the time of writing.

TABLE 1   Order of publications and manuscripts of Marx's 'Capital project'

		Publication 1st edition (German)	Main manuscript by Marx (of 1st edition)	Order of ms
1	Capital I	1867 (Marx)*	1866–67†	4
2	Capital II	1885 (ed. Engels)	1865; 1877–81	3/5
3	Capital III	1894 (ed. Engels)	1863–65	2
4	Capital I	penultimate draft‡	1863–64	1
5	Results∗	1933 (published ms.)	1864	1

*   2nd edition (Marx) 1872; 3rd edn. (Engels, using Marx's notes) 1883; 4th edn. (Engels) 1890.
†   For much of its Part One redrafting his 1859 work, and for much of the current Parts Two to Six redrafting his 1863–64 manuscripts (see Vollgraf 2012, and Hubmann and Roth 2013).
‡   Blended into the final draft of 1866–67, except the next text (see Vollgraf 2012).
∗   "Results of the direct production process".

The order here is particularly important because, as MEGA editor Vollgraf indicates, with the drafts for Capital of 1864–81 Marx started in fact a conceptually new project, in contradistinction to his 1857–63 project. The two "differ in content and structure" (Vollgraf 2018, p. 71).

It is most likely that if Marx had lived longer, he would have rewritten his drafts for Volumes II and III in line with his new 1866–67 Capital I findings.

In §§2–4 I will draw on the works of rows 1–3 of the table, and also that of row 5, "Results of the direct production process".

1.5   Marx as continuous critic of Marx

Marx's two main projects and the continuous redrafting and re-conceptualisations of his texts (continued after 1867 – see especially MEGA II.4.3; II.7; II.11 and II.14) show how Marx was continuously his own main critic. This shows his thorough scientific attitude. It is most likely that had he lived longer this would have been prolonged. In my view, therefore, the best tribute to Marx is to not only interpret his texts (with all their problems – §1.2) but to be a critic of Marx in his vein and go on to reconstruct and expand his project. The worst attitude, alien to Marx, is to consider his writings handed down as the final truth.

1.6   Marx's 'averages' account in Capital I

A final issue on which I will draw in the rest of this essay – an issue that has received too little attention in the literature – regards Marx's 'averages' account in Capital I especially. I stressed this in a 2004 article. It was greatly highlighted again by Vollgraf (2012, pp. 50–1). He indicates that Marx was influenced by the Belgian mathematician and statistician Quételet, who in a work of 1835 was the first to apply 'averages' in social science.

Below (§3) we will see the import of the averages account in Parts Four and Five of *Capital I*, which are especially crucial for his conceptualisation of value. Marx starts from social averages, moves to deviation from and changes of averages, and then returns back to (new) social averages.

To be sure, this averages account of individual capitals is not the same as a macroeconomic account. Besides, Marx is very explicit that only in *Capital II*, Part Three (where he presents his reproduction schemes) does he move from the individual capital to the "total social capital" – or what since 1933 is called 'macroeconomics' (Marx 1893 [1885^1] EBF, especially pp. 427–30 and 469–70).

2 The static conceptualisation of value: averages (*Capital I*, Part One)

2.1 *Elements of the initial static or average account of value: Chapter 1*

In *Capital I*, ch. 1, section 1, Marx posits the duality of the use-value and the value of commodities, and along with it the duality of concrete labour and abstract labour. In a commodity producing society, products not only have some use-value (usefulness) – which is the product of concrete labour – but also an exchange-value. The dualities introduced here are core to all of his further exposition in *Capital*.

(a) *The value of commodities and the concept of abstract labour*. This is how 'abstract labour' and 'value' are introduced for the first time:

> If then we disregard the use-value of commodities, only one property remains, that of being products of labour. (...) If we make abstraction from its use-value, we abstract also from the material constituents and forms which make it a use-value. (...) [With it] the useful character of the kinds of labour embodied in them also disappears {*aufgelöscht*: dissolves} this in turn entails the disappearance of the different concrete forms of labour. They can no longer be distinguished, but are altogether reduced to the same kind of labour, human <u>labour in the abstract</u>. (Marx 1890^4 [1867^1] EBF, p. 128; cf. 1890^4 [1867^1] MEW, p. 52. Below I abbreviate the references as MEW for the German, and EBF for the English Ben Fowkes translation. Superscripts after a publication year always refer to the edition of a work.)

Thus, Marx continues, disregarding the usefulness of commodities:

> There is nothing left of them ... but the same phantom-like objectivity; they are merely congealed quantities of homogeneous human labour, i.e., of human labour-power expended without regard to the form of its expenditure. All these things <u>now tell us</u> {*stellen nur noch dar*: are exhibited only as} that human labour-power has been expended to produce them, human labour is accumulated {*aufgehäuft*: amassed} in them. As crystals of this social substance, which is common to them all, they are values – <u>commodity values</u> [*Warenwerte*]. (Marx, EBF, p. 128; MEW, p. 52).

After this he indicates: "The progress of the investigation will lead us back to exchange-value as the necessary mode of expression, or form of appearance, of value" (ibid.). (In his chapter 1, section 3, and chapters 2–3). Somewhat further on we have the one and only time that Marx uses the term measure(ment) of value in the fifty pages of chapter 1:

> How is the magnitude of this value to be measured? By means of the quantity of the 'value-forming {*bildenden*: constituting} substance', the labour contained in the article. This quantity is <u>measured by its duration</u>, and the labour-time is itself measured on the particular scale of hours, days, etc. (Marx, EBF, p. 129; MEW, p. 53)

(*b*) *Socially necessary labour-time and the intensity of labour*. Next the terms 'average', 'socially necessary labour-time' and 'intensity of labour' are introduced for the first time.

> The total labour-power of society, which is manifested {*sich darstellt*: is exhibited} in the values of the world of commodities, counts here as <u>one homogeneous mass of human labour-power</u>, although composed of innumerable individual units of labour-power.[5] Each of these units is the same as any other, to the extent that it has the character of a <u>socially average</u> unit of labour-power and acts as such; i.e., only needs, in order to produce a commodity, the labour time which is <u>necessary on an average</u>, <u>or</u> in other words is <u>socially necessary</u>. Socially necessary labour-time is the labour-time required to produce any use-value <u>under the conditions</u>

---

5 The term "unit" in this and the following sentence brings in a certain emphasis that is not in the German text. Marx has, literally, "individual labour powers" (MEW, p. 53).

of production normal for a given society and with the average degree of skill and intensity of labour prevalent in that society. (...) What exclusively determines the magnitude of the value of any article is therefore the amount of labour socially necessary, or the labour-time socially necessary for its production. (Marx, EBF, p. 129; MEW, pp. 53–4).

(c) The productive power of labour. A final general concept regarding Marx's conceptualisation of the value of commodities, is that of the "productive power of labour" (German: *Produktivkraft der Arbeit*), which should be distinguished from "labour-power". Note that the term *Produktivkräfte* dates back to the 1845–46 *German Ideology* (in MECW 5 it is translated as "productive forces"). Unfortunately, the translator of *Capital* has withheld the concept from English readers, translating the phrase as "productivity of labour" – a concept that Marx also uses, but the two are definitively not the same.[6] The concept of the "productive power of labour" will also play an important role in §3 below (dynamics), and it is essential to distinguish it from the "intensity of labour" introduced above. Henceforth I will correct the translator's error by amending his "productivity of labour," putting *productive power of labour* between asterisks. Marx writes:

> The value of a commodity would therefore remain constant, if the labour-time required for its production also remained constant. But the latter changes with every variation in the *productive power of labour*. This is determined by a wide range of circumstances; it is determined amongst other things by the workers' average degree of skill, the level of development of science and its technological application, the social organisation of the process of production, the extent and effectiveness of the means of production, and the conditions found in the natural environment. (...) The value of a commodity, therefore, varies directly as the quantity, and inversely as the *productive power* of the labour which finds its realisation {*verwirklichenden*: actualisation} within the commodity. (Marx, EBF, pp. 130–1; MEW, pp. 54–5).

So far Chapter 1's section 1. Anticipating §3 (dynamics), I record that Marx first introduced the average intensity of labour and next, as distinguished from it, the productive power of labour.

---

[6] In the earlier translation by Moore and Aveling (originally 1887) the same mistake is made: their translation is "productiveness" (see MECW 35, p. 50).

(*d*) *Complex 'empowered labour' and the reduction to simple labour.* Section 2 expands on the duality of labour as producing use-values and as producing the value actualised in commodities. I focus on one main issue, namely Marx's conceptualisation of 'simple average labour'. He writes according to the translator:

> But the value of a commodity represents {*stellt da*: exhibits} human labour pure and simple {*schlechthin*: plainly}, the expenditure of human labour in general {*überhaupt*}. (...) It is the expenditure of simple labour-power, i.e., of the labour-power possessed in his bodily organism by every ordinary man, on the average, without being developed in any special way. *Simple average labour*, it is true, varies in character in different countries and at different cultural epochs, but in a particular society it is given. More complex labour counts only as *intensified*, or rather *multiplied* simple labour, so that a smaller quantity of complex labour is considered equal to a larger quantity of simple labour. (EBF, p. 135; cf. MEW, p. 59)

As a translation from the German, the last dotted text is utterly wrong. The German reads: "Kompliziertere Arbeit gilt nur als *potenzierte* oder vielmehr *multiplizierte* einfache Arbeit .." (MEW, p. 59). That is: "More complex labour counts only as *empowered* or rather *multiplied* simple labour ...".[7] In §3.1 we will see the relevance of this amended translation. Here I record the order of Marx exposition: he first introduces the average intensity of labour (EBF, p. 129; MEW, pp. 53–4), and after his introduction of the concept of the 'productive power of labour' (EBF, p. 130; MEW, p. 54) he now introduces the concept of 'empowered labour'. Immediately after this Marx writes:

> Experience shows that this reduction [of empowered into simple labour] is constantly {*Beständig*: continually} being made.[8] A commodity may be the outcome of the most complicated labour, but through its *value* it is posited as equal to the product of simple labour, hence it represents {exhibits} only a specific quantity of simple labour ... The various proportions in which different kinds of labour are reduced to simple labour as their unit of measurement are established by a social process that goes on behind the backs of the producers; these proportions therefore

---

7   Again, in the Moore and Aveling translation we have roughly the same mistake: "Skilled labour counts only as simple labour intensified, or rather, as multiplied simple labour ..." (MECW 35, p. 54).
8   It seems to me that 'constant' has too much the connotation of a constant factor (*Konstant* in German), though English writers are often not precise in this respect.

appear to the producers to have been handed down by tradition. <u>In the interests of simplification</u>, we shall henceforth view every form of labour-power directly as simple labour-power; by this we shall simply be <u>saving ourselves the trouble of making the reduction</u>. (Marx, EBF, p. 135; cf. MEW, p. 59)

I have nothing against Marx's concept of 'empowered labour': it is a great and utmost important concept (as we will see in my §3). However, his concept of "reduction" requires a brief comment. Marx does not tell how this reduction of labour-power is operationalised. My problem is not that he glosses over this at this point (Chapter 1). The problem is that in all three volumes of *Capital* he never returns to this matter. The extent to which this is important depends on whether at some stage one would want to apply this empirically and operationalise it. I think that this simplification precludes the adding up of labour-times before settling the trouble of making the reduction.[9] Indeed, I think that this simplifying abstraction (here: assumption) makes a quantitative procedure at the empirical level of adding up concrete premarket hours of labour very dubious.

(e) *Labour creates purely social value in the form of commodities (labour is not itself value)*. In Chapter 1, sections 3–4, it becomes clear how we must read the earlier sections in retrospect. Within the space constraints for this essay I merely highlight two conclusions of Marx from section 3 ("The value-form, or exchange value"). In this section Marx sets out how the value of commodities appears in relations of exchange. At the opening of this section he writes:

> Commodities (…) only appear as commodities, or have the form of commodities, in so far as they possess a double form, i.e., natural form and value form. (…) Not an atom of matter enters into the objectivity of commodities as values (…) <u>their objective character as values is therefore purely social</u>. (Marx, EBF, pp. 138–9; cf. MEW, p. 62)

Thus, to be sure, when we perceive a single commodity (bread or a car) there is no way to detect its value from that perception. As such, its value seems supersensuous. The value character of commodities emerges {*hervortreten*} only in their relation to other commodities (EBF, pp. 141–2; MEW, p. 65) and in partic-

---

9 However, actually settling the trouble might then take one into Adam Smith's labour-commanded waters, or the realm of J.M. Keynes's wage unit.

ular in their manifestation (*Gestalt*) of the commodities' common value-form, that is, the money form (EBF, p. 139; MEW, p. 62; MEW, p. 75 and EBF, p. 162; MEW, p. 84). Early on in this section Marx concluded already:

> Human labour-power in its fluid state, or human labour, creates value, but is not itself value. It becomes value in its coagulated state, in objective form. (Marx, EBF, p. 142; cf. MEW, p. 65)

Thus the value of commodities is *explained* by labour-time.

2.2 Money as the measure of value in practice: Chapters 2–3

The current subsection is not relevant for the remainder of this essay. However, regarding Marx's conceptualisation of value I cannot neglect to focus the reader's attention to Chapters 2–3 of *Capital I*, Part One. Each one of the Parts of *Capital* constitutes a unity.

Marx started Ch. 1, section 1, with the exchange-value of commodities. He systematically introduces this concept in section 3, where he also posits *the form* of money – expanding on the latter's broad social implications in section 4.

The relatively brief Ch. 2 on the process of exchange, introduces social actors of exchange and the action of society to turn a particular commodity into the general equivalent 'money' (EBF, p. 180) within a society of generalised commodity production (EBF, p. 187). In sum it posits the *prevalence* (*Dasein*) of money in practice.

Money itself (i.e., its systemic existence) is derived in Ch. 3. Notably it is systematically derived from exchange, just as the commodity and value were derived from exchange. It is only later (that is in all the rest of *Capital*) that the role of the money-form of value, that is money's role in production and in the full circuit of capital will become explicit. But in order to comprehend this role, Ch. 3 is absolutely crucial.

Here I restrict myself to one brief quotation from its section 1 ("The measure of values"):

> Money as a measure of value is the necessary form of appearance of the measure of value which is immanent in commodities, namely labour-time. (Marx, EBF, p. 188; MEW, p. 109)

Marx starts his exposition in this chapter with the sentence: "Throughout this work I assume that gold is the money commodity, for the sake of simplicity" (ibid). Whereas this was not strange in 1867, it has nevertheless been controversial among Marxian scholars. I refer to three contrary positions, each one plausible in itself, that are in the end, in my view, nevertheless complementary. These are Campbell 1997, Williams 2000 and Bellofiore 2005.

2.3 Some concluding remarks on the social dimensions adopted by Marx

The result of Part One is that in all of *Capital* value entities are expressed in a monetary dimension (using some currency standard such as £); the same applies to all numerical examples.[10] Throughout Marx adopts two main social dimensions, namely labour-time and monetary value. "Labour, creates value, but is not itself value." It is important to (re)emphasise the latter since in some interpretations of Marx's *Capital* 'value' is itself taken to have a labour-time dimension. Those same accounts often adopt the term 'labour values' – a term *never* used in *Capital*.[11] At the level of the production of capital (*Capital I*) Marx aims to *explain* value and surplus-value (in the monetary dimension) in terms of labour-time (in Parts Three to Five, 350 pages) – an explanation in terms of labour-time does, of course, not mean that value actually ever discards its monetary dimension.[12]

3 The dynamic conceptualisation of value: deviation from averages (*Capital I*, Part Four)

3.1 *The dynamics as presented in* Capital I, *Part Four*

Marx's major dynamic conceptualisation of value is in *Capital I*, Part Four ("The production of relative surplus-value"). Starting from averages, he next considers changes in the value of commodities due to changes in labour's productivity. There are two factors affecting such changes. Each of these were already briefly treated in the book's Ch. 1 (§2.1 above under *b* to *d*).

(*a*) *The intensity of labour*. Taking the degree of "empowerment of labour" as given (see under heading *b* below), the productivity of labour will change with the "intensity of labour", that is, the effort and strain of labour, as initiated

---

10 Elson (1979) pointed this out.
11 For example, Schefold (who is generally well acquainted with the field) does presume this. Thus, in his introduction to *Capital III*, Schefold (2004, p. 874) erroneously writes "Arbeitswerten (wie Marx sie nannte)" {"Labour-values (as Marx called them)"}. Possibly Marx used this expression in some writing prior to *Capital* – Schefold cites no source – but that would surprise me very much.
12 Reuten 2004, §1.1 traces the dimensions and measures adopted by Marx in Parts Three to Five of *Capital I*. [Chapter 8 of the current book.]

by some capitalist in some sector. Along with it Marx introduces the concept of the *"degree of density"* of labour, implying that clock-time is an insufficient measure.[13] He treats this matter in Part Four, chapter 15 (ch. 13 of the German edition). He writes:

> It [intensification of labour] imposes <u>on the worker</u> an increased expenditure of labour within a time which remains constant, <u>a heightened tension of labour-power</u>, and a closer filling-up of the pores of the working day, i.e., a condensation of labour, to a degree which can only be attained within the limits of the shortened working day. This compression of a greater mass of labour into a given period now counts for what it really is, namely an increase of the quantity of labour. In addition to the measure of its 'extensive magnitude', <u>labour-time now acquires a measure of its degree of density</u>.[14] (...) the same mass of value is now produced for the capitalist by, say, 3⅓ hours of surplus labour and 6⅔ hours of necessary labour, as was previously produced by 4 hours of surplus labour and 8 hours of necessary labour. (Marx 1890⁴ [1867¹] EBF, p. 534; cf. Marx 1890⁴ [1867¹] MEW, pp. 432–3)

According to Marx, however, differences in the intensity of labour tend to be levelled out by way of competition between workers. I add that this may perhaps seem obvious within some sector (branch) of production, though less so between sectors of production. Given the current skills of labour, a levelling out between sectors would seem a medium or long run matter. As long as this is not effectuated we would have diverging rates of surplus-value between sectors.

(*b*) *The empowerment of labour.* The second factor affecting changes in the productivity of labour is the "empowerment of labour". It is treated in chapter 12 (chapter 10 of the German edition), where Marx systematically introduces the "productive power of labour" (German: *Produktivkraft der Arbeit*). Again the English translator renders *Produktivkraft* into 'productivity'. In all quotations below I amend this, as marked by asterisks (*). Marx writes:

> increase in the *productive power of labour* (...) cannot be done except by an alteration in his [the labourer's] tools or in his mode of working, or

---

13   Throughout the 1861–63 manuscript he uses the term "condensation" instead of "density" (MECW 33, pp. 382–7).

14   Before the phrase "degree of density", the translator adds: "intensity, or".

both. (...) By an increase in the *productive power of labour*, we mean an alteration in the labour process of such a kind as to <u>shorten the labour-time socially necessary for the production of a commodity</u>, whence a smaller quantity of labour acquires the power of producing a greater quantity of use-value. (Marx, EBF, p. 431-amended; MEW, p. 333)

And:

The technical and social conditions of the labour process and consequently the mode of production itself must be revolutionized before the *productive power of labour* can be increased. (Marx, EBF, p. 432-amended; MEW, p. 334)

Regarding the "empowerment of labour" the following is the key sentence:

The labour operating at this exceptional productive power acts as <u>empowered labour</u>; it creates in equal periods of time greater values than average social labour of the same kind. (Marx, my translation of MEW, p. 337; cf. EBF, p. 435)[15]

Fowkes – and hence all English language readers – completely misses the point because he translates the German "potenzierte Arbeit" by "intensified labour" so muddling it with the distinction that I introduced above under (a).[16]

This beyond average value-creating empowerment of labour cannot be simply measured in clock-time. (The latter's insufficiency is the one similarity between the intensity and the empowerment of labour.) Marx continues:

Hence, the capitalist who applies the improved method of production, appropriates as surplus-labour a greater portion of the working-day than the other capitalists in the same business. (...) On the other hand, however, this extra surplus-value vanishes, as soon as the new method of production is generalized .... (Marx, EBF, p. 436; cf. MEW, p. 337)

---

15   The German text reads: "Die Arbeit von ausnahmsweiser Produktivkraft wirkt als potenzierte Arbeit oder schafft in gleichen Zeiträumen höhere Werte als die gesellschaftliche Durchschnittsarbeit derselben Art" (MEW, p. 337). This text is identical in the first edition of *Capital I* (MEGA II/5). (In Reuten 2017, I translated 'potenzierte' as 'potentiated' instead of 'empowered'. [Ch. 15 of the current book].)

16   The same applies for the Moore and Aveling translation: "The exceptionally productive labour operates as intensified labour ..." (MECW 35, p. 323).

This is quite right. Note, however, that Marx feels (rightfully) constrained to exhibit a change in the social-average productive power as a change *within one sector* of production. He (rightfully) *posits no mechanism for generalisations of the productive powers* between sectors. (Anticipating §4, it can already be remarked that would such a mechanism exist, it might perhaps imply an equalisation of compositions of capital?!)

In the absence of such a mechanism and given the value-generating empowerment, Marx's exposition here *implies divergences in rates of surplus-value between sectors*. These stem from diverging technical changes, a factor independent of the intensity of labour, even if the two can be combined – as Marx indicates.[17]

3.2   *The new matter about technique related empowerment of labour: comparison with 1861–63 and 1864 manuscripts*

All the evidence that we have establishes that Marx developed his insights regarding the "empowerment of labour" related to technique only in 1866–67 when he worked on the final draft for the first edition of *Capital I*. Regarding the 1861–63 text this can be checked since we have these texts: MECW 30 and 34 (based on MEGA II/3). Because the 1863–64 penultimate draft for Capital I was blended into the ultimate draft, except for the 1864 *Results* (§1.4, Table 1), the latter might provide a further indication. In this text Marx presents a quite extensive treatment of technical change. Nevertheless, as in the earlier manuscripts, he here treats only the intensity of labour.

3.3   Capital I, *Part Four: return to averages*

In Chapter 17 of Part Five (German edition ch. 15) – synthesising Parts Three and Four – the main focus is again on social averages (this also applies for the next and last chapter of this Part). Given Marx's method in *Capital I* there is nothing wrong with this. For the purposes of this essay I merely record that he continues to make a clear distinction between the intensity and the productive power of labour. Thus he writes that at a given average real-wage rate per "normal working day", the rate of surplus-value depends on:

(1) the length of the working day, or the extensive magnitude of labour, (2) the normal intensity of labour, or its intensive magnitude, whereby a given quantity of labour is expended in a given time and (3) the *pro-

---

17   For more details about the issues of this subsection see Reuten 2017, §3.2–§3.4. [Ch. 15 of the current book.]

ductive power* of labour, whereby the same quantity of labour yields, in a given time, a greater or a smaller quantity of the product, depending on the degree of development attained by the conditions of production. (EBF, p. 655; cf. MEW, p. 542)

Marx emphasises strongly that the three determinants mentioned in this passage are not only variable, but also may occur separately or in several combinations. In what follows this passage, he analyses each of these in turn, in four separate sections. Marx here usually assumes that the determinants have been generalised across the economy, whereas the previous chapters (briefly discussed in §3.1) also treated (the initiation of) changes.

4 Manifestation of value in prices of production (the *Capital III* manuscript for its Part Two)

Capital III presents "The manifestations (*Gestaltungen*) of capitalist production."[18] Engels turned this title of Marx in his manuscript into: "The production process as a whole." In this section I briefly present the third main stage of Marx's conceptualisation of value: the "transformation" of the value of commodities into "prices of production" (Part Two of the book).[19]

4.1 Marx's 1864–65 manuscript for Capital III: prices of production

At the very beginning of Part Two (in the manuscript the full Part is one single chapter), Marx immediately delimits the scope of his theorising about the rate of surplus-value. He writes:

> In this chapter {i.e., Part} we ... assume that the degree of exploitation of labour, i.e., the rate of surplus-value, and the length of the working day, is the same in all the spheres of production .... (Marx 1894, EDF, p. 241).

Below I use the following notation: s = surplus-value; v = the wages sum; s' = the rate of surplus-value (s' = s/v); c = constant capital (means of production used up); c/v = the 'composition of capital' (abbreviated CC); r' = the rate of profit (r' = s(c+v)). Subscripts i and j refer to any sector. Later on I use p for the post-transformation profits.

---

18 Cf. Marx {1864–65 ms} 2016 EBF, p. 47. Fowkes translates *Gestaltungen* as "forms".
19 For further details, comments and page references to the manuscript, see Reuten 2018, §2.

In Ch. 8 Marx sets out the following prepositions, indicating a hypothetical state *prior* to the transformation:

[A] Commodities are sold "at their values".
[B] Rates of surplus-value are equalised. $\quad s'_i = s'_j$
[C] Compositions of capital diverge. $\quad (c/v)_i \neq (c/v)_j$
[D] Hence [A-C] equal capitals produce unequal $\quad [s/(c+v)]_i \neq$
surplus-value or profit. $\quad [s/(c+v)]_j$
Therefore we obtain diverging rates of profit. $\quad r'_i \neq r'_j$
(See *Table 2*, left box: '*Capital I* in apparent hindsight'.)
[E] Yet, in fact, we have (tendentially) equalised profit $\quad r'_i = r'_j$
rates.

Hence this set of presuppositions [A–E] is incompatible. At least one of these must be wrong.

In Ch. 9 Marx introduces the new concept of 'production price', which is predicated on preposition [E]. The production price is a "transformation of value". Here he sets out three numerical schemes. The first and the second scheme apply presuppositions [A]–[D]. The third scheme applies [B]–[C] and [E] and introduces prices of production. For the sake of brevity, *Table 2* compresses these three schemes to one single and reduced one.

TABLE 2   *Reduced transformation scheme: expressions in money*

	Capital I in apparent hindsight					*Capital III* after transformation				
	c	v	s	c+v+s	r' = s/(c+v)	c	v	distribution ρ	c+v+ρ	π = ρ/(c+v)
low CC	70	30	30	130	30%	70	30	30 − 10	130 − 10	20%
average CC	80	20	20	120	20%	80	20	20	120	20%
high CC	90	10	10	110	10%	90	10	10 + 10	110 + 10	20%
total	240	60	60	360†	20%	240	60	60	360‡	20%

† values
‡ prices of production

Thus Marx drops sales at value (presupposition A), introduces production prices instead, and thereby gets rid of diverging profit rates (presupposition D). He does this with hardly any argument. Note that he maintains the *production* of surplus-value, which is now redistributed as profits p.

However, presupposition [A] is not abandoned altogether. Marx posits two aggregate equalities: that of aggregate surplus-value and profits, and that of aggregate values and production prices (see the bottom row of Table 2).

For Marx's exposition in Ch. 10 of how this transformation actually comes about as a process, I refer to Reuten 2018, §2.4. Here I focus on one main aspect of it. Marx writes about the constellation prior to the transformation and the surplus-value *produced* after it:

> [E]quality in the *grade of exploitation of labour* or the *rate of surplus-value* (...) presupposes competition among the workers and an equalisation that takes place by their continuous migration from one sphere of production to another. (Marx {1864–65 ms}1993[1] MEGA, p. 250, my translation; cf. Marx {1864–65 ms} 2016, EBF, p. 286 and Marx 1894, EDF, p. 275)

Thus regarding the rate of surplus-value he has merely the intensity of labour in mind, because only this would be relevant for the migration.

5 Incompatibilities: interpretation versus reconstruction

5.1 *Incompatibilities*

Many commentators of Marx have rightly pointed to the defects of this transformation (Marx was aware of quite a number of them), as well as its incompatibilities with his *Capital I* text. This is not the place to review these defects, and there is not one independent review of the positions that I could refer to. A novice reader of Marx might perhaps start with the now 'classic' Sweezy 1968 [1942], pp. 109–30.

5.2 *A reconstruction*

We have seen that in *Capital I*, after the dynamic account of Part Four, Marx in Part Five returns to the account of average "socially necessary labour time". There is nothing wrong with this. However, when considering different spheres of production as in (the draft for) *Capital III*, these averages are inadequate as the (presumably structural) between-sector deviations from the average are the crux. Marx's inter-sector differing compositions of capital are one part of the relevant matter. The other part regards the differing technique related empowerment of labour, whence rates of surplus-value differ between sectors (§3.1). However, in the *Capital III* draft for Part Two Marx neglects this, which is even more remarkable because in Part Three he directly associates the composition of capital with the productive power of labour.[20] (I write that he 'neglects' it; perhaps he was not yet aware of it – see the following subsection.)

In Reuten 2017 (§4) it is shown that it is not difficult to reconstruct Marx's account of value in *Capital III*, Part Two. In brief: cross out the "*re*distribution" of surplus-value and cross out "prices of production". We have *differing productive powers of labour* between sectors that in equilibrium – because of intra-labour competition regarding the intensity of labour (effort and strain) – reduce to *differing empowerments of labour*. The latter are associated with technique-determined differing compositions of capital. As a result the rates of surplus-value differ between sectors. In equilibrium we have thus equalised rates of profit.

Hence the stylised example of *Table 2* turns simply into that of *Table 3*.

TABLE 3.   '*Capital III*, Part Two, reconstructed in face of *Capital I*: expressions in money

	c	v	s	c+v+s	r' = s/(c+v)	s/v
low cc	70	30	20	120	20%	67%
average cc	80	20	20	120	20%	100%
high cc	90	10	20	120	20%	200%
total	240	60	60	360†	20%	100%‡

† values
‡ average

---

20 In Part Two, Ch. 9, we read: "The specific degree of development of the social *productive power of labour* differs from one particular sphere of production to another, being higher or lower according to the quantity of means of production set in motion by a certain specific amount of labour ... Hence its degree of development depends on how small a quantity of labour is required for a certain quantity of means of production. We therefore call capitals that contain a greater percentage of constant capital than the social average ... capitals of *higher* composition." (EDF, pp. 263–4; cf. MEW, p. 173).

In Part Three, Chapter 13, Marx identifies the productive power of labour even more directly with the composition of capital: "... it has been shown to be a law of the capitalist mode of production that its development does in fact involve a relative decline in the

Thus the core matter is that capitalists are out to raise the accumulation of capital by way of raising the rate of surplus-value via technical change, that is, change of the empowerment of labour associated with the productive powers. This is in line with all of Marx's exposition in *Capital I*.[21]

All along we have the dimension of value as expressed in money. Furthermore, this reconstruction can be directly applied empirically, with two qualifications. Firstly, we have to neglect Marx's "reduction to simple labour" (§2.1 above, under *d*). As indicated, Marx himself never returned to this matter – and it also plays no role in his transformation to prices of production. Secondly, the distinction between the intensity and the empowerment of labour is important, but the intensity of labour is very difficult to measure in an operational way, and especially so between sectors. Thus I assume (as does Marx) that in the *long* run it is levelled out between sectors. (I am not saying that the intensity of labour should be neglected, it is an important field for empirical research.)

5.3   *Philological puzzles*

The final point regards the question why Marx, as well as Marxian political economists working in his tradition, never came up with the simple reconstruction set out above.

It seems that – as indicated in §3.2 – the technique determined empowerment of labour was only developed by Marx during 1866–67. We might then hypothesise that he left for later the working out of its consequences for his '*Capital III*' draft. (We can be glad that he gave priority to the far more important reproduction schemes of *Capital II*, where we find his foundation of macroeconomics *avant la lettre*.)

---

relation of variable capital to constant, and hence also to the total capital set in motion. (...) This progressive decline ... is identical with the progressively rising organic composition, on average, of the social capital as a whole. It is just another expression for the progressive development of the social *productive power of labour* ..." (EDF, p. 318; cf. MEW, p. 222).

Regarding the productive power of labour (*Produktivkraft der Arbeit*) Fowkes, the translator of the 'Capital III' manuscript, makes the same mistake again (Marx {1864–65 ms} 2016; EBF).

21 In an interesting paper Smith (2002, p. 158) rightfully points out that "innovation trajectories" diverge between sectors and he creatively 'reconstructs' their theorisation in terms of structural "surplus profits from innovation" at the level of *Capital III* – over prices of production. In face of the divergent empowerment of labour associated with productive powers, this can now be theorised in terms of super-profits associated with super rates of surplus-value.

Against this hypothesis weights a letter he wrote to Engels on 30 April 1868. Here he starts out from the presupposition of equalised rates of surplus-value between sectors.[22] Marx apparently continued to have in mind the ideas about the transformation found in the 1861–63 manuscripts, as well as his *Capital I*, Part Five 'return to averages' account. Apparently Marx's mind was fixed on equalising rates of surplus-value.

At least at that time. There is a small manuscript of six pages – published for the first time in 2003 – that dates probably from 1878 (see Vollgraf and Roth with Jungnickel 2003, p. 697). Consider the following two passages:[23]

> *For [the] calculation of the rate of profit that the social capital yields it was assumed* {angenommen}, *1) that the rate of surplus-value* {is} *uniform for the different heaps of capital* {Kapitalmassen} *in different branches of industry, 2) and neglecting turnover, i.e., the turnover of the social capital over the year posited* = *1*. <u>In fact for the different heaps of capital different rates of surplus-value</u> *and different turnover times.* (Marx {1878ms; emphases in italics are Marx's} 2003, p. 158, my translation)

The clarification following it (after seven printed lines on the calibration of turnover times) is very interesting. Note Marx's usage of the term pure (*rein*) which he reserves for law-like entities.

> These are just differences {Differenzen} emerging from the pure economic conditions, namely *different* {verschiedne} *magnitudes of the capitals invested in business sectors*, <u>*different rates of exploitation of labour-power*</u>, *different turnover times*. However [there are] other aspects of the equalisation such as unattractiveness, danger and standing of the work. (Marx {1878ms} 2003, p. 158, my translation)[24]

---

22 In this letter Marx sets out his transformation of value to prices of production in about 50 printed lines, including the following key phrases: "... assuming *the rate of surplus value*, i.e., the exploitation of labour, as *equal*, the production of value and therefore the production of surplus value and therefore the *rate of profit* are *different* in different branches of production. ... this means that the *price determination* of the commodities must *deviate* from their *values*. ... The price ... which divides up the social surplus value equally among the various masses of capital in proportion to their sizes, is the *price of production* of commodities, the centre around which the oscillation of the market prices moves" (MECW 43, pp. 23–4).

23 It is extremely difficult to translate these texts. Marx's texts are unpolished and continuously mixed with shorthand phrases. Insertions in square brackets are from the MEGA editors. Insertions in braces with German original terms are mine.

24 A few more comments are in Reuten 2009, pp. 227–8, from which the text above is taken. [Chapter 14 below.]

As for the 1864–65 *Capital III* manuscript or the 1868 letter, this text cannot be taken as definitive. The greatness of Marx was that for him nothing was definitive (see §1.5). This is what I have learnt, and what all interpreters of Marx could learn from him.

Summary

In the methodological stages approach of Marx, he starts in chapter 1 of *Capital I* with a static and averages conceptualisation of the value of commodities. Positing a distinction between the use-value and the value of commodities, and abstracting from the concrete aspect of labour creating use-value, the remaining aspect of qualitatively homogeneous value is determined by qualitatively homogenous social average labour – the quantity of commodities' value being determined by the amount of time this social average labour is used for their production. Marx arrives at this in the first two sections of the chapter, where he also specifies the determinants he posits as constant in this (what I have called 'static') approach. These are the intensity of labour and the empowerment of labour – the latter itself being determined by the "productive power of labour" which includes technology and techniques. In the last two sections of the chapter, and continuing in chapters 2 and 3, he derives the exchange-value of commodities, the concept of money, and finally money as the measure of value in practice (§2).

In Part Four of *Capital I* Marx gets to what I have called the 'dynamics' of his conceptualisation of value. Here he considers changes and variations between sectors of production of, first, the intensity of labour and, secondly, the "productive powers" determined empowerment of labour. Each one of these implies, firstly, that a clock-time measure of labour-time is an insufficient measure of the immanent value of commodities and, secondly that the rates of surplus-value diverge between sectors of production (initially also within sectors of production). A specific, though most important, point is that he posits no mechanism for between sector generalisations of the productive powers – hence neither for the empowerment of labour. In Part Five Marx returns to the averages account. I indicated that all the information that we have establishes that Marx developed his insights regarding the technique related 'empowerment of labour' only in 1866–67, when he worked on the final draft for the first edition of *Capital I*. This applies for Part Four as well as for Part One (§3).

In §4 I very briefly summarised Marx's transformation of values into prices of production, as written in 1864–65. In face of the foregoing sections the most important point is that Marx keeps here the rates of surplus-value as equalised between sectors of production. In fact *this* is what made him construct the prices of production framework (given the rather evident diverging compositions of capital and equalising rates of profit).

Section 4 concluded that Marx's *Capital I* and the 'Capital III' manuscript views are incompatible (unless we would assume equalising productive powers and compositions of capital across sectors – which is contrary to all the empirical evidence that we have hitherto). On basis of *Capital I* Part Four, however, a most simple reconstruction is obvious: erase the 1864–65 equalised rates of surplus-value and erase its prices of production.

Given that Marx was a continuous critic of Marx (§1), it is proper – as an interpretation – to give dominant weight to his last version of *Capital I*, and his last brief manuscript on the matter of 1878 in which he seems to widen his perspective towards sector-wise diverging rates of surplus-value. However, for those that would not want to swallow this brief manuscript, I propose the reconstruction indicated without that manuscript. In this way the whole of *Capital* makes sense – that is within its constraints.

References

A General references to Marx's and Engels's works

MECW (*Marx Engels Collective Works*). http://hiaw.org/defcon6/works/cw/index.html
MEGA (*Marx-Engels-Gesamtausgabe*). https://mega.bbaw.de/de/struktur/ii-abteilung
MEW (*Marx-Engels Werke*). https://marx-wirklich-studieren.net/marx-engels-werke-als-pdf-zum-download/
MIA (*Marx-Engels Archive*). https://www.marxists.org/archive/marx/index.htm
Regarding the *Marx-Engels Gesamtausgabe* (MEGA), the first number in Roman refers to the division of the MEGA (in the current article this is always division II, on *Capital* and the preparations for it); the second number in Arabic refers to the volume number (some volumes are again subdivided, in which case we have, e.g., MEGA II/4.2, where the last digit is the subdivision). There is also an earlier German collective works series around (the *Marx-Engels Werke*, MEW, which is fully available online). Quite a number of these works (not all of the MEGA) are available in English translation as the *Marx Engels Collective Works* (MECW).

B All other references

General note. Superscripts after a year of publication refer to the edition of a work. For references to Marx the date in braces indicates the (probable) year of the manuscript, the year following it is the first year of publication.

Bellofiore, Riccardo 2005, 'The monetary aspects of the capitalist process in the Marxian system: an investigation from the point of view of the theory of the monetary circuit', in *Marx's theory of money: modern appraisals*, edited by Fred Moseley, London: Palgrave Macmillan, pp. 124–39.

Campbell, Martha 1997, 'Marx's theory of money: a defense', in *New investigations of Marx's method*, edited by Fred Moseley and Martha Campbell, Albany, NJ: Humanities Press, pp. 89–120.

Elson, Diane 1979, 'The value theory of labour', in *Value: the representation of labour in capitalism*, edited by Diane Elson, London: CSE Books, pp. 115–80.

Hubmann, Gerald, and Regina Roth 2013, 'Die "Kapital"-Abteilung der MEGA – Einleitung und Überblick', in *Marx-Engels Jahrbuch 2012/13*, Berlin: Akademie Verlag, pp. 60–9.

Marx, Karl {1864 ms}[1933^1] MEGA. 'Resultate des unmittelbaren Produktionsprozesses'.[25] In *Ökonomische Manuskripte 1863–1867, Teil 1.* (Manuskripte 1864/65 zum 1. und 2. Buch des „Kapital"). *MEGA II/4.2*:24–131.

Marx, Karl {1864 ms}[1933^1] MECW. 'Results of the direct production process'. Translation of Marx {1864 ms}[1933^1] MEGA by Ben Fowkes. *MECW* Vol. 34:355–466.

Marx, Karl {1864–65 ms}1993^1 MEGA. *Ökonomische Manuskripte 1863–1867, Teil 2: Manuskript 1863/65 zum 3. Buch des „Kapital"*, arranged and edited by Manfred Müller, Jürgen Jungnickel, Barbara Lietz, Christel Sander and Arthur Schnickmann. *MEGA II/4.2*, Berlin: Dietz Verlag.

Marx, Karl {1864–65 ms} 2016 EBF. *Marx's economic manuscript of 1864–1865*. Translation of Marx {1864–65 ms}1993 MEGA by Ben Fowkes, edited by Fred Moseley, Leiden: Brill.

Marx, Karl {1878 ms} 2003^1 MEGA. 'Über Profitrate, Kapitalumschlag, Zins und Rabat'.[26] Edited by Carl-Erich Vollgraf and Regina Roth with collaboration of Jürgen Jungnickel, in *MEGA II/14*, Berlin: Akademie Verlag, pp. 155–62.

Marx, Karl 1890^4 [1867^1] MEW. *Das Kapital, Kritik der Politischen Ökonomie; Erster Band, Der Produktionsprozeß des Kapitals*, 4th edition, edited by Friedrich Engels, MEW, Volume 23, Berlin: Dietz Verlag.

Marx, Karl 1890^4 [1867^1] EBF. *Capital: a critique of political economy, vol. I*. Translation of Marx 1890^4 MEW by Ben Fowkes, Harmondsworth: Penguin Books, 1976.

Marx, Karl 1893^2 [1885^1] EBF. *Das Kapital, Kritik der Politischen Ökonomie, Zweiter Band, Der Zirkulationsprozess des Kapitals*. Edited by Friedrich Engels, MEW, Vol. 24, Berlin: Dietz Verlag. Referred to in the translation by David Fernbach, *Capital: a critique of political economy, volume II*, Harmondsworth: Penguin Books, 1978.

---

25   First published in German and Russian in *Arkhiv Marksa i Engelsa*, vol. II (VII), Moscow 1933.
26   On the rate of profit, turnover of capital, interest and discount.

Marx, Karl 1894 MEW. *Das Kapital. Kritik der politischen Ökonomie. Dritter Band, Der Gesamtprozeß der kapitalistischen Produktion.* Edited by Friedrich Engels, MEW Volume 25, Berlin: Dietz Verlag.

Marx, Karl 1894 EDF. *Capital: a critique of political economy, volume III.* Translation of Marx 1894 MEW by David Fernbach, Harmondsworth: Penguin Books, 1981.

Reuten, Geert 1993, 'The difficult labour of a theory of social value: metaphors and systematic dialectics at the beginning of Marx's *Capital*', in *Marx's method in Capital: a re-examination*, edited by Fred Moseley, Atlantic Highlands, NJ: Humanities Press, pp. 89–113.[27]

Reuten, Geert 2004, 'Productive force and the degree of intensity of labour – Marx's concepts and formalizations in the middle part of *Capital I*', in *The constitution of capital: essays on volume I of Marx's 'Capital'*, edited by Riccardo Bellofiore and Nicola Taylor, London: Palgrave Macmillan, pp. 117–45.

Reuten, Geert 2009, 'Marx's general rate of profit transformation: methodological, theoretical and philological obstacles – an appraisal based on the 1864–65 manuscript of *Das Kapital III*', in *Re-reading Marx: new perspectives after the critical edition*, edited by Riccardo Bellofiore and Roberto Fineschi, London: Palgrave Macmillan, pp. 211–30.

Reuten, Geert 2017, 'The productive powers of labour and the redundant transformation to prices of production: a Marx-immanent critique and reconstruction', *Historical Materialism*, 25(3): 3–35.

Reuten, Geert 2018, 'The redundant transformation to prices of production: a Marx-immanent critique and reconstruction', in *Marx's 'Capital': an unfinished and unfinishable project?*, edited by Marcel van der Linden and Gerald Hubmann, Leiden: Brill, pp. 157–94.

Schefold, Bertram 2004, 'Einführung zu MEGA II/15', in *Das Kapital, Kritik der politischen Ökonomie, Dritter Band*, MEGA II/15, pp. 871–910.

Smith, Tony 2002, 'Surplus profits from innovation: a missing level in *Capital III*?', in *The culmination of capital: essays on volume III of Marx's 'Capital'*, edited by Martha Campbell and Geert Reuten, London: Palgrave Macmillan, pp. 149–73.

Sweezy, Paul M. 1968 [1942], *The theory of capitalist development*, New York: Modern Reader Paperbacks.

Vollgraf, Carl-Erich 2012, 'Einführung zu MEGA II/4.3', in *MEGA* II/4.3, pp. 421–74.

Vollgraf, Carl-Erich 2018, 'Marx's further work on *Capital* after publishing volume 1: on the completion of Part II of the MEGA²', in *Marx's 'Capital': an unfinished and unfinishable project?*, edited by Marcel van der Linden and Gerald Hubmann, Leiden: Brill, pp. 56–79.

---

27 For internet access to the publications of Reuten, see http://reuten.eu (type the year of publication in the search box).

Vollgraf, Carl-Erich, and Regina Roth (with collaboration of Jürgen Jungnickel) 2003, 'Introduction, contextualization, and notes on the genesis and handing down of the MEGA II/14 texts', in *MEGA II/14*: 381–489, Berlin: Akademie Verlag, pp. 56–79.

Williams, Michael 2000, 'Why Marx neither has nor needs a commodity theory of money', *Review of Political Economy*, 12(4): 435–51.

CHAPTER 3

Dialectical Method

1998 article, originally published in *The handbook of economic methodology*, edited by John Davis, Wade Hands and Uskali Mäki, Cheltenham: Edward Elgar, pp. 103–7.
(For its abstract see the Abstracts of all chapters, p. 2.)

∴

Of the main philosophical traditions, the dialectical has been only modestly influential in the economics methodology. With few exceptions, the applications of dialectics to economics are restricted to scholars who have in some way been influenced by the work of Marx (1818–1883). There is, however, no *a priori* reason why a dialectical method should be restricted to a Marxian orientation.

The dialectical method, in the modern sense, derives from the work of Hegel (1770–1831) who aimed at critically synthesising rationalism and empiricism. Both rationalism and empiricism conceive the world in terms of a subject–object or thought–reality dualism, and both reduce the foundation of knowledge to one of these poles. Hegel's project was to transcend the one-sidedness of these philosophies; that is, to overcome them without losing sight of them. This aim Hegel shares with Kant (1724–1804). However, the latter's philosophy is considered insufficient, in that it does not overcome dualism: it separates the form from the content of knowledge, it poses a conceptual apriorism and it postulates a 'thing in itself' which we cannot know.

Today, dialectics is in fact a family name for a variety of strands, as are rationalism and empiricism. Two main strands are *historical dialectic* and *systematic dialectic*. The first applies to the study of society and its philosophy, arts and science – or, more specifically, an economy and its economics – in their historical emergence. Popular accounts of dialectics often stress this first strand, owing to the two circumstances that Marx is often introduced by way of an historical materialist view of society (see the entry 'Marx's Method'),[1] Hegel by way of his work on the philosophy of history (Hegel 1837). (Note that this dialectic also figures prominently in Popper's depiction of Hegel and Marx.) In what follows I emphasise the systematic dialectics. The primary sources for this dialectic are

---

1 This refers to an entry in the Handbook in which the current article appeared. [Ch. 4 below.]

Hegel's two works on logic (see particularly Hegel 1817). Below I merely highlight a few elements of it in so far as they relate to some of the problems that face the mainstream philosophy of economics.

I start by outlining an economic example, so as to bring to the fore some of the issues that systematic dialectics aims to deal with. Consider a simple model of investment (I), which is dependent on consumption (C), the money supply (M) and government expenditure on education (G). So we have $I = aC + bM + cG$. Suppose that the model is made operational, and particular values for the parameters a, b and c are estimated. A relevant question would then be: are these variables equally 'important'? In the usual economic models approach this would be answered by pointing out their *quantitative* difference, by the size of the variables times their parameters. But a prior question is: can a *qualitative* order of significance be assigned to these variables? Then at least one such ascription would be in terms of their *necessity* or their *contingency* with respect to the economic system that we are theorising. Suppose that qualitative analysis has shown that both consumption and banking are necessary to investment – that is, they are a condition of the existence of investment – whereas we could still have investment without government expenditure on education. Then the latter's qualitative importance would not be reflected in its quantitative significance. Although the government expenditure may thus quantitatively codetermine the level of investment, the question would be: to what extent does this determine the *concept* of investment – that is, what investment *is* conceived as something that is systematically interconnected with other phenomena?

Although these and similar questions seem very relevant to our theorising as regards the economy and society, they appear difficult to answer within the discourse of a mainstream economics framework. The main problem is that, in contradistinction to systematic dialectics, it lacks a systemic hierarchy of determinations. More specifically, first, it lacks systematically related conceptual layers or levels of abstraction: once defined within an argument, a concept retains its meaning – it is fixed and cannot be developed (although concepts may change over the history of a discourse). For the dialectician, on the other hand, definitions are merely useful as an initial starting point; processes of reconceptualisation are the kernel of a dialectical argument. Second, it lacks the notion of a system as determined by interconnected *necessary* entities, as opposed to merely contingent aspects, that is, necessary to the very existence of the system as a self-reproducing entity as a whole. Indeed, one aim of dialectical research is to differentiate the necessary from the contingent. Here the notions of 'system' and 'whole' depend much on our perspective. While the aim is to widen the perspective from all possible angles – that is, those necessary to the object of inquiry – we may still want to restrict the analysis *pro tempore* to more narrow points of view (the jargon for which is 'a moment'), as long as we are *explicitly* aware of the ties of these to greater wholes. (Cf. Ollman 1993.)

In general, a systematic-dialectical presentation (*Darstellung*) can be characterised as a movement from an abstract-universal starting point to the concrete-empirical, gradually concretising the starting point in successive stages, thus ultimately aiming to grasp the empirical phenomena in their systemic interconnectedness. We cannot fruitfully proceed from the starting point by immediately subsuming single empirical phenomena – things, human relations, processes and so on – as particulars under this universal since this provides merely empty truth. Such subsumption might indicate what these phenomena have in common, but not what, if anything, *unites* them systemically: how they are interconnected. Further, it is the *difference* between phenomena which determines them; but this difference also fails to say what, if anything, unites them systemically. As long as we have not specified both differentiation and unification of related phenomena, we have provided no concrete determination. It is this double determination (*difference in unity*) that systematic dialectics seeks. As Hegel expresses it, "The truth of the differentiated is its being in unity. And only through this movement is the unity truly concrete." At the starting point: "difference is still sunk in the unity, not yet set forth as different" (Hegel 1833, p. 83). I will briefly expand on the starting point and the way to proceed from it.

For any dialectical presentation the starting point, or point of entry, is crucial (as it is for any theory). The starting point of its presentation is a universal, all-embracing abstract concept which is proposed as rendering the comprehension of the object totality (in Hegel's *Logic*, the ubiquitous starting point is "being"). Such an all-embracing concept seems in a way hopelessly true (everything is a being). So why seek more when we have the all-embracing concept in our hand? Notwithstanding that we have posited a putatively all-embracing concept, we clearly need to seek more concrete content.

Further reflection reveals that such a concept does not represent the truth in its full, mundane richness. Remaining at the same all-embracing *level* of abstraction ('flatly', as in a conventional economic model), the category from which we started is seen to contain its *negation* or its opposite, a category contrary to it ("nothing" at the beginning of Hegel's *Logic*). But this differing contrast is equally hopelessly omnipotent and true: insufficient. This apparent negative result may have a positive outcome if we find a category uniting as well as concretising both of our earlier concepts ("becoming" at the beginning of Hegel's *Logic*).

In either case (negation and concretisation) opposed concepts are applied to the *same* entity, and in this specific sense Hegel calls these opposites 'contradictions'. It is the purpose of the dialectical presentation to resolve the contradiction (opposition) from which we start ("the essence of philosophy consists precisely in resolving the contradiction of the Understanding" – Hegel 1833, p. 71).

Next to the differentiation of the systemically necessary from the contingent, negation and concretisation are two important principles that drive the dialectical presentation forward towards ever more empirically concrete levels so as to arrive at the concrete comprehension of the object of inquiry. Thus the presentation moves forward by the transcendence of contradiction and by providing the ever more concrete *grounds* – the conditions of existence – of the earlier determination. This forward movement does not ignore the earlier determination, rather, it overcomes the opposite moments (identity–difference, universal–particular) of the earlier determination, so as to posit them at a conceptually more concrete level: the ground provides the unity of the opposed moments. But, at the same time, that is a further, more concrete determination of the *difference*, a difference previously posited only in itself (*an sich*, potentially, implicitly) as it now appears. So the differences that were previously not set forth as such now come into existence (that is, a more concrete existence, yet still abstract in the sense of not being fully developed). The ground at this new level itself then gains momentum; it is itself an abstract existent showing the contradiction that it cannot exist for itself (*für sich*, actually), whence the presentation has to move on in order to ground it in its turn, so as to provide *its* conditions of existence (Hegel 1817, §120–4; 1833, pp. 81–3). And so on, until the presentation claims to have reached the stage where it comprehends the existent as actual, as actuality (*Wirklichkeit*), in the sense that its conditions of existence have now been determined such that it is indeed actual, concrete, self-sufficient or endogenous existence, which requires no external or exogenous determinants for its systemic reproduction. (Note that, in many mainstream economic models, some of the essential determinants are treated as exogenous.)

By having reconstituted the empirical 'facts' which were at the base of the initial inquiry, the dialectical presentation then is a conceptualisation of the concrete in successive steps (levels of abstraction) ultimately gaining full comprehension. If successful, the presentation is able to grasp the concrete as an interconnected self-sufficient system (and ideally it is also a self-determining system).

Returning to our earlier economic model example, one category of mainstream economic models ('rationalist') is indeed devised for conceptual exploration. However, the aim here is the exploration of the implications of (axiomatic) definitions: they are not devised for an internal conceptually layered *development*, even less so in the perspective of systemic necessity (interconnection) or contingency. The other category of models ('empirical') is generally not devised to set up an empirically concrete self-sufficient system. The 'endogeneity' or the 'exogeneity' of variables does not pertain to their systemic necessity or contingency.

This article ends with a few remarks on a controversial issue: Hegel's idealism (see for example, Norman 1976, ch. 6; Forster 1993). It was said at the beginning of this article that Hegel's dialectic aims to transcend the subject–object dualism of both rationalism and empiricism. Dualisms and oppositions, consequently, play a major role in his dialectic. Hegel often refers to dualisms and oppositions in terms of contradictions.

From the point of view of mainstream methodology (rationalist or empiricist), it is tempting either to see Hegel advancing a rationalist logic or to see him describing oppositions in empirical reality. From the point of view of rationalism, it is the interdependence of opposed concepts (such as buyer and seller, or truth and error) that is highlighted: they necessarily form a unity in the sense that one concept can have no existence without the other (the concept of buyer just by itself would then be a contradiction). From the point of view of empiricism, real entities in conflict are characterised by interdependent opposed concepts (master–slave, bourgeoisie–proletariat); again, the one entity can have no real existence without the other (when there are no subjects, there are no kings). Even if (one of) these two senses of opposition may make sense to many, Hegel holds that the two can be shown to be the same: the activity of consciousness posits the object of knowledge *as* an object of knowledge. Since he develops this insight from the Idea as a union of subjectivity and objectivity, his philosophy is termed 'Absolute Idealism'.

Reader's guide. Hegel (1817) is the primary source for systematic dialectics: most difficult, yet most fruitful. Hegel (1812) covers the same structure in more detail. Hegel (1833) is a somewhat easier primary source; pages 53–86 of the English translation provide a nice gist of Hegel's logic. Norman (1976) provides a lucid critical introduction to Hegel's thought in 125 pages (recommended). Forster (1993) introduces Hegel's method in 40 pages. Ollman (1993) is a lucid account of how the dialectical method may be deployed in practice, first at an introductory and then at a more advanced level. The book finishes with a number of illuminating case studies. Reuten and Williams (1989), Part One, pp. 3–49, sets out a systematic-dialectical method; the other parts apply this to the capitalist economy, state and economic policy. Smith (1990) provides a systematic-dialectical account of Marx's *Capital*; Chapter 1 gives a good outline of Hegel's dialectical method; Chapter 3 sets out Hegelian, objections to Marx's *Capital*.

References

Forster, Michael 1993, 'Hegel's dialectical method', in F.C. Beiser (ed.), *The Cambridge companion to Hegel*, Cambridge: Cambridge University Press.

Hegel, G.W.F. 1812, *Wissenschaft der Logik*, Engl. transl. (1969) of the 1923 Lasson edition, A.V. Miller, *Hegel's science of logic*, Atlantic Highlands, NJ: Humanities Press, 1989.

Hegel, G.W.F. 1817, *Enzyklopädie der Philosophischen Wissenschaften im Grundrisse I, Die Wissenschaft der Logik*, Engl. transl. of the third edition (of 1830), T.F. Geraets, W.A. Suchting and H.S. Harris, *The encyclopaedia of logic*, Indianapolis: Hackett Publishing Company, 1991.

Hegel, G.W.F. 1833, *Einleitung in die Geschichte der Philosophie*, ed. J. Hoffmeister, 1940; Engl. transl. T.M. Knox and A.V. Miller, *Introduction to the lectures on the history of philosophy*, Oxford: Clarendon Press, 1985.

Hegel, G.W.F. 1837, *Vorlesungen über die Philosophie der Geschichte*, 3rd edn., ed. J. Hoffmeister, 1955; Engl. transl. selections, H.B. Nisbet (1975), *Lectures on the philosophy of world history, introduction: reason in history*, Cambridge: Cambridge University Press, 1984.

Norman, Richard 1976, *Hegel's Phenomenology: a philosophical introduction*, Atlantic Highlands, NJ: Humanities Press.

Ollman, Bertell 1993, *Dialectical investigations*, London: Routledge.

Reuten, Geert, and Michael Williams 1989, *Value-form and the state; the tendencies of accumulation and the determination of economic policy in capitalist society*, London: Routledge.

Smith, Tony 1990, *The logic of Marx's Capital: replies to Hegelian criticisms*, Albany: State University of New York Press.

CHAPTER 4

Marx's Method

1998 article, originally published in *The handbook of economic methodology*, edited by John Davis, D. Wade Hands, and Uskali Mäki, Cheltenham: Edward Elgar, pp. 283–7.
(For its abstract see the Abstracts of all chapters, p. 2)

⁞

Karl Marx (1818–1883) was not only an economist but also a sociologist, philosopher and political activist. Although he is perhaps best known for a political pamphlet, *The Communist Manifesto*, written in 1848 jointly with Friedrich Engels, his main scientific work is an economic analysis of capitalism, as laid down in *Das Kapital*, a treatise of 2200 pages in three volumes (1867, 1885, 1894 – the latter two posthumously edited by Engels). The method of the latter work will be the main focus of this article.

Marx's *Capital* is an investigation of the characteristic form of the capitalist mode of production. It proceeds by presenting a movement from abstract to concrete (complex) categories. Starting with an analysis of the commodity, exchange and money, he develops the social forms of capital and capitalist production, showing how these are reproduced by definite social relations (Volume I). Having constituted capital as a social form distinct to this mode of production he traces its internal structure of circulation and reproduction (Volume II), and moves on to the dynamics of the market and production, the connection between the industrial and the financial system and distribution (Volume III). What is the method adopted by Marx in this presentation?

Before explicating key terms such as 'mode of production', 'social form' and 'abstract–concrete', let us first consider Marx's view on the study of history: 'historical materialism'. A brief pronouncement of it is to be found in the Preface to his *Critique of Political Economy* (1859), where Marx states that legal relations and political institutions are to be comprehended from "the material conditions of life", and that the "anatomy" of the latter "has to be sought in political economy". Thus

> in the social production of their existence, men inevitably enter into definite relations, which are independent of their will, namely relations of production appropriate to a given stage in the development of their

material forces of production. The totality of these relations of production constitutes the economic structure of society, the real foundation, on which arises a legal and political superstructure and to which correspond definite forms of social consciousness. The mode of production of material life conditions the general process of social, political and intellectual life. (Marx 1859, pp. 20–1)

If we turn to Marx's main work, *Capital*, the text quoted above seems hardly helpful. We can see *why* Marx undertook the study of "the economic structure" of capitalist society, but not *how*. However, from Marx's writings, especially the critiques of his political economic predecessors, three main methodological principles can be discerned. First is the difference between general and determinate categories, the former applying to societies – or more particularly, to productive activity – generally, the latter to historically specific "modes" or "social forms" of production (Murray 1988, ch. 10). Thus capitalism is regarded as a particular social form of production with specific determinate categories applicable to it. In this context Marx criticises, for example, Smith and Ricardo for applying determinate 'capitalist' economic categories to other (previous) social formations, thus muddling the understanding of their specificity. The concept of 'social form' is indeed a key to Marx's work. In capitalism, human labour and its products necessarily take the 'value-form' (money), and this form begets so much a life of its own that it dominates the content (even if the latter – labour, production, the product – remains a necessity). The form, money, has become the subject and object of this mode of production. From this springs Marx's famous account of alienation and money-fetishism: human relations have become (like) relations between things (*Capital I*, ch. 1; also *Economico-philosophical Manuscripts of 1844*).

This takes us to the second methodological principle: immanent exposition and critique. Whereas 'mere criticism' takes some prescriptivist stand, external to the object of inquiry, an immanent critique takes its stand from within the object of inquiry, showing its internal inconsistencies and contradictions. This 'method of critique' considers that its object of inquiry is reflexive; it conceives that what is investigated is already a social reality which has its own self-interpretation. Marx's *Capital*, then, is an immanent exposition and critique of a social reality (capitalism) as well as of the theoretical expression of capitalist social relations in the discourse of political economy. This aspect of Marx's method, brilliantly set out by Benhabib (1986, chs. 1–4), is indicated in the subtitle of *Capital*, *"A critique of political economy"*, as well as by the appearance of the term 'critique' in many other titles of Marx's writings.

A third methodological principle is the requirement for a hierarchy of determinations within the set of determinate categories, although this also applies to those general categories that remain at work along the determinate ones. Since in Marx's presentation the capitalist mode of production is shown to be an organic unity, "knowledge of it must take the form of a *system* of related categories rather than a series of discrete investigations" (Arthur 1992, x; cf. Marx's Introduction, 1953). More specifically Marx sets out, as already indicated, a system of categories layered from abstract to concrete and complex. Thus in the course of *Capital* we are gradually led into ever more concrete levels of abstraction, each made explicit by a conceptual 'transformation' (*Verwandlung*). The famous value-price transformation (conversion) is merely one of many; whilst one can apply quantitative operations *at* some definite level of abstraction, some scholars doubt if it makes sense at all to apply them *between* levels of abstraction: see, for example, Smith 1990, pp. 169–71.

Most commentators agree that Marx's method in *Capital* is indeed a movement in stages from abstract to concrete categories. There is, however, disagreement on the status of each of the levels, as well as on the mode of progression from one level to the other. For a long time the method has been looked upon as a logical-historical approach (an interpretation propagated by Engels), or as a method of successive approximation where one starts with simplifying assumptions that are gradually being dropped (propagated by Sweezy 1968 [1942]). Other interpretations have focused on the particular dialectic adopted by Marx (see, for example, the contributions and references in Moseley 1993; Moseley and Campbell 1997; Arthur and Reuten 1998; Norman and Sayers 1980) and which some argue to be a 'systematic dialectic'. The former two interpretations do not deny Marx adopting a dialectic; it is, however, de-emphasised in their accounts.

Anyway, it should be stressed that the presentation in *Capital* is not a deductive argument, nor does the movement from abstract to concrete mean that the former is non-empirical. Indeed, Volume III seems to get to an empirical level – as it is commonly understood – and mainstream economists therefore have always felt more at ease commenting on this rather than the earlier two volumes. However, the 'abstract' Volume I is loaded with often very detailed empirical descriptions and references to statistical reports. How are we to account for this?

Consider the abstract categories of *Capital I* that refer to relations *within* a historically determinate mode of production, that is, the capitalist. Take for example 'surplus-value'. Then the *phenomenal empirical* expressions of such a category may be visible (for example, struggle over the length of the working day), to the extent that the *categorical* development to the concrete is a simple expression of that abstract category; not, however, to the extent that the categorical development is a complex one, especially where the totality of the system inverts its appearances (as with interest or 'productivity of capital') or reverses its dynamic (as in the case of tendencies and countertendencies). The empirical references at each stage, then, must be carefully selected accordingly. Now of course, at first sight, this seems to have a circular flavour (note, though, that such empirical references are not meant to be a proof: they are, at that stage, illustrations). However, and this is the important point, for Marx it is, at any stage, the apparent *insufficiency* in comprehending more complex empirical phenomena that must drive the presentation forward to the more complex concrete categories. But cannot we then dispense with the abstract categories once we have reached their concretisation? No, the point is that the concrete categories derive meaning from their *interconnection* with the abstract categories, their "inner structure". At the end of the movement from abstract to concrete, "the concrete is concrete because it is the concentration of many determinants". (These issues are elaborated upon in Marx's Introduction to the *Grundrisse*, 1953, written in 1857, from which the last sentence has been quoted.)

Regarding Marx's method there are, as indicated, three strands of interpretation, and the extent to which Marx may be considered an heir of Hegel's dialectic has always been controversial. Two factors have contributed to this controversy. The first is the order of and delay in the appearance in print of Marx's work, both in the original German and in English translation. For brevity, I will merely give two examples. In 1932, two philosophically and anthropologically important works of Marx appeared in German: *The German Ideology* (with Engels) and the *Economico-philosophical Manuscripts* of 1844 (English translation 1938–63). A key 1857–58 manuscript, the *Grundrisse*, drafting *Capital* in a rather dialectical style, received its full German publication in 1953 and its English version only in 1973 (its Introduction had appeared in a German journal in 1903). Thus several times a new Marx seems to be on the stage, and in particular the 1932 and 1953 works quite changed the dialectical interpretation.

The second factor is that, throughout his writings over a period of 40 years, Marx was not consistent in his appreciation of Hegel's dialectic (he in fact reread some of Hegel's work several times). For some authors (for example, Althusser 1965) there appears to be "an epistemological break" in Marx's work: later on in his life he is supposed to have taken a radical break from the human, anthropological and Hegelian orientation of his youth. Arthur (1986) convincingly argues for a continuity both in terms of method and general problematic of the research programme. With this, Arthur does not deny Marx's radical critique of Hegel. As Murray (1988, p. 221) expresses it in an important study of Marx's method, "Hegel was Marx's chief mentor and antagonist". Whereas Murray de-emphasises the Hegelian dialectic for Marx's method (similarly, for example, Mattick 1993), Tony Smith (1990) in a most original contribution has shown how the whole of *Capital* can be read as a systematic dialectic (see the entry, 'Dialectical Method').[1] Still others take the position that *Capital* provides important systematic-dialectical and form-theoretical outlines that need, however, reconstruction and further development (Backhaus 1969; Reuten and Williams 1989; Arthur 1993; Reuten 1995).

This takes us, finally, into the issue that Marx's method and theory cannot be equated with Marxian method and Marxian theory. Marx laid the foundations for a particular tradition of several methodological styles of research. However much these styles may diverge, they have in common the three general methodological characteristics set out earlier on: (1) the difference between general and historically determinate categories, (2) the method of immanent exposition and critique, and (3) setting out a system of determinate interconnected layers of categories for concretely grasping empirical reality. For better or worse, this distinguishes the Marxian tradition from mainstream approaches to methodology.

Reader's guide. Marx's texts on method have been collected in Carver (1975). Marx's method must, of course, be judged from his own work. The first chapters of Capital especially are difficult, but they are essential to the appreciation of the method. Arthur (1992) provides in 15 pages a good and accessible introduction to the work, emphasising various methodological aspects. Some recent methodological assessments are in the collections edited by Moseley (1993), Bellofiore (1998), Moseley and Campbell (1997), and Arthur and Reuten (1998); earlier ones are Mepham and Ruben (1979) and Schmidt (1969), the latter with by now 'classical' contributions from, for example, Backhaus, Iljenkow and Zelený. Bonefeld et al. (1992) extends from Marx to recent Marxian theory.

References

Althusser, Louis, and Etienne Balibar 1965, *Lire le Capital*, vols. I and II, Paris: Maspero; Engl. transl. Ben Brewster, *Reading Capital*, London: New Left Books, 1970.

Arthur, Christopher J. 1986, *Dialectics of labour: Marx and his relation to Hegel*, Oxford: Basil Blackwell.

---

[1] This refers to an entry in the Handbook in which the current article appeared – see ch. 4 above.

Arthur, Christopher J. 1992, 'Introduction', in C.J. Arthur (ed.), *Marx's Capital: a student edition*, London: Lawrence & Wishart.
Arthur, Christopher J. 1993, 'Hegel's *Logic* and Marx's *Capital*', in F. Moseley (ed.), *Marx's method in 'Capital'*, Atlantic Highlands, NJ: Humanities Press.
Arthur, Christopher J., and Geert Reuten (eds) 1998, *The circulation of capital: essays on volume two of Marx's 'Capital'*, London: Macmillan.
Backhaus, Hans-Georg 1969, 'Zur Dialektik der Wertform', in A. Schmidt (ed.), *Beiträge zur marxistischen Erkenntnistheorie*; Engl. transl. M. Eldred and M. Roth 1980, 'On the dialectics of the value-form', *Thesis Eleven*, 1: 99–120.
Bellofiore, Riccardo (ed.) 1998, *Marxian economics: a reappraisal*, volumes I and II, London: Macmillan.
Benhabib, Seyla 1986, *Critique, norm, and utopia*, New York: Columbia University Press.
Bonefeld, Werner, Richard Gunn, and Kosmas Psychopedis (eds) 1992, *Open Marxism*, Volume I and II, London: Pluto Press.
Carver, Terrell (ed.) 1975, *Karl Marx: texts on method*, Oxford: Blackwell.
Likitkijsomboon, Pichit 1992, 'The Hegelian dialectic and Marx's *Capital*', *Cambridge Journal of Economics*, 16(4): 405–19.
Marx, Karl 1859, *Zur Kritik der Politischen Ökonomie*, MEW 13, Berlin: Dietz Verlag. 1974; Engl. edn Maurice Dobb. transl. S.W. Ryazanskaya, *A contribution to the critique of political economy*, London: Lawrence & Wishart, 1971.
Marx, Karl 1867; 1885; 1894, *Capital: a critique of political economy*, vols. I–III (German originals I: 1867^1, 1890^4; II: 1885^1, 1883^2; III: 1894), trans. Ben Fowkes (I) and David Fernbach (II and III), Harmondsworth: Penguin Books, 1976, 1978, 1981.
Marx, Karl 1932, *Economico-philosophical manuscripts* in *Early writings*, trans. Rodney Livingstone and Ted Benton, Harmondsworth: Penguin Books, 1975 (includes 'Critique of Hegel's doctrine of the state', the 'Theses on Feuerbach', and the 1859 Preface mentioned in the text).
Marx, Karl 1953, *Grundrisse: foundations of the critique of political economy (rough draft)*, trans. Martin Nicolaus, Harmondsworth: Penguin Books, 1973.
Mattick, Paul 1993, 'Marx's dialectic', in F. Moseley (ed.), *Marx's method in 'Capital'*, Atlantic Highlands, NJ: Humanities Press.
Mepham, John, and David-Hillel Ruben (eds) 1979, *Issues in Marxist philosophy, volume I: dialectics and method*, Brighton: Harvester.
Moseley, Fred (ed.) 1993, *Marx's method in 'Capital': a re-examination*, Atlantic Highlands, NJ: Humanities Press.
Moseley, Fred, and Martha Campbell (eds) 1997, *New investigations of Marx's method*, Atlantic Highlands, NJ: Humanities Press.
Murray, Patrick 1988, *Marx's theory of scientific knowledge*, Atlantic Highlands, NJ: Humanities Press.
Norman, Richard, and Sean Sayers 1980, *Hegel, Marx and dialectic: a debate*, Brighton: Harvester.

Reuten, Geert 1993, 'The difficult labour of a theory of social value: metaphors and systematic dialectics at the beginning of Marx's *Capital*', in F. Moseley (ed.), *Marx's method in 'Capital'*, Atlantic Highlands, NJ: Humanities Press.

Reuten, Geert 1995, 'Conceptual collapses: a note on value-form theory', *Review of Radical Political Economics*, 27(3): 104–10.

Reuten, Geert, and Michael Williams 1989, *Value-form and the state; the tendencies of accumulation and the determination of economic policy in capitalist society*, London: Routledge.

Schmidt, Alfred (ed.) 1969, *Beiträge zur marxistischen Erkenntnistheorie*, Frankfurt a.M.: Suhrkamp.

Smith, Tony 1990, *The logic of Marx's Capital: replies to Hegelian criticisms*, Albany: State University of New York Press.

Sweezy, Paul M. 1942, *The theory of capitalist development*, New York: Modern Reader Paperbacks.

CHAPTER 5

The interconnection of Systematic Dialectics and Historical Materialism

2000 article, originally published in *Historical Materialism*, 7, pp. 137–65. (For its abstract see the Abstracts of all chapters, p. 2.)

Preface

This chapter is placed at this point of the book because its main section 2 regards Marx's method in all of *Capital*. Within the systematic of the book section 3 would belong to Part B of the book (*Capital*, Volume I).

The article includes comments to an article by Patrick Murray (2000). Murray re-commented in his 'Reply to Geert Reuten' (*Historical Materialism*, 10, 2002, pp. 155–76).

Contents

1 Introduction: Marxian discourse   77
2 Historical Materialism overarching Systematic Dialectics; and vice versa   77
    2.1 Introduction: critique and historical materialism   79
    2.2 Systematic dialectics: what to show   81
    2.3 Systematic dialectics: how to show   83
    2.4 The two starting points of dialectical research   84
    2.5 Two circles   86
    2.6 Conclusion: the relation of historical materialism and systematic dialectics   90
3 Abstract labour: interpretation versus reconstruction   91
    3.1 Abstract labour: a general or/and a determinate notion?   91
    3.2 A flaw in the standard answer to the Ricardian interpretation   96
    3.3 Conclusion: phenomenology, systematic dialectics and its starting point   97
Summary and conclusions   99
References   100

1   Introduction: Marxian discourse[1]

This article discusses some recent developments in the Marxian theory of value, called 'value-form theory', which have gone along with a methodical shift from a linear logic and Historical Dialectic to a dialectical logic and Systematic Dialectic within the Marxian paradigm.[2] In order to appreciate these developments it is useful to make two introductory remarks on, first, some peculiarities of the Marxian discourse and, second, about discrepancies in Marx's *Capital*.

It is common scientific practice for new theoretical developments and findings in a field to be presented both in contrast with the received view and in reference to early originators of those developments and findings. A peculiarity of the Marxian paradigm is that this practice is on top combined with enduring reference to Marx's work, especially *Capital*. This might be considered normal practice to the extent that the Marxian paradigm, of course, originates with Marx. Nevertheless, there is both a difference in frequency and depth here. In neoclassical economic research for example, reference to the early originators such as Jevons, Walras, Edgworth and Marshall are not pronounced.

This practice amongst Marxists has both advantages and disadvantages. One advantage is that this common reference point, and its language, contributes to its interdisciplinary aims. Specialists in varied fields such as philosophy, economics, sociology and political science have to make an effort to translate their findings into the common language. Apparently, it also provides an indicator of how the paradigm is developing. The disadvantage is that Marxists are often inclined to reinterpret Marx in the light of their own findings, thus contributing to a lack of clarity and to unnecessary hermeneutic controversy. This last is strengthened by the fact that quite some Marxists also have a genuine historiographic interest in the work of Marx, extending well beyond 'mere' reference to his work.[3]

---

1   I am most grateful to Tony Smith for his detailed comments on an earlier version of this paper. I also benefitted from comments by Chris Arthur, Sebastian Budgen and Andrew Brown. I thank Rebecca Burke for helping me to improve the English. Of course, I remain responsible for content and style. Finally I thank Patrick Murray for a number of fruitful conversations on the issues discussed in this article.
2   Systematic dialectic originates with Hegel's works on logic (1812, 1817), which is quite different from Hegel's historical dialectic (1837) and from his dialectical theory of society (1821). One important reason for insisting on the term 'systematic' dialectics is to precisely to differentiate it from a historical dialectic. (See also Norman 1976, and the debate in Norman and Sayers 1980; Norman adopts the term 'conceptual dialectic' instead of 'systematic dialectics'.) Arthur 1997 provides a good overview of the differences between these within the Marxian paradigm. See also Smith 1999 and Arthur 1998a.
3   This seems unavoidable, given the first mentioned advantage. For a common interdisciplin-

These introductory remarks form the first background to this article. The second set of introductory remarks relates to the fact that in both fields examined in this article – method and the theory of value – there is considerable unclarity, if not inconsistency, in the work of Marx. In orthodox interpretations of Marx's work, these shortcomings have been attributed to 'unnecessary' Hegelian jargon that can, without loss of content, be dismissed. Contemporary value-form theoreticians working with the method of systematic dialectics, however, hold that Marx's most important contribution lay precisely in these two fields, and involves a paradigmatic break from Classical Political Economy. Paradigmatic breaks imply inconsistencies, since they necessarily have to be cast – in part – in terms of the 'old' language.[4]

From this perspective it is not surprising that twentieth-century Marxian theory has been divided into different strands of thinking about the two key issues of method and value.[5] The fact that these different strands can take inspiration from the work of Marx or even base their theories on Marx's, is not therefore a matter of discursive reading. Even if Marx adopts the method of systematic dialectics – as I hold – his presentation in *Capital* is often defective in that respect, leaving room for linear-logical methodical orientations to develop from it. Even if Marx lays the foundation for a theory of social form (under capitalism the value-form) he presents alongside it other, more Ricardian, lines of thought, opening the way for a respectable Ricardian-Marxist theory of value to develop from his work. Indeed, the current state of Marxian theory shows that there are several lines of argument in *Capital* from which several different theories can be developed.

In Issue 6 of *Historical Materialism*, Patrick Murray explained how the concept of 'social form' is a key to the understanding of Marx's *Capital*, especially the theory of value. I fully agree, though disagree that this leaves no room for other than form theoretical interpretations. I will show in Section 3 of this article that Murray's reading of *Capital* cannot explain how other – often fundamentally different – interpretations could ever make sense. In fact, Murray's article

---

ary language to exist, references must indeed refer to more than page numbers: one has to 'translate' the referenced text. Most Marxists do this because it is a genuine requirement of the paradigm to have studied the works of Marx. This is in contradistinction, for example, to neoclassical economists who are less likely to study seriously the founders of their paradigm.

4 See Reuten 1993. [Chapter 6 of the current book.]
5 There are also important divides over the theory of cyclical economic development and crises; these can be traced to the former divides – the argument for this goes beyond the confines of this paper.

is an intervention in the development of current Marxian theory – to which, seen as reconstruction, I subscribe.

In Section 2 I argue that Murray's interpretation is based on a questionable view of the method of systematic dialectics, which he sees as based on presuppositions (specified below). Apparently he needs this view for his interpretation of Marx's value theory. Murray's view of systematic dialectics seems to mix up the different phases of dialectical research. (I suggest that Marx's *Capital* does the same, thus seeming to verify Murray's argument.)

Murray rarely refers to historical materialism explicitly, yet it is crucial to his argument. One of my objectives in Section 2 is to set out the relation between historical materialism and systematic dialectics. I assume that for readers of *Historical Materialism* I need not outline the method of historical materialism, and so devote more space to that of systematic dialectics. I conclude that in one respect historical materialism is synthesised into the method of systematic dialectics but, in another, historical materialism overarches systematic dialectics. This articulation of the two methods takes into account ideas of a century-long development of Marxian method and theory (though this article provides not even the rudiments of their historiography). Marx's *Capital*, I will indicate, navigates between the two methods – this idea is implicitly shared by Murray – but it does not sharply bring out this articulation.

2   **Historical Materialism overarching Systematic Dialectics; and vice versa**

2.1   *Introduction: critique and historical materialism*
Before going into differences of and disputes over Marx's method, it is worth noticing that one aspect is in fact undisputed, which is that it is a 'method of critique'. Defenders of all methodological strands in Marxism agree that this is either a central or subsidiary part of the(ir) method. Thus, they agree to Marx's methodological requirement – to a large extent taken over from Hegel – of describing the object of enquiry from within: driving *the object's* (society, the economy, or theories thereof) own standards and processes/arguments to their logical conclusions, and thus assessing the object internally (instead of externally as would 'criticism' as opposed to 'critique').[6]

---

6 How much Marx succeeded in this can be seen from the view of Marx's contemporary, Freiligrath who considered *Capital* a manual for business managers (as narrated by Mehring 1973 [1918], p. 346).

The subtitle of Marx's *Capital* reveals what it does in this respect; it is 'a critique of political economy'. Herewith, Marx had a double object: critique of the economy, and critique of the economists (in the German 'Kritik der politischen Ökonomie' it is even clearer that the object is two-fold).

Anticipating one of the conclusions of this article, I should like to stress an important corollary of the method of critique. The Marxian paradigm is one approach, along many others, to the study of current society. A fruitful development of the paradigm requires that the method of critique be applied not only to current capitalism and current orthodox social sciences, but – in the face of the particular reference practice amongst Marxians, mentioned in the Introduction – also to the work of Marx.

Looking back to Marx's *Capital* it is obvious that there are outlines of the method of systematic dialectics to be found in the work. A matter of controversy, though, is where its starts, and whether this method is perhaps combined with another method, or other methods.

Throughout his work Marx adopts three distinct approaches: historical materialism, critique (as briefly outlined above), and systematic dialectics.[7] How do these relate, particularly in *Capital*?

Historical materialism includes an approach to the study of history that without doubt takes distance from Hegel's historical dialectic (rightfully so in my view). In the context of this article, I will not much amplify on this approach. I merely emphasise that for the study of a particular 'historical material constellation' such as capitalism, Marxists make use of its results. First, the historical materialist method should enable to differentiate 'transhistorical notions' from 'historically specific categories'.[8] In Murray's terminology, these are 'general abstractions' versus 'determinate abstractions'.[9] This differentiation is a far from easy task. All the same, it is crucial to the Marxian method. I will come back to this in Section 3.

Second, historical materialism, apparently (see below), puts a constraint on the analysis and exposition of a particular 'historical material constellation', namely the requirement to set out how a particular society reproduces itself materially, its particular way of 'sociation'.[10] Marx: 'The mode of production of material life conditions the general process of social, political and intellectual

---

7   Cf. my 1998a. [Chapter 4 of the current book.]
8   Reuten 1988a, pp. 47–8; Reuten and Williams 1989, pp. 38, 55–6.
9   See Murray 1988, ch. 10. Following Mészáros (1970, p. 79) Arthur calls them 'first order mediations' versus 'second order mediations' (1986, pp. 11–12).
10 Reuten 1988a, pp. 47–8; Reuten and Williams 1989, p. 56.

life.'[11] Murray calls this constraint the 'general phenomenology', comprising 'the truth of historical materialism' and he insists that it is '*a presupposition*' for the systematic dialectic.[12] In the remainder of this section I will set out why I disagree with Murray's point of view.

Apart from what I have indicated so far, historical materialism provides no methodological indication of *how* to set up the study of a particular 'historical material constellation'. The method of 'critique' provides a further inkling, but it, too, does not indicate a starting point or the way of proceeding from it.

I would suggest (although I lack solid evidence) that this is the reason why Marx in his preparations for the writing of *Capital* returned to the study of Hegel's *Logic*. The systematic dialectic set out there provides a method for the exposition of the object of inquiry (in this case the capitalist mode of production) 'from within'.[13] Thus, systematic dialectics is also a particular method of 'critique'.[14]

2.2 *Systematic dialectics: what to show*

In outline, systematic dialectics aims to 'show' its object of inquiry – in the case of *Capital*, the capitalist mode of production. Why would one have to show something that is already there before our eyes? Because we may perceive its outcomes before our eyes, but not how it works; we may perceive the outcomes but not know how these come about and how these are interconnected; we may not perceive the structure and the processes reproducing that structure. Systematic dialectics aims to show the essential working of the object: the whole in essence.[15] The whole in essence is the interconnection of all the moments

---

11   Marx 1871 [1859¹], pp. 20–1.
12   Murray 2000, pp. 38–9.
13   Hegel's object of inquiry here, to be sure, is in a different realm; the object of inquiry of his logic is thought, it is a 'self'-understanding and next 'self'-comprehension of thought; this is relatively 'easy' since subject and object are one.
14   One may contest the systematic-dialectical character of Marx's *Capital* and at the same time highlight its method of critique, as, for example, Mattick Jr. 1993 does. Generally, of course, 'critique' is not restricted to dialectics or to Hegelian and Marxian traditions.
15   That is, systematic dialectics as developed for the social realm. Hegel's logic (as developed for the realm of thought) unfolds a 'doctrine of comprehension' (*Begriff*) from a 'doctrine of essence'. Regarding the development of this dialectic for the social realm, I hold that a science of (capitalist) social relations cannot reach further than comprehension of its object-totality ('essence'). Relatedly, contradiction is persistent and irreducible characteristic of the actual existent. See Reuten and Williams 1989, pp. 26–7, for some amplification on this issue.

necessary for the *reproduction* of the object.[16] The emphasis on reproduction reveals that we are dealing with an organic whole, therefore "knowledge of it must take the form of a *system* of related categories rather than a series of discrete investigations".[17] The emphasis on 'necessary' reveals that we are out to lay bare first of all the continuous moments rather than the merely contingent expressions. That is, we are out to *distinguish* aspects and expressions that could come and go without affecting the reproduction of the system, from all the necessary moments the lack or distortion of which would make the system, the object, fall apart.[18]

This provides a first guide for systematicity: we have a guide for *what* to show (but not yet for *how*). Obviously, this guide pertains to what Murray calls the phenomenological question: What is it?[19] Perhaps we merely use different jargon here, but for me phenomenological research is a mainly *analytic* stage of inquiry prior to the research of the dialectical *Darstellung* (positing, positioning, presentation).[20] The analysis of this prior stage results in abstractions and ultimately ends up with an 'abstract universal'. Thus the phenomenological research is the prior stage that Marx refers to as *Forschungsweise*, 'the way of inquiry'.[21] Conversely, the distinction of necessary moments from contingencies, set out in the previous paragraph, goes at the heart of the systematic dialectics proper: it is the result of the research of the dialectical *Darstellung* at each of its successive stages.

---

16   'A *moment* is an element considered in itself, which can be conceptually isolated, and analysed as such, but which can have no isolated existence' (Reuten and Williams 1989, p. 22).
17   Arthur 1992, p. x; cf. Marx's *Grundrisse* Introduction.
18   Just to present the reader a picture: the capitalist mode of production (CMP) would fall apart without the moment of technical change or without the moment of a credit system. Nevertheless *within* the CMP technical change or the credit system could, contingently to the CMP – thus without it falling apart – take several historically specific guises. This differentiation between necessary and contingent moments/aspects/expressions is not to say that contingencies are unimportant in everyday life. They may be damned important. The capitalist system can do without wars, but wars crucially affect life. The concepts of necessity and contingency thus relate to a particular object of inquiry.
19   Murray 2000, p. 37.
20   I adopt the term 'analysis' in a broad sense (cf. also its use in Marx's *Capital*). Thus, the stage of phenomenological analysis involves more than 'analysis' in the narrow sense of merely indicating *difference*, it also involves provisional outlines of the inseparability of phenomena (see also §2.3 and §2.4 below).
21   Marx 1973 [1857], p. 102. (*Contribution to the critique ...*)

2.3 Systematic dialectics: how to show

How then? Foremost this is a *synthetic* process: synthesis of the object of inquiry as a whole.[22] It has two requirements going on at the same time. First, simpler categories come before complex ones. Thus we have a succession in stages from the 'simple' to the complex (in the end, complex reality, "the concentration of many determinants").[23]

The difficulty, however, lies in the second requirement, which is that we equally have a movement from abstract to concrete concepts.[24] Here, the dialectical layering of concepts comes in. Since we set out to present the whole, we cannot *just* start from one simple aspect of it (what simple aspect would we choose? – is this a matter of arbitrary choice?). If you want to present the whole, you must start from the whole. That is, you must start from the abstract whole (in other terms, the abstract universal, where 'universal' refers to the object of inquiry, i.e., the whole – in the case of *Capital*, an abstract concept of the capitalist mode of production). Of course, the abstract whole also appears simple. In its simplicity it exhibits abstract unity. Equally, the abstract whole lacks concrete richness (diversity), and it also appears to lack concrete material foundations; it is unclear (or perhaps implicit) how it is reproduced. Concretisation, foundation and reproduction are the aspects of the one process that drives the systematic dialectic forward in stages. In the case of *Capital* these stages of movement are each time explicitly marked as a conceptual 'transformation' (*Verwandlung* – 'conversion' is perhaps a better translation).[25] This movement goes on until in the end, hopefully, one has been able to show how the initial object of inquiry reproduces itself in essence.

---

22 Murray 2000 indicates this synthetic course; however, I would want to rephrase the way he sets this out. Note that 'synthesis' should not be taken in the narrow logical positivist meaning of synthetic statements (i.e., empirical statements), but in the broader philosophical meaning of connection, bringing parts together (in contradistinction to analysis).

23 Marx 1973 {1857–58}, p. 101. (*Grundrisse*.)

24 Murray seems to reduce these two requirements to one aspect: "The orderliness requirement ... [calls] for the introduction of concepts *synthetically*, that is, in order of their conceptual concreteness: simpler categories come before more complex ones" (Murray 2000, p. 38).

25 Indeed, the famous value–price transformation is merely one of those. It seems to me a fundamental mistake to treat these stages and their conversions as if they were *analytical* and thus – as in the value–price 'transformation problem' – treat the categories of an earlier more abstract exposition as if they were *actualities*. Therefore, also, whilst one can apply quantitative operations at some definite level of abstraction, it makes no sense at all to apply them between levels of abstraction. This issue has been very clearly pointed out by Smith 1990, pp. 169–71.

Still, prior to that, at each of the stages referred to, we have reference to the totality, though in degrees of abstractness. In the case of Marx's *Capital*, therefore, it may seem that after the completion of each Volume, and often after the completion of its Parts, we are done. Of course, Volume I presents the totality. Of course, Volume II, Part One or Part Three presents the totality et cetera, but each time richer, more concrete, more materially founded, showing more how it reproduces itself.[26]

All this is further complicated by the conflicts and contradictions inherent to the object of inquiry and the conceptualisation of it.[27] In the context of this article I refrain from going into those.[28]

2.4 The two starting points of dialectical research

Up until now I have provided in outline the answer to the *how?* question: the question as to how systematic dialectics shows us the object of inquiry. Above I only briefly touched on the phenomenological analytic stage of inquiry prior to the synthetics of the dialectical *Darstellung* (end of §2.2). Nevertheless, here, it seems, lies the source of the basic disagreement between Murray and myself;

---

26 Since any major stage of the presentation (e.g. the Parts in Marx's *Capital*) is of the whole, it *must* show an *apparent* completeness. For me, one mark of the good quality of a systematic-dialectical work is that each time when you get to a new stage you are caught by surprise: 'Gosh, I thought that the foregoing was all there is to say, but now it appears that there is more to it'. The necessity of the next moment is only demonstrated when we arrive at that new moment. From this perspective one can understand why readers of *Capital* at the beginning of the twentieth century (and still today) believed that the first Volume is sufficient – in a way, it is! Or why some may believe that the current Volumes I–III are sufficient. However, the same happens within Parts. A striking example of this is the famous 'tendency for the rate of profit to fall', (Volume III, Part Three, Chapters 13–15), for which one group of readers can believe that all is said in chapter 13, another that 13+14 is sufficient, whereas few seem to get to 15 where the theory is developed into a theory of cyclical development. I say that high-quality systematic dialectics *must* give each time the impression of completeness, in the last case completeness within the 'moment' of the 'tendency for the rate of profit to fall'. *Therefore* this dialectics is difficult. Relatedly, it is often difficult, especially the early parts of such a work, because of the struggle for a language positing the whole.

27 'Contradiction' has a complex meaning within the paradigm. A simpler term would be 'paradox' although this term does not cover the complexity of the former. A simple example of a contradiction inherent to capitalist reality is that 'free competition' bears in it its dissolution, in that firms will always try to ologopolise and monopolise markets, thus (partly) extinguish free competition.

28 See the amplification on these issues in for example Reuten and Williams 1989, pp. 3–33. See also the outlines of systematic dialectics in Arthur 1997, pp. 21–32, Arthur 1998a, pp. 447–52 and Smith 1993, pp. 15–36. Brief accounts are in Reuten 1998a and 1998b [Chapters 4 and 3 of the current book.]

'here' or perhaps rather in the connection (or intersection?) of the analytic and the synthetic stages. Once more, this is also the stage where the methods of historical materialism and systematic dialectics touch.

Murray rightfully observes: "systematic-dialectical presentation (or systematic dialectics) is the name for the most appropriate way to present the findings of phenomenology. So, dialectical presentation is rooted in experience; it is not a matter of spinning webs *a priori*."[29] Indeed, dialectical research has two starting points: one is non-systematic and often informal – analytical phenomenological research; the other is systematic, the formal starting point of which is the abstract universal – the starting point of the synthetic systematic-dialectical research and its presentation (*Darstellung*). The first research stage starts from empirical reality, the phenomena – from what one in ordinary language calls 'the concrete', but what Marx prefers to call the "imagined concrete"; this stage of thorough analysis results in abstractions and ultimately ends up with an 'abstract universal'. The second research stage takes its start from the latter, gradually concretising it systematically (as set out in §2.3), until in the end it reaches back to the empirical reality that can now be comprehended in its concrete manifoldness. Or as Marx expressed it: "Along the first path the full conception was evaporated to yield an abstract determination; along the second, the abstract determinations lead towards a reproduction of the concrete by way of thought."[30]

The first research stage may, but need not, have been reported on in phenomenological writings, expressed in hopefully a 'normal' systematic organisation of the material. These are the reports of what Hegel called the act of 'understanding' instead of 'dialectical reason'.[31] They range from newspaper reports to historical investigations and highbrow philosophical work. Phenomenological research, however, also consists in the study of such reports, as well as in the study of new empirical material. Their digestion, i.e., phenomenological research, often takes the course of a "chaotic conception of the whole"[32] in ways that one can hardly report on. We try this analysis, fail and move on to the next, fail again then return to the former, and so on. Nevertheless, for a dialectician, this research might also take the shape of 'essays' (try-outs) in dialectics.

---

29   Murray 2000, p. 37. I take it that the most appropriate way to present the findings of phenomenology' is not to be read as implying that it is 'merely' a matter of presentation. The dialectical exposition involves a research stage itself, as amplified upon below.
30   Marx 1973 {1857–58}, p. 100. (*Grundrisse*.)
31   See also Smith 1999, p. 220.
32   Marx 1973 {1857–58}, p. 100. (*Grundrisse*.)

I believe that Marx's work prior to the 1859 *Critique of Political Economy*, or perhaps prior to the *Grundrisse*, must be located in the research domain mentioned in the previous paragraph.

2.5   *Two circles*

In dialectical research and dialectical presentation, then, we see two circles going on.[33] One is the empirical circle from empirical reality via its working up by phenomenological research to 'abstract determination' and back via systematic dialectics to empirical reality (comprising the two research stages).

The other is a circle that systematic dialectics proper goes through (i.e., the second research stage) – from abstract universal to concrete manifoldness.[34] But why is this a 'circle'? The appraisal of any systematic-dialectical presentation lies in whether or not it succeeds in providing the foundation for its starting point within the systematic-dialectical presentation itself. (Thus, its foundations do not rest in presupposed unquestionable axioms, as in the mathematical-analytical way of proceeding; nor do they rest in the first research stage – the context of its discovery so to say.) Foundation, concretisation and reproduction, we have seen, are the aspects of the same systematic-dialectical process, or movement. Thus, foundation also comes down to whether the abstract starting point and the movement from it 'generates' its own existence – its truth – in the sense that it generates all the moments necessary for its existence, thus the object-totality as a self-reproducing entity. Of course, we must require this, since the object-totality in question, the capitalist system, is in reality a self-reproducing entity today. So, the possible truth of the starting point, the first level of abstraction, lies in the second and so forth. Equally, the possible truth of any intermediate moment lies in all the others. In this sense all moments are part of one and the same circle.[35]

Murray objects to "this two-way directionality of dialectical systematicity".[36] In order to flesh this out, I want to consider an example from the structure of *Capital*. At the end of Volume I, although accumulation of capital has been presented, it appears that accumulation can in fact have no existence since the social circulation of capital has not been presented yet (Volume II). Of course, I suppose, we had in Volume I an inkling of accumulation. But it turns out that at that point accumulation is still abstract, because insufficiently founded (thus, its full reproduction is lacking: it appears that we were shown merely

---

33   Murray (2000, pp. 37–8) in my view insufficiently differentiates these two.
34   This one, I suppose, is in fact the point of attack for Murray.
35   Arthur (1998a, p. 448) aptly refers to "a *circuit* of reproduction" instead of a circle.
36   Murray 2000, p. 38.

one moment of accumulation'. Thus the existence of accumulation 'presupposes' (*i.e., requires*) its further foundation in circulation. But, of course, when we get to circulation, that 'presupposes' (*i.e., requires*) accumulation. And so on. In the previous two sentences I used the term 'presupposition' that Murray stresses, even if it risks confusion. 'Presupposition' in this sense of requirement is quite different from presupposition in the sense of postulates, assumptions, axioms.[37] As indicated, systematic dialectics does not presuppose, assume, the truth of the starting point: its truth has to be proven in the course of the presentation. Similarly, here, at a level more concrete than the starting point, accumulation is not presupposed – in the sense of assumed – to exist, rather the truth of the existence of accumulation has to be proven in the further course of the presentation (e.g. circulation) – although the prior presentation may already have shown part of the evidence for its existence. Thus the systematic starting point of *Capital* is ultimately only grounded when all the moments necessary for the reproduction of the system have been presented. At that point (level) we can be said to have provided the full foundation for the starting point, and we have come full *circle*.

The "inseparability of multiple aspects of the object under examination", writes Murray, "introduces a *circularity* into a systematic-dialectical presentation that seems disturbing".[38] His criticism becomes a bit obscure when he adds: "it is at this point that Marx parts company with the Hegelian notion of systematic dialectics". He continues:

> Marx does not leave the circle of Hegelian systematic dialectics unbroken; famously he objects to the 'presuppositionlessness' of Hegelian systematic dialectics and insists that science has premises, which he and Engels sketched in *The German Ideology*.[39]

One page further on, he specifies these premises as follows:

> human beings are needy, self-conscious, symbolizing, social, sexually reproducing animals who are in (and of) non-human nature, which they purposively transform according to their perceived wants.[40]

---

37 When Murray writes "Marx's whole presentation of the commodity and generalized simple commodity circulation presupposes capital and its characteristic form of circulation" (p. 41), then this risk being read in rather an analytic way.
38 Murray 2000, p. 38.
39 Murray 2000, p. 38.
40 Murray 2000, p. 39. It is relevant to note that exactly the same point is made by Hegel is

This is what Murray calls the "general phenomenology", which comprises historical materialism.[41] Earlier on he indicates:

> In *Capital*, Marx offers both a general phenomenology of the human predicament [the premises just cited] and a specific phenomenology of the plight of humanity under capitalism.[42]

First of all, it should be noted that this "general phenomenology" is perplexingly thin. But that is not the point for now.[43] More to the point is that Murray provides no reference for his statement that Marx 'objects to the "presuppositionlessness" of Hegelian dialectics'. I assume there is none.

However, in his scholarly 1988 book, Murray does provide a seemingly relevant citation. Its context, though, is that of history, historiography and historical materialism – quite different from systematic dialectics. He writes:

> Marx's criticisms of speculative method and the philosophical anthropology of absolute idealism establish a context for his attack on speculative historiography and for his own materialism. To see this connections, let us consider a celebrated passage from the *German Ideology* in which Marx expounds his historical materialism at the expense of speculative historiography: 'With the presuppositionless Germans we must begin with ascertaining the first presuppositions of all human existence, therefore also of all history, namely the presupposition that man must be in a position to live in order to "make history"'.[44]

As Murray himself indicates, this objection to 'presuppositionlessness' is set out in criticism of speculative historiography. First, no one would claim that this,

---

his *Phenomenology*. Thus, quite apart from the argument below, it is not clear that Marx "parts company" with Hegel in this respect. I thank Tony Smith for drawing my attention to this.

41 Murray 2000, p. 39.
42 Murray 2000, p. 38.
43 Nor that he says that these premises "are given by nature" (pp. 38 and 41). I suppose that this (panlogic) is a slip of the pen.
44 Murray 1988, p. 6. The Marx citation is from *The German Ideology*, cf. the Arthur edition p. 48. Commenting on page 126 of his book on the same passage Murray writes: "The 'presuppositions' set forth in this subsection [the History subsection of the chapter on Feuerbach] *cannot* be taken as constituting real scientific knowledge, because they all fall within the logic of general abstractions. Marx explains at length that general abstractions, taken independently of determinate abstractions, have little scientific worth."

including Hegel's own writings on history, is 'systematic dialectics'. Second, historiography – including the historical materialist – indeed cannot do without presuppositions. And this equally counts for phenomenology generally.

Thus, first, there seems to be no textual evidence that Marx for his dialectical *Darstellung* "parts company with the Hegelian notion of systematic dialectics" in this respect, and "objects to the 'presuppositionlessness' of Hegelian dialectics". Second, I fail to see how Marx "parts company" since the presentational structure of *Capital* is like that of a systematic-dialectical circle/circuit. What is more, if a dialectical systematic presentation is complete, or even quite a way on the track (Murray and I agree that *Capital* is not complete),[45] it *must* have the bite of 'too' true, and of 'how can I break into this damn circle?'[46] Marx was well aware of this. In the Postface to the second edition of *Capital* he writes:

> Of course the method of presentation must differ from that of inquiry. The latter has to appropriate the material in detail, to analyse its different forms of development and to track down their inner connection. Only after this work has been done can the real [*wirkliche*, i.e., actual] movement be appropriately presented. If this is done successfully, *if the life of the subject matter* is now reflected back in the ideas, then it may appear as if we have before us an *a priori* construction.[47]

Nevertheless, I understand, I think, what seems disturbing. 'Circularity' is a sin in conventional linear logic, and I guess that Murray lets himself be affected by this (his) term. I reply on two planes. First, if the reality of capitalism is such that it is a self-reproducing entity, we cannot escape from describing it as self-reproducing. Of course, it is an organic entity, and a writer is constrained to represent the organic in the pages of a book with a beginning and end page even if in fact all the arguments, as representations of real moments, hang together synchronically, rather than in the apparent page sequence.[48] We can do no better than describing the organic intention in terms of the metaphor of a circle.

Second, I am not enchanted by the axiomatic deductive method of conventional logic – and orthodox scientific practise (and neither is Murray). Why do we have to accept axioms, postulates, assumptions? What is their foundation?

---

45 Cf. Murray 2000, p. 38.
46 One can always break into the circle, and one must keep on trying so as to improve it. It is a human enterprise and open to failure.
47 Marx 1873, p. 102; first English emphasis added.
48 I owe this point to discussion with Christopher Arthur.

Any mainstream economic paper, for example, – the field I know best – starts with those, and together with the conventional rules of deduction the conclusions follow by inexorable logic. I am not saying that this necessarily produces nonsense; of course, the merit of such procedures depends on the merit of the assumptions – but here lies the weak point.[49] If assumptions are without foundation then the derived argument is circular in them.

2.6 Conclusion: the relation of historical materialism and systematic dialectics

It can now be seen why I took up some space to set out the difference between the two stages of dialectical research: (i) the analytical stage of history and phenomenology, and (ii) the synthetic stage of systematic dialectics. The first necessarily involves presuppositions. The second is – subject to failures – presuppositionless.[50] The first stage is indispensable to the second. I hope to have shown that historical materialism is therefore indispensable to systematic dialectics.

Returning to the second stage, if the object of inquiry is to reproduce itself, it must, of necessity, at least reproduce itself materially. Thus, this reproduction must be part and parcel of the systematic-dialectical presentation. It is also the case that historical materialism provides an obvious guide and check for systematic dialectics. At some point all of the 'general' trans-historical requirements (Murray's general phenomenology) must be incorporated into the systematic-dialectical presentation in their determinate *social form* (specific phenomenology).

But next, the findings of historical materialism are also overarching to systematic dialectics regarding transitions between modes of production. In his *Grundrisse* Marx writes:

> our method indicates the points where historical investigation must enter in ... Just as, on one side the pre-bourgeois phases appear as *merely historical*, i.e., suspended presuppositions, so do the contemporary conditions of production likewise appear as engaged in *suspending themselves* and hence in positing the *historic presuppositions* for a new state of society.[51]

---

49   See Reuten 1996 for a methodological appraisal in this respect of neoclassical economics.
50   Nevertheless, like any scientific endeavour, systematic dialectics 'presupposes' language as a medium of thought and reality. This is not Murray's point, but it is far reaching and worth reminding.
51   Marx 1973 {1857–58}, pp. 460–1.

Historical materialism overarches systematic dialectics to the extent that the latter cannot but present one subject-matter at a time (e.g. capitalism); it can present *extant* contradictions and conflict and the way they are settled within the system, but it is unable to present transitions from one system to another.[52]

My criticism of Murray thus amounts to his mixing up the two stages of dialectical research. If he had argued that Marx's *Capital* does not adopt the method of systematic dialectics I would have disagreed since that cannot be sustained in general. If he had argued that *Capital* is often defective in this respect, he would have found me on his side.[53] Instead he redefines systematic dialectics into what he names "Marxian systematic dialectics", which, apparently, is what Marx does. This largely immunises *Capital* against improvements. My disagreements with Murray on the issue of 'abstract labour', taken up in the next section, follow from this.

3 Abstract labour: interpretation versus reconstruction

3.1 *Abstract labour: a general or/and a determinate notion?*

In Reuten 1993, I set out elements of a critique of Marx – critique in the sense indicated in §2.1 – especially concerning the theory of value in the first chapter

---

52 That is, inter-system transitions. It can theorise intra-system transitions. Against the background of the systematic of necessary moments and of contradictions remaining untranscended by these, it can next analyse their historically contingent transcendences: shifts, conjunctural settlements, regimes (see Reuten and Williams 1989, pp. 26–7, 30–2, 42, 46).

53 Marx's *Capital* is not impeccable from the point of view of this method. Within a general systematic-dialectical structure we find a number of deficient transitions as well as many historical excurses that are not explicitly accounted for as such and that seem to replace systematic argument. Tony Smith (1990), analysing *Capital* from a systematic-dialectical point of view, has set these out in detail. The inadequacies, according to Smith, occur especially onwards from Volume I, Part Four (Smith 1990, chs. 7–9). In many respects I consider Smith's work a reconstruction instead of an interpretation: in my view, the dialectical deficiencies in *Capital* are even greater than those suggested by Smith. Generally, one can say that the several Parts of *Capital* diverge in dialectical rigour. For Volume II, for example, Arthur (1998b) can show the magnificent systematic dialectics of its first Part (the circuits of capital), whereas I show that for its last Part (Three, on social reproduction) it is trifling (Reuten 1998c [Chapter 11 of the current book]). Especially for Volumes II and III this may be due to the draft character of the writings (Part Three of Volume II, was the last part of *Capital* that Marx worked on before his death). But this excuse cannot apply to Volume I. Nevertheless, even if there are these deficiencies, there is indeed ample room for reconstruction. Next to Smith's a recent outstanding example of this is Chris Arthur's outline of a reconstruction of the three volumes of *Capital* in terms of the triadic logic of universal, particular and individual (Arthur 2002).

of *Capital I*.⁵⁴ Murray rightfully notes my conclusion that Marx, whilst laying the foundation for a theory of social value – a value-form theory – at the same time does not completely break with the naturalistic Classical labour theory of value.⁵⁵ Murray also rightfully notes that I see this critique in line with the project of *Capital*.

I argued especially that while Marx sets out elements of a value-form theory in that chapter, he nevertheless *also* relies on labour-embodied notions. The same point was already made by Rubin in his essays of 1928. However, we see in Marx not the Ricardian naturalistic labour-embodied notion, but rather a more complicated 'abstract labour' concept. Specifically, I argued that Marx's theory in part may usefully be labelled an 'abstract-labour-embodied' theory, thus indicating his half-way break with the Classical naturalistic labour-embodied theory.⁵⁶ Regarding the introduction of the concept of abstract labour, I quoted the following passage from Marx:

---

54 That article had a second aim – understanding the development of the Marxian theory of value in its *current* state – to which I will return later on.

55 On the basis of my brief exposition of Marx's method of critique in §2.1 – a methodological requirement, it should be stressed, running along others – one can see how difficult it is to disentangle *critique*, in this case his critique of classical political economists, and *break*. In fact, this may provide Murray with an additional argument against me, although I contest that for the time being.

56 It may be useful to briefly amplify on the terminology used in this section (especially the issues under 2–4 in this note, are treated in more detail in my 1993 paper).

1. The classical labour-embodied theory of value is called *naturalistic*, first, because it relies on a prerequisite of all social formations (by 'nature'), that is, the requirement of labour for the production of goods (under this aspect naturalistic is the same as a-historical). At the same time, as Marx 1976 [1867] notes (p. 174), Classical Political Economy fails to provide arguments why this general prerequisite should become the benchmark for production and exchange particularly in the capitalist social formation and why, in this mode of production, it takes the *form of value*. Second, this theory of value is called 'naturalistic' because physicalist notions (especially embodiment) are used to constitute a social concept, i.e., value (under this aspect naturalistic is the same as physical). Thus, hours of physical work are conceived to be literally incorporated in physical goods as values. Under these two aspects together, the naturalistic labour-embodied theory of value conceives of a particular *social* process of production and exchange – as well as their particular social form, i.e., value – as a purely physical-material process applicable to all social formations.

2. The standard Ricardian and Ricardian-Marxist labour-embodied theory of value – the concrete-labour-embodied theory – takes it that different *concrete* labour hours (that is labour hours in their manifold heterogeneous qualities) can be added up and that these constitute value.

3. For the *abstract-labour-embodied* theory of value it is not concrete heterogeneous but abstract homogeneous entities that go into the determination of value ('crystals of

> If we make abstraction from its [the commodity's] use-value, we abstract also from the material constituents and forms which make it a use-value. ... The useful character of the kinds of labour embodied in them also disappears; this in turn entails the disappearance of the different concrete forms of labour. They can no longer be distinguished, but are altogether reduced to the same kind of labour, human labour in the abstract.[57]

Second, with the introduction of the concept of value, abstract labour is further specified as:

> merely congealed quantities of homogeneous human labour, i.e., of human labour-power expended without regard to the form of its expenditure. All these things now tell us is that human labour-power has been expended to produce them, human labour is accumulated in them. As crystals of this social substance, which is common to them all, they are values – commodity values [*Warenwerte*].[58]

And somewhat further on:

> How is the magnitude of this value to be measured? By means of the quantity of the 'value-forming [*bildenden* i.e., constituting] substance', the labour contained in the article. This quantity is measured by its duration, and the labour-time is itself measured on the particular scale of hours, days etc.[59]

Murray agrees that the concept of abstract labour set out here is indeed a *general*, trans-historical, instead of a historically *determinate* notion. We also agree

---

social substance'). This takes place via, what may be called, a reductive abstraction. (Marx can be interpreted to hold this view, even though there is also a value-form theoretic line of argument in Marx.)

Those who subscribe to the theories under 2 or 3 often seem to identify labour and value.

4. In the *abstract-labour theory of value* (for which there are certainly important roots in Marx, but which I take to be a development from Marx's theory) the concept of abstract labour refers to *abstraction in practice*, that is in the market, by which concrete labour is actually reduced to and homogenous money. Thus in the market and via the market, labour is actually reduced to and treated as abstract in the sense of a merely money-producing entity (at least potentially so).

57 Marx 1976 [1867, 1890], p. 128; ch. 1, sect. 1 (*Capital I*).
58 Ibid.
59 Marx 1976 [1867, 1890], p. 129; ch. 1, sect. 1 (*Capital I*).

that both the concepts of value and use-value are meant to be determinate.[60] However, the concept of value especially suffers here from the *general* abstract-labour notion. If so, we cannot say that we are here on the track of a theory of the particularly capitalist kind of *social form*. Yet Murray and I also agree about the requirement of setting out a theory of social form instead of adopting formless general notions.

One part of the way out here for Murray is to make the concept of abstract labour a determinate one, which he calls "practically abstract labour" emphasising that, in capitalist society, labour is treated as abstract in practice.[61] I could not agree more.[62] I would also agree to distinguish two concepts, one general (abstract labour) and one determinate (practically abstract labour). This then would be one element for a *reconstruction* of a truly social Marxian abstract-labour theory of value.

However, Murray makes the astonishing move of delivering this as an *interpretation* of Marx's theory. He interprets Marx's *one* term of abstract labour to have *two* separate meanings, one general and one determinate (can we choose at will?). For an interpretation of the current text of *Capital* this just runs too fast. He writes:

> But by 'practically abstract' labour, *a term of my own device* for which there is ample warrant in Marx's thoughts and words, I mean labour that a society treats as abstract ... This, then, is a historically determinate social sort of labour, *which shows* that Marx's theory of value is not 'asocial' but a theory of social form.[63]

Murray's evidence for the 'ample warrant' is both scarce and ambiguous.[64]

---

60 In recent work Murray (1998) has insightfully stressed the determinate character of the concept of use-value.
61 Murray 2000, p. 43 ff.
62 In fact I adopted this determinate concept of 'actual abstraction' or 'abstraction in practice' in a 1988 paper (Reuten 1988a, pp. 52–3) and also used it in the 1993 one, as Murray acknowledges. See also Reuten and Williams 1989, pp. 62–5. Note that some authors in a similar context have used the term 'real abstraction' – see Taylor (2000, pp. 71–3) for a critique of this last.
63 Murray 2000, pp. 43–4, emphasis added. He provides one reference for 'the ample warrant', namely to the *Grundrisse* (Marx 1973, pp. 104–5). He might also have referred to the 1859 *Critique* (Marx 1971 [1859, 1897], p. 30) or even more to the point (?) the first edition of *Capital I* (Marx 1978 [1867], pp. 136–7). But especially the latter would bring up the question of why Marx deleted this for later editions. Murray would have to explain this.
64 Apart from the single reference mentioned in the previous note, he provides later on one other reference for his view. He considers "the passage in *Capital* that most compellingly

So he interprets Marx's term of abstract labour to have two different meanings. In the last section of his article Murray then writes:

> I agree with Reuten that an abstract labour-embodied [i.e., abstract-labour-embodied] theory is an asocial one that represents no fundamental break with classical political economy. ... Where Reuten's reasoning goes wrong, I believe, is in its failure to recognize that there are *two* concepts in play in Chapter One, the general concept of abstract labour and the concept of 'practically abstract' labour.[65]

Have I gone wrong? I thought that Marx does not explicitly differentiate these concepts; I thought that Marx does not devote two terms to them in the way

---

supports the present interpretation" (Murray 2000, p. 50), to be from the beginning of Chapter 1, Section 4 on fetishism:

"The mystical character of the commodity does not ... proceed from the nature of the determinants of value. For ... however varied the useful kinds of labour, or productive activities, it is a physiological fact that they are functions of the human organism, and that each such function, whatever may be its nature or its form, is essentially the expenditure of human brain, nerves, muscles and sense organs." (Marx 1976 [1867, 1890], p. 164)

Murray concludes: "In other words, Marx flatly asserts that value, or the fetish character of the commodity, is *not* a consequence of 'abstract labour', that is, labour does not produce value *simply because* it can be viewed as an expenditure of human capacities" (2000, pp. 50–1). I find it not very convincing to derive a core argument from something that is *not* said. Quite apart from this, however, I concluded in my 1993 paper that Marx's text is ambiguous or unclear and that "therefore there is room for several interpretations as well as lines of research developing from *Capital*." Murray acknowledges several times that my aim indeed was to point out ambiguity. This ambiguity is brought out very well in the continuation from the previous quote that Murray next cites, and that for him is the crucial one:

Whence, then, arises the enigmatic character of the products of labour, as soon as it assumes the form of a commodity? Clearly it arises from this form itself. The equality of the kinds of human labour takes on a physiological form in the equal objectivity of the products of labour as values; the measure of the expenditure of human labour-power by its duration takes on the form of the magnitude of the value of the products of labour; and finally the relationship between the producers, within which the social characteristics of their labours are manifested, takes on the form of a social relation between the products of labour. (Marx 1976 [1867, 1890], p. 164)

Murray (2000, p. 51) comments: "There it is. Value is a consequence of the peculiar social form of wealth and labour in societies where wealth generally takes the form of commodities." Yes. No, no! The ambiguity is precisely that once you have adopted from the previous sections the idea 'value = (abstract) labour as measured by labour-time' you will see this idea confirmed here!

65   Murray 2000, p. 56.

Murray does. Murray is quite right to point this out and I fully agree with him. But where Murray goes wrong is to propose this as an interpretation instead of a (welcome) reconstruction.

3.2   *A flaw in the standard answer to the Ricardian interpretation*
Why do I insist on this, when at the same time I myself hold a value-form theory distanced from labour-embodied theories of value? If Marx's theory is not ambiguous, Murray has a problem. He then must be able to explain why so many Marxists and non-Marxists read a labour-embodied theory of value in Marx's text (be it concrete-labour-embodied or abstract-labour-embodied).

The dubious standard answer to this question on the part of those criticising labour-embodied notions was always that Marx had been read with 'Ricardian' preconceptions in mind. Murray also takes this position. I doubt if this standard answer ever made rudimentary sense. At most it would apply to *economists* that had a university education in economics prior to 1920. Until 1910–20 most economists, at least in Britain, were still being educated with Ricardo (1817) or Mill's (1848) version of his approach serving as their manual. In other countries such as the US, Austrian blends like Taussig's (1911) should have done the same work. But for those trained after that time the standard answer cannot even begin to make sense. In the period since then few (Marxian) economists, and even fewer Marxian philosophers or sociologists have read Ricardo. Even fewer have read it prior to Marx's work.

There remains the answer that students turn to Marxism and the reading of Marx after prior digestion of an introduction such as Sweezy's *The Theory of Capitalist Development* of 1942 (to which Murray refers) that did the 'harm'. I find this unconvincing. It assumes what has to be proven, namely that an introduction such as Sweezy's does no justice to Marx.

Against this background, I set myself the task of finding out if the first chapter of Marx's *Capital 1*, contrary to my own earlier readings, might perhaps consistently be read from a labour-embodied point of view – this is what my 1993 article addresses. To my own surprise – at that time – I found that it can. Moreover, I realised that the crucial value-form theoretic Section 3 can be skipped as a tedious historical account of the emergence of money.[66] Indeed

---

66   In a footnote (p. 61, note 77) Murray writes: "It's a telling fact about Reuten's essay that he does not talk about section 3." I do on page 100, but let's leave that aside. Indeed, for value-form theory this section and the next one is the heart of the matter. However, in my essay I was searching for a labour-embodied theory which indeed is absent from this section; on the other hand, once you have a labour-embodied theory in mind at that point, section 3 need not be inconsistent with it (although it must seem overdone from that perspective and therefore raise questions).

I concluded that, to say the least, Marx's theory of value is ambiguous, and that there is room for at least two lines of argument in Marx's text, an abstract-labour-embodied theory and a value-form theory.

Murray comments on this, a bit hidden in a footnote: "Even if Reuten's suspicions about Marx are unsustainable, he sheds light on how Marx came to be so widely misunderstood, including by Marxists."[67] Murray's roundabout 'interpretation' in fact confirms my 'suspicions'.

Once again, if Murray's interpretation is unambiguously obvious, he needs to explain other prevailing interpretations.

3.3   *Conclusion: phenomenology, systematic dialectics and its starting point*
For Murray's reading of abstract labour to make sense (which I contest) Marx must conflate the stages of dialectical research, as indicated in §2; that is, "Marx's" systematic dialectics interpolates phenomenological research into the systematic dialectics. If that were so, Murray could make an argument for "Marx's" two-fold use of the term 'abstract labour': as general and determinate. However, that is still unconvincing since at other places in *Capital I*, Chapter 1 Marx carefully and explicitly distinguishes his use of general versus determinate categories. Why not then for this crucial concept of abstract labour?

In my 1993 article I indicated that it is not clear where in *Capital* we should trace the formal starting point of the *systematic-dialectical* presentation, and that the earlier sections of the book set out preparatory (phenomenological?) notions.[68] Arthur refers in this respect to the very interesting interpretation by Banaji, who suggests that we have in *Capital* two starting points:[69] one the immediacy of 'the commodity' as a preparatory analytic point of departure, the other of universality in abstract form, i.e., 'value' as the synthetic point of departure.[70] The former would then be a short cut representation of the first dialectical research stage mentioned in §2.4.[71]

Banaji's interpretation, however, does not take away the point of Marx's insufficient break with the classical naturalism. Banaji writes that the social properties of the commodity

---

67   Murray 2000, p. 57, note 63.
68   Reuten 1993, pp. 95–6.
69   Banaji 1979, esp. pp. 36–40. Cf. Arthur 1997, p. 26.
70   Banaji 1979, p. 39, comments: 'As something universal, however, the latter *presupposes nothing* – except, Marx will say, the *historical process* through it has come about (which is why 'the dialectical form of presentation is only correct when it knows *its own limits*', GKP, p. 945).'
71   See also Taylor (alias Mostyn) 2000, pp. 19–24 and 64–5.

appear initially as a sort of 'content' 'hidden within' their 'form of appearance', exchange-value. Insofar as Marx, both in Section 1 and later, calls this 'content' *value* (cf. *Capital I*, p. 139 [which is at the beginning of Section 3]: "We started from exchange-value ... in order to track down the value that lay hidden within it"), it is easy to fall into the illusion of supposing that value is something actually contained in the commodity. For example, it is easy to suppose that Marx means by value (as quite clearly he did *at one stage*) "the labour objectified in a commodity", and then from there to proceed to the more general identification of labour with value which I.I. Rubin quite correctly polemicised *against*.[72]

Is this incomplete break with the classical naturalism a defect of Marx's theory in *Capital*? Quite so, in my view. However, the fruitfulness of great scientific work lies not in the consistency of its reasoning – although that helps. It rather lies in its exposition of the limits of previous thought and the degree of its break with that. Marx's break with past thought, especially Classical Political Economy, is obvious. To expect that such a break can be thoroughly 'clean', consistent and unambiguous is to neglect two points: first, one (in this case Marx) cannot but start thinking in terms of past thought (and for the hypothetical case in which one would start thinking in a void, we cannot even see that it is a break); second, and relatedly, communication (writing) of the break has to take place in a language close to the language of the old view (otherwise, again, it can even not be perceived as a break).

Fundamental breaks are bound to be inconsistent. Only once we command the new language of the break, can we, in retrospect, detect the inconsistencies and the remainders of the old thought and language. For our awareness of Marx's break we are greatly assisted by the fact that, after Marx, economics saw another break, that of Marginalist and Neoclassical Economics' utility theory, which was equally based on naturalism, this time that of the immediate use-aspect of commodities. Paraphrasing Banaji[73] we might say that it is not remarkable that Marx left an incomplete and at points ambiguous work, 'but that close to four generations of Marxists' put more effort in interpretation and reinterpretation than in reconstruction and development of the programme.

---

72 Banaji 1979, p. 31.
73 Banaji 1979, p. 40.

Summary and conclusions

The issues discussed in this article – critique, systematic dialectics in relation to historical materialism and social-form theory – can be seen as constituting one interconnected research programme. Marx magnificently brought these together into one. The complications of carrying out this programme are enormous. In the case of Marx, the drafts, changed plans, redrafts and rechanged plans, including rewrites of already published work, abundantly testify this. From his personal history and scholarship, it is obvious that he would have continued trying to make improvements had he lived longer.

Marx provided elements for a theory of the social form of capitalist entities, including a value-form theory. This was a most important breakthrough. However, this ought not obscure the fact that Marx's break from Classical Political Economy is incomplete.

Equally, but the two points really are one, Marx laid down the track for developing a critique on the basis of a systematic-dialectical account of society in its historicity. The two are one since social form theory accounts for the historicity (nevertheless, historical materialism overarches systematic dialectics trans-historically). Marx's accomplishment here is, in my view, tremendous. Yet the project of *Capital* in this respect is far from either complete – as Marx knew very well – or dialectically impeccable – of which he was equally conscious.[74] Neglecting this would prevent the improvement of the project.

In this light my disagreements and agreements with Patrick Murray can be summarised in the following eight points.

Method: systematic dialectics and historical materialism
1. Murray proposes a particular view about the relation between historical materialism (HM) – he rather refers to phenomenology – and systematic dialectics (SD): (a) HM is a presupposition for SD; (b) Phenomenology and SD are developed alongside each other in *Capital*.
2. If my view of systematic dialectics differs from Murray's, then I am obliged to set out how HM and SD relate. This is what I have done in §2.
3. (a) Murray's interpretation of Marx's method in *Capital* can perhaps be sustained in the face of the content of *Capital*. (b) It is, however, inconsistent with Marx's (few) mature writings on method, i.e., those from the *Grundrisse* Introduction onwards.

---

74 See, for example, Smith 1990 (pp. 124, 236) and Oakley 1983 (pp. 94–8).

4. (a) My interpretation of Marx's method in *Capital* makes sense in face of his mature writings on method. (b) My interpretation of this method is inconsistent with at least some parts of *Capital*.

Value-form theory: interpretation, reconstruction
5. If what Murray has to say about 'abstract labour' and value-form theory is not a reconstruction but an unambiguous interpretation, then he is obliged to explain why (abstract-)labour-embodied interpretations nevertheless have been overwhelming.
6. My interpretation of the text on abstract labour and value-form theory explains the development of Marxian theory in the twentieth century.
7. If Murray cannot furnish the explanation sub 5, then his view amounts to a reconstruction instead of an interpretation. As a reconstruction I agree with him in outline (subject to the methodical frame).
8. Neither of us is happy with the (abstract-)labour-embodied strands of the twentieth-century development of Marxian theory. Provided the lack of explanation sub 7, we seem to agree on the need for reconstructing the theory, in either way of method (1 or 2).

I thank Murray for challenging me to set out the relation between historical materialism and systematic dialectics. I believe that the issue between us of interpretation versus reconstruction is surmountable. Dialecticians insist on the inseparable connection of method and content. Our disagreements on method are important – though, weighed against mainstream methods based on a 'linear' logic, they are very moderate indeed. Since we share so much on the issue of content (social form), I feel that there is a firm basis for overcoming the methodological issues in further discussion.

References

Arthur, Christopher J. 1986, *Dialectics of labour: Marx and his relation to Hegel*, Oxford: Basil Blackwell.
Arthur, Christopher J. 1992, 'Introduction' to *Marx's Capital: a student edition*, edited by C.J. Arthur, London: Lawrence & Wishart.
Arthur, Christopher J. 1997, 'Against the logical-historical method: dialectical derivation versus linear logic', in Moseley and Campbell (eds) 1997, pp. 9–37.
Arthur, Christopher J. 1998a, 'Systematic dialectic', *Science & Society*, 62(3): 447–59.
Arthur, Christopher J. 1998b, 'The fluidity of capital and the logic of the concept', in Arthur and Reuten (eds) 1998, pp. 95–128.

Arthur, Christopher J. 2002, 'Capital in general and Marx's *Capital*', in Campbell and Reuten (eds) 2002, pp. 42–64.

Arthur, Christopher, and Geert Reuten (eds) 1998, *The circulation of capital: essays on volume II of Marx's 'Capital'*, London: Macmillan.

Banaji, Jairus 1979, 'From the commodity to capital: Hegel's dialectic in Marx's *Capital*', in Elson (ed.) 1979, pp. 14–45.

Campbell, Martha, and Geert Reuten (eds) 2002, *The culmination of capital: essays on volume III of Marx's Capital*, London: Palgrave Macmillan.

Davis, John, D. Wade Hands, and Uskali Mäki (eds) 1998, *The handbook of economic methodology*, Cheltenham: Edward Elgar.

Hegel, G.W.F. 1812[1], 1831[2], *Wissenschaft der Logik*, Engl. transl. of the 1923 Lasson edition, A.V. Miller (1969), *Science of logic*, Atlantic Highlands, NJ: Humanities Press, 1989.

Hegel, G.W.F. 1817[1], 1830[3], *Enzyklopädie der Philosophischen Wissenschaften im Grundrisse I, Die Wissenschaft der Logik*, Engl. transl. of the third edition, T.F. Geraets, W.A. Suchting, and H.S. Harris, *The encyclopaedia logic*, Indianapolis: Hackett Publishing Company, 1991.

Hegel, G.W.F. 1821[1], 1970[7], *Grundlinien der Philosophie des Rechts* oder *Naturrecht und Staatswissenschaft im Grundrisse*, Engl. transl. T.M. Knox (1942), *Philosophy of right*, Oxford: Oxford University Press, 1967.

Hegel, G.W.F. 1837[1], 1840[2], 1955[4], *Vorlesungen über die Philosophie der Geschichte*, ed. J. Hoffmeister 1955, Engl. transl. selections, H.B. Nisbet (1975), *Lectures on the philosophy of world history, introduction: reason in history*, Cambridge: Cambridge University Press, 1984.

Marx, Karl 1873, Postface to the second edition of *Capital I* (see Marx 1976).

Marx, Karl 1971 [1859[1], 1897[2]], *Zur Kritik der Politischen Ökonomie*, MEW 13, Berlin: Dietz Verlag, 1974; English edition Maurice Dobb, translated by S.W. Ryazanskaya, *A contribution to the critique of political economy*, London: Lawrence & Wishart.

Marx, Karl 1973 [1953[2], 1939–41[1]], {written 1857–58}, *Grundrisse der Kritik der Politischen Ökonomie (Rohentwurf)*, Engl. transl. (1973) Martin Nicolaus, *Grundrisse*, Harmondsworth: Penguin/NLB.

Marx, Karl 1976 [1867[1], 1873[2], 1890[4]] *Das Kapital, Kritik der politischen Ökonomie, Band I, Der Produktionsprozess des Kapitals*, Engl. transl. Ben Fowkes (1976), *Capital: a critique of political economy, volume one*, Harmondsworth: Penguin/NLB.

Marx, Karl 1978 [1867[1] first edn.] *Das Kapital etc.*, 'Anhang, Die Wertform' (pp. 764–84; dropped in subsequent editions), Engl. transl. M. Roth and W. Suchting, 'The valueform', *Capital & Class*, 4 (1978): 134–50.

Marx, Karl, and Friedrich Engels 1974 [1902/24[1], 1932[2], 1965/66[3]] {written 1845–46}, *Die Deutsche Ideologie: Kritik der neuesten deutschen Philosophie* etc., Engl. transl. of 3rd edn. W. Lough, C. Dutt, and C.P. Magill, edited by C.J. Arthur (1970), *The German ideology*, Part One (with selections from Parts II–III), London: Lawrence & Wishart, 1974.

Mattick Jr., Paul 1993, 'Marx's dialectic', in Moseley (ed.) 1993, pp. 115–33.

Mehring, Franz 1973 [1918], *Karl Marx, Geschichte seines Lebens*, Dutch authorised translation, Jan Romein (1921), Nijmegen: SUN, 1973.

Mészáros, István 1970, *Marx's theory of alienation*, London: Merlin Press.

Mill, John Stuart 1966 [1848^1, 1871^7], *Principles of political economy, with some of their applications to social philosophy*, Toronto: University of Toronto Press.

Moseley, Fred (ed.) 1993, *Marx's method in 'Capital': a re-examination*, Atlantic Highlands, NJ: Humanities Press.

Moseley, Fred, and Martha Campbell (eds) 1997, *New investigations of Marx's method*, Atlantic Highlands, NJ: Humanities Press.

Murray, Patrick 1988, *Marx's theory of scientific knowledge*, Atlantic Highlands, NJ: Humanities Press.

Murray, Patrick 1998, 'Beyond the "commerce and industry" picture of capital', in Arthur and Reuten (eds) 1998, pp. 33–66.

Murray, Patrick 2000, 'Marx's "truly social" labour theory of value: part I, abstract labour in Marxian value theory', *Historical Materialism*, 6: 27–65.

Norman, Richard 1976, *Hegel's phenomenology: a philosophical introduction*, Atlantic Highlands, NJ: Humanities Press.

Norman, Richard, and Sean Sayers 1980, *Hegel, Marx and dialectic: a debate*, Brighton: Harvester Press.

Oakley, Allen 1983, *The making of Marx's critical theory: a bibliographical analysis*, London: Routledge & Kegan Paul.

Ricardo, David 1951 [1817^1, 1821^3], *On the principles of political economy and taxation*, in P. Sraffa (ed.), *The works and correspondence of David Ricardo, volume I*, Cambridge: Cambridge University Press.

Reuten, Geert 1988a, 'Value as social form', in Williams (ed.) 1988, pp. 42–61.

Reuten, Geert 1988b, 'The money expression of value and the credit system: a value-form theoretic outline', *Capital & Class*, 35: 121–41.

Reuten, Geert 1993, 'The difficult labour of a theory of social value: metaphors and systematic dialectics at the beginning of Marx's *Capital*', in Moseley (ed.) 1993, pp. 89–113.

Reuten, Geert 1996, 'A revision of the neoclassical economics methodology: appraising Hausman's Mill-twist, Robbins-gist, and Popper-whist', *Journal of Economic Methodology*, 3(1): 39–67.

Reuten, Geert 1998a, 'Marx's method', in Davis et al. (eds) 1998, pp. 283–7.

Reuten, Geert 1998b, 'Dialectical method', in Davis et al. (eds) 1998, pp. 103–7.

Reuten, Geert 1998c, 'The status of Marx's reproduction schemes', in Arthur and Reuten (eds) 1998, pp. 187–229.

Reuten, Geert, and Michael Williams 1989, *Value-form and the state; the tendencies of accumulation and the determination of economic policy in capitalist society*, London: Routledge.

Rubin, Isaak Illich 1972 [1928³], *Ocherki po teorii stoimosti Marksa*, Gosudarstvennoe Izdatel'stvo, Moscow 1928, Engl. transl. Miloš Samardžija and Fredy Perlman, *Essays on Marx's theory of value*, Detroit: Black & Red.

Smith, Tony 1990, *The logic of Marx's Capital: replies to Hegelian criticisms*, Albany: State University of New York Press.

Smith, Tony 1993, 'Marx's *Capital* and Hegelian dialectical logic', in Moseley (ed.) 1993, pp. 15–36.

Smith, Tony 1999, 'The relevance of systematic dialectics to Marxian thought: a reply to Rosenthal', *Historical Materialism*, 4: 215–40.

Sweezy, Paul M. 1968 [1942], *The theory of capitalist development*, New York: Modern Reader Paperbacks.

Taussig, Frank W. 1917 [1911¹, 1915²], *Principles of economics*, second edn., Volumes I and II, New York: The Macmillan Company.

Taylor, Nicola (alias Nicola Mostyn) 2000, 'Abstract labour and social mediation in Marxian value theory', unpublished thesis, Murdoch University, School of Economics.

Williams, Michael (ed.) 1988, *Value, social form and the state*, London: Macmillan.

PART B

Capital I – outlines and comments

∴

Contents
6. The difficult labour of a theory of social value: metaphors and systematic dialectics at the beginning of Marx's *Capital* (1993) p. 107.
7. Money as constituent of value: the ideal introversive substance and the ideal extroversive form of value in Marx's *Capital* (2005) p. 135.
8. Productive force and the degree of intensity of labour: Marx's concepts and formalisations in the middle part of *Capital I* (2004) p. 153.
9. The inner mechanism of the accumulation of capital: the acceleration triple; A methodological appraisal of Part Seven of Marx's *Capital I* (2004) p. 181.

Chapters 6–7 are on Part One of *Capital*, Volume I.
Chapter 8 is on Parts Three to Five of Volume I.
Chapter 9 is on Part Seven of Volume I.

Note on the editions of *Das Kapital I* and *Capital I*.
   Marx's 1st German edition is from 1867 and the 2nd from 1873. Engels brought out a 3rd edition in 1883 and a 4th in 1890. The 3rd edition was translated into English by Samuel Moore and Edward Aveling (1887) and the 4th by Ben Fowkes (1976).

CHAPTER 6

The difficult labour of a theory of social value; metaphors and systematic dialectics at the beginning of Marx's *Capital*

1993 article, which was originally published in *Marx's method in 'Capital': a re-examination*, edited by Fred Moseley, Atlantic Highlands, NJ: Humanities Press, pp. 89–113.
 (For its abstract see the Abstracts of all chapters, p. 3.)

Contents

Introduction   108
1   Systematic dialectic   109
2   Marx's method in *Capital*   112
   2.1   Kinds of interpretation   112
   2.2   Systematic dialectic in *Capital*?   113
3   The starting point of *Capital* and the theory of value   115
   3.1   A systematic starting point   115
   3.2   Abstract labour and value   116
      A   Abstract labour   116
      B   Value   118
   3.3   Embodiment: more than a metaphor?   119
   3.4   Value-form and value form   120
4   Labour-embodied versus abstract-labour theory of value: some current controversies   122
   4.1   Interpretations of Marx's theory of value   122
   4.2   Labour-embodied theories of value   123
      A   Concrete-labour-embodied   123
      B   Abstract-labour-embodied   123
      C   Substance of value in the labour-embodied theories   124
   4.3   The abstract-labour theory of value: abstraction in practice   125
   4.4   Substance and the measure of time: real abstractions   126
5   Reconstructing abstract labour within a systematic-dialectical view   127
Conclusions   131
References   132

Introduction[1]

Although the science of nature, it seems, first got off the ground from a social-scientific impetus,[2] eighteenth- and nineteenth-century social scientists felt constrained to cast their theoretical innovations in terms of metaphors borrowed from the natural sciences, in particular physics (see Mirowski 1990). The birth of Marxist social science in the nineteenth century is no exception in this respect. This is remarkable because Marx was very aware of the naturalism of classical political economy. Borrowing metaphors from physics, it is true, need not be naturalistic. Nevertheless, metaphors may be dangerous (as Hegel observed) if perhaps unavoidable. Within Marxist social science, I will argue, the metaphor *substance of value* as introduced by Marx (1867|1976) has played a very dubious role. It seems that this metaphor came to be taken for a real embodiment – at least within one important strand of Marxism. Of course, because our thinking is so tied to our language, it is always difficult to disentangle metaphoric language from what we really think. It is, however, important to try to be conscious of the metaphors and their purport.

Although the metaphor *substance of value* was used by Marx (1867|1976), not without a Hegelian undertone, his linking it to embodiment seems to derive from classical political economy. I argue that the combination of (1) the substance metaphor and the classical embodiment remnant with (2) the only implicit method of *Capital* and, in particular, the unclarity as to the type of abstractions used by Marx, gave rise to an extensive period of birth of a true theory of social value (a theory of value as a purely social institutional phenomenon). I take such a theory to be in the spirit of Marx's theory in *Capital*. Despite Marx's explicit rejection of classical naturalism, the actual content of *Capital* often seems to bear the remnants of such a naturalism, which can be explained from his lack of clarity as to the extent of the break with his predecessors (which is a common occurrence among path-breaking theoreticians).

---

[1] I am grateful to Chris Arthur, Martha Campbell, Mino Carchedi, Paul Mattick Jr., Patrick Murray, Fred Moseley, and Tony Smith for the intensive and enjoyable conference discussion of an earlier version of this paper, which has also benefited from comments by Michael Williams and Alexander van Altena, and further from a second-round comment by Fred Moseley.

[2] Paolucci (1974, p. 108) indicates how Francis Bacon was inspired by Machiavelli, who had taken the laws of statecraft as statecraft really is rather than as it ought to be. Cf. Mattick Jr. 1986, p. 113, on the natural law metaphor taken from "the medieval Christian picture of God as lawgiving sovereign of creation".

I examine to what extent Marx's theory may indeed be considered a labour-embodied theory of value and to what extent labour is seen to be a substance of value (§3). Then I consider how this has affected current Marxist theory of value, especially in its varieties of the labour-embodied and the abstract-labour theories of value. These theories contain, in my view, a number of defects that may be traced back to the substance of value view (§4). Finally, I provide an outline of how these defects might be overcome (§5). I hope to show that interpreting the type of abstractions that Marx uses is crucial to the examination of his value theory. Are these dialectical abstractions or some sort of analytical abstractions? An answer to this question is complicated by the fact that Marx is hardly explicit about his method. His attitude vis-à-vis Hegel's logic is an especially ambivalent one. First, I briefly set out my view of this dialectical logic (§1). This will be the vantage point for the examination of Marx's theory of value (§2) as well as for my view on a possible reconstruction of the labour theory of value (§5). I also make a number of general remarks on Marx's method in *Capital*.

1 Systematic dialectic

That Marx's method remains only implicit in *Capital* has always complicated the discussion of the work both among and between supporters and opponents. There seems to be no way out of this dilemma apart from making one's own methodological inclinations explicit: Inasmuch as empirical observations are theory laden (Popper), theoretical evaluations will be methodologically laden. My own methodological inclinations, however – as inspired by Hegel's logic – are not totally farfetched with respect to Marx. Marx has repeatedly stressed his own indebtedness to this dialectical logic. (See, e.g., Arthur 1986, Echeverria 1978, Murray 1988, Smith 1990, and the contributions in the collection by Schmidt 1969.) The Introduction to the *Grundrisse* (Marx 1857|1973) provides a statement of a number of the characteristics of systematic dialectics. In other works, however, Marx often seems to distance himself from this approach. The brief outline of the method of systematic dialectic below may prove to be difficult when abstracting it from the content of the theory. In order to give a more complete picture, I include certain concepts that are less relevant for the issues discussed in the sections that follow (these paragraphs are starred [*] in case the reader wishes to skip them).

Systematic dialectic or *conceptual dialectic* refers to the dialectic as developed in Hegel's logic (Hegel 1817 1975), which is a logic of dialectical conceptual development. This dialectic should be distinguished definitively from a theory of dialectical historical development (as in Hegel's philosophy of history) or a theory of historical development of concepts (as introduced in Hegel's history of philosophy).³

The starting point of the presentation of the systematic-dialectical theory (*Darstellung*) is an abstract universal notion – an abstract all-embracing concept. This starting point itself is the result of a process of inquiry, of critical appropriation of empirical perceptions and existing theories (of them). This abstract notion is the starting point of explicit theorisation and its presentation (cf. Marx 1867|1976, p. 102; 1857|1973, p. 100). Thinking cannot conceivably make anything of such an abstract universal notion, other than by thinking its abstract negation and its abstract particularisation. In both cases (negation and particularisation), opposed concepts are applied to the same thing or notion, and in this specific sense these opposites are contradictions. In this sense also, to think these things and notions is to articulate their doubling that is, the universal doubles into the universal and an opposite universal, or into universal and particular. (The value–use-value opposition is an example of the former; the opposition of universal and particular labour – amplified upon below – or in simpler terms the animal–cat opposition, are examples of the latter.)

*Two further remarks concerning these oppositions should be made. First, it is precisely the purpose of the presentation to resolve the contradiction from which we start; it is this process of thought that should render comprehension of reality. "The essence of philosophy consists precisely in resolving the contradiction of the Understanding" (Hegel 1833|1985, p. 71). Second, to immediately subsume single empirical phenomena as particulars under universals provides only empty abstractions. One reason for this is that such subsumption may indicate what such phenomena have in common, but not what, if anything, unites them, how they are interconnected. Another is that it is the difference between phenomena that determines them; but this difference also does not say what, if anything, unites them. As long as we have provided no difference-in-unity we have provided no concrete determination. It is this double determination (difference-in-unity) that systematic-dialectical thinking seeks. As Hegel expresses it: "The truth of the differentiated is its being in unity. And only through this movement is the unity truly concrete." Whereas at first, at the starting point: "difference is still sunk in the unity, not yet set forth as different" (Hegel 1833|1985, p. 83).

---

3 The remainder of this section draws on a section on method in Reuten 1988. An extensive discussion is in Reuten and Williams 1989, part 1.

*The object of the presentation is to grasp the phenomena from which we start in our perception as concrete, that is, as the "concentration [*Zusammenfassung*] of many determinations, hence unity of the diverse" (Marx 1857/1973, p. 101). But that may only be possible to the extent that these are phenomena necessary to the existent, rather than contingent ones. (For example, if we have established monetary policy to be necessary to the existent, then credit restrictions or open market policy may be only contingent.) Contingent phenomena cannot be explained as codetermining the internal unity of many determinants – thus not as necessary – but only as an external determinant. (In this article, however, I will not reach this stage of contingency of phenomena.)

A further characteristic of the method of systematic dialectic is that the argument is not based on rules of axiomatic deductive nomological systems. All axioms are eschewed. Rather, anything that is required to be assumed, or anything that is posited immediately (such as the starting point), must be grounded. But it should not be grounded merely abstractly (i.e., giving the arguments in advance), because this always leads to regress. That which is posited must be ultimately grounded in the argument itself, in concretising it. Therefore, the intrinsic merits of the presentation – and not some external criterion – have to convince the reader of the adequacy of the presentation. Thus the presentation moves forward by the transcendence of contradiction and by providing the ever more concrete grounds – the conditions of existence – of the earlier abstract determination. In this forward movement the conditions of existence of earlier abstract determination do not dissolve, but transcend the opposite moments (identity–difference, universal–particular) of the abstract determination. (A moment is an element considered in itself that can be conceptually isolated and analysed as such but that can have no isolated existence.)

*Thus the previous conceptualisation of abstract determinations as moments is not negated, but rather transcended in the ground; or the ground provides the unity of the opposed moments. But at the same time it is a further, more concrete determination of the difference, a difference previously posited only in itself (*an sich*, potentially, implicitly), as it now appears. So the differences that were previously not set forth as such now come into (abstract) existence. The ground at this new level itself then gains momentum; it is itself an abstract existent showing the contradiction that it cannot exist for itself (*für sich*, actually). The presentation has to move on in order to ground it in its turn, so as to provide its conditions of existence (Hegel 1817/1975, pp. 120–4; 1833/1985, pp. 81–3). And so on, until the presentation claims to have reached the stage where it comprehends the existent as actual, as actuality (*Wirklichkeit*), in the sense that its conditions of existence have now been determined such that it is indeed actual, concrete, self-reproducing, or endogenous existence, which requires no external or exogenous determinants for its systematic reproduction.

The presentation then is one of conceptual reproduction of the concrete in successive steps (levels of abstraction); if successful, the presentation is able to grasp the concrete as mediated by the theory (that is, to theoretically reconstitute the empirical 'facts', which were at the basis of the initial inquiry). Such a process of inquiry and reconstruction can, of course, never be posited as definitive and completed.

*Levels of abstraction may further be characterised by degree of necessity versus degree of contingency of the elements theorised. It is the purpose of the theory to single out which elements of the object of inquiry may be theorised as necessary to the object, and which elements are (merely) contingent. Of course, the more the presentation moves toward lower levels of abstraction, the more (historically) contingent elements have to be incorporated.

2   Marx's method in *Capital*

2.1   *Kinds of interpretation*

I have indicated that Marx is hardly explicit about the method he uses in *Capital*. The scarce explicit remarks, moreover, are open to different interpretations. Of course, such interpretations are linked to the understanding of the content. In this respect the history of Marxism has resulted not only in various fashions (such as those led by Bernstein or Althusser) but also in specific research programs (linked to minor groups, e.g., around Lukács and Korsch or Gramsci).

In general, interpretations can be of three sorts, and one can find all three within the Marxist tradition. The first allots authority to, in this case, *Capital* and sticks in an exegetic way to the text. In terms of the development of a scientific programme this is not very fruitful. The second is historiographic, and for this critical approach one cannot normally stick to a single text. The third type of interpretation is heuristic. Under the heuristic approach, *Capital* has proved to be a fruitful source. (Indeed, this is what makes a work a classical text.)

Aspects of these three approaches, in general, cannot be kept separate. The historiographer, for example, will at some point be faced with exegetic questions, and good theoretical history will end up with either heuristically interesting questions or heuristically interesting loose ends. My remarks in the remainder of this section and the next derive primarily from the heuristic interest.

2.2 Systematic dialectic in 'Capital'?

Is Marx's method in *Capital* systematic dialectic? And if not, what kind of dialectic is it? Even if I were able to answer this question, this is not the place to do so in a well-balanced and well-documented way. (One need only consult the scholarly works of Murray 1988 and Smith 1990 to see that the issue is quite complicated.) In §3 I consider, from a limited point of view, only one aspect of the question: How can we evaluate the very beginning of *Capital*, that is, the starting point, in terms of a systematic dialectic? However, these considerations do not provide an answer to the question of the systematic-dialectical character of *Capital* as a whole. For several reasons, there cannot be a simple yes or no answer to this question.

Hegel's logic is not a philosophy of social science or of political economy in particular. It is propaedeutic to that philosophy, which needs to be developed on the basis of that logic. There are several ways to do this, and the choice is connected to one's view of the object realm of the science. However, the object realm is inseparable from the content of the science. Further, these ways are tied not only to the object realm but also to one's view (vision) of the state of the science in relation to the phenomena (although this is closely related to the object realm).[4]

It follows that the philosophy and methodology of a science cannot be developed in separation from the content of the science. Both Hegel and Marx seem to have been well aware of this point. (And I am very much aware of it from my own research experience.) Nevertheless, I believe that much of the trouble with Hegelian Marxism is due to an exaggerated puritanism in this respect. I want to make a plea for making the philosophy and methodology of systematic-dialectical social science explicit. However, this can never be a once-and-for-all matter. It can never be more than a temporary state of the art since it is necessarily linked to (one's view of) the state of the science. Marx, for example, might have written such a treatise after the completion of the *Grundrisse* (i.e., more than the current Introduction) and a new one after the completion of Volume 1 of *Capital* and another new one after the completion of Volume 3 of *Capital*.

There are indeed several ways to proceed from Hegel's dialectical logic. For example, within an agreed movement from abstract to concrete categories, as well as an agreement that Hegel's *Begriff*'s logic cannot be applied or developed immediately to the social science of capitalism, Murray (1988) stresses general

---

4   If we are primarily interested in historiographic questions with respect to Marx's *Capital*, then the relevant phenomena are those of 1850.

versus determinate abstractions and their development, Smith (1990) a triadic development, and Reuten and Williams (1989) systemic necessity versus contingency as well as negation and particularisation.[5] In their works these authors do not deny the importance of that which is stressed by the others; only the emphasis is different.[6]

In *The Philosophy of Right*, originally published in 1821, Hegel does develop *Begriff*'s logic into social science (i.e., in his theory of the state). It is a social-scientific work into which Hegel develops his own logic. Although *The Philosophy of Right* contains, in my view, a number of outstanding insights (especially in the Introduction), it does not live up to Hegel's logic. At least it can be highly criticised from the point of view of Hegel's logic. For example, it does not (cf. Smith 1990) follow a strict triadic movement even if the three parts do so, the movements within the parts definitely do not. Hegel leaves no room for the articulation of general versus determinate abstractions (cf. Murray 1988), and the articulation of the necessary versus the contingent is far from sound (cf. Reuten and Williams 1989).[7]

I will not blame anyone for not seeing a systematic conceptual development in Marx's *Capital*. When I first read the work, I knew little about dialectics and conceptual development, and my reading was a flat one. A later reading though – with some knowledge of dialectics – did not convey to me more than three broad levels of abstraction in line with the three volumes of *Capital*. Nevertheless, and perhaps paradoxically, certain moments in Marx's *Capital* contain a conceptual development. In general, this applies to his concept of tendency and, in particular, that of the tendency of the rate of profit to fall. But in a recent reading of the first three chapters of Volume 1 (undertaken in writing this essay), I once again found them very disappointing in terms of systematic conceptual development.

---

5 Reuten and Williams 1989 – note, however, that this work is not an interpretation of Marx, although it owes a lot to Marx.

6 In Murray's (1988) work, 'contradiction' and its developmental powers are far less prominent than in either Smith (1990) or Reuten and Williams (1989). In both Murray and Smith, the concept of form is treated differently than in Reuten and Williams. Form is at the very basis of Reuten and Williams; it is developed as expressions of form, whereas both Murray and Smith allow for forms of form. As an interpretation of Marx, forms of form is correct, though I think it is a confusing concept.

7 Two examples that spring to mind are Hegel's view on the male-female functions, divisions, and roles, and the role of the monarch. Even if Hegel's views on these issues can be explained in terms of the culture of his time, and even if in his time (around 1800) his views were far from conservative, they are still inadmissible if we take his own logic seriously: The systemic necessity of the roles referred to is not developed in Hegel's *Philosophy of Right* (1821|1967).

3 The starting point of *Capital* and the theory of value

3.1 A systematic starting point

The opening sentences of *Capital* are:

> The wealth of societies in which the capitalist mode of production prevails appears as an 'immense collection of commodities' [quoted from Marx 1859|1971]; the individual [*einzelne*] commodity appears as its elementary form. Our investigation therefore begins with the analysis of the commodity. (Marx 1867|1976, p. 125)

Is this the systematic starting point of a dialectical systematic presentation? It might be argued that the first section of Marx's chapter, as well as the very important second one on the double character, introduce a number of preparatory notions; therefore, the actual starting point would be the third section, which again starts off with the commodity (cf. Murray 1988, ch. 12; see also Eldred and Roth 1978). But even so, is this, the commodity, the most abstract all-embracing concept for the capitalist mode of production? I doubt it. For example, does it embrace in itself a notion of the activity of creation of useful objects in capitalist form? The commodity is certainly a ubiquitous phenomenon. Marx certainly develops from it the form of capitalist production (from Chapter 4 onwards). Nevertheless, from a systematic-dialectical point of view, this is not convincing.

I think that Marx does what he says he does (see the quotation above): analyse. In fact, he repeats several times statements to that effect. What kind of analysis is this? It is certainly not the kind of axiomatic analysis that proceeds from definitions. Marx does not define. (At one place in the English translation the word occurs – "as it has just been defined" – but in German the word is *bestimmt*, i.e., determined.) What Marx seems to do, at least in Part One, is conceptual analysis rather than dialectical conceptual development. Again, there is a process, but it seems to go from simple (rather than abstract) to complex concepts. Each time it seems to be the analysis of concepts that keeps the process moving. It is not an internal proceeding from contradictions and their transcendences (negation or particularisation). (Note that the latter proceeding would not exclude the analysis of moments – but then moments would need to have been posited as such.)

I do not think that my interpretation in this respect is fundamentally different from either Smith's (1990) or Murray's (1988), although the emphases are somewhat different. Further, Marx's 'Notes on Wagner' do not falsify such a reading. Smith quotes from this text:

> In the first place I [Marx] do not start out from 'concepts' hence do not start out from 'the concept of value' ... What I start out from is that simplest social form in which the labour-product is presented in contemporary society, and this is the 'commodity'. (Smith 1990, p. 23; cf. Murray 1988, pp. xvii, 143)

In the next subsections I further consider Marx's conceptual analysis, especially focusing on the type of abstractions that are being used.

3.2   *Abstract labour and value*
In the first two sections of Chapter 1 of *Capital* Marx introduces the twin concepts of abstract labour and value. They seem to exist by way of a transformation whose character is hardly expanded upon.

A   Abstract labour
When the term abstract labour is introduced for the first time, Marx refers to a transformation:

> If then we disregard the use-value of commodities, only one property remains, that of being products of labour. But even the product of labour has already been transformed in our hands. [*Jedoch ist uns auch das Arbeitsprodukt bereits in der Hand verwandelt.*] If we make abstraction from its use-value, we abstract also from the material constituents and forms which make it a use-value. ... The useful character of the kinds of labour embodied in them also disappears; this in turn entails the disappearance of the different concrete forms of labour. They can no longer be distinguished, but are altogether reduced to the same kind of labour, human labour in the abstract. (Marx 1867|1976, p. 128)

Here abstract labour is not posited as universal labour in contradiction with particular labour (the universal–particular contradiction referred to above). Rather, the particular labour appears to be abstracted away. We have a transformation that seems to be established via a *reductive abstraction*: The disregarding of use-values, the abstraction from use-value, and the disappearance of the useful character of labour give rise to the reduction to abstract labour. I propose to call this (reductive) abstract labour Λ. This abstraction is conveyed by way of a (metaphorical) reference to a transformation in the sense of a transubstantiation (the phrase "transformed in the hand" undoubtedly stresses the connotation of the German term *Verwandlung* when signifying the change of the eucharistic elements at their consecration in the Mass – in the priest's hand).

Anticipating the discussion of the current abstract-labour theory of value in §4 below, it may be observed that at this point there is no reference to the market – thus no reference to a real abstraction or an abstraction in practice.[8]

However, from the middle of the second section of Chapter 1 onward, abstract labour is (also) treated as a *simplifying abstraction* (or a simplifying assumption):

> In the interests of simplification, we shall henceforth view every form [*Art*, i.e., kind] of labour-power directly as simple labour-power; by this we shall simply be saving ourselves the trouble of making the reduction. (Marx 1867|1976, p. 135)

The extent to which this is important depends not only on how much of a labour-embodied theory one wants to read in Marx (see below) but also on whether at some stage one would want to apply the theory empirically. I think that within a labour-embodied theory this simplification precludes the adding up of labour-time before settling the trouble of making the reduction. (However, actually settling the trouble would then take one into Smithian (1776|1933) labour-commanded waters, or the realm of Keynes's, 1936, wage unit.) Indeed, I believe that this simplifying abstraction (assumption) makes a quantitative procedure at the empirical level of adding up concrete premarket hours of labour very dubious.

If i and j are particular (concrete) kinds of labour, and if we consider that labour only under the aspect of being particulars, then their respective labour hours (L_i and L_j) cannot be added up. (For reasons of simplicity all my equations below are restricted to two kinds of labour, i and j. Of course, they hold for the set of all kinds of labour.)

If α_i and α_j are discounting coefficients and if Λ is (reductive) abstract labour as indicated above, then we may write $\alpha_i L_i + \alpha_j L_j = \Lambda$. Next, we may make the simplifying assumption $\alpha_i = \alpha_j$ (= 1), but this does not get us to the concrete

---

8 Later on there is such a reference: "But the act of equating tailoring with weaving reduces the former in fact to what is really equal in the two kinds of labour, to the characteristic they have in common of being human labour" (Marx 1867|1976, p. 142). However, if one wishes to read an abstract-labour theory of value in the first chapter of *Capital*, it might then be argued that a real abstraction is implicit in the transformation referred to in Marx 1867|1976, p. 128. Indeed, the concept of commodity is clearly connected to the market and exchange: "In order to produce the latter [commodities], he must not only produce use-values, but use-values for others, social use-values" (Marx 1867|1976, p. 131).

empirical level.[9] For that we need a procedure to quantify the discounting coefficients. It is hard to see how this could be done prior to the market.

(In §5 I show how, because of the dialectical contradiction of particular labour being universal labour at the same time, the labour-time i and j can in principle be added up as labour hours in the abstract (l): $l_i + l_j = l$, even though we cannot add them up as particulars L. This may be done on the basis of a dialectical abstraction rather than on the basis of a (Marxian) reductive abstraction.)

B   Value

Is value an entity that exists prior to exchange? (This question is discussed again when I examine current Marxist theories of value.) I think that Marx takes it as such, although there are a number of texts that would refute this view. This is how 'value' is introduced for the first time. Abstract labour is further specified as:

> merely congealed quantities of homogeneous human labour, i.e., of human labour-power expended without regard to the form of its expenditure. All these things now tell us that human labour-power has been expended to produce them, human labour is accumulated in them. As crystals of this social substance, which is common to them all, they are values – commodity values [*Warenwerte*]. (Marx 1867|1976, p. 128)

And somewhat further on:

> How is the magnitude of this value to be measured? By means of the quantity of the 'value-forming [*bildenden*, i.e., constituting] substance', the labour contained in the article. This quantity is measured by its duration, and the labour-time is itself measured on the particular scale of hours, days, etc. (Marx 1867|1976, p. 129)

From this and other passages there seems hardly any doubt that there is some kind of labour-embodied view of value (see below) and that it is seen to exist

---

9   Musgrave (1981) distinguishes three kinds of assumptions: negligibility, domain, and heuristic. The simplification at hand does not say that the theory applies only to cases where $\alpha_i = \alpha_j$ (domain assumption). I assume that it also does not say that we can neglect the differences between the concrete labours because they have a negligible effect with respect to the problematic the theory addresses (negligibility assumption). Thus the simplification at hand might be a heuristic assumption, one that plays a role in one stage of a theory but must then be dropped in a later stage (as in the method of successive approximation).

prior to exchange. Nevertheless, although value exists prior to exchange, it is always objectified:

> Human labour-power in its fluid state, or human labour, creates value, but is not itself value. It becomes value in its coagulated state, in objective form. (Marx 1867|1976, p. 142)

Thus value is identified with the (reduced) abstract labour Λ, insofar as it is objectified or expended. Quite another issue is that exchange-value (the forms of exchange-value) is the only mode of expression or form of appearance of value (which is the subject of section 3, Chapter 1 of *Capital*).

The problem with this concept of value is that it relies on an abstract entity, the reduced abstract labour, but it is also given – already at this level – a fairly concrete meaning, especially because of what is added on measurement. It is not made clear, however, how we can undertake this measurement ("on the particular scale of hours, days, etc.") prior to the market because we are left in doubt about the actual discounting to simple labour.

3.3 Embodiment: more than a metaphor?

What do we make of all the natural-physical references that Marx uses in order to explain what he means by abstract labour and value, such as "crystals of this social substance", "congealed quantities of ... labour", and indeed the notion of "labour embodied" itself? (All these appear for the first time in Marx 1867|1976, p. 128, but are used throughout Chapter 1.) Are they merely metaphors? The following quotation seems to point at a 'merely' interpretation:

> Not an atom of matter enters into the objectivity of commodities as values; in this it is the direct opposite of the coarsely sensuous objectivity of commodities as physical objects ... However, let us remember that commodities possess an objective character as values only insofar as they are all expressions of an identical social substance, human labour, that their objective character as values is therefore purely social. (Marx 1867|1976, pp. 138–9)

The least we can say is that – apart from in this quotation and a few other places – the metaphors have somewhat taken over the presentation.

In sum, I think we can safely say that Marx presents an abstract-labour-*embodied* theory of value. This term may seem confusing with respect to the labour-embodied versus abstract-labour debate. My reason for introducing it is not to arrive at a synthesis. The point is that, on the one hand, Marx does not propose to add up concrete labour hours $L_i + L_j$ into an L that is taken for the sum of these concrete labour hours (= concrete-labour-embodied). Instead he starts off from abstract entities ("crystals of social substance"):

$$\Lambda_i + \Lambda_j = \Lambda \tag{1}$$

In objectified form these are values. The abstract entities Λ_i and Λ_j are homogenous. These seem to be equivalent to:

$$\alpha_i L_i + \alpha_j L_j = \Lambda \tag{2}$$

The L_i and L_j are not homogenous. Thus from (1) and (2) we have:

$$\alpha_i = \Lambda_i / L_i \tag{3}$$

which is the value productivity of concrete particular labour i. (Thus when Marx says value is labour he means presumably that value is simple labour.) {2023 note: This sentence is imprecise. It should have been: Thus when Marx refers to value creating labour, he presumably means value creating simple labour – cf. the last but one quotation from page 142.} By simplifying assumption, equation (2) reduces to:

$$L_i + L_j = \Lambda \tag{4}$$

(The simplifying assumption does *not* say $L_i + L_j = L$.) Thus, on the one hand, we have a reductive abstraction coupled with a simplifying assumption: By way of reductive abstraction we got to abstract entities (Λ); concrete entities (L_i) may actually be discounted to the abstract entities (or the other way around). On the other hand, these entities are taken to be premarket entities, which come into existence in production. As objectified they are values, and this constitutes value as an embodiment. It is a secondary question if the discounting will be seen to be possible prior to exchange. Whatever the answer is, this will not affect the embodied character of the abstract entities.

3.4 *Value-form and value form*

Marx goes to great lengths to develop the form of appearance of value from the simple form to the money form (section 3 of Chapter 1 of *Capital I*). The upshot of this is the demonstration that Ricardian value (L_i, L) does not appear immediately, and that the "whole mystery of the form of value lies hidden in this [the simple] form" (Marx 1867|1976, p. 139), not in the money form. (The latter point bears political importance also, in relation to Marx's polemic against Proudhon.) Although I do not wish to dispute the importance of these issues, the stress on these (also in terms of mere length of text) has underrated the importance of the value-form itself. This may sound cryptic. The point is that *value form* has two meanings (which I distinguish by hyphenating one of the meanings as explained below). Let me say first that the two meanings have led to different interpretations of Marx as well as to certain political practices evolving from it. Consider, for example, the following quotations:

> I-A: "Therefore they [commodities] only appear as commodities, or have the form of commodities, insofar as they possess a double form, i.e., natural form and value form." (Marx 1867|1976, p. 138)
> I-B: "The price or money-form of commodities is, like their form of value generally, quite distinct from their palpable and real bodily form; it is therefore a purely ideal or notional form." (Marx 1867|1976, p. 189)
> II: "Hence, in the value-relation, in which the coat is the equivalent of the linen, the form of the coat counts as the form of value." (Marx 1867|1976, p. 143)

Let us say, for the sake of argument – I do not agree with it – that *value* is a genus and that *exchange value* is its species. In quotations I-A and I-B it is clear that value form refers to the genus value. This is clear from the context, and in I-B it says so explicitly: "value generally". Thus we are referred to value as a form itself. In quotation II, "form of value" refers to the species. Although in these quotations the context helps us out, this is often not the case. (The formulations in German do not shed light here; Marx always uses the term *Wertform*.) I am not sure that Marx was aware of this problem with the term *value form*. (But perhaps I say so only because I myself have struggled with it so much.) Anyway, I propose to write *value-form* for meaning I and *value form* for meaning II.[10]

Two final remarks. First, it seems that in much of Marxist writing the problems of the value form have been stressed at the expense of the problems of the

---

10 In order to emphasise the possible confusions, I give a few more examples:

   A. 'Human activity takes on the form of value' = 'Human activity takes on the value-form'. An abstract (activity) takes on a particular – historically specific – form (the value-form).

   B. Were value assumed to be a trans-historical (which I do not so assume), only then might one speak of 'the form value' = 'the value form', as in: 'The capitalist form of value is money' = 'The capitalist value form is money'.

   C. 'The money-form and the capital-form are [particular] value forms', or, 'The form of money is a [particular] form of value'. [*footnote continued on next page*]

value-form. Second, a related issue that I have not been able to analyse properly is Marx's usage of the terms form, expression, and appearance. He just seems to treat them as synonyms.

4 Labour-embodied versus abstract-labour theory of value: some current controversies

4.1 *Interpretations of Marx's theory of value*

Although the first chapter of *Capital*, discussed in the previous section, is value theoretical, it is not Marx's complete theory of value. The theory extends throughout the three volumes. Much debate has been centred around the consequences of the introduction of the general rate of profit in Volume 3 (the so-called transformation problem). I will not concentrate on this part of the debate but rather proceed to the scope of the transformation alluded to in Chapter 1 of Volume 1 (i.e., the introduction of the concept of abstract labour as identified with value) {2023 note: for 'identified' read 'associated'} and the related methodological questions of abstraction. Indeed there are many transformations in *Capital*, each located at particular levels of abstraction. All those are important, though not every one of them is equally easy, or difficult, to grasp. In this respect I agree with Tony Smith when he writes:

> Most Marxist and non-Marxist accounts [of *the* Volume 3 transformation] have concentrated exclusively on the problems involved in establishing the quantitative identity of values and prices, surplus value and profits.
>
> It is true enough that Marx himself directed considerable attention to these equations. But there is much in his theory that points away from granting them a place of absolute centrality. Consider, for example, the relationship between 'expanded accumulation' and 'simple reproduction'. No Marxist has ever claimed to prove that the sum total of values accumulated in expanded accumulation equals the sum total reproduced in simple reproduction. No non-Marxist has ever claimed to refute Marx based on a proof of the non-equivalence of these magnitudes. Indeed the question of the mathematical relationship between the two magnitudes hardly makes sense. (Smith 1990, p. 171)

D. 'Money is a form value' is very confusing, because it can be read as in (B) or (C). The same goes for: 'The money form of value' (i.e., 'the money-form of value', or, 'the money form-of-value').

There are two main accepted interpretations of Marx's theory of value: a *labour-embodied* theory of value and an *abstract-labour* theory of value. It is shown in the following subsections that these may usefully be subdivided. The differences between them are much obscured by the fact that the same terms are attributed different meanings in each of them. After expounding some problems with each of these interpretations in the remainder of this §4, I then indicate in §5 how a Marxist labour theory of value might be reconstructed along systematic-dialectical lines.

4.2   Labour-embodied theories of value

4.2.A. Concrete-labour-embodied. Marx's text in *Capital* opens up the way to a concrete-labour-embodied theory of value: $L_i + L_j = \Lambda$. Marx's simplifying assumption, $\alpha_i = \alpha_j$, is then taken for a negligibility assumption and not for a heuristic assumption (in Musgrave's, 1981, sense, see note 9 on p. 118). It is then only a small step to get to the immediately empirical observable $L_i + L_j = L$, where L_i and L are taken to be values (so-called 'labour values', measured in concrete labour-time).

Simple as it is, there are three problems related to this theory: (1) It is not clear exactly how this is a theory of capitalism (rather than a trans-historically universal theory); (2) as an interpretation of Marx it is not clear how this theory is different from Ricardo's (it is indeed near to a Sraffian theory, where instead of the force of theoretical abstractions we have the force of just adding up: vectors); and (3) it is not obvious how this theory can be developed so as to be sufficiently explanatory.

4.2.B. Abstract-labour-embodied. As I have indicated in §3.3, an interpretation of *abstract-labour-embodied* seems near to what Marx was getting at. But I believe that there are too many problems to stick with it. The problem is not so much that of the reductive abstraction $\Lambda_i + \Lambda_j = \Lambda$ (although I do have methodological objections to it). This need not prevent it from being developed into a consistent and applicable theory. The difficulty, however, is that the Λ is taken to be value, and that value is taken to be a premarket entity. It is not clear how we can ever make this theory operational. If we say, with Marx, that the former equation may be transformed into $\alpha_i L_i + \alpha_j L_j = \Lambda$, where the dimensions are so-called simple labour, then this seems an acceptable link from the abstract to the concrete level. At an abstract level of the development of this theory it is, of course, permissible (within this methodological approach) to assume the discounting coefficients to be one: $L_i + L_j = \Lambda$. That is by way of successive approximation. But one clearly cannot stick to this. If one does stick to it, the theory reduces to the concrete-labour-embodied theory. Thus at some stage a procedure has to be developed for getting to the discounting coefficients. It has not been shown how this can be done prior to the market. Indeed, if we need the market to get to the coefficients, then we can no longer hold that value (Λ) is a premarket entity.

4.2.C. Substance of value in the labour-embodied theories. I believe that the labour substance metaphor has much bedevilled the Marxist theory of value, and as I have indicated, the metaphor originates with Marx. (Of course, in this respect he was a child of his times.) Apart from anything else, both the concrete- and abstract-labour approaches will have to deal at some point with the transformation problem (i.e., the problem related to the introduction of the general rate of profit). The point is that within the labour-embodied approach one has labour embodied at the abstract beginning and at the concrete end (in whatever way the end is the result of 'redistribution'). Labour embodied thus seems to be 'conserved' within the modifications proposed by the theory – modifications proposed either to capture real processes or to be a stage in, for example, successive approximation. This bears a resemblance to the classical physics conservation principle from which, according to Mirowski (1990), classical political economy borrowed.[11] Thus we seem to have a substance theory of value together with a notion of conservation of this substance that is carried over from the one (analytical) level of abstraction to the next. Thus there is a particular ontology of conservation (of labour-embodied 'value') behind this theory. Moving from one level to the other does not involve a transformation in the sense of a "transubstantiation" (cf. Marx 1867|1976, p. 128, quoted in §3.2). Thus although *the* transformation relates to the move to a specific level of abstraction – the concrete appearances – this does not involve a transformation of substance.

What reason would this labour-embodied strand of Marxism have for sticking to the substance metaphor? Clearly the effect of it has been the theory's focus on physical entities rather than the social form of those in capitalism (or rather than a focus on entities having a double form – use-value and value, physical and social – as the dialectical value-form theory would have it). The substance-embodied metaphor seems very much a "negative heuristic" (Lakatos 1974), which should save the priority Marxists give to production. Indeed, the stress on production is in my view one of the strong points of the Marxist paradigm. However, as I will show, it seems possible to theorise production and to give it a central place even if we cut loose the substance-embodied part of the

---

11 On redistribution, see Fine and Harris (1979), as well as the critique (on the manuscript) by Himmelweit and Mohun (1978). Note that within the usual algorithms the concrete-labour-embodied theory is formally equivalent to a technical coefficients framework (see Gerstein 1976). This is also the point of the Steedman (1977) 'Marx after Sraffa' critique.

theory. This would open the way for a truly social labour theory of value, which may be said to originate in outline with Marx, but which he did not complete (and which Marxists neglected to complete).

4.3 The abstract-labour theory of value: abstraction in practice

In one variety of the abstract-labour theory of value there is a shift in the status of the abstractions used in the theory. The theoretical abstractions are themselves taken to be a kind of mirror of the abstractions that people make in everyday life. Such a view would, of course, fit a materialist philosophy, but it is not restricted to it. The theory of value of this approach seems to have certain roots in Marx's theory in *Capital*, though I am inclined to see it more as a development from it. There is some question about the unity of this approach, and it is certainly not a fully developed theory (see, e.g., De Vroey 1982; Gleicher 1983, 1985; Eldred 1984; and Bellofiore 1989, who expand on this question).[12] I think that with my distinction between concrete- and abstract-labour-embodied I have clarified the differences between them. However, the result is that what is called the abstract-labour theory of value is now even more obscure and even less of a fully constructed theory.

In this approach, the concept *abstract labour* (also) refers to an 'abstraction in practice' (cf. Marx 1859|1971, p. 30) or a 'real abstraction' (Himmelweit and Mohun 1978, p. 75) or a 'concrete abstraction'. Thus it is argued that in the market, concrete labour (the labour of a carpenter or an information worker) actually takes the form of abstract labour expressed in money. Thus the actual abstraction in the market is that concrete labour is reduced to homogenous money; this is so at the input side of the production process (wages) as well as at the output side. The products of concrete labour are homogenised into money when concrete labour is commensurated as or converted into abstract labour.

Abstract-labour-*embodied* theoreticians (§4.2B) may not disagree with the argument so far, but the point is – further expanded upon below – that this view also entails a shift in the very concept of value. Within the abstraction-in-practice view, value is bound to be established in the market (hence a market concept) rather than having existence prior to it. This does not necessarily

---

12 References to the germinal literature of this approach are given by these authors as well as by Reuten and Williams 1989, p. 64. Although most adherents of a Hegelian-Marxist dialectic incorporate elements of this theory in theirs (e.g. Arthur, Backhaus, Eldred, Hanlon, Kleiber, Roth, Reuten and Williams), it is surely not the case that most abstract-labour theoreticians adhere to a Hegelian-Marxist dialectic. Conversely, not all of the latter seem to take the nonembodied abstract-labour view.

imply that this theory underrates the importance of production. Theoreticians within this approach will say that the defect of Sraffian or neo-Ricardian economics is its reduction of production to technical coefficients, that is, to techniques. They say that the production process is of primary importance. It is not clear, however, how this statement fits the importance they allot to exchange and the market.

4.4 Substance and the measure of time: real abstractions

One determination of the concept of the abstraction *labour* and *abstract labour* is the question of whether it is a trans-historical or general abstraction, as opposed to a determinate abstraction particular to capitalism or, more generally, commodity-producing modes of production (cf. Murray 1988, ch. 10; and Arthur 1986, 11–12 on first-order and second-order mediations). Arthur (1986, pp. 12–19, cf. p. 47) points out how Marx in the *Economic and philosophic manuscripts of 1844* – in contradistinction to *Capital* – uses the term *labour* in a determinate sense. I would prefer to conceptualise labour as a determinate abstraction particular to capitalism, for example.

If we say that labour is needed to produce commodities, this is not very telling. It is more telling if we say that a certain amount of labour is needed to produce a commodity. Labour under the aspect of time is certainly a determinate abstraction. There are numerous cultures in which the aspect of time is of no importance in connection with the activity of labour. Anyway, there are good reasons to believe that labour under the aspect of time is at least determinate to a commodity-producing society if not just a capitalist society. (Cf. Mirowski 1990, 1991, on all kinds of standardisation with the emergence of the market – pounds of apples, etc.) Mirowski's argument could be extended to argue that labour under the aspect of time is equally a standardisation that emerged with the institutionalisation of the labour market. If this makes sense, then stories such as Adam Smith's (1776|1933, vol. 1, pp. 41–2) on beaver and deer hunters of the "early and rude state of society" for whom "the quantities of labour necessary for acquiring different objects seems to be the only circumstance which can afford any rule for exchanging them for one another" are merely part of a method of theoretical history – as Skinner (1985, p. 29) suggests.[13]

---

13   Cf. also Marx (1867|1976, p. 164): "In all situations, the labour-time it costs to produce the means of subsistence must necessarily concern mankind, although not to the same degree at different stages of development." In a footnote he adds that among the ancient Germans the size of a piece of land was measured according to the labour of a day. However, such were accidental personal not standardised measures; cf. Mirowski 1991.

It is now tempting to say that labour under the aspect of time, that is, labour-time, is a real capitalist abstraction (and perhaps also a real abstraction in other commodity-producing societies). However, there may be a problem of logical order here. Why would labour-time be a real social abstraction? Not for its own sake. Pounds of apples (apples are never identical) have become a real social abstraction because apples are sold on the institutional market (i.e., they take the value-form). Similarly, I would argue, labour-time is a real social abstraction *because* labour (labour-power) is sold on the market (i.e., because labour has taken the value-form). Therefore the concept of value is prior to that of labour-time.

Thus we have two real social abstractions. First, human activity takes the value-form. (Within the history of capitalism up to now, certain activities have been excluded; increasingly, however, household and leisure-time activities are at least being calculated in terms of value.) Second, because human activity takes the value-form, that activity is considered to be labour under the aspect of time, that is, labour-time.[14]

But what does it mean to say that labour-time is 'embodied' in a commodity? Or that labour is the 'substance' of value? Clearly labour-time is not some stuff that we find in the commodity (or even 'beyond' it: I consider that even within a classical essence-appearance model at least some stuff/substance is not meant to be the essence). Thus *embodiment* and *substance* seem to be metaphors. In general there is nothing wrong with using metaphors to get an idea across. However, the metaphor may be misleading and go on to live a life of its own. In this case I think that within much of Marxism these metaphors have been taken literally. (Of course, Marx's language gave rise to this. He took distance from the classical presentation in this respect, but he kept on using the metaphor.)

The point is that the real abstractions referred to are *social* issues.

5 Reconstructing abstract labour within a systematic-dialectical view

This section provides some elements of a methodological outline of how a social labour theory of value may be derived from Marx's theory by way of

---

14 Therefore we can, as a representation of these real abstractions, formally write ml (where m is the monetary expression of labour, and l is labour). This is further explained in §5. (The argument in Reuten and Williams 1989, ch. 2, §16, for writing ml is somewhat obscure. I thank Alexander van Altena for pointing this out to me.)

reconstructing that theory. It is not an interpretation of Marx's theory. The reconstruction is one along the lines of a systematic dialectic as briefly introduced in §1. I confine myself to a few stages of such a theory. The systematic context is set out in Reuten and Williams (1989, ch. 1); my remarks expand on the concepts of abstract labour and value set out in that work.

In §3 I indicated how Marx derives the concept of abstract labour. He does this on the basis of a reductive abstraction, not a dialectical logical abstraction. Marx arrives at his concept of abstract labour in abstraction from particular and concrete labour: The latter is reduced to elements making up human labour in the abstract, metaphorically referred to as crystals of social substance. As this objectified social substance, they are value(s) (Λ in the notation introduced in §3.2).

It was also indicated that the concrete labour L_i and L_j cannot be added up as particulars. However, because of the dialectical contradiction of particular labour being simultaneously universal labour, the labour-time i and j can in principle be added up as labour hours in the abstract (l): $l_i + l_j = l$, even though we cannot add them up as particulars L. Similarly we can add up acres of land even if we know their qualities to be different; the same goes for pieces of fruit. But this is a dialectical logical abstraction and not a simplification. Within an approach of dialectical conceptual development, l_i and l_j may have abstract existence as l. But this very approach purports to concretise this abstract existence to the level of concrete and phenomenal existence. At the abstract level it is not impossible to quantify, but any such quantification will have only abstract meaning – and sometimes makes hardly any sense.[15] To take an example: The abstract 'animal' has concrete existence as my cat Mitzy or as the fly she is catching; it is not impossible to think of them as two animals and to add them up as such. But we cannot add them up as particulars. Also, many mathematical operations make no sense: Half a cat plus half a fly do not make one animal. The dialectical contradiction is that Mitzy is a cat and an animal at the same time. A fly and a cat cannot be added up as particulars, but only in the abstract.

Thus we have the dialectical contradiction $L_i \cdot \times \cdot l$ (where $\cdot \times \cdot$ indicates dialectical contradiction).[16] At this level, $l_i + l_j = l$ is fairly empty; it is indeed an abstract statement, a statement at the abstract level of theory. (Though the statement

---

15 Reuten and Williams (1989) aim to show how the abstract category l develops, via the existence of the market and the complex of market relations, into the more concrete category of ml.

16 We can look at this contradiction both as particular labour L_i under the aspect of universal labour l, i.e., $l(L_i)$, and as universal labour under the aspect of particular labour, i.e., $L_i(l)$. Using this notation we may write: $l(L_i) + l(L_j) = l$. However, $L_i(l) + L_j(l) = L$ makes no sense.

is true and remains true even if we move to concrete levels of the theory: In fact we do speak in practice of US labour expended.) In the market, people do not reckon in terms of the abstract l. Nor do they reckon in terms of concrete L_i's because these cannot be added up. Because production inputs and outputs diverge (and because in capitalist production such divergence itself is not the aim, it is production for others) they have to be reduced to a common denominator, which is value. Value is thus constituted as universal as opposed to the particularity of the physical inputs and outputs. (Note that in this view, labour, even l or l objectified, is not value. Here the theory clearly diverges from Marx's.)[17] In the market, value actually gets shape in its expression in terms of money. If we restrict ourselves to the output, and to the value-added component, we may write m for the monetary expression of labour, as it is actually realised in the market. Thus m is also the value productivity of labour. In the market then, the contradiction $L_i \cdot \times \cdot l$ is transcended at a more concrete level into what I provisionally call mL_i (but should call ml_i as indicated below). mL_i is a sum of money (in terms of dollars, for example, though this belongs to an even more concrete level of the theory). In the market, labour actually takes the value-form. Thus labour is actually converted (transformed) into an abstract entity. It is actual and capitalist abstract labour, which is capitalist value. (This opens up an enormous terminological confusion, because here and in the abstract-labour-embodied theory the same words are used to denote different concepts. This is, however, inevitable if one wants to keep in touch with everyday language.)

Perhaps a somewhat subtle differentiation (that is, for the current purposes) is that in the market the $L_i \cdot \times \cdot l$ contradiction is transcended by way of positing it, more concretely, in the abstract moment (l) of the contradiction. Thus we should write ml_i.

At a somewhat more concrete level we may have diverging monetary expressions of labour, whence we have $m_i l_i$. (In Reuten and Williams 1989, ch. 2, it is explained how this expression bears on the aggregate income $Y = ml = \Sigma\, m_i l_i$.)

In comparison with the abstract-labour-embodied theory, the upshot of all this is that the simple labour discounting that bedevils the theory pertains to a process that actually takes place in the market ($m_i; m_j$). Of course, the current theory maintains that value has no existence prior to the market. But this is far from saying that it does not affect production. In Reuten and Wil-

---

17 [2023 note: Regarding this last sentence I do not recall what I meant here in 1993. Anyway, in *Capital I*, ch. 1, section 3 Marx writes: "Human labour-power in its fluid state, or human labour, creates value, but is not itself value. It becomes value in its coagulated state, in objective form" (1867/1976, pp. 138–9).]

liams (1989, pp. 66–8)[18] it is explained how the commensuration in the market ($m_i l_i$) is anticipated by capital and so gives rise to what we have called an 'ideal pre-commensuration' in production (properly written $m_i{'}L_i$). Thus the labour process is in fact calculated in terms of value (i.e., money).

Let me summarise the different views in terms of the symbols that have been used (3§2-A; §3.3; §5).

A. The systematic-dialectical reconstruction states:
$$l_i + l_j = l \qquad (5)$$
Equation (5) makes sense to the extent labour is considered as universal. The expression is rather empty and in that sense is an abstract statement (of universal labour in the abstract). In this view the following equation make no sense.
$$L_i + L_j = L \qquad (6)$$
Equation (6) makes no sense in this view because we cannot add up different labour as particular labour. The following equation is considerably more concrete than equation (5):
$$m_i l_i + m_j l_j = ml \qquad (7)$$
This equation (7) represents the expression for real abstract labour. It is also the expression for value (in terms of money).

B. The concrete-labour-embodied view states:
$$L_i + L_j = \Lambda \qquad (8)$$
or alternatively
$$L_i + L_j = L \qquad (9)$$
If there is a concept of abstract labour at all in this view, then this is Λ. All the quantities in equations (8) and (9) are in terms of value, measured in hours.

C. The abstract-labour-embodied view states:
$$\Lambda_i + \Lambda_j = \Lambda \qquad (10)$$
Equation (10) is the expression for abstract labour = value (abstract labour is the result of a reductive abstraction). Equation (10) is equivalent to or may be transformed into:
$$\alpha_i L_i + \alpha_j L_j = \Lambda \qquad (11)$$
where the dimensions are simple labour = value, measured in hours. Only by simplifying (heuristic) assumption does (11) reduce to (8).

---

18   See also Reuten 1988, 53–55.

Conclusions

It is somewhat grandiose to say that *Capital* was an effort at developing systematic dialectics for social science – beginning with political economy – in confrontation with Hegel's work. (But then the qualifications in this respect as set out by Murray 1988 and Smith 1990 seem plausible.) I have shown that a reconsideration of the first chapter of *Capital* reveals that Marx embarked on a different track from Hegel's logic. Marx felt that this method would have to be developed in the practice of research (cf. Murray 1988). However, as with all founders of new paradigms, Marx's exact break with the previous paradigm(s) is unclear, and here this applies to both the method and the content. Therefore there is room for several interpretations as well as lines of research developing from *Capital*. And, for the time being, this does no harm: I sympathise with Feyerabend's anarchistic view even if I myself have rather definite inclinations as to the way in which the paradigm might fruitfully develop.

Systematic-Dialectical interpretations of Marx have always been in a minority. The majority of the Marxist tradition indeed took the dialectic for Hegelian claptrap. Heuristically the question of how far Marx reached in developing systematic dialectics is not very important – though it is interesting from a historiographic point of view. What is important is that, from it, a systematic-dialectical social science may be (further) developed. If we take this project seriously, then one of its targets should be a critical study of *Capital* from that perspective. The critique of *Capital* in this chapter then has been a critique of Marx with (as far as I am concerned) Marx.

A systematic-dialectical study of current society would have to be a four-stage project. These stages are those that I consider the stages of a systematic-dialectical methodology.

The first step is a critical phenomenal analysis, which would need to concentrate on phenomena as reported in newspapers and everyday conversations rather than their filtered reports in books and journal articles. It is not obvious, for example, that labour–capital class or exploitation issues are the *phenomena* that require explanation rather than the phenomena, for example, of third-world catastrophes, oppression of women, unemployment, racism, the ecological environment, unequal distribution of income, and authoritarian relations. I am not saying in advance that the latter phenomena cannot be grasped in terms of the capital relation; I am saying that we need to step back regularly in order to think over our theory.

The second step is to reanalyse the analyses of those phenomena, as well as the existing systematic outlines in books and journal articles. This includes a critical study of philosophy and social science in perspective of the analysis carried out in the first step. The abstract determination should result from this.

Third is the reproduction of the concrete from the abstract determination in the second step.

And the fourth step is the critique of the analyses done in the second step.

All this may sound familiar, but it has to be carried out as an ongoing project. We cannot – ever – just take for granted what has been accomplished yesterday.

In this chapter I have picked out some value-theoretical issues of the second step mentioned. I have suggested that although Marx provided the rudiments of a theory of social value (which nobody after him took any further), he was enmeshed in the physical substance–embodiment metaphor inherited from Hegel (substance) and classical political economy (embodiment). The Marxist tradition, rather than taking off from Marx in this respect, seems to have 'fetishised' the metaphor (which is remarkable in the face of the antinaturalism that is one of the main characteristics of the Marxist tradition). This seems related to the priority Marxists give to the theorisation of production. Indeed, this is the strong point of the Marxist paradigm in comparison with any other. However, with it Marxism has tended to theorise the economy in one-sided physical terms. I believe that the metaphor has prohibited the breakthrough to a true theory of social value. It may be added that no other paradigm in economics has been able to undertake this breakthrough. I have indicated how the ground may be cleared for developing a social labour theory of value. Within such an approach it seems possible to dispense with the metaphor and the related concept of value without, however, cutting loose from the theorisation of production.

References

Arthur, Christopher J. 1986, *The dialectics of labour: Marx and his relation to Hegel*, Oxford: Basil Blackwell.

Bellofiore, Riccardo 1989, 'A monetary labour theory of value', *Review of Radical Political Economics* 21 (Spring-Summer): 1–25.

De Vroey, Michel 1982, 'On the obsolescence of the Marxian theory of value: a critical review', *Capital & Class* 17: 34–59.

Echeverria, Rafael 1978, 'Critique of Marx's 1857 introduction', *Economy and Society* 7(4) (November): 333–65.

Eldred, Michael 1984, 'A reply to Gleicher; history: universal concept dissolves any concept!', *Capital & Class* 13: 135–40.

Eldred, Michael, and Mike Roth 1978, *A guide to Marx's 'Capital'*, London: CSE Books.

Fine, Ben, and Laurence Harris 1979, *Rereading 'Capital'*, London: Macmillan.
Gerstein, Ira 1976, 'Production, circulation and value', *Economy and Society* 5(3): 243–91.
Gleicher, David 1983, 'A historical approach to the question of abstract labour', *Capital & Class* 21: 97–122.
Gleicher, David 1985, 'A rejoinder to Eldred, abstract labour, the Rubin school and the Marxist theory of value', *Capital & Class* 24: 147–55.
Hegel, G.W.F. 1821/1967, *Grundlinien der Philosophie des Rechts* oder *Naturrecht und Staatswissenschaft im Grundrisse*, translated by T.M. Knox as *Hegel's philosophy of right*, Oxford: Oxford University Press, 1967.
Hegel, G.W.F. 1833/1985, *Einleitung in die Geschichte der Philosophie*, edition J. Hoffmeister 1940 as translated by T.M. Knox and A.V. Miller, *Introduction to the lectures on the history of philosophy*, Oxford: Clarendon Press, 1985.
Hegel, G.W.F. 1817/1975, *Enzyklopädie der Philosophischen Wissenschaften im Grundrisse I, Die Wissenschaft der Logik*, Engl. transl. of the third edition by W. Wallace, *Hegel's logic*, London: Oxford University Press, 1975.
Himmelweit, Susan, and Simon Mohun 1978, 'The anomalies of capital', *Capital & Class* 6: 67–105.
Keynes, John Maynard 1936, *The general theory of employment, interest and money*, London: Macmillan.
Lakatos, Imre 1974, 'Falsification and the methodology of scientific research programmes', in *Criticism and the growth of knowledge*, edited by I. Lakatos and A. Musgrave, Cambridge: Cambridge University Press.
Marx, Karl 1857/1973, *Grundrisse der Kritik der politischen Ökonomie* {draft of 1857–58, published 1939} as translated by Martin Nicolaus, *Grundrisse*, Harmondsworth: Penguin, 1973.
Marx, Karl 1859/1971, *Zur Kritik der Politischen Ökonomie* (MEW 13) as translated by S.W. Ryazanskaya and edited by Maurice Dobb, *A contribution to the critique of political economy*, London: Lawrence & Wishart, 1971.
Marx, Karl 1867/1976, *Das Kapital I*, quoted from the 4th edition of 1890, MEW 23, as translated by Ben Fowkes, *Capital I*, Harmondsworth: Penguin, 1976.
Mattick Jr., Paul 1986, *Social knowledge: an essay on the nature and limits of social science*, Armonk, NY: M.E. Sharpe
Mirowski, Philip 1990, 'Learning the meaning of a dollar: conservation principles and the social theory of value in economic theory', *Social Research* 57(3): 689–717.
Mirowski, Philip 1991, 'Postmodernism and the social theory of value', *Journal of Post Keynesian Economics* 13(4): 565–82.
Murray, Patrick 1988, *Marx's theory of scientific knowledge*, Atlantic Highlands, NJ: Humanities Press.
Musgrave, Alan 1981, 'Unreal assumptions in economic theory: the F-twist untwisted', *Kyklos* 4/3: 377–87.

Paolucci, Henri 1974, 'Truth in the philosophical sciences of society, politics and history', in *Beyond epistemology: new studies in the philosophy of Hegel*, edited by F.G. Weiss, The Hague: Martin Nijhoff.

Reuten, Geert 1988, 'Value as social form', in *Value, social form and the state*, edited by Michael Williams, London: Macmillan.

Reuten, Geert, and Michael Williams 1989, *Value-form and the state; the tendencies of accumulation and the determination of economic policy in capitalist society*, London: Routledge.

Schmidt, Alfred (ed.) 1969, *Beiträge zur Marxistischen Erkenntnistheorie*, Frankfurt am Main: Suhrkamp.

Skinner, Andrew 1985, 'Introduction', in Adam Smith, *The wealth of nations*, Harmondsworth: Penguin.

Smith, Adam 1776/1933, *An inquiry into the nature and causes of the wealth of nations*, vols. 1 and 2, London: Dent & Sons.

Smith, Tony 1990, *The logic of Marx's 'Capital': replies to Hegelian criticisms*, Albany, NY: State University of New York Press.

Steedman, Ian 1977, *Marx after Sraffa*, London: New Left Books.

CHAPTER 7

Money as constituent of value; the ideal introversive substance and the ideal extroversive form of value in Marx's *Capital*

2005 article, originally published in *Marx's theory of money: modern appraisals*, edited by Fred Moseley, London/New York: Palgrave Macmillan, pp. 78–92.
(For its abstract see the Abstracts of all chapters, p. 4.)

Contents

Introduction   136
1   The monetary dimension   137
   1.1   Form, prevalence, systemic existence   137
   1.2   Extroversion   137
   1.3   The introversive and the extroversive constituent of value   138
   1.4   From a simple to an enriched notion of value   139
2   Very abstract labour   140
   2.1   False analogies – abstract labour and abstract timber – and the disappearance of the simplified notion of abstract labour   140
   2.2   Immanent substance and immanent measure – abstract labour and method   142
3   Money's measuring: ideal transubstantiation   144
   3.1   Idealities   144
   3.2   Marx's notion of 'measurement': 'verwandeln' and standardised measurement   145
   3.3   Imaginary measurement by imaginary money   147
   3.4   Extroversive hypostasisation   148
4   An introversive regress: bullion   148
Summary and Conclusions   149
References   150

Introduction[1]

In the first volume of *Capital* Marx introduces 'money' in Chapter 1 (section 3) and then reintroduces it in Chapter 3. At first sight the second introduction seems merely a superfluous excursion at this point since in the remainder of the book Marx apparently does not 'do' anything with it. He returns to money only in *Capital II* (Part Two) and then again in *Capital III* (Parts Four and Five). This may be one reason why the Chapter 3 introduction has for a long time been much neglected.

Over the last 15 years commentators of Marx have tended to focus on the aspect of the 'commodity money' basis in Marx's theory. This is relevant for the current Marxian theory of capitalism, but it is irrelevant for the historical assessment of an author writing in the second half of the nineteenth century.[2] Yet another issue is the methodological question of why Marx – given that commodity money basis – postpones a full account of credit money till later in the work. Here I ally myself with Campbell who argues that this issue should be assessed from within Marx's method and systematic, especially the gradual movement from relatively simple to complex concepts and accounts.[3]

In this essay I provide a novel interpretation of the relation between the two introductions of money referred to (Chapter 1 and Chapter 3 of *Capital I*). In particular I will argue that Chapter 3 sheds indispensable light on what happens in Chapter 1; Chapter 1 is a one-sided account that gets complemented in Chapter 3. A neglect of the core aspect that I will emphasise about Chapter 3

---

[1] The first version of this chapter was presented at the 2003 conference of the *International Symposium on Marxian Theory*. I am grateful for the comments by its participants (Christopher Arthur, Riccardo Bellofiore, Suzanne de Brunhoff, Martha Campbell, Duncan Foley, Claus Germer, Makoto Itoh, Costas Lapavitsas, Pichit Likitkijsomboon, Fred Moseley, Patrick Murray, Anitra Nelson, and Tony Smith).

[2] It is obvious that a Marxian theory of pure credit-money can be constructed. See Williams (2000), Realfonzo and Bellofiore (1996), Bellofiore and Realfonzo (1997), Bellofiore (2004); see also Reuten and Williams (1989: Chapter 2 and Chapter 8, §4). However, pure credit-money cannot be introduced early on in *Capital*: an implantation of the stuff of *Capital III*, Parts Four and Five early on in *Capital I* would demolish the complete systematic structure of the work, and hence it would require a complete reconstruction (although there is also a class of reconstruction that does not affect the systematic structure of the work). Even if Marx had introduced money as finance early on in *Capital I* (say after Part Two) he still would have had to present a general account of money earlier, and it is this general account of Part I that I am concerned with in the rest of this chapter.

[3] Campbell (1997, 1998, 2002). See also Williams (2000).

must have consequences for all further interpretations of the book; however, I cannot deal with that issue here.[4]

This essay is historiographic and hence I abstain from presenting my own (value-form theoretical) views. Thus there is no question of agreement or disagreement with Marx involved other than internal critique.

I refer to the German *Das Kapital I* by (1867G – quoted from the 4th edition of 1890) and to the English Fowkes translation by (1867F – as translated from the 4th edition). Unspecified page references (e.g. 180) are always to the latter. Note that Chapters 1–3 together constitute Part One of the book.

1 The monetary dimension

1.1 *Form, prevalence, systemic existence*

The standpoint of Chapter 1 of *Capital I* is 'the commodity'. The relatively brief Chapter 2, on the process of exchange, introduces social actors of exchange and the action of society to turn a particular commodity into the general equivalent 'money' (180) within a society of generalised commodity production (187). Thus Chapter 2 posits the *prevalence (Dasein)* of money in practice. Whereas Chapter 1 already posits *the form* of money, money itself (i.e., its systemic existence) is derived in Chapter 3. Notably it is systematically derived from exchange, just as the commodity and value were derived from exchange. Behind it is a notion of dissociate production, but this is implicit.[5] It is only later that the role of value, that is money's role in production and the full circuit of capital, will become explicit (that is in all the rest of *Capital*). But in order to comprehend this role, Chapter 3 is absolutely crucial.

1.2 *Extroversion*

Throughout Chapter 3 Marx frequently uses the term *veräußerlichen* for 'to sell', which literally means 'to outer' or 'outering'. Nevertheless, the normal German

---

4 In previous work (esp. Reuten 1989, 1993 and 2000) I suggested that whereas Marx made a fundamental 'break' from Classical Political Economy there are (inevitably) Classical/Ricardian remnants in his work. (See Murray's 2000a critique of my 1993 paper, my reply (2000), and Murray's rejoinder in 2002). A restudy of a number of German texts of *Capital* (together with insights from Hegel's work) makes me conclude that there are fewer such remnants than I thought before. See Reuten (2004), which, next to the current chapter, is a key to this. [For the 2004 article see Chapter 8 of the current book.]

5 Chapter 2 – prior to the introduction of capital in Chapter 4 – nevertheless posits an anticipation of dissociated production.

term would be *verkaufen* (a term that he also uses; the difference is lost in the English translation). He also uses *entäußeren* for the same, as well as other terms with the same root of *außer*, especially *Außdruck* (expression; compare the roots *außer*, outer, utter). This homology is also lost in the translation.

The term 'outer' prepares one, of course, for an 'inner' or 'immanent'. Moreover, against the background of Marx's familiarity with Hegel's philosophy, the terms are rather heavy; they point at 'moments' that can be distinguished but that inseparably belong together.

At the end of the first section of Chapter 3 of *Das Kapital I* Marx writes (1867G: 118; italics added): "Die Preisform schließt die *Veräußerlichkeit* der Waren gegen Geld und die Notwendigkeit dieser *Veräußerung* ein." Fowkes translates (198) as: "The price-form therefore [?] implies both the exchangeability of commodities for money and the necessity of exchanges." Apart from the 'therefore' this translation is defendable, but it completely loses the connection pointed out above. A more literal translation would be: "The price-form implies/entails the 'extroversibility' of commodities for money as well as the necessity of this 'extroversion'." But without explication this would not make sufficient sense in English.[6]

1.3   *The introversive and the extroversive constituent of value*

In Marx's view money is one *constituent* of value (he does not use exactly this formulation). The immanent or introversive constituent of value is undifferentiated 'abstract labour' (Chapter 1), its extroversive (*außer*) constituent is money (Chapter 3); but these two *inseparably* belong together. Money is the *necessary* form of expression of value (*Außdruck*). That is, *value has no existence without money*.[7] This is the end-result of Part One.

---

6   Translation necessarily involves interpretation. Translators are confined to rely on the common interpretation of their day, and therefore a novel interpretation must have consequences for the translation.
7   My thoughts are intuitive without expressing them. My face is that due to its expression; when my skin has been injured by fire, my face is still my face, and yet not. It seems to me that the *innere-äußere* opposition is in between:
   internal – external (inadequate because of its 'exogenous' connotation)
   impressive – expressive
   introversive – extroversive
   implosive – explosive (if we could cut their connotations of destruction).
   For Hegel especially, inward–outward would have to be added. Marx evades *innere* in the current context (he uses it in *Capital I*, Part Seven), and adopts instead 'immanent' (*immanent*). Henceforth I adopt the terms of immanent/introversive and extroversive.

Another way of saying that value has no existence without money is to say that value is *without exception* of monetary dimension.[8] In fact this is already the outcome of Chapter 1. Its Section 3 presents the *formation* of the form of money; or one could say it posits the *form* of extroversion (*Veräußerlichung*) which is the starting point for Chapter 3.[9]

Marx introduces the concept of 'value-form' in Chapter 1. After that the term moves to the background in the sense that it is only sporadically used. The reason is that in Chapter 3 the concept is concretised into its monetary expression. Key to this concretisation is money's role as *measure* of value as well as the meaning of 'measure' (see §3 below).

1.4 From a simple to an enriched notion of value

Section 1 of Chapter 3 sets out the 'function' of money as 'measure *of* values'. This may give the (false) impression of there 'being' value entities independently of the 'measure', that is independently of money. If Marx had started here from scratch and considered the measurement of a use-value in terms of money, the problem would not have arisen. In fact he considers *commodities*.

If my interpretation as set out in §1.3 is accepted we move from a simplified notion of value (Chapter 1) to an enriched one (that of the full Part One),

---

8 Value's monetary *dimension* does not imply that it only exists in monetary shape. Entities in capitalism (e.g. machines) may have a value of monetary dimension without being money. Equally things may be of monetary dimension (e.g. machines as functioning means of production) without having a price: things have a price only when they are offered for sale. Within the circuit of capital $M-C_i...P...C_j'-M'$ the $C_i...P...C_j'$ is ideally accounted in monetary dimension. This ideality may be exciting (as it should be) but it is not surprising. Every businessman, accountant or auditor knows that most of the balance sheet of an enterprise is made up in terms of an ideal monetary dimension (the balance sheet is a static version of the circuit of capital).

9 See also Arthur's excellent study (2004, pp. 36–8). He writes: "to be a commodity involves *all* the determinations of chapter 1 including those of Section 3 on its *form*, in which it is shown that an adequate expression of the value of commodities requires the existence of money". See also Arthur 2005. The notion that value has no existence without money is also key to Murray 2005 although he arrives at this from a different angle from the one proposed in the current chapter. Elson 1979 is an inspiration for the research reported in the current chapter. "Marx's examples", she wrote, "are always couched in money terms, *never* in terms of hours" (p. 139). In fact the same applies for Marx's equations (Reuten 2004). Elson notes that "values cannot be calculated or observed independently of prices" but she also thought that "in *Capital* Marx does not highlight the conceptual distinction which he makes between an 'immanent' or 'intrinsic' measure, and an 'external' measure, which is the mode of appearance of the 'immanent' measure" (1979, p. 136). In fact the German text is rather explicit. With her "Marx does not highlight the conceptual distinction which he makes", she showed great intuition.

each indicated with one term 'value' (§2.2 below). Evidently, we cannot but start Chapter 3 with the simple notion of value inherited from the previous chapters. Therefore, there might at first sight appear to be two lines of reasoning in Chapter 3: labour-time and money. Near to the opening of Chapter 3 Marx writes (188): "Money as a measure of value is the necessary form of appearance of the measure of value which is immanent in commodities, namely labour-time." The first line of reasoning is an obvious reference back to the Chapter 1, what I call, simple–abstract 'immanent' or introversive notion of value with its immanent measure, namely labour-time. The other line posits that money is 'the necessary form of appearance' of that immanency. The commodity, and hence value, has *no existence* without money: "products of labour ... taking the form of commodities implies their differentiation into commodities and the money commodity" (188n).

The monistic focus on the introversive notion of value in much of the Marxian economics after Marx is certainly also due to Marx's presentation of the matter, especially his particular way of moving from simplified determinations to complex ones.[10] However, because of the inseparability of the introversive and the extroversive constituents of value, monistic phrases such as 'labour-values', or conversely, 'value-prices' do not fit Marx's theory and hence are never used in *Capital*.

2 Very abstract labour

2.1 *False analogies – abstract labour and abstract timber – and the disappearance of the simplified notion of abstract labour*

The (false) impression of there being value entities independently of the 'money measure' is reinforced by (false) analogies with other types of measurement. When we measure the length of a table with a metre stick, the table's length exists independently of the stick.[11] The analogy is false because the table is fully constituted as material/substance (introversive) *and* form (extroversive). There is no obvious unique way to measure the length of the *material* of the table (i.e., the length of the timber and nails, say). Surely we can in principle measure the length of two odd pieces of freshly cut timber – in this sense we have measurables – but we cannot add those up in a unique sensible way because of their unequal shapes.

---

10   Without helping us by saying what he is doing.
11   Its length *in metres* does *not* exist independently of the stick (or rather the metric system), but that is not my point here.

To redress the analogy: there is no obvious unique way to measure the 'introversive substance' of value. You cannot add up nails and timber to measure the length of a table, or at least these would be awkwardly related. The same goes for concrete labour in connection to value.

In Chapter 1, therefore, Marx takes recourse to the notion of 'abstract labour' as a simplified constituent of value (it would be misleading to call this even an abstract substitute measure).[12] It is most telling that after this chapter the term 'abstract labour' disappears, with four exceptions. In face of the Marxian discourse of the last 20 years this cannot be stressed enough.[13]

When in Chapter 1 Marx presents the commodity, he *posits* their being and prevalence (*Dasein*). In fact their existence is only *grounded* when he gets to their production in Parts Three to Five (though even this grounding is still a simplified one). In a different jargon: their production is presupposed (the presupposition being grounded later). Similarly, when presenting the commodity in Chapter 1 Marx presupposes the money measure that is only grounded (still simple) in Chapter 3. Abstract labour foreshadows the money measure.

---

12   I still think that it is to the point to conceive of 'abstract labour' as a foreshadow of *money* (as I did in previous work). But this notion has proved to be confusing in debates with those labour-embodied proponents who think in terms of 'abstract-labour-embodied' and from which I distance myself (see Reuten 1993 [chapter 6 of the current book]). In previous work I adopted for abstract labour the composite mL (where m is the monetary expression of labour; and L in fact added-up concrete labour). As an interpretation of Marx this is wrong. (At least it is wrong to use Marx's term abstract labour for mL; mL is value-added which is a more concrete notion.) After the initiating Chapter 1 this notion (and the term) 'abstract labour' is superseded and should not be used any more.

In my view many, if not most, of the problems for the interpretation of Chapter 1 have to do with the difference between abstract and concrete labour. *Capital* was not written (Marx thought) for philosophically educated readers. The meaning of 'abstract labour' is not easy. In the course of explaining it, Marx, I think, felt constrained to take recourse to all kinds of non-rigorous approximations, analogies and examples. However, these are overcome section-wise. Once the later section is comprehended it makes no sense to phrase that non-rigorously. (Didactics may require one to explain the mathematical notion of fraction by example of a cake. It is expected that when we get to fractional exponential growth, the thinking in terms of cakes is past.)

13   To my knowledge 'abstract labour' is further used: once in Chapter 2, twice in Chapter 3 (1867F: 209, 240) and once in Chapter 8 (1867F: 308) (German edition Chapter 6), all in Volume I. There are no occurrences in Volumes II or III. There is also an occurrence in the *Results* (1867F: 992–3).

Relatedly the term labour as 'substance' disappears after Chapter 3. There are two exceptions for Volume I: 18 (672), 23 (715); one exception for Volume II: 19 (462); four exceptions for Volume III: 8 (248), 48 (961, 964, 968) (references are by chapter and page number of the English texts in the Fowkes/Fernbach translation).

The term 'homogeneous labour' equally disappears after Chapter 3 (without exception to my knowledge).

Column 2 of *Table 1* (p. 143) provides a schematic outline of the determinations of value. Column 1 sets out a hypothetical analogy with another realm. Several entries in the Table will be expanded upon later.

2.2   *Immanent substance and immanent measure: abstract labour and method*

We saw that money is the necessary expression of value: only with money do we arrive at the extroversive form of immanent substance: that is, the determinate 'being' of commodities. There cannot be a privileging of the one over the other (analogously: when we consider a specific table there is no point in privileging the 'introversive' timber and nails over the 'extroversive' creative act of formation of that table or vice versa; the one without the other is not-table – see Table 1 on p. 143). In other words, 'value' and the 'commodity' are not fully constituted in Chapter 1: they are merely as an initiating simplification.

Marx's method is one of conceptual *progression* from simple to complex determinations. In the case at hand Chapter 1 establishes introversive notions of the commodity; at that level of the presentation the commodity has no determinate existence, but rather 'prevalence' (*Dasein*). The commodity of simple circulation is fully posited only with its extroversive notions in Chapter 3 (completing Part One).

Marx's immanent measure of value in Chapter 1 – time of 'abstract labour' – is *very* abstract. It does not provide a measure of value in the sense that we (nowadays) usually use the term measure. Many commentators have brushed away this problem by identifying value and 'abstract labour time'![14] 'Abstract labour' cannot be measured (in terms of time) with more sense than a table's timber as abstracted from, for example, anything but its length. But for the latter this does not provide the full constitution of a table (merely substance); for the former this does not constitute value (merely substance).

I use the term 'very abstract labour' because in the literature on Marx, or developments from his work, the term 'abstract labour' has become somewhat worn out: it seems often identified with a *quantitative part of concrete(!) labour*: (1) producing at average conditions of production (hence, it is said, 'necessary'); (2) for the product of which there is demand (hence, it is said, 'necessary'); (3) that contributes to production in a particular sense, or 'productive' labour (hence, it is said, 'necessary'). These issues can be announced; however, there is no way of *knowing* them or measuring them prior to the market. Thus abstract labour has no determinate existence. Abstract labour has a dimension of time but, paradoxically, it cannot be measured unless we *assume* that abstract labour equals concrete labour (thus abstract from abstract labour).

---

14   See also Reuten (1999).

TABLE 1 *A hypothetical analogy for the measurement of material 'tables' and of social ideal 'value'*†

TIMBER AND TABLES	LABOUR AND VALUE
We begin by a *simplifying* abstraction and reduce (e.g.) 'tables' to a material substance that they have in common, **timber**; we consider this as a 'moment' of tables.	We begin by a *simplifying* abstraction and reduce 'value' to a social substance that entities of value have in common, **labour**; we consider this as a 'moment' of value.
'**Timber**': substance of *tables*. *Introversive moment* for the constitution of tables.	'**Labour**': substance of *value*. *Introversive moment* for the constitution of value.
Tables are not timber as such. (Further: considering timber under the aspect of length does not imply that 'length of timber' is the measure for tables.)	Value is not labour as such. (Further: considering labour under the aspect of time (labour-time) does not imply that 'labour-time' is the measure of value.)
The length of timber is a quality necessary for the being of tables – at least provisionally.*	The time of labour is a quality necessary for the being of value – at least provisionally.*
'Tables' (at the level of abstraction reached so far): tables are constituted by an *introversive moment* of substance (timber) and an *extroversive moment* of form (actually: the creative material act of making).	'Value' (at the level of abstraction reached so far): value is constituted by an *introversive moment* of substance (labour) and an *extroversive moment* of form (actually: *ideal commensuration by money*).
All tables have timber in common – at least provisionally (i.e., at the current level of abstraction*); but they are *not* fully constituted by timber.	All value has labour in common, at least provisionally (i.e., at the current level of abstraction*); but it is *not* fully constituted by labour.
'Tables' are material realities. (In principle tables can be trans-historical material realities.)	'Value' is an ideal reality. (Moreover, it is a social-historical ideal reality.)
* Provisionally: we can have plastic tables.	* Provisionally: the form allows for an extroversive hypostasisation – value without labour substance (see §3.4 below).
Once we have reached beyond the early simplification it makes no sense to measure conceptually enriched tables by measuring length of timber: *length of tables ≠ length of timber*	Once we have reached beyond the early simplification it makes no sense to measure conceptually enriched value by measuring time of labour: *quantity of value ≠ time of labour* (value ≠ abstract labour-time)

† I do not want to suggest that Column 1 sets out the appropriate way for knowing what tables are, and how they should be measured; the message is that inasmuch as it makes no sense to measure the length of fully constituted tables by the timber, it makes no sense to measure value by labour-time.

Rather, value is fully constituted only when we have money; money in the market measures 'abstract labour' and so determines 'abstract labour' so to speak; however (!), at this point the term 'abstract labour' is superfluous: we have value. (Of course, it may be added, 'value' itself is an abstraction in practice.)

The notion of very abstract labour implies that Chapter 1 does not present a 'labour theory of value' (a term not used by Marx) in any quantifiable sense. From this again derives the conclusion that abstract labour, *a fortiori*, cannot be quantitatively implanted into lower levels of abstraction (and – to repeat – Marx does not do this).

The warning regarding the Chapter 1 notions of value and labour also applies to 'money' within Chapter 3. It seems that for Marx a thing's 'being' the measure of value (Section 1) and its being the means of circulation (Section 2), constitutes it as being money. The heading of Section 3 is: 'Money'. It means that only in that section money becomes constituted (though simple). This gives rise to a considerable language problem (as always in systematic dialectics) of how to talk about the entity prior to it (i.e., without running into artificial language). In the first two sections of Chapter 3 Marx often uses the term 'gold', but frequently also 'money' even if money has not yet been fully constituted – merely a simplified constituent.

Of course, this problem applies to 'capital' in all of *Capital*. Each time (section, chapter, part, volume) we are further introduced into it. It is misleading to think of any early presentation as 'truth'; it is also misleading to cite it in that way. Until the completion it is always partial ("the whole is the truth", wrote Hegel).

3 Money's measuring: ideal transubstantiation

3.1 *Idealities*

In this section I expand on the core of Chapter 3: 'money's measuring'. I begin with a fairly long quotation from early on in the chapter, which I take to be programmatic. It shows, first, that the *value* of an entity is a purely ideal form of its existence (this denies ontologically real 'embodiment'); second, the measurement in terms of money (gold) is an *ideal* act: it is performed through an *imaginary* equalisation with money (gold); third, as a result the second performance can be established by imaginary money. I amplify on the first two issues in §3.2 and on the third in §3.3.

The price or *money-form* of commodities is, *like their form of value generally* [wie ihre Wertform überhaupt] quite distinct from their palpable and real bodily form; it is therefore a purely *ideal* or notional form [nur ideelle oder vorgestellte Form – 'vorgestellte', i.e., 'imagined']. Although invisible, the value of iron, linen and corn exists in these very articles [Dingen]: it is signified [vorgestellt, i.e. 'imagined'] through their equality with gold, even though this relation with gold exists only in their heads, so to speak [ihre Gleichheit mit Gold, eine Beziehung zum Gold, die sozusagen nur in ihren Köpfen spukt, i.e., their equality with gold, a relation to gold, even though this only haunts their heads, so to speak]. The guardian of the commodities must therefore lend them his tongue, or hang a ticket on them, in order to communicate their prices to the outside world. Since the expression of the value of commodities in gold is a purely ideal act [ideelles], we may use purely imaginary [nur vorgestelltes] or ideal gold to perform this operation ... In its function as measure of value, money therefore serves only in an imaginary or ideal capacity [als nur vorgestelltes oder ideelles Geld, i.e., as merely imaginary or ideal money]. (1867F: 189–90; 1867G: 110–11; emphasis added)[15]

3.2   *Marx's notion of 'measurement': 'verwandlen' and standardised measurement*

When Marx refers to money's measurement, he refers to an abstract genus. This is a problem for us. In everyday language and practice money is so much an ('imagined') concrete entity, that we tend to immediately give it the content of *our* particular money – the North Americans think of their dollars, many Europeans of euros, and so on. 'Money', however, is the abstract general of these. This is a main difficulty of Chapter 3. If this is not grasped then Marx's distinction between measure of value and standard of price becomes a superficial one.[16] Marx points this out, but not clearly enough. It is important to stress this because it underlines the conceptual progress made in Chapter 3.

Usually when we think of a measure we think of a standard. However, when Marx says 'money measures value' he means that it establishes the *commen-*

---

15   Fowkes misses the qualification of 'equality' into 'relation'. His suppression of the 'haunting' (*spukt*) is an obvious intervention in the text. It is also not clear why Fowkes is not consistent about 'imaginary'/'imagined' where Marx is consistent about it (*vorgestellt*).
16   The 'standard of price' may be some (nominal) quantum of gold when a commodity money regime prevails, or a specific nominal accounting unit (dollar, euro) when a regime of pure credit-money prevails (as after the Bretton Woods demise of the mid-1970s). Standards of price are linked in their exchange rates.

suration (i.e., homogenisation).[17] That is to say, the value-form determination is concretised as *money measure*. On the other hand, the 'taking measure' (and ticketing) of the value of a commodity is established in terms of a standard of price. The distinction between this 'measurement in general' and the specific 'taking measure' by way of a particular standard is most important. (Marx's terminology might seem idiosyncratic in current language. However, in Hegel's Logic (both its versions) we have a similar usage of the term 'measure'. In hindsight this also sheds light on Marx's usage of 'immanent measure' for the Chapter 1 moment of value.)

> As the measure of value it [money] serves to convert [verwandeln, transform] the values of all the manifold commodities into prices, into imaginary *quantities of gold* {that is, money in general}; as the standard of price it [money] ... measures, on the contrary, *quantities of gold by a unit* quantity of gold [Goldquantum]. (1867F: 192; 1867G: 113; emphasis added)[18]

The second phrase, about the standard, specifies a unit (quantum) for the measurement of the quantity in the first phrase. For the *second phrase* we can use the analogy of (say) length measurement: as a standard of length a particular rod (named metre or yard) measures 'entities of length' by a unit of length (one metre or one yard). As the standard of price, some particular money (named dollar or euro) measures quantities of money (a pile of notes or coins) by a unit of price (one dollar or one euro).

For the *first phrase*, as already indicated (§2.1), the analogy would be false. Prior to the measurement we have 'entities of length' (such as tables). For the commodities, prior to the measurement, we merely have the 'introversive substance', which is a *purely ideal or imagined* introversive substance (cf. the quote in §3.1).[19]

The act of measurement by money (i.e., prior to the actual exchange) ideally 'transubstantiates' commodities into form-determined entities and *hence* commensurate or homogeneous (cf. the quotation from 1867F: 192 given above).

---

17 A homogenisation that is foreshadowed in the term 'abstract labour'. But this *is not* a homogenisation: it is a (very) abstract notion.

18 My interpolations in square brackets derive directly from the (German) text; interpolations in curly brackets are interpretative.
    Note again that Marx, of course, departs from the Chapter 1 'immanent value' – a notion that is now, with the extroversion, transformed into a more concrete concept of value.

19 I use this term 'substance' because Marx uses it. But even when prefixed by 'purely ideal' the term risks giving rise to notions of 'embodiment' (expanded upon in Reuten 1993) [Chapter 6 of the current book].

This is like a miracle. But just as most Catholics that go to church every week or perhaps every day may not be very attentive any more to the miraculousness of the (ideal) transformation of bread and wine into the body of Christ, we are, when we mundanely buy our daily bread, usually not very attentive to the miraculous ideal transubstantiation as performed by the lady in the baker's shop.

This transubstantiation in reference to the Catholic celebration is one connotation of the German term *Verwandlung* (and its verb *verwandeln*). Transformation and to transform is perhaps the preferable translation (unfortunately, it is not consistently adopted). Thus money's measurement per-forms the value-homogeneity of commodities. Or we could also say: money turns the hopelessly abstract immanent notion of 'abstract labour' into extroversive form, and therewith into a potential concretum (concretum, that is when the salto mortale is completed into the metamorphosis C–M). Without this 'measurement *überhaupt*', standards of price (or standards of value) make no sense.

Thus value is, in *both* its constituents (introversive and extroversive), imaginary or ideality. Although it is beyond the subject of this chapter, I should add that ideality can have real effect. In this case this is – as far as I am concerned – the point. (See Murray 2000b and 2004 on subsumption.)

3.3 Imaginary measurement by imaginary money

I now turn to the third aspect of the 'programmatic' quotation (§3.1). If we restrict the discussion (as I have done so far) to money as measure of value, Marx goes as far as one could go in the commodity-money based monetary regime of his day (though see §4) that is, within the restriction – much emphasised by Campbell 1997 – of simple commodity circulation, namely, prior to the introduction of capital into the presentation, and hence prior to the introduction of money as finance. In hindsight it is easy (but a-historical) to criticise almost all of monetary theory prior to, say, 1973 for allotting a major role to metal in the top of the money pyramid.

If we compare the current 'pure credit-money' regime with a 'pure commodity money' regime the crucial step is not the demise of the Bretton Woods regime (the controlled international gold–dollar standard); the latter is the tail. Crucial is the (national) irredeemability of banknotes and the prevalence of 'money of account' at all: imaginary money (cf. Marx's treatment of money of account in Section 3 of Chapter 3).[20] Thus the ideal or imaginary *Verwandlung*

---

20   In this context Marx's 'inverse quantity theory of money' is important (the quantity of money is determined by the price level).

is accomplished by ideal or imaginary money (or – from a perspective of pure credit-money – by nominal money).

3.4 *Extroversive hypostasisation*

One culmination of Marx's treatment of money as measure is the 'imaginary measurement by imaginary money' mentioned above. A second one is the hypostasisation of money as extroversive measure, whence entities (as including insensuous ones) can take the price-form without having value (196).

> The possibility ... of a quantitative incongruity between price and magnitude of value ... is inherent in the price-form itself. This is not a defect, but, on the contrary, it makes this form the adequate one for a mode of production whose laws can only assert themselves as blindly operating averages between constant irregularities. (196)

However, the possibility of incongruity may go further than these irregularities. Marieken, Faust or a modern business manager can sell their souls. With the money they can buy indulgences or 'goodwill':

> Things which in and for themselves are not commodities, things such as conscience, honour, etc., can formally speaking, have a price without having a value. (197)

Whereas in their simplicity the introversive determinations of Chapter 1 are necessary – as Marx frequently repeats – the extroversive determinations are equally necessary. However, because it is inherent to the latter that these do not stick to the former, the extroversive measure hypostases.

The upshot is a shift in the connection between the Chapter 1 'simple value' and the Chapter 3 price constituting 'value'. Whilst money necessarily measures value, it can also measure nullities.

4   An introversive regress: bullion

The weakness of Marx's presentation dated 1867 (1890^4) is not at all, in my view, that he starts his account of money as measure with commodity money: the development of money of account from it is fine. The weakness is rather that when he gets to the final subsection of the chapter, 'World Money', he makes the impression of presenting the empirical prevalence of 'world money' in the shape of gold/silver (especially for settling international payments) as an argument for his starting point in commodity money. And instead of *theorising* that prevalence, he just describes it: money "falls back into its original form as precious metal in the shape of bullion" (240). What is more, he explicitly presents a regression to Chapter 1:

> In the world market ... money functions to its full extent as the commodity whose natural form is also the directly [unmittelbar, i.e., immediate] social form of realisation [Verwirklichungsform, i.e., form of actualisation] of human labour in the abstract. (1867F: 240–1; 1867G: 156 – underlining added)

Quite aside from my methodological critique above, this quotation provides a textual confirmation of the main thesis of this chapter about the relation between Chapters 1 and 3, including the *ex ante* immeasurability of abstract labour (in the usual sense of measurement). By itself abstract labour is not actual. Note first that we have here one of the two occurrences of 'abstract labour' in this chapter (and in all of the 2,000 pages to come there is just one recurrence). Note also that the two corrections in the translation above are crucial. 'Immediateness' refers to an abstract, yet underdeveloped or defective account. 'Realisation' in this context is most confusing, as in some Marxian accounts the term refers to 'sale'. Instead, Marx says, bullion is *being* the immediate form of human labour in the abstract. Directly following the text just quoted Marx writes: "Its mode of existence [*seine Daseinsweise*] becomes adequate to its concept." Mere *Dasein* is another reference to defectiveness. Thus bullion *is* the immediate form of abstract labour. I add: bullion itself.

Thus the Chapter 1 'abstract labour' is *only mediately measurable* – we necessarily require money: money measures abstract labour. The one exception to this necessary mediation (in 1867) is the labour producing the commodity 'bullion'; because bullion as world money functions as general means of payment and general means of purchase, we have an immediate social form of actualisation of abstract labour. (Today, of course, there is no exception.)

Summary and Conclusions

Value constitutes the historically specific *social form* of production in capitalist societies. Part One of *Capital I* introduces the concept of value by way of an analysis and synthesis of simple commodity circulation: that is, commodity circulation in abstraction from capital, the production of capital and the development of the circuit of capital (the subject – briefly – of the remainder of the work).

Although this social form has real (ontological) effect in shaping the material production in capitalist societies, it is an *ideal* form in the sense that it is insensuously permutated to entities and processes. It has sensuous existence only in money and artefacts of accounting, themselves physically separate from those entities and processes, although utterly meaningless without the latter.

In the interpretation of Part One of *Capital I* set out here, the *ideal immanent (or introversive) substance of the value* of commodities is 'abstract labour' (*sic*). Its qualitative measure (i.e., the immanent measure of value) is 'time' of abstract labour. This is what I called the simple-abstract notion of value (of Chapter 1). It is defective and it has no real ideal existence (no ideal existence in practice).

This simple notion is complemented in Chapter 3 by the *ideal extroversive form of the value* of commodities: money. It is only henceforth that 'value' has been fully constituted. Money establishes the actual homogeneity of commodities and is the only one actual ideal measure of value (adopting a particular standard).

The introversive substance and the extroversive form of value are *inseparable*. *Value* cannot be concretely measured without money; any effort to do so comes down to a Ricardian 'timber-nail tale' of measurement. However, we have seen that this inseparability is not symmetrical: money can measure, and purchase, nullities.

Once we are past Chapter 3, any talk in terms of abstract-labour(-time) is a regress to a simplification – i.e., simple or underdetermined value. Marx, though, does not make this mistake.

References

Superscripts indicate first and other relevant editions; the last mentioned year in the bibliography is the edition cited.

Arthur, Christopher J. 2004, 'Money and the form of value', in Bellofiore and Taylor (eds 2004), pp. 35–62.
Arthur, Christopher J. 2005, 'Value and money', in Moseley (ed.) 2005, pp. 111–23.
Arthur, Christopher J., and Geert Reuten (eds) 1998, *The circulation of capital: essays on volume II of Marx's 'Capital'*, London: Macmillan.
Bellofiore, Riccardo 2004, 'Marx and the macro-monetary foundation of microeconomics', in Bellofiore and Taylor (eds) 2004, pp. 170–210.
Bellofiore, Riccardo 2005, 'The monetary aspects of the capitalist process in the Marx-

ian system: an investigation from the point of view of the theory of the monetary circuit', in Moseley (ed.) 2005, pp. 124–42.

Bellofiore, Riccardo, and Riccardo Realfonzo 1997, 'Finance and the labour theory of value: toward a macroeconomic theory of distribution from a monetary perspective', *International Journal of Political Economy*, 27/2.

Bellofiore, Riccardo, and Nicola Taylor (eds) 2004, *The constitution of capital: essays on volume I of Marx's 'Capital'*, London: Palgrave Macmillan.

Campbell, Martha 1997, 'Marx's theory of money: a defense', in Moseley and Campbell (eds) 1997, pp. 89–120.

Campbell, Martha 1998, 'Money in the circulation of capital', in Arthur and Reuten (eds) 1998, pp. 129–58.

Campbell, Martha 2002, 'The credit system', in Campbell and Reuten (eds) 2002, pp. 212–27.

Campbell, Martha, and Geert Reuten (eds) 2002, *The culmination of capital: essays on volume III of Marx's 'Capital'*, London: Palgrave Macmillan.

Elson, Diane 1979, 'The value theory of labour', in *Value: the representation of labour in capitalism*, edited by Diane Elson, London: CSE Books.

Marx, Karl 1867^{1}G/1890^4, *Das Kapital, Kritik der politischen Ökonomie, Band I, Der Produktionsprozeß des Kapitals*, MEW 23, Berlin: Dietz Verlag, 1973.

Marx, Karl 1867^{1}F/1890^4, *Capital, a critique of political economy, volume I*, trans. of the 4th German ed. by Ben Fowkes, Harmondsworth: Penguin Books, 1976.

Moseley, Fred, and Martha Campbell (eds) 1997, *New investigations of Marx's method*, Atlantic Highlands, NJ: Humanities Press.

Moseley, Fred (ed.) 2005, *Marx's theory of money: modern appraisals*, London: Palgrave Macmillan.

Murray, Patrick 2000a, 'Marx's "truly social" labour theory of value: abstract labour in Marxian value theory (part one)', *Historical Materialism* 6: 27–66.

Murray, Patrick 2000b, 'Marx's "truly social" labour theory of value: abstract labour in Marxian value theory (part two)', *Historical Materialism* 7: 99–136.

Murray, Patrick 2002, 'Reply to Geert Reuten', *Historical Materialism* 10.1: 155–76.

Murray, Patrick 2004, 'The social and material transformation of production by capital: formal and real subsumption in "Capital volume I"', in Bellofiore and Taylor (eds) 2004, pp. 243–73.

Murray, Patrick 2005, 'Money as displaced social form: why value cannot be independent of price', in Moseley (ed.) 2005, pp. 50–64.

Realfonzo, Riccardo, and Riccardo Bellofiore 1996, 'Marx and money', *Trimestre* 29/1–2: 189–212.

Reuten, Geert 1988, 'Value as social form', in *Value, social form and the state*, edited by Michael Williams, London: Macmillan, pp. 42–61.

Reuten, Geert 1993, 'The difficult labour of a theory of social value: metaphors and systematic dialectics at the beginning of Marx's *Capital*', in *Marx's method in Capital: a re-examination*, edited by Fred Moseley, Atlantic Highlands, NJ: Humanities Press, pp. 89–113.

Reuten, Geert 1999, 'The source versus measure obstacle in value theory', *Rivista di Politica Economica* 89/4–5: 87–115.

Reuten, Geert 2000, 'The interconnection of systematic dialectics and historical materialism', *Historical Materialism* 7: 137–66.

Reuten, Geert 2004, 'Productive force and the degree of intensity of labour', in Bellofiore and Taylor (eds) 2004, pp. 117–45.

Reuten, Geert, and Michael Williams 1989, *Value-form and the state; the tendencies of accumulation and the determination of economic policy in capitalist society*, London: Routledge.

Williams, Michael 2000, 'Why Marx neither has nor needs a commodity theory of money', *Review of Political Economy* 12/4: 435–51.

CHAPTER 8

Productive force and the degree of intensity of labour; Marx's concepts and formalisations in the middle part of *Capital I*

2004 article, originally published in *The constitution of capital: essays on volume I of Marx's 'Capital'*, edited by Riccardo Bellofiore and Nicola Taylor, London: Palgrave Macmillan, pp. 117–45.
(For its abstract see the Abstracts of all chapters, p. 4.)

Contents

Introduction   153
1   The production of capital   153
   1.1   A comment on dimensions: monetary value and labour-time   155
   1.2   The terrain of the middle part of 'Capital I'   159
2   Determinants of (the rate of) surplus-value   161
   2.1   The rate of surplus-value   161
   2.2   The 'productive force' of labour   166
   2.3   A formal and immanent-reconstructive intermezzo on capitalist revolutions in the productive force of labour   168
   2.4   Degree of intensity of labour   172
   2.5   Once again, the value of labour-power and the wage rate   176
Summary and conclusions   178
References   179

Introduction[1]

The first volume of Marx's *Capital* (1867^1; 1890^4) is subtitled "The production process of capital". This reveals the twofold object of the book of, first, an outline of the capitalist *form* of production – i.e., in contradistinction to other

---

[1] I am grateful for the stimulating comments by Chris Arthur, Riccardo Bellofiore, Martha Campbell, Fred Moseley, Patrick Murray, Tony Smith, and Nicola Taylor. I also thank my University of Amsterdam colleague Mark Blaug for his comments.

modes of production – and, second, the production of capital itself – i.e., its continuity. There are again two aspects to this object. The one is highlighted in the 'middle part' of the book – Parts Three to Six – on the production of surplus-value. It sets out how the production of surplus-value (profit) is the motive force of capital, how surplus-value is actually produced and so how capital grows. The second aspect is the resulting process of accumulation of capital – treated in the 'end part' of the book.

In this essay I survey the middle part of *Capital I*, therein especially focusing on Marx's formalisations. As will be seen, he formalises explanatory *results* rather than either 'explanatory *processes*' or 'mechanisms'. Absent from the formalisations are Marx's key concepts such as: productive forces, labour productivity, extensity and intensity of labour, and the value of labour-power (or the wage rate). Therefore, also, these formulas are deprived of heuristic inspiration.[2]

In §2 I follow the text of this middle part and make some elementary beginnings for an immanent reconstruction of Marx's formalism. As to the content of this reconstruction I restrict myself to the key concepts mentioned in the previous paragraph. By 'immanent' reconstruction I mean that I base myself on Marx's concepts – that is qua intention: even an immanent reconstruction cannot be but interpretative. The idea of an immanent reconstruction is not to further develop the theory at hand, but to understand it better – thus my intentions are historiographic.[3]

The general conceptual terrain of the middle part of *Capital I* will briefly be surveyed in §1 (only the first subsection goes beyond an immanent reconstruction).

Apart from 'normal' historiographic accounts of Marx's texts, the reader will find quite a bit of comparison between Marx's German text and its English translation by Ben Fowkes. Some of this comparison is critical of the translation. However, I should like to voice my high esteem for the translator. I know by experience how difficult it is to write in a foreign language. Translation, however, is a far more difficult task. It is just *inevitable* – especially with authors

---

[2] Other formalisations of Marx, such as his reproduction schemes, have been heuristically inspiring (see Reuten 1998) [Chapter 11 of the current book]. In effect, within the Marxian tradition the *Capital I* formulas have mostly been replicated instead of enriched. I make no plea for any formalism to dominate the enquiry or its presentation. Opting myself for a systematic-dialectical methodology, I believe nevertheless that, in many instances and *at one and the same* conceptual level (especially for the analysis of a dialectical 'moment'), formal treatments may provide helpful tools.

[3] Of course, a better understanding might, next, play a role in the further development of a theory, or even a reconstruction in the sense of a new construction.

such as Marx – that the translator interprets the text. This may not be a problem so long as we have fairly standard interpretations on which the translator can rely. However, as soon as interpretations shift then the particular translation of key terms may no longer be obvious.

All page references to *Capital I* in the Fowkes translation of its fourth edition are denoted by an *F* followed by a page number. Those to the fourth German edition of *Das Kapital I* are denoted by a *G* and page number (*MEW* edition). Sometimes I also refer to the earlier English Moore and Aveling translation (of the third edition), as indicated by *MA* and page number. Throughout this essay I insert quite a few footnotes. Of these, notes 4–5, 8, 14, 20, 38, 40 and 43 are introductory; the others are for the specialist.

1 **The production of capital**

1.1 *A comment on dimensions: monetary value and labour-time*
I begin with a brief comment on the 'dimensions' in which Marx casts his analysis of the process of production of capital. Note first his particular level of abstraction here: his analysis deals with an average production process – in regard to the quantity and quality of both the means of production used and the labour used, and in regard to their organisation.[4] [2023 remark: Most of

---

4 In effect, he abstracts from intra-branch and inter-branch differences [except in ch. 12], including differing production periods and compositions of capital (dealt with in Volume III, Parts One and Two). He also assumes that the output produced will be sold – or at least that any discrepancy in this respect is the average one (the complications, especially in the context of accumulation of capital are dealt with in Volume II, Part Three). He assumes that there is no difference between production time and labour-time – or, he assumes that this difference indeed is the average one (further dealt with in Volume II, Part Two). Finally, he abstracts from finance and banking – or he assumes that its functions are integrated into the average capital that he treats (explicitly dealt with in Volume III, Parts Four and Five).

At the current level of abstraction Marx achieves, in effect, similarities to a macroeconomic treatment (the concept of macroeconomics dates only from the 1930s), without however losing the connection to microeconomic processes. I say 'similarities' – it is not macroeconomic; if that term were applicable it would be for Part Three of *Capital II* when Marx explicitly considers "the functioning of the social capital – that is of the total capital" (Marx 1885, p. 468). (For the latter interpretation as the construction of a macroeconomics, see Reuten 1998, esp. pp. 190–5.)

One implication of dealing with the average production process is that 'labour' always means 'socially necessary labour', that is, (1) it is of average skill and dexterity; (2) it produces at the prevailing productive forces; (3) any supply/demand discrepancies are either abstracted from or considered to be the average ones.

the time Marx indeed treats averages. However, not so in Chapter 12 (ch. 10 of the German edition). I regret that the current article neglected this. The non-average account here is treated in Chapter 2 (2019) and Chapter 15 (2017) of the current book.]

One of Marx's greatest insights, in my view, is that he comprehends the capitalist production process as a unity of labour process and of {ideal} valorisation process.[5] In the opening Chapter 7 of the middle part Marx writes:

> Just as the commodity itself is a *unity of* use-value and value, so the process of production must be a *unity of labour process and process of creating value*. (...)
>
> The production process *as a unity of labour process and process of creating value*, is a process of production of commodities; *as a unity of labour process and process of valorisation*, it is a capitalist process of production, or the capitalist form of the production of commodities. (F, 293 and 304 – amended;[6] G, 201 and 211)

Thus Marx is pointing out here the specific capitalist value-form of production. Expressed otherwise, we have a unity of a process of physical production (labour process) and a process of {ideal} value augmentation (valorisation process). We have two things coinciding, as unity. As simple as this may appear in practice (it is happening all the time in capitalist enterprises), its analysis is complex especially dimensionally: we have value categories (homogenous); time (homogenous); heterogenous physical inputs and outputs; and labour that can be conceived of in terms of homogenous time, but that is itself heterogenous.

Throughout this middle part Marx, as we will see, uses two dimensions for his analysis in general and his representations/equations in particular: a value dimension and a labour-time dimension. Without exception the value entit-

---

5 'Valorisation', i.e., value augmentation. The interpolation of 'ideal' will be explained later on.
6 For the first starred text Fowkes has "unity formed of" for "Einheit von" ('formed of' has some connotation of separate elements); for the second starred text he has "unity composed of the labour process and the process of creating value" for *"Einheit von Arbeitsprozeß und Werthildungsprozeß"*. Fowkes makes better English, but it seems especially important here not to add 'the' before 'labour process' as this may suggest (as for my first amendment) that it is pre-given; Marx's view is that the character of the labour process itself is affected by it being a valorisation process – thus the latter is not just added on to the first.

Similarly, for the first starred text after the ellipsis, Fowkes has "considered as the unity of the labour process and the process of creating value" for *"Als Einheit von Arbeitsprozeß und Wertbildungsprozeß"*; the last amendment is alike.

ies are expressed in *monetary* terms (£); the same applies to all numerical examples.[7] It is necessary to emphasise this since in some accounts of Marx's theory, 'value' is itself taken to have a labour-time dimension. This is a wrong account of Marx's *Capital* (those same accounts often adopt the term 'labour values' – one that is never used in *Capital*). As we will see, Marx, at the level of abstraction of *Capital I*, aims to *explain* value (monetary dimension) in terms of labour-time – therewith, of course, value is not discarded of its monetary dimension. (Value is the abstract counterpart of price, at the level of abstraction – *Capital I* – where the distinction between surplus-value and profit is still implicit; the distinction is also not yet relevant – Marx reaches this by presenting the average capital.)

Besides the two dimensions mentioned, Marx adopts an intuitive notion of physical labour productivity increase: increases in the number of use-values (goods) produced by a unit of labour (but he always ends up by expressing these use-values in terms of price multiplied by quantity).[8]

The main problem in understanding Marx's texts (beginning with Part One of *Capital I*) is that he proceeds, step-wise, to find an endogenous dimensional reference point (or reference points), one that is (or are) *internal to his object of enquiry*, one that is (are) key to the functioning of his object of enquiry.[9] Its core terms, in Marx's view, are the monetary dimension and the time dimension. The early parts of each of the three volumes of *Capital* theorise the interconnection of these dimensions in increasing complexity and concretion (Volume I, Parts One and Two; Volume II, Part One; Volume III, Part One) ending up with *the* measure of capital, the rate of profit over time. Thus we end up with the connection of the monetary dimension with the time dimension in general, not the particular *labour*-time (of *Capital I*). However, that does not mean that labour-time becomes irrelevant at the *Capital III* level of analysis, just that we reach an overarching category.

The labour and labour-time category retains relevance at any level of abstraction in three respects. First, for the grand organisation of the production

---

7 Elson (1979) pointed this out.
8 Without value imputation (i.e., prices), the notion of physical productivity must, of course, be intuitive, because different use-values cannot be added up.
9 In contradistinction to external constructs, such as – later on in history – Fisher's index numbers, or Sraffa's standard commodity (both analytical commodity baskets). These are measures or devices of the analyst; they do not actually play a role in the functioning of the object of enquiry. (Though for index numbers we have a case of reflexivity, in that after their 'invention' they may be adopted in practice – e.g. some consumer price index in wage bargaining.)

process (the technique adopted) and, related, the planned organisation of the intensity of labour (say 'speed'). Second, for the common day to day organisation of production on the production floor, the management of output per labourer, i.e., per unit of labour-time. Third, the renumeration of labour-time, i.e., the wage rate. With the first and third fixed for any time being, the second determines the level of output and so profits. Earlier I wrote that Marx adopts in his analysis an 'intuitive' notion of physical labour productivity increase. At the point of production there is nothing intuitive about it.

In Marx's choice of categories and dimensions, and especially in the particular way he phrases his theory, there are undoubtedly also other issues at stake. For one, Marx (1867^1;1890^4) intervenes in the discourse of the Ricardian economics of his day (with its 'labour-embodied' theory of value), at times radically breaking away from it (his value-form theory), at others operating within it or at least at its margins. An additional problem here is that Marx sometimes, misleadingly, speaks about values (the explanandum) as "expressions" of labour (the explanans). (In the same vein a neoclassical economist might, also misleadingly, speak about prices as "expressions" of utility or preferences.) Apart from the few remarks in the next paragraph, I will not comment on these aspects in the remainder of this essay (for more see my 1993, Murray's 2000a comment on it, my 2000 reply, and Murray's 2002 rejoinder).

I take the circuit of capital {M – C ... P ... C' – M'}, i.e., its growth via the stages of investment (M–C), production (C–P–C') and sales (C'–M'), to be an interconnected process. From the perspective of the valorisation (i.e., augmentation) of capital, the 'moments' of the circuit (M–C; C–P–C'; and C'–M') can be distinguished but not separated. Thus valorisation of capital, the 'production' of capital, is the unity of this process. To stress this is in part a value-form theoretical development from Marx (i.e., with Marx beyond Marx – see e.g. Reuten and Williams 1989 and much of the work of Christopher Arthur, Tony Smith and Patrick Murray; see also Nicola Taylor 2004).[10] This development builds on *one* of the theoretical lines in *Capital*. On the other hand, Marx often tends, so it seems, to attribute a predominance to the 'moment' of production, especially when he is discussing production. His terminology of 'production' of surplus-value and 'production' of capital (apparently in abstraction from the other moments) seems to reflect this attributed predominance. In face of the unity of this process, I consider Marx's terminology misleading. For the

---

10 This does not imply that these authors agree with the particular way I briefly phrase this here.

value-form theoretical view, more specifically, there is properly speaking no production of 'value'; we have value inputs (M–C) and the valorisation result in C′–M′, i.e., when commodities are validated and commensurated in the market in terms of money. In between (C–P–C′) this result is *anticipated* upon, hence in production we merely have an 'ideal' pre-commensuration, or an anticipated imputation of value.[11] Hence we have no production *of* value, but physical production *in terms of* value. Having said this, I will for the purposes of this essay – and apart from a few reminders in footnotes – just report Marx's own terminology in this respect.

1.2 The terrain of the middle part of 'Capital I'

In this subsection I briefly survey the general terrain of the middle part of *Capital I* (Parts Three to Six, over 400 pages), against the background of Part Two.[12][13]

Capital, writes Marx in Part Two of *Capital I*, is "the unceasing movement of profit-making" (F, 254). We have a movement from money (M) into more money: M ... M+ΔM. But "unless it takes the form of some commodity, it does not become capital" (F, 256). Marx expresses this in the formula M–C–M′ (where C is the value of a commodity, or of commodities, and M′=M+ΔM). This is a formula of exchange derived from the simpler M–C–M. The latter is a strange act, namely buying (M–C) in order to sell (C–M). It is an 'inversion' of C_i–M–C_j, i.e., selling C_i in order to buy a qualitatively different C_j (F, 258). Here, money is merely a facilitator – it does not really matter. In the strange, inverted, form M–C–M, though, money is all that matters; however, it makes sense only as M–C–M′, that is, when the end result is an increment (ΔM), a 'surplus-value' as Marx calls it. In M–C–M′ value is

> the subject of a process in which, while constantly assuming the form in turn of money and commodities, it changes its own magnitude, throws off surplus-value from itself considered as original value, and thus valorises itself independently. For the movement in the course of which it

---

11　Usually capitalist firms, their management and their shareholders and other financiers do not worry about this. It is especially in times of crises that balance sheets are shown to be 'anticipations'. The notion of 'anticipation' and 'ideal pre-commensuration' is amplified upon in Reuten 1988, pp. 53–5 and Reuten and Williams 1989, pp. 66–8. See also Taylor 2004.

12　However, for the purposes of this essay I abstain from a specific treatment of the relatively short Part Six on 'Wages' (chapters 19–22, together about 35 pages). See Bellofiore 2004.

13　The next three paragraphs of this subsection are adapted from Reuten (2003a).

adds surplus-value is its own movement, its valorisation is therefore self-valorisation. (F, 255)

So capital is a movement of self-valorising value, of throwing off surplus-value.[14] Part Two is closed off with the introduction of a particular commodity and commodity market, that of labour-power. The existence of this market is predicated on the workers' lack of means of production. We also have a brief introduction of the value of labour-power, i.e., the wage, which in principle should be sufficient to reproduce labour-power. How much is 'sufficient' depends on physical, historical and moral elements (F, 272–5).

In the middle part of *Capital I* (Parts Three to Six) we see "not only how capital produces, but how capital is itself produced" (F, 280). That is, how surplus-value (ΔM) is produced – thus the (potential) expansion of capital. How can surplus-value be explained? Reconsider M–C–M′. "The change in value of the money ... cannot take place in the money itself ... The change must therefore take place in the commodity ..." (F, 270). Hence the key to M–C–M′ lies in C. In an analysis of the production process, Marx next shows how this is the site were the value of C is turned into C′.

In the exchange M–C, capital in money-form is turned into capital in commodity-form: means of production and labour-power. Means of production bought are static elements; they have on average a fixed technical lifetime and have their value transferred to the product, whence Marx terms the part of capital laid out on it *constant capital* (F, 311–17).[15] Labour-power, or labour capacity, is exchanged against the wage; so the labourer sells its capacity to labour (for the time agreed by contract). A change in C can only be engendered by this *active* living element, labour. And since this capacity is in principle variable, both in time (length of the working day) and in intensity – as we will see in more detail later on – Marx terms the part of capital laid out on it *variable capital*. During production, labour is "subordinated" to capital: "the worker works under the control of the capitalist ... the product is the property of the capitalist and not that of the worker" (F, 291–2). In labour resides the potential to produce a surplus-product, or, in value-terms: surplus-value. Thus labour

---

14 Note that the concept of 'profit' has been 'bracketed' – until *Capital III* – and replaced by the both simpler and more abstract notion of 'surplus-value'.

15 Means of production derive their value – we might add – not from the process of production in which they figure as means of production, but from the process of production in which they were produced; labour-power is not produced for sale in a capitalist process of production (Reuten 1988 and Reuten and Williams 1989, ch. 1, §9; see also Taylor 2004).

potentially generates a surplus-value beyond the wage – or, from the point of view of the capitalist, a surplus-value beyond the capital advanced. Marx calls the ratio between the amount of surplus-value and the capital laid out in wages the "rate of surplus-value" or the "degree of exploitation of labour-power by capital" (F, 320–7).

Part Three is on "The production of absolute surplus-value" (Chapters 7–11, about 150 pages). Central to it is the increase in the rate of surplus-value through extension of the working day. In my view this part serves didactic purposes, similarly to Marx's recurrent procedure of starting with "simple reproduction" (stationary state) before setting out "expanding reproduction". In this case it allows Marx to introduce systematically both the concept of "the value of labour-power" and the drive for increase in the rate of surplus-value. This didactic procedure of Marx also has a surprise effect. How could we still have – as happened in Marx's day – an increase in the rate of surplus-value, or perhaps a constant rate, when we have a decrease of the working day?

This question is the core issue treated in Part Four on "The production of relative surplus-value" (Chapters 12–15, some 215 pages). Both regular "revolutions in the productive forces" and increases in the intensity of labour (each with very different effects as we will see in §2) allow for a constant or even an increasing rate of surplus-value along with a decreasing length of the working day. Both of these are core to the capitalist mode of production.

The synthetic Part Five bears the dull but appropriate title of "The production of absolute and relative surplus-value" (Chapters 16–18; it is a relatively short part, extending to 30 pages).

In sum, for the explanation of surplus-value (and the rate of surplus-value), Marx posits four factors:
1. The magnitude of the value of labour-power;
2. The length of the working day;
3. The productive force of labour;
4. The intensity of labour.

He deals with the first two in Part Three (see §2.1 below) and the next two in Part Four (see §2.2 and §2.4). Sections 2.3 and 2.5 provide reconstructions of Marx's formal explanatory treatment.

2 Determinants of (the rate of) surplus-value

2.1 *The rate of surplus-value*

Part Three, "The production of absolute surplus-value", begins with two chapters setting out the distinctions between the 'Labour process and the valorisation process' (Chapter 7) and between 'Constant capital and variable capital' (Chapter 8) – briefly discussed in §1.2 above.[16] In Chapter 9 Marx formalises these distinctions, decomposing capital advanced (Z) into constant capital (c) laid out on means of production, and variable capital (v) expended on labour-power (F, 320–1).[17] The starting point for his formalisation (equations M–1 to M–5 below) is a (stylised) empirical reference:

> The surplus-value generated in the production process by Z, the capital advanced, i.e., the valorisation of the value of the capital Z, presents itself to us first as the amount by which the value of the product exceeds the value of its constituent elements. (F, 320 – C amended into Z, cf. the previous note)

Capturing this, Marx *formally* starts with a number of identities and definitions.

$$Z = c + v \qquad \text{[accounting identity] (M–1)}$$

As valorised Z is 'transformed' into:

$$Z' = (c + v) + s \qquad \text{[accounting identity] (M–2)}$$

where s is surplus-value. Thus in Z-Z' we have the abbreviated formula of the production by and of capital.

Henceforth all of Marx's equations/representations are indicated with M–. Unless made explicit otherwise, the dimension of all equations is monetary (as indeed Marx has it explicitly in terms of pounds, £; cf. also pp. F 327–29 where Marx, using empirical cases, derives s from business accounts.). All equations apply to a definite time period (a production period); I have refrained from adding on time subscripts as these would be uniform for all equations (up to equation 14). For each equation I indicate their analytical status in square

---

[16] All chapter indications refer to the English editions of Capital I. The English editions break up the German 4th chapter into three (Chapters 4–6). Hence from Chapter 7 onwards, the equivalent German chapter should be counted two back.

[17] Fowkes uses the symbol C for capital advanced (instead of my Z). This is confusing because the German M–C–M' formula is G–W–G'. In the chapter at hand Marx uses for 'capital advanced' the symbol C in German (i.e., not 'W', see G, 226 ff.) – which, if it were related to the formula, would seem nearer to the (English) M than to C. This makes a difference which actually gets lost in both the translations (cf. MA, 204 ff.).

brackets; the particular terms are mine (M–2, for example, is named 'a tautology' by Marx – F, 320).

Marx calls 'the new value created' (y) 'the value-product' and the output (x) 'the value of the product'.[18]

$$y \equiv v + s \qquad \text{[definition] (M–3)}$$

$$x \equiv (c + v) + s \qquad \text{[definition] (M–4)}$$

The s over v proportion is called 'the rate of surplus-value' (e).

$$e \equiv s/v \qquad \text{[definition] (M–5)}$$

As a ratio of equal dimensions $e \equiv s/v$ is, of course, a dimensionless number. Crucially from a theoretical point of view Marx (F, 324–6) casts the "same" ratio (F, 326) in terms of 'surplus labour' (SL) and 'necessary labour' (NL).[19]

$$e^* \equiv SL/NL \qquad \text{[definition] (M–6)}$$

$$e = e^* \qquad \text{[explanatory device] (M–7)}$$

Thus he posits e^* as an explanation for e. There is a difficulty here. So far, there is nothing in itself wrong with positing the one ratio as an explanation for the other, or with positing surplus labour(-time) as an explanation for surplus-value. There is a problem, however, if the explanans (e^*, or SL) cannot

---

18 The right-hand sides of (M–3) to (M–6) are Marx's (the symbols y, x, e, and e* are mine). Although it is not important in the context of the problematic of the current essay, it should be noted that soon in this Chapter 9 Marx abstracts from fixed capital, thus interprets both Z and c as circulating capital (F, 321). Next, and until the second section of Chapter 15, Marx also sets c=0 (F, 324). However, the context here and in the Chapters 10–14 rather points at moving 'constant capital' to the background: "In order that variable capital may perform its function, constant capital must be advanced … appropriate to the special technical conditions of each labour process" (F, 323).
19 'Surplus labour' and 'necessary labour' are 'the labour expended' during 'surplus labour-time' and 'necessary labour-time' (F, 325). Thus we see Marx making the distinction of 'labour' and 'labour-time', anticipating his discussion of 'intensity of labour' in later chapters (see §2.4 below). It seems, though, that for the time being we can treat the concepts as similar, especially for a discussion of the average capital.

The term 'necessary labour' should be distinguished from the term 'socially necessary labour' as referred to in note 4; the similarities of these terms is 'inconvenient', as Marx remarks in a footnote (F, 325, n. 5).

be measured independently of the explanandum (e, or s). This is not uncommon in science, but it is nevertheless a problem and far from a perfect situation.[20]

So far we have entities (c, v, s) that are, in principle, observable and measurable. However, *by themselves* (in isolation from the already known s/v ratio, one that can be measured) SL and NL cannot be measured. Another observable and measurable entity might be the labour-time of workers, e.g. 10 hours a day. Given a particular length of the working day we could, analytically, divide that up into one part in which an amount of value is produced equivalent to wages (equivalent to variable capital, v) and call this 'necessary labour(-time)' (NL), and another part in which an amount of value is produced equivalent to the surplus-value (s) and call this 'surplus labour(-time)' (SL). This is in fact what Marx does (F, 329–31).[21]

Another way to think about this is that (M–6) together with (M–7) simply makes explicit the idea that at a given wage per day, an extension of the working day results, in general, in an increased value-product. On this account (M–6) with (M–7) have elementary explanatory meaning.[22]

Early on in the last chapter of Part Three, Chapter 11, Marx provides a decomposition of the surplus-value in his earlier representations.[23]

---

20 Incidentally it may be noted that for the present-day mainstream in economics, a paradigm emerging soon after 1867, and aiming to explain prices or demand in terms of utility – and later on in terms of preferences – a similar problem applies: the explanans cannot be measured independently of the explanandum (of course this does not make Marx's problem more comforting).

21 Possibly one could argue that in this respect Marx is near to an abductive (Peirce) or a retroductive (Lawson) proceeding. An uncompromising empiricist would consider it doubtful if (M–6) adds anything explanatory to (M–5). What it achieves, in effect, is to breach the idea that the wage is the equivalent of the labour delivered. In whatever way this may be appraised – and in reference back to the misconceived notion of 'labour values' (see section 1.1, just after note 7) – Marx endeavours to provide an explanation of surplus-value in terms of labour(-time). To conceive of value itself in terms of labour(-time) is to collapse the explanation – and Marx definitely does not do this.

22 Though it is either analytical or largely intuitive. Let TL be total labour-time. Then we can rewrite (M–6) into: $e^* \equiv (TL - NL)/NL$, with TL in principle observable and NL unobservable. Now we could posit: s varies with TL, ceteris paribus. This may make analytical sense if the theory makes sense. However, Marx has yet to unpack a host of other factors affecting s (in all the rest of *Capital* at least), so that the 'ceteris paribus' makes no empirical sense.

23 Marx in a change of notation has $S = (s/v)V$ and $S = P(a'/a)n$ where P is the wage rate per day ($= \underline{w}$ in my notation).

$$s = (\underline{s}/\underline{v})v \qquad \text{[definition] (M–8)}$$

$$s = \underline{w}(a'/a)n \qquad \text{[explanatory device] (M–9)}$$

where:

s	= the mass of surplus-value;
v	= variable capital;
$\underline{s}$	= surplus-value per worker per average day;
$\underline{v}$	= variable capital advanced per worker per day (hence in fact the equivalent of the wage rate per day);
$\underline{w}$	= the wage rate per day ('the value of one individual labour-power');
a′	= surplus labour (surplus labour-time);
a	= necessary labour (necessary labour-time);
a′/a	= the average 'degree of exploitation';
n	= the number of workers employed (i.e., measured in days);
s/v	= the average rate of exploitation per worker per day (but as this is a dimensionless ratio it may as well be applied to any other time unit).

(Hence the underlined symbols in M–8 and M–9 are in value per time dimension; a′ and a in time dimension. This way we end up with the monetary value dimension for s – at least if we interpret Marx's "the number of workers employed" for n (F, 418) as workers days, which can readily be inferred from the context.)

Note that as ratios we have the equalities of

$$e \equiv s/v = \underline{s}/\underline{v} = a'/a \qquad \text{[recapitulation of explanatory device] (10)}$$

The $\underline{s}$ in the $\underline{s}/\underline{v}$ of (M–8) cannot be measured independently of s and v. Similarly the a′/a of (M–9) cannot be measured independently of s and v. (See the comment on (M–6) and (M–7) above.)

Anticipating Marx's discussion of absolute and relative surplus-value in Part Five, I add on a definition here (equations 11 or 12 are not Marx's):

$$wL \equiv v \qquad \text{[definition] (11)}$$

where w is the wage rate per hour and L the amount of *labour hours hired*. Hence we may rewrite (M–9) as

$$s = e^{*}(wL) \qquad \text{[explanatory device] (12)}$$

Marx writes: "the mass of surplus-value $\{s\}$ is determined [*bestimmt*] by the product of the number of labour-powers $\{L\}$ and the degree of exploitation of each individual labour-power $\{e^*\}$ ... We assume throughout, not only that the value of an average labour-power $\{\underline{w}\,?\}$ is constant, but that the workers employed by a capitalist are reduced to average workers" (F, 418; G, 322; symbols in curled brackets added).

The advantage of this notation (12) is that the number of hours hired (L) – as well as their remuneration (w) – has been made explicit. It seems that in his representation (M–9) Marx tried to bring this in – unsuccessfully though, since the working day itself is a variable (cf. Marx's $\underline{w}$ and n). On the other hand, in equation (12) we seem to have lost Marx's distinction between labour-power (L) and labour (L).[24] Or at least, this is now merely implicit.[25] In that respect, representation (12) – to be found in much of contemporary Marxian theory – is defective.[26] Later on we will retrieve Marx's labour–labour-power distinction (§2.3 and §2.5).

2.2 The 'productive force' of labour

Part Four of *Capital I* presents "The production of relative surplus-value". In its first Chapter 12 Marx introduces a key factor into his presentation: "change in the productive force of labour".[27] Before going into this, a note on translation is required. In the context of production we will generally need to differentiate between changes that have to do with the exertion of labour only, or mainly, and changes that have to do with the interconnection of changes in the means of production, technology and the exertion of labour. It seems to me that in the German text Marx makes important differentiations in this respect. Fowkes translates the German *Produktivkraft* by "productivity".[28] This is unfortunate, as Marx sometimes also uses the term *Arbeitsproduktivität* (labour productivity) –

---

24 In fact Marx's $s = \underline{w}(a'/a)n$ also does not bring out the distinction between labour and labour-power (the same applies to all of Marx's equations in *Capital*) although this one does make explicit the *value* of (a day's) labour-power.

25 The reader may observe that the same happens in Sraffian types of approach.

26 As including some of my own earlier work.

27 Earlier on it was sometimes briefly anticipated.

28 Most of the time at least – e.g. on page F, 453 2nd paragraph, Fowkes translates Produktivkraft into "productive power" and on page F, 508 it is translated into "productive forces" (cf. G, 407). Not only do we lose terminological connections, the English text also makes connections that are absent from the German (esp. with the German term *Produktivität der Arbeit* and when Fowkes translates this into "productivity of labour", "productivity" being his most frequent translation for "*Produktivkraft*"). We have the same problem in the *Results* (translated by Livingstone). Moore & Aveling (*Capital I*) translate *Produktivkraft* into "productiveness" (at least those instances I have checked). [*Continued on next page.*]

this will be seen to be especially important in the context of his presentation of 'intensity' of labour, discussed in the next subsection. In all of the following texts I will amend the translation for *Produktivkraft* into 'productive force' (marked *...* – I use the same mark for any other amendments, as specified in footnotes).²⁹

In Chapter 12 Marx writes:

> Hitherto, in dealing with the production of surplus-value ... we have assumed that the mode of production is given and invariable. ... The technical and social conditions of the process and consequently the mode of production itself must be revolutionized *so as to increase the productive force of labour* .... (F, 431–2 amended;³⁰ G, 333–4).

Introducing this by way of an example Marx wrote:

> increase in the *productive force* of labour ... cannot be done except by an alteration in his [the labourer's] tools or in his mode of working [*Arbeitsmethode*], or both. Hence the conditions of production of his labour, i.e., his mode of production, and the labour process itself, must be revolutionized. By an increase in the *productive force* of labour, we mean an alteration in the labour process of such a kind as to shorten the labour-time socially necessary for the production of a commodity, *hence a smaller quantity of labour acquires the force* of producing a greater quantity of use-value. (F, 431 amended;³¹ G, 333)

Productivity (it seems to me) has an imprecise meaning.³² I am pretty sure that Marx always reserves his term *Produktivkraft* (productive force) for – as he says

---

Generally there are two translation options for the term *Kraft* as in *Produktivkraft*: power and force. The former is adopted in the *Grundrisse* translation (productive power) and the latter in *The German Ideology* and the 1859 *Critique* Introduction (productive force).

29 Note that I do not claim to make better English than Fowkes.

30 For the starred text Fowkes has 'before the productivity of labour can be increased" for "um die Produktivkraft der Arbeit zu erhöhn".

31 For the first and second starred text Fowkes has 'productivity' for 'Produktivkraft'. For the third he has 'and to endow a given quantity of labour with the power ...' for '*ein kleineres Quantum Arbeit also die Kraft erwirbt*'. My point for this amendment is not only the reference to shortening of the labour day, but foremost the *reversion* of the apparently active element – with Fowkes's 'endow', labour seems to be put is the passive position.

32 In both mainstream and in much of Marxian economics it loosely refers to a combination of effects of technological change and effectiveness of labour. (I will come back to this in §2.4.)

in this quotation – the production of a greater quantity of use-value by a smaller (or by the same) quantity of labour (and it usually goes along with price decrease). My hypothesis is that the notion of 'socially necessary labour-time' – see the quotation – is associated with this notion of productive force and that, in this context, 'productive force' must be taken as average.

In the subsequent chapters of Part Four (13–15) Marx further conceptualises the development of productive force by way of a historical description of the development of 'tools', via manufacture, into (Chapter 15, section 1) 'machinery and large-scale industry'. Generally Marx associates an increase in productive force with changes in the organisation of the labour process (e.g. related to scale and division of labour and to changes in the composition of capital).[33]

2.3 A formal and immanent-reconstructive intermezzo on capitalist revolutions in the productive force of labour

It is not until Chapter 18 (i.e., the last chapter of Part Five) that Marx returns to his formulas for the rate of surplus-value, however, without improving on the previous ones – i.e., those discussed in §2.1 above. Nevertheless, in view of the conceptual progress made by Marx so far (Chapter 11 to Chapter 15, section 2), there is reason to do so. (Marx does not do it here and does not return to it in similar contexts later on.)

We saw that the potential of labour for producing use-values (the potential use-value productivity) is affected by the productive force; today economists would say: the state of technology and its implementation. Thus given that state, any labour is potentially exerted at a particular productive force.

A revolution in the productive force of labour can be envisaged as a change in technological trajectory (T) – think of grand technologies such as that of steam engine, electricity, petrol motor, computer. They get started in particular branches and then are gradually diffused throughout all or most of the branches in the economy. Let us simplify a trajectory (i) into a certain value c of specific means of production that could potentially be worked up by an amount of average labour (measured in time).

$$T_i \supseteq \ll c/L \gg \qquad \text{[definition of approximation]} \quad (13)$$

Thus c/L stands for a certain value (£) of means of production that could be worked up by a particular amount of labour in a definite period of time. (*Ana-*

---

[33] The concept of the 'composition of capital', the c/v ratio, is mostly only implicit in Part Four (it is alluded to in Chapter 15 – F, 571 and 577–8). It makes proper appearance in Part Seven. See Reuten 2004b. [Chapter 9 of the current book.]

lytically we might put L to unity, e.g. an hour, whence we have, e.g., £10 per labour hour.) The guillemets here, indicate the specificity of means of production and labour; ⊇ is the sign for 'contains or equals'. Within a trajectory we have bounded variations in c/L ratio's coming about in tranches (blocks) of diffusion (variations say of a range of 40% – in the analytical example ranging from £10/hr to £14/hr, coming about in e.g. 5 tranches). We call any one such tranche a *state* of the technological trajectory (ST), or a *state* of the development of the productive forces:[34]

$$ST_{i(t)} \supseteq \text{«}c/L\text{»}_{(t)} \qquad \text{[definition] (14)}$$

The subscript (t) stands for that particular state of trajectory (i) – it also stands for a definite period in time (e.g. 1850–1860) in a region (e.g. Great Britain and France).

Let us now consider production (recall that the accounting dimension of the production process is a monetary one).[35]

$$x = \text{«}c/L\text{»}_{(t)} L^\beta \quad [\beta>1]^{36} \qquad \text{[determination; step of heuristic approximation] (15)}$$

Hence, as before, x is the gross output in value terms (e.g. £). «c/L» is the quantity of means of production in value terms *that could, potentially, be worked up* by a quantity of labour (hours). The c is some value of means of production *at the point when workers enter the business gate* (at the point where they enter 'the hidden abode of production' – F, 280). Thus «c/L» is for example (£40mln)/(4mln potential labour hours).[37] The outer right-hand L in repres-

---

34 The 40% range is one in the absence of inflation or deflation of prices. Remember that c is in value terms. States of the trajectory are associated with a dissemination of the technology over a new tranche of branches in the economy.

35 In this accounting the management of firms anticipates sales and so carries out a commensuration of heterogeneous entities (means of production, labour in process) before the deed so to speak, and thus carries out 'an ideal pre-commensuration'. Cf. the last paragraph of §1.1 above.

36 Obviously for β=1 we would merely have a reproduction of the value of means of production, i.e., without any value added.

37 It may be misleading to add: (£40mln)/(4mln potential labour hours) = £10 per potential labour hour, as we did in the analytical example. «*c/L*» is fixed plant-wise, hence the average or modal «*c/L*» is fixed. Underlying L is a technical matrix with, in its column, the number of workers simultaneously required to operate the means of production at a point in time, and with, in the rows of the matrix, the duration of the production process (in hours). (Of course, «*c/L*» is only relatively 'fixed'. We may have major restructuring/reor-

entation (15) is the actual labour employed (measured in hours), i.e., actual labour-time. The factor β in L^β is *the actual exerting power* of labour (per hour). For the time being we take β to be a (stylised) *constant*, as attached to the productive force «c/L»$_{(t)}$.

I make a strict distinction between, first, the productive force of labour («c/L»$_t$), second, labour-power in the conventional sense (the L in «c/L»), i.e., a potential, and third, the 'actual exerting power of labour' (L^β) – this distinction is returned to in §2.5.[38] Apart from the value of labour-power (see §2.5) we have herewith collected all of the main variables that Marx adopts in his Part Four analysis of relative surplus-value. [2023 note: except the 'potentiated' (or 'empowered') value-productivity of labour – cf. chapters 2 and 15 of the current book.]

Before further commenting on β in the next subsection, we may proceed with a simple example (simple purely illustrative numbers). Let «c/L» = £40mln/(4mln labour hrs). Let β=1.16 (at L=4mln hrs). Then, because $4^{1.16}$=5, x = £50mln. Assume the average wage rate to be £1.50. From Marx's equation (M–4) and definition (11) we have the accounting identity:

$$s = x - (c + wL)$$

$$s = £50m - [£40m + (£1.50)(4m)] = £50m - [£40m + £6m] = £4m$$

$$x = c + wL + s = £60m + £6m + £4m$$

---

ganisations of capital – i.e., of plants or clusters of plants – which in effect introduce new states of the trajectory.)

38   I have been following so far (and will below) Marx's *Capital I* simplification (generally) of abstracting from means of production that last beyond the production period. (Including those we would simply have «K/L»$_{(t)}L^\beta$ – see Reuten 2002.) For readers familiar with neoclassical economics, it should be noted that representation (15) may look like a particular 'production function'. However, its conceptualisation (especially as to what are variables and as to how a 'technique' is defined) is different from orthodox meanings:

– *c* are *specific* means of production (measured in monetary terms: prices times quantities);
– the concept of c/L is that of a plant (or plants), and thus is incompatible with marginalist notions as including marginal productivity (see also the previous footnote);
– c/L is taken to be 'almost' fixed in the short run: «c/L» (the guillemets should be warning for that); thus we are within a particular *state* of a technological trajectory – in which only moderate variations in c/L (say within a 8% bound) can be profitably applied (that is macroeconomically; micro variations may be larger).
– there is no blue book of techniques that can profitably be used – no substitution in the orthodox sense – we are on a one-way trajectory. [*Continued on next page.*]

So this gets us back to Marx's type of example. In fact my statement 'let $\beta=1.16$' is analogous to statements of his, such as 'if 1 hour's labour is exhibited in 6d', where d is a monetary unit.[39]

Indeed all of Marx's formulas are *results*. The advantage of a representation such as (15) is that we see some more of the explanatory dynamic behind those results; an explanatory dynamic that Marx sets out in his text.

As indicated, in Parts Three ⊃ Six of *Capital I* all of Marx's focus is on the rate of surplus-value. In terms of the formalisation of the current subsection we have for that rate:[40]

$$e = \frac{s}{v} = \frac{\{«c/L»_{(t)}\}\{L^{\beta-1} - 1\}}{w} - 1 \qquad \text{[explanatory device] (16)}$$

Thus at the *prevailing* productive force of labour $«c/L»_{(t)}$, the rate of surplus-value depends positively on the actual exerting power of labour' β, and negatively on the wage rate w. So far β is a constant power. Note that it cannot be directly measured independently of surplus-value (s).[41]

According to Marx the main concomitant of revolutions in the productive forces is a decrease in the value of commodities. To the extent that these are wage goods, such revolutions allow for nominal wage decrease at any level of real wages. Thus *between states* of technological trajectories we have, *ceteris paribus* (specifically the factors affecting the subsumption of labour), the rate of surplus-value pushed up. Indeed this, for Marx, is the heart of the production of relative surplus-value. Thus we have

---

(For some other differences in this respect between the neoclassical and the Marxian approach see Smith 1997. See also Smith 2004 for contrasts with Neo-Schumpeterian views.)

39 E.g. F, 433. Instead of 'exhibited' Fowkes has 'embodied' for 'stellt sich dar' (G, 335). 'Embodied' rings, of course, Ricardian bells (perhaps it should, perhaps not; in some contexts Marx uses the term *verkörpert*, i.e., embodied).

40 Representation (16) is derived as follows:
$x = «c/L»_{(t)} L^\beta$
$s = x - (c + v)$
$s = \{«c/L»_{(t)} L^\beta\} - \{c + wL\}$
$$e = \frac{s}{v} = \frac{\{«c/L»_{(t)} L^\beta\} - \{c + wL\}}{wL} = \frac{\{«c/L»_{(t)} L^{\beta-1} - c/L\}}{w} - 1$$

41 Though one might devise experiments ('slow down'), or adopt indirect measures for changes in β.

$$w = w^* + f(\Delta \text{ST}_{(t)}) \qquad [f' < 0] \qquad (17)$$

where w^* summarises the labour market aspects of the general state of subsumption of labour.[42]

2.4 Degree of intensity of labour

We now proceed from the point where we left Marx's text prior to the reconstructive intermezzo of the previous subsection. Note first that Marx *up to this point* – as he reminds us early on in the section now under discussion – conceptualised increase in the production of relative surplus-value as being engendered by increase in the use-value productivity of labour. *"The same amount of labour-time adds the same value* as before to the total product, but ... is spread over more use-values. Hence the value of each single commodity falls" (F, 534 – italics added).[43]

In section 3(c) of Chapter 15, Marx presents the concept of 'intensity of labour'.[44]

> ... something we have already met with, namely the intensity of labour, develops into a phenomenon of decisive importance. Our analysis of absolute surplus-value dealt primarily with the extensive magnitude of labour, its duration, while *the degree of its intensity* was treated as a given factor. We now have to consider the inversion [*Umschlag*] of extensive magnitude into intensive magnitude, or magnitude of degree. (F, 533 amended;[45] G, 431)

---

42 The further determination of the state of subsumption is beyond the confines of this paper (see Murray 2000b and 2004). The prevailing rate of unemployment is merely one obvious factor affecting w^*.

43 This is based on a number of assumptions that Marx repeats over and again. Next to the three assumptions associated with the concept of 'socially necessary labour' (see note 4) it is assumed that competition results in the pushing down of prices when productivity rises spread over branches of production.

44 Here he introduces it systematically – the term was used five times before in passing: in Chapter 1 (F, 129; G, 153), Chapter 7 (F, 303; G, 210), Chapter 11 (F, 424; G, 328) and Chapter 14 (F, 460; G, 361 and F, 465; G, 365). In two other instances Marx uses in German the term 'potenzierte Arbeit' which both Moore/Aveling and Fowkes render into 'intensified labour' (F, 135; MA, 51; G, 59; and F, 435; MA, 302; G, 337). [This last rendering is wrong, as it does not regard 'intensity of labour' – see Chapters 2 and 15 of the current book.]

45 For the starred text Fowkes has "its intensity" for "der Grad ihrer Intensität". The insertion of the German for 'inversion' is by Fowkes. It seems to me that *Umschlag* is rather a heavy term, pointing to a new moment. Other candidates for the translation would be 'break' (as in 'break in the weather') or 'turn' (as in 'turn in the relationship').

Marx directs our attention here both by the terms 'decisive importance' and 'inversion/break' [*Umschlag*]. Thus next to the magnitude of labour (L), Marx introduces its degree of intensity. In fact part of my reason for introducing the formalisation of §2.3 is to be able to put sharp focus on this. In terms of my representation (15) or (16) a change in the 'actual exerting power of labour', the β in L^β, is at stake. Henceforth I will call this the 'degree of intensity of labour'.[46] Marx – as he does often when introducing an important new concept – uses a number of adjectives to stress the concept. Here is a key formulation – it is also a key citation for the current article:

> ... the development of *the productive force and the economisation of the conditions of production* imposes on the worker an increased expenditure of labour within a time ... This compression of a greater mass of labour into a given period now *counts for what it really is, namely an increase of the quantity of labour*. In addition to the measure of its 'extensive magnitude', *labour-time now acquires a measure of its *degree of density**. ... The same mass of value is now produced for the capitalist by, say, 3⅓ hours of surplus labour and 6⅔ hours of necessary labour, as was previously produced by 4 hours of surplus labour and 8 hours of necessary labour. (F, 534 amended and italics added;[47] G, 432–3)

Thus we see a crucial conceptual progress (concretisation) in comparison with the earlier simpler (more abstract) conception summarised at the opening of this subsection: *no longer do we have the simple parallel between value and labour-time*.[48]

---

46 I challenge the reader who is not convinced by my L^β representation to come up with an alternative representation for the italicised text in the next quote.

47 For the first starred text Fowkes has "the development of productivity and the more economical use of the conditions of production" for "der Entwicklung der Produktivkraft und der Ökonomisierung der Produktionsbedingungen". For the second he has 'intensity, or degree of density' for "*das maß ihres Verdichtungsgrads*".

Concerning the term 'measure' a general warning – for all of *Capital* – is appropriate. The meaning of the German term '*maß*' is complicated. The relevant meaning *here* seems near to 'grade' or 'degree' – or 'measure' as in the phrase 'to considerable measure'. (For at least some explication of the term see Inwood 1992, p. 240.)

48 Or 'socially necessary labour-time' (see note 4). For the purposes of the current essay I will not quarrel with historiographers who argue that *Capital* is based on a linear logic (instead of a systematic-dialectical) and that already in the first section of Chapter 1 Marx writes: "Socially necessary labour-time is the labour-time required to produce any use-value under the conditions of production normal for a given society and with the average degree of skill and intensity of labour prevalent in that society" (F, 129; G, 53). At that point

Marx indicates as main factors bringing about this intensity increase, an increase in the speed of the machines, and the same worker having to supervise or operate a greater quantity of machinery (F, 536). In the remainder of the section he cites reports as evidence for this process.

The issue is taken up further in the synthetic Part Five – apart from a brief passage in Chapter 16 (F, 646) mainly in its Chapter 17. Note that all along Marx's primary problematic is not so much the determination of the magnitude of value, but rather the relative magnitudes of surplus-value and the price of labour-power.[49] At a given average real wage rate per 'normal working day', the latter relative magnitudes depend on:

> (1) the length of the working day, or the extensive magnitude of labour, (2) the normal intensity of labour, or its intensive magnitude, whereby a given quantity of labour is expended in a given time and (3) the *productive force* of labour, whereby the same quantity of labour yields, in a given time, a greater or a smaller quantity of the product, depending on the degree of development attained by the conditions of production. (F, 655 amended;[50] G, 542)

All these three are variable, and next Marx analyses their variation in turn. I focus on the intensity of labour (section 2 of Chapter 17).

> ... if the length of the working day remains constant, a day's labour of increased intensity will be incorporated *in an increased amount of value*, and, assuming no change in the value of money, in an increased amount of money. ... A given working day, therefore, no longer creates a constant value, but a variable one .... (F, 661 – italics added;[51] G, 547)

> we cannot know what he means by 'degree of intensity'; he subsequently 'blends out' the intensity issue and returns to it systematically in Chapter 15.
>
> I just wrote 'no longer do we have the simple parallel between value and labour-time'. In fact we see breaks in this parallel (conceptual progress) here in *Capital I* and in all the volumes of *Capital* (particularly also in Parts Two and Three of *Capital II*). There is no particular dichotomy in this respect between Volumes I and III (and even less so two algorithms). Nevertheless, as indicated in §1.1, labour-time for Marx remains all along an important reference point for the analysis of (changes in) the capitalist production process.

49 The upshot of this is, in my view, that when we have reached the introduction of the concept of profit (in Volume III), profit/wage ratios are affected by the factors mentioned in the next quote.
50 For the starred text Fowkes has 'productivity' for 'Produktivkraft'.
51 The italicised text reads in German: 'in höherem Wertprodukt' – literally: in an increased

So far this repeats – though in a very clear formulation – the inversion/break indicated above. However, in two subsequent statements Marx (I think) muddles the issue for the inattentive (preoccupied?) reader. Here is the first one.

> Whether the magnitude of the labour changes in extent or in intensity, there is always a corresponding change in the magnitude of the value created, independently of the nature of the article in which that value is *exhibited*. (F, 661 amended;[52] G, 548)

Although to the letter of the text there is nothing to complain about, it might (carelessly) be read as a repetition of the conceptualisation cited at the very opening of this subsection. In fact the 'magnitude of labour' has now been cut loose from labour-time; labour-time no longer 'corresponds' to value (at least not diachronically).

Such a (careless) reading and its implication might be reinforced by the next, and final, text of this section in Chapter 17:

> If the intensity of labour were to increase simultaneously and equally in every branch of industry, then the new and higher degree of intensity would become the normal social degree of intensity, and would therefore cease to count as an extensive magnitude. (F, 661–2; G, 548)

Again, to the letter this is fair enough – as well as consistent with Marx's general approach. However, it seems to de-emphasise the conceptual progress "of decisive importance".[53] To the extent that over time (diachronically) we have recurrent increases in the "normal social degree of intensity", the value-producing potential of labour cannot be measured diachronically by labour-time independently of the value produced.[54] (By itself this does not make the explanatory power of the theory useless; it makes it more problematical.)

---

value-product (y in equation M–3). The same for 'value' in the next sentence. The same for the *first* term 'value' in the next citation.

52   For the starred text Fowkes has 'embodied' for 'sich darstellen'.
53   Marx continues immediately after the text just quoted: "But even so, the intensity of labour would still be different in different countries, and would modify the application of the law of value to the working days of different nations. The more intensive working day of one nation would be represented by a greater sum of money than the less intensive day of another nation" (F, 662). Systematically this international context is irrelevant here. Relevant would be to say that 'the law of value' does not apply, generally, over time (i.e., not diachronically).
54   Thus 1 hour of $\text{SNLT}_{(t)} \neq \text{SNLT}_{(t+1)}$ (where SNLT is socially necessary labour-time).

As indicated, Marx returns to his formula for the rate of surplus-value in the final Chapter, 18, of Part Five. It is a mystery why he, after making subtle distinctions in the previous chapters, relapses into the simple s/v result and its 'surplus-labour' over 'necessary labour' counterpart.

The intensity matter is returned to in Chapter 25 of Part Seven, "The general law of capitalist accumulation", however, without much further development (F, 788–9 and 793).[55]

It is obvious that in terms of the reconstructive formalisation of the previous subsection Marx's new "normal social degree of intensity" of labour would be posited in terms of changes in the degree β in L^β associated with a state of the 'productive forces' or the state of a trajectory. Of course, this does not increase the explanatory power of the theory; it does focus, though, on the conceptual development (and it may help developing it further).

2.5 Once again, the value of labour-power and the wage rate

From all of the middle part of *Capital I* – indeed all of the book – it is obvious that Marx always conceives of wages, and the value of labour-power, in terms of *days* or weeks. Indeed this directs all his theorising about absolute and relative surplus-value. Theoretically this seems as poignant as an engraved *Gestalt* (in the sense of Kuhn). On the one hand this is understandable historically, that is from the perspective of the practice of the second half of the nineteenth century (including struggles over the length of the working day and the working week); the perspective of if, and how well, one can live off a day's or a week's wage. On the other hand, however, this is difficult to understand given that it is Marx's aim to set out 'capital' and its development from *its* perspective, i.e., immanently.

Whereas Marx's conceptualisation of labour-power is fine as and when he introduces it in Part Three (absolute surplus-value), there is a problem when he moves to Part Four (relative surplus-value) and introduces shortening of the working day. The daily value of labour-power is by itself not of interest to capital, but rather the value of labour-power per hour of labour-time (that is the value of labour-power relative to the actual time of employment).

Reconsider Marx's equations (cf. §2.1)

$$s = (\underline{s}/\underline{v})v \qquad (\text{M}-8)$$

$$s = \underline{w}(a'/a)n \qquad (\text{M}-9)$$

---

[55] There are also a couple of related passages in the Results (included in Marx 1867|1890 F: 987, 991–2, 1021, 1024–6; cf. 1034–5).

and the added

$$\text{wL} \equiv \text{v} \tag{11}$$

$$\text{s} = \text{e}^*(\text{wL}) \tag{12}$$

Recall that the underlined symbols are in per day terms, and w and L in per hour terms. If s would be measured over a year (for example), n would have to be the 'number of workers times the number of labour days in a year'. (If s would be measured over one turn-over time of capital, n would have to be the 'number of workers times the number of days of turn-over time'.)[56]

Let the value of labour-power per day, $v_{LP}\text{-}d = \underline{w}$; the length of the working day = w_D (i.e., a number of hours). Recall that w = the wage per hour, and L the number of hours worked. Thus we have:

$$w \equiv \underline{w}/w_D \qquad \text{[definition]} \tag{18}$$

$$L \equiv n(w_D) \qquad \text{[definition]} \tag{19}$$

hence

$$wL = \underline{w}n \qquad \text{[implication]} \tag{20}$$

Thus there is no problem to translate wL into Marx's terminology of 'the value of labour-power'. But what is labour-power in these 'different' frames? Labour-power is the potential to perform labour (for a day says Marx) at some definite extensity (i.e., a number of clock hours) and intensity. What do we lose if we reduce this to intensity per hour? Nothing (note that for Marx a substitution between extensity and intensity is possible). Then we can interpret L as a number of labour-power per hour (labour potential) and L^β as labour actually exerted at some degree of intensity.

Here is the rephrase. Workers sell their labour-potential L (= labour-power) by the hour.[57] In production it is exerted *at* a prevailing productive force (*Produktivkraft*) *with* a certain degree of intensity L^β (= labour).

---

56 Of course, relevant for capital is the investment of (variable) capital including Sundays so to speak.
57 Irrespective of the fact that depending on labour contracts this may go in packages (e.g. 40 hours a week).

All this merely makes more explicit what is in Marx's text. It also makes more explicit that the only directly measurable entities are all value entities, as well as total labour-time (extensity). All other 'labour' entities, including the intensity of labour (L^β) cannot be directly measured independently of the value entities and of labour extensity.

Summary and conclusions

Key to the production process of capital – the subject of *Capital I* – is the production of surplus-value. The middle part of the book explains how it is produced. Marx comprehends the capitalist production process as a unity of labour process and of valorisation process – this sets the frame for his analysis, including its dimensions. He starts from value entities, always in monetary dimension, and aims to explain these in terms of: (1) productive forces ('techniques of production' – this term is anachronistic); (2) extensity of labour; (3) intensity of labour; (4) the value of labour-power. The point of the 'unity' view is the interaction, the melding, of the two processes – the valorisation process affects the content of the labour process and this works back again on valorisation.

In line with his general method, Marx starts this middle part with an abstract and simple account – the production of absolute surplus-value. In effect this means that he treats all but factor (2), the extensity of labour, as constant. Next – under the head of the production of relative surplus-value – he brings in variations in the other three factors mentioned.

Unfortunately, when it comes to Marx's formalisation of his analysis – the main subject of this essay – he sticks *in effect* to the simple account ($e = e^*$, i.e., $s/v = sL/NL$ – §2.1). It is not obvious that he sticks to the simple account, because once we accept $e = e^*$ as a useful explanation it remains in force after the complications have been brought in – now other variables have an effect *on* the e^* ratio. This is why I have complained that Marx formalises results instead of explanatory processes (or mechanisms).

I have shown that it is not too difficult to 'immanently reconstruct' Marx's formalisation such that all four factors are captured (see equation 16 in §2.3). Its upshot is a reconceptualisation of Marx's 'value of labour-power' into a value per unit of time, a wage rate (§2.5). The corollary advantage of the latter concept is that it matches the perspective of capital – which fits Marx's general approach in *Capital* of presenting an immanent analysis of capital.

Comments on the secondary literature have been beyond the confines of this essay. Some of that literature misconceives Marx in making 'him' identify value with a labour(-time) dimension (hence the collapse of any explanatory force of his theory in this respect). Perhaps Marx misled the superficial reader with his, in effect, dimensionless ratios. However, he *always* casts value in monetary terms.

As to the explanatory force of $e = e^*$ (in either its simple or its complex representation) I indicated that the explanans (e^*, or surplus labour in relation to total labour) cannot be measured independently of the explanandum (e, or surplus-value in relation to the value-product). Marx was well aware of this measurement problem – highlighted in the variability of labour intensity – as well as, of course, the main further inversions/breaks to come in the later volumes of *Capital* (much of which had been drafted before 1867).

References

Superscripts indicate first and other relevant editions; the last mentioned year in the bibliography is the edition cited.

Arthur, Christopher, and Geert Reuten (eds) 1998, *The circulation of capital: essays on volume II of Marx's 'Capital'*, London: Macmillan.

Bellofiore, Riccardo 2004, 'Marx and the macro-monetary foundation of microeconomics', in Bellofiore and Taylor (eds) 2004, pp. 170–210.

Bellofiore, Riccardo, and Nicola Taylor (eds) 2004, *The constitution of capital: essays on volume I of Marx's 'Capital'*, London: Palgrave Macmillan.

Elson, Diane 1979, 'The value theory of labour', in *Value: the representation of labour in capitalism*, London: CSE Books.

Inwood, Michael 1992, *A Hegel dictionary*, Oxford: Blackwell.

Marx, Karl 1867[1], 1890[4] G, *Das Kapital, Kritik der politischen Ökonomie, Band I, Der Produktionsprozeß des Kapitals*, MEW 23, Berlin: Dietz Verlag, 1973.

Marx, Karl 1867[1], 1883[3] MA, *Capital, a critical analysis of capitalist production, volume I*, trans. of the 3rd German ed. by Samuel Moore and Edward Aveling (1886[1]), London: Lawrence & Wishart, 1974.

Marx, Karl 1867[1], 1890[4] F, *Capital, a critique of political economy, volume I*, trans. of the 4th German ed. by Ben Fowkes, Harmondsworth: Penguin Books, 1976.

Marx, Karl 1885[1], 1893[2], ed. F. Engels, *Das Kapital, Kritik der politischen Ökonomie, Band II, Der Zirkulationsprozeß des Kapitals*, MEW 24, Berlin: Dietz Verlag, 1972, (first Engl. trans. by Ernest Untermann 1907), second Engl. trans. by David Fernbach, *Capital, a critique of political economy, volume II*, Harmondsworth: Penguin Books, 1978.

Marx, Karl 1894, ed. F. Engels, *Das Kapital, Kritik der politischen Ökonomie, Band III, Der Gesamtprozeß der kapitalistischen Produktion*, MEW 25, Berlin: Dietz Verlag 1972, (first Engl. trans. by Ernest Untermann, 1909), second Engl. trans. by David Fernbach, *Capital, a critique of political economy, volume III*, Harmondsworth: Penguin Books, 1981.

Marx, Karl 1933, *Results of the immediate process of production*, Engl. trans. by Rodney Livingstone, Appendix in *Capital, volume I*, Harmondsworth: Penguin Books, 1976.

Moseley, Fred (ed.) 1993, *Marx's method in 'Capital': a re-examination*, Atlantic Highlands, NJ: Humanities Press.

Murray, Patrick 2000a, 'Marx's "truly social" labour theory of value: part I, abstract labour in Marxian value theory', *Historical Materialism* 6: 27–66.

Murray, Patrick 2000b, 'Marx's "truly social" labour theory of value: part II, how is labour that is under the sway of capital *actually* abstract?', *Historical Materialism* 7: 99–136.

Murray, Patrick 2002, 'Reply to Geert Reuten', *Historical Materialism* 10.1: 155–76.

Murray, Patrick 2004, 'The social and material transformation of production by capital: formal and real subsumption in *Capital volume I*', in Bellofiore and Taylor (eds) 2004, pp. 243–73.

Reuten, Geert 1988, 'Value as social form', in *Value, social form and the state*, edited by Michael Williams, London: Macmillan, pp. 42–61.

Reuten, Geert 1993, 'The difficult labour of a theory of social value: metaphors and systematic dialectics at the beginning of Marx's *Capital*', in Moseley (ed.) 1993, pp. 89–113.

Reuten, Geert 1998, 'The status of Marx's reproduction schemes: conventional or dialectical logic?', in Arthur and Reuten (eds) 1998, pp. 187–229.

Reuten, Geert 2000, 'The interconnection of systematic dialectics and historical materialism', *Historical Materialism* 7: 137–66.

Reuten, Geert 2002, 'Marxian macroeconomics: some key relationships', in *Encyclopedia of macroeconomics*, edited by Brian Snowdon and Howard Vane, Aldershot: Edward Elgar, pp. 469–80.

Reuten, Geert 2003a, 'Karl Marx: his work and the major changes in its interpretation', in *A companion to the history of economic thought*, edited by Warren Samuels, Jeff Biddle and John Davis, Oxford: Blackwell, pp. 148–66.

Reuten, Geert 2004b, 'The inner mechanism of the accumulation of capital: the acceleration triple', in Bellofiore and Taylor (eds) 2004, pp. 274–98.

Reuten, Geert, and Michael Williams 1989, *Value-form and the state; the tendencies of accumulation and the determinati-on of economic policy in capitalist society*, London: Routledge.

Smith, Tony 1997, 'The neoclassical and Marxian theories of technology: a comparison and critical assessment', *Historical Materialism* 1: 113–33.

Smith, Tony 2004, 'Technology and history in capitalism: Marxian and neo-Schumpeterian perspectives', in Bellofiore and Taylor (eds) 2004, pp. 217–42.

Taylor, Nicola 2004, 'Reconstructing Marx on money, and the measurement of value', in Bellofiore and Taylor (eds) 2004, pp. 88–116.

CHAPTER 9

The inner mechanism of the accumulation of capital: the acceleration triple; a methodological appraisal of 'Part Seven' of Marx's *Capital I*

2004 article, originally published in *The constitution of capital: essays on volume I of Marx's 'Capital'*, edited by Riccardo Bellofiore and Nicola Taylor, London: Palgrave Macmillan, pp. 274–98.
 (For its abstract see the Abstracts of all chapters, p. 5.)

Contents

Introduction   182
1   **Part Seven within the systematic of *Capital* Volume I**   182
   1.1   Part Seven in the German and English editions   182
   1.2   A cursory survey of Part Seven   183
   1.3   The assumptions delineating the level of abstraction   183
2   **Transformation of surplus-value into capital**   186
   2.1   The drive for and the force for accumulation   186
   2.2   The dynamics of accumulation introduced: productive forces and accelerated accumulation   186
3   **'The general law of capitalist accumulation'**   190
   3.1   Interdependency of wage rate and rate of exploitation – 'the law of capitalist production'   190
   3.2   Increasing capital composition – the acceleration triple   193
   3.3   Progressive growth – a dialogue on limitations of the theory so far   197
      A   Progressive growth   197
      B   Continuous accelerated accumulation with pauses   198
      C   Periodic changes   198
      D   Once again progressive growth   198
      E   Cyclical path as characteristic   199
      F   Wages   199
   3.4   The final two sections   200
Summary and methodological conclusions   202
References   204

Introduction

In this essay I discuss Marx's theory of the accumulation of capital in Part Seven of Volume I of *Capital*, especially in reference to its methodological status. The accumulation of capital – or the conversion of surplus-value into capital – is one of the two aspects of "The production process of capital" (the subtitle of the book), the other aspect being the production of surplus-value, treated in the middle part of the book.

Starting from simplified notions of accumulation, Marx gradually explicates the complex dynamics of an interconnected triple accelerator of: increasing accumulation of capital, increasing productive forces of labour, and an increasing composition of capital. All along, however, his focus is methodologically restricted to the 'inner mechanism' of capital accumulation (as explained in §1 below); I will indicate that this is important for understanding what Marx can (or is able to) achieve here.

We will see – in §3 – that Marx introduces an idea of cyclical accumulation of capital. The character of this cyclical accumulation has been an issue of debate within the Marxian tradition and amongst historians of thought. It is shown that Marx does not introduce a 'labour-shortage' theory of the cycle. In fact he does not present a theory of the cycle at all: in *Capital I* cyclical accumulation is introduced by way of an empirical reference. (I do not argue that the later Marxian theory of cyclical labour-shortage makes no sense; I argue that Marx does not introduce it in this book – the same applies for a theory of cyclical under-consumption; in fact, he never introduces these theories in either of the volumes of *Capital*.)

In this essay my concern is the methodological status of the final text of the book and not its genesis. Where required I compare the *Capital I* text with the text of *Das Kapital I*.[1] For reasons of space I abstain from specific comments on interpretations in the secondary literature.

1 Part Seven within the systematic of *Capital* Volume I

1.1 *Part Seven in the German and English editions*

The most general theoretical conclusions that Marx draws in *Capital I* on the process of accumulation of capital can be found in Chapter 24, Section 4 (the

---

[1] I have great respect for the translators. Translators have to rely on contemporary text interpretations. When interpretations shift, earlier translations will inevitably become defective. Here lies a fundamental difference between an original text and a translation (of course a translation itself may be reinterpreted).

factors determining the extent of accumulation of capital) and the first four sections of Chapter 25 ('The general law of capitalist accumulation'). These will be discussed in §2–§3 below. The corresponding chapters in the German edition are 22 and 23 – the difference is due to a reordering by Friedrich Engels for the English edition (1886) of the book. With some reluctance I follow this English convention for my chapter references – with apologies to those who read *Das Kapital* or its other language translations.

Engels also broke up the German Part Seven into two parts: Part Seven encompassing the systematic chapters 23–25 (German 21–23) and Part Eight the historical chapters 26–33 (German 24–25). When I refer to 'Part Seven' I mean the three systematic chapters – with the same apologies.

1.2   *A cursory survey of Part Seven*
"Earlier we considered how surplus-value arises from capital; now we have to see how capital arises from surplus-value. The employment of surplus-value as capital, or its reconversion into capital, is called accumulation of capital" (725).[2] In Part Seven of *Capital I*, from which this quote is taken, Marx first sets out the elementary shape of accumulation: extension or growth of capital. Next he shows how this growth accelerates in combination with the development of the productive forces of labour (§2 below). And finally he introduces another accelerator: the technical composition of capital (§3 below). All along his focus is on the dynamic consequences of this triple interaction on the capital–labour relation, and particularly on their propagation of a reserve army of unemployed labour which is a necessary condition for continuous accumulation of capital.

1.3   *The assumptions delineating the level of abstraction*
Since around 1990, Marx scholars have increasingly come to appraise Marx's *Capital* as a systematic-dialectical work (to be distinguished from historical dialects – both of these different types of dialectics find their modern roots in Hegel).[3] Relevant for this essay is not so much the dialectic (I will not stress that) but the systematic, which is a systematic of, in principle, rigorous levels of

---

[2] All unspecified numbers, like this one, are page references to the English edition of *Capital I* in the Fowkes translation (Marx 1867[1]; 1390[4] F). Where the context requires it, I specify with a prefix "F", e.g. F, 725. Page references to the German edition of the work are always prefixed by a "G", e.g. G, 668 (Marx 1867[1]; 1890[4] G).

[3] See Reuten (2003) for a brief history of the methodological appraisal of *Capital*, as well as for references to the literature. [Chapter 1, §2, of the current book.] A problem in this appraisal is, first, that Marx experimented with the method so as to find his own way with it – but was hardly explicit about this; second, that he did not complete *Capital* (even less its planned continuations). Another problem is the status of 'Part Eight' of *Capital I*, which does not fit

abstraction running both in terms of the terrain analysed and synthesised (see below) and in terms of the movement from simple determinations to complex ones (both within and across these terrains).

In considering the meaning of Marx's statements about the effects of the accumulation of capital – including cyclical aspects – it is of preeminent importance to list the assumptions on which these statements are based, assumptions that delineate Marx's level of abstraction. Here I list the assumptions relevant for the Part Seven chapters.[4]

1. Earlier (Part Four) Marx explicitly considers an average capital (thus abstracting from intra- and inter-branch differences, including differing production periods and compositions of capital – dealt with in Volume III, Parts One and Two). In Part Seven, however, he deals with average *changes* in the composition of capital. Although much of Part Seven can still be read in terms of the average capital the analysis *leans*, and sometimes explicitly, towards a macroeconomic treatment.[5]

2. In the introduction to Part Seven Marx indicates that he assumes capital to pass "through its process of circulation in the normal way".[6] The 'normal way' implies that commodities produced are sold "at their value" (709–10). (This again implies that production and sales are carried out at the normal profit, or the normal surplus-value.) 'Normal' also implies, as Marx states, abstraction from any supply/demand discrepancies of the commodities produced. (He will explicitly introduce changes in the reserve of labour though, without considering their effect on the demand for commodities.)

3. Marx also abstracts from differentiations of capital into industrial capital, commercial capital, finance and banking and from landed property. Hence abstraction is made from the "various mutually independent forms" into which surplus-value is fragmented, "such as profit, interest ... rent" (709–10).[7]

Immediately following this, Marx makes a formal methodological statement:

---

the systematic (see Smith 1990, pp. 133–5 for a scholarly account; see Murray 2000 and 2002 for qualifications of the appraisal).

4 Others are listed in my 2004a (footnote 4) [Chapter 8 of the current book, p. 155.] In comparison to those, Marx now considers average changes in the composition of capital. He also states explicitly: that some share of surplus-value is accumulated (or consumed); that, generally and on average, there is some reserve army of labour; that wages are variable (within limits).

5 Though it is not macroeconomic – see my 2004a, footnote 4, and Bellofiore 2004, section 5.

6 He refers to Volume II for its analysis. Discrepancies especially are dealt with in Part Three of that volume.

7 For the analysis of "these modified forms of surplus-value" he refers to Volume III.

"Hence we initiate the accumulation abstractly, that is, merely as moment of the immediate process of production" (my translation of the German text p. 590).[8]

Both of the English translations miss the term "moment" and (therefore) its reference to the subject matter of Volume I; that is, *its* level of abstraction.[9] A 'moment' is a systematic-dialectical notion, referring to a type of analysis. First, it is the analysis of a constituent (in this case accumulation) that is not yet fully constituted (indeed, in the abstract perspective posited by, and extending through Volume I, we cannot yet grasp accumulation concretely). Second, a moment can have no isolated existence (it obviously cannot be isolated from everything presented so far in Volume I but, more importantly in the current context, it also has no existence in isolation from the presentation still to come in the following Volumes). Indeed it is the analysis of something abstract.[10]

Next, Marx makes a second methodological remark, this time relating to the content of his particular abstractions. He says that we can nevertheless consider accumulation merely as moment of the current level of abstraction; in other words, it is adequate to do this provisionally (*vorläufig*), since dropping the assumptions 2 and 3 would hinder a pure (*reine*) analysis of accumulation:

> A pure analysis of the process, therefore, demands that we should, provisionally, disregard all phenomena that conceal the workings of its inner mechanism. (F, 710 amended; G, 590)

Fowkes has 'exact' instead of 'pure' for *reine*; and he has 'for a time' instead of 'provisionally' for *vorläufig* (and Moore has the same). The "inner" here refers, in my view, to the 'immediate process of production', that is, the capital–labour relation in general. In reference back to the first methodological remark, this does *not* mean that the "inner mechanism" can have an isolated existence, *nor* that 'the inner working' would be unaffected (qualitatively or quantitatively) by the successive introduction into the presentation of additional phenomena (cf. the inner–outer pair in Hegel's *Logic*).[11]

---

8 "Wir betrachten also zunächst die Akkumulation abstrakt, d.h. als bloßes Moment des unmittelbaren Produktionsprozesses." As emphasised in '*The Results*' (published in 1933 – Appendix in the Penguin edition of *Capital I*) the 'immediate' refers to the *Capital I* level of abstraction.
9 Cf. Marx 1883^3 MA: 530 and 1890^4 F: 710.
10 On the notion of 'moment' see also Reuten and Williams 1989, p. 22.
11 To stay close to the metaphor, we could analyse the inner working of the heart and the blood circulation; but each of these 'inner' parts of the body stands in a physical and social

In other (non-dialectical) words, Marx's assumptions here are not negligibility assumptions, but heuristic assumptions.

2 Transformation of surplus-value into capital

2.1 *The drive for and the force for accumulation*

Accumulation of capital is the reconversion of surplus-value into capital. Its degree thus depends, *ceteris paribus*, on the part of surplus-value accumulated as capital. On the one hand this is the capitalist's "act of will" and "drive towards self-enrichment" (738–9). On the other hand, Marx indicates (739), with

> the development of capitalist production ... competition subordinates every individual capitalist to the immanent laws of capitalist production, as external and coercive laws. It compels him to keep extending his capital, so as to preserve it, and he can only extend it by means of progressive accumulation.

Nevertheless, "with the growth of accumulation and wealth, the capitalist ceases to be merely the incarnation of capital"; "there develops in the breast of the capitalist a Faustian conflict between the passion for accumulation and the desire for enjoyment" (740–1).

2.2 *The dynamics of accumulation introduced: productive forces and accelerated accumulation*

In this and the following section I summarise a number of Marx's statements in a formal way. At the same time, I try to stay as close as possible to Marx's text; of course, any reading and summarising is necessarily interpretative. Although I use a mathematical form (equations), what I do is not mathematics but rather the adoption of a shorthand notation for purposes of precision and logical consistency checking.

I keep the equations as simple as possible, that is in so far as Marx's text allows. Marx is not always explicit about whether the relations he posits are

---

relation to its external surroundings; the body's interaction affects the actual blood circulation and we may, for example, lose blood. Thus the body and its surroundings affect the blood circulation qualitatively and quantitatively. What is more, the heart and the blood circulation have no meaningful existence without the 'outer' body. That is to say, concretely commodities are not produced 'at their value' (et cetera) and this fact affects 'their' production and the accumulation of capital.

linear or non-linear. Whenever that is unclear I just phrase the relation as a function ($A = f(B)$). Determination should be read from right to left; if no determination is posited I use a ≡ sign. An unspecified change in a variable is indicated by the prefix Δ. Thus $\Delta A = A_t - A_{t-1}$. Rates of growth are indicated by a circumflex. Thus $\hat{A} = \Delta A/A_{t-1}$.

In this essay all capitalised symbols refer to values in monetary terms (thus calculated in a monetary dimension, e.g. £). All time indices have been suppressed; thus, for A read A_t (unless otherwise indicated). Time refers to a calendar period (t), for example a year.

Marx introduces the dynamics of accumulation of capital in the fourth section of Chapter 24. Without always being very explicit about this, he now introduces fixed capital (i.e., capital that is only in part 'consumed' within the production period). I use the symbol K for capital. In order to keep transparent the connection with Marx's concepts and symbols as used in the middle part of *Capital I* (see Reuten 2004a) [ch. 8 of the current book], I adopt as simplification the total constant capital (K_c) to be a multitude (μ) of the circulating constant capital C.[12] Note that μ may be taken as a temporary constant, but it is in fact variable and part of Marx's dynamics.

$$K \equiv \mu C + V \qquad [\mu > 1] \qquad \text{[definition] (1)}$$

Marx starts (747) by taking the accumulation of capital (ΔK) to be a given fraction ($\mathring{a}$) out of surplus-value (S):

$$\Delta K = \mathring{a}S \qquad [0 < \mathring{a} \leq 1] \qquad \text{[determination] (2)}$$

The magnitude of surplus-value depends on the rate of surplus-value (e) and on the magnitude of the initial capital:[13]

$$S = f(e; K) \qquad [f' > 0]^{14} \qquad \text{[determination] (3)}$$

Or also:

---

12   $K \equiv K_c + K_v$. More precisely we should have $K \equiv (\mu C_f + \tau C_c) + \upsilon V$, where: C_f is the component of instruments of labour; C_c the component of circulating constant capital; and τ and υ turn-over coefficients (Marx introduces turn-over time only in *Capital II*, Part Two).

13   In the middle part of *Capital* the rate of surplus-value (e) has been explained by e^*, the rate of surplus labour to necessary labour (see my 2004a). On pages 751–2 Marx sets out why $\Delta K=f(K)$ is false (or perhaps we should say a false start – see the next section).

14   $f' > 0$ means that there is a positive relation between S and each of e and K.

$$S = f(\Delta e) \qquad [f' > 0] \qquad \text{[determination] (3')}$$

(Marx is not explicit about time – the focus of Volume II. Nevertheless, it should be noticed that if we consider a production period, S is an 'end of period' result, K a 'begin of period' stock and e a *process variable*, conditioned by the value of labour-power *and the labour process*. Having analysed the latter we may, for the sake of heuristic simplicity, take e each time again as a given. Being a process variable, there is nevertheless also a result for e (in the magnitude of surplus-value S). A difficulty in Marx's text is that he sometimes switches between these two notions of e without notification.)[15]

Next, in refocusing his conclusions from Parts Three to Five towards the accumulation of capital, Marx considers the effect of changes in the productive forces of labour (pfl)[16] that press down commodity prices (indicator Π):[17]

$$\Delta\Pi = f(\Delta pfl) \qquad [f' < 0] \qquad \text{[determination] (4a)}$$

Increasing productive forces have a twofold effect on accumulation. First, because the physical surplus product increases, capitalists 'may' buy the same consumption basket with a smaller "consumption-fund", hence the "accumulation-fund" may increase. Thus the fraction $å$ in equation (2) is turned into a variable depending on the development of the productive forces ('may' depending on the 'drive' and force for accumulation, which I abbreviate as dfa):[18]

$$å = f_1(dfa) + f_2(\Delta\Pi) \qquad [f_1' > 0; f_2' < 0] \qquad \text{[determination] (5)}$$

---

15   The reconstruction in my 2004a [ch. 8 of this book] tried to take account of this. In terms of that chapter, we each time take *beta* as given.

16   The *effect* of rising 'productive forces' is a *potential* rise in productivity of labour (see also my 2004a). If Marx had lived 100 years later, he would perhaps have cast this in terms of techniques of production. Note that in this Section he abstracts from the value composition of capital (or perhaps, he considers such changes in 'technique' that leave unaffected the *value* of means of production).

17   I take Π to be some composite indicator for prices (at the level of *Capital I*, i.e., on the basis of its assumptions, and particularly in abstraction from strictly monetary determinations of the price level). Today it might perhaps be interpreted as a particular price index.

   Equations with a number plus letter, e.g. (4a), will be amended in the course of the argument – into e.g. (4b). Capitalised equation indicators – e.g. (A) – are derived from other ones.

18   Pages 752–3. Note again the assumptions. It is only in *Capital II*, Part Three, that Marx considers the problems of sectoral adaptation of such switches from consumption to accumulation. In fact Marx's labour theory of value allows him to stylise all kinds of complications into a tractable shape.

Thus:

$$\mathring{a} = f(dfa; \Delta pfl) \quad [f' > 0] \quad \text{[reduced form of 4 \& 5] (A)}$$

The second effect is on the rate of exploitation. Let us first simply translate the value of labour-power per day (v_LP) into the wage rate per hour (W) given some length of the working day (h).

$$W \equiv v_LP / h \quad \text{[definition] (6)}$$

Thus to the extent that the working day is a constant, we can use the wage rate and the v_LP interchangeably.[19] Marx posits:

$$\Delta e = f(\Delta W) \quad [f' < 0] \quad \text{[determination] (7)}$$

Of course we know that this determination is defective and represents *merely one factor* (Marx 'freezes' changes in the labour process, including the intensity of labour). The value of labour-power (and the wage rate) is made up of a given 'real' component (some basket of commodities w) and a price component.

$$W \equiv w\Pi \quad \text{[definition] (8)}$$

Thus:

$$\Delta W = f(\Delta pfl) \quad [f' < 0] \quad \text{[reduced form of 4 \& 8] (B)}$$

Therefore the change in productive forces similarly affects the value of labour-power (or W) – the production of relative surplus-value, treated in Parts Four and Five. Hence the nominal wage is pressed down, and the rate of surplus-value up. All this *ceteris paribus*, we should add (see the next sections).

Taking (1)–(8) together we see how, *ceteris paribus*, the accumulation of capital (ΔK) depends on, first, K and the initial C/V division (eqn. 1) – to which we will return in §3 – and second on the development of the productive forces (Δpfl). Or, more precise, starting from an initial rate of growth of accumulation ($\underline{K}$), a change in that rate depends on changes in the productive forces:[20]

---

19 I expanded on this in §2.5 of my 2004a. [See ch. 8 of the current book.]
20 For the productive forces I have used, in my 2004a, the shorthand «C/L», or «K/L» if we include fixed capital. Although I believe that representation to be close to Marx, also for

$$\Delta \hat{K} = f(\Delta pfl) \qquad [f' > 0] \qquad \text{[reduced form of 2–8] (C)}$$

Marx calls this "accelerated accumulation" (e.g. 753; this terminology became fashionable in mainstream economics around 1935). Therefore:

> science and technology are formative [*bilden*] to a potential expansion of capital, independent of the prevailing magnitude of the functioning capital. (F, 754; translation amended, cf. G, 632)[21]

In the next pages Marx clarifies that changes in the productive forces also impact on the replacement investment (and that it has depreciative effects); thus the change in *pfl* spreads gradually over the existing capital (753–4).

3   'The general law of capitalist accumulation'

3.1   *Interdependency of wage rate and rate of exploitation – 'the law of capitalist production'*

I now turn to Chapter 25 of *Capital I*, "The General Law of Capitalist Accumulation": the investigation of "the influence of the growth of capital on the fate of the working class". Its "most important factor", Marx writes, "is the composition of capital, and the changes it undergoes in the course of the process of accumulation" (762). Since Marx, for the purposes of his first section, takes the 'composition of capital' as constant, I just present two definitions and postpone their discussion until later (§3.2). The 'value composition of capital' (*vcc*) is the ratio of constant capital (C) to variable capital (V).

$$vcc \equiv C / V \qquad \text{[definition] (9)}$$

(In terms of equation (1): $vcc = \{(K/V) - 1\}\{1/\mu\}$.)

The 'organic composition of capital' (*occ*) is the ratio of the value of the means of production (C) to the labour working up those means of production (l) – the latter measured in hours.

---

the current Part (e.g. "the value and mass of the means of production set in motion by a given quantity of labour increase as the labour becomes more productive" – 754; cf. 759), I refrain from adopting it here.

21   The translation misses both the 'formative' (*bilden*, rendered as 'give') and the 'potential' (*Potenz*). Of course, they have to be *applied* for valorisation. (See also Smith 2004 and Murray 2004.)

$$\text{occ}_l \equiv C / l \qquad \text{[definition] (10)}$$

(In terms of equation (1): $\text{occ}_l = \{(K - V)/l\}\{1/\mu\}$.)

When the term 'composition of capital' is used without further specification, Marx writes (762), the organic composition is meant. As indicated, in this section he sets these constant – the same applies for the productive forces. (Recall that a circumflex stands for rate of growth.)

$$v\hat{c}c = 0 \qquad \text{[heuristic assumption] (11a)}$$

$$o\hat{c}c = 0 \qquad \text{[heuristic assumption] (12a)}$$

$$\Delta\Pi = f(\Delta\text{pfl}) = 0 \qquad \text{[heuristic assumption] (4b)}$$

Marx notices (763):

> If we assume that, while all other circumstances remain the same, the composition of capital also remains constant ... then the demand for labour, and the fund for the subsistence of the workers, both clearly increase in the same proportion as the capital, and with the same rapidity.

Hence $\hat{L} = \hat{V} = \hat{K}$. Next he sets out how this, and especially the proportional growth of the middle term, is unlikely. Marx takes the 'value of labour-power' to be a historical datum around which the actual price of labour-power fluctuates. $w^*\Pi$ stands for this datum and $w'\Pi$ for the negative or positive fluctuation around it.[22]

$$W \equiv w\Pi \equiv (w^* + w')\Pi \qquad \text{[definition] (13)}$$

Therefore:

$$\hat{W} = \hat{w} \qquad \text{[reduced form of 4b and 13] (D)}$$

Wages may fluctuate because the growth in K may outrun the growth of labour-power (i.e., the supply), so inducing rising wages (763, 769). Accumulation then

---

22 See also Bellofiore 2004. Marx began the text discussed in §2.2 above, by addressing wage reduction, thus dropping his previous assumption "that wages were at least equal to the value of labour-power" (747–8).

still goes on but at a lower rate (since the wage rise affects the rate of surplus-value and hence S). With the decreased rate of growth of accumulation, wages will decrease (770). Thus we have the relations (14) and (15a).

$$\hat{w} = f(\hat{I}) \qquad [f' > 0] \qquad\qquad [\text{determination}] \quad (14)$$

where $\hat{I}$ is the growth in the "demand for workers" (763). This relation, including its 'right to left' determination, is of *key* importance to *all* of Marx's further reasoning in this chapter, including his critique of 'Malthusian' doctrines (§3.3 below). This cannot be stressed too much. Marx amplifies on it at the beginning of the next section, where he refers approvingly to Adam Smith (not only is he usually 'moderate' in tributes to Smith, it is also one of the scarce 'in text' references – i.e., instead of in a footnote):[23] it is not the absolute magnitude but "the degree of rapidity of that growth" in accumulation which is relevant for a rise of wages (772).

Marx posits *in this section* (763, indeed it is conditioned by 12a – cf. 772):

$$\hat{I} = \hat{K} \qquad\qquad [\text{determination}] \quad (15a)$$

And hence:

$$\hat{w} = f(\hat{K}) \qquad [f' > 0] \qquad\qquad [\text{reduced form of 14 \& 15a}] \quad (E)$$

Marx lays particular stress on this relation by his formulation: "To put it mathematically: the rate of accumulation is the independent, not the dependent variable; the rate of wages is the dependent, not the independent variable" (770).

Thus whereas the nominal wage is affected by the productive forces (equation B), the real wage is affected by the rate of accumulation (therefore also the nominal wage, *ceteris paribus*, the productive forces).

Hence we have, what Marx calls, *the law of capitalist production* (771), that is, the rate of growth of the real wage ($\hat{w}$) depends via the rate of growth in accumulation (eqn. D) and the ratio of accumulation ($\mathring{a}$ in eqn. 2) on the rate of surplus-value (eqn. 3):

$$\hat{w} = f(\Delta e) \qquad [f' > 0] \qquad\qquad [\text{reduced form of 2–3, 4b, 9–15a}] \quad (F)$$

---

23 That is, in the theoretical sections of *Capital*.

This is very interesting. We have the apparent paradox that an increase in the rate of exploitation generates an increase in the real wage rate. In fact it would seem (on the basis of the current conditions and *ceteris paribus* qualifications, especially 12a and 4b) that given some rate of exploitation, the real wage rate stabilises at some level at which its rate of growth has become zero (or oscillates around that point). "The rise of wages is therefore confined within limits that not only leave intact the foundations of the capitalist system, but also secure its reproduction on an increasing scale" (771); that is, most briefly, a positive rate of exploitation.

3.2   Increasing capital composition – the acceleration triple

In Section 2 of Chapter 25 Marx introduces the variation in the composition of capital, notably its increase.

Marx's definitions of his three variants of the capital composition (we have talked about two of them) are not crystal clear. Their interpretation is of some importance to the interpretation of *Capital III*, Part Three – where the composition of capital reappears. However, for the general interpretation of the current Chapter 25, Marx's specific definitions are not very important. He knows that each concept has its limitation, and he just shifts terms according to the state of his analysis (even if not always consistently).

Non-controversial is the value composition of capital (vcc), which is defined as (762):

$$vcc \equiv C/V \qquad \text{[definition] (9)}$$

Marx writes about the 'technical composition of capital' (tcc): "As material, as it functions in the process of production, all capital is divided into means of production and living labour-power. This latter composition is determined by the relation between the mass of the means of production [mp] employed on the one hand, and the mass of labour necessary for their employment on the other [l]" (762). Thus we can safely render:

$$tcc \equiv mp/l$$

Of course this is no more than an intuitive notion, as especially mp cannot be measured without prices. Controversial is the term 'organic composition of capital' (occ). Marx writes a bit cryptically: "There is a close correlation between the two [i.e., vcc and tcc]. To express this, I call the value composition of capital, in so far as it is determined by its technical composition and mirrors the changes in the latter, the organic composition of capital" (762). It seems to me that two interpretations square with Marx's text:

$$\text{occ}_y \equiv C/(V+S) \qquad \text{[definition] (16)}$$

$$\text{occ}_l \equiv C/l \qquad \text{[definition] (10)}$$

Note that over time this occ_l does not reflect change in the *tcc* to the extent that productivity rise is translated in price decrease (of means of production). The *vcc* and the occ_y bear similar problems in different ways.[24]

The differences are relevant in so far that each concept has its limitations. First, the *vcc* is not independent of wage changes (wage changes affect the ratio; and a wage change – as we will see – may be the effect of an initial change in the *vcc*). Thus it is no purely socio-technical ratio. Hence Marx evidently also needs another concept, which he reaches via the (intuitive) *tcc*. The occ_y seems useful to the extent that wage changes (and hence V) are directly translated into changes in surplus-value (S). However, Marx is concerned about another variable, namely the intensity of labour, and the occ_y is not independent of intensity changes, whereas the occ_l is (at least if l is measured in constant intertemporal clock hours – that is how I take it). Each of the concepts is relevant depending on the particular analysis.

Marx, throughout this chapter, is concerned with "the average ... composition of the total social capital" (762–63).

Now that these terminological issues have been addressed, I return to Marx's Section 2 where he introduces increase in the composition of capital. Thus:

$$\hat{vcc} > 0 \qquad \text{[thesis] (11b)}$$

$$\hat{occ} > 0 \qquad \text{[thesis] (12b)}$$

> ... the development of the productivity of social labour becomes the most powerful lever of accumulation. ... Apart from natural conditions ... the level of the social productivity of labour is expressed in the relative extent of the means of production that one worker, during a given time, with the same degree of intensity of labour-power, turns into products. (F, 772–3; G, 650)

However, and as we will see in the next section in some more detail, this is not a linear process (774):

---

[24] Marx was well aware of this, and points at it several times (e.g. 774). See Fine and Harris (1979, pp. 58–61) for a different interpretation/reconstruction building on this problematic.

The relative magnitude of the part of the price which represents the value of the means of production, or the constant part of the capital, is in direct proportion to the progress of accumulation, whereas the relative magnitude of the other part of the price, which represents the variable part of the capital, or the payment made for labour, is in inverse proportion to the progress of accumulation.

From the remainder of the section (and the next) it is obvious that Marx takes these proportions as variable, thus:

$\hat{C} = \varphi'\hat{K}$ [φ' variable and $\varphi' > 1$]   [determination]^{25} (11c)

$\hat{V} = \varphi\hat{K}$ [φ variable and $\varphi < 1$]   [determination] (11c')

(The implication is a modified version of equation (E).) On the same page Marx writes about "the variable part of capital ... that this by no means thereby excludes the possibility of a rise in its absolute magnitude" (thus $\varphi > 0$). He also writes that these changes "provide only an approximate indication of the change in the composition of its material constituents" (i.e., the *tcc*) because of the price changes that go along with "the increasing productivity of labour" (774). (Thus implicitly he says that these price changes may unevenly affect the two components.)

This increasing productivity along with increasing productive forces and the changing composition of capital is the main theme of the rest of this section. Without deriving further conclusions, Marx connects the changing capital composition with the production of relative surplus-value (Part Four) and price decrease (Chapter 24, discussed in my §2.2). Recall the synthetical equation:

$\Delta\hat{K} = f(\Delta pfl)$ [f' > 0]   [reduced form of 2–8] (C)

First Marx posits the mutual dependency of these two factors, in fact already anticipated by the end of Chapter 24, Section 4. Because of this mutual dependency "it appears" [*erscheint*] – this is no delusion – that "All the forces of labour project themselves as forces of capital ..." (F, 756 amended; cf. G, 634). Here he writes:

---

25   The determination here or in the next equation lies in the variable φ' which represents the result of capitalist behaviour directed at accelerating accumulation.

all methods of raising the social productive forces that grow up on this basis [capitalist production] are at the same time methods for the increased production of surplus-value, or surplus product, which is in its turn the formative element of accumulation. They are, therefore, also methods for the production of capital by capital, or methods for its accelerated accumulation. (F, 775 amended; G, 653)

Next he connects these methods for accelerating the accumulation of capital with the composition of capital (776):

These two economic factors [eqn. C] bring about, in the compound ratio of the impulses they give to each other, that change in the technical composition of capital by which the variable component becomes smaller and smaller as compared with the constant component.

Thus we have the triple accelerating growth of:

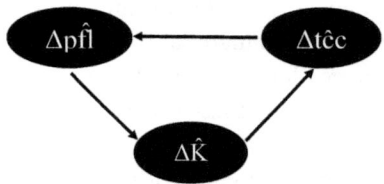

The working out of this schema is postponed until Marx's (and my) next section.

The remainder of the current section is devoted to the 'tendency to centralisation of capital'. In the face of Marx's method it is rather surprising to find that here, as it is a phenomenon related to the competition *between* capitals, which should have been dealt with in or after Part Two of *Capital III*. Marx is aware of the limitations of his analysis (777): "The laws of this centralisation of capitals ..., cannot be developed here. A few brief factual indications must suffice" (these are provided in about three pages).[26] I merely note that Marx (here) does not treat centralisation in reference to the cycle.

---

26 I am not suggesting that anything introduced should be grounded at that same level of abstraction. I question the systematic need for introducing it at all here. There is no need. (In fact it plays a role in the rhetoric of the brief Chapter 32 – a chapter loaded with assertions instead of arguments.)

3.3   *Progressive growth – a dialogue on limitations of the theory so far*
It is obvious from the text of Chapter 25, and especially Section 3, that Marx struggles with the dynamics consequent on the rising composition of capital. In a dialogue-like fashion he moves from argument to counter argument (though in the sub-headings below I have made this process more explicit than it is in Marx's presentation).

Before reporting on this 'dialogue' I should make a terminological point. Readers of *Capital* may wonder why Marx when addressing 'unemployment' apparently uses such bombastic terminology: 'reserve army of labour', 'surplus population', or 'redundant working population'. He may have had his reasons for the particular choice, but the simple point is that in his day the term 'unemployment' (or its German equivalent) just did not exist.[27]

A. *Progressive growth*. Marx begins by setting out the (general?) effect of a rising capital composition on labour:

> the demand for labour ... falls progressively with the growth of the total capital, instead of rising in proportion to it, as was previously assumed [Section 1]. ... and at an accelerated rate ... With the growth of the total capital, its variable constituent ... does admittedly increase, but in a constantly [*beständig*: continuously] diminishing proportion. (781–2; G, 658)[28]

Hence the ceteris paribus relation of Section 1

$$\hat{I} = \hat{K} \qquad \text{[determination] (15a)}$$

is modified into an exponential relation: l increases with K, but at a decreasing rate:

$$\hat{I} = \hat{K}^{\varphi} \qquad [\varphi \text{ variable and } 0 < \varphi < 1] \qquad \text{[determination] (15b)}$$

Similarly:

$$\hat{V} = \hat{K}^{\varphi''} \qquad [\varphi'' \text{ variable and } 0 < \varphi'' < 1] \qquad \text{[determination] (11d)}$$

---

27   Rodenburg 2006 provides further details (e.g. p. 2).
28   Here and elsewhere I insert the German term *beständig*. For 'constant' in the mathematical sense of unchanging, the German would likely be *Konstant* (or perhaps *gleichbleibend* or *unveränderlich*).

B. Continuous accelerated accumulation with pauses. It is, however, more complicated, as the acceleration seems to occur with intervals: "The intermediate pauses in which accumulation works as simple extension of production on a given technical basis are shortened" (782). Apart from this, the "accelerated relative diminution of the variable component [of capital] ... produces ... a relatively redundant working population" (782). (Thus he implicitly assumes something near to constant population growth, or at least one that does not decelerate to the extent that accumulation accelerates.)

C. Periodic changes. Next he qualifies this (782–3, italics added):

> If we consider the total social capital ... the movement of its accumulation sometimes causes periodic changes (...); in all spheres, the *increase* of the variable part of the capital, and therefore of the number of workers employed by it, is always connected with violent fluctuations and the *temporary production of a surplus population*, whether this takes the more striking form of the extrusion of workers already employed or the less evident, but not less real, form of a greater difficulty in absorbing the additional working population through its customary outlets.

This sentence contains some cryptic elements, but the idea seems clear. In a half-page footnote he shows census figures of employment for 1851 and 1861, diverging branch-wise. Note that the periodic changes or fluctuations are not theorised but implanted into the presentation.[29]

Thus under *A* (and next *B*) Marx posits a specified recapitulation of his theory of Section 2. The fluctuations (*C*), however, do not fit the theory developed so far.

D. Once again progressive growth. Then again he redresses (783–4, italics added):

> The working population ... produces both the accumulation of capital and the means by which it is itself made relatively superfluous; and it

---

29 Not only would an "increase ... in the rapidity of the change in the organic composition of capital" (783) itself require explanation, more important is that it does not explain cyclical turning points, nor why 'pauses' would be associated (if so) with downturns and increasing surplus population (if so). A theory can be constructed on the basis of these elements (and others – see *Capital III*, Part Three), but Marx does not do it here.

does this *to an extent which is always increasing.* This is a law of population peculiar to the capitalist mode of production ...

E. *Cyclical path as characteristic.* But once more he shifts perspective (785–6, italics added; cf. G, 661–2):

> The path characteristically described by modern industry, which takes the form of a decennial cycle (interrupted by smaller oscillations) of periods of average activity, production at high pressure, crisis, and stagnation, *depends* on the constant [*beständigen*: continuous] formation, the greater or less absorption, and the reformation of the industrial reserve army (...) Just as the heavenly bodies always repeat a certain movement, once they have been flung into it, so also does social production, once it has been flung into this movement of alternate expansion and contraction. Effects become causes in their turn, and the various vicissitudes of the whole process ... take on the form of periodicity.

This is interesting, but in fact Marx appends an empirical phenomenon to the theory without explaining it, i.e., without theory (the metaphor is a phenomenal analogy, no analogous explanation). In particular, Marx does not tell how the phases of this 'path' relate to the development of capital composition or all of – what I have called – the 'acceleration triple'. It is interesting because he posits the obvious limitations (empirically) of the theory so far (good scientific practice).

F. *Wages.* A final issue enters the dialogue, namely wage increase.[30] Marx denies any relation between population growth and the decennial cycle (he cites Malthus: 'From the nature of a population, an increase of labourers cannot be brought into market in consequence of a particular demand till after the lapse of 16 or 18 years ...' – 787). He also rejects the doctrine that 'restraint' on the part of the working population should be the remedy for the diminution of the 'surplus population' and so the impulse to (real) wage increase (798). Instead Marx posits: (1) the dynamic of capitalist production – with its main element

---

30 All along Marx is aware that wage changes affect the value composition of capital (788–9). Aside from the general line of the argument – but important in itself – Marx indicates that "with the progress of accumulation" wages may increase along with increasing intensity of labour. This is not particularly related to the cycle, moreover intensity increase generally reinforces the 'production of a relative surplus population' – i.e., relatively less labour working at higher intensity.

of a rising composition of capital – creates a 'relative surplus population' (the 'progressive growth' thesis – A and D in the dialogue); (2) wage changes do *not* depend on the absolute level of the surplus population, *nor* on the absolute level, or state, of the accumulation of capital: they depend (Adam Smith's insight) on the *change* in the demand for labour. Thus (790):

> Taking them as a whole, the general movements of wages are exclusively regulated by the expansion and contraction of the industrial reserve army, and this in turn corresponds to the periodic alternations of the industrial cycle. They are not therefore determined by the variations of the absolute numbers of the working population, but by ... the extent to which it is alternately absorbed and set free.

It may be tempting to read into this quote (and the following) – as many have done – a 'labour shortage' theory of the cycle (in which case, to begin with, the first sentence would have to be a tautology). No, the first part of the first sentence makes Adam Smith's point, and the second part *refers* to the periodic cycle. Marx does not posit the wage rate mechanism to *explain* the cycle; the wage movements *correspond* to it (and if, instead, he believed wage movements to be causative he would certainly have said so). The second sentence combats the Malthusian doctrine.

The next quote (equally from page 790) follows the same pattern – ending with a reference to the generational (16 or 18 year lapse) versus the decennial issue.

> The appropriate law for modern industry, with its decennial cycles and periodic phases ... is the law of the regulation of the demand and supply of labour by the alternate expansion and contraction of capital ... It would be utterly absurd, in place of this, to lay down a law according to which the movement of capital depended simply on the movement of the population.

Thus, wages are not determining for they are determined by the growth of accumulation of capital.

3.4   *The final two sections*

The final two section of Chapter 25 contain no new theoretical analysis. Section 5 (some 70 pages) provides empirical illustrations for the theses advanced in the chapter. Section 4 begins with a number of 'surplus population' distinctions (floating, latent and stagnant). Then Marx summarises the 'general law' –

the cycle, though, does not appear in this summary. We have the one moment of the acceleration triple and their effect on the working population.

Marx sets out that on the one hand (for those employed), the worker is degraded to "an appendage of a machine" and alienated from "the intellectual potentialities of the labour process in the same proportion as science is incorporated in it as an independent power" (a conclusion from the middle part of the book). Therefore, "in proportion as capital accumulates, the situation of the worker, be his payment high or low, must grow worse". On the other hand (for those not employed), we have "an accumulation of misery" for the surplus population (799).

Why does Marx, in this section, posit 'the general law' apparently unqualified? In the concluding section I expand on theory-systematic aspects; here I address but one theory-empirical aspect.

On the basis of the triple acceleration theory developed through into Section 3, the demand for labour should fall progressively with the growth of capital. However, Marx knows that empirically the development is cyclical. Thus his theory is incomplete (it might be wrong of course). This theoretical problem might have been overcome by combining his theory with, what was later called, a 'labour-shortage' theory of the cycle.[31] He seems to have the material before him to posit such a theory, but he does not do it.[32] Instead he makes an empirical reference to the cycle.

But this empirical attitude seems to work in two ways. On the one hand, Marx is aware of 'a ten-year cycle' (in fact, Marx was one of the first to put it on the economists' research agenda). On the other hand, the empirical facts of his day all pointed in the direction of increasing degradation and increasing misery of the working population. Faced with this, the triple accelerator of increasing accumulation and increasing composition of capital together with increasing labour productivity (the reverse of Ricardo) seemed of great explanatory power.

Still, in Section 4 Marx inserts a, seemingly fairly weak, warning about the generality of the law: "Like all other laws, it is modified in its working [*Verwirklichung*] by many circumstances, the analysis of which does not concern us

---

31   A major proponent is Itoh (1988, ch. 9). For references see Clarke (1994), who – to be sure – does not take this view.

32   Cf. the relations posited in Section 1, my §3.1. Recall what Marx said about equation (E): "the rate of wages is the dependent, not the independent variable". As we know from *Capital III*, Part Three – drafted before the publication of *Capital* I – his theory of the acceleration triple can be developed into a theory of the cycle (see Reuten 2004b, for the textual evidence based on Marx's manuscripts [Chapter 17 of the current book]).

here [*nicht hierher gehört*]" (798; G, 674). Note that the warning in the German text is much stronger. In the latter it is not, say, the 'precise working' that gets modified, but its 'reality' its 'actualisation' (*Verwirklichung*).³³

Summary and methodological conclusions

Throughout the three volumes of *Capital* Marx presents the dynamics of the accumulation of capital in a number of steps. These represent, firstly, a movement from 'inner determinations' to 'outer determinations' (not less important). The inner determinations are discussed in *Capital I* and in §1.3 I set out the delineation of the latter's terrain. Secondly, both between and within the terrains, these steps also represent a movement from simple accounts to more complex ones.

In §2 and §3 we have seen how Marx proceeds in this respect. He first discusses the effect of changing productive forces of labour on the acceleration of accumulation (keeping real wages and the composition of capital constant and neglecting any problems of the growth of labour) (§2.2). Next he discusses the effect of accumulation of capital on the growth of labour employment and the possible real wage changes along with it – resulting in an oscillating growth in the real wage rate determined by an oscillating growth rate of exploitation (here keeping constant the productive forces, prices and the composition of capital) (§3.1). Finally he drops all the assumptions just mentioned (keeping intact those set out in §1.3) and so arrives at, what I have called, the acceleration triple of capital accumulation, productive forces of labour and composition of capital (§3.2). Taking their multiple interaction together at first seems to result in a continuously growing 'surplus population' (unemployment is the later term). As Marx sets out, however, this is contrary to the empirical observation of a fairly regular cyclical movement. Thus the theory is incomplete. Because, in Marx's view, a theory of the cycle cannot be developed at this level of abstraction (more is needed: the terrains and concepts developed in Volumes II and III of *Capital*); instead he just appends empirical observations to the theory developed so far and postpones explanation (and synthesis).

All this is theoretically and historically (1867^1; 1890^4) most exciting. From the point of view of a systematic-dialectical methodology (and many other meth-

---

33   With Hegel's *Logic* in mind the qualification is even heavier. (Moore & Aveling's translation – Marx 1883³ MA: 603 – is the same: 'working'.)

odologies) all this is fine. We reach a point at which the presentation so far is insufficient, so we must go on (in this case to the analysis to be covered in other volumes of *Capital*). It is also acceptable, at this point, to *blend out* (or bracket) the insufficiency, on the condition that it is made crystal clear that this 'blending out' is procedural. Marx is reluctant to do this (the blending out) in his Section 3 of Chapter 25 (§3.3 above); but he does do it in his summarising Section 4. In the latter section Marx also gives a procedural warning, but in the English text this warning is greatly deemphasised (§3.4 above). However, to fully understand the warning (in both languages) the reader must remember that about 90 pages earlier Marx signals that he is presenting a *"pure* analysis of the process" which "demands that we should, provisionally, disregard all phenomena that conceal the workings of its inner mechanism" (710). (English readers were not much helped by the translators rendering of *reine Analyse* into 'exact analysis'.) What is more, to understand that 'inner' and 'outer' mechanisms are necessarily *inseparably* connected, the reader has to have at least 'leafed' through Hegel's *Logic*.[34]

This must give rise (and has given rise) to misunderstandings about Marx's "general law of capitalist accumulation". The neglect that Marx's general law is merely posited as a "moment", has been fostered by the view Engels expressed in his Preface to the English edition of *Capital I* (1886): namely, that Volume I is "in a great measure a whole in itself, and has for twenty years ranked as an independent work". Although, strictly speaking, the indication 'whole *in itself*' is correct, Engels's statement carries the impression that a missing of Volumes II and III is no big deal.

As indicated, in Volume I Marx does not present – and methodologically could not present – a theory of capital centralisation or a theory of the cycle. *A fortiori* he presents no labour-shortage theory of the cycle. In §3.3 (especially its heading F) I have provided textual evidence for my interpretation. What is more, only a little reconstruction of the relationships that Marx posits might generate a cyclical *pattern*. It would be a grave underestimation of Marx (and all of his insights on dynamics point against it) to believe that he was not aware of this. He just did not want to posit this theory, at the level of the 'pure' 'inner mechanism' of the production process of capital.

---

34   This is a paraphrase of Marx in a letter to Engels at the time (1858) when he drafted *Capital*.

References

Superscripts indicate first and other relevant editions; the last mentioned year in the bibliography is the edition cited.

Bellofiore, Riccardo 2004, 'Marx and the macro-monetary foundation of microeconomics', in Bellofiore and Taylor (eds) 2004, pp. 146–69.
Bellofiore, Riccardo, and Nicola Taylor (eds) 2004, *The constitution of capital: essays on volume I of Marx's 'Capital'*, London: Palgrave Macmillan.
Clarke, Simon 1994, *Marx's theory of crisis*, London: Macmillan.
Fine, Ben, and Laurence Harris 1979, *Rereading Capital*, London: Macmillan.
Itoh, Makoto 1988, *The basic theory of capitalism*, London: Macmillan.
Marx, Karl 1867¹, 1890⁴G, *Das Kapital, Kritik der politischen Ökonomie, Band I, Der Produktionsprozeß des Kapitals*, MEW 23, Berlin: Dietz Verlag, 1973.
Marx, Karl 1867¹, 1883³ MA, *Capital, a critical analysis of capitalist production, volume I*, trans. of the 3rd German ed. by Samuel Moore and Edward Aveling (1886), London: Lawrence & Wishart, 1974.
Marx, Karl 1867¹, 1890⁴ F, *Capital: a critique of political economy, volume I*, trans. of the 4th German ed. by Ben Fowkes (1976), Harmondsworth: Penguin Books, 1976.
Murray, Patrick 2000, 'Marx's "truly social" labour theory of value: part I, abstract labour in Marxian value theory', *Historical Materialism* 6: 27–66.
Murray, Patrick 2002, 'Reply to Geert Reuten', *Historical Materialism* 10: 155–76.
Murray, Patrick 2004, 'The social and material transformation of production by capital: formal and real subsumption in "Capital volume I"', in Bellofiore and Taylor (eds) 2004, pp. 243–73.
Reuten, Geert 2003, 'Karl Marx: his work and the major changes in its interpretation', in *A companion to the history of economic thought*, edited by Warren Samuels, Jeff Biddle, and John Davis, Oxford: Blackwell, pp. 148–66.
Reuten, Geert 2004a, 'Productive force and the degree of intensity of labour', in Bellofiore and Taylor (eds) 2004, pp. 117–45.
Reuten, Geert 2004b, '"Zirkel vicieux" or trend fall? The course of the profit rate in Marx's "Capital III"', *History of Political Economy* 36(1): 163–86.
Reuten, Geert, and Michael Williams 1989, *Value-form and the state; the tendencies of accumulation and the determination of economic policy in capitalist society*, London: Routledge.
Rodenburg, Peter 2006, *The construction of instruments for measuring unemployment*, PhD thesis, University of Amsterdam, School of Economics.
Smith, Tony 1990, *The logic of Marx's Capital*, Albany: State University of New York Press.
Smith, Tony 2004, 'Technology and history in capitalism: Marxian and neo-Schumpeterian perspectives', in Bellofiore and Taylor (eds) 2004, pp. 217–42.

PART C

Capital II – outlines and comments

⁝

Contents
10. Marx's *Capital II*, The circulation of capital – general introduction (with Christopher Arthur; 1998) p. 207.
11. The status of Marx's reproduction schemes: conventional or dialectical logic? (1998) p. 219.
12. Some notes on Marx's macroeconomics *avant la lettre* (2023/2014) p. 261.

CHAPTER 10

Marx's *Capital II*, The circulation of capital – general introduction

(*with Christopher Arthur*)

1998 article, originally published in *The circulation of capital: essays on volume II of Marx's 'Capital'*, edited by Christopher Arthur and Geert Reuten, London: Macmillan, pp. 1–16. [The overview of that book's articles has been omitted.]
 (For its abstract see the Abstracts of all chapters on p. 5.)

General note. The essays in that 1998 book were written well before the 2008 MEGA edition of Marx's 1868–1881 manuscripts for *Capital II*.

Contents

Preliminary remarks   207
1   The interconnection of Book I and II of *Capital*   208
2   Schematic outline of *Capital II*   213
3   German and English editions, the manuscripts and Engels's editorial work   214
4   Influence of *Capital II*   215
References   216

Preliminary remarks

To understand how the life and growth of capital related to the exploitation of people was Marx's aim in his great work, *Capital*. But for a comprehensive account of the logic of capital's life process it was necessary to go beyond the dynamic of class struggle at the point of production elucidated in the first volume of the work. Marx discerned three complementary aspects of capital's movement which he treated in three books: the production of capital (1867); the circulation of capital (1885); and "the process as a whole" (including distribution) (1894).
 In 1978, Ernest Mandel introduced a new English translation of the second book, *Capital II*, referring to it as "the forgotten book" of *Capital*, while a reviewer of the translation (Tom Kemp) called it "the unknown volume". This is something of an exaggeration, for it was here, in the final part of this book,

that Marx introduced his 'Schemes of Reproduction' which influenced both Marxian and orthodox economics in the first decades of the twentieth century. Nevertheless, such debate as has taken place on the book has been mostly restricted to that final part. In any event, it would certainly be right to say that, of the three books of *Capital*, the second is the least known and has been least studied over the last 50 years. Yet there is much to learn from in doing so.

Here, in a collection of original essays, a group of specialists in the field range over the whole of *Capital II*, bringing to bear on various of its chapters the latest methodological resources, textual scholarship, scientific criticism and accumulated knowledge of Marxian theory. The result, we hope, will repair the unjustified neglect of Book II in the literature and awaken new interest in it, for our work fills a gap in scholarship, in that there is not a single volume on *Capital II*. Furthermore, even the existing textbooks and commentaries on Marx's economics as a whole limit the amount of space given to it compared with the first and last books.

This collection of articles, the only book so far specifically devoted to considering problems in Book II of *Capital*, is especially thorough on the methodological aspects of that work. However, it is not a textbook as such, working through the whole of Marx's argument from beginning to end, but a sequence of essays 'at the frontier', with individual authors selecting what seemed to them the most interesting issue to address, although every part of the text is treated by one or other contributor, and the articles are in that way beautifully complementary.

The first versions of the articles were discussed at the International Symposium on Marxian Theory V, a six-day working conference devoted to *Capital II*, held at Mount Holyoke College (Massachusetts) in 1995. Subsequent revisions are the result of it.[1] We provide in the following sections a general introduction to *Capital II* (which naturally reveals our own view on matters at issue in Marxian theory). Next, we give some information on the manuscripts and editions of Book II. Then we comment briefly on its reception in various traditions of economic thought. Finally, we preview the articles presented here [omitted in the current book].

1   The interconnection of Book I and II of *Capital*

Even if we neglect Marx's *Theories of surplus-value* (which some consider the fourth Book of *Capital*) the (remaining) three books cover some 2,200 pages,

---

[1] Other papers from the ISMT are collected in Moseley 1993 and Moseley and Campbell 1997; a

which implies a demanding architectonic. The outward systematic is in its books, next parts and then chapters. The main inward systematic is organised in the books and their parts rather than the chapters. As it happens, Books I–III now coincide with the published Volumes I–III, even if Marx himself at various points in time had different expectations on this matter. (More on this below: note that, while in this chapter we consistently use 'book' instead of 'volume', some authors prefer the latter term or like to use the terms interchangeably; indeed, except when studying the 'making' of *Capital*, the terms can be used interchangeably, but it is important to understand that, when Marx in his correspondence refers to what will be in 'Volume 2', this does not refer to 'Volume 2' as given to us by Engels but to Engels's Volumes 2 *and* 3.)

The title of Book II, "The process of circulation of capital", is clearly intended to be complementary to that of Book I, "The process of production of capital". These titles indeed represent the subject matter. However, since Marx starts Book I with *commodities*, and over and again returns to what "appears as" capitalism's "elementary form", the subject matter is easily misunderstood. (See Chapter 3 by Murray.) Nothing could be more wrong than to think that Book I is about the production of commodities, and Book II about their circulation. This is not so at all. The subject matter throughout is clearly signalled by Marx to be *capital*; this is what is produced, circulated and distributed. The circulation of commodities is thus incorporated within the circulation of capital, just as the production of commodities is studied in relation to the production and reproduction of capital.

Book I gives a thorough analysis of simple commodity circulation before it turns to capitalist production of these commodities. Only at the end of Part Two of this Book do we "leave this noisy sphere, where everything takes place on the surface and in full view", to enter "the hidden abode of production". Here we see "not only how capital produces but how capital itself is produced" (Marx 1867[1], 1890[4], pp. 279–80). It was necessary to follow this sequence for production of capital is necessarily production of value, a form originally constituted in exchange:

> To develop the concept of capital it is necessary to begin not with labour but with value, and, precisely, with exchange value in an already developed movement of circulation. It is ... impossible to make the transition directly from labour to capital. (Marx 1953, p. 259)[2]

---

fourth book is in process. [2023 note: From 1993 to 2014 the group published 11 books on Marx's *Capital* – see https://chrisarthur.net/international-symposium-on-marxian-theory-ismt/.]

2 This book of Marx, the *Grundrisse*, written in 1857–58, is a rough draft of *Capital* in rather

Equally Book II is not about such circulation of commodities as distinct from their production; rather it is about the social circulation of *capital*; as such this circulation includes the time spent in the production process, already partially analysed in Book I. Book II (Part One), under the headings of the three interconnected circuits of money capital, productive capital and commodity capital, *reconceptualises* the circulation process from Book I, only now as thoroughly transformed from a 'shallow' perspective which understands it to be about *commodities* simply to a 'deeper' view which reconceptualises it as the bearer of the part of the *capital* circuit, whose movement subsumes that of money and commodities under the drive for valorisation. (Cf. Murray 1998 and Arthur 1998.)

All the attention in Book I was on the significance of production for capital's valorisation: that is for value augmentation geared to the growth of capital: accumulation. Even if this analysis of capitalist production already stamps Marx's critique of classical political economy (cf. Mattick 1998) – classical political economy neglected the capitalist form of production, as does neoclassical economics today – Marx shows the insufficiency of just remaining at that level of analysis. Thus he takes on the investigation of production and capital's valorisation in the perspective of the circulation of capital.

Although Book II embodies the requirement for such a transition from Book I, we are rather short of methodological statements by Marx on it. It is worth quoting a relevant passage at the end of the first edition of *Capital 1*, dropped in subsequent editions.[3] In this passage Marx gives a final numerical example of the production of surplus-value (in iron-smelting) and then concludes:

> Sold by the capitalist at its value, the iron realizes a surplus-value of £1000, corresponding to the unpaid labour materialized in the value of the iron. But for this to come about the iron must be *marketed*. The immediate result of capitalist production is the *commodity* ... pregnant with surplus-value. We are thus thrown back on our point of departure, the commodity, and with it to the sphere of circulation. What we have to deal with in the

---

dialectical style. It made an impact with the 1953 German publication and again with its much-delayed 1973 English translation.

3 It was probably dropped for the second edition partly because of its absurdity as a tailpiece to the chapter on colonisation and partly because Marx felt embarrassed that he had not yet produced the promised book on the circulation of capital. Obviously, this paragraph is also a remnant of the famous 'missing chapter' on 'the immediate results of commodity production' (included as an appendix to the 1976 English translation of Book I – cf. p. 975).

following book, however, is no longer *simple commodity circulation*, but *the circulation process of capital*. (Marx 1867[1], 1st edn., p. 619)

This is because we now have to deal with the circulation, not of commodities as uncomprehended givens, but of commodities "pregnant with surplus-value", that is, products of capital, and therefore shapes of capital's reproduction.

Of course, right from the start of Book I, Marx presupposes what he will later prove: that there is no such thing as generalised circulation of commodities as a free-standing phenomenon; rather generalised commodity circulation presupposes capitalist production and hence is determined as an aspect of the circulation of capital (Marx 1885, p. 117). In Book II, however, Marx is not dealing, as he was at the start of Book I, with the circulation of money and commodities *as surface phenomena*, but as *forms of capital's self-positing movement*: for capital to be what it is, for it to exist and survive, it has to go through the phases, the metamorphoses, of being money capital, of being capital in production, of being commodity capital and recycling the movement over again. So in Book II Marx is in a way running over the Book I ground at a more comprehensive, that is concrete, level of conceptualisation (just as Hegel often represents material in his dialectical expositions at more concrete levels). Hence in Book II such matters as 'turnover time' obviously require discussion of time in production along with time spent on the market.

In sum, when Marx entitles Book II "The process of circulation of capital" this does not refer to circulation in its narrow sense, in which it is *contrasted* with the production process, it refers rather to the *whole process* of capital's movement through such phases. In the last Part of the book this becomes a study of the revolutions of the entire social capital, articulated through interchanges between its key particularisations.

In the jargon of modern orthodox economics, by this Marx apparently takes the analysis into 'macroeconomics'. Indeed he does so, and Marx may therefore be considered a founder of a particular macroeconomics (cf. Reuten 1998). Nevertheless to see merely that would be to miss important conceptual differences between Marx and modern orthodox economics, for much of *Capital II*, especially Part Two on the turnover of capital, would nowadays be classified as business economics. And to further complicate the comparison, much of that same part – together with the other two – would nowadays be classified as monetary economics (cf. Campbell 1998). Leaving aside what analysis Book I exactly presents (in orthodox jargon it is a blend of social economics, microeconomics and business economics) the Book II 'macroeconomics' incorporates and surpasses it. All this, of course, makes Book II into a fruitful source of theoretical inspiration along paths barely explored. At the same time problems of incommensurability between Marxian and orthodox economics are revealed. (The incommensurability is highlighted if we consider the orthodox search for micro-foundations of macroeconomics: in the Marxian case – dialectical interpretations of Marx especially would emphasise this – the Book II 'macro' analysis rather provides the foundation for Book I!)

While both books posit that capital's production and circulation are inseparable, the emphasis is certainly different in the two books. A lot of things 'set at zero' in Book I are indeed to do with markets (for example, sale is assumed to be no problem) and are addressed in Book II (notably the problem of exchange between 'departments' producing means of production and 'departments' producing means of consumption). Conversely the second book holds at zero many of the problems of production such as the struggle over wages and the working day.

In Book I, Marx considered the "immediate production process of capital" as a unity of the labour process and the valorisation process, the result being not merely a product but a commodity containing surplus-value.[4] Therewith the production process constitutes a process of production and accumulation of capital itself, subject to the realisation of this surplus-value.[5] Marx assumed in this book that there was no problem about it, that the capitalist was able to sell the product at its value and that he found in the market material means of production needed to continue production. The formal and material changes undergone by capital in the sphere of circulation distinct from the immediate production process were not examined, the only act of circulation dwelt on in Book I being the purchase and sale of labour-power as the basic premise of capitalist production.

However, the immediate production process has to be understood as located within the circuit of industrial capital as a whole. Whereas in Book I the argument went from exchange down to production and back to circulation, as a result of just that discussion we grasp capital "as this unity-in-process of production and circulation" (Marx 1953, p. 620). In Book II, Marx studies 'circulation' in this totalising sense.

---

4 Thus Marx indicates the *duality* of capitalist production: it is a contradictory process of producing useful objects (labour process) and at the same time of producing value and surplus-value (valorisation process). The latter, however, dominates the former. (See Reuten and Williams 1989, ch. 1; and Murray 1998 pointing out that the 'real subsumption' of labour indeed affects the labour process and the kind of commodities being produced).

5 Moseley (1998) points out that Marx, with his Reproduction Schemes of Part Three, and against Smith's 'dogma' in this respect, shows how the annual production indeed reproduces capital.

2 Schematic outline of *Capital II*

Marx's *Capital* Book II, "The circulation process of capital", is divided into three main parts. In Part One, Marx considers the metamorphoses capital undergoes in its circuit, namely as money capital, production capital and commodity capital. Of course, in normal conditions, this sequence is expanded into a regular imbricated set of sequences such that at any given time a different component of the total capital is present in each form.

In Part Two, Marx examines the circuit as a turnover. He shows how various components of capital (for example, so-called 'fixed' and 'circulating') complete their circuit at different rates; he argues that the influence of the circuit's periodicity, and the varying ratios of such components, must affect the annual rate of surplus-value. In both these parts capital as such is treated; but it is not considered as a system of capitals; however, the reproduction of any given capital is necessarily bound up with the reproduction and circulation of the total social capital.

Thus in Part Three, when Marx considers reproduction, he examines the revolution of this totality which necessarily includes not only the intertwining of each individual capital circuit with others but the whole circulation of commodities, those commodities bought by the workers to maintain themselves as well as those means of production capitals sell to each other. On this basis Marx distinguishes two "departments" of production: those producing means of production and those producing means of consumption. This very division, as well as the analysis of the relations between these departments, is one of the enduring achievements of Marx's work.

The relatively 'technical' character of much of Book II misled Engels, for one, into thinking that the argument concerns only relations between capitals; this is a grave mistake, for class relations are integral to capital and thus the matters dealt with here stand in intimate connection with its class basis; for example, capital's concern with shortening turnover time has consequences for the intensity of labour, and the very choice of criterion for discriminating departments is rooted in the necessary reproduction of class relations (as Mattick 1998 points out).

Even if this Book II study is still one at a relatively abstract level, the *phenomenal* expressions of the abstract categories developed may be visible to the extent that the concrete is a simple expression of the abstract categories – but not if in this process of concretion the system inverts its fundamental logic in its appearances (for example, in interest or 'productivity of capital') or reverses its dynamic (for example, in the case of tendencies and countertendencies). Tony Smith (1998) shows how many of the categories developed in Marx's Book II indeed find phenomenal expression; hence he can show how much of the Book II analysis can help us in understanding current developments in capitalism such as 'flexible production'.

3   German and English editions, the manuscripts and Engels's editorial work

Marx himself managed to publish only the first book of *Capital*: "The process of production of capital" (1867^1; 1873^2). Book II "The Process of Circulation of Capital" appeared posthumously, edited by Friedrich Engels from Marx's manuscripts, as was the third book (1885 and 1894). A work that is sometimes considered as Book IV, *Theories of surplus-value*, published in three volumes, was also edited from Marx's manuscripts, this time by Karl Kautsky (1904/10). An argument for not considering it as Book IV is that the material from which it was drawn is too rudimentary and lacks a concept for its presentation.[6]

As far as Book II is concerned, the following German and English editions are the most relevant. In German: the first edition by Engels was published in Hamburg in 1885; a second edition by Engels, with minor changes, appeared in 1893; this second edition is the basis for volume 24 of the *Marx-Engels Werke* (*MEW*), Berlin; the original manuscripts for Book II will shortly be published in the *Marx-Engels Gesamtausgabe* (*MEGA*), Berlin and Amsterdam. In English: the first English translation by E. Untermann was published by Kerr & Co, in 1909; it is the basis of subsequent Moscow editions. A new translation by D. Fernbach appeared in 1978 (New York and London). Fernbach's translation is generally preferable, but it should always be checked against the other. The English *Marx Engels collected works* will shortly provide a revised version of the old Moscow edition (as its volume 36). But our information is that the changes to the translation will not be as extensive as might be justifiable, although we may expect the provision of useful editorial notes, as in the new edition of Book I published as Volume 35 (1996) of the *Collected works*.

Marx referred to the three parts of *Capital* as 'books'. While Book I appeared on its own in 1867 as 'Volume One', Marx *at that time* intended to publish both subsequent books in one volume. But after Marx's death in 1883, Engels found so much material to hand for these books that he published them as separate

---

6   See Oakley 1983, pp. 124–5. Up to at least 1877, Marx indeed planned to redraft the latter material for a fourth book: letters to Kugelman, 13 October 1866, to Meyer, 30 April 1867, and to Schott, 3 November 1877.

volumes. Thus, as we have already indicated, the upshot is that 'books' correspond exactly with 'volumes'.[7]

As Engels explains in his preface to the second edition of *Capital II*, the material from which he reconstructed Book II consists of several drafts attempted by Marx (Notebooks I–VIII, written between 1865 and 1878; however, Engels mainly used the drafts of 1870 (II), 1877 (V) and 1878 (VIII).) It will eventually be possible for all to study what a fist he made of it when the original manuscripts are published in the new *MEGA*. Thus far only the first full draft dated 1865 (not used by Engels) has appeared. (One aspect of it is treated in Arthur 1998, Appendix B.)

It is worth nothing that Book II comprises Marx's final thoughts on capital for the various drafts Engels used were composed more than five years after the draft of Book III (1865). It follows that thoughts developed in Book II may well have to be taken into account when evaluating Book III.[8]

4   Influence of *Capital II*

Some comments on the influence of Book II on Marxian and orthodox economic theory would be appropriate here. However, as the material for this might cover a chapter or even a full book in itself, we merely provide some references to the literature. As we have already indicated, it was Part Three of the book that had the most impact, whereas the other two parts were rather neglected.[9]

As to Part Three (on the 'macroeconomic' departmental division and reproduction schemes) we may mention four main lines of influence. They all arose in the first decades of the twentieth century. The first author to adopt Marx's

---

[7] However, this does not excuse David Fernbach's altering Engels's preface to Volume Two without notice by changing the term 'book' to 'volume' throughout his translation of it. Incidentally, for purely external reasons, part of Engels's preface to *Capital II* gives an explanation of the uniqueness of Marx's theory of surplus-value in which he clarified the point that labour as value-creating activity cannot have a value of its own; only labour-power can. Note that the 1978 English translation by D. Fernbach misses matter in this passage: "labour-power for labour as the value-creating property" (p. 99) should read "labour-power. By substituting labour-power for labour as the value-creating property".

[8] A concise source in English on the various drafts for *Capital* is Oakley (1983). Evidently it deserves reconsideration on the basis of the new source material not available to Oakley.

[9] We may mention just one exception: Moggridge (biographer of Keynes and editor of his collected works) indicates that Keynes used Marx's capital circuit approach in his 1933 lectures. See Moggridge (1976, p. 104); Keynes (CW, XIII, p. 420); cf. CW, XXIX, pp. 81–2, where Keynes writes on the same issue in the preparation of his *General Theory*.

reproduction schemes in his own work back in 1894 was Tugan-Baranowski, and he subsequently influenced orthodox approaches to the business cycle. Within this line we also have the construction of orthodox macroeconomics and growth theory.[10] The work of Kalecki deserves special mention, as in many respects his work is within the Marxian tradition: certainly Marx's reproduction schemes influenced his approach to economics.[11] The second line is within Marxian economics where Hilferding and Luxemburg were among the first to adopt the analysis.[12] A third, and rather surprising, line is the adoption of the schemes in the USSR economic planning of the 1920s.[13] However from this line there is a direct link to the last one, input–output analysis. Leontief, a Soviet emigrant to the USA, founder of this approach within orthodox economics for which he was granted a Nobel Prize, apparently got the idea from his Soviet education.[14] (The above is merely a preliminary guide for the interested reader, and the list of references in the notes is not meant to be exhaustive.)

References

Note 1: All years in brackets are the original dates of publication as referred to in the text; editions quoted from may differ and are provided where appropriate.
Note 2 of 2023: The introduction above has cross-references to the chapters of the 1998 volume. Its title and the relevant articles are therefore included below.

Arthur, Christopher J. 1998, 'The fluidity of capital and the logic of the concept', in Arthur and Reuten (eds) 1998, pp. 95–128.
Arthur, Christopher J., and Geert Reuten (eds) 1998, *The circulation of capital: essays on volume II of Marx's 'Capital'*, London: Macmillan.
Campbell, Martha 1998, 'Money in the circulation of capital', in Arthur and Reuten (eds) 1998, pp. 129–58.

---

10 Domar in his seminal paper (1946), for example, refers to Marx. See further the papers in Horowitz (1968), Mandel (1978), Howard and King (1989), and Kurz (1995).
11 See Kalecki (1954, ch. 3 and 1968); cf. Sawyer (1985, ch. 8). Incidentally, according to Harcourt (1982, p. 270), Robinson over the years came "to prefer Kalecki's version of the central propositions of the *General Theory* to Keynes's version because they are placed in the context of Marx's schemes of reproduction and a theory of cyclical growth". According to her account, Robinson, after reading Volume Two, liked to tease Harrod by telling him that his growth theory was already there, in Marx's last chapter (Robinson 1953, p. 17).
12 See Mandel (1978); and Howard and King (1989).
13 See, for example, Desai (1979, ch. 17).
14 See Lange (1959, ch. 3); Jasny (1962); Stone and Stone (1977).

Desai, Meghnad 1979, *Marxian economics*, Oxford: Basil Blackwell.
Domar, Evsey D. 1946, 'Capital expansion, rate of growth and employment', *Econometrica*, 14; reprinted in Amartya Sen (ed.), *Growth economics*, Harmondsworth: Penguin, 1970.
Harcourt, Geoffrey C. 1982, 'The Sraffian contribution: an evaluation', in *Classical and Marxian political economy*, edited by Ian Bradley and Michael Howard, London: Macmillan.
Horowitz, David (ed.) 1968, *Marx and modern economics*, New York/London: Monthly Review Press.
Howard, Michael C., and Jesse E. King 1989; 1992, *A history of Marxian economics, vol. I, 1883–1929, vol. II, 1929–1990*, London: Macmillan.
Jasny, Naum 1962, 'The Soviet balance of national income and the American input-output analysis', *L'industria* 1: 51–7.
Kalecki, Michał 1954, *Theory of economic dynamics*, New York: Augustus Kelley.
Kalecki, Michał 1968, 'The Marxian equations of reproduction and modern economics', *Social Science Information* 7.
Kurz, Heinz D. 1995, 'Marginalism, classicism and socialism in German-speaking countries 1871–1932', in *Socialism and marginalism in economics 1870–1930*, edited by I. Steedman, London: Routledge.
Lange, Oscar 1966 [1959/1962], *Introduction to econometrics*, 2nd edn, trans. by E. Lepa, Oxford: Pergamon Press.
Mandel, Ernest 1978, 'Introduction' to Marx 1885, English trans. David Fernbach, pp. 11–79.
Marx, Karl 1867¹, 1890⁴, *Das Kapital, Kritik der politischen Ökonomie, Band I, Der Produktionsprozess der Kapitals; MEW* 23; English trans. Ben Fowkes, *Capital, a critique of political economy, volume one*, Harmondsworth: Penguin Books, 1976.
Marx, Karl 1867, 1st edn., *Das Kapital, Kritik der politischen Ökonomie, Erster Band Hamburg 1867, Marx-Engels Gesamtausgabe*, Abteilung II, Band 5, Berlin: Dietz Verlag, 1983.
Marx, Karl 1885¹, 1893², ed. F. Engels, *Das Kapital, Kritik der Politischen Ökonomie, Band II, Der Zirkulationsprozess des Kapitals, MEW* 24, Berlin: Dietz Verlag, 1972; English trans. Ernest Untermann 1907; David Fernbach, *Capital, a critique of political economy, vol. II*, Harmondsworth: Penguin Books, 1978.
Marx, Karl 1894, ed. F. Engels, *Das Kapital, Kritik der Politischen Ökonomie, Band III, Der Gesamtprozess der kapitalistischen Produktion, MEW* 25, Berlin: Dietz Verlag, 1972; English trans. Ernest Untermann 1909; David Fernbach, *Capital, a critique of political economy, vol. III*, Harmondsworth: Penguin Books, 1981.
Marx, Karl 1904/10, 1996/62 {written 1861–63} ed. K. Kautsky, *Theorien über den Mehrwert* (1904/10); 2nd edn (1996/62) by Institut für Marxismus-Leninismus, *Theorien über den Mehrwert Teile I, II, III, MEW* 26.1, 26.2, 26.3, Berlin: Dietz Verlag, 1965/68

English edn: *Theories of surplus-value, part I*, ed. S. Ryazanskaya, trans. Emile Burns (1963); *Part II*, ed. and trans. S. Ryazanskaya (1968); *Part III*, ed. S. Ryazanskaya and Richard Dixon, trans. Jack Cohen and S. Ryazanskaya (1971), London: Lawrence & Wishart.

Marx, Karl 1953, *Grundrisse; foundations of the critique of political economy (rough draft)* (original German publication 1953), trans. Martin Nicolaus, Harmondsworth: Penguin Books, 1973.

Mattick Jr., Paul 1998, 'Economic form and social reproduction: on the place of "book II" in Marx's critique of political economy', in Arthur and Reuten (eds) 1998, pp. 17–32.

Moggridge, Donald E. 1976, *Keynes*, London: Fontana/Collins.

Moseley, Fred (ed.) 1993, *Marx's method in 'Capital': a re-examination*, Atlantic Highlands, NJ: Humanities Press.

Moseley, Fred (ed.) 1998, 'Marx's reproduction schemes and Smith's dogma', in Arthur and Reuten (eds) 1998, pp. 159–86.

Moseley, Fred, and Martha Campbell (eds) 1997, *New investigations of Marx's method*, Atlantic Highlands, NJ: Humanities Press.

Murray, Patrick 1998, 'Beyond the "commerce and industry" picture of capital', in Arthur and Reuten (eds) 1998, pp. 33–66.

Oakley, Allen 1983, *The making of Marx's critical theory*, London: Routledge.

Reuten, Geert 1998, 'The status of Marx's reproduction schemes: conventional or dialectical logic?' in Arthur and Reuten (eds) 1998, pp. 187–229.

Reuten, Geert, and Michael Williams 1989, *Value-form and the state; the tendencies of accumulation and the determination of economic policy in capitalist society*, London: Routledge.

Robinson, Joan 1953, *On re-reading Marx*, Cambridge: Students Bookshop Ltd.

Sawyer, Malcolm C. 1985, *The economics of Michał Kalecki*, London: Macmillan.

Stone, Richard, and Giovanna Stone 1961, 1977, *National income and expenditure*, 2nd edn, London: Bowes.

CHAPTER 11

The status of Marx's reproduction schemes; conventional or dialectical logic?

1998 article, originally published in *The circulation of capital: essays on volume II of Marx's 'Capital'*, edited by Christopher Arthur and Geert Reuten, London: Macmillan, pp. 187–229.
 (For its abstract see the Abstracts of all chapters, p. 6.)

General note. This chapter was written well before the 2008 MEGA edition of Marx's 1868–81 manuscripts for *Capital II*.

Contents

Introduction   220
1   The notebooks for the chapters on reproduction and circulation   221
2   Simple reproduction   223
   2.1   The construction of a macroeconomics   223
   2.2   A two-sector macroeconomic model   227
   2.3   Further assumptions   228
   2.4   The schema of simple reproduction and the condition for simple reproduction   229
   2.5   The value of the total product and the value product of labour   231
   2.6   Money circulation and 'the widow's cruse'   233
   2.7   Maintenance of fixed capital and disproportionate production   234
   2.8   Conclusions to the model for simple reproduction   234
3   Expanded reproduction   235
   3.1   The general frame for the analysis: general assumptions and abstractions   235
   3.2   The schemes for expanded reproduction   237
   3.3   A formal recapitulation of the model for expanded reproduction: conclusions   248
4   Marx's method for the theory of reproduction and circulation of the social capital   251
   4.1   Precursor to the modern conventional economic modelling   252
   4.2   First and second thoughts on systematic dialectics   253

Conclusions 257
References 257

Introduction[1]

[2023 note: This introduction unfortunately omits that the main part of the article (§2–§3) regards a general analysis of Marx's reproduction schemes.]

Marx's *Capital* is an unfinished project, in the narrower sense of the plan for the work with this title, dating from 1862, and even more so in the wider sense of a theory of the interconnection of economy and state and of the development of world capitalism. The evaluation of what is there, obviously depends on the method adopted by Marx, but opinions diverge on the interpretation of that method.[2]

Some prefer to read Marx in a 'conventional' way, as adopting a method of inquiry in line with formal logic; that is, not different *in principle* from approaches of modern orthodox economics. In this case one has to 'neglect', 'de-emphasise', 'purify it from' some supposedly superfluous jargon of Marx, stemming from his flirtation with an obscure dialectics. One finds such a position held by people ranging from adversaries and sympathetic critics to scholars themselves working in the Marxian tradition. Others see Marx adopting a systematic-dialectical method, in line with – though not necessarily the same as – Hegel's dialectical logic (1812, 1817).[3] Here most commentators agree that Marx's *Capital* did not reach a full systematic-dialectical presentation and that the work requires reconstruction and further development.[4]

---

1 Drafts of this paper were presented at the *International Symposium on Marxian Theory* (South Hadley, 1995), the *European Conference of the History of Economics* (Lisbon, 1996), and the *Workshop Models as Mediators in the Practice of Economic Science* (Amsterdam, 1996). I thank Christopher J. Arthur, Martha Campbell, Mino Carchedi, Paul Mattick Jr., Fred Moseley, Patrick Murray, and Tony Smith as well as Francisco Louçã and Margaret Morrison for their comments. Finally, I thank my colleagues in the *Amsterdam University Research Group into the History and Philosophy of Economics* for their discussions; this paper has benefited particularly from comments by Marcel Boumans and Mary Morgan. [Added note: This article was written well before the 2008 MEGA edition of Marx's 1868–81 manuscripts for *Capital II*.]
2 Strictly the material for such interpretation comprises the three books of *Capital* (1867, 1885, 1894) and perhaps also the material for the planned fourth book, the *Theories of surplus-value* (1904/10). Various other works, however, may be relevant.
3 This position is most vehemently argued for by Smith (1990, 1993). Whereas he considers his work 'an interpretation', I see it as an original reconstruction.
4 Most of these authors at the same time emphasise the value-form theoretical elements in

Both groups can find support for their position in quotations from Marx concerning his relation to Hegel's dialectic, spread out over the course of his writing life. It is useful then to study the texts of *Capital* and see if these resolve the matter. This is the aim of the case study reported in this article. However, the reader interested in decisive answers only can stop reading here: it will appear that the case presented below is compatible with both positions.

The systematic presentation of Marx's *Capital* is organised in its parts rather than its chapters (eight parts for Book I, three for II and seven for III). The second book of *Capital*, "The process of circulation of capital" (1885), is made up of parts on the circuits of capital, the turnover of capital, and the reproduction and circulation of capital. In this article I investigate the methodological status of this last part: "The reproduction and circulation of the total social capital".

As indicated, of particular interest is the question to what extent we find in this Part a (systematic) dialectics going on, or rather some other method, perhaps the groundwork for a modelling approach as adopted by much of modern orthodox economics. As will be argued towards the end of this article, a case can be made for this latter thesis of a modelling approach. The questions then remain how it differs – if at all – from modern orthodox modelling approaches and how this approach might fit – if at all – into a systematic-dialectical methodology. In order to put those questions into perspective, and prior to outlining the case, I first provide some information on the case material.

1 The notebooks for the chapters on reproduction and circulation

Both Book II and Book III of *Capital* were edited by Engels from Marx's notebooks. These notebooks differ in status from notes to preliminary drafts to revisions of the various drafts. Generally it seems that Book II has more the status of reordered though barely edited notebooks than Book III. Many of the Book II chapters show signs of being a first study of the subject; their analytical rigour and depth differ greatly, and some parts are very repetitious. One may speculate as to how the work might have looked if Marx had drafted it for publication. Engels, anyway, did not consider it his task to rewrite the material (see Engels's preface).

Marx: for example, Backhaus (1963, 1992); Eldred (1984); Eldred et al. (1982/1985); Reuten and Williams (1989); Reuten (1993, 1995); Williams (1998). Arthur (1993) is a most important development.

The material for Part Three, on reproduction and circulation, was taken from Notebooks II (written in 1870), and VIII (1878) – see Engels's preface (in Marx 1885, pp. 103–4).[5] The 1878 Notebook VIII, redrafting the part on reproduction, was probably the last work Marx undertook for *Capital* (see Oakley 1983, pp. 101–3).

All the quotations below are from the Penguin edition in Fernbach's translation; all page references are preceded by a Roman number, indicating the notebook from which it is taken. For example II:109 means that the quotation is from Notebook II, page 109 in the Penguin edition (Marx 1885). Part Three is made up of four chapters: Chapter 18: Introduction (8 pages); Chapter 19: Former Presentations of the Subject (33 pages); Chapter 20: Simple Reproduction (97 pages); Chapter 21: Accumulation and Reproduction on an Expanded Scale (35 pages).

Chapter 19 deals mainly with the theories of Quesnay and Smith. The piece on Quesnay and his *Tableau economique* is relatively brief.[6] Whilst he considers the Physiocratic system "the first systematic conception of capitalist production", he sees in Smith vis-à-vis the Physiocrats on the one hand progression – for his generalising *"avances primitives"* and *"advances annuelles"* into 'fixed' and 'circulating' capital – and on the other retrogression consisting in "the acceptance and the perpetuation of the concepts of 'fixed' and 'circulating' as decisive distinctions" (VIII:438).[7]

The introductory chapter 18 sets out the interconnection of the subject under investigation with the analysis of Book 1 of *Capital* ("the immediate production process of capital") as well as with Parts One and Two of the present Book II: (1) "the various forms that capital assumes in its circuit, and the various forms of this circuit itself"; (2) "the circuit as a periodic one, i.e., as a turnover". In Book 1, "the capitalist production process was analysed both as an isolated event and as a process of reproduction: the production of surplus-value and the production of capital itself". Parts One and Two dealt with "no more than an individual capital, the movement of an autonomous part of the social capital". However, Marx continues, "the circuits of individual capitals are interlinked, they presuppose one another and condition one another, and it is precisely by

---

5 Thus, according to Engels's information, Notebook VIII was written in 1878. However, the text contains references to two 1879 works, one of which was *The Nation* of October 1879 (p. 591). [Added note: From the *MEGA* editors we now know that Marx worked on this Notebook until 1881.]

6 It is more extensively dealt with in *Theories of Surplus Value*, Part One (Marx 1904/10, pp. 308–44; 378–80) where we also find a representation of the *Tableau*. On Marx's appreciation of and inspiration from Quesnay, see Gehrke and Kurz (1995, esp. pp. 6–9 and 80–84).

7 See further Moseley (1998).

being interlinked in this way that they constitute the movement of the total social capital" (11:427–9).

Thus this is what is presented in Chapters 20 and 21: "the circulation process of this total social capital" which, taken in its entirety, is "a form of the reproduction process" (11:430). These two chapters will be discussed in the next two sections. Note that in what follows I will frequently use the term 'model' for Marx's representations of reproduction. It is taken to be a general term that can be adopted in dialectical as well as non-dialectical discourses – each time, however, with different qualifications. I will come back to this in the last section.

2 Simple reproduction

2.1 *The Construction of a Macroeconomics*

Perhaps the most important aspect of the chapters on reproduction is to be found in the opening section of Chapter 20: here we find in fact the construction of a macroeconomics, the "functioning of the social capital", as Marx calls it, the movement of individual capitals being "an integral link in the movement of the total capital". We have, on the one hand, the elements of production of the individual capital, "in so far as they are of the objective kind", forming a component of the social capital; and, on the other hand,

> the movement of the part of the social commodity product that is consumed by the worker in spending his wage, and by the capitalist in spending surplus-value, not only forms an integral link in the movement of the total product, but is also interwoven with the movements of the individual capitals, so that its course, too, cannot be explained by being simply presupposed. (11:469)

The problem of reproduction, then, is: "How is the *capital* consumed in production replaced in its value out of the annual product, and how is the movement of this replacement intertwined with the consumption of surplus-value by the capitalist and of wages by the workers?" (11:469).

Whereas Marx's solutions to the problem are of interest – as we will see – the major achievement is the particular posing of the problem. Of course, many aspects of the problem may be obvious from the standpoint of the end of twentieth-century economics. It is therefore useful to quote three opinions from a time when Keynes's macroeconomics had been on the scene for only a few years, and these issues were less evident:

> "Marx ... developed the fundamental scheme describing the interrelation between consumer and capital goods industries." (Leontief 1938, p. 93)
> "His theory is probably the origin of macro-economics." (Klein 1947, p. 154)
> "the theory adumbrated in Volume Two of *Capital* has close affinities with Keynes." (Robinson 1948, p. 103)

Whilst it is perhaps arbitrary where we locate 'the' origin of macroeconomics (Klein) – Quesnay and Ricardo certainly also provided seminal elements – it is certain that Marx conceived the multiple dimensions of the problem: material and value, as well as production and circulation in their several aspects. In this respect we see here the culmination of both Marx's value-form theory (*Capital*, I) and the theory of the metamorphoses of capital and their circuits (*Capital*, II, Part One). We see this in the extract from Marx given above, and it is even more obvious one page further on in the text:

> As long as we were dealing with capital's value production and the value of its product individually, the natural form of the commodity product was a matter of complete indifference for the analysis, whether it was machines or corn or mirrors .... But this purely formal manner of presentation is no longer sufficient once we consider the total social capital and the value of its product.... [The latter's movement is] conditioned not just by the mutual relations of the value components of the social product hut equally by their use-values, their material shape. (II:470)

Thus we see the construction of not only a macroeconomics, but a particular macroeconomics emphasising the twofold conflicting guises of the capitalist economy – value and use-value – for which at least temporary modes of operation have to be established (modes which Marx shows to be ridden with contradictions, as manifest especially in economic crises). Thus we have, on the one hand, use-value, the material component of production necessary for 'natural survival' – however much shaped by the actual capitalist mode of production. On the other hand, we have value (ultimately money profits), driving and shaping the course of production, necessary for 'capitalist survival'. But for capitalism the two are one; the one has no existence without the other.

This twofold macroeconomics contrasts sharply with the post-Keynes orthodox macroeconomics approaches dichotomising the problem into two separate sides, or reducing the problem to one of its sides (either monetary or physical, the latter homogenised via index numbers).

For the further construction of the macroeconomics model Marx operates in two stages. Starting in Chapter 20 with a model of 'Simple Reproduction', where capitalists consume all surplus-value, he considers in Chapter 21 'Expanded Reproduction'; that is, the realistic situation where capitalists accumulate (part of) the surplus-value. This is a very remarkable procedure, one which he had also adopted in the earlier parts of the book (see especially its Chapter 2). Marx emphasises over and over again that accumulation of capital is essential to the system. At the very end of the book he states forcefully that simple reproduction is "incompatible with capitalist production from the very start" (VIII:596). So why start with something that is alien to the object of inquiry? What kind of abstraction or kind of simplification is this? Indeed for a simplification we might expect simplification to what is essential. Or is Marx rather cutting up the problem into (non-essential) parts that can be analysed separately?

> **a**[8] "Simple reproduction on the same scale seems to be an abstraction, both in the sense that the absence of any accumulation ... is an assumption foreign to the capitalist basis, and in the sense that the conditions in which production takes place do not remain absolutely the same in different years (which is what is assumed here) .... But since, when accumulation takes place, simple reproduction still remains a part of this, and is a real factor in accumulation, this can also be considered by itself." (VIII:470–71)

Some pages later the point is stated again, but now in terms of the Faustian conflict between the capitalist passion for accumulation and the desire for consumption, alluded to in Part Seven of *Capital I* (740–1): "Simple reproduction is oriented by nature to consumption as its aim .... In so far as simple reproduction is also part of any reproduction on an expanded scale, and the major part at that, this motive remains alongside the motive of enrichment as such and in opposition to it" (VIII:487). As we will see below (towards the end of §3) simple reproduction, even if "foreign to the capitalist basis", appears to be the sea on which accumulation moves.

The opening section of Chapter 20 contains another assumption disregarding an essential characteristic of capitalism:

> **b** "Moreover, we assume not only that products are exchanged at their values, but also that no revolution in values takes place in the components of the productive capital." (II:469)

---

8   Successive abstractions/assumptions are indicated in bold letters throughout this essay.

This assumption is maintained throughout the remainder of the book.[9] Its first part (exchange at values) is not surprising: it fits into the general systematic of *Capital,* and is in fact dropped in Part Two of Book III. The question is whether dropping this assumption would affect the macroeconomic construct as well as the particular 'schema' to be developed later on. The answer is no; hence any divergence of price from value is *irrelevant* for the problem at stake:

> In as much as prices diverge from values, this circumstance *cannot exert any influence* on the movement of the social capital. *The same mass* of products is exchanged afterwards as before, even though the value relationships in which the individual capitalists are involved are no longer proportionate to their respective advances and to the quantities of surplus-value produced by each of them. (II:469; emphasis added)[10]

The second part of the assumption is remarkable to the extent that in *Capital I,* "revolution in values" has already been shown as essential to the system. However, this part of assumption **b** is evidently of different status from the previous one, **a**. With it the very construction of the macroeconomics is at stake. Whereas the distinction related to **a** is relevant for the problem, it seems to be made for heuristic reasons. For **b**, however, Marx holds that for the problem at hand the issue of 'revolutions in value' is *irrelevant,* or neglectable:

> As far as revolutions in value are concerned, they change nothing in the relations between the value components of the total annual product, as long as they are generally and evenly distributed. In so far as they are only partially and unevenly distributed, they represent disturbances which, *firstly,* can be understood only if they are treated as *divergences* from value relations that remain unchanged; *secondly,* however, given proof of the law that one part of the value of the annual product replaces constant capital, and another variable capital, then a revolution ... would alter only the relative magnitudes of the portions of value that function in one or the other capacity. (II:469–70)

---

9   The same assumption was already posited at the opening of Ch. 1 (II:109) and reasserted in Ch. 2 (V:153). Next the assumption is relaxed in the same chapter (V:162) and further discussed again in Ch. 4 (V:185–9).
10 Incidentally this seems relevant for some interpretations of the Book III value to price transformation.

In other words, even unevenly distributed 'revolutions in value' – though affecting the magnitudes of the components of (social) capital – would not change the particular macroeconomic *interconnections* between constant and variable capital (as well as between them and surplus-value) in the way they will be seen to be set out by Marx.

2.2 A two-sector macroeconomic model

The next phase for constructing the model is central to Marx's approach. He constructs a two-sector macroeconomics model – as far as is known, the first in the history of economics, even if the inspiration for thinking in *similar abstract* categories may have come from Quesnay (1759). The model is composed of two 'departments'. Department I is the sector producing means of production, department II the one producing consumption goods. At the same time this composition fits Marx's particular value-theoretical distinction between constant capital and variable capital.

> c   "The society's total product, and thus its total production process, breaks down into two great departments:
>
>   1. *Means of production:* commodities that possess a form in which they either have to enter productive consumption, or at least can enter this.
>   2. *Means of consumption:* commodities that possess a form in which they enter the individual consumption of the capitalist and working classes.
>
> In each of these departments, all the various branches of production belonging to it form a single great branch of production ... The total capital applied in each of these two branches of production forms a separate major department of the social capital." (II:471)

In the text there follow definitions of variable and constant capital (471–2) which emphasise again the twofold character of capital: its material constituent and its value constituent.

So we have three sets of abstractions (retained throughout this volume – Book II – as well as Book III): First the abstraction of the macroeconomic categories of total product, total production process and social capital; second, the division of these categories into two material functional forms (means of production and means of consumption) – which is a *generic* abstraction, applicable in principle to all modes of production; third, we have the *determinate* abstraction, particularly applicable to the capitalist mode of production, of the division of the same categories into their value constituents (constant capital, variable capital, surplus-value) and which, at the same time, reflects the class division in this society.[11] Together these constitute a major analytical and synthetical achievement.

2.3 Further Assumptions

d Apparently so as to reduce the problem to its bare elements, Marx next assumes temporarily (that is, throughout the earlier sections of Chapter 20, as well as in most of Chapter 21) that there is no fixed capital or, equally, that all fixed capital is used up during the production period (VIII:473). Note that we still have a *flow* both in value (constant capital) and in the 'natural form' of means of production.[12]

e It is further assumed that for both departments the rate of surplus-value (s/v) is equal, constant and given (100 per cent). This assumption is maintained throughout this Part. Although it is not commented upon (it is treated at length in both Book I and Book III of *Capital*), it seems a simplifying device without particular relevance to the problem at hand.

f The next assumption concerns the value composition of capital ($c/(c + v)$), which is, for each department, taken as equal, constant and given. This assumption is maintained throughout Chapter 20, but relaxed several times in Chapter 21. Marx comments:

> What is arbitrarily chosen here, for both departments I and II, is the ratio of variable capital to constant capital; arbitrary also is the identity of this ratio between the departments ... This identity is assumed here for the sake of simplification, and the assumption of different ratios would not change anything at all in the conditions of the problem or its solution. (VIII:483)

In fact both simplifications **e** and **f** can be made because their possible departmental divergences do not fundamentally affect the problem. This is related to the more severe assumption **b**: the possible divergences at hand would not affect the interconnection between the departments – yet to be developed. (From the point of view of method, all this is most important: the transform-

---

11 See Murray (1988, Ch. 10) for the difference between generic and determinate abstraction.
12 If we had capital fixed for more than one production period, this would not affect the problem for the value calculations (as long as we refrain from investigating the rate of profit: cf. VIII:597); that is in case of simple reproduction and its schema. For expanded reproduction this would be different as part of surplus-value would get accumulated into fixed capital – more than the expanded flow of constant capital. (Cf. Robinson 1951, p. 16, discussing Luxemburg's schemes.)

ations in *Capital* are systematic, not historical. Thus, for example, the value–price transformation in Book III is conceptual and cannot be said actually to affect the size of the departments.)

A final assumption, which is maintained throughout the Part, is made explicit much further on in the text:

g   "Capitalist production never exists without foreign trade .... Bringing foreign trade into an analysis of the value of the product annually reproduced can ... only confuse things ... We therefore completely abstract from it here." (VIII:546)

This is again an assumption of simplification of the type 'neglectable' for the current problematic.

2.4   *The schema of simple reproduction and the condition for simple reproduction*

Schema ch. 20 presents the departmental schema and the numerical example, that is used throughout this chapter – in the dimension of money, that is £ or $ and so on – (VIII:473).

Schema ch. 20. General numerical schema for simple reproduction

	c		v		s		x	
I	4000	+	1000	+	1000	=	6000	(means of production)
II	2000	+	500	+	500	=	3000	(means of consumption)
	6000	+	1500	+	1500	=	9000	(social gross product)[13]

where:
I   = department I, producing means of production (6000);
II = department II, producing means of consumption (3000);
c   = constant capital, the value of the means of production applied;
v   = variable capital, the value of the social labour-power applied;

---

13   Here the fourth column is total gross production (including intermediate production) and the third row is total gross expenditure (including intermediate expenditure). So for the shape of a modern Leontief input–output table (derived from the schema), one has to rotate the schema 90 degrees to the west, and move the initial third row to the outer east, with c_1 (4000) and c_2 (2000) remaining in the first quadrant of intermediate expenditure and production.

s = surplus-value, the value that is added by labour minus the replacement of the variable capital advanced. (Cf. 11:472.)

Although Marx does not comment on the numbers in the schema, they do not seem arbitrary. In an earlier chapter (Ch. 17, 11:397–8) Marx quotes an estimate of the ratio of the total capital stock and the total consumption for Britain and Ireland (as reported by Thompson 1850). This ratio amounts to 3.[14] A similar ratio in the schema above is 2. However fixed constant capital has been excluded for the time being.

Generalising the schema, Marx uses the notation:[15]

$$\text{I}c + \text{I}v + \text{I}s = \text{I}$$
$$\text{II}c + \text{II}v + \text{II}s = \text{II}$$

In what follows, I adopt the notation that has become conventional in modern Marxian economics:

$$c_1 + v_1 + s_1 = x_1 \qquad (A)$$
$$c_2 + v_2 + s_2 = x_2 \qquad (B)$$
$$\overline{c + v + s = x} \qquad (C)$$

For simple reproduction, then,

$$x_1 = c \quad \text{or equally,} \qquad (D)$$
$$x_2 = v + s \qquad (E)$$

Analysing at length the mutual exchange between the departments, which is "brought about by a money circulation, which both mediates it and makes it harder to comprehend" (VIII:474), Marx derives the following proportionality condition for simple reproduction (VIII:478):

$$v_1 + s_1 = c_2 \qquad (F)$$

He does not use the term equilibrium, but talks of "proportionate part", and holds that the proportionate part on the left side of (F) "must be equal" to the proportionate part on the right side (VIII:474, 478). The result is:

---

[14] Or three times the year's labour of the community ... "Tis with the proportions, rather than with the absolute accurate amount of these estimated sums, we are concerned" (William Thompson, *An Inquiry into the Principles of the Distribution of Wealth*, London 1824/1850, quoted by Marx 1885, p. 398).

[15] Although Marx uses his notation throughout the text, for example for the derivation of conditions of reproduction (see below), a full schema, like this one, is always cast in numerical terms.

The new value product of the year's labour that is created in the natural form of means of production (which can be broken down into $v + s$) is equal to the constant capital value c in the product of the other section of the year's labour reproduced in the form of means of consumption. If it were smaller than IIc [that is, c_2], then department II could not completely replace its constant capital; if it were larger, then an unused surplus would be left over. In both cases, the assumption of simple reproduction would be destroyed. (VIII:483–4)

Note that condition (F) and the conditions (D) and (E) each imply each other. Representation (F) specially emphasises the interconnection between the two departments as revealed in their mutual exchange.

2.5   *The value of the total product and the value product of labour*
In an alternative formulation the concept of value-added is brought to the fore:

> On the premise of simple reproduction ... the total value of the means of consumption annually produced is equal to the annual value product, i.e., equal to the total value produced by the labour of the society in the course of the year, and the reason why this must be the case is that with simple reproduction this entire value is consumed ... for the capitalists in department II, the value of their product breaks down into $c + v + s$ [that is, $c_2 + v_1 + s_2$], yet, considered from the social point of view, the value of this product can be broken down into $v + s$. (II:501–2)

Marx formalises this as:[16]

$$x_2 = (v_1 + s_1) + (v_2 + s_2) \tag{G}$$

which has condition (F) at its base.

On the same theme (remember that the numerical schema for department II runs: $2000_c + 500_v + 500_s = 3000_x$) Marx writes:

> As far as the constant value component of this product of department II is concerned ... it simply reappears in a new use-value, in a new natural form, the form of means of consumption, whereas it earlier existed in the form of means of production. Its value has been transferred

---

16   In his notation: $\text{II}_{(c+v+s)} = \text{II}_{(v+s)} + \text{I}_{(v+s)}$.

by the labour process from its old natural form to its new one. But the *value* of this two-thirds of the value of the product, 2000, has not been produced by department II in the current year's valorisation process. (II:503)

Hence, again, the importance of formula G.[17]

Conversely, for department I ($4000_c + 1000_v + 1000_s = 6000_x$) the 4000 constant capital

is equal in value to the means of production consumed in the production of this mass of commodities, a value which reappears in the commodity product of department I. This reappearing value, which was not produced in the production process of department I, but entered it the year before as constant value, as the given value of its means of production, now exists in that entire part of the commodity mass of department I that is not absorbed by department II. (II:498)

Thus we have $c_1 + v_1 + s_1 = x_1 = c_1 + c_2$. Or, in terms of the circuits of *Capital II*, Part One:

$$
\begin{array}{cccccccc}
\text{M} & - & \text{C} \;\{\text{MP} \quad ;\text{LP}\} & \ldots \text{P} \ldots & \text{C}' \;\{\text{MP} & = & x_1\} & - \quad \text{M}' \quad \text{(H)} \\
| & & | \qquad\qquad | & & | & & & | \\
5000 & & 4000c_1 \quad 1000v_1 & & 4000x_1 + 1000x_1 + 1000x_1 & & & 6000
\end{array}
$$

These distinctions gain even more force when explicitly linked to the twofold character of capitalist economic entities, central to Marx's theory (cf. *Capital I*, Ch. 1):

Thus the difficulty does not lie in analysing the value of the social product itself [$c + v + s = 9000$]. It arises when the *value* components of the social product are compared with its *material* components.

---

17   Or in Keynesian symbols: $C = Y$. The question is whether the circuit aspect indicated in the quotation above can be grasped from the Keynesian formula. In the post-Keynes economics there is an ambiguity (at least) as to the meaning of Y. It is considered both 'real' net income as deflated by an index number (value-added in terms of a commodity index) and output (product) as deflated by an index number. This is not meant to be a 'contradiction' – in the post-Keynes economics these are both conceived of as commodity bundles, in each case looked upon from a different aspect. Note that to Keynes himself these indexes would have been a horror: he called them "conundrums".

> The constant portion of value, that simply reappearing, is equal to the value of the part of the social product that consists of means of *production*, and is embodied in this part. The new year's value product = $v + s$ is equal to the value of the part of the annual product that consists of means of *consumption*, and is embodied in this. (II:506; cf. 504)

This is even more forcefully expressed in a later notebook:

> The overall annual reproduction [$c + v + s = x$], the entire product of the current year is the product of the useful labour of this year [$L^u \to x$]. But the value of this total product is greater than the portion of its value which embodies the annual labour, i.e., the labour-power spent during this year [$L^v \to v + s = y$]. The *value product* of the current year, the value newly created during the year in the commodity form [y], is smaller than the *value of the product*, the total value of the mass of commodities produced during the year [x]. (VIII:53)

Here we see the distinction related to the twofold character of the labour process as technical and valorisation process.

2.6 Money circulation and 'the widow's cruse'

Throughout the text much emphasis is on the money circulation within and between the two departments (see also Campbell 1998); a recapitulation is on pp. 491–2; cf. Ch. 17 on the same issue. Especially here we may notice similarities with Quesnay's 'zigzag' in his *Tableau economique*.[18]

In the course of outlining money circulation, Marx formulates the so-called 'widow's cruse' argument – derived in Keynes's *Treatise on Money* (1930) and in Kalecki's 'A macroeconomic theory of business cycles' (1935) and which in Kaldor's (1955/56, p. 85) well-known paraphrase of Kalecki runs: "capitalists earn what they spend, and workers spend what they earn". Marx: "*it is the money that department I itself casts into circulation that realises its own surplus-value*" (VIII:495; his emphasis). And in more general terms (cf. Chapter 17, II:409):[19] "In relation to the capitalist class as a whole, however, the proposition that it

---

[18] In general, however, there is quite a conceptual distance between Quesnay's *Tableau* and Marx's schemes. See also Marx's version of the *Tableau* (1904/10, pp. 308, 378).

[19] Thus Kaldor is wrong when he writes that "this model" [that is, 'his' model] "is the precise opposite of the Ricardian (or Marxian) one" (1955/56, p. 85). See also the end of his footnote 1.

must itself cast into circulation the money needed to realise its surplus-value ... is not only far from paradoxical, it is in fact a necessary condition of the overall mechanism" (VIII:497).

2.7 Maintenance of fixed capital and disproportionate production

In Section 11 of Chapter 20, Marx drops assumption d and considers the effect of the incorporation of fixed capital for his model. Thus in terms of annual reproduction he incorporates constant capital components whose life is longer than a year (cf. VIII:525). For the individual capital, "the part of the money received from the sale of commodities, which is equal to the wear and tear of the fixed capital, is not transformed back again into ... productive capital ... it persists in its money form", that is, hoard formation, to be expended when the fixed capital components have to be replaced (VIII:526). Thus the commodity value "contains an element for depreciation of ... fixed capital" (VIII:528).

For simple reproduction, then, as a "precondition", the annual total of fixed capital to be renewed "has to be equal to the annual wear and tear". "Such a balance accordingly appears as a law of reproduction on the same scale" (VIII:540). Next Marx discusses the two cases in which this equality does not hold. In the first case, fixed capital has to be renewed, for which there has been insufficient production; thus "there would be an insufficient amount of reproduction, quite independent of the monetary relations" (VIII:543). "The reverse happens in the second case, where department I ... has to contract its production, which means a crisis" (VIII:544). Marx emphasises that such "disproportionate production of fixed and circulating capital" ("a factor much favoured by the economists in their explanation of crises") can "arise from the mere *maintenance* of the fixed capital", that is with simple reproduction. "Within capitalist society ... it is an anarchic element" (VIII:545).

2.8 Conclusions to the model for simple reproduction

The first major achievement of the chapter on simple reproduction is the construction of a macroeconomics generally, with its particular emphasis on the twofold character of the capitalist mode of production. This leads Marx to the – now familiar – distinction between "value of the product" (production value) and "value product" (value-added), The second major achievement is to grasp the macroeconomic relations in terms of a two-sector system fitting Marx's approach of general and determinate abstractions. And the third is the general thread in Marx's analysis: to search for the necessary interconnections between the two departments of production. Therefore, rather than the two equations $x_1 = c$, or $x_2 = v + s$, it is the equation $v_1 + s_1 = c_2$ that is central to the analysis [for these equations see p. 230 above]. We will see in §3 that a similar equation also provides the guiding thread for Marx's analysis of the macroeconomics of expanded reproduction.

3 Expanded reproduction

More so than in the previous chapter (Ch. 20), the last chapter (Ch. 21) has the character of an unfinished draft. A main part of the text is a meticulous analysis of how economic growth (twofold) is possible at all. What are the conditions? The import one gets from it is that the two-department abstraction (carried on from the previous chapter) is a powerful analytical instrument. For example, in the course of the analysis Marx is able to grasp all kinds of spiral (multiplier) effects, such as on page 580, where, starting from an accumulation in department I, there results an overproduction in department II, whence a spiral effect influences department I. At times the two-department division is further differentiated (subdivisions within departments) so as to get to grips with particular problems. Perhaps most importantly, his use of the two-department abstraction indeed brings to the fore the problematic of the twofold character of capitalist entities, processes and relations. With the exception of this last issue, Marx's end result seems generally not too complicated – as judged from the point of view of the end of twentieth century economic theory on cycles and growth. However, even if that maturation required some 80 years, the real trail-blazing activity was the way in which the problem of this dynamics of the capitalist economy was posited by Marx.

3.1 *The general frame for the analysis: general assumptions and abstractions*

The chapter on expanded reproduction starts with an analysis of fixed constant capital and the addition to it, which from the side of individual capitals runs in gradual lumps of hoarding (depreciation allowances) and discrete dishoarding (investment); within a department and its branches, one section of capitalists will be engaged in stages of the former ("one-sided sale"), while another section actually buys additional elements of constant capital ("one-sided purchase") (VIII:565–70).[20]

> The fact that the production of commodities is the general form of capitalist production already implies that money plays a role, not just as means

---

20   These monetary aspects are dealt with in detail by Campbell (1998).

of circulation, but also as money capital within the circulation sphere, and gives rise to certain conditions for normal exchange that are peculiar to this mode of production, i.e., conditions for the normal course of reproduction, whether simple or on an expanded scale, which turn into an equal number of conditions for an abnormal course, possibilities of crisis, since, on the basis of the spontaneous pattern of this production, this balance itself is an accident. (VIII:570–1)

However, Marx's aim for this chapter is *not* the analysis of crises, but rather the accidental balance. (In this respect the point of application is similar to that of the 'equilibrium' growth models of Harrod and Domar.) To this end he assumes, even for the case of expanded reproduction, that

    h   "balance exists ... that the values of the one-sided purchases and the one-sided sales cover each other." (VIII:570)
    i   In the same vein, Marx assumes a sufficient monetary accommodation for expanded reproduction (VIII:576).
    j   A further delimitation of the problematic is revealed in the assumption of a sufficient labour force; that is, that "labour-power is always on hand" (VIII:577).

The last assumption, however, is not an analytical one, as Marx for its explanation refers back to *Capital I*.

Nevertheless a problem of potential imbalance – or, rather, of potential overproduction – is central to reproduction on an expanded scale insofar as we consider either a transition from simple to expanded reproduction or a transition to further expansion, that is, to a higher growth path. Marx states: "in order to make the transition from simple reproduction to expanded reproduction, production in department I must be in a position to produce *fewer* elements of constant capital for department II, but all the more for department I" (VIII:572). In effect, then, department I would substitute spending part of surplus-value (s_1) to means of consumption (some equivalent part of c_2) for spending it on additional means of production (which are now to that equivalent available in commodity form from department I). Department II would thus be stuck with a commodity stock to that equivalent: "There would thus be an overproduction in department II, corresponding in value precisely to the expansion of production that took place in department I" (VIII:580).

The 'normal' reaction would be for department II to cut back production, which would be fine if it were to the extent of the means of production they could not get from department I anyway. However, given their overproduction, they might want to cut back production more than that, and thus buy even less means of production: "The over-production in department II might in fact react so strongly on department I ... [that the] latter would thus be inhibited even in their reproduction on the same scale, and inhibited, moreover, by the very attempt to expand it" (VIII:530). We thus have a real paradox. Marx brings up the problem and refers back to it several times, but does not analyse it any further: from the text it is clear that he purposefully wants to abstract from any crisis elements so as to set out the situation of accidental balance (assumption **h**).

3.2 The schemes for expanded reproduction

In setting out expanded reproduction, Marx proceeds on the basis of – apart from the assumptions **h** to **j** just mentioned – the earlier assumptions **b** to **g** [pp. 225 and 227–29 above] (assumption **a** was the one of simple reproduction). However, assumption **f**, about the composition of capital, is sometimes relaxed so as to allow for divergent compositions as between the departments; nevertheless, within a department it remains constant. Apparently, Marx does not aim to set out the transition from simple to expanded reproduction. Indeed, he assumes that:

    k   there has "already been reproduction on an expanded scale" (VIII: 566).

For the analysis of expanded reproduction, Marx uses three numerical schemes, which I refer to as Schemata A, B and C.[21] Marx treats *Schema A* very briefly, and its analysis is apparently a preliminary one (omitted here). Below I present an outline of *Schema B*, which is also the best worked out case in Marx's text. Towards the end of this section I make some remarks on *Schema C*.

Once again these schemes are in numerical form; each with different starting values. For all schemata it is at first sight unclear why these specific starting values in particular have been chosen – only towards the end of the chapter does it become clear that they are meant to be representative cases for three particular circumstances. (Quite apart from this it is also obvious from the text that Marx tried to employ 'easy numbers' for his calculations.)

Each schema (A, B, C) is presented for a sequence of periods, each representing the *production* in that period. At the end of each period capitalists in

---

21   In the text these are mentioned as follows: Schema A = "schema a" (pp. 581–5); Schema B = "first example" (pp. 586–9); Schema C = "second example" (pp. 589–95).

each department make plans ('arrangements') to accumulate capital for an expanded production in the next period (= *intended exchange arrangement*). Thus they aim to use more means of production (c) and labour-power (v) than they did in the running period. However, these plans may not match, for example, the means of production that have actually been produced in the running period, thus there might be over- or underproduction in comparison with these plans. Thus especially for the case of underproduction there may be bottlenecks preventing steady growth. At the end of each period then the confrontation of the realised *production* and the *intended exchange arrangement* gives rise to some *actual exchange arrangement* which is the basis for the next round of production.

Once we are in a situation that the *intended* exchange arrangements match the *actual* arrangements (and therefore also production), and no new changes in parameters occur, we are on a steady growth path. I will call a situation of a fixed set of parameters a 'regime'. Marx then analyses the transition from one regime to another by varying just one parameter, which is the rate of accumulation out of surplus-value for department I (α_1). Particularly he assumes that in department I half of surplus-value is being accumulated; the rate for the other departments stays, as intended, initially at the old rate (in the proportions of the existing compositions of capital in each department).[22]

In the *way* Marx makes his model work (at least for Scheme B, as we will see) there is only one period of *transition* from the old regime to the new one. Hence starting from a steady state regime in period 1, and changing the regime at the end of that period (intended), a new steady state will already be reached in period 3.

Thus we have the sequence as set out in the table on p. 239.

Although I interpret the starting situation (period 1) of each schema as one of proportionality for a specific steady state growth path, Marx does not say this explicitly. Nor does he calculate the steady state parameters for the starting situation (as I will do below). (And as we see later on, his omission to do this may have put him on the wrong track for his conclusions from the model.)

The schemes of production (Ba, Be, Bh) that I present below are identical to the ones that Marx gives. The other schemes (Bb, Bc, Bd, Bf, Bg) are presented by Marx in different and varying formats.

---

22 See pages 586 and 590. Note that for the preliminary Schema A, Marx assumes an intended rate of accumulation of 50% for *both* departments (p. 582). As we will see, that has no effect on the actual rate of accumulation for department II.

Periodisation of the transition between steady states

a.	*period 1*	*production old regime – steady state*
b.	end period 1	intended arrangement for old regime (would old regime have continued; matches a)
c.	end period 1	intended arrangement for new regime (would have to match a)
d.	end period 1	actual arrangement for new regime (= basis for production period 2)
e.	*period 2*	*production new regime – transition*
f.	end period 2	intended arrangement for new regime (would have to match e)
g.	end period 2	actual arrangement for new regime (= basis for production period 3)
h.	*period 3*	*production new regime – steady state*

The following notation is used:
- g = rate of growth;
- u = surplus-value consumed by or via capitalists ('unproductive consumption');
- Δc = surplus-value accumulated in constant capital;
- Δv = surplus-value accumulated in variable capital.

Thus we have for surplus-value (s)

$s = u + \Delta c + \Delta v$

The actual rate of accumulation out of surplus-value (α) is defined as:

$\alpha = (\Delta c + \Delta v) : s$

- α' = rate of accumulation for the old regime;
- α = rate of accumulation for the new regime;
- α^p = the *intended*, or *planned*, rate of accumulation.

The parameters for Marx's scheme (old regime) are only explicit by his numbers. These are for the composition of capital:

$$c_1 : (c_1 + v_1) = \gamma_1 \quad = 0.80 \qquad (7)^{23}$$
$$c_2 : (c_2 + v_2) = \gamma_2 \quad = 0.67 \qquad (8)$$

---

23 Representations (1) to (6) regard definitions that are stated in §3.3.

For the rate of surplus-value:

$$s_1 : v_1 = \varepsilon \qquad = 1 \qquad (9)$$
$$s_2 : v_2 = \varepsilon \qquad = 1 \qquad (10)$$

For the rate of accumulation out of surplus-value:

$$(\Delta c_1 + \Delta v_1) : s_1 = \alpha_1 \qquad = 0.45 \qquad (11)$$
$$(\Delta c_2 + \Delta v_2) : s_2 = \alpha_2 \qquad = 0.45 \qquad (12)$$

Where Δc and Δv have the same proportions as in (7) and (8):

$$\Delta c_1 : (\Delta c_1 + \Delta v_1) = \gamma_1 \qquad = 0.80 \qquad (13)$$
$$\Delta c_2 : (\Delta c_2 + \Delta v_2) = \gamma_2 \qquad = 0.67 \qquad (14)$$

Thus there is no technical change – at least no change in the value composition of capital (assumption **b**).

The remainder of (potential) surplus-value is the 'unproductive consumption' (u) by or via capitalists:

$$u_1 = (1 - \alpha_1) s_1 \qquad (15)$$
$$u_2 = (1 - \alpha_2) s_2 \qquad (16)$$

Thus 'hoarding' is set aside, that is all incomes are expended – at least in the aggregate. (In his text, however, Marx devotes considerable attention to hoarding, for example in the opening section of Chapter 21. Indeed, he conceives of hoarding as crucial to the circulation and reproduction process – see Campbell 1998.)

Schemas B: Expanded Reproduction

I reiterate that for the model below the ratios $c/(c+v)$ and s/v are given and constant. Thus once we have a starting value for e.g. c the numerical values for the other variables follow. *Scheme Ba* sets out the starting point.

Scheme Ba. Period 1: Production old regime – steady state (VIII:586)

	c		v		s		x	growth rate: 9.1%
I	4000	+	1000	+	1000	=	6000	(means of production)
II	1500	+	750	+	750	=	3000	(means of consumption)
	5500	+	1750	+	1750	=	9000	(social gross product)

Since $(x_1-c)/c = (6000-5500)/5500 = 9.1\%$, *Schema Ba* might be a schema of proportionality for a steady growth path of $g = 9.1\%$, if $\alpha_1' = 45.5\%$; $\alpha_2' = 27.3\%$; with

$\Delta c_1/s_1 = 36.4\%$; $\Delta c_2/s_2 = 18.2\%$; and for both departments $\Delta v/s = 9.1\%$. (Marx does not calculate these ratio's.) Equivalently: for such a steady state growth the ratio c_1/c_2 is fixed so that we can find $\Delta c = \Delta c_1 + \Delta c_2$. Next, given $c/(c+v)$ we also find $\Delta v_1 + \Delta v_2 = \Delta v$ From these values then we derive the necessary rates of accumulation $\alpha_1' = (\Delta c_1 + \Delta v_1)/s_1 = 45.5\%$ and $\alpha_2' = (\Delta c_2 + \Delta v_2)/s_2 = 27.3\%$.

Accordingly, had the old regime continued, we would have had the *Scheme Bb*'s intended exchange arrangement at the *end* of period 1 (Marx does not mention this).

Scheme Bb. End period 1: Intended exchange arrangement for old regime (would old regime have continued; matches schema Ba)

	c		v		u		Δv		Δc		x	$(\Delta c + \Delta v)/s$
I	4000	+	1000	+	545	+	91	+	364	=	6000	$\alpha_1 p' = 45.5\% \, [= \alpha_1']$
II	1500	+	750	+	545	+	68	+	137	=	3000	$\alpha_2 p' = 45.5\% \, [= \alpha_2']$
	5500	+	1750	+	1091*	+	159	+	500*	=	9000	

* rounding off

In *Schema Bb*, the u, Δv and Δc are the (intended) destination of the total of profits s. *Schema Bb* matches Schema Ba, so the intended exchange arrangement can also be the actual exchange arrangement ($x_1 = 6000 = c + \Delta c$ and $x_1 = 3000 = v + u + \Delta v$).

The part of the surplus product that is accumulated (Δc and Δv) seems to have a different status from the other components (c, v, u). Although Δv in particular is materially produced within the period under consideration, this part of (potential) surplus-value is only realised within the next, when the extra labour-power is hired (VIII:580–1). The realisation of Δc can be conceived of in the same way (VIII:575). Thus the realisation of these components of scale increase, in a way lags behind. Of course, it applies to all components, and not just the last-mentioned, that their production and circulation – even within a period under consideration – involves complex intertemporal processes:

> The continuous supply of labour-power on the part of the working class in department I, the transformation of one part of departments I's commodity capital back into the money form of variable capital, the replacement of a part of departments II's commodity capital by natural elements of constant capital IIc [that is, c_2] – these necessary preconditions all mutually require one another, but they are mediated by a very complic-

ated process which involves three processes of circulation that proceed independently, even if they are intertwined with one another. The very complexity of the processes provides many occasions for it to take an abnormal course. (VIII:571)

Nevertheless the lagging behind of realisation, Marx concludes, is not the vital point of difference between simple and expanded reproduction:

> Just as the current year concludes ... with a commodity stock for the next, so it began with a commodity stock on the same side left over from the previous year. In analysing the annual reproduction – reduced to its most abstract expression – we must thus cancel out the stock on both sides ... and thus we have the total product of an average year as the object of our analysis. (VIII:581)

Now instead of carrying on at the old regime (Schema Bb) at the end of period 1, department I decides to increase the rate of accumulation (department II intends to maintain the old rate). Thus Marx fixes $α_1 = 50\%$ per cent and then analyses the transition numerically. For this he takes as starting point the condition for simple reproduction $(v_1 + s_1 = c_2)$, *gradually* developing this in the course of the examples into a condition for expanded reproduction.

> It is self-evident that, on the assumption of accumulation, $I_{(v + s)}$ [that is, $v_1 + s_1$] is greater than II_c [that is, c_2], ... since (1) department I incorporates a part of its surplus product into its own capital and transforms ... $[Δc_1]$ of this into constant capital, so that it cannot simultaneously exchange this ... for means of consumption; and (2) department I has to supply the material for the constant capital needed for accumulation within department II $[Δc_2]$ out of its surplus product. (VIII:590).

Thus we have:

$$(v_1 + s_1) - Δc_1 = c_2 + Δc_2 \qquad\qquad\text{(I)}$$

or

$$(v_1 + u_1) + Δv_1 = c_2 + Δc_2 \qquad\qquad\text{(J)}^{24}$$

---

24 This also derives from the balance equation:
$x_1 = (c_1 + Δc_1) + (c_1 + Δc_2)$
or from:
$x_2 = (v_1 + u_1 + Δv_1) + (v_2 + u_2 + Δv_2)$

In further presenting the numerical schemes, I will indicate for each schema whether it satisfies this condition. Marx does not do this. Again he derives generalisations *from* his numerical schemes. Thus they are not illustrations, but rather heuristic tools. So, for schema Bb, above, we have the condition satisfied, as 1000 + 545 + 91 = 1500 + 136. Following on from the change in the rate of accumulation ($\alpha_1 = 50\%$) we get, instead of this schema, the following intended arrangement at the end of period 1 (*Scheme Bc*).

Scheme Bc. End of period 1: intended arrangement for new regime (would have to match Ba)

	c	v	u	Δv	Δc	x	$(\Delta c + \Delta v)/s$
I	4000 +	1000 +	500 +	100 +	400 =	6000	new regime: $\alpha_1^p = 50\%$
II	1500 +	750 +	545 +	68 +	137 =	3000	old regime: $\alpha_2^p = 27\%$
	5500 +	1750 +	1045 +	168 +	537 =	9000	

With these plans (*Scheme Bc*) there is imbalance, the intended arrangement does not match production (Ba):

$(v_1 + u_1) + \Delta v_1 < c_2 + \Delta c_2$ \hfill [1600 < 1637]

This situation cannot be. There are fewer means of production on offer (6000) than there is intended demand for (5500 + 537). Conversely there are more means of consumption on offer (3000) than the intended demand (1750 + 1045 + 168). So what happens? In fact Marx lets the course of development be dictated by department I as they hold the means of production. (Note that it is assumed there are no price changes.) Thus department I fulfils its plans and department II is stuck with a shortage of means of production (37), plus an equivalent unsold stock of commodities for consumption. However, it will then hire proportionally less extra labour-power (from 68 to 50) giving rise to an extra stock of 18. (Thus we have the paradox for department II: eager to expand at overcapacity. If department II were to react to its overcapacity by decreasing demand for means of production from department I, we would have the same paradox for department I. In sum, a downward spiral would be plausible. Cf. §3.2.) Marx shortcuts the transition, apparently because he wants to make the strongest possible case for 'balance', by assuming that department II capitalists absorb the stock of means of consumption (37 + 18) by consuming it unproductively, thus realising their surplus-value to that extent. (We see the 'widow's cruse' in effect – §2.6.) Thus we get the arrangement of *Scheme Bd* (the differences from the previous Scheme Bc are in italics).

Scheme Bd. End of period 1: actual arrangement for new regime (= basis for production period 2)

	c		v		u		Δv		Δc		x	(Δc + Δv) / s
I	4000	+	1000	+	500	+	100	+	400	=	6000	$\alpha_1 = 50\%$
II	1500	+	750	+	600	+	50	+	100	=	3000	$\alpha_2 = 20\%$
	5500	+	1750	+	1100	+	150	+	500	=	9000	

(where condition (J) is met: 1000 + 500 + 100 = 1500 + 100).

Scheme Bd is the 'rational' reaction for department II to have; $\alpha_2 = 20\%$ being the result. In effect the plan for department I to increase the rate of accumulation out of surplus-value, results in a decreased rate for department II (and this, according to Marx, is the only way in which an (extra) expansion can come about: VIII:572). For the next period the production is as in *Scheme Be*.

Scheme Be. Period 2: production new regime – transition (VIII: 587)

	c		v		s		x	growth rate
I	4400	+	1100	+	1100	=	6600	$g_1 = 10\%$
II	1600	+	800	+	800	=	3200	$g_2 = 6.7\%$
	6000	+	1900	+	1900	=	9800	

Consequently in *Scheme Be* the rate of growth for department I has increased, to 10% and that for II has decreased to 6.7% (both initially at 9.1%).

For the end of period 2 (*Scheme Bf*), Marx then (implicitly) assumes that department II intends to reach the old rate of accumulation out of surplus-value ($\alpha_2' = 27.3\%$; $\Delta c_2/s_2 = 18.2\%$, that is, 146) and moreover to catch up with the former level of accumulation (in means of production 36). Thus the intended Δc_2 becomes 146+36=182. Department I maintains $\alpha_1 = 50\%$.

Scheme Bf. End of period 2: intended arrangement for new regime (would have to match Be)

	c		v		u		Δv		Δc		x	(Δc + Δv) / s
I	4400	+	1100	+	550	+	110	+	440	=	6600	$\alpha_1^p = 50\%$
II	1600	+	800	+	527	+	91	+	182	=	3200	$\alpha_2^p = 34\%$
	6000	+	1900	+	1077	+	201	+	622	=	9800	

In *Scheme Bf*, again $(v_1 + u_1) + \underline{\Delta} v_1 < c_2 + \Delta c_2$ [1760 < 1782], and again department I can dictate the course and again department II absorbs the potential overproduction (22 plus 11, since labour-power hired decreases proportionally). Accordingly we have the exchange arrangement of *Scheme Bg* (differences from schema Bf in italics).

Scheme Bg. End of period 2: arrangement for new regime (= basis for production period 3)

	c		v		u		Δv		Δc		x	$(\Delta c + \Delta v)/s$
I	4400	+	1100	+	550	+	110	+	440	=	6600	$\alpha_1 = 50\%$
II	1600	+	800	+	560	+	80	+	160	=	3200	$\alpha_2 = 30\%$
	6000	+	1900	+	1110	+	190	+	600	=	9800	

(Where condition J, i.e., $(v_1 + s_1) - \Delta c_1 = c_2 + \Delta c_2$ is met: 1100+550+110=1600+160.)

In *Scheme Bg* Department II has recovered part of the former level of accumulation, but not all. As a result the schema for the next period is that of *Scheme Bh*.

Scheme Bh. Period 3: production new regime (new steady state) (VIII:588)

	c		v		s		x	growth rate
I	4840	+	1210	+	1210	=	7260	$g_1 = 10\%$
II	1760	+	880	+	880	=	3520	$g_2 = 10\%$
	6600	+	2090	+	2090	=	10780	

With *Schema Bh* we are at the new steady state growth path. From now on all entries can increase at a growth rate of 10% ($g = 10\%$ for both departments). Department II cannot catch up with accumulation any further, so α_2 stays at 30%. (Though for this example it will have caught up in effect after two more periods, since the growth rate has risen.) Marx calculates the schema for three more periods (VIII:589). So much for Schemas B.[25]

---

25   In the literature the object of Marx's reproduction scheme is variously appreciated, especially the status of its 'accidental balance'. In my view Marx sets out the best possible case

As has been said above, Marx's schemes are not illustrations; they are tools for arriving at a generalisation. He (implicitly) applies the formula $(v_1 + s_1) - \Delta c_1 = c_2 + \Delta c_2$ (condition J) in all his examples, and explicitly derives it from them (pp. 590 and 593). Nevertheless, at the very end of the text (595–7), when Marx is preparing to draw general conclusions from his schemes, he once again falls back on the modified simple reproduction condition $v_1 + s_1 = c_2$ (condition F). Why? The easy answer is to refer to the unfinished shape of the text: it

---

for capitalism (a case that lives up to the system's self-image), showing how unlikely it would be for its conditions to be met. As will be shown in more detail below, the difference between the 'intended' or 'planned' and the realised rate of accumulation is central to Marx's account. (In later theories of the business cycle a similar difference is that between 'ex ante' and 'ex post' variables.) Closest to my own account is that of Desai (see below). A review of that literature is beyond the scope of this chapter therefore I restrict myself to a few comments on three well known scholars in the field.

I cannot agree with Foley's (1986, p. 85) interpretation of what Marx is doing: it is not the case that Marx's *initial* schemes (period 1) were meant to represent reproduction for the *new* rate of accumulation (which they clearly cannot, as Marx indicates). Foley suggests that Marx merely wanted to find an adequate schema for 'period 1' and that the "discrepancy" between the initial schema and the rate of accumulation "annoyed Marx", and that he therefore "devoted several pages of his notes to the attempt to find a schema that would exhibit proportional expanded reproduction". No, Marx analyses the *process of change* following on from a change in the rate of accumulation.

Koshimura (1975, pp. 17–19) equally neglects the transitional process.

Morishima (1973) hardly analyses the properties of Marx's schemes of expanded reproduction or the transitional process (pp. 117–20), concerned as he is to "replace" Marx's "special investment function" (department I's rate of accumulation determining the course) by what he considers the "more reasonable" case for which capitalists of departments I and II "have the same propensity to save" (p. 122). Whilst this precludes him from getting grips with the logic of the schemes themselves, his exercise is of interest. In Morishima's reconstruction the model is one of unstable growth (with, depending on the compositions of capital, either explosive oscillations or monotonic divergence from the balanced grow path – p. 125). The account of Harris (1972) is along similar lines.

Desai (1979, pp. 147–53, 161–71) – although he takes a somewhat different view of the periodisation from that outlined above – appreciates the 'ex ante' versus 'ex post' character of Marx's schemes. His account de-emphasises the level of abstraction at which the schemes operate and, consequently, we differ about the interpretation of the aim of the schemes. Desai also thinks that the dimensions of the schemes are 'labour-values' (so does Mandel 1978, p. 38) and that the schemes fail "to pose the problem of expanded reproduction in the price domain". On the first point he is wrong (at least, Marx says otherwise, for example on p. 473) and on the second he neglects Marx's view about its irrelevance for the problem at hand (see my comment on assumption f). Finally, and relatedly, he neglects Marx's emphasis on the twofold character of the entities he deals with. Therefore I cannot agree that Marx's problematic is "entirely confined to the circuit of commodity capital". (I do not want to disclaim the Marxian theories of these three authors in this field; however, I am concerned here strictly with Marx's reproduction theory.)

was perhaps meant to be followed by a piece indicating the relevant difference between the conditions for simple and expanded reproduction.

However, there is another explanation, which directly relates to Marx's examples. Note that his generalisations (595–7) follow just after setting out the schema that is set out below, *Schema C* (590–95). The problem is not so much that he takes the formula $v_1 + s_1 = c_2$ for a *starting point* of the analysis. Indeed, with *Schema C*, Marx takes an example for which this formula does *not* apply in the initial situation – as it did for Schemata B and A.[26] The point is that *Schema C* is an unlucky example (though, since Marx neglects to calculate the relevant *initial* properties of his schemes – especially the rates of accumulation and growth – he seems unaware of this). In fact, with his *Schema C*, he describes the transition to a *decreasing* rate of accumulation and growth, whilst it is apparently meant to describe (further) expansion, taking off with a rate of accumulation of 50% for department I as in all his examples.

Schema C: Expanded Reproduction; Production, Period 1, Initial Situation

	c		v		s		x	growth rate: 9.1%
I	5000	+	1000	+	1000	=	7000	(means of production)
II	1430	+	286*	+	286*	=	2002	(means of consumption)
	6430	+	1286	+	1286	=	9000	(social gross product)

* Marx has 285 here.

---

26 Schema A has the same relevant properties as Schema B, except that it is somewhat simpler as the compositions of capital are equal. Its initial make-up is:

Schema A: expanded reproduction; production, period 1, initial regime

	c		v		s		x
I	4000	+	1000	+	1000	=	6000
II	1500	+	375*	+	375*	=	2250
	5500	+	1375	+	1375	=	8250

* Marx has 376, apparently to facilitate the calculations.
This might be a scheme of proportionality for a steady growth path of g = 9.1% (6000–5500/5500), if for both departments $\Delta c/s$ = 36.4%; $\Delta v/s$ = 9.1%; hence α' = 45.5% (Marx does not mention this). The new rate of accumulation increases to α_1 = 50%. Note that for the new regime (end period 1) it just happens to be the case that $v_1 + u_1 = c_2$. But the same

Schema C might be a schema of proportionality for a steady growth path of $g = 8.9\%$ if for both departments $\Delta c/s = 44.3\%$; $\Delta v/s = 8.9\%$; hence $\alpha' = 53.2\%$ (Marx does not calculate these ratios). The new rate of accumulation *decreases* to $\alpha_1 = 50\%$.

For our purposes we do not need to go through this example any further (in the end, the new growth rate will slow down to 8.3%). Indeed, for the new situation, $(v_1 + u_1) < c_2$ (that is, $1500 < 1430$). What *is* relevant, however, and whence we have potential *overproduction* in department I, is that $(v_1 + u_1) + \Delta v_1 > c_2 + \Delta c_2$ (that is, $1000 + 500 + 83 > 1430 + 127$, thus $1583 > 1557$).

3.3 A formal recapitulation of the model for expanded reproduction: conclusions

Marx's main tool, as has been indicated, is numerical schemes with some elementary formalisation. Thus, although we do not find the formalisation given below in the text, this *type* of formalisation may be said to be in their spirit.

Apart from the properties of the model for expanded reproduction described below, we have the following assumptions, as discussed earlier on:
– prices do not change (or prices are equal to values) (assumption **b**);
– there is no fixed capital (or it is used up within the production period) (assumption **d**);
– there is no foreign trade (assumption **g**);
– monetary accommodation is sufficient (assumption **i**);
– sufficient labour-power is available (assumption **j**).

Below the assumptions and equations marked * are identical to the ones for simple reproduction. (Symbols are defined at the beginning of §2.4 and in §3.2 below the table 'Periodisation of the transition between steady states' [see p. 239].)

We have the system:

$$c_1 + v_1 + s_1 = x_1 \qquad (1)^*$$
$$c_2 + v_2 + s_2 = x_2 \qquad (2)^*$$
$$c + v + s = x \qquad (3)^*$$

There are three definitions for aggregation:

$$c_1 + c_2 = c \qquad (4)^*$$
$$v_1 + v_2 = v \qquad (5)^*$$
$$s_1 + s_2 = s \qquad (6)^*$$

---

applied to Scheme B! Apparently Marx is then led to take this formula – much akin to the simple reproduction condition (F) – as the starting point for his analysis.

We have four equations fixating the dynamics of the structure of production: in each department, one for the value composition of capital ($c/(c + v)$) and one for the rate of surplus-value (s/v):

$$c_1 : (c_1 + v_1) = \gamma_1 \qquad (7)^*$$
$$c_2 : (c_2 + v_2) = \gamma_2 \qquad (8)^*$$
$$s_1 : v_1 = \varepsilon \qquad (9)^*$$
$$s_2 : v_2 = \varepsilon \qquad (10)^*$$

(These 10 equations, together with the condition $v_1 + s_1 = c_2$ (condition F) comprise the model for *simple reproduction* analysed in §2.)

The ratios γ and ε may in principle be estimated; here, however, they are fixed, for analytical purposes.

For the model of *expanded reproduction* the crucial element is α, the rate of accumulation out of surplus-value (commented upon below), which is defined as follows:[27]

$$(\Delta c_1 + \Delta v_1) : s_1 = \alpha_1 \qquad (11)$$
$$(\Delta c_2 + \Delta v_2) : s_2 = \alpha_2 \qquad (12)$$

Where Δc and Δv have the same proportions as in (7) and (8):

$$\Delta c_1 : (\Delta c_1 + \Delta v_1) = \gamma_1 \qquad (13)$$
$$\Delta c_2 : (\Delta c_2 + \Delta v_2) = \gamma_2 \qquad (14)$$

Thus there is no technical change – at least no change in the value composition of capital (assumption **b**).

The remainder of (potential) surplus-value is the 'unproductive consumption' (u) by or via capitalists:

$$u_1 = (1 - \alpha_1) s_1 \qquad (15)$$
$$u_2 = (1 - \alpha_2) s_2 \qquad (16)$$

Thus 'hoarding' is abstracted from.

The rates of accumulation, α_1 and α_2, may in principle be estimated (elsewhere Marx further theorises α as a necessary force in capitalism). Here, however, α_1 is fixed, for analytical purposes; α_2, on the other hand, is taken for a *semi-variable*. Its starting intended value is that of the previous period (see below), but within the period it acts as a *result*. Unproductive consumption u_2 varies accordingly. In this way, Marx's account short-cuts adaptation after any changes in the system ($\alpha, \gamma, \varepsilon$); it also precludes downward spiral effects: effective overproduction is ruled out. Any potential overproduction (given a rate of

---

[27] Marx uses the term this way (VIII: 595); α is linked to capital accumulated ($c + v$, abstracting from fixed capital) via equations (7) to (10).

accumulation α_1) is absorbed via the adaptation in α_2: either by unproductive consumption (for means of consumption) or by accumulation (for means of production).[28]

Finally expanded reproduction and proportionality is defined by the condition:
$$(v_1 + s_1) - \Delta c_1 = c_2 + \Delta c_2 \qquad (17) = (J)[29]$$
It centres the analysis on the interconnecting exchanges between the two departments.

So we have 17 equations and 19 unknowns, leaving two degrees of freedom. Similarly as for simple reproduction it is within the logic of Marx's reasoning to start from a given accumulation of capital in each department, from which follow numerical values for the other variables (given some initial value for α_2, that is, intended accumulation in department II). However, as α_2 is a semi-variable (its intended value may not be equal to its realised value, or its 'ex ante' value may not be equal to its 'ex-post' value), condition (17) may be violated.

Thus, in the face of the pattern for α, γ and ϵ, the starting values c_1 and c_2 – or $(c_1 + v_1)$ and $(c_2 + v_2)$ – determine the course of things, notably smooth adaptation or *potential* overproduction in department I or department II, with their potential downward spiral effects. Each time condition (17) may turn out to be an inequality 'at the end' of the period, the resulting accumulation of capital ('ex post') thus determining the course for the next period. The following three cases can be distinguished:[30]

(1) Potential overproduction in department II (cf. Schemata A and B), if:[31]
$$(v_1 + u_1) + \Delta v_1 < c_2 + \Delta c_2 \qquad \text{(Marx has } v_1 + u_1 = c_2\text{)}$$
(2) Smooth adaptation, if:
$$(v_1 + u_1) + \Delta v_1 = c_2 + \Delta c_2$$
(3) potential overproduction in department I (cf. Schema C), if:
$$(v_1 + u_1) + \Delta v_1 > c_2 + \Delta c_2$$

---

28 The latter happens in Schema C. Whereas Marx lets department I dictate the course of things (α_1 fixed) – and whilst that may make sense within his line of thought – either or both of α_1 and α_2 might in principle be taken as semi-variables (with 'ex ante' and 'ex post' divergences).

29 It can be derived directly from either $x_1 = c + \Delta c$ or $x_2 = v + u + \Delta v$.

30 As I have indicated in §3.2 (under Scheme Bb, just after condition J [pp. 242–43 above]), Marx sets out the interconnection in his numerical schemes; not quite, however, as generalisations. Nevertheless the latter are not difficult to derive from his schemes.

31 I did not say much about the preliminary Schema A (see footnote 26 – p. 247 above).

In effect the process of adaptation runs as follows. Ensuing upon a (positive) change in the rate of accumulation from a previous α´ to a new intended increased α (requiring a relative increase of department I), (new) proportionality is established via a readaptation of the rates of accumulation α_1 and α_2. In Marx's model the period of transition is short-cut by a pre-emptive readaptation for especially α_2, thus absorbing any overproduction and evading downward spirals.

In other words, upon the change of α_1' to α_1 the Δc_1 (that is, $\alpha_{1*}\gamma_{1*}\, s_1$) is a constant fraction of c_1, whence we have a constant rate of growth for department I. However $(v_1 + u_1) + \Delta v_1$ [that is, $v_1 + (1-\alpha_1)s_1$] is also a constant fraction of c_1; at the same time it determines $c_2 + \Delta c_2$ [that is, $c_2 + \alpha_2 + \alpha_2(\gamma_{2*}s_2)$]: the extra production of means of production in department I that it does not use up itself – department II cannot have more, only less; however, given the α_2 planned, it absorbs what is available. Therefore department II becomes chained to the growth rate of department I. (In this process of adaptation, department I thus dictates the course. The ownership of means of production for producing means of production is thought of as crucial: department II cannot expand unless I does.)

More so than the chapter on simple reproduction, the chapter on expanded reproduction reveals the defects of an unfinished draft and an unfinished analysis. Guiding Marx's generalisations is an adjustment of the condition for simple reproduction. However, the adjustment is not carried through to its full extent; it is nevertheless effected in the numerical schemes. Even if unfinished, the power of the model is revealed very well. Heuristically it also leaves plenty of room for further analysis of dynamic processes. At the core of the model are the same fundamental macroeconomic abstractions, developed into a two-sector approach, as those of simple reproduction (equations (1) to (3)). Generally Marx succeeds in showing convincingly that, even abstracting from all sorts of further complications, proportionality between the two sectors – or generally, steady-state growth – is most unlikely. In the process of transition from one growth path to another, we saw in effect, as an interesting digression (?), the 'widow's cruse' mechanism: 'capitalists earn what they spend, and workers spend what they earn'.

4 Marx's method for the theory of reproduction and circulation of the social capital

With the case material of the previous sections we are now prepared to return to the initial questions in the introduction. What is the method adopted by

Marx in the Part of *Capital* II, on reproduction and circulation of the social capital? Is the method akin to a modelling approach as we find it in modern orthodox economics? Does the approach fit into a systematic-dialectical methodology? We can be relatively brief in answering the first question. The second will take more time.

4.1   Precursor to the modern conventional economic modelling

Marx's text abounds with elements demonstrating similarities to modern economic modelling approaches. We find a set of explicit assumptions delineating the problematic in its – purposefully – case elements. We are then left with a set of variables and parameters ready for analysing the properties of their interconnection. Generalisations concerning the problematic can be drawn from this analysis. Although the main tool for the analysis is a numerical schema, we also find an elementary formalisation.[32] The approach also contains a heuristic: the findings of an earlier model – simple reproduction – can be carried over to be adjusted for a model dealing with different or more complex phenomena: expanded reproduction.

If we add to this that a dialectics, at least a dialectical jargon, is almost absent from this text, at least apparently so (see below), it is no wonder that of all of Marx's economics this Part especially has much influenced orthodox economics. Of course, that is not just a matter of method. It is also the case that the content of the approach, the construction of a particular macroeconomics, was seen to be fruitful, especially for the theory of the business cycle and of economic growth.

So is this a decisive case for defending the thesis that Marx adopts a method of inquiry in line with formal logic, that is, not different *in principle* from modern orthodox economics approaches? The textual evidence certainly favours this view (this may, of course, be different for other cases).[33]

---

32   Numerical analysis in this field of economics was usual practice until the work of Kalecki (this is set out by Boumans 1997).

33   Moreover, this conclusion is not inconsistent with the view of Marx adopting a 'historical materialist' method of inquiry or a 'historical dialectics'. Historical materialism or historical dialectics might affect (1) the frame within which one places *Capital*, that is, this study of capitalism; (2) the particular questions addressed by Marx; (3) the way of attacking those questions (see, for example, the discussion about a given accumulation of capital and the prevailing ownership of means of production within the context of the degree of freedom in the models of simple and expanded reproduction, as well as the priority given to department I within the dynamics of the latter model in Section 3.3); (4) his ontological and epistemological views; and (5) the categories he adopts (historically specific). All these, however, need not affect his method of reasoning, verification and presentation.

A next question is whether there are any important differences distinguishing Marx's modelling approach from the conventional. In this respect I may emphasise that Marx, as we have seen, adopts as a methodological requirement a particular abstraction procedure: the particular *designation of his representations* at an early phase of the exposition is intended to *anticipate later expositions*, earlier abstractions remain in force at later stages, albeit in modified form. We have seen this prominently in the carrying over of the condition for simple reproduction to expanded reproduction. This is in fact the case for many of the representations in *Capital II*: they are still applicable, in modified form, when their underlying simplifying assumptions are dropped (for example, v:162).

From the perspective of a systematic-dialectical methodology (see below) this requirement is no surprise. Most of the reviewers of Marx that question his systematic *dialectics* have at the same time no doubt that he adopts a systematic in his work. Even if dialectics and its particular way of logical proceeding are suppressed, the methodological requirement for abstractions (in anticipation of later exposition) enforces a *systematic* for presentation, as well as an order for the process of model building. In this case, as with a systematic dialectics, the process of discovery cannot be the same as the process of presentation (an issue much stressed by Marx; see his 1873 Postface to the 2nd edition of *Capital I*).

4.2 First and second thoughts on systematic-dialectics

Let us now consider arguments stemming from this case for the view that Marx adopts a systematic-dialectical method. Two relevant issues will be discussed: first the general point of the (in)compatibility of 'model building' within a systematic-dialectical approach; second the specific point of the notebook status of the text.

For the *first* point I start with a contentious thesis: even if Marx's method were systematic-dialectical, it would not prevent the conceiving of *Capital* as a model of the capitalist economy.[34] In this view, the term 'model' is itself neutral as to a particular logic and method of constructing models. However, since the capitalist system entails contradictory entities, relations and processes, a dialectical logic is most appropriate, as it is able to grasp contradictions. Hegel's

---

34   Many Marxian scholars, though certainly not all, would hesitate to adopt the term 'model' for Marx's or perhaps their own work, even if they do not consider Marx or themselves as working in a systematic-dialectical tradition. This is because they seem to identify economic modelling with some of the modern 'analytical' exaggerations of starting by just 'any' set of assumptions and playing on it with a mathematical tool kit.

logic, in this view, is the proper logic of and for capitalism.³⁵ Several layers (Parts) of *Capital* can next usefully be seen as 'sub-models', the one presented in this article being a case of such a sub-model. In dialectical jargon it would be called a *moment*; that is, "an element considered in itself, which can be conceptually isolated, and analysed as such, but which can have no isolated existence" (Reuten and Williams 1989, p. 22). Indeed the great advantage of a systematic-dialectical method is that it is called upon to connect its 'sub-models' within the systematic whole.³⁶ If my initial thesis of conceiving the whole of *Capital* as a model is for some unacceptable, we may restrict the matter to conceiving particular moments as dialectical models, our case being a possible example.

This view, however, if useful at all, seems not particularly illuminating for the case at hand: a systematic-dialectical logic seems largely absent from it. Undoubtedly that is the first impression one gets from the text, but rather than leaving the point at that, let us list what one might expect for a systematic-dialectical text.

(1) An abstract-general starting point. Of course, for the case at hand this cannot be an all-embracing starting point, as we are already under way (Part Three of *Capital II*). However, the case as a 'moment' may have its own relatively abstract-general starting point. This can be well defended by the macroeconomic abstractions that Marx starts with.

(2) The positing of contradictions. Absent (but see below).

(3) The transcendence of contradiction. Consequently absent.

(4) Along with 2–3, a gradual conceptual progress, in layers of abstraction, towards concretisation, distinguishing necessary from contingent moments. Although apparently not *along with* 2–3, one can show that aspects of this are happening in the text: notably the very move from simple to expanded reproduction (even if we were not to agree with Marx that the former is in some way essential – he *does* argue for it); and along with it there is obviously conceptual progress on the notions of reproduction and circulation, including money (even if this has not been emphasised in the present article); indeed, after Part

---

35 See Arthur (1993). This reference to Arthur is not meant to imply that he shares this view of models. Of course, these issues can be taken separately. One can hold that Hegelian dialectics is the proper logic for capitalism, while denying that it is compatible with 'modelling'.

36 Note that economists, and perhaps scientists generally, trained in mathematical and formal logical traditions of thought, may find it difficult that dialectical sub-models from different layers (levels of abstraction) are conceptually different from each other. To put it in orthodox language: if chapter 1 of a systematic-dialectical work, seemingly, defines money, the term 'money' may have a different meaning (richer, less abstract) some chapters later on. Thus in fact 'definitions' are not fixed in a dialectical method.

Three, we have a better grasp of Part One. A possible distinction between necessary and contingent moments, however, is awkward in the text, especially if we consider 'balance' and the 'normal imbalance' or even crisis. The text is unclear on this point. On the one hand Marx convincingly shows the 'knife edge' of balance, whereas on the other at least a degree of balance must prevail for the system to exist at all (necessity). Of course, this would have been an obvious point for grasping dialectically. So perhaps we can grant this point, though, to say the least, with a dialectics suppressed.

(5) Along with 2–3, showing the systematic interconnection of what is theorised, within the whole of the object of inquiry. Again, although apparently not *along with* 2–3, the interconnection is shown: first that with the earlier parts of *Capital II*, as well as with *Capital I* (see Arthur and Reuten 1998), secondly within the theory at hand (Part Three) the interconnection of the elements theorised ranks high.

(6) Points 1–5 together determine the systematic for the proceeding. Generally transcendence of contradiction and the new problems created by it show the insufficiency of the previous theorisation, and hence the way to proceed. Given the absence of contradiction and transcendence, at least explicitly, this kind of systematic seems absent from the text (even if there is the systematic of 'anticipative abstraction' referred to above).

Thus, on second thoughts, considering the six points together, perhaps the case is not that clear-cut methodologically? It is even less so if we bear in mind the emphasis in the text on the twofold character of the entities (material, value – cf. §2.1 and §2.5). This, in retrospect, seems very much to guide Marx's approach in this part, at least as far as the positing of the problems is concerned (in my view, the citations given in §2.5 are the most thought-provoking of the whole text). The twofold character seems after all central to Marx's schemes (which is no surprise in the face of the rest of *Capital*, especially Book I, Chapter 1).[37] Unfortunately, and this is perhaps misleading, the theme is not carried through systematically – at least not in a clear way. Manifestly so, not only do the major entities discussed (c_2, v_1, and so on) have a twofold character (value, material), but there is also a 'redoubling' in that they stand for two material guises, and their two value forms (for example, c_2 is means of production as well as means of consumption – emphasised in the guises it goes through in the capital circuit). This might have been expressed in a different notation, perhaps akin to the circuit models of Part One.

---

37   Even if that chapter in particular is a major achievement, one may have some dialectical complaints to make about it (see Reuten 1993).

It must be emphasised that none of this affects the fact that within a dialectical presentation one can build in analytical 'moments'. *Within* its restrictedness there is nothing wrong with formal logic or a formal model. They are indispensable tools in research practice; formal logic and formal modelling can have a proper place within systematic dialectics (cf. Reuten and Williams 1989, p. 27). Rather it is the other way around that is difficult.

So where does this leave us? From point, 1–6 above we saw that, dialectically, a main defect of the text is that contradictions and their transcendences are not made explicit, and do not explicitly lead the systematic conceptually. However, at the same time, there *is* the emphasis in the text on the twofold character of entities, which is the major contradiction of the system. In the text it is perhaps too often expressed abstractly, rather than at the level of concreteness that we have already attained. Nevertheless this is an obvious anchor for a systematic-dialectical presentation. All this, however, does not lead to the conclusion that this *is* a systematic-dialectical text. It is not. However, there are arguments for conceiving it as *compatible* with a systematic-dialectical method.

This takes us to the *second* point, which can be dealt with briefly: the notebook status of Book II of *Capital*. It is rather speculative to argue about something that *might* have been if … Nevertheless, to answer the leading question of this article, this notebook status must be taken into account. All the more so since it is not only that, as we have just concluded, the Part Three text we have considered is compatible with a systematic-dialectical approach, but we also have the textual evidence of *Capital I*, and of Part One of *Capital II* (see Arthur 1998) which are written in a dialectical vein, even if perhaps not perfectly from several points of view. I have no doubt whatsoever (partly because of personal experience) that a dialectical presentation is often preceded by an *analytical* stage of inquiry: even more so for the study of new problems. The dialectical hard work lies in the way of *systematising* the material one has at hand. Indeed empirical inquiry and analytical inquiry are the building stages and material for a systematic-dialectic. From this we cannot answer the question whether Marx intended a systematic-dialectical presentation, let alone that of how the *kind of analysis* we find in the Book II manuscripts might have been incorporated in a dialectical presentation. It is rather that this notebook status strengthens the conclusion that the text we have considered is compatible with a systematic-dialectical methodology.[38]

---

38   Note that systematic-dialectics may not be inconsistent with historical dialectics in the same five ways as indicated in note 33. However, in this case, these five issues cannot be isolated from the specific systematic-dialectical reasoning, verification and presentation (starting point, contradiction, conceptual development, levels of abstraction, and so on).

Conclusions

This case is fascinating. We see the construction of a macroeconomics with a powerful two-department division. We see the core problems related to the fact that a capitalist economy must materially reproduce itself for survival (generic) but cannot, inherently, do this without being a monetary economy at the same time (determinate). The two processes may not coincide. Consequently we see the 'knife edge' of balanced growth together with the potentialities for economic crisis, and thus the important groundwork for later theory on business cycles. Methodologically the case is just as intriguing. It is a wonderful work from the formal-logical conventional modelling point of view. How, then, may the case fit other apparently systematic-dialectical parts of *Capital*? As I have indicated, the text *is not* systematic-dialectical, although it contains elements for developing such an approach. While the text is *compatible* with both methodological positions, the better arguments are on the conventional modelling side.

References

Note 1: All years in brackets are the original dates of publication as referred to in the text; the edition quoted from may differ and is provided where appropriate.
Note 2: Several references are to articles in the book in which the current article initially appeared (at the time of writing available as their earlier drafts).

Arthur, Christopher J. 1993, 'Hegel's *Logic* and Marx's *Capital*', in Moseley (ed.) 1993, pp. 63–87.
Arthur, Christopher J. 1998, 'The fluidity of capital and the logic of the concept', in Arthur and Reuten (eds) 1998, pp. 95–128.
Arthur, Christopher J., and Geert Reuten (eds) 1998, *The circulation of capital: essays on volume II of Marx's 'Capital'*, London: Macmillan.
Backhaus, Hans-Georg 1969, 'Zur Dialektik der Wertform', in *Beiträge zur Marxistischen Erkenntnistheorie*, edited by Alfred Schmidt, Frankfurt a.M.; Engl. trans. M. Eldred and M. Roth, 'On the dialectics of the value-form', *Thesis Eleven* 1 (1980): 99–120.
Backhaus, Hans-Georg 1992, 'Between philosophy and science: Marxian social economy as critical theory', in *Open Marxism: volume 1, dialectics and history*, edited by Werner Bonefeld, Richard Gunn, and Kosmas Psychopedis, London: Pluto Press, pp. 54–92.
Boumans, Marcel 1997, 'Built-in justification', *Amsterdam working papers in the history and methodology of economics*, University of Amsterdam, Faculty of Economics.

Campbell, Martha 1998, 'Money in the circulation of capital', in Arthur and Reuten (eds) 1998, pp. 129–57.

Desai, Meghnad 1979, *Marxian economics*, Oxford: Basil Blackwell.

Eldred, Michael 1984, *Critique of competitive freedom and the bourgeois democratic state*, Copenhagen: Kurasje.

Eldred, Michael, Marnie Hanlon, Lucia Kleiber, and Mike Roth 1982/85[1], 1984[2], 'Reconstructing value-form analysis 1–4', *Thesis Eleven* 4, 1982; 7, 1983; 9, 1984; 11, 1985; modified as 'A value-form analytic reconstruction of "Capital"' Appendix to Eldred 1984, pp. 350–487.

Foley, Duncan K. 1986, *Understanding Capital: Marx's economic theory*, Cambridge, MA: Harvard University Press.

Gehrke, Christian, and Heinz D. Kurz 1995, 'Karl Marx on physiocracy', *The European Journal of the History of Economic Thought* 2/1: 53–90.

Harris, Donald J. 1972, 'On Marx's scheme of reproduction and accumulation', *Journal of Political Economy* 80 (3–1): 503–22.

Hegel, G.W.F. 1812, 1831, *Wissenschaft der Logik*, Engl. trans of the 1923 Lasson edn. A.V. Miller, *Hegel's science of logic*, Atlantic Highlands, NJ: Humanities Press, 1989.

Hegel, G.W.F. 1817, 1830, *Enzyklopädie der Philosophischen Wissenschaften in Grundrisse I, Die Wissenschaft der Logik*, Engl. trans of the 3rd edn, T.F. Geraets, W.A. Suchting, and H.S. Harris, *The encyclopaedia logic*, Indianapolis: Hackett Publishing, 1991.

Horowitz, David (ed.) 1968, *Marx and modern economics*, New York: Monthly Review Press.

Kaldor, Nicolas 1955/56, 'Alternative theories of distribution', *Review of Economic Studies* 23: 94–100; reprinted in Amartya Sen (ed.), *Growth economics*, Harmondsworth: Penguin Books, 1970, pp. 81–91.

Kalecki, Michal 1935, 1952, 'A macroeconomic theory of business cycles', *Econometrica* July; revised as 'The determinants of profits', in *Theory of economic dynamics*, New York: Kelley, 1969.

Koshimura, Shinzaburo 1975, *Theory of capital reproduction and accumulation*, edited by J.G. Schwartz, Engl. trans. Toshihiro Ataka, Dumont Press Graphix, Kitchener (Ontario); first published, in Japanese, in 1956.

Klein, Lawrence R. 1947, 'Theories of effective demand and employment', *The Journal of Political Economy* April; reprinted in Horowitz 1968, pp. 138–75.

Leontief, Wassily 1938, 'The significance of Marxian economics for present-day economic theory', *American Economic Review Supplement* 28 (1), March; reprinted in Horowitz 1968, pp. 88–99.

Mandel, Ernest 1978, 'Introduction' to Marx 1885, English trans. D. Fernbach, pp. 11–79.

Marx, Karl 1867[1], 1890[4], *Das Kapital, Kritik der politischen Okonomie, Band I, Der Produktionsprozess der Kapitals*, Engl. trans. Ben Fowkes, *Capital, a critique of political economy, volume one*, Harmondsworth: Penguin Books, 1976.

Marx, Karl 1885[1], 1893[2], ed. F. Engels, *Das Kapital, Kritik der Politischen Ökonomie, Band II, Der Zirkulationsprozess des Kapitals*, MEW 24, Berlin: Dietz Verlag, 1972; Engl. trans. Ernest Untermann, 1907; David Fernbach, *Capital, a critique of political economy, vol. II*, Harmondsworth: Penguin Books, 1978.

Marx, Karl 1894, ed. F. Engels, *Das Kapital, Kritik der Politischen Ökonomie, Band III, Der Gesamtprozess der kapitalistischen Produktion*, MEW 25, Berlin: Dietz Verlag, 1972; Engl. trans. Ernest Untermann 1909; David Fernbach, *Capital, a critique of political economy, vol. III*, Harmondsworth: Penguin Books, 1981.

Marx, Karl 1904/10, 1956/66, ed. K. Kautsky, *Theorien über den Mehrwert* (1904/10); selections first translated 1951 by G.A. Bonner and E. Burns; 2nd edition (1956/66) by Institut für Marxismus-Leninismus, *Theorien über den Mehrwert Teile I, II, III*, MEW 26.1, 26.2, 26.3, Berlin: Dietz Verlag, 1973, 1972, 1972; Engl. edn: *Theories of surplus-value, part I*, ed. S. Ryazanskaya, trans. E. Burns (1963); *part II*, ed. and trans. S. Ryazanskaya (1968); *Part III*, ed. S.W. Ryazanskaya and R. Dixon, trans. J. Cohen and S.W. Ryazanskaya (1971), London: Lawrence & Wishart, 1969, 1969, 1972.

Morishima, Michio 1973, *Marx's economics: a dual theory of value and growth*, Cambridge: Cambridge University Press.

Moseley, Fred (ed.) 1993, *Marx's method in 'Capital': a re-examination*, Atlantic Highlands, NJ: Humanities Press.

Moseley, Fred 1998, 'Marx's reproduction schemes and Smith's dogma', in Arthur and Reuten (eds) 1998, pp. 159–85.

Murray, Patrick 1988, *Marx's theory of scientific knowledge*, Atlantic Highlands, NJ: Humanities Press.

Oakley, Allen 1983, *The making of Marx's critical theory: a bibliographical analysis*, London: Routledge & Kegan Paul.

Reuten, Geert 1993, 'The difficult labour of a theory of social value: metaphors and systematic dialectics at the beginning of Marx's *Capital*', in Moseley (ed.) 1993, pp. 89–113.

Reuten, Geert 1995, 'Conceptual collapses: a note on value-form theory', *Review of Radical Political Economics* 27(3): 10z–10.

Reuten, Geert, and Michael Williams 1989, *Value-form and the state; the tendencies of accumulation and the determination of economic policy in capitalist society*, London: Routledge.

Robinson, Joan 1948, 'Marx and Keynes' (in Italian for *Critica Economica*), in Joan Robinson, *Collected economic papers I* Oxford, 1950; reprinted in Horowitz 1968, pp. 103–16.

Robinson, Joan 1951, 'Introduction' to Rosa Luxemburg (1913), *The accumulation of capital*, London: Routledge and Kegan Paul, 1971, pp. 13–28.

Smith, Tony 1990, *The logic of Marx's Capital: replies to Hegelian criticisms*, Albany: State University of New York Press.

Smith, Tony 1993, 'Marx's Capital; and Hegelian dialectical logic', in Moseley (ed.) 1993, pp. 15–36.

Williams, Michael 1998, 'Money and labour-power: Marx after Hegel, or Smith plus Sraffa?', *Cambridge Journal of Economics* 22(1): 187–98.

CHAPTER 12

Some notes on Marx's macroeconomics *avant la lettre*

The notes below (merely five pages) are written for this book, though they derive mainly from my 2014 article 'Marx' macro-economie *avant la lettre*' that appeared in the Netherlandic journal *Tijdschrift voor Politieke Economie* (TPE-digitaal), 8(3): 97–114.

Contents

Introduction 261
1   'The general law of capitalist accumulation' (*Capital I*, Part Seven)   262
2   'The reproduction and circulation of the total social capital' – the reproduction schemes (*Capital II*, Part Three)   263
References   264

Introduction

Some of the previous chapters alluded to the parts of Marx's *Capital* where he adopts macrosocial and macroeconomic analysis and exposition of the capitalist mode of production: either in some detail or in passing.[1] The current notes expand on some aspects. Although in light of the systematic of the current book these would belong in its Part A (on the three volumes of *Capital*) I decided against that, as this would have required too much detailed anticipation.

In his *Capital* Marx sets out important foundations for 'macroeconomics'. However, because the term macroeconomics dates from 1933 (Ragnar Frisch), this relates to a macroeconomics *avant la lettre*. Lawrence Klein (1980 Nobel Prize winner for his work on macroeconometric models) wrote in 1947: "His [Marx's] theory is probably the origin of macro-economics" (p. 154). I will refer subsequently to Marx's *Capital I* theory of capital accumulation (§1), and his

---

1   In some detail: ch. 11, §2.1–§2.2, §2.8 and conclusions; in passing: ch. 1, summary of §4; ch. 2, §5.3; ch. 9, §1.3; ch. 10, §1 and §4.

Capital II theory of reproduction of the total social capital (§2). Marx's macroeconomic treatment can also be found in *Capital III*, especially its Part Three on the rate of profit cycle, that will be covered in the next part of the current book.

Because we are considering a nineteenth-century work, I will first say something about the terminology. Current key terms such as investment, unemployment and the business cycle hardly existed in Marx's days. Investment was referred to by 'capital accumulation' and for unemployment Marx used the terms 'redundancy' or 'reserve army'.[2] Before Marx, the 'business cycle' was probably not even experienced as a phenomenon (according to Schumpeter – see §1). Marx uses several terms to indicate the phenomenon (such as: periodicity, periodic phases, cycle, alternate expansion and contraction, fluctuations).

1 'The general law of capitalist accumulation' (*Capital I*, Part Seven)

Business cycles are an important part of current macroeconomic studies. Recall the following two elements of *Capital I*, Part Seven (chapter 9 above).

(a) Marx 'lifts' the accumulation of capital and technological change to a social level (in what I called the 'acceleration triple'). He is in fact the first economist to introduce technical change at a macroeconomic level. Furthermore, Marx has been praised for connecting his theory of accumulation with the centralisation of capital.[3]

(b) He describes the course of capitalist development as a cyclical one (citations reproduced from Chapter 9 above).

> The path characteristically described by modern industry, which takes the form of a decennial cycle (interrupted by smaller oscillations) of periods of average activity, production at high pressure, crisis, and stagnation, depends on the constant [*beständigen*] formation, the greater or less absorption, and the reformation of the industrial reserve army (...) Just as the heavenly bodies always repeat a certain movement, once they

---

2 In the 600 pages of Smith's *Wealth of Nations* (1776) the term 'invest' is used only once (in passing, at the end of the work); in Ricardo's *Principles* (1817) the term does not occur. The term 'unemployment' emerges around 1895 and in 1911 it appears for the first time in the *Encyclopaedia Britannica* (Rodenburg 2006, p. 2).

3 See, for example, Landreth and Colander (1994, pp. 203–4). It was also one of the reasons why Marx (after Keynes and Smith) was quoted as number three in the top economists of the second millennium in a poll by Reuters of December 1999 among economists specialised in international economics (Friedman, Schumpeter and Galbraith held positions 4–6).

have been flung into it, so also does social production, once it has been flung into this movement of alternate expansion and contraction. Effects become causes in their turn, and the various vicissitudes of the whole process ... take on the form of periodicity. (Marx, *Capital I*, pp. 785–6)

The appropriate law for modern industry, with its decennial cycles and periodic phases ... is the law of the regulation of the demand and supply of labour by the alternate expansion and contraction of capital ... It would be utterly absurd, in place of this, to lay down a law according to which the movement of capital depended simply on the movement of the population. (Marx, *Capital I*, p. 790)

Note that Marx here describes this cycle empirically, he does not go into the theoretical explanation of cyclical phases and their turns in terms of the 'acceleration triple'. Schumpeter (himself a major twentieth-century business cycle theoretician) comments:

We find practically all the elements that ever entered into any serious analysis of business cycles, and on the whole very little error. Moreover, it must not be forgotten that the mere perception of the existence of cyclical movements was a great achievement at the time. Many economists who went before him had an inkling of it. In the main, however, they focused their attention on the spectacular breakdowns that came to be referred to as "crises". And those crises they failed to see in their true light, that is to say, in the light of the cyclical process of which they are mere incidents. (...) Marx was, I believe, the first economist to rise above that tradition and to anticipate – barring the statistical complement – the work of Clément Juglar. Though, as we have seen, he did not offer an adequate explanation of the business cycle, the phenomenon stood clearly before his eyes and he understood much of its mechanism. Also like Juglar, he unhesitatingly spoke of a decennial cycle "interrupted by minor fluctuations". ... This is enough to assure him high rank among the fathers of modern cycle research. (Schumpeter 1943, pp. 40–1).

2 'The reproduction and circulation of the total social capital' – the reproduction schemes (*Capital II*, Part Three)

The macroeconomic character of Marx's 'reproduction schemes' was discussed in Chapter 11 above.[4] This section adds some casual information.

---

4 The chapter's §2.1–§2.2, §2.8 and the conclusions.

The first is on Marx's term "scheme". In economics the term "model" came into fashion only after 1950. One major twentieth-century founder of macroeconomics and of model building, Tinbergen (the first Nobel Prize laureate in economics – in 1969), in his early work, used the term 'schema' for the later term 'model' (Boumans 1992, p. 39 ff.).

Marx's schemes of reproduction (first published in 1885) played an important role in the development of (early) Marxian theory (e.g. works of Bauer, Luxemburg, Grossman, and Kalecki). The schemes also influenced non-Marxian theories of cyclical development – mainly through Tugan-Baranowski, the first author to take up the schema in his own work in 1894.[5] Tugan-Baranowski, in turn, directly or indirectly influenced business cycle authors such as Aftalion, Cassel, Keynes, W. Mitchell, Spiethoff and Schumpeter (see Reijnders 1998 and Allisson 2021). Another major development from Marx's schemes is that of 'input–output analysis', developed by Leontief (1941, 1953) – for which he was granted the 1973 Nobel Prize in economics.[6]

Klein (mentioned in the Introduction) remarks about Marx's schemes: "Marx laid the groundwork for a complete equation system to determine the level of income (effective demand) but did not build the complete system" (1947, pp. 167–8). In 1974 Samuelson (economics Nobel Prize laureate 1970) writes: "On the basis of his schemes of reproduction one can claim immortal fame for Marx" (1974).

References

Allisson, François 2021, 'Tugan-Baranovsky and the West', *Russian Journal of Economics* 7(1): 19–33. https://www.researchgate.net/publication/350527728

Boumans, Marcel 1992, *A case of limited physics transfer: Jan Tinbergen's resources for re-shaping economics*, Amsterdam: Amsterdam: Thela Thesis/Tinbergen Institute.

Frisch, Ragnar 1933, 'Propagation problems and impulse problems in dynamic economics', in *Economic essays in honour of Gustav Cassel*, London: George Allen & Unwin, pp. 171–205.

Horowitz, David (ed.) 1968, *Marx and modern economics*, New York/London: Monthly Review Press.

---

5 Especially in the theoretical chapters of the 1894 work.
6 This analysis is used still today in the National Account Statistics of most OECD countries. For the link between Marx's schemes and the Leontief input–output analysis, see Lange (1959, ch. 3).

Klein, Lawrence R. 1947, 'Theories of effective demand and employment', *Journal of Political Economy*, April; reprinted in Horowitz (ed.) 1968, pp. 138–75.

Landreth, Harry, and David Colander 1994, *History of economic thought*, 3rd edition, Boston: Houghton Mifflin.

Marx, Karl, *Capital*, volumes I–III, first published in German 1867, 1885 and 1894, English translation by Fowkes and Fernbach, Harmondsworth: Penguin Books, 1976 (from the 4th German edition), 1978 (from the 2nd German edition) and 1981.

Reijnders, Jan 1998, 'Tugan-Baranowsky's breakthrough in business cycle theory', in *History of Continental economic thought*, edited by J. Glombowski, A. Gronert and H. Plasmeijer, Marburg: Metropolis, pp. 211–38.

Rodenburg, Peter 2006, *The construction of instruments for measuring unemployment*, Amsterdam: Thela Thesis/Tinbergen Institute.

Samuelson, Paul A. 1974, 'Insight and detour in the theory of exploitation: a reply to Baumol', *Journal of Economic Literature* 12(1): 62–70.

Schumpeter, Joseph A. 1943[1], 1954[4], *Capitalism, socialism and democracy*, London/New York, Taylor & Francis e-Library, 2003.

Smith, Adam 1776[1], 1791[6], *An inquiry into the nature and causes of the wealth of nations*, volumes I and II, London: Dent & Sons, 1933.

Tugan-Baranovsky, Mikhail 1894, *Industrial crises in contemporary England, their causes and influences on national life*, St. Petersburg: Skorokhodov (in Russian). [2nd Russian edition, 1900, 3rd Russian edition, 1914, German edition, 1901, French edition, 1913].

PART D

Capital III – outlines and comments

∴

Contents

13. Marx's *Capital III*, the culmination of capital (2002) p. 269.
14. Marx's rate of profit transformation: methodological, theoretical and philological obstacles (2009) p. 282.
15. The productive powers of labour and the redundant transformation to prices of production: a Marx-immanent critique and reconstruction (2017) p. 305.
16. The notion of tendency in Marx's 1894 law of profit (1997) p. 337.
17. "Zirkel vicieux" or trend fall? The course of the profit rate in Marx's *Capital III* (2004) p. 365.
18. Accumulation of capital and the foundation of the tendency of the rate of profit to fall (1991) p. 390.
19. From the "fall of the rate of profit" in the *Grundrisse* to the cyclical development of the profit rate in *Capital* (with Peter Thomas; 2011) p. 413.
20. Destructive creativity; institutional arrangements of banking and the logic of capitalist technical change (1998) p. 431.
21. The rate of profit cycle and the opposition between Managerial and Finance Capital; a discussion of *Capital III* Parts Three to Five (2002) p. 448.

Chapter 13 provides a brief outline of *Capital*, Volume III in the light of the earlier two volumes.

Chapters 14 and 15 are on Part Two of Volume III.

Chapters 16–19 are on Part Three of Volume III; the last one compares the Volume III text with the corresponding text of the *Grundrisse* and an 1861–63 manuscript.

Chapter 20 is on, or develops from, Parts Two, Three and Five of Volume III.

Chapter 21 is on Parts Three to Five of Volume III.

Chapters 16–21 treat different aspects of, or expand on, Part Three of Volume III. Given that these chapters were published separately in journals or book collections, it is inevitable that at least a summary of Part Three appears in all these six chapters.

CHAPTER 13

Marx's *Capital III*, the culmination of capital; Introduction

2002 article, originally published in *The culmination of capital: essays on volume III of Marx's 'Capital'*, edited by Martha Campbell and Geert Reuten, London/New York: Palgrave Macmillan, pp. 1–15. The article's final section 3 (introduction to the essays of the 2002 book) has been omitted.

(For its abstract see the Abstracts of all chapters, p. 7.)

Contents

1 "The shapes of the whole process": interpretation and reconstruction   269
2 *Capital III* in light of the first two volumes   273
     2.1 Levels of abstraction   273
     2.2 From *Capital I* and *II* to *Capital III*   274
     2.3 The seven Parts of *Capital III*   275
References   278

This introductory chapter starts with a brief discussion of why writing about Marx's *Capital III* is not only interpretative – this is true for any work – but is also bound to be reconstructive. The next section outlines a general overview of *Capital III*'s seven Parts in the light of the earlier two volumes.[1]

1   "The shapes of the whole process": interpretation and reconstruction

The first volume of Karl Marx's life work *Das Kapital* was published in 1867[1]. When Marx died in 1883 at the age of 64, he left Volumes II and III as unfinished

---

[1] The following authors contributed to the 2002 book: Christopher Arthur, Riccardo Bellofiore, Martha Campbell, Paul Mattick Jr, Fred Moseley, Patrick Murray, Geert Reuten and Tony Smith. Initial versions of the papers were discussed at a week-long working conference at the University of Amsterdam in July 2000. (The authors are part of the International Symposium on Marxian Theory, see https://chrisarthur.net/international-symposium-on-marxian-theory-ismt/.)

manuscripts, which range anywhere from mere notes or outlines to text all but ready for publication. The manuscript for Volume III is a single draft, and, relative to the other volumes, an early one, having been written between 1863 and the end of 1865. It was not until 30 years later, in 1894, that the third volume was published in German; like the second (1885), it was edited by Friedrich Engels. One year after the 1894 publication Engels himself died at the age of 75.[2]

These few biblio-biographical facts are relevant to the interpretation of *Capital* since, for Marx, architectonic and *Darstellung* (presentation) are an essential stage of scientific work. Almost certainly, if Marx had lived long enough to publish Volumes II and III himself, they would have been quite different from the works we now have.[3] Most likely also their difference would have led, in turn, to another revision of Volume I (which Marx had already changed between the first edition and the second of 1873).[4]

The reading of any text, complete or incomplete, of course, involves interpretation – behind the author's back so to speak. There are, however, three particular reasons to be extra cautious in the case of Marx's works. First, as Engels says of his editing in his Preface to *Capital III*:

> I confined this simply to what was most necessary, and wherever clarity permitted I retained the character of the original draft, not even deleting certain repetitions where these grasped the subject-matter *from a different angle or expressed it in another way, as was Marx's custom*. (Engels 1894F, p. 93, emphasis added)

---

2   Regarding the current German and English editions of the book, a transcription of the Volume III manuscripts, from which Engels did his editorial work, was published in 1992 in the *Marx–Engels Gesamtausgabe* (Marx 1894M). The widely used German text identical to Engels's edition of 1894 is published in the *Marx–Engels Werke* (Marx 1894G). The first English translation, by Ernest Untermann, appeared in 1909; a current edition based on it is published by Lawrence & Wishart/Progress Publishers (Marx 1894U). It is also available on disc (Marx 1894D) with full search possibilities, although with different page numbers. A second English translation, by David Fernbach, was published in 1981 (Marx 1894F). It is currently more widely used than the former, which does not imply that the translation is always superior – translation necessarily implies interpretation.

3   That is, if he had lived long enough, and also had enough energy. Marx's last work on *Capital*, which is a draft for the third part of Volume II, probably dates from 1878 (see Oakley 1983, pp. 101–3). After that time his faculties for creative scientific work gradually faded away.

4   Engels remarks in his Preface to the third edition that Marx indeed intended 'to rewrite a great part of the text of the first volume'.

Such repetitions appear not only in Volume III of *Capital* but in the earlier volumes as well. Apart from those related to the draft character of the text, they are due to aspects of Marx's method. In particular, he emphasises throughout the double character of entities in capitalism (material shape and capitalist value-form) and the related differentiation between 'general' (transhistorical) and 'determinate' (capitalist) categories.[5] Further, as Marx's presentation proceeds, it discloses new features of the entities under consideration, so that these are continually reconceptualised (and 'redefined' so to say). Apart from such aspects of method, however, Marx often obviously struggles with the material at hand, either to *find* the most appropriate way of presenting it, *or* indeed to present it from different angles because there *is* more than one appropriate aspect.

Second – and related to the first point – in the view of all the contributors to this [2002] book at least, Marx makes a fundamental break with the political economy and philosophy of his time.[6] Without implying that all my co-authors (see note 1) share this view, I also hold that the initiator of a break can never realise it completely. Because initiators are brought up in the tradition from which they break, their work is shaped by the central concerns of that tradition, and they must, to a considerable extent, speak in its language. Especially in the case of *Capital III*, these central concerns arise, in large part, from Ricardo's theory.[7] It is left to the heirs, setting out from different questions, to unfold all that the break entails – or retreat from it. Hence 'interpreting' the work of the initiator of a break is bound to be an unfolding or a retreating reconstruction. It follows also that there may not be full consistency in the initiator's work. As regards 'interpretation' then, it is generally easier to see a particular interpretation confirmed by the texts than to see it not falsified.

In view of the foregoing, the contributors to this book adopt different stances towards the interpretation of Marx. At one end, Tony Smith (2002) holds that any interpretation of Marx's texts is always a reconstruction. At the other, in Fred Moseley's view (2002), Marx's aims are clear enough to allow for an interpretation close to the intention of the author. Others see a need for reconstruc-

---

5 See Murray (1988) on general versus determinate categories; see also his 2002. Mészáros (1970, p. 79) calls these first order versus second order mediations (cf. Arthur 1986, pp. 11–12).
6 'Break' in the fundamental sense of epistemological rupture (*césure*).
7 This necessary double-mindedness can be detected in both the most heatedly discussed parts of the book, especially the value to price transformation and the tendency of the rate of profit to fall, and those that have attracted less attention, e.g. on rent. See also, concerning especially Marx's theory of value, Reuten 1993, 2000. [Chapters 6 and 5 of the current book.]

tion for several reasons: because of defects in, or of, acknowledged, concurrent theoretical lines in Marx's writing (the presence of different lines is not by itself a problem) and because certain abstract treatments by Marx require further mediation and concretion.

The third reason to be extra cautious in the interpretation of Marx's work, particularly *Capital III*, is more straightforward: the text is clearly influenced by Engels's editing. This should not be read as a criticism of Engels; it is only because of his dedication that Volumes II and III were published at all. As already noted, *Capital III* was published in 1894, eleven years after Marx's death and nine years after the publication of Volume II. In its Preface Engels explains why there was such a delay: political activities, other theoretical work, his health; but the main reason appears to have been the state of Marx's draft for Volume III.[8] Given the state of the manuscript, Engels could never have been successful in all respects. For example, one might complain that he should have taken out repetitious parts (which would have implied a choice of emphasis), that he should not have included chapters that obviously were just notes (which might have concealed the intended architectonic) or that he should have been more specific in indicating his own alterations and interpolations (which might have marred the continuity of the text). In any case, it must be recognised that Engels left his mark on the text.[9] In his Preface Engels writes: 'Wherever my alterations or additions are not simply editorial in character ... I have put the entire passage in pointed brackets and indicated it with my initials' (Engels 1894F, p. 93).[10] We may grant that this was Engels's intention but dispute his claim to have observed the limits he set.[11]

By way of illustration, attention is drawn here just to one point: the subtitle of Volume III. It is notorious that for the English edition of Volume I, Engels changed Marx's subtitle from *The production process of capital* to *The process of capitalist production*. These are, of course, quite different issues.[12] In line

---

8   Deciphering Marx's handwriting, apparently, was only a minor problem, although, Engels tells us, before he could work on it, he first had to dictate the entire manuscript – note that the book in its final shape contains some 900 printed pages.

9   For a fuller discussion see Vollgraf and Jungnickel (1944), Vygodskij (1995) and Heinrich (1996). See also Arthur (1996) as well as Oakley (1983, pp. 125–6).

10 Fernbach, in his English translation for the Pelican edition, adds here the misleading footnote (which does not appear in the German edition or the Untermann translation): "In the present edition, all Engels's substantial interpolations in the main body of the text are placed simply in parentheses and followed by initials" (p. 93). "All" creates the impression of an extra check, which obviously is not the case.

11 See, for example, the discussion of the text of Part Three (Reuten 2002) [Chapter 21 of the current book.]

12 It should be noted, however, that this alteration is given some justification by the French edition of 1872, which Marx authorised.

with his revision of the subtitle of Volume I, Engels imposed on Volume III the subtitle *The process of capitalist production as a whole* (*Der Gesammtprozeß der Kapitalistischen Produktion*). Marx's own title in his draft of Volume III is different; it is "The shapes of the whole Process" ("Die Gestaltungen des Gesammtprozeß"). Marx says in his introduction that this meant the 'unity' of the first two books.[13] Engels gives credence to his subtitle by inserting (unmarked) the first three sentences of the opening chapter of Volume III.[14]

This collection of studies [the 2002 book] is based on Marx's *Capital III* as edited by Engels. The authors do not take the view that the 'real' text (whatever real may mean in this context) is that of Marx's manuscripts. The manuscript of 1864–65, for example, is a work on its own (as are those of e.g. 1857–58 and 1861–63) and they should be the subject of a study of their own. Nevertheless, although the *Capital III* text is our platform, some of us, from that platform, further develop Marxian theory in reference to later, e.g. twentieth century, works, while others for their purposes refer back to earlier work of Marx, including the published manuscripts just mentioned.

2   *Capital III* in light of the first two volumes[15]

2.1   *Levels of abstraction*

Descriptions of the interconnection of the three volumes of *Capital* and relatedly of Marx's general method are bound to be reconstructive as well as controversial. Among the authors of this book [2002], at least, there is agreement about three interdependent aspects of Marx's method. First, the dialectic is not unnecessary jargon that could be dispensed with, but key to the understanding of *Capital*. Nevertheless views differ as to differences between the (systematic) dialectics of Hegel and Marx.[16] Second, all authors agree that the

---

13   This formulation, in fact, goes back to the 1861–63 draft (MECW 33, p. 69). At that time the main title was still to be "Capital and Profit".

14   More accurately the first three and a half sentences of the chapter (i.e., down to "production process" in the fourth sentence). Cf. *Collected Works* (MECW) Vol. 37: 3, 30 and Marx–Engels *Gesamtausgabe* (MEGA) Vol II. 4.2: 7. (Thanks to Chris Arthur for pointing this out.)

15   In this section I provide a brief overview of *Capital III* in relation to Volumes I and II. Although I try not to impose too forcefully my own opinions about the work as a whole, this account reflects my own views and not those of all my co-authors.

16   These differences and systematic dialectics itself are not spelled out much in the current book [2002]. See the essays by the same authors in Moseley (ed. 1993) and Moseley and Campbell (eds 1997) and Bellofiore and Finelli (1998). Earlier works are Arthur (1986), Mur-

movement in *Capital* is from abstract and simple categories to concrete and complex ones, and is marked by conceptual levels of abstraction/concretion. Nevertheless there are different views about what this implies, especially about whether and how the later more concrete levels modify the earlier and more abstract ones.[17] Third, all agree that these levels are marked by the Parts within each of the volumes of *Capital*, many of which are also conceptual conversions or transformations.[18] Nevertheless views may differ as to whether these can be 'defined' into each other (as in a linear or formal logic) allowing perhaps also for quantitative 'translations' between levels.[19]

In addition, all the authors [see note 1] emphasise – although with different accentuations – that the monetary value-form is key to the understanding of *Capital*. These general agreements, it should be noted, differentiate the current work from what may be considered its complement: the collection of articles edited by Bellofiore (1998a; 1998b).[20]

2.2 From Capital I and II to Capital III

Marx's *Capital* is an exposition of the logic of capital – its production and reproduction. The work describes the object of enquiry from within, developing the object's own standards and processes to its logical conclusions, and thus assessing the object internally. In *Capital I*, after having established the capitalist social form – the value-form, and its expression in money and capital itself – capital's *need* for labour for the production of value and surplus-value is developed in extenso. Capital's need can be fulfilled because of its social *dominance* over labour – dominance, since capital is also the social materialisation of property in the means of production. For this reason, capital can impose its

---

ray (1988), Reuten and Williams (1989) and Smith (1990; 1993). See also the more recent Arthur (1998; 2000), Murray (2000a; 2000b), Reuten (1998; 2000) and Smith (1999). Note that in Paul Mattick's view Marx's break with Hegel is such that the term 'systematic dialectic' is not appropriate (see Mattick 1986; 1993).

[17] Engels says, in his Preface to the English edition of 1886, that *Capital I* is "in a great measure a whole in itself". If "in itself" is, dialectically, meant as "implicitly" this is fine. As such, however, it is insufficient. When we still lack essential determinations (such as the rate of profit at the level of *Capital I*) because they have not yet been shown to exist, we lack essential understanding of the whole. In the end the comprehension of the concrete, when that state has been reached, informs the abstract.

[18] The last Part of *Capital I*, in particular, seems to be an exception – it is pretty clearly a digression from the systematic ordering (see Smith 1990 on the explanation for this exception).

[19] In this book Moseley (2002) argues that this can be done.

[20] An earlier collection on Volume III is edited by Eberle (1973) – its main focus is 'the' transformation problem.

form on society. Therefore also we have the social production of capital. The German subtitle of Volume I brings out this double meaning very well: *Der Produktionsprozeß des Kapitals*, where *des* means both the process of production 'of' and 'by' capital, i.e., need and dominance.

Having established this in Volume I, capital can move on, so to say, to its own workings in Volume II and III (in jargon: its own business). Labour moves to the background. It literally scarcely makes an appearance, except for a few instances such as in the circuit of capital, where labour occurs as only a formal element (Vol. II, Part One), or the social reproduction of capital where labour appears merely in its function of buying part of the consumer goods produced (Vol. II, Part Three).[21]

Consequently, whenever Marx discusses aspects of crisis and the cycle of production in *Capital II* and *III*, it is no longer in terms of a shortage or abundance of labour as in Volume I.[22] Rather it is from the standpoint of the dominance of *capital*: in terms of *its movement* from slack to overproduction – predicated on the movement of production of surplus-value in relation to capital investment (Vol. II, Part Three; Vol. III, Part Three); or even more sublimated, in terms of the *shortage or abundance of money capital* – seemingly disconnected from production (Vol. III, Part Five).

2.3 The seven Parts of Capital III

The first three Parts of *Capital III*, 15 chapters in all, are on aspects of the rate of profit of 'capital in general'.[23] From the concepts of surplus-value and the rate of surplus-value – treated at length in the first volume – Marx develops in Part One the core concepts of profit and the rate of profit. They are effects or results of the whole process at any point in time – and as such the concentration of many determinants – but simultaneously they are decisive or causative for the reproduction of capital; they are capital's continuity measures. "The rate of profit is the motive power of capitalist production, and nothing is produced save what can be produced at a profit."[24]

Part Two shows one side of the dynamics of this continuity, that is, how the competition between capitals for the highest rate of profit, results in an aver-

---

21 See the papers in Arthur and Reuten (eds 1998).

22 I say *aspects* of crisis and the cycle of production because for Marx a *systematic* treatment of these goes beyond the three volumes (see e.g. 1894U, p. 358).

23 This concept of 'capital in general' is expanded upon by Chris Arthur (2002a). In an alternative usage of the term, we leave 'capital in general' behind – and go to the level of 'many capitals' – as soon as we take into account differences among sectors in organic composition and turnover times of capital.

24 Marx 1894M, p. 333; 1894U, p. 269; 1894F, p. 368 (translation amended).

aging out of the rate of profit. The flow of capital from branches producing at a relatively lower profit rate, to branches producing at a higher, thus results tendentially in the establishment of a *general* rate of profit, which, as before, is both effect and cause. Along the way it is shown how the concept of price, as developed in Volume I, gets modified.

Thus we see, first, how the oneness of the capitalist social form, that is the oneness, or one-dimensionality, of the value-form as expressed in prices (established in Volume I), brings forth a common measure, or scale, for capitalist success: the rate of profit, which is money over money. Next we see how this measure – generalising prices into prices of production, that is prices formed in terms of the rate of profit – tendentially brings forth a common quantity on this scale.

Whereas Part Two sets out, so to speak, the synchronic dynamics of capitalist continuity – although this is a synchronic process in time – Part Three presents the diachronic dynamics of continuity, that is the development of the general rate of profit itself. Thus within the synchronic tendency to the formation of a general rate of profit, that rate itself changes diachronically – and again we have a further determining moment of the production of surplus-value.

This diachronic dynamic is the culmination of Marx's architectonic of 'capital in general. Its basis is the profit-enforced introduction of cost-reducing techniques of production, which are reflected in a rising organic composition of capital, and which generate rate of profit increases to the *initiating* capital but simultaneously operate as a drain on the *average* rate of profit. With this capital goes through treadmill-like cyclical movements in which valorisation of capital gets expressed in devalorisation, and accumulation of capital in devaluation.

Up to this point capital was presented as an organic unity: (1) of capitals in synchronic concurrence (competition) for profit (Part One);[25] (2) synchronically establishing their general rate of profit (Part Two).[26] This has been based on (reading backwards through *Capital*) the presentation of capital (3) as synchronically connected in its material constituents, that is, the means of production and means of consumption both in their material character and as values (Vol. II, Part Three); (4) as synchronising its diachronic movement so as to trim the time that capital is tied up in the phases of its circuit (Vol. II, Part Two); (5) diachronically moving through the stages by which it is posited and reposited

---

[25] 'Competition' and 'concurrence' meaning a joint operation, which is the etymological root of both.

[26] Again, these synchronies are dynamic synchronical processes in time. Synchronics and diachronics are thus a matter of emphasis.

as capital, from the money form of capital (M), to its commodity form (C), to its *valorising* productive form (P) to an ideally valorised new-commodity form (C') and back to the *valorised* money form (M'), that is, in

M–C ... P ... C'–M'

or from any other point of departure, constituting the circuit of capital (Vol. II, Part One). (6) Nevertheless, capital is an organic unity that has only apparent self-subsistence. To be more than a formal 'organic' unity it needs the other of and for itself, that is the subsumption of labour as its valorising foundation so as to exist and generate fruit (Vol. I).[27]

At the level of capital in general all this culminates in the forces raising the value productivity of labour by revolutionising the 'technical' constituents of the labour process. The concomitant accelerating valorisation for the revolutionising 'echelons' of capital goes along with devalorisation and devaluation of capital as a whole, giving rise to crises and cycles in accumulation (Part Three).

Even if capitals are invested in different branches of production, and competing, they are all alike up to this point in Marx's presentation in that they go through the same process of valorisation and its cycle. In Parts Four to Six this unity seems to fall apart: capital in general separates into functionally different factions of capital. In Part Four capital divides into Industrial Capital, Commercial Capital and Money-dealing Capital. Though functionally different they are still alike in that they all equally share, tendentially, in the one for all general rate of profit. Note also that in hindsight this division is implicit in the 'synchronising diachronic' of the second part of *Capital II*.

The rigorous split seems to occur in Part Five when Marx, via a number of intermediate steps, develops what now is called Finance Capital. This he initially counterposes to the management of functioning capital. At this stage of the analysis these factions are in conflict and it is their relative power (as well as the stage of the cycle) that decides their shares in the general rate of profit. With Marx's 'presentation' of share capital, however, the counterposition seems to supersede into the dominance of Finance Capital.[28] Thus we see capital 'actually' developed into (M) → (M + ΔM), as money breeding money, into this 'irrational form' as Marx calls it, which is anticipated early in Volume I. In interest-bearing capital, which is capital in its most fetishistic form, we see

---

27   On the concept of subsumption in *Capital*, see Murray 1998 and 2000b.
28   This description is, I believe, fair to Marx but a very idealised one. First, it requires a regrouping of the order of the chapters; second, the state of the manuscript at times does not even reach the status of an analysis, let alone the systematic required for dialectical presentation. (See further Campbell 2002 and Reuten 2002.)

another culmination of capital and of *Capital*. It is reinforced by another culmination that is unfolded along with it, the development of money into credit money, which also hints back to the starting point of *Capital*. Capital develops into itself (but see the previous note).

One might wonder what, qua presentation equally underdeveloped, Part Six on land and ground rent should add to this. From one point of view Marx 'merely' treats an important phenomenal shape of his time. There are, however, two other reasons – not particularly emphasised by Marx – why this part deserves to be placed at the very end. The first reason is in line with the general argument of *Capital*: 'even' nature must take on the form of value, and in so far as it can be appropriated it can be capitalised. (The 'even' needs qualification, of course, as, already, even labour-power and its labour have taken on the form of value.) The second reason apparently tempers the 'conclusion' of the previous part, of capital developing into itself: capital can mould nature – and labour – but it is ultimately limited by them. Capital cannot reproduce land or nature. Marx does not emphasise this particular point explicitly, but uses it to develop the category of monopoly and monopoly profits generally. The category of monopoly may be seen as positing capital's mirror for the capital-form of the monopoly over the means of production generally.

The last part, Part Seven, consists of five relatively short and diverse chapters that cap off Volume III's presentation of the shapes of capital and of its valorisation (interest, profit of enterprise, and rent). In addition, they emphasise Marx's fundamental point that capitalism is a historically specific and mutable mode of production that conceals its class structure. These chapters might be considered as outlines for setting out the concrete manifestations of the whole.

References

Note 1. Superscripts indicate first and other relevant editions; unless otherwise indicated the last mentioned year in the bibliography is the edition cited.
Note 2 of 2023: The introduction above has cross-references to the chapters of the 2002 volume. Its title and the respective articles are therefore included below.

Arthur, Christopher J. 1986, *Dialectics of labour: Marx and his relation to Hegel*, Oxford/ New York: Basil Blackwell.
Arthur, Christopher J. 1996, 'Engels as interpreter of Marx's economics', in *Engels today: a centenary appreciation*, edited by C.J. Arthur, Basingstoke: Macmillan.
Arthur, Christopher J. 1998, 'Systematic dialectic', *Science & Society* 62(3): 447–59.
Arthur, Christopher J. 2000, 'From the critique of Hegel to the critique of capital', in

The Hegel–Marx connection, edited by T. Burns and I. Fraser, Basingstoke: Macmillan, pp. 105–30.

Arthur, Christopher J. 2001, 'The spectral ontology of value', *Radical Philosophy* 107: 32–42; reprinted in Andrew Brown, Steve Fleetwood and John Roberts (eds), *Critical realism and Marxism*, London/New York: Routledge.

Arthur, Christopher J. 2002a, 'Capital in general and Marx's *Capital*', in Campbell and Reuten (eds) 2002, pp. 42–64.

Arthur, Christopher J., and Geert Reuten (eds) 1998, *The circulation of capital: essays on volume II of Marx's 'Capital'*, Basingstoke: Macmillan.

Bellofiore, Riccardo (ed.) 1998a, *Marxian economics: a reappraisal (volume 1)*, London/New York: Macmillan/St. Martin's Press.

Bellofiore, Riccardo (ed.) 1998b, *Marxian economics: a reappraisal (volume 2)*, London/New York: Macmillan/St. Martin's Press.

Bellofiore, Riccardo, and Roberto Finelli 1998, 'Capital, labour and time: the Marxian monetary labour theory of value as a theory of exploitation', in Bellofiore (ed.) 1998a, pp. 48–74.

Campbell, Martha 2002, 'The credit system', in Campbell and Reuten (eds) 2002, pp. 212–27.

Campbell, Martha, and Geert Reuten (eds) 2002, *The culmination of capital: essays on volume III of Marx's 'Capital'*, London/New York: Palgrave Macmillan.

Eberle, Friedrich (ed.) 1973, *Aspekte der Marxschen Theorie I; Zur methodischen Bedeutung des 3. Bandes des 'Kapital'*, Frankfurt am Main: Suhrkamp.

Engels, Frederick 1894F, 'Preface to *Capital III*' (see Marx 1894F).

Heinrich, Michael 1996, 'Engels' edition of the third volume of *Capital* and Marx's original manuscript', *Science & Society* 60(4): 452–66.

Marx, Karl 1867^1; 1890^4, *Das Kapital. Kritik der Politischen Ökonomie, Band I, Der Produktionsprozeß des Kapitals* (MEW 23); English transl. of the 4th edition by Ben Fowkes, *Capital, a critique of political economy, volume I*, Harmondsworth: Penguin, 1976.[29]

Marx, Karl 1885^1, 1893^2, ed. F. Engels, *Das Kapital, Kritik der Politischen Ökonomie, Band II, Der Zirkulationsprozeß des Kapitals* (MEW 24), English trans. (Ernest Untermann 1907^1), David Fernbach, *Capital, a critique of political economy, volume II*, Harmondsworth: Penguin, 1978.

Marx, Karl 1894G, ed. F. Engels, *Das Kapital; Kritik der Politischen Ökonomie, Band III, Der Gesamtprozeß der kapitalistischen Produktion* (MEW 25), Berlin: Dietz Verlag, 1972.

---

29   There is also an English translation of the 3rd edition (by Samuel Moore and Edward Aveling, first published in 1887).

Marx, Karl 1894U, *Capital, a critique of political economy, volume III, The process of capitalist production as a whole*, trans. of 1894G (Ernest Untermann, 1909¹), London, Lawrence & Wishart, 1974.

Marx, Karl 1894F, *Capital, a critique of political economy, volume III*, trans. of 1894G (David Fernbach, 1981¹), Harmondsworth: Penguin, 1981.

Marx, Karl 1894M, *Ökonomische Manuscripte 1863–1867* [Transcription of manuscript for *Das Kapital III*, 1894G], eds M. Müller, J. Jungnickel, B. Lietz, C. Sander and A. Schnickmann, *MEGA*, Vol. II. 4.2 (1992).

Marx, Karl 1894D, *Capital III* [Disc version of 1894U], K. Marx and F. Engels, Classics in Politics, London: The Electronic Book Company [ElecBook].

Marx, Karl, and Frederick Engels, *Collected works* (MECW), London/New York/Moscow: Lawrence & Wishart/International Publishers/Progress Publishers.

Marx, Karl, and Friedrich Engels, *Marx–Engels Gesamtausgabe* (MEGA), Berlin/Amsterdam: Dietz Verlag/Internationales Institut für Sozialgeschichte Amsterdam.

Marx, Karl, and Friedrich Engels, *Werke* (MEW), Berlin: Dietz Verlag.

Mattick Jr., Paul 1986, *Social knowledge: an essay on the nature and limits of social science*, London: Hutchinson.

Mattick Jr., Paul 1993, 'Marx's dialectic', in Moseley (ed.) 1993, pp. 115–34.

Mészáros, István 1970, *Marx's theory of alienation*, London: Merlin.

Moseley, Fred (ed.) 1993, *Marx's method in 'Capital': A Re-examination*, Atlantic Highlands, NJ: Humanities Press.

Moseley, Fred 2002, 'Hostile brothers: Marx's theory of the distribution of surplus-value in volume III of *Capital*', in Campbell and Reuten (eds) 2002, pp. 65–101.

Moseley, Fred, and Martha Campbell (eds) 1997, *New investigations of Marx's method*, Atlantic Highlands, NJ: Humanities Press.

Murray, Patrick 1988, *Marx's theory of scientific knowledge*, Atlantic Highlands, NJ: Humanities Press.

Murray, Patrick 1998, 'Beyond the "commerce and industry" picture of capital', in Arthur and Reuten (eds) 1998, pp. 33–66.

Murray, Patrick 2000a, 'Marx's "truly social" labour theory of value: abstract labour in Marxian value theory, part I', *Historical Materialism* 6 (Summer 2000): 27–65.

Murray, Patrick 2000b, 'Marx's "truly social" labour theory of value: abstract labour in Marxian value theory, part II', *Historical Materialism* 7 (Winter 2000): 99–136.

Murray, Patrick 2002, 'The illusion of the economic: the trinity formula and the "religion of everyday life"', in Campbell and Reuten (eds) 2002, pp. 246–72.

Oakley, Allen 1983, *The making of Marx's critical theory: a bibliographical analysis*, London: Routledge & Kegan Paul.

Reuten, Geert 1993, 'The difficult labour of a theory of social value: metaphors and systematic dialectics at the beginning of Marx's "Capital"', in Moseley (ed.) 1993, pp. 89–113.

Reuten, Geert 1998, 'Marx's method', in *The handbook of economic methodology*, edited by J. Davis, W. Hands and U. Mäki, Cheltenham: Edward Elgar, pp. 283–7.

Reuten, Geert 2000, 'The interconnection of systematic dialectics and historical materialism', *Historical Materialism* 7 (Winter 2000): 137–65.

Reuten, Geert 2002, 'The rate of profit cycle and the opposition between managerial and finance capital: a discussion of *Capital III*, parts Three to Five', in Campbell and Reuten (eds) 2002, pp. 174–211.

Reuten, Geert, and Michael Williams 1989, *Value-form and the state; the tendencies of accumulation and the determination of economic policy in capitalist society*, London/New York: Routledge.

Smith, Tony 1990, *The logic of Marx's Capital: replies to Hegelian criticisms*, Albany, NY: State University of New York Press.

Smith, Tony 1993, *Dialectical social theory and its critics: from Hegel to analytical Marxism and postmodernism*, Albany, NY: State University of New York Press.

Smith, Tony 1999, 'The relevance of systematic dialectics to Marxian thought: a reply to Rosenthal', *Historical Materialism* 4: 215–40.

Smith, Tony 2002, 'Surplus profits from innovation: a missing level in *Capital III*?', in Campbell and Reuten (eds) 2002, pp. 149–73.

Vollgraf, Carl-Erich, and Jürgen Jungnickel 1994, 'Marx in Marx's Worten? – Zu Engels' Edition des Hauptmanuskripts zum dritten Buch des *Kapital*', *MEGA-Studien* 2: 3–55.

Vygodskij, Vitalij 1995, 'Was hat Engels in den Jahren 1885 und 1894 eigentlich veröffentlicht? – Zu dem Artikel von Carl-Erich Vollgraf und Jürgen Jungnickel „Marx in Marx's Worten?"', *MEGA-Studien* 1: 117–20.

CHAPTER 14

Marx's rate of profit transformation: methodological, theoretical and philological obstacles – an appraisal based on the text of *Capital III* and manuscripts of 1864–65, 1875 and 1878

2009 article, originally published in *Re-reading Marx: new perspectives after the critical edition*, edited by Riccardo Bellofiore and Roberto Fineschi, London/New York: Palgrave Macmillan, pp. 211–30.
(For its abstract see the Abstracts of all chapters, p. 7.)

Contents

Introduction 283
§1 The published drafts for Part Two of *Das Kapital III* 284
§2 A note on Marx's method in *Capital* 285
§3 A formal presentation of alternative interpretations of the *Das Kapital I* categories from the perspective of those of the *Das Kapital III* manuscript 285
 §3.1 Rate of surplus-value and rate of profit 285
 §3.2 [CC-1] Method of Concretion at Volume I level: abstract explanandum 287
 §3.3 [CC-2] Method of Concretion at Volume III level: concretion 288
 §3.4 [CP-1] Method of Completion at Volume I level: partial explanation of "concretum" 290
 §3.5 [CP-2] Method of Completion at Volume III level: completion 291
 §3.6 Some conclusions and a preview 293
§4 The 1864–65 manuscript and the text of *Capital III* Part Two 294
 §4.1 General outline 294
 §4.2 Chapter 8: the problematic 296
 §4.3 Chapter 9: a cheerful accommodation for the inconsistency 296
 §4.4 Chapter 10: gloomy reflection 298
§5 Notes on a small 1878 manuscript: diverging rates of surplus-value 300
Conclusions 301
References 302

Introduction[1]

In Part Two of the third volume of *Capital* Marx addresses the famous transformation of the rate of surplus-value into the general rate of profit. This article discusses Marx's 1864–65 manuscript on this issue – the text that Engels (selectively) used for his edition of *Das Kapital III*. We shall see that this text is a research manuscript rather than a near to final presentation of the matter, and that Engels polished away this preliminary status of the manuscript – in this I merely confirm the view of the *MEGA* editors.

The assessment of Marx's transformation procedure very much hinges on our view of the method that he adopted. Two main alternative interpretations of the method are set out in §3 below. Even if only one of those would make Marx's transformation procedure methodologically legitimate, we shall see in §4 of this essay that, paradoxically, it is not obvious that Marx intended to adopt this method. Thus the main object of this essay is to lift the discussion on the 'transformation problem' to a more fundamental level.

References without mention of author (e.g. M:272 or E:208) are to works of Marx as follows (full references are in the bibliography).
M   Marx (1992M/1864–65): main manuscript for 'Das Kapital III' (*MEGA*);
E   Marx (1894E/~1864–65): *Das Kapital III* as edited by Engels (*MEW*);
F   Marx (1894F/~1864–65): *Capital III* in the Fernbach translation.
The first date is the date of first publication; the second one indicates the year(s) of composition of the manuscript. A tilde ~ before the second date means that the text, as edited by Engels, is roughly based on that manuscript.

Within citations italics are always in the original. Any underlining is my emphasis. Unproblematic insertions in quotations are in square brackets. Comments are in curly brackets. The indication 'mt' after a page number (for example 370-mt) means 'my translation'. Within my translations the original German term also appears, in case, in curly brackets.

---

[1] I am grateful for the comments and discussion provided by the participants of the 2006 ISMT meeting in Bergamo – esp. Christopher Arthur, Riccardo Bellofiore, Roberto Finelli, Roberto Fineschi, Rolf Hecker, Michael Heinrich, Fred Moseley, Patrick Murray, Regina Roth, Tony Smith, and Massimiliano Tomba. I have also added the completely new section 4 (against which, due to space limits, other parts of the original paper were removed).

§1 The published drafts for Part Two of *Das Kapital III*

Engels edited the text of Part Two of *Das Kapital III* from a 1864–65 manuscript of Marx. For the main argument of this essay it is important that this manuscript thus dates from before the final manuscript of 1866–67 for the first edition of *Das Kapital I* (1867).[2]

The transcript of the German 1864–65 manuscript was first published in 1992 (*MEGA* II/4.2). There is no (published) English translation.[3] A 1857–58 manuscript, the *Grundrisse*, contains notes concerning the problematic of this part.[4] A more mature – though relatively short – draft dates from 1861–63, first published in 1980 (*MEGA* II/3.5), first English translation 1991.[5]

Other relevant texts, published for the first time in 2003, can be found in *MEGA* II/14. This includes a substantial manuscript dating from 1875 as well as four shorter texts from (probably) 1871?, 1873–75?, 1877–82 and 1878? (see §5 for a note on especially this last manuscript).[6]

A final number of eleven draft texts for *Das Kapital III* (dating from 1867–68) is to be published in *MEGA*'s II/4.3. Herewith the publication of Marx's manuscripts for the work will be complete (Vollgraf and Roth 2003, p. 382).

From reading the 1864–65 manuscript it is obvious that it reports preliminary investigations; it includes 'try outs' together with mistakes of which the author at some point becomes aware. In Engels's manner of carrying out his editorial work, this investigative character of the text has been polished away; hence it has seemed for over a century that much of *Das Kapital III* (and *II*) was in a rather finalised state – as including its Part Two. I am, of course, not the first to observe this (see e.g. Vollgraf and Jungnickel 1994 and Heinrich 1996; cf. Roth 2009 and Heinrich 2009). In fact, there was no simple solution to the problem that faced Engels: most of the drafts were not in a readable state for non-specialists. The problem is that, given the solution he adopted, he gave very ill warning as to his interventions.[7]

---

2   Kopf et al. 1983, pp. 15*–16*.
3   [2023 note. Since 2015 there is one by Ben Fowkes: *Marx's economic manuscript of 1864–1865*, Leiden: Brill.]
4   Relevant are esp. pp. 373ff. and 434ff. of the English edition.
5   For a comparison: the 1861–63 draft consists of 35 printed pages (*MEGA*); the 1864–65 draft has 285 printed pages (*MEGA*); the final text of *Das Kapital III*, as edited by Engels is 164 pages (*MEGA*) (220 pages in the *MEW* edition).
6   The annotations to the texts (e.g. text variations, crossing outs, dating and contextualisation) by Vollgraf and Roth are of superb scrutiny and scholarship.
7   Heinrich (1996) writes about the whole of the manuscript for *Das Kapital III*: "there are modi-

§2 A note on Marx's method in *Capital*

Although in my view, the project of Marx's *Capital* is based methodologically on a development from Hegel's Systematic Dialectics (cf. Arthur 2009), the main argument of this essay can do without this stringent position. Instead, I just emphasise one, less controversial, aspect of Marx's method in *Capital*, namely that it proceeds by way of *conceptual development*. Between the three volumes of *Capital*, as well as within each one, we have a movement of 'levels of abstraction', running from abstract, relatively indeterminate, general and simple concepts to increasingly concrete, determinate, particular and so complex concepts. At the earlier levels, certain complexities are suppressed, or 'bracketed'. Each time it is the 'insufficiency' of the earlier presentation that drives on to the introduction of further complexities. (For the purposes of this essay, these levels of abstraction may even be interpreted in terms of a movement from 'simple models' to 'complex models' in the course of which initial ceteris paribus assumptions are increasingly dropped.)

§3 A formal presentation of alternative interpretations of the *Das Kapital I* categories from the perspective of those of the *Das Kapital III* manuscript

§3.1 *Rate of surplus-value and rate of profit*

In this section I use the following four main concepts and definitions. Circulating capital (k):

$$k_i = c_i + v_i \qquad \text{[definition]} \quad (1)$$

where c and v are the parts invested in means of production and in labour-power (the wages sum of wl). For simplicity, we abstract throughout, like Marx,

---

fications to the original text on practically each page that have not been indicated. Hardly one paragraph remained as Marx had written it. Engels's modifications are not confined to 'stylistic' matters. ... [T]he 1894 edition was an extensive adaptation of Marx's manuscript, and Engels did not inform the readers about the true extent of his adaptation. ... The interventions ... offer solutions for problems which the manuscript left open ... and in some passages they even change the argumentation of the original text, if this obstructs Engels' interpretations" (pp. 456, 459, 464). See also the extensive comments by Vollgraf and Jungnickel (1994) about Engels's mark on the text ("Engels left only few of Marx's sentences untouched" – p. 47-mt).

from fixed capital and from differences in turnover time.[8] The subscript i refers to a specific sector of production (later, the subscript j will refer to any other sector).

The rate of surplus-value (s'):

$$s'_i = f(e^*_i) \qquad \text{[explanation – pro memory] (2a)}$$
$$s_i = s'_i v_i \qquad \text{[explanation; here reduced to definition] (2b)}$$

(where e^* is the ratio of 'surplus labour' and 'necessary labour').

Capital I posits surplus-value (s) and its increase as the driving force of capital. The focus of the middle part of *Capital I* is the *explanation* of surplus-value in terms of labour-time and of the productive forces of labour operating on the means of production.[9] The *rate* of surplus-value (s') is the concentration of these explanatory determinants. Here, as for Marx in the *Kapital III* manuscript, all this explanation is assumed. Thus we have s' as a determinant for s. It remains to be seen (cf. the subsections below) *how* it is also a determinant for profit (r) and the rate of profit (r'):

$$r'_i = r_i/k_i \qquad \text{[definition] (3)}$$

The spectrum of wages is posited synchronically equal for all sectors ($w_i = w$), hence:

$$wl_i = v_i \qquad \text{[approximation] (4)}$$

For the sake of brevity, I posit throughout this section a number of assumptions without further argument. For our purposes there are three types: 'simplifications' serve to make a problem tractable; the same applies to 'stage simplifications' (these, however, are dropped in a later stage); 'approximations' {Annäherungen} set out the uninhibited result of forces (tendency laws).

The assessment of Marx's general rate of profit transformation in the 1864–65 draft for Part Two of *Das Kapital III* depends very much on the view of how the categories presented in this part are connected to those of *Capital I*. We shall see (§4) that Marx is aware of the importance of the connection, and how he hes-

---

8   Relating to (uniform) turnover time, there is a problem with equation (1) that I set aside for the purposes of this essay (see Reuten 2006).

9   Marx's explanation is discussed in Reuten 2004. [Chapter 8 of the current book.]

itates about the Part Two consequences (his self-interpretation!) for the, then, draft of *Das Kapital I*. Both in order to shortcut the discussion in the next section (§4), and because the categorical connections are not obvious, the current section sets out a brief formal presentation of the two main alternatives (§3.2–§3.5). Note that a formal presentation necessarily loses conceptual richness; on the other hand, once quantitative matters are involved – as is the case – it is a means of precision.

For the purposes of this section I reduce Marx's complex method of many stages (levels of abstraction) to simply *two* stages: that of *Capital I* and of Part Two of *Capital III*. The movement to the later stage is one of increasing determination (concretion or completion).

In considering surplus-value and production, we can, of course, not get around exchange and prices. We assume that 'market prices' converge to what I provisionally call 'supply prices' (and what Marx will call "production prices" in *Capital III*). We want to explain production ($x = pq$) in terms of these convergence prices (p). In principle we can adopt two methods, and we can take these as possible interpretations of the two stages referred to. I call them 'the method of concretion' (§3.2–§3.3), and 'the method of completion' (§3.4–§3.5). For both methods, we shall be concerned throughout with *synchronic* matters only (some synchronic uniformity of sectors of production may go along with diachronic change).

§3.2 [CC-1] **Method of Concretion at Volume I level: Abstract explanandum**
Before we get to the explanation of the prices p, we first explain an abstract approximation of them, labelled 'pi' (π), whence we also have an abstract approximation of production: πq. Thus we have an abstractum or a theoretical construct. (This may be interpreted as a systematic-dialectical stage; or also as a theorisation of variables constructed in an (ideal) experimental constellation, so reaching ceteris paribus conditions.) In brief we posit:

$$\pi_i q_i = k_i + s'_i v_i \qquad \text{[explanation of a construct/abstractum]} \quad (5)$$

Via the moment of $s'_i v_i$ this incorporates the explanation represented by equations (2a and 2b). We proceed by adding two simplifying assumptions. First, that of synchronically uniform rates of surplus-value:

$$s'_i = s' \qquad \text{(for all i)} \qquad \text{[simplification or approximation]} \quad (6)$$

A key question is whether this is indeed a simplifying assumption or rather an approximation of a systemic force (see §3.3, §4.1 and §5). Second, that of synchronically uniform compositions of capital:

$$(k/v)_i = k/v \quad \text{(for all i)} \qquad \text{[stage simplification] (7)}$$

Dividing (5) through v_i, and making use of (6) and (7), we have:

$$\pi_i q_i / v_i = k/v + s/v \quad \text{(for all i)} \qquad \text{[implication] (8)}$$

Because $wl_i = v$ (eqn. 4), then substituting wl_i for v_i, and multiplying by w, we also have:

$$\pi_i q_i / l_i = k/l + s/l \quad \text{(for all i)} \qquad \text{[implication] (9)}$$

In the way I have presented it here, it is the *implication* of the construct that its prices (π) are proportional to labour commanded (Smith) as well as to labour embodied (Ricardo).

Even if Marx introduces the (general) rate of profit only in *Capital III*, another *implication* is that we have *uniform rates of profit* since (cf. eqn. 3):

$$r'_i = s' v_i / k_i = s'/(k_i/v_i) = s'(k/v) \qquad \text{[implication] (10)}$$

(This is roughly how I interpreted *Capital I* until my study of the 1864–65 manuscript discussed in this essay.[10] In §4 we will see that this interpretation makes Marx's *Das Kapital III* manuscript transformation procedure methodologically mistaken.)

§3.3 [CC-2] *Method of Concretion* at Volume III level: concretion

We drop the construct π and proceed to 'production prices' (p). We assume that real market prices converge to these production prices ('centres of gravitation').

Variant (a)
Marx (at some point, see §4.2-§4.3) defines this constellation as follows.
• Analogous to the πq equation (5):

$$p_i q_i = k_i + s'_i v_i \qquad \text{[explanation] (11)}$$

---

[10] I feel constrained to stress that an interpretation may be truthful as an interpretation, but that this does not imply that the interpreter agrees with what is interpreted.

Via the moment of $s'_i v_i$ this again incorporates the explanation represented by equations (2a and 2b).
• Rates of profit converge to uniform rates:

$$r'_i = r' \quad \text{(for all i)} \qquad \text{[approximation]} \quad (12)$$

• Non-uniform compositions of capital (thus 7 is dropped). Hence in general:

$$(k/v)_i \ne (k/v)_j \qquad \text{[empirical observation]} \quad (13)$$

• Uniform rates of surplus-value (thus 6 is maintained):

$$s'_i = s' \quad \text{(for all i)} \qquad \text{[simplification or approximation]} \quad (6) = (14)$$

Because of the diverging k/v there is no labour-commanded or labour-embodied proportionality for the production prices p (we merely have $p_i q_i / v_i = (k/v)_i + s'$). Marx is aware and explicit about this. Rather more problematical is that the combination of the three restrictions (12), (13) and (14) is impossible.

$$r'_i = s' v_i / k_i = s' / (k/v)_i \qquad \text{[implication]} \quad (15)$$

Thus $r'_i \ne r'_j$. We can have uniform profit rates only with either (1) both of s' and (k/v) uniform (the πq constellation) or (2) both of them non-uniform.

Variant (b): reconstruction of variant (a)
The obvious way to mend the incompatibility is to reconstructively drop the (simplifying) assumption of uniform rates of surplus-value (14).[11] So we have:

$$s'_i \ne s'_j \qquad \text{[empirical observation]} \quad (14^*)$$

Whence we derive:

$$r'_i = r' = (s'_i v_i)/k_i \quad \text{(for all i)} \qquad \text{[implication]} \quad (15^*)$$

---

11 The theoretical ground for this reconstruction is in the productive force and the degree of intensity of labour (cf. *Capital I*, Ch. 15) as discussed in Reuten (2004, esp. pp. 136–41). [Chapter 8 of the current book, §2.4.]

In this reconstruction the *micro* equality of profits and surplus-value ($r = s$) is maintained;[12] by implication we also have the macro $R = S$. Each at this level.

Variants (a) and (b)
Instead, Marx endeavours to get around the incompatibility via a macro-micro détour in which he transposes quantities between the two levels, and that in effect results in:

$$r'_i = r' = [(s'v_i)+\delta_i]/k_i \qquad \text{['methodologically illegitimate détour']} \quad (15^{**})$$

(with the aggregate sum of the δ_i amounting to zero).

However, within the constellation of the Concretion Method this is methodologically illegitimate (though not for the reasons usually stated). Since the two explananda πq and pq are non-identical, transposition of quantities from the one to the other level makes no sense. (Certainly, it does make sense to apply the qualitative conclusions from the earlier level to quantification *at* the lower level – that is, as long as any ceteris paribus conditions of the earlier level allow for it.)

§3.4 [CP-1] *Method of Completion* at *Volume I* level: partial explanation of 'concretum'

There is also a very different interpretation of what happens at *Capital I* level. In this alternative we have no π construct but we rather start immediately with the convergence price p (and hence pq), thus prices of production – even if these are explicitly called like this only at Volume III level. However, given that we have the same set of simplifying assumptions as in [CC-1] (equations 6 and 7) we have approximations for the explanation of p, leaving some of p unexplained. (In §4.4 we shall see that Marx at some point leans to this (self-)interpretation. Fred Moseley (e.g. Moseley 2000) seems to be proposing something similar. For each I am not sure they would draw all of the consequences.) Thus p is explained in successive stages, here reduced to two. Until we reach full explanation we have an unexplained part u.

$$p_i q_i = k_i + s'_i v_i + u_i \qquad \text{[partial explanation]} \quad (16)$$

As in CC-1 the moment of $s'_i v_i$ incorporates the explanation represented by equations (2a and 2b). Again, we proceed by adding on the two simplifying

---

12   That is, prior to the introduction of finance and interest.

assumptions of synchronically uniform rates of surplus-value and of synchronically uniform compositions of capital:

$s'_i = s'$ (for all i)   [simplification/approximation] (6 =) (17)

$(k/v)_i = k/v$ (for all i)   [stage simplification] (7 =) (18)

Here, however, we have from the beginning no labour-commanded or labour-embodied proportionality because of the factor u:

$(p_i q_i)/v_i = k/v + s/v + u_i/v_i$ [implication] (19)

(cf. 8 and 9 above). It has been argued (e.g. by Moseley) that *Capital I*, merely provides a partial explanation of prices (in a different way, of course, nor does CC-1 provide a full explanation).[13]

§3.5   [CP-2] **Method of Completion** at Volume III level: completion
Rates of profit converge to uniform rates:

$r'_i = r'$ (for all i)   [approximation] (12) = (20)

Hence we have for (what is now explicitly thus called) prices of production:

$p_i q_i = k_i + r_i$ [accounting identity / empirical observation] (21)

$p_i q_i = k_i + r' k_i$ [putative explanation] (22)

This is a putative explanation pending the determination of r'. Again, we have non-uniform compositions of capital (thus the simplifying assumption of equation 18 is dropped):

$(k/v)_i \ne (k/v)_j$ [empirical observation] (13) = (23)

The uniform rates of surplus-value thesis of equation (17) is maintained; however, given equation (22) it is considered to play no (new) role *at the current level*.

$s'_i = s'$ (for all i)   [simplification/approximation] (17)

---

[13]   As a corollary it may be noted that, as against CC-1, there is at *this* point no implication of (implicit) uniform profit rates.

Reordering equations (20)–(22) we have:

$$r'_i = r' = r_i/k_i \quad \text{(for all i)} \qquad \text{[implication] (24)}$$

Because the *pq* in the two price equations (16) and (22) are on the same plane, it is now methodologically legitimate to transpose quantities from the one level to the other (CP-1 and CP-2). (Cf. the Marx/Engels (in)famous aggregation tables of *Capital III*, chapter 9.)

Substituting (16) and (2b) into (21) we have:

$$r_i = s_i + u_i \qquad \text{[implication] (25)}$$
$$r_i = s'_i v_i + u_i \qquad \text{[implication] (26)}$$

In fact, this is a shortcut for Marx's aggregation tables. However, it deserves a serious warning (and here the usual critiques come in), namely that it is *assumed* that the unexplained factor of u_i concerns, and so is to be allotted to, profits rather than (in part) any other factor in equation (16).

We now aggregate surplus-value (*S*) and profits (*R*):

$$S = \Sigma s_i \qquad \text{[aggregation] (27)}$$
$$R = \Sigma r_i \qquad \text{[aggregation] (28)}$$

Next it is posited that *S* explains, and fully determines, *R*:

$$R = S \quad \text{(right to left determination)} \qquad \text{[derived explanation] (29)}$$

(The explanation is derived from the set of equations (1)–(4) and (16)–(28).)

We also aggregate equation (25) into:

$$R = S + U \qquad \text{[aggregation] (30)}$$

Because theoretical priority is given to (29) we have:

$$U = 0 \qquad \text{[theory decision] (31)}$$

Finally, the sector u_i's are determined via the rate of profit criterion. From (24)–(26) we have:

$$r'_i = r' = (s'v_i + u_i)/k_i \qquad \text{[implication] (32)}$$

Hence:

$$u_i = r'k_i - s'v_i \qquad \text{[implication]} \quad (33)$$

§3.6 Some conclusions and a preview

1. The last equation (33) is the *'tache de beauté'* of this CP set up. The u_i's are determined by the 'general rate of profit', instead of the rate of profit being fully determined by explanatory entities. Two objections may be raised against this alleged blemish. One is that we have a simultaneous determination. The other, as argued by Marx, is that, at a still lower level of abstraction, the u_i's are determined by competition (see §4.3).

2. Remind Marx's equation (15**) from CC-2 that I qualified as 'methodologically illegitimate' (a qualification that I maintain, that is within the Concretion Method). We had:

$$r'_i = r' = [(s'v_i) + \delta_i]/k_i \qquad (15^{**})$$

Its outward appearance is similar to (32).

3. In Variant (b) of CC-2, i.e., my reconstruction of Variant (a), we have the rate of profit fully determined without any transformation 'problem':

$$r'_i = r' = (s'_i v_i)/k_i \qquad (15^*)$$

4. In my view CC-1 is the better *interpretation* of *Das Kapital I*, published by Marx in 1867!, and revised shortly before it. In my view CP-2 is the better *interpretation* of Marx's manuscript for Part Two of *Das Kapital III*, written in 1864/65! (at least up to some point of the manuscript – see §4.4).

5. How is this so? This is methodologically inconsistent! Yes. Because of this problem, the following section (§4) is rather complex. My hypothesis is as follows. The 1864–65 manuscript for Part Two initially followed the path of the 1861–61 manuscript, which is in line with CP-2 – i.e., the 'chapter 9' transformation procedure (see §4.3). Then, reflecting on this transformation procedure in Marx's 'chapter 10', Marx got increasingly worried about what he had been doing in terms of his manuscript for *Das Kapital I* (see §4.4).[14] (Engels, however, in his editing of the 1864/65 manuscript for 'his' *Das Kapital III* polished away these worries whence we have the 'CP-2' result.)

---

14 Another problem is that the penultimate manuscript for *Das Kapital I* is missing. We just do not know to what extent – if at all – Marx adapted his text as a consequence of the worries mentioned.

6. Each of [CC-1 with CC-2] and [CP-1 with CP-2] is consistent. The usual post-Marx solutions to the transformation problem obviously took Engels's version of *Das Kapital III* for granted, and then combined the 'theoretical domain' of CC-1 with that of CP-2, which is methodologically inconsistent. If one would want to use the 'domain' CP-2 (not only for a solution to the transformation problem but also for any other quantitative matters) then one is bound to CP-1.

§4 The 1864–65 manuscript and the text of 'Capital III' Part Two

§4.1 *General outline*

Regarding Part Two (originally one 'chapter') of the 1864–65 manuscript Engels left unchanged the main chapter *structure* of the text for his *Capital III* edition (chapters 8–12); however, there are changes of order within the chapters as well as texts that have disappeared altogether. For the reader's convenience, I therefore refer in this section to the *Capital III* chapters.

At the very opening of Part Two (Chapter 8) we immediately find the crucial assumption of a uniform rate of surplus-value, for all of Part Two (M:212; E:151; F:241).[15] It is repeated regularly throughout the part. According to this manuscript it is not just a simplifying assumption but rather a *law*. In 'Chapter 10' Marx writes that competition between labourers gives rise to:

> a general rate of surplus-value – tendentially that is, as for all economic laws; we posit it as a *theoretical* simplifying presupposition; in fact it is the actual presupposition of the capitalist mode of production even if inhibited by practical frictions ...; in theory we assume that the laws of the capitalist mode of production develop in their pure form {rein}. (M:250-mt; cf. E:184, F:275)

Given this assumption/law the terrain of the problematic for Part Two is defined by the prevalence of non-uniform compositions of capital (ratios of k/v) between sectors of production, or also non-uniform turnover times of capital – which offers the same problematic (M:216). Thus whereas *Capital I*, Parts Four, Five and Seven treat the diachronic change of the capital composition (with any divergences between sectors 'bracketed') the current part makes the reverse assumption: constant though diverging.

---

15 I write "uniform"; the manuscript has "constant" and "given". The manuscript has "chapter"; Engels apparently forgot to change this into "part".

Part Two comprises three main chapters (chs. 8–10) that in my view should be considered together (the two smaller chapters (11–12) may be regarded as 'addenda'). I begin with a brief outline of these three chapters before discussing some of the details.

In Chapter 8 Marx sets out the constellation that results from the assumptions just indicated. These together with the assumption that commodities are sold 'at their values' [presumably equation (5)] would result in differing rates of profit between sectors (M:223–4) [cf. equation (10)]. This constellation, however, does not exist in reality (M:229–30). Hence the presentation is insufficient.

Therefore the next chapter (Chapter 9) must widen the theoretical terrain. Marx introduces a new concept 'production price'; "its presupposition is the existence of a *general rate of profit*" (GRP) (M:234). Thus Marx *posits* in Chapter 9 the 'production price' [cf. equation (11)/(22)]. He indicates that this is "a transformation of value" ("eine verwandelte Form des Werths" – M:239; E:173) but nevertheless carries out a quantitative *substitution* between the two levels of abstraction! This is a problem *if* his method is the Method of Concretion (§3.2–§3.3), which is the hypothesis from which I start.

The point is that the status of *this* transformation is very different from the *purely conceptual* one that Marx presented in Part One and in which no quantitative differences are involved. Consider e.g. the following quotation from its Chapter 2:

> while surplus-value and profit are in fact the same – they are *numerically* identical – profit is still for all that a transformation {verwandelte Form} of surplus-value ... (M:64; cf. E:58, F:139)

Or from Chapter 1:

> Materially {Stoff; stofflich} considered ... the *profit* ... is not different from the *surplus-value* itself. Hence its absolute magnitude is not different from the magnitude of the surplus-value (...) it is however a *transformation* {verwandelte *Form*} of the latter ... (M:8–9-mt)[16]

For the Part One transformation no new quantitative determinations come in. However, as Marx is well aware, for his Part Two transformation we do have different quantities ($\pi_i q_i \neq p_i q_i$ and $k/v \neq k_i/v_i$ and $s' v_i \neq r' k_i$), at least for the micro

---

[16] This text appears on the opening pages (2–3) of the manuscript; apparently it is omitted in Engels's text.

level. Thus he substitutes quantities of a theoretically insufficient constellation (πq) into that of a theoretically enriched, more concrete, constellation (pq). On the basis of the Method of Concretion this would be very awkward. Then the problem is not primarily that the two famous conditions of aggregation (of $\Sigma\pi q$ = Σpq and $R=S$) are mathematically incompatible (as stressed in the literature on the issue). No, the primary problem is that of conceptually incompatible quantities.[17] (Note that for post-Marx solutions to 'the' transformation problem, there is potentially the same pitfall.)

It is especially in Chapter 10 that Marx reflects on, and questions, what he accomplished in the previous chapters, including the consequences for his self-interpretation of the concept of value set out in his manuscripts.

§4.2   *Chapter 8: the problematic*

I now move on to the relevant details. I begin by recapitulating the important point about Chapter 8 that was been made above. This chapter sets out the following five assumptions/theses (M:223–4, 229–30):

[A]   assume commodities are sold 'at their values' [presumably πq; cf. equation (5)];
[B]   assume equalised rates of surplus-value [$s'_i = s'_j$];
[C]   we have diverging compositions of capital [$(k/v)_i \ne (k/v)_j$];
[Dᵃ]   hence [A-C] equal capitals produce unequal surplus-value or profit [$(s/k)_i \ne (s/k)_j$];
[Dᵇ]   therefore we have diverging rates of profit [$r'_i \ne r'_j$];
[E]   in fact, however, we have (tendentially) equalised profit rates [$r'_i = r'_j$].

These five assumptions/theses are inconsistent. At least one of them must be wrong, it remains to find out which one(s). Analytically, I repeat analytically, this set up might make sense. (Chapter 8 makes sense generally – also in that there are no deviations from the later *Capital I* terminology.)

§4.3   *Chapter 9: a cheerful accommodation for the inconsistency*

Chapter 9 sets up a *possible* constellation accommodating for the inconsistency (this is my interpretation); however, in any case it is obvious that the text is investigative (*Forschung*) not presentational (*Darstellung*).[18] As it turns out Marx's set up is much along the lines of his earlier 1861–63 manuscript.

---

17   A similar critique was made earlier by Hartmann (1970, p. 370): "The mistake made by Marx was the mistake of viewing a transcendentally early (category) as identical to a transcendentally late one." Smith (1990, p. 168) adds: "This goes against one of the basic canons of systematic theories of categories." (Hartmann is cited from Smith.)

18   Cf. Vollgraf and Roth 2003, p. 385.

The chapter starts by repeating the assumption about the rate of surplus-value [B above]. Marx also introduces a number of simplifying assumptions such as the full and linear depreciation of fixed capital within the year, and equal turnover times (M:230–1).

Next he sets out the famous three schemes (M: 231–3). (The first and the second scheme apply assumptions/theses [A]-[D];[19] the third scheme is the one were Marx introduces prices of production as diverging from value [equation (11)/(16)]). He drops sales at value [A], introduces (instead) production prices and so gets rid of diverging profit rates [D^b]. He does so without hardly any argument:

> Their presupposition [i.e., of production prices] is the existence of a general rate of profit ... In reality the very different profit rates ... are by way of *competition* equalised into a *general rate of profit* ... (M:234-mt; cf. E:167, F:257)

Note that he maintains the disproportional production of surplus-value [D^a] (M:234–5).

However, [A] is not really dropped. At this point in the text Marx posits one of the famous two aggregate equalities – that is, that of 'values' and production prices (perhaps $\Sigma pq = \Sigma \pi q$). The aggregate equality of profits and surplus-value ($R = S$) is posited throughout.[2c]

As indicated, from the point of view of the Method of Concretion (§3.3), these equalities make no sense. Not so much because of an analytical mistake (the standard critique), but because of a methodological mistake: the 'values' [πq] ('values' in Marx's terminology at this point) have no concrete existence, hence they are quantitatively incompatible with (more) concrete existence. From the point of view of the Method of Completion (§3.5) there would not be such problem; however, at this point in the text I am still assuming Marx has adopted the Method of Concretion.

Finally, for Chapter 9 I draw attention to the passage where Marx seems quite happy about what he has achieved so far, declaring that the current presentation "reveals for the first time ... the inner connection" between value and production price, and between surplus-value and profit (M:245; cf. E:178 and F:268).

---

19 In the second scheme the silly addition of profit rates (to 110%) is Engels's (F:256).
20 When he posits $\Sigma pq = \Sigma \pi q$ (presumably) he feels there is a difficulty (M:236–7; E:169; F:259); M:241–3 on the same theme.

§4.4   *Chapter 10: gloomy reflection*

In Chapter 10, however, the scene seems much more gloomy and dismal. After two pages connecting the two chapters, Marx posits two research questions, one immediately after the other (I call these Question 1 and Question 2):

> {Question 1} The really difficult question here is this: how does this equalisation of profits or this emergence {Hertstellung} of the general profit rate come about, since it is evidently a result and cannot be a point of departure.
>
> It is clear first of all that an assessment of commodity values, e.g. in money, can only be the result of their exchange, and that, when we presuppose such assessment, we have to consider them as the outcome of *actual exchanges of commodity value against commodity value*. {Question 2:} But how could this exchange of commodities against their actual values have come about? (M:250-mt; cf. E:183–4, F:274–5)

It is especially at this point in the text that the reader (I) may start doubting if Marx indeed *aims to adopt* (remember this is a research manuscript) the Method of Concretion. Note the "actual exchanges" ("wirklicher Austausche"), which especially for a Hegel inspired scholar cannot leave room for compromises. So do we bid 'πq' farewell?

Marx devotes about 20 pages to Question 2, before he gets to the first. The answer to Question 1 (M:269–70; E 205–7; F:297–8) is rather limited. We learn mainly that capital moves from low to high profit rate spheres and that the thus affected supply in relation to demand establishes the transformation of values into production prices. This answer is far more problematical than it might perhaps seem at first sight. (The process briefly described *here* is not problematical – such movement of capital and labour is also part and parcel of classical political economy, and of many economics paradigms after it.) The problem is that Marx must rely, so it seems, on a *historical* process to set out a *systematic* problem! The movement of capital is a continuous *systemic* process. However, the implication of Marx's set up is that the GRP 'transformation' is of the past. Marx is aware of this, as we can infer from the fact that he realises that Question 1 cannot properly be answered before Question 2.

By this time – that is, when he finally gets to Question 1 (page M:269) – I guess that Marx had run out of steam as a result of being disillusioned by the consequences of his Chapter 9 outline (1864–65) – that is, the answer to Question 2.

On to Question 2: how could the *actual* exchange of commodities against their *actual* values $\{\pi q\}$ have come about? Marx repeats (M:250) that such exchange (given the equalised rate of surplus-value assumption, as he once again stresses) would result in unequal rates of profit – which is counterfactual.[21] Obviously, the production prices of the research manuscript for Chapter 9 put the (current) *Capital I* Chapter 1 presentation – of commodity exchange according to value – into question in a rather disastrous way.[22] It is clear from the text that Marx was much bothered by this. My reading is that Marx sets out, in a unsystematic way, a number of analytical consequences of where he has got to, together with some possible ways out. We find, for example, a model-like case in which workers own the means of production and exchange products according to their value; then a move to a 'historical transformation'; next a long détour on *market* value and supply and demand generally, without coming to the point (in his work of 1896, all this was rightfully ridiculed by Böhm-Bawerk in this context).[23]

The 'try out' of the historical transformation especially is inconsistent with the Chapter 9 procedure.[24]

On page M:267 (E:203; F:294) Marx finally arrives at a systematically and thus methodologically relevant statement. Note that he uses the kind of 1859 (or 1867) terminology of exchange (Engels puts the following in the past tense suggesting an even more direct reference to *Capital I*, Chapter 1):

> In considering money, it is assumed that commodities are sold at their values, because there is no foundation {Grund} to consider prices deviating from value since <u>the concern is just the changes in form that commodities have to undergo</u> when they are turned into money and then transformed back into commodities again. ... <u>it is completely irrelevant for them *as such*</u> [the commodities] <u>whether the realised commodity price is *below* or *above* their value</u>. The *value* of the commodity as groundwork {Grundlage} remains important, since money can only be developed <u>conceptually</u> from this foundation {Fundament}, and *price*, in its gen-

---

21 Note that for the following 20 pages Engels maintains the structure of Marx's text.
22 Instead of *Capital I*, Chapter 1, we can take the 1859 *Critique* as a reference point. On page M:257 (E:191–2) Marx refers to this work (note that the 1864–65 manuscript for *Capital I* is lost – see Kopf et al. 1983, pp. 15*–16*).
23 Böhm-Bawerk, of course, read the text as a final document – that is, as polished by Engels.
24 Engels, on the other hand, seems to have liked the idea. It has given rise to a historical, as against systematic, interpretation of *Capital I*, Chapter 1 – rightly criticised by Arthur (1997). Such an interpretation, however, cannot save the Chapter 9 procedure (even neglecting the latter's internal problems of the two conditions).

eral concept {seinem allgemeinen Begriff nach}, is only *valeur monetisie* [monetised value; the two words appear in French]. (M:267-mt; cf. E:203, F:294–5)

Methodologically this is fine. I believe this sheds light on what Marx (with the 1859, or later, text in his mind) intended to do in the 1867 text. It is a *conceptual* presentation in stages of complexity. So, finally, it seems that Marx leans back to the Method of Concretion?

In fact, Marx shows here himself (implicitly that is) that the Chapter 9 procedure makes no methodological sense. An abstract magnitude of value cannot be put into quantitative equality with the magnitude of some concretum.

I round off this section with a comment on Engels's editorial work. Quite apart from all my methodological critique on Chapter 9 as addressed above, Engels seems to have misjudged Marx's own critique on that chapter in his Chapter 10 manuscript (and Engels's polishing work made all this worse). Thus Engels provided intelligent people like Böhm-Bawerk with plentiful opportunities to point out inconsistencies, inconsistencies that Marx himself in fact laid bar.

§5   Notes on a small 1878 ms.: diverging rates of surplus-value

My suggestion that Marx was not happy with the Chapter 9 manuscript is sustained by the fact that Marx kept returning to the matter in manuscripts from much after the publication of *Capital I* (see §1) even if without substantial progress (that is, in the MEGA II/14 manuscripts). However, I should like draw attention to a hint in Marx's final manuscript on the issue (Marx 2003f/1878?).[25] This is a small manuscript of six pages dating probably from 1878 (see Vollgraf and Roth 2003, p. 697). Consider the following passages:[26]

> For [the] calculation of the rate of profit that the social capital yields it was assumed {angenommen}, 1) that the rate of surplus-value uniform for the different heaps of capital {Kapitalmassen} in different branches of industry, 2) and *neglecting* turnover, i.e., the turnover of the social capital over the year posited = 1.

---

25   If we neglect the 25 lines of algebra which is the content of a manuscript from probably 1877–82.
26   It is extremely difficult to translate these texts. Marx's texts are unpolished and continuously mixed with shorthand phrases.

> In fact for the different heaps of capital *different rates of surplus-value and different turnover times*. (158-mt)

The clarification following it (after seven, printed, lines on the calibration of turnover times) is very interesting. Note Marx's usage of the term pure (*rein*) which he reserves for law-like entities.

> These are just differences {Differenzen} emerging from the pure economic conditions, namely *different {verschiedne} magnitudes of the capitals invested in business sectors, different rates of exploitation of labour-power, different turnover times*. However [there are] other aspects of the equalisation such as unattractiveness, danger and standing of the work. (158-mt)

This text is ambiguous. With some hesitation I opt for the interpretation that the text emphasised by Marx in the last quotation, sums up the pure conditions. (In the alternative interpretation the two assumptions of the first citation would presumably be the 'pure conditions'. However, it would then be most puzzling how these could turn in their exact opposite.)

Remember the first quotation in §4.1 [p. 294 of the current book] from the 1864–65 manuscript (its p. 250) where Marx posited the *uniform* (general) rate of surplus-value as part of the 'pure' constellation. Thirteen years later, if my interpretation above is correct, *non-uniform* rates of surplus-value are seen to be part of the theoretically *pure* constellation – whereas the competition between labourers has become a subordinate factor. Then even Marx's reason for the troubling 1864–65 Chapter 9 type of procedure evaporates.

Conclusions

We have seen that the assessment of Marx's GRP transformation procedure in Chapter 9 of his 1864–65 research manuscript for *Das Kapital III* hinges on the interpretation of the general method that he adopts for the three volumes of *Capital*. If the adopts the Method of Concretion (cf. §3.3) then the procedure is illegitimate. The problem centres on the two equations for 'value' and 'price of production', each posited at a different level of abstraction. Then the mistake is to transpose quantities between these levels. If Marx adopts the Method of Completion (§3.5) the procedure is legitimate, though not without problems. More important, it would make much of *Capital I* problematical.

We have seen that in the course of writing Chapter 10 of the research manuscript for *Das Kapital III*, Marx becomes increasingly worried about the consequences of Chapter 9. For over 15 pages it seems that Marx is leaning towards the Method of Completion. However, towards the end of Chapter 10, Marx's apparently reverts to the Method of Concretion, so leaving the Chapter 9 procedure in the air. This conclusion applies to the manuscript. On basis of 'Engels's' text (as well as his interpretation of Part One of *Capital I*) the Method of Completion is fairly consistent for most of Part Two of *Capital III*.

The problem for the interpretation of Marx's work, and for the further development of Marxian theory after Marx, is not that Marx encountered a big problem that he did not solve. The problem is that Engels in his editorial work polished away most of Marx's worries and so made it appear as if *Das Kapital III* was a near to final texts instead of a research manuscript on this issue.

We also saw (§3.3) that the very reason for Marx's troubling 1864–65 Chapter 9 type of procedure is in fact the thesis of a uniform rate of surplus-value. If that thesis is dropped there is in fact no transformation 'problem'. In reference to Marx's brief last manuscript on the issue (§5), we saw that there is some (thin) evidence that Marx might have been about to set on this track.

References

Arthur, Christopher J. 1997, 'Against the logical-historical method: dialectical derivation versus linear logic', in Moseley and Campbell (eds) 1997, pp. 9–37.

Arthur, Christopher J. 2009, 'The possessive spirit of capital: subsumption/inversion/contradiction', in Bellofiore and Fineschi (eds) 2009, pp. 148–62.

Bellofiore, Riccardo, and Nicola Taylor (eds) 2004, *The constitution of capital: essays on volume 1 of Marx's 'Capital'*, Basingstoke: Palgrave Macmillan.

Bellofiore, Riccardo, and Roberto Fineschi (eds) 2009, *Re-reading Marx: new perspectives after the critical edition*, Basingstoke: Palgrave Macmillan.

Hartmann, Klaus 1970, *Die Marxsche Theorie*, Bonn: Walter de Gruyter & Co.

Heinrich, Michael 1996, 'Engels' edition of the third volume of *Capital* and Marx's original manuscript', *Science & Society* 60(4): 452–66.

Heinrich, Michael 2009, 'Reconstruction or deconstruction? Methodological controversies about value and capital, and new insights from the critical edition', in Bellofiore and Fineschi (eds) 2009, pp. 71–98.

Kopf, Eike, Willi Bang, Joachim Conrad, and Edgar Klapperstück (with collaboration of Liesel Hanemann 1983, Einleitung zu MEGA II/5, pp. 1*–55*.

Marx, Karl 1867/1866–67 {4th edn 1890}, *Das Kapital; Kritik der Politischen Ökonomie, Band I, Der Produktionsprozeß des Kapitals*, MEW 23, Berlin: Dietz Verlag.

Marx, Karl 1894E/~1864–65,[27] ed. F. Engels, *Das Kapital, Kritik der Politischen Ökonomie, Band III, Der Gesamtprozesz der kapitalistischen Produktion*, MEW 25, Berlin: Dietz Verlag.

Marx, Karl 1894F/~1864–65, idem, Engl. transl. David Fernbach, *Capital: a critique of political economy, vol. III* (1981), Harmondsworth: Penguin.[28]

Marx, Karl 1894M/1864–65, see Marx 1992M/1864–65.

Marx, Karl 1980/1861–63, *Zur Kritik der politischen Ökonomie (Manuskript 1861–1863)*, MEGA II/3.5, eds. Hannes Skambraks, Hannelore Drohla, Bernd Fisher, Carl-Erich Vollgraf (with Jutta Laskowski and Anna Maria Rambaum), Berlin: Dietz Verlag.[29]

Marx, Karl 1980F/1861–63, idem Engl. transl. Ben Fowkes, *Economic manuscript of 1861–1863 (continuation)* (1991), *Marx–Engels collected works*, volume 33, New York: International Publishers.

Marx, Karl 1992M/1864–65, 'Das Kapital (Ökonomisches Manuskript 1863–65), Drittes Buch', in *Ökonomische Manuskripte 1863–67*, MEGA II/4.2, eds. Manfred Müller, Jürgen Jungnickel, Barbara Lietz, Christel Sander and Arthur Schnickmann, Berlin: Dietz Verlag.

Marx, Karl 2003f/1878?, 'Über Profitrate, Kapitalumschlag, Zins und Rabat' (edited by Carl-Erich Vollgraf and Regina Roth with collaboration of Jürgen Jungnickel) MEGA II/14, Berlin: Akademie Verlag, pp. 155–62.

Moseley, Fred 2000, 'The new solution to the transformation problem: a sympathetic critique', *Review of Radical Political Economics* 33(2): 282–316.

Moseley, Fred (ed.) 2005, *Marx's theory of money: modern appraisals*, London/New York: Palgrave Macmillan.

Moseley, Fred, and Martha Campbell (eds) 1997, *New investigations of Marx's method*, Atlantic Highlands, NJ: Humanities Press.

Reuten, Geert 2004, 'Productive force and the degree of intensity of labour: Marx's concepts and formalizations in the middle part of *Capital I*', in Bellofiore and Taylor (eds) 2004, pp. 117–45.

Reuten, Geert 2005, 'Money as constituent of value: the ideal introversive substance and the ideal extroversive form of value in *Capital*', in Moseley (ed.) 2005, pp. 78–92.

Reuten, Geert 2006, 'On the quantitative homology between circulating capital and capital value – the problem of Marx's and the Marxian notion of "variable capital"', paper presented at ISMT-15 and at the 2006 Historical Materialism Annual Confer-

---

27   A tilde ~ before the second date means that the text, as edited by Engels, is roughly based on that manuscript.
28   First Engl.transl. Ernest Untermann 1909.
29   MEGA: *Marx–Engels–Gesamtausgabe* (1975–1997 Dietz Verlag, Berlin; 1998-current Akademie Verlag, Berlin).

ence. https://reuten.eu/2006-on-the-quantitative-homology-between-circulating-capital-and-capital-value/

Roth, Regina 2009, 'Karl Marx's original manuscripts in the Marx-Engels-Gesamtausgabe (MEGA)', in Bellofiore and Fineschi (eds) 2009, pp. 27–49.

Smith, Tony 1990, *The logic of Marx's Capital: replies to Hegelian criticisms*, Albany: State University of New York Press.

Vollgraf, Carl-Erich, and Jürgen Jungnickel 1994, 'Marx in Marx's Worten? – Zu Engels's Edition des Hauptmanuskripts zum dritten Buch des *Kapital*', *MEGA-Studien* 2: 3–55.

Vollgraf, Carl-Erich, and Regina Roth (with collaboration of Jürgen Jungnickel) 2003, 'Introduction, contextualisation, and notes on the genesis and handing down of the MEGA II/14 texts', in *MEGA II/14*, Berlin: Akademie Verlag.

CHAPTER 15

The productive powers of labour and the redundant transformation to prices of production: a Marx-immanent critique and reconstruction

2017 article, originally published in *Historical Materialism* 25(3): 3–35.
(For its abstract see the Abstracts of all chapters, p. 8.)

It will be seen that in this article Marx's German 'potenzierte Arbeit' is translated as 'potentiated labour'. In my 2019 essay (Chapter 2 above) I adopted the translation of 'empowered labour'.

Contents

Introduction   306
1   Method and dimensions   309
2   Marx's 1864–65 General Rate of Profit transformation   311
3   'Productive powers', 'intensity of labour' and the rate of surplus-value in *Capital I*   314
    §3.1   Preliminary remarks   314
    §3.2   The productive powers of labour: degree of value-generating potencies of labour   316
    §3.3   Intensity of labour: degree of value-generating density of labour   319
    §3.4   Separate and combined average variations in productive power and intensity   320
    §3.5   A digression on 'potentiated labour' in Chapter 1   321
    §3.6   Conclusions   322
4   An immanent reconstruction: the 1864–65 GRP transformation in face of *Capital I*   324
    §4.1   Introduction   324
    §4.2   Main elements for a reconstructive account of the GRP as a stage of concretisation   325
    §4.3   Implications of the reconstruction   326
    Summary and conclusions   327
    Appendix (to §4). Core analytics of an immanent reconstruction of the GRP transformation in face of *Capital I*   329

A§1 Preliminary remarks 329
A§2 Analytics of technical change along with increasing productive powers, and associated with varying organic compositions of capital 329
References 334

Introduction[1]

In this article I revisit what probably is the main theoretical problem in *Capital*, namely the transformation of the *Capital I* value concepts into the 'prices of production' of *Capital III*, Part Two. Marx's own approach to this transformation, and its implications, was subsequently dubbed the 'transformation problem'.

Marx sets out this transformation in an 1864–65 research manuscript of 'Capital III'. At this time *Capital I* existed in a draft form that differed from the version that was actually published in 1867. In the 1864–65 manuscript some key 'Capital I' concepts – referring to averages of the capitalist economy at large – are transformed into concepts referring to the particular sectors (or branches) of production. Here he posits a configuration of so-called 'prices of production', defined by ratios of capital and wages (capital compositions) which diverge in each sector, equalised rates of surplus-value, and equalised profit rates. After Marx's death in 1883, Engels edited and published this research manuscript in Part Two of *Capital III* (1894). Soon after, however, it was discovered that Marx's transformation contains a serious flaw (see §2 below). This flaw, and later formal-analytical extensions of it, came to be known as 'the Marxian transformation problem'. I agree with many of the formal-analytical criticisms, and it is not my intention to repeat them here.[2] Note though that the

---

[1] This article is a revised and briefer version of a chapter that appears in *Marx's Capital: An Unfinished and Unfinishable Project?*, edited by Marcel van der Linden and Gerald Hubmann (Leiden: Brill). The first version was presented at a conference, under the same title, organised by the Berlin-Brandenburgische Akademie der Wissenschaften and the International Institute of Social History, Amsterdam, on 9–11 October 2014. I thank the participants for their discussion of that paper. In rewriting the text for that chapter (the second version), I benefitted especially from the comments by Chris Arthur, the main commentator at the conference. I also benefitted from a written comment by Fred Moseley, from oral and written comments by Boe Thio, and from Jurriaan Bendien's correspondence and copy-edits (all these scholars participated in the conference). The current third version has greatly benefitted from comments by the *Historical Materialism* editors and by three anonymous reviewers, for which I am grateful.

[2] For an overview, see Schefold 2004.

scholarly transformation controversy mainly concerns issues that Marx himself never dealt with. In that sense these are *external* criticisms, although this does not disqualify them.

My own aim in this article is to set out an *immanent* critique of the way in which Marx posited the transformation in 1864–65. For this immanent critique, I rely on the 1866–67 thoroughly-reworked version of *Capital I* (§3). In a reconstruction (§4) I transcend the transformation as a concretisation of the *Capital I* concepts of value and surplus-value. This concretisation makes the (current *Capital III*) concept of prices of production redundant, as a result of which the transformation problem evaporates. Instead of dual accounts for values and prices of production, my reconstruction posits one single account.[3] My argument focuses on the frail constraints of the transformation procedure posited by Marx himself, and thus interprets the problem to be wider in scope than in the usual appraisals.

In *Capital I*, Part Four, Marx presents the determinants of relative surplus-value and the concomitant rate of surplus-value, a major one being the 'productive powers' of labour (also translated as 'productive forces'). He associates sectoral divergences in the productive powers with divergent *value-generating potencies* of labour. Given the other determinants of the rate of surplus-value, we then obtain diverging rates of surplus-value. In the 1864–65 research manuscript of 'Capital III', however, Marx posits equalised rates of surplus-value, either because he had not yet developed the *Capital I* notion just referred to, or because he disregarded this productive-powers determinant for unknown reasons.

My reconstruction shows how, predicated on this productive-powers determinant, diverging rates of surplus-value are associated with diverging compositions of capital and equalising rates of profit, maintaining throughout the monetary-value dimensions of *Capital I*. Since in the reconstruction 'prices of production' are redundant, that monetary-value dimension also captures balanced and non-balanced prices generally.

In line with Marx's own view in the 1864–65 manuscript, the received view on the transformation is that the texts for *Capital III* put the argument of *Capital I* into question. Inverting that interpretation, I will show that the later finalised *Capital I* theory instead puts the drafts for the *Capital III* transformation into question.

---

3   On very different grounds, and without considering prices of production as a redundant concept, a single-system account is also proposed by the TSSI school ('temporal single-system interpretation'). See e.g. Moseley 2015, Chapter 9 for references on the TSSI school.

After some methodological and value-theoretical remarks (§1) followed by a summary of the transformation problematic (§2), I will focus on the concept of relative surplus-value in *Capital I*'s Part Four (§3). With that background, I then provide the main elements for a Marx-immanent reconstruction which transcends the transformation (§4).

The admittedly difficult and controversial idea I propose is that Marx himself posited the *problematic* in such a way, the better that a transformation *problem* could emerge which remains irresolvable because of its deficient premises. Thus, more than a hundred and twenty years after 1894, I want to argue that the problematic may well have been wrongly posited by Marx himself in his drafts, and therefore by his latter-day critics as well. In that case, the difficult challenge for us is to transcend the way the issue was originally framed.

Because the dating of Marx's manuscripts for *Capital* is important to this article, relevant dates are presented in *Table 1*.

TABLE 1 Marx's work on Capital from 1863 to 1867

Volume	Dating	Draft	Remarks
C I	1863–64	penultimate draft	lost or blended into the final draft (see §2)
C III	1864–65	first full research ms.	
C II	1865 early 1866	first research ms.	Engels convinces Marx that he should bring out C-I, even when C-II and C-III are not completed
C I	1866–67	final draft first edition	

SOURCE: VOLLGRAF 2012[4]

Making the argument in this article necessarily involves quite a number of terminological references, as well as citations from German and English texts,

---

[4] Between 1868 and his death in 1883, Marx's continuation of *Capital* is very briefly as follows (for details, see Vollgraf 2018):
On Capital I: second edition (of 1872); preparation third edition (of 1883); French edition (of 1872–75).
On Capital II: 1868–70 and 1877–81.
On Capital III: conceptual, mathematical and comparative statistical studies (no new drafts).

for which I adopt some conventions. I render the German noun *'Darstellung'* as *'exposition'*, and use 'exhibit' to refer to the setting-out of this exposition. With regard to Marx's research manuscripts, the German noun *'Forschung'* is rendered as *'investigation'* and I use 'write', 'set out' or variants thereof for the setting-out of this investigation. Within cited passages, the italics are always an emphasis in the original. Underlining indicates my own emphasis. Unproblematic insertions in quotations are rendered in square brackets. My own comments are in braces. The abbreviation 'mt' after a page number (e.g. 370-mt) denotes my own translation. Within my translations, an original German term is likewise inserted within braces. References to the published texts of *Capital* are rendered in italics. When I refer to manuscripts prior to it, these are non-italicised in quotation marks ('Capital I', 'Capital III').

1 Method and dimensions

To place the argument in its appropriate theoretical context, I will first make five relevant points about Marx's method and the value-theoretical dimensions which he uses.

1. In *Capital*, Marx's methodology of exposition involves different stages. He moves from the production of capital (Book I), to capital's circulation which includes the realisation-conditions of production (Book II), and finally to the concretisation of the former two stages, distinguishing on the one hand capital in its particular material manifestation (*Gestaltungen*) of sectors of production, and on the other its functional forms, such as industrial capital and finance capital (Book III). Although in my view there are good reasons for interpreting Marx's method as a systematic-dialectical one, the argument of the current article does not rely on that interpretation.[5] I want to emphasise here only that – contrary to most 'economic modelling' approaches – Marx's method is one in which the general statements established within *each* one of these three stages must be claims to *general* truth. In particular, if for example a level III statement would turn out to be inconsistent with a level I statement, one of those statements must be false. (As regards a core theme in my argument in this article, for example, we cannot combine the first-stage general statement that the production of commodities and commodity transactions is determined by their value – as explained by labour-time – and a next-stage general statement that,

---

5 For various accounts of the systematic-dialectics, see the contributions in Moseley and Smith (eds) 2014.

instead, commodity production and transactions are determined by prices of production that are only partly determined in that way. Similarly, we cannot combine the initial general statement that capitalist production is motivated by the production of surplus-value only, with another general statement that it is determined by an *amalgamation* of surplus-value and a capital-size related profit-levelling (dis)agio.) In brief: the abstract statements must be true statements; they must, without additional qualification, cover the richer and more-concrete statements.

2. In Marx's way of exposition of the production process in *Capital I* – the production of surplus-value and therefore of capital – he is able to abstract from ('bracket') all kinds of factors that do not affect this core matter (including the realisation restrictions in *Capital II*, and the financiers' share in surplus-value in *Capital III*). In this way he can show how labour is the overall determinant for the production of surplus-value and capital.

3. The first chapter of *Capital I* is complex.[6] In my view, it ought to be read in the context of the Ricardian labour-embodied theory of value which predominated in those days (recall the subtitle of *Capital I*).[7] A main result of that chapter is that he breaks away from Ricardianism. For example, implicitly opposing Ricardo, Marx writes:

> Human labour-power in its fluid state, or human labour, creates value, but is not itself value. It becomes value in its coagulated state, in objective form {i.e., commodities}. (Marx 1976 [1890^4], p. 142)

Thus the value of commodities is *explained* by labour-time. However, a full comprehension of this chapter requires a reading interconnected within the full Part One (i.e., Chapters 1–3), as including especially Chapter 3 on money.

4. It follows from this Part One that in *Capital I*, as for all of *Capital*, value entities are expressed within a monetary dimension (using some currency standard such as £); the same applies to all numerical examples.[8] It is important to emphasise this since in some interpretations of Marx's theory, 'value' is itself taken to have a labour-time dimension (those same accounts often adopt

---

6 Marx himself admits that the chapter is complicated – see his Foreword to the first edition (1867).
7 A distinction ought to be made between, first, the dominance of a school of thought (here, the Ricardian one) in university teaching and in common appraisal and, second, research leading to new thought that might perhaps become a new dominant school in teaching and appraisal later on. There are considerable time lags between the two.
8 This was pointed out by Elson (1979).

the term 'labour values' – one that is never used in *Capital*).⁹ At the expositional level of the production of capital (*Capital I*) Marx aims to *explain* value and surplus-value (within a monetary dimension) in terms of labour-time (in Parts Three to Five, 350 pages) – an explanation in terms of labour-time does, of course, not mean that *value* ever discards its monetary dimension.¹⁰

5. Even if Marx breaks with Ricardo (point 3 above), for some, including myself, this break is not complete.¹¹ Whereas I am a proponent of a value-form theoretical interpretation and reconstruction of *Capital I*, Part One, that is not relevant for my argument in this article.¹² This article is not about *Capital I*, Part One as such, and it mainly builds on its Parts Three to Five, in which such disputed matters are absent or not prominent. What is more, the reconstruction that I propose in §4 should fit any interpretation of the value-theoretical categories. For each interpretation, the reconstruction does away with dichotomous 'value'–'prices of production' algorithms, and results in a continuity of the concept of value for each of *Capital*'s levels of exposition. This conceptual continuity *includes* all specific and concrete market phenomena in terms of balanced or imbalanced market prices (*Capital II*, Part Three and *Capital III*, Part One). However, it *excludes* 'prices of production' and hence dual-account systems.

2   Marx's 1864–65 General Rate of Profit transformation

In this article I shall refer to the field of *Capital III*, Part Two, as 'the general rate of profit transformation' (abbreviated as 'GRP transformation'). In the research

---

9   For example, Schefold (who is generally well acquainted with the field) does presume this. Thus, in his introduction to *Capital III*, Schefold erroneously writes "Arbeitswerten (wie Marx sie nannte) [Labour-values (as Marx called them)]" (Schefold 2004, p. 874). Possibly Marx used this expression in some writing prior to *Capital* – Schefold cites no source – but that would surprise me very much.

10 In §1.1 of Reuten 2004, I trace the dimensions and measures adopted by Marx in the explanatory Parts Three to Five of *Capital I*. [See Chapter 8 of the current book.]

11 See the references in Reuten 1988 and 1993 [for the latter see Chapter 6 of the current book]; here I merely mention the pivotal paper by Backhaus 1969 (English translation 1980). However, the value-form theoretic critique does not dispute Marx's explanation of surplus-value in terms of labour-time (that is, at least, my own take on value-form theory). Regarding Part One's Chapter 3, a main problem is that Marx's theory of 'commodity money' is clearly a nineteenth-century theory that is not applicable in the current age (see Campbell 1997, Williams 2000 and Bellofiore 2005 – these are contrary positions, though in my view in the end complementary ones).

12 I should add here that in the opinion of one anonymous reviewer, it is relevant.

manuscript for it, of 1864–65, Marx sets out a concretisation of his 'Capital I' categories, in face of the tendency toward equalisation of rates of profit between sectors, or to the formation of a 'general rate of profit' (GRP).[13] In face of the 'Capital I' concepts of value and surplus-value, Marx refers to this concretisation as a 'transformation'.

I assume that many readers have at least a general acquaintance with Marx's GRP transformation (that is, of Engels's rendering of it in his edition of *Capital III*) and with its problems: 'the transformation problem(s)'. In brief, Marx posits the relationships between sectors of production as: (1) equal or equalising rates of profit; (2) diverging compositions of capital; and (3) equal or equalising rates of surplus-value. He then feels (reluctantly) constrained to drop his 'Capital I' commodity sales at value, and to introduce 'production prices' instead.[14]

The standard critique of Marx's GRP transformation procedure is that it is a 'halfway house'. He transforms *Capital I* output quantities into *Capital III* output quantities, neglecting to apply that transformation to the inputs.[15] He therefore obtains incorrect results (especially regarding the simultaneous aggregate equalities of, on the one hand, the commodity values and the prices of production of commodities, and on the other, surplus-value and profit). This critique is accurate (though see footnote 3), and it has been extensively dealt with already in the literature.[16]

However, in a way this was not Marx's problem, since he (mistakenly) neglected it, or was not aware of it.[17][18] Elsewhere, I approach the matter rather

---

13 The research manuscript is published in *MEGA II/4.2* (1993). Engels's editorial work is published in *MEGA II/14* (2003). *MEGA II/15* (2004) contains the critical edition of *Das Kapital III* of 1894.

14 Reuten 2018, section 2, provides an overview and a critical discussion of that text. Reuten 2009 discusses the transformation issue mainly in methodological terms. [Chapter 14 of the current book.]

15 Here I refer to the published versions (*Capital I*, *Capital III*) as they appeared for the reader at the time of publication of the third Volume. In his Foreword to the latter, Engels provides the reader no hint concerning the order in which Marx wrote the published manuscripts – see Table 1 above (even though some readers might perhaps have inferred this from Engels's Foreword to *Capital II*).

16 See the overview by Schefold (2004, pp. 875–95).

17 Perhaps he was aware of it in other contexts (see e.g. his 1861/63 discussion of Bailey in the *Theories of surplus-value*, *MECW* 32, pp. 352–3; I thank Jurriaan Bendien for pointing this out). Marx seems nearly aware of it in his manuscript for *Capital III*, 'Chapter 12' (M:283; cf. E:217, EF:309) – see the next footnote for these shorthand references.

18 In this section I use the following shorthand references: M = Marx 1993 (Marx's 1864/65 research manuscript for *Das Kapital III*, *MEGA* II/4.2); MF = Marx 2015 (Fowkes's

from the perspective of the problems that Marx *was* aware of in the 1864–65 manuscript.[19] There it is set out how Marx is sceptical and worries about his transformation, the main point being that his transformation cannot simply be combined with his text for 'Capital I' – i.e., its draft at the time (1864–65). Howard and King (1989, p. 37) comment: "Engels accepted Marx's defective solution to the transformation problem uncritically. He did not, indeed, follow up or even comment upon the uncertainties expressed by Marx himself concerning the volume III solution." In my view Marx's own worries overarch those of the post-Marx criticisms: even if he would not have made the formal mistake of neglecting the transformation of inputs, his own problems with the manuscript would still prevail. These problems are not resolved in the standard post-Marx solutions to the transformation problem.

In the remainder of the current section I merely focus on one passage, from what became Chapter 10 of *Capital III*, where Marx writes that equality in the rate of surplus-value is not just a simplifying theoretical presupposition, but rather a *law* which is predicated on competition between workers:

> [E]quality in the *grade of exploitation of labour* or the *rate of surplus-value* (...) presupposes competition among the workers and an equalisation that takes place by their continual migration from one sphere of production to another. (MF:286-amended; M:250; cf. E:184, EF:275)[20] [See footnote 18 for these shorthand references.]

Anticipating §3 and §4, I indicate already here that I have no problems with this competition determinant of the rate of surplus-value (concerning the 'intensity of labour'). In this manuscript, however, Marx neglects the productive-powers determinant of the rate of surplus-value that we find in Part Four of *Capital I*, which has nothing to do with competition between workers (see §3.2). However, we do not know what manuscript of 'Capital I' Marx had before him in 1864–65. The draft of 1863–64 for *Capital I* is either lost (as

---

translation of the former); E = Marx 1964 (Engels's 1894 edition of *Das Kapital III*, *Marx-Engels-Werke* Band 25); EF = Marx 1981 (Fernbach's translation of the former: *Capital III*).

19 In Reuten 2018 (section 2). [Not included in the current book.]

20 Marx continues: "A general rate of surplus-value of this kind – as a tendency, like all economic laws – is presupposed by us as *theoretical* simplification; but in practice it is an actual presupposition of the capitalist mode of production, even if inhibited to a greater or lesser extent by practical frictions .... In theory we presuppose that the laws of the capitalist mode of production develop in their pure form." (Translation amended.)

much was suggested previously by the MEGA II/5 editors),[21] or – and this is the recent expert opinion – it was blended (*verschnitten*) into the final version compiled for the printer (as convincingly argued by MEGA II editor Vollgraf).[22]

3 'Productive powers', 'intensity of labour' and the rate of surplus-value in *Capital I*

§3.1 *Preliminary remarks*

Six preliminary remarks are in order here:

1. In the next section (§4), I present an immanent reconstruction of the GRP problematic – 'immanent' in the sense that I base myself on Marx's own text. Divergent rates of surplus-value in different sectors of production are at the core of this reconstruction. In §3, I therefore reconsider Marx's exposition of surplus-value and the rate of surplus-value in *Capital I*, in order to argue that the key to the solution of the transformation problematic is found in *Capital I*, Parts Four and Five, on the production of relative surplus-value.

2. Recall Marx's exposition of surplus-value in *Capital I*, in which he draws a distinction between absolute surplus-value (Part Three) and relative surplus-value (Part Four), each predicated on some given real wage per working day. Then the *absolute surplus-value* varies with the length of the working day. The *relative surplus-value* varies with the production costs of the wage bundle. Thus, at a given length of the working day (and hence with a given absolute surplus-value), the surplus-value in its aspect of relative surplus-value may increase, when the value of commodities that make up the wage bundle decreases (and vice versa).

3. Recall from my §1 that 'value' has a monetary dimension, and that Marx aims to *explain* value and surplus-value in terms of labour-time.

4. It is relevant to emphasise that, in most of *Capital I*, Marx reasons from economic averages – including their change.[23] This applies especially also for most of what Marx develops in the 350 pages of Parts Three to Five, where he

---

21 See Kopf, Bang, Conrad and Klapperstück 1983, pp. 15*–16*.
22 Vollgraf 2012, p. 465; his full argument can be found on pp. 464–7.
23 I stressed this in Reuten 2004, but it is emphasised much more by Vollgraf (2012, pp. 450–1). He points to Marx's acquaintance with the work of Quételet, a Belgian mathematician and statistician who in a work of 1835 was the first to apply "averages" in social science. Vollgraf also quotes Marx on Quételet from the 1863–65 manuscript (p. 879). In a footnote in *Capital I*, Marx refers in passing to Quételet (Marx 1867, p. 261, n. 8; Marx 1962 [1890], p. 342, n. 8; Marx 1976 [1890], p. 440, n. 1).

discusses (changes in) the 'average' production of surplus-value and the average capital. Marx repeats over and again that he is only considering averages (also alternated with the term 'normal'). Except when he discusses *changes* (especially in productive powers), differences between sectors are bracketed out.

5. It is just as relevant that the concept of the 'composition of capital' (the c/v ratio) makes its proper appearance only in Part Seven of *Capital I*. In the relevant Parts Four and Five, the capital composition is mostly only implicit (it is alluded to in Part Four's Chapter $15^{Ger.13}$).[24] Notably it is not alluded to in Chapter $12^{Ger.10}$ on the productive powers of labour, where the discussion in the next subsection (3§2) starts.

6. From the 1845/46 *German Ideology* onwards, Marx adopts the term *Produktivkräfte* (in MECW 5 it is translated as 'productive forces'). Regarding the standard English translation of *Capital I* by Ben Fowkes, I note here that he translates the German *Produktivkraft der Arbeit* as 'productivity of labour'.[25] This does not cover the meaning of the term. It is moreover unfortunate, because Marx sometimes also uses the term *Arbeitsproduktivität* (labour productivity). In all of the following citations, I have amended the translation for *Produktivkraft* to 'productive power' (marked *...*); I use the same mark for any other amendments of the translation. Fowkes also misses the related term *potenzierte Arbeit* (see below). The same applies for the Moore and Aveling translation. These remarks highlight that the art of translation is inevitably also one of interpretation. All English citations below have been checked against the German.

---

24 Marx 1962 [1890^4], pp. 466–7 and 473–4; Marx 1976 [transl. 1890^4], pp. 571 and 577–8. Superscripts 'Ger' followed by a number, refer to the chapter in the German edition.

25 Most of the time at least – e.g. on page F:453, second paragraph, Fowkes translates *Produktivkraft* as "productive power", and on page F:508 it is translated as "productive forces" (cf. M^4:407). Not only do we lose terminological connections, the English text also makes connections that are absent from the German (especially with the German term *Produktivität der Arbeit*, and when Fowkes translates this as "productivity of labour", "productivity" being his most frequent translation for *"Produktivkraft"*). We have the same problem in the *Results* (translated by Livingstone). Moore and Aveling (*Capital I*, edition of 1887) translate *Produktivkraft* as "productiveness" (at least in those instances that I have checked). Generally there are two translation options for the term *Kraft* as in *Produktivkraft*: power and force. The former is adopted in the *Grundrisse* translation (productive power) and the latter in *The German Ideology* and the 1859 *Critique* Introduction (productive force). I do not mind which single translation is adopted, provided that the translation is consistent. In what follows I use "productive power". At the end of Chapter $12^{Ger.10}$ Marx refers to Richard Jones, who uses the term "productive powers". Marx in his German text translates this as "Produktivkräfte", which is one reason for me to incline toward the "productive powers" translation.

References in this section are as follows: M^1 = Marx 1867^1 (*Das Kapital I*, first edition 1867, MEGA II.5); M^4 = Marx 1962 (*Das Kapital I*, fourth edition 1890, *Marx-Engels-Werke* Band 23); MF = Marx 1976 (*Capital I*, fourth edition 1890 in the Fowkes translation). All key quotations in this section have also been checked against the first German edition of *Capital* (1867), because that is nearest to the 1864–65 manuscript. Chapter references are to the English editions, with those of the German editions as superscript (e.g. Chapter 15$^{Ger.13}$).

§3.2   *The productive powers of labour: degree of value-generating potencies of labour*

I will now show how Marx posits *diverging rates of surplus-value* between sectors of production according to the development of the productive powers. Marx systematically introduces the 'productive power' of labour in Part Four, Chapter 12$^{Ger.10}$.|26

> [I]ncrease in the *productive power* of labour (...) cannot be done except by an alteration in his [the labourer's] tools or in his mode of working, or both. Hence the conditions of production of his labour, i.e., his mode of production, and the labour process itself, must be revolutionized. By an increase in the *productive power* of labour, we mean an alteration in the labour process of such a kind as to shorten the labour-time socially necessary for the production of a commodity, *hence a smaller quantity of labour acquires the force* of producing a greater quantity of use-value. (MF:431 amended; M^4:333)

In other words, the effect of such a change is that one worker works up more means of production. Marx considers the transition from the one state of the productive powers to a new one as initiated by some individual capitalist.[27] As regards the labour producing at the increased productive power, he states the following key sentence:

---

26   Earlier (Chapter 1) he wrote: "*The productive power of labour* is determined by a wide range of circumstances; it is determined amongst other things by the workers' average degree of skill, the level of development of science and its *technological applicability*, the social organisation of the process of production, the extent and effectiveness of the means of production, and the conditions found in the natural environment" (MF:130 amended; M^4:54).

27   MF:433–6; M^4:335–8.

The labour operating at this exceptional productive power acts as potentiated labour; it creates in equal periods of time greater values than average social labour of the same kind. (My translation; cf. MF:435.)[28][29]

Die Arbeit von ausnahmsweiser Produktivkraft wirkt als potenzierte Arbeit oder schafft in gleichen Zeiträumen höhere Werte als die gesellschaftliche Durchschnittsarbeit derselben Art. (M^4:337; M^1:257)[30]

Therefore, the above-average potentiated labour – labour with extra value-generating potencies – cannot be simply measured in clock-time. Note that Marx thus draws a distinction between the 'value productivity of labour' (the value produced per unit of time) – the last quotation – as opposed to labour's 'use-value productivity' (the physical quantity of commodities produced per unit of time) – the last-but-one quotation. Marx continues:

> Hence, the capitalist who applies the improved method of production, *appropriates as surplus-labour* a greater portion of the working-day than the other capitalists in the same business. He does as an individual what capital itself taken as a whole does when engaged in producing relative surplus-value. On the other hand, however, this extra surplus-value vanishes, as soon as the new method of production is generalized ... (MF:436; M^4:337)

Thus Marx feels (rightfully) constrained to exhibit a change in the socially-average production power as a change within one sector of production (of course other changes may occur in other sectors). Note that whereas he suggests a generalisation of the implementation of productive powers within a sector, he (rightfully) posits no mechanism for inter-sectoral generalisations of the development of the productive powers (equalisation of compositions

---

[28] Fowkes (Marx 1976, p. 435) renders this as: "The exceptionally productive labour acts as intensified labour; it creates in equal periods of time greater values than average social labour of the same kind." We find the "intensified" also in the earlier translation by Moore and Aveling (Marx 2010 [1887], p. 323). This is wrong, also because it risks making a confusing reference to the treatment of 'intensity of labour' discussed in Chapter $15^{Ger.13}$. Marx, as we will see, carefully distinguishes the two.

[29] Instead of "potentiated labour", an alternative translation for "potenzierte Arbeit" might perhaps be "exponentiated labour". [In my 2019 – ch. 2 above – I used the term empowered labour.]

[30] In the first edition, there are two emphases: "Die Arbeit von *ausnahmsweiser* Produktivkraft wirkt als *potenzirte* Arbeit oder schafft in gleichen Zeiträumen höhere Werthe als die gesellschaftliche Durchschnittsarbeit derselben Art" (M^1:257).

of capital?!). However, *given the value-generating potencies, this implies divergences in rates of surplus-value between sectors* – that is, under the condition that there are diverging productive powers of labour. Thus whereas there seems to be no direct measure for the comparison of the physical use-value productivity of labour *between* sectors of production (indirectly there is one – see §3.3), there is a measure for the value productivity of labour between sectors, which is the value-added per unit of labour-time. Given the real-wage rate per unit of labour-time, this value productivity can be measured by the rate of surplus-value.

Note that in the last quotation, Marx posits the 'exceptional' and 'vanishing' character of the implied divergences in rates of surplus-value (apparently due to competition). However, this circumstance is not obvious. The point is that, in the current exposition, Marx is not explicit about the composition of capital. Should a change in productive powers in a sector go along with an above-total-economy-average c/v, then the extra surplus-value or some of it will *not* vanish, whence we have persistent sectoral diverging potencies of labour and concomitantly diverging rates of surplus-value. (See §4 – and in more detail the Appendix, section A§2.)

The concept of 'potentiated labour' reoccurs one more, relevant, time in *Capital I* (Chapter 15^{Ger13}):[31]

> Machinery produces relative surplus-value, not only by ... cheapening the commodities that enter into its [labour-power's] reproduction, but also, when it is first introduced sporadically into an industry, by converting {*verwandlen*} the labour employed by the owner of that machinery, into *potentiated* labour ... During this transitional period, while the use of machinery remains a sort of monopoly, profits are exceptional {*außerordentlich*} ... (MF:530 amended; M⁴:428–9; M¹:333)[32]

In the same chapter (15$^{Ger.13}$), we find another reference to divergent sectoral rates of surplus-value related to the productive powers:[33]

> The use of machinery for the exclusive purpose of cheapening the product is limited (...) by the difference between the value of the machine and the value of the labour-power replaced by it. Since <u>the division of the day's</u>

---

31 In §3.5 I will refer to another, different occurrence.
32 The latter (Marx 1867¹) has several terms emphasised, including "potentiated" (*potenziert*) and "transitional".
33 I thank Boe Thio for drawing my attention to this passage.

work into necessary and surplus-labour differs ... *simultaneously* in different branches of industry ..., it is possible for the difference between the price of the machinery and the price of the labour-power replaced by that machinery to *vary very much* (...) [It] determines the cost to the capitalist of producing a commodity, and influences his actions through the pressure {Zwangsgesetze} of competition. (MF:515–16 amended; M^4:414; M^1:321)[34][35]

Comment. Overall, we find in *Capital I* three types of statements and arguments about generalisations and averages:
- First, *generalisations* (which are applicable in each case). For example, in capitalism, production takes the form of commodity production; or, value takes the form of monetary value.
- Second, *averages accounts*. In *Capital I*, these are most often social averages (for the economy at large). A problem with Marx's terminology is that he often conflates 'general' and 'grand average' throughout his research manuscripts and final texts – sometimes explicitly.[36][37]
- Third, *distinctions within the averages*. In *Capital I*, Marx mostly summarises these later on in the text, in terms of averages (for the distinctions above, we will see this in §3.4).

Each time, the reader has to be very alert about the type of statement Marx is actually making. Thus, in the quotations that I provided above, Marx sets out sectoral distinctions and, in particular, differences in rates of surplus-value. These are, of course, levelled out in an averages account. One of my main points is that when we get to sectors of production in a *systematic* way (the concretisation of *Capital III*, Part Two), all these sectoral distinctions – including diverging rates of surplus-value – must regain account.

§3.3 Intensity of labour: degree of value-generating density of labour

In Chapter 15$^{Ger.13}$ of Part Four, Marx systematically introduces the 'intensity of labour'. One important point about it is that, once again, labour-time cannot be

---

34   The latter text (Marx 1867^1) has several phrases emphasised.
35   The text that I emphasised reads in German (in full): "<u>Da die Teilung des Arbeitstags in notwendige Arbeit und Mehrarbeit</u> in verschiednen Ländern <u>verschieden ist</u>, ebenso in demselben Lande zu verschiednen Perioden oder während derselben Periode <u>in verschiednen Geschäftszweigen</u>; ..."
36   As in the title of *Capital III*, Chapter 9, which is identical in the research manuscript: "Formation of a general rate of profit (average rate of profit), and ...".
37   One reason might be that Marx is only gradually making up his mind about the importance of averages – see Vollgraf 2012, referred to in the first footnote of §3.1.

simply measured in terms of clock-time. Now, however, for reasons other than those for changes in productive powers. He writes:

> It [intensification of labour] imposes <u>on the worker</u> an increased expenditure of labour within a time which remains constant, <u>a heightened tension of labour-power</u>, and a closer filling-up of the pores of the working day, i.e., a condensation of labour, to a degree which can only be attained within the limits of the shortened working day. This compression of a greater mass of labour into a given period now counts for what it really is, namely an increase of the quantity of labour. In addition to the measure of its 'extensive magnitude', <u>labour-time now acquires a measure of its *degree of density*</u>*.[38] (...) The same mass of value is now produced for the capitalist by, say, 3⅓ hours of surplus labour and 6⅔ hours of necessary labour, as was previously produced by 4 hours of surplus labour and 8 hours of necessary labour. (MF:534 amended; M⁴:432–3)

Marx next uses terms like "degree of power exerted [*Grad der Kraftäußerung*]", "energy of labour" and "discipline" (MF:535; M⁴:433). In brief, it concerns the effort and strain of labour. In so far as there are intra-sector or inter-sector differences in intensity, and *to the extent* that it is the intensity that affects divergences in the intra-sector or inter-sector rates of surplus-value, these are likely to be levelled out by intra-labour competition. From *this* perspective, and this one only, the Marx of 1864–65 is quite right to posit equalised rates of surplus-value (see the quotation in §2).

§3.4 *Separate and combined average variations in productive power and intensity*

In Chapter 17$^{Ger.15}$ of Part Five – synthesising Parts Three and Four – the main focus is on social averages (this also applies for the next and last chapter of this Part, which I will not discuss here). Marx indicates that at a given average real-wage rate per 'normal working day', the rate of surplus-value depends on:[39]

---

38   "Neben das Maß der Arbeitszeit als 'ausgedehnter Größe' tritt jetzt das Maß ihres Verdichtungsgrads." Concerning the term 'measure', a general warning – for all of *Capital* – is appropriate: the meaning of the German term '*maß*' is complicated. The relevant meaning *here* seems near to 'gradation' or 'degree' – or 'measure', as in the phrase 'to considerable measure' (for at least some explication of the term, see Inwood 1992, p. 240).

39   Next to the normal sales of commodities at their value, Marx assumes that the price of labour-power may at times be above its value, but not below it.

(1) the length of the working day, or the extensive magnitude of labour, (2) the normal intensity of labour, or its intensive magnitude, whereby a given quantity of labour is expended in a given time and (3) the *productive power* of labour, whereby the same quantity of labour yields, in a given time, a greater or a smaller quantity of the product, depending on the degree of development attained by the conditions of production. (MF:655 amended; M⁴:542)

Marx emphasises strongly that the three determinants mentioned in this passage are not only variable, but also may occur separately or in several combinations. In what follows after this passage, he analyses each of these in turn, in four separate sections. Marx here usually assumes that the determinants have been generalised across the economy, whereas the previous chapters that I discussed (§3.2 and §3.3) also treated (the initiation of) changes.[40]

§3.5 A digression on 'potentiated labour' in Chapter 1

By itself, the notion of different value-generating potencies of labour (§3.2) is not a novel issue within Marx's systematic of *Capital I*. In its Chapter 1 he uses a similar notion:

> *Simple average labour* ... varies ... at different cultural epochs ... but in a particular society it is given. ... More complex labour counts only as *potentiated* or rather *multiplied* simple labour, so that a smaller quantity of complex labour *is equal* to a larger quantity of simple labour. (...) In the interests of simplification, we shall henceforth view every *kind* of

---

[40] Marx opens the first section by stating: "A working day of given length always creates the same amount of value, no matter how the productivity of labour, and, with it, the mass of the product and the price of each single commodity produced may vary." (MF:656; M⁴:543.) Given Marx's earlier exposition (§3.2 above) I take it that he refers to the social averages of labour-time and value. The first section ends with a preview in which Marx moves beyond averages: "I shall show in *Book III** that the same rate of surplus-value may be expressed in the most diverse rates of profit, and that <u>different rates of surplus-value</u> may, under certain conditions, be expressed in the same rate of profit." (MF:660; M⁴:546–7; M¹:423.) Concerning the last phrase of this sentence: at this point Marx does not seem worried about differing rates of surplus-value. In the second section, he writes: "Increased intensity of labour means increased expenditure of labour in a given time. (...) Whether the magnitude of the labour changes in extent or in intensity, there is always a corresponding change in the magnitude of the value created, independently of the nature of the article in which that value is *actualised* {*sich darstelt*}." (MF:660–61, amended; M⁴:547–8.) Marx does not posit (here) a tendency toward equalisation of the intensities, but in the following he is perhaps near to suggesting it: "If the intensity of labour were to increase

labour-power directly as simple labour-power; by this we shall simply be saving ourselves the trouble of making the reduction. (MF:135 amended;[41] M⁴:59; cf. M¹:204[42])

Note that Marx introduced the *intensity* of labour six pages earlier on (MF:129) – distinguishing between degree of skill and intensity. The similarity of the Chapter 1 and the Chapter 12$^{Ger.10}$ notions is that the *same* clock-time of different kinds of labour creates *different* quantities of value (due to different labour potencies). The reduction matter in the quotation's last sentence is perhaps acceptable as a simplification in Chapter 1; the problem is rather that Marx never returns to it.[43]

§3.6 Conclusions

With the composition of capital still being implicit, Parts Three to Five of *Capital I* are mainly an exposition of *the determinants of* the average rate of surplus-value, and changes in that rate. The first determinant is the average real-wage rate per working day of labour of average quality. The further determinants are: (1) the length of the working day; (2) the intensity of labour; and (3) the productive power of labour. These further determinants can arise either separately or in several combinations.

The intensity affects the 'density' of labour, while in contrast the productive powers affect its 'potency'. Each of the *non-generalised changes* in the intensity or the productive power of labour mean that the *value* produced in one hour of labour diverges between capitals (whether intra-sectoral or inter-sectoral).

Differing intensities of labour can be presumed to be equalised due to competition between workers. However, there is apparently no mechanism

---

simultaneously and equally in every branch of industry, then the new and higher degree of intensity would become the normal social degree of intensity, and would therefore cease to count as an extensive magnitude." (MF:661–2; M⁴:548.) I suppose that the last "extensive" is a mistake and that it should instead read "intensive".

41   Fowkes has "intensified" for the German "potenzierte". In a similar passage in Marx's 1859 *Critique*, where the German text has "einfache Arbeit auf höherer Potenz" (Marx 1859, p. 19), Ryazanskaya translates this more appropriately as "simple labour raised to a higher power" (Marx 1971 [1859], p. 31).

42   There are some deviations between the German editions.

43   In Reuten 1993 [ch. 6 of the current book] it is shown that this reduction precludes the interpretation that Marx would hold any simple pre-market labour-embodied theory of value, because there is no other way to make the reduction than via the labour market.

for the equalisation of productive powers (or techniques) between sectors. Hence Marx does not posit it: he can only exhibit the matter for single sectors. Given the extra value-generating potencies of labour as associated with above-average productive powers (§3.2), this is a key point, because in this way we obtain diverging rates of surplus-value between sectors, that is, when the development of the productive powers is unequally diffused across the economy.

Addendum. Given Marx's exposition of the productive powers recapitulated above, it is relevant to now briefly refer back to the 1864–65 GRP manuscript. Because, as indicated in §2, the 1363–64 draft for *Capital I* is missing, we do not know if the conceptualisation from 1867 presented in §3 is richer than that in the missing manuscript, which is the one that Marx presumably had in mind when he wrote the GRP manuscript.

However, all the evidence that we have points out that Marx developed his insights regarding the technique related 'potency of labour' only in 1866–67 when he worked on the final draft for the first edition of *Capital I*. Regarding the 1861–63 text this can be checked, since we have these texts: MECW 30 and 34 (based on MEGA II/3). Further, of the 1863–64 penultimate draft for Capital I we do have the 1864 *Results* (MECW 34, pp. 355–466). In this text Marx presents a quite extensive treatment of technical change. Nevertheless, as in the earlier manuscripts, he here treats only the intensity of labour.

The term 'productive powers' (or also 'technology') is mentioned several times in Chapters 1–2 of the 1864–65 manuscript (i.e., Parts One to Two of the current *Capital III*).[44] However, in those passages Marx keeps the rate of surplus-value constant.[45] The notion of (extra) value-generating potencies of labour or a variant thereof is not mentioned.

It is appropriate to indicate though that Marx in this 1864–65 manuscript considers specific sectors of production to have developed some specific 'gradation' in the development of the productive powers of labour. Next he associates this gradation with the proportions of the composition of capital:

> [T]he specific development of the social productive power of labour in each particular sphere of production varies in degree relative to how large

---

44 Chapter 1 (Part One): MEGA II.4.2, pp. 78–9, 81–2, 103, 108–9, 112, 114–23; Chapter 2 (Part Two): MEGA II.4.2, pp. 241–3, 247.

45 See especially his statement on pages 110, 118 and 164 (Chapter 1/Part One) and 212 (Chapter 2/Part Two).

a *quantity of means of production is set in motion* by *a certain quantity of labour* ...; such capitals as contain a larger quantity of constant capital ... than the social average capital are called capitals of *higher* composition ...[46]

Finally – keeping the rate of surplus-value uniform – he associates these grades and proportions with the deviations of production prices from values.[47]

4 An immanent reconstruction: the 1864–65 GRP transformation in face of *Capital I*

§4.1 *Introduction*

Although value is produced by labour and labour only, diverging productive powers of labour (and perhaps concomitantly diverging compositions of capital) mean that value and surplus-value cannot be simply explained in terms of labour clock-time.

When we leave the social-averages account, and move to the presentation of sectors of production with their distinct 'gradation' in the development of the productive powers of labour (i.e., the expositional level of 'Capital III, Part Two'), it is far from obvious to posit equalised rates of surplus-value between sectors. Nevertheless, as we have seen (§2) this is what Marx does in the GRP manuscript. In that manuscript, he decisively posits the uniformity of rates of surplus-value for all sectors as predicated on the *competition between workers*. Hence it would seem that (in 1864–65, though not so in 1867) rates of surplus-value *uniquely* reflect the physical *intensity* aspect of the exploitation of labour, leaving no room for its productive-powers aspect.

Workers, from their own perspective, have an interest in: the real wage (the value of labour-power), the length of the working day and the intensity of labour. These determine the degree of physical exploitation, and these can be supposed to be levelled out by competition among workers. The final determinant of the rate of surplus-value, i.e., the productive powers, is apparently of no

---

46 He writes this in the text that became Chapter 10 of *Capital III*: MEGA II/4.2, p. 241, my translation; cf. Fowkes's translation (Marx 2015) p. 276; cf. *Das Kapital III, Marx-Engels-Werke* Band 25, p. 173; *Capital III*, Fernbach translation, pp. 263–4. I have amended Fowkes's translation (admittedly from one sentence of about 125 words), the most important point being that he once again has "productivity" instead of "productive power"; later he also misplaces the term "degree".

47 *Idem*.

importance for their competition (it is the capitalists' thing, so to speak). This is the key point neglected by Marx in his 1864–65 GRP transformation, whence he posits equalised rates of surplus-value.

As far as I am aware, this position of Marx has never been questioned in the main debates on 'the' transformation problem.[48]

§4.2   *Main elements for a reconstructive account of the GRP as a stage of concretisation*

The core of a Marx-immanent reconstruction of the GRP problematic is simple.
– First, we posit a tendency to between-sector equalisation of profit rates.
– Second, we posit compositions of capital diverging between sectors.
– Third, we posit diverging rates of surplus-value between sectors, predicated on diverging productive powers and potencies of labour. (Generally, an increase in the rate of surplus-value in a sector concomitant on an increase in the composition of capital is a *condition* for such a technical change.)
– Fourth, we maintain the *Capital I* concept of value.

I claim that there is no friction between these four theses. We thus have no GRP transformation problematic, and much of what is written in Part Two of *Capital III* is redundant, including the concept of prices of production. Because of the maintenance of the *Capital I* concept of value, any value-theoretical duality between *Capital I* and *Capital III* is eliminated. Therefore, output transformation or input transformation is also redundant. In brief, we have continuity of the concept of value for each of *Capital*'s expositional levels.

Generally speaking, the systematic insufficiency, or incompleteness, of Marx's 1864–65 draft for *Capital III* is that he moves to a consideration of sectoral differences without having concretised his 'Capital I' account of *social average* production into sectors of production. Thus he skips a step, and is so bound to phrase the matter immediately (i.e., non-mediated) in terms of market-supply phenomena (which, I might add, for a major conceptual transformation, seems not quite fitting for the Marxian paradigm).

Hence the reconstructed conceptual progress, or concretisation, of *Capital III*, Part Two, that I propose, concerns, first, the explicit introduction of a

---

48   However, prior to those main debates (prior to the publication of *Capital III*) two authors, George Stiebeling (1890) and Julius Wolf (1891), anticipated in fairly general terms the relevance of the productive powers for divergent sectoral rates of surplus-value. They expressed their views in connection with Engels's (1885) 'prize essay contest' about the consistency of 'the law of value' in face of divergent sectoral compositions of capital. (These texts are discussed in Reuten 2018, Appendix.) Their contributions were inaptly ridiculed by Engels in his Preface to *Capital III*.

general (i.e., average) rate of profit, and second, abandoning the *Capital I* production averages, so that we have differentiated sectors of production. That is also Marx's aim.

In particular, this reconstructed concretisation moves from the explanation of the social average surplus-value produced (*Capital I*) to the explanation of the sectors' *production* of surplus-value. In a way, this is formally in line with Marx, be it that in the 1864–65 manuscript he *implicitly* posits that this matter requires no concretisation: rates of surplus-value tend to equalise between sectors.

The concretisation also includes the explicit introduction of the composition of capital (c/v) – which was mostly only implicit in Part Four of *Capital I* (see §3.1 point 4).

The Appendix below sets out this reconstruction in more detail, making use of some simple formalisations. It treats especially increasing productive powers in one sector in comparison with the economy as a whole, along with the three cases of constant, increasing and decreasing compositions of capital.

To understand the context of this reconstruction correctly, I should make the following explicit. More so than Marx in the current context, I put emphasis on the point that the social development of the productive powers of labour – that is, technology as well as its potential application in techniques – is the product of labour and labour only.[49] However, capital appropriates these and the management of capital decides which particular techniques are actually applied and specifically developed (by labour) for specific production processes. Thus, in as much as labour produces capital – via the production of surplus-value and capital's appropriation of it – it produces the potential technical forms of the production processes and hence labour's productive power. In brief, in capitalism the development of the productive powers of labour takes the value-form.

§4.3 *Implications of the reconstruction*

The reconstruction strengthens Marx's explanation of surplus-value. The central idea is the diverging value-generating potencies of labour between sectors, associated with diverging states of the productive powers between sectors. There are five implications:

---

49   I make a distinction, as Marx does, between 'technology' (knowledge about and search for potential techniques) and 'technique' (the particular application of technology in production). It is akin to Schumpeter's and Christopher Freeman's distinction between 'invention' and 'innovation' (see Reuten and Williams 1989, pp. 80 and 119–21).

1. Contrary to the 1864–65 GRP manuscript for *Capital III*, we have no transformation of value concepts, no dual account systems, and no artificial value and surplus-value adjusting transfers that would question the status of the *Capital I* determinations.

2. The reconstruction maintains the monetary value account – established in *Capital I* – throughout the terrains of each of the levels of the three volumes of *Capital*, as including the exposition of all specific and concrete market phenomena in terms of balanced or imbalanced market prices. Again, it merely excludes prices of production and hence the implied account duality.

3. The reconstruction does not affect the determination of average surplus-value by the average exploitation of labour as set out in *Capital I*.

4. Given the real wage, the length of the working day (or year) and the intensity of labour, the production of surplus-value in each one sector is determined by the value-generating potencies of labour. Sectoral divergences of the latter are predicated on the degree of diffusion of the productive powers of labour. In other words, these are predicated on the degree of diffusion of technology into techniques applied in each sector – technology and techniques themselves being the product of social labour.

5. The 'productive powers' component of surplus-value and the rate of surplus-value has explanatory power. However (and as far as I can see now) it can be measured only indirectly (this is a defect, even if it also applies to many accepted theories in the social and natural sciences).

Summary and conclusions

I revisited what probably is the main problem with Marx's *Capital*, namely the concretising transformation of the *Capital I* value concepts into the prices of production of *Capital III*, Part Two – dubbed the 'transformation problem'. As a quantitative transformation, it posits dual account systems.

In what became Part Two of *Capital III*, and in the 1864–65 research manuscript for it, Marx set out a number of constraining incompatible presuppositions for that transformation. Key presuppositions are the sale of commodities 'at their values' and equalised rates of surplus-value. To get rid of the incompatibility of presuppositions, Marx then abandons the first one, although he is hesitant to do so, because of its severe implications for his (draft stage) *Capital I* exposition (§2).

In the 120-year history of the appraisal of that transformation, the main focus has been on the analytical shortcomings of *that* transformation (shortcomings which I do not question, given the way it was posited). That appraisal leaves the constraints as finally posited by Marx untouched. In this article, I have set out a Marx-immanent critique of his positing of these constraints, and especially the presupposition of equalised rates of surplus-value.

To achieve this, I scrutinised Marx's exposition of surplus-value and the rate of surplus-value in *Capital I* – especially Parts Four and Five – an exposition which I accept. In brief, given a real wage, the rate of surplus-value is determined by (1) the length of the working day; (2) the intensity of labour; and (3) the productive power of labour. Changes in each of these three can arise either separately or in various combinations. In these Parts, Marx presents these in terms of social averages and their changes (§3).

Key to the defect of Marx's 1864–65 transformation is its disregard of the development of the productive powers of labour that is presented in the 1866–67 thoroughly reworked version of *Capital I*. In the latter we find that while there are mechanisms for the equalisation of wages between sectors, the working day and the intensity of labour, there is no mechanism for the equalisation of the productive powers between sectors. Marx justifiably does not posit the latter (§3.2). In particular, he does not posit an equalisation of the composition of capitals. Confronted by the transformation problem, the heart of the matter turns out to be that Marx's *Capital I* associates diverging productive powers of labour with diverging *value-generating potencies* of labour (§3.2).

In the reconstruction which I set out in §4 (and in more detail in the Appendix), I carry over these *Capital I* notions to the level of concretisation in 'Capital III'. Marx's transformation (and its problem) is then transcended into a concretisation of the averages account of *Capital I*, especially with regard to divergences between sectors in their productive powers, and the concomitant value-generating potencies of labour. Because of these divergences, we have divergent rates of surplus-value. This concretisation is consistent with diverging composition of capitals and equalising or equalised rates of profit. Thus, the transformation of the *Capital I* concept of value into 'prices of production' becomes redundant. The result is a continuity of the concept of value for each of *Capital*'s levels of exposition.

With *Capital I* in retrospect, and equipped with the reconstruction, we can see that Marx's 1864–65 GRP constraints posit the matter in a static way: we have divergent sectoral compositions of capital. However, dynamically considered, we have diverging compositions of capital *because* diverging rates of surplus-value are their condition.

Appendix (to §4). Core analytics of an immanent reconstruction of the GRP transformation in face of *Capital I*

A§1   Preliminary remarks

In §4 I proposed a reconstruction of Part Two of *Capital III* in face of Part Four of *Capital I*. In this Appendix I set out a simple formalisation of the analysis that underlies this reconstruction. It builds on the between-sectors diverging rates of surplus-value that Marx introduced in *Capital I* at a point when he digressed from his averages account of that book (cf. §3). It is appropriate to build on that because the GRP transformation is pre-eminently about between-sector differences.

Recall the four main elements of the reconstruction summed up at the beginning of §4.2. Given a tendency to equalisation of rates of profit, I focus on two variables in terms of *Capital I*'s monetary-value dimension. First, the rate of surplus-value and its divergence between sectors as determined by the productive powers. Given Marx's mature exposition of these (1867), it is far from obvious to posit equalised rates of surplus-value between sectors as he did in an earlier research manuscript (1864–65). Second, the organic composition of capital (c/v), which was mostly only implicit in Part Four of *Capital I* (see §3.1 point 5).

With regard to details of the reconstruction, I will add a terminological point. Just as Marx did *at the start* of his GRP manuscript, I treat surplus-value as being identical to profit. My reason is that the distribution of surplus-value to financiers has not yet been introduced. However, because the reconstruction makes 'prices of production' redundant, surplus-value keeps on being identical to profit prior to the explicit introduction of finance.

A§2   Analytics of technical change along with increasing productive powers, and associated with varying organic compositions of capital

I set out a brief point-wise presentation of the main elements of the reconstruction. Generally, there are three possibilities regarding the combination of increasing productive powers of labour (PPL) and of the organic composition of capital (CC): first, a constant CC; second, an increasing CC; third, a decreasing CC. I consider each of these in turn.

1. The productive powers in a sector increase along with a constant CC

If the PPL rise while the CC is constant, the change is without costs. I suppose that this is what Marx generally had in mind in *Capital I*, Parts Four and Five. In this case, we have – after competitive adaptation – *a pure*

decrease in the value of commodities and so an increase in relative surplus-value (that is, to the extent that the commodity at hand makes part of the wage bundle).
- Upon introduction of the new technique, the initiator makes an extra surplus-value due the increased value-generating potencies of labour, that is, at a constant market price. Along with it, the initiator's rate of profit rises above the average.

PPL↑, CC constant → s'_I↑ and $r'_I > r'_S = r'_E$ (1)

(From here on I use the following notation: s = surplus-value; s' = rate of surplus-value; r' = rate of profit; subscripts: I = initiator; S = sector; E = economy.)
- Competitors follow suit, and because of the above-average rate of profit there will also be an extra investment (by the initiator, competitors or entrants) which forces the market price downward.[50] This price decrease devalues the initial extra value-generating potency of labour. I call this a 'devaluation', because an increased value-generating potency results in fact in a revaluation.

competition → p↓ → $s'_I = s'_S = s'_E$ (result of devaluation) and $r'_I = r'_S = r'_E$ (2)

- The result is a normal, and ultimately generalised, increase in relative surplus-value; that is, to the extent that the commodity at hand makes, directly or indirectly, part of the wage bundle.

p↓ (relative surplus-value↑) → **generalised s'↑ and r'↑** (3)

This part of the concretisation is directly in line with Marx's *Capital I*, Part Five (moreover, there is no problem of different CC).

---

50   I draw a distinction between *production-process competition* and *market competition*. Only additional supply of the commodity at hand (predicated on extra investment) will *ceteris paribus* lower the market price. The above-average rate of profit (predicated on the production-process competition) induces this extra investment, and hence this market competition. In case the new technique requires an increase in scale, we would have already upon its initiation an extra investment and an additional supply, and some downward pressure on the market price. This qualification also applies for the next two cases. (I disregard any market-strategic-pricing considerations, which would belong at a more concrete level of the exposition.)

2. The productive powers in a sector increase along with the CC increasing

In the second case the PPL increase in a sector along with a rise in CC. *A capitalist introduces a CC-raising technique only if this raises the **rate of surplus-value** such that the rate of profit rises as a result* (or remains at least constant). Thus, the expectation of a rise in the rate of surplus-value is a condition for a rising CC. This is a very simple point, but a key one for the whole discussion.[51]

2-a. For analytical reasons, I start by considering the period before any competitor has adopted the new technique; along with it I assume *constant* market prices.[52]

- Upon the introduction of the CC-raising technique (as predicated on increasing PPL), the initiator obtains an extra surplus-value due to the increased potencies of labour (this is in line with Marx 1867).[53] Along with it, the initiator's rate of profit moves above the average.

$$\text{PPL}\uparrow, \text{CC}\uparrow \rightarrow s'_I\uparrow \text{ and } r'_I > r'_S = r'_E \qquad (4)$$

- Because of constant market prices, the increase in PPL has no effect on the relative surplus-value. In fact, the absolute surplus-value increases without an increase in the length of the working day.[54] I call this '*compressed absolute surplus-value*'.

2-b. We now drop the assumption of a constant market price, and consider effective production-process competition. Again, for the initiator we have:

$$\text{PPL}\uparrow, \text{CC}\uparrow \rightarrow s'_I\uparrow \text{ and } r'_I > r'_S = r'_E \qquad (5)=(4)$$

- Now competitors follow suit, and extra investment (by the initiator, competitors or entrants) forces the market price down, thereby devaluing *some* of the initial extra value-generating potency of labour.

---

51 Within any other theoretical constellation – (including the ones that I contest) and in whatever way profits are explained – an expected rise in profits such that the rate of profit remains at least constant is also a condition.

52 In order to keep the presentation concise, I will disregard, for this and the next point, any market-strategic considerations for gaining an increased market share. These are relevant for a further concretisation, although they do not inherently pertain to changes in productive powers, because 'market share competition' – e.g. a (temporary) price-decreasing one – might occur independently of it.

53 Thus the aggregate surplus-value increases. This is not different for Marx's presentation in *Capital I*, Chapter 12$^{\text{Ger.10}}$ (§3.2 above).

54 The qualification about this type of absolute surplus-value was pointed out by Chris Arthur in the conference discussion, based on an earlier version of this paper.

- Extra investment (and price decrease) continues up to the point where the sector rate of profit (r_S) is averaged out.[55] Given the increase in CC, this averaging-out of the sector's rate of profit will be reached at a point where the sector *rate of surplus-value* is higher than the economy average rate ($s'_S > s'_E$); hence, the value-potency of labour is devalued up to that point. Thus the extra value-potency of labour (and hence the increased sector rate of surplus-value) will not completely vanish, since there is no capitalist motive or force or mechanism for any further price decrease that would push the rate of profit below the average.

competition $\to p\downarrow \to s'_I = s'_S > s'_E$ (result of partial devaluation)
and $r'_I = r'_S = r'_E$ (6)

- The result is a *combination* of, first, an *increase in the 'compressed absolute surplus-value'* for this sector (due to the lasting increase in labour potency for this sector) and, second, an economy-wide *increase in relative surplus-value* (to the extent that the price decrease affects the wage bundle).

- *sector effect:*
  $p\downarrow \to s'_I = s'_S > s'_E$ (partial devaluation) and $r'_I = r'_S = r'_E$ (7a)
- *economy-wide effect (as including on the sector at hand):*
  $p\downarrow$ **(restricted relative $s\uparrow$)** $\to$ **generalised $s'\uparrow$ and $r'\uparrow$** (at $r'_I = r'_S = r'_E$) (7b)

Recall from §3.2 that such changes and divergences in the rate of surplus-value between sectors are in line with Marx's 1867 Part Four exposition. However, at that point in the 1867 exposition, he has the CC and the rate of profit implicit; we now have made these explicit, so concretising the exposition at a 'Capital III' level. Marx probably assumed that the 'compressed absolute surplus-value', i.e., the increased potency of labour, would vanish (see the third citation in §3.2), because he implicitly held the CC unchanged. In that case, we have the constellation set out under point 1 above.

3. The productive powers in a sector increase along with the CC decreasing
The case of an increase in PPL along with a decrease in the CC has effects similar to case 1 (although now CC diverge across the economy).

---

55 All these are notions of pure theory (in an equilibrium framework the final match will be exact). In practice all such investments are more or less rough guesses or expectations.

- The initiator's introduction of a new technique:

$$\text{PPL}\uparrow, \text{CC}\downarrow \to s'_I\uparrow \text{ and } r'_I > r'_S = r'_E \tag{8}$$

- Competition and extra investment:

$$\text{competition} \to p\downarrow \to s'_I = s'_S < s'_E \text{ (result of devaluation) and } r'_I = r'_S = r'_E \tag{9}$$

Now the equalisation of the rate of profit is reached at a sector rate of surplus-value below the average one ($s'_S < s'_E$).

- To the extent that the lower sector price affects the wage bundle, we have a generalised increase in relative surplus-value, and hence a generalised increase in the rate of profit.

$$p\downarrow \text{ (relative surplus-value}\uparrow) \to \text{generalised } s'\uparrow \text{ and } r'\uparrow \tag{10}$$

See §4.3 of the main text for the conclusions.

Addendum on the status of a transformation. In line with what Marx wrote about this, Part One of 'Capital III' can be characterised as a conceptual transformation.[56] Concomitant on making the driving force of 'the rate of profit' explicit, this transformation concerns mainly the transformation of the concept of surplus-value into profit – each one value concepts.

Part Two in fact makes it explicit that the driving force of the rate of profit entails that capitals move from low- to high-rate-of-profit sectors, so establishing a tendency to equalisation of rates of profit (the 'general rate of profit'). It is somewhat arbitrary whether in the reconstruction presented above, this should still be called a transformation. We have no new transformation of an earlier *value* concept (as in Part One). If anything, we have transformations of the *physical* guise of capital (producing e.g. soap instead of sweets).[57]

---

56   Chapter 1: "Materially {*Stoff; stofflich*} considered ... the *profit* ... is not different from the *surplus-value* itself. Hence its absolute magnitude is not different from the magnitude of the surplus-value (...) it is however a *transformation* {*verwandelte Form*} of the latter ..." (M:8–9-mt; cf. MF:50)↔(Marx 1993 and Marx 2015). Engels omits this text in *Capital III*.

57   I have no objection in principle to calling this a (particular) transformation. In reference to a comment by one of the reviewers for *Historical Materialism* I add that I would even have no objection to calling the resulting constellation one of 'prices of production', were it not that the history of Marxian political economy has been such that this name now stands for quite some more: value adjustments and dual systems.

References

Backhaus, Hans-Georg 1969, 'Zur Dialektik der Wertform', in *Beitrage zur Marxistischen Erkenntnistheorie*, edited by Alfred Schmidt, Frankfurt: Suhrkamp. Translated by M. Eldred and M. Roth, 'On the dialectics of the value-form', *Thesis Eleven*, 1, 1980, pp. 90–120.

Bellofiore, Riccardo 2005, 'The monetary aspects of the capitalist process in Marx: a re-reading from the point of view of the theory of the monetary circuit', in *Marx's theory of money: modern appraisals*, edited by Fred Moseley, Basingstoke: Palgrave Macmillan.

Campbell, Martha 1997, 'Marx's theory of money: a defense', in *New investigations of Marx's method*, edited by Fred Moseley and Martha Campbell, Atlantic Highlands, NJ: Humanities Press.

Elson, Diane 1979, 'The value theory of labour', in *Value: the representation of labour in capitalism*, edited by Diane Elson, London: CSE Books.

Engels, Friedrich 1885, 'Vorwort' to *Das Kapital II* (see MEGA II/13); 'Preface' to *Capital II* (see Marx 1978).

Engels, Friedrich 1894, 'Vorwort' to *Das Kapital III* (see Marx 1964); 'Preface' to *Capital III* (see Marx 1981).

Howard, Michael C., and John E. King 1989, *A history of Marxian economics: volume I, 1883–1929*, London: Macmillan.

Inwood, Michael 1992, *A Hegel dictionary*, Oxford: Blackwell.

Kopf, Eike, Willi Bang, Joachim Conrad, and Edgar Klapperstück 1983, 'Einleitung zu MEGA II/5' (see MEGA II/5, pp. 1*–55*).

Marx, Karl 1859, *Zur Kritik der politischen Ökonomie*, MEGA II/2; *Marx-Engels-Werke* Band 13, available at: https://marxwirklichstudieren.files.wordpress.com/2012/11/mew_band13.pdf.

Marx, Karl 1867[1], *Das Kapital. Kritik der politischen Oekonomie. Buch I: Der Produktionsprocess des Kapitals* [first edition], Hamburg: Verlag von Otto Meissner (see MEGA II/5).

Marx, Karl 1962 [1890[4]], *Das Kapital, Kritik der Politischen Ökonomie; Erster Band, Der Produktionsprozeß des Kapitals*, fourth edition, edited by Friedrich Engels, in *Marx-Engels-Werke* Band 23, Berlin: Dietz Verlag.

Marx, Karl 1964 [1894], *Das Kapital, Kritik der Politischen Ökonomie; Dritter Band, Der Gesamtprozeß der kapitalistischen Produktion*, edited by Friedrich Engels, in *Marx-Engels-Werke* Band 25, Berlin: Dietz Verlag.

Marx, Karl 1971 [1859], *A contribution to the critique of political economy*, edited by Maurice Dobb and translated by S.W. Ryazanskaya, London: Lawrence & Wishart.

Marx, Karl 1976 [1890[4]], *Capital: a critique of political economy, volume one*, translated by Ben Fowkes from the fourth German edition (see Marx 1962), Harmondsworth: Penguin.

Marx, Karl 1978 [1885], *Capital: a critique of political economy, volume two*, translated by David Fernbach from the German edition, Harmondsworth: Penguin.

Marx, Karl 1981 [1894], *Capital: a critique of political economy, volume three*, translated by David Fernbach from the German edition (see Marx 1964), Harmondsworth: Penguin.

Marx, Karl 1993, research manuscript for *Capital III* of 1864–65, MEGA II/4.2.

Marx, Karl 2010 [1887], *Capital: a critical analysis of capitalist production, volume 1*, edited by Frederick Engels, translated by Samuel Moore and Edward Aveling, *MECW 35* (digital edition), London: Lawrence & Wishart.

Marx, Karl 2015, research manuscript for *Capital III* of 1864–65 (see Marx 1993), translated from MEGA II/4.2 by Ben Fowkes, *Marx's economic manuscript of 1864–1865*, edited and with an introduction by Fred Moseley, Leiden: Brill.

MEGA II/2,[58] *Ökonomische Manuskripte und Schriften, 1858–1861 (einschl. Zur Kritik der politischen Ökonomie, 1859)*, Berlin: Dietz Verlag, 1980.

MEGA II/4.2, *Ökonomische Manuskripte 1863–1867, Teil 2: Manuskript 1863/65 zum 3. Buch des „Kapital"*, arranged and edited by Manfred Müller, Jürgen Jungnickel, Barbara Lietz, Christel Sander, and Arthur Schnickmann, Berlin: Dietz Verlag, 1993.

MEGA II/4.3, *Ökonomische Manuskripte 1863–1867, Teil 3: Manuskripte 1867–68 zum 2. und 3. Buch des „Kapital"*, arranged and edited by Carl-Erich Vollgraf with Larisa Mis'kevic, Berlin: Akademie Verlag, 2012.

MEGA II/5, *Das Kapital. Kritik der Politischen Ökonomie. Erster Band*, Hamburg 1867, Berlin: Dietz Verlag, 1983, available at: http://telota.bbaw.de/mega/.

MEGA II/13, *Das Kapital. Kritik der politischen Ökonomie. Zweiter Band*. Herausgegeben von Friedrich Engels. Hamburg: Verlag von Otto Meissner, 1885, arranged and edited by Izumi Omura, Keizo Hayasaka, Rolf Hecker, Sejiro Kubo, Akira Miyakawa, Kenji Mori, Sadao Ohno, Regina Roth, Shinya Shibata, and Ryojiro Yatuyanagi, Berlin: Akademie Verlag, 2008, available at: http://telota.bbaw.de/mega/.

MEGA II/14, *Manuskripte und redaktionelle Texte zum dritten Buch des „Kapitals", 1871 bis 1895*, arranged and edited by Carl-Erich Vollgraf and Regina Roth, with Jürgen Jungnickel, Berlin: Akademie Verlag, 2003.

MEGA II/15, *Das Kapital. Kritik der politischen Ökonomie. Dritter Band, Herausgegeben von Friedrich Engels. Hamburg 1894*, arranged and edited by Regina Roth, Eike Kopf, and Carl-Erich Vollgraf, with Gerald Hubmann, Berlin: Akademie Verlag, 2004, available at: http://telota.bbaw.de/mega/.

Moseley, Fred 2015, *Money and totality: a macro-monetary interpretation of Marx's logic in Capital and the end of the 'transformation problem'*, Leiden: Brill.

Moseley, Fred, and Tony Smith (eds) 2014, *Marx's Capital and Hegel's Logic*, Leiden: Brill.

---

58   For the complete list of works of MEGA II, see http://mega.bbaw.de/struktur/abteilung_ii.

Reuten, Geert 1988, 'Value as social form', in *Value, social form and the state*, edited by Michael Williams, London: Macmillan, available at: http://reuten.eu.

Reuten, Geert 1993, 'The difficult labour of a theory of social value: metaphors and systematic dialectics at the beginning of Marx's *Capital*', in *Marx's method in Capital: a re-examination*, edited by Fred Moseley, Atlantic Highlands, NJ: Humanities Press, available at: http://reuten.eu.

Reuten, Geert 2004, 'Productive power and the degree of intensity of labour: Marx's concepts and formalizations in the middle part of *Capital I*', in *The constitution of capital: essays on volume I of Marx's 'Capital'*, edited by Riccardo Bellofiore and Nicola Taylor, Basingstoke: Palgrave Macmillan, available at: http://reuten.eu.

Reuten, Geert 2009, 'Marx's rate of profit transformation: methodological, theoretical and philological obstacles', in *Re-reading Marx: new perspectives after the critical edition*, edited by Riccardo Bellofiore and Roberto Fineschi, Basingstoke: Palgrave Macmillan, available at: http://reuten.eu.

Reuten, Geert 2018, 'The redundant transformation to prices of production: a Marx-immanent critique and reconstruction', in *Marx's Capital: an unfinished and unfinishable project?*, edited by Marcel van der Linden and Gerald Hubmann, Leiden: Brill.

Reuten, Geert, and Michael Williams 1989, *Value-form and the state; the tendencies of accumulation and the determination of economic policy in capitalist society*, London: Routledge.

Schefold, Bertram 2004, 'Einführung zu MEGA II/15', in *Das Kapital, Kritik der politischen Ökonomie, Dritter Band*, MEGA II/15, pp. 871–910.

Stiebeling, George C. 1890, *Das Werthgesetz und die Profit-Rate; Leichtfaßliche Auseinandersetzung einiger wissenschaftlicher Fragen; Mit einem polemischen Vorwort*, New York: Heinrich, available at: http://library.fes.de/pdf-files/bibliothek/bestand/a79-03605.pdf.

Vollgraf, Carl-Erich 2012, 'Einführung zu MEGA II/4.3', in MEGA II/4.3, pp. 421–74.

Vollgraf, Carl-Erich 2018, 'Marx's further work on *Capital* after publishing volume 1: on the completion of section II of the MEGA²', in *Marx's Capital: an unfinished and unfinishable project?*, edited by Marcel van der Linden and Gerald Hubmann, Leiden: Brill.

Williams, Michael 2000, 'Why Marx neither has nor needs a commodity theory of money', *Review of Political Economy* 12(4): 435–51.

Wolf, Julius 1891, 'Das Rätsel der Durchschnittsprofitrate bei Marx', *Jahrbücher für Nationalökonomie und Statistik*, III. Folge 57, Band II, pp. 352–67, available at: <http://www.digizeitschriften.de/download/PPN345616359_0057/log76.pdf.

CHAPTER 16

The notion of tendency in Marx's 1894 law of profit

1997 article, originally published in *New investigations of Marx's method*, edited by Fred Moseley and Martha Campbell, Atlantic Highlands, NJ: Humanities Press, pp. 150–75.
(For its abstract see the Abstracts of all chapters p. 8.)

Contents

Introduction   337
1   The concept of 'tendency': some general notions   339
　1.1   Universal versus Social-General theories and tendencies versus trends   339
　1.2   Tendencies: laws as 'normic laws'   340
　1.3   Tendencies: powers, effects and phenomenal results   342
2   The case of Marx's tendency law of profits   346
　2.1   Chapter 13, The Law Itself   347
　2.2   Chapter 14, Counteracting Factors   352
　2.3   Conclusions to the chapter on the counteracting factors   355
　2.4   Chapter 15, Development of the Law's Internal Contradictions   357
3   Marx's and Marxian theory: concluding remarks   358
　3.1   General conclusions to the case   358
　3.2   Marxian theory and empirical research: some further and tentative concluding remarks   360
References   361

Introduction[1]

In economics and other social sciences it is difficult to make explanatory general theories that are empirically falsifiable and empirically corroborated

---

1   I would like to thank Chris Arthur, Martha Campbell, Paul Mattick Jr., Patrick Murray, Fred Moseley and Tony Smith for the provocative as well as enjoyable discussions at the 'International Symposium on Marxian Theory IV'. I am grateful to Fred Moseley for a second-round comment. This paper has also much benefitted from the stimulation and the thorough comments of Mary Morgan.

(Popper). Current mainstream economists deal with this difficulty by just evading it: (a) They refrain from formulating general empirical theories; (b) Consequently the notion of 'law' has by and large disappeared from the economics jargon; (c) Adopting a deductive method they construct mathematical economic models – these are not empirically tested, however, they are 'applied'.

In some of the recent methodological literature it is being suggested that the classical notion of 'tendency' or 'tendency law' might be fruitful for developing explanatory devices in economics and other social sciences (Bhaskar 1979, Lawson 1989, Hausman 1992).[2] In this essay I want to look at the actual usage of the concept of tendency in economics' history, for which I have selected as a case a well known as well as controversial theory, that is, Marx's 1894 Law of Profit (the three chapters on the tendency of the rate of profit to fall in Volume III of *Capital*).

In mainstream economics, indeed the notion of tendency (if not taken as identical to 'trend') merely prevails in its history. Between 1900 and 1940 the concept disappeared from the center of mainstream theorising. Marshall (1890, p. 26) still held that: "Nearly all laws of science are statements of tendencies." A number of marxists, on the other hand, have kept on using notions of tendency – though rarely in constructing new theories.

What is a tendency? The notion of tendency is by no means a clear cut and univocally used concept. Blaug (1992) and Hausman (1992), for example, take it merely to be a *ceteris paribus* statement. I think that such a notion loses a lot of what is interesting about the tendency concept (see Reuten 1995 for a critique of Hausman). The least one can say is that tendencies are about 'forces' and (their) 'expressions', or about 'powers' and (their) 'outcomes' – be it natural or social forces/powers (for the purposes of this essay I will use these pairs from now on interchangeably). The main divergent notions are to either see powers as tendentially in operation (thus to link 'tendency' to some power entity) *or* to see the outcome as a tendential occurrence. I will briefly expand on these and similar conceptual issues in §1. It is my contention, however, that full clarity on such issues cannot be gained by talking *about* them. The case of Marx's law of profit, then, must have the double object of both finding out about Marx's notion of tendency and clarification of possible notions of tendency (§2). As we will see there appears to be room for more than one notion of tendency in

---

2　Bhaskar 1975 and Cartwright 1989 suggest that the concept of tendency might be useful to grasp explanation in the sciences generally.

Marx. Whilst this is a difficulty for interpreting the content of Marx's theory of profit, it makes the case interesting for exploring the notion of tendency – and perhaps learning from it.

A crucial question, of course, is how we can do empirical research on the basis of tendency laws. Although this is not the subject of this article, I will make, in §3, a few tentative remarks on this issue. Indeed this question motivates my concern for the notion of tendency law. Law? Isn't that a concept that we had happily extinguished from economic research? Yes. With it, indeed, theoretically informed explanation of empirical phenomena: mainstream economics is left with an ever so more elegant but sterile formal framework cut loose from reality (cf. Rosenberg 1992).

1 The concept of 'tendency': some general notions

1.1 *Universal versus Social-General theories and tendencies versus trends*
For a start I want to have two issues out of the way. The first is that tendencies *are* not trends. A trend is a statistical device imposed on or/and observed from empirical figures. On the other hand tendencies might be, but need not be, causative for trends. This needs emphasising because some current mainstream economists as well as some philosophers of science (e.g. Popper 1957) mix up tendency and trend.

The second is that, in this essay, I am not concerned with so called 'trans-historical laws' (sometimes, confusingly, called for short 'historical laws'), I make a distinction between (1) trans-historical universal theories ('all human beings are mortal'), (2) historicist theories ('feudalism necessarily develops into capitalism') and (3) social-general theories ('within the domain of capitalism: if prices go up demand slows down'). All natural scientific theories are in fact of a trans-historical kind (evolutionary theories might be classified separately). Some psychological and social theories might be trans-historical. By their *aims* e.g. Freud's, and Maslow's theories are trans-historical. Much of neoclassical economics is by its *aim* trans-historical (as against the modern neoclassical institutionalism).

Much of the 'floor' for the mainstream discussion of laws in the social sciences (including economics) has been set by Popper's *The Poverty of Historicism* (1957). For the time being I share his queries about historicist theories in this work. However, in taking 'trans-historical' (i.e., universal) theories for the prototype of scientific theories generally, I think he goes much too far. Many (if not most) empirically interesting social scientific theories are of the 'social-general' type.

This needs emphasising, because my 'tendency case', discussed in Section 2, is of a social-general type theory. In his *Capital* Marx sets out a theory that is particular to the capitalist mode of production.[3]

1.2 Tendencies: laws as 'normic laws'

In the Introduction I referred to problems of the application of a positivist methodology in economics (either in a verificationist or falsificationist variety). Since the 1980s such problems have been well documented in the economics methodology literature. Some years before that, Bhaskar (1975, 1979) provided a rigorous critique of empiricist positivism, centering the discussion on the notions of law and tendency. The kernel of this critique is rather simple.

The foremost problem lies in positivism's bequest of the Humean concept of law, that is, that laws are constant conjunctions of events (plus some disputed contribution of mind). Though a constant conjunction of events is not always considered as a sufficient condition for a law, it is generally considered as at least a necessary condition. Related to this concept of law is the notion that laws find phenomenal expression as events or states of affairs, and that only the phenomenal is real (Bhaskar 1975, p. 64; 1979, p. 158).[4]

Thence the first principle of the positivist account of science is "*the principle of empirical-invariance*, viz. that laws are or depend upon empirical regularities". From this derive theories of causality, explanation, prediction, the symmetry of prediction with explanation, the development of science, etc. The second is "*The principle of instance-confirmation* (or falsification), viz. that laws are confirmed (or falsified) by their instances" (Bhaskar 1979, p. 159; cf. 1975, p. 127). From this derive various theories of demarcation and scientific rationality.

The kernel of Bhaskar's critique lies in his application of the distinction between closed and open systems. In the natural sciences (apart from astronomy) experimental situations have the character of closed systems, and it is only in such situations that a *constant* conjunction of events can occur. Outside it, in the open system of the "real world", disturbing or counteracting forces

---

[3] There are a few exceptions to this: sometimes he discusses the historical emergence of an institution; only rarely does he make a remark about a future society. These exceptions, however, do not concern the systematic of the general theory and have the status of illustrations (Smith 1990). Generally, in his work, Marx conceptually differentiates his categories into trans-historical ones and those applied to a particular epoch or mode of production (see Murray 1988, ch. 10, on determinate abstractions and Arthur 1986, pp. 11–12 and *passim*, on first-order and second-order mediations). In my case of §2 there are no such exceptions: all abstractions are determinate ones.

[4] The latter are 'empirical results' in the terminology of my next §1.3.

operate. (Thus, for example, the law of gravity will only be related to a constant conjunction in cases where there are no disturbing factors.) Laws then must either be restricted to closed systems (whence they are not universal or general laws), or the empirical status of laws in open systems must be doubted. In the first case the question is why the empirical should be privileged in closed systems:

> The empiricist is now caught in a terrible dilemma: for to the extent that the antecedents of law-like statements are instantiated in open systems, he must sacrifice either the universal character or the empirical status of laws. If, on the other hand, he attempts to avoid this dilemma by restricting the application of laws to closed systems (e.g. by making the satisfaction of a ceteris paribus clause a condition of their applicability), he is faced with the embarrassing question of what governs phenomena in open systems. (Bhaskar 1975, p. 65)

Thus the argument is that from the perspective of empiricism there are no universal or general laws. But even if pure positivism is inapplicable, could not a pragmatic *attempt* be made to apply their criteria? – as some methodologists have in fact claimed (for example Klant 1972; 1984 and Blaug 1980; 1992). This would be decisive to the extent that with the positivist methodological criteria the object of study would get reduced to, or identified with, its empirical manifestations (cf. Bhaskar 1979, p. 167).

For science to be an intelligible activity, Bhaskar argues, the invariance principle must be dispensed with.[5] For Bhaskar the status of laws in both the natural and the social sciences is similar. They are tendencies, or as he also calls them: normic laws.[6] The crucial point is that laws are not open system empirical *regularities* and that open system empirical regularities are not laws: On the one hand, counteraction both by different laws and by accidental/contingent events may prevent the phenomenal expression of normic laws. On the other hand empirical regularities may be the joint outcome of the operation of several laws, or indeed be accidental or contingent; that is there may be empirical regularities for which there is no natural or systemic necessity.

---

5 This is what he himself does in expounding his own transcendental realist philosophy of science. However, to agree with Bhaskar's critique of empiricist positivism, one need not subscribe to that philosophy.
6 Note that the basis of *his* argument for this is an ontological distinction of causal laws from patterns of events (Bhaskar 1975, p. 66; 1979, pp. 11–14). For a critique see Reuten and Williams 1988, pp. 20–2.

But the similar status of laws in the natural and the social sciences (naturalism) does not imply that social objects can be studied in the same way as natural objects (scientism). The point, mentioned in almost every elementary economics textbook, is that the social sciences do not have the opportunity (ontologically or because of moral objections) to experiment. The domain of social science is not more complex than that of the natural sciences: they are both open systems; *ceteris paribus* and probability are not the unique inventions of economists. Nevertheless, natural scientists, if their conceptual apparatus is similar, may reach agreement on the events produced in an experimental situation (on their relevance and interpretation, different schools may diverge). However, the absence of closed systems in the social sciences seems to imply that there are no decisive test situations for social scientific theories. If that is so, the conclusion to draw from this is not that there are no social laws. There are laws in both the natural and the social sciences but they are tendential. The difference between natural and social science is that the conditions for the identification of laws are different (Bhaskar 1979, p. 163).

In summary: If one identifies laws with constant conjunctions of events then there are no non-superficial general laws, in natural science or in social science. This does not imply that there can be no laws (this would only be the case if the invariance principle were taken as axiomatic); it only implies that laws (which are always tendential) are *not immediately manifest* in open systems.

1.3   *Tendencies: powers, effects and phenomenal results*

This concept of laws as tendential laws, expounded in the previous subsection, appears to be akin to that of J.S. Mill. Bhaskar (1979, p. 161) seems to deny this; of course, the philosophical foundation of such a concept may be different for them. For those methodologists writing on the issue of tendencies J.S. Mill is a common reference point. In this subsection, in order to further clarify different notions of tendency, as briefly set out in the Introduction, I will reformulate in my own words what I take to be the gist of Mill's view on tendencies in his 1836 Essay on method (reprinted in his 1844 collection of Essays). My reformulation is restricted to some points relevant to the current discussion. For reasons that will become clear later on, I will make a strict difference between a result and an effect of a tendency. Mill does not always make this strict difference (cf. 1836, pp. 337–8). Nevertheless this is an interpretation of Mill.

In the essay Mill seems to make no distinction in ontological status between the natural and the social to the extent that in both domains certain 'powers' or 'forces' are operative that produce *results* (phenomenal). Some results are more complicated than others in that many different powers rather than one or a few different powers are operative so as to produce a result. If we had a full picture of the world[7] we would have for the sum of all powers (P) and results (R):

$$P(1, ...n) \to R(1, ...n) \tag{a}$$

For each result taken in isolation (e.g. the Result numbered 127) we would know its cause or causes, for example,

$$P(2) \text{ and } P(7) \text{ and } P(8) \to R(127) \tag{b}$$

Now step aside from this case of a full picture. Suppose that in reality we already have grounds to know that P(i) is an operative causal power (borrowed from other sciences or ascertained via induction from within political economy), though we do not know (all of) 'its' results. We don't even know if there exists at all a *result* (phenomenal) produced by just this one cause. Then let us take P(i) in isolation (because we don't have a full picture and we wish to study causes one at a time – Mill 1836, p. 322). Now suppose we have information about the working of P(i). In this case we may have grounds to argue that P(i), in isolation, *tends* to produce or *tendentially* produces an *effect* F(j):

$$P(i) \text{-}t\to F(j) \tag{c}$$

(where -t→ stands for tendency; or perhaps rather 'tendential operation')

Note that both effects and results are occurrences even if we may not be able to perceive the *effect* (thus there may not be an *immediate* empirical counterpart for an effect). Note also that there is *no* principal difference between the latter case of isolation (b) and the former full picture case (a). In fact the full picture case (a) should have been written as:

$$P(1, ...n) \text{-}t\to R(1, ...n) \tag{d}$$

In the case of *result* R(127), in representation (b), we had three different causes P2, P7, P8 *each* producing a *tendency* towards some *effect*, perhaps counteracting each other, the outcome of which is *result* R(127).

---

7 According to Mill we may hope to reach such an (ideal) full picture via an 'upwards' process of induction and a 'downwards' process of deduction (Mill 1836, pp. 324–5).

Thus we had, for example:

$$\left.\begin{array}{l} P(2)\text{-}t\to F(12) \\ P(7)\text{-}t\to F(17) \\ P(8)\text{-}t\to F(18) \end{array}\right\} R(127) \qquad (e)$$

In view of the ontological status of tendencies (see below), it is to be noted that for Mill effects may not be less true than results: "That which is true in the abstract, is always true in the concrete with proper *allowances*." (Mill 1836, p. 326)
So far my interpretation of Mill.

In discussing tendencies and the related concepts, one may first of all make a difference between their status as either epistemological or ontological or onto-epistemological (by the latter I refer to those philosophies (of science) that principally do not want to make a separation between epistemology and ontology – e.g. Hegelian dialectics). If one makes a separation between epistemology and ontology, then the least problematic of the 'tendency related concepts' is that of the phenomenological empirical 'result'. One might claim existence for the latter, even if we might not be able to perceive it in the absence of thought and theory and their cultural mediation (e.g. snow and sorts of snow, or a rate of profit and sorts of rates of profit). 'Results' have at least an onto-epistemological existence. In an onto-epistemological framework 'results' and all the other concepts – powers, tendencies and effects – are in fact all equally problematic. These problems are 'solved' in the presentation of their systematic connection – which is a presentation of both theoretical and methodological content. (For the purposes of this essay I will not dwell any more on this onto-epistemological position – see Reuten and Williams 1989, Part One; Smith 1990; 1993; Arthur 1993.) I will proceed by making an (as if) separation between epistemology and ontology.

Far more problematic then, is the status of the concepts of power, tendency and effect. Least problematic is the notion of 'power'. Usually one makes ontological existence claims for 'powers' (forces, motives), that is, if one has at least some aim for explanation. What about tendencies and effects? It is clear that one can be an ontological realist for powers and results, whilst merely allotting an epistemological status for tendencies and effects (they are merely theoretical devices). Ruben (1982, pp. 49–56) claims that this holds for Marx. In his interpretation of Marx, tendencies are merely theoretical simplifications in the face of a lack of 'full' knowledge of all the relevant conditions – tendency claims are in principle replaceable by claims about the conditions sufficient for the occurrence of the kind of event in question. ... Under such ideal epistemic conditions, laws entail categorical claims about what actually does occur, and not just what tends to occur ... (p. 51)

In terms of the representations above, Ruben's interpretation would mean that Marx might agree with representation (a), though not with representation (d). Nevertheless, Ruben writes, "At any given stage in our acquisition of knowledge, we may have to accept laws of tendencies as the best we can do for the present ..." (p. 55).

Anticipating the next section (§2) I can merely say that Ruben's interpretation is interesting, but that other interpretations equally fit the text. Marx (1894F, p. 318) uses, for example, the phrase of "an actual tendency of capitalist production".

Mill indeed seems an ontological realist about tendencies and effects. (As is Bhaskar – the latter, however, conceives of effects and results as in different ontological layers.)

These issues of ontology make up half the story of the different notions of tendencies. The other half is about the proper 'place' for 'tendency' in a representation similar to (e) above. There are two main possibilities here. (Note that in my Mill representations I did not want to take sides as to these possibilities. It is even possible that Mill takes in fact a third, intermediate position, between the two ones indicated below.)

First. In representation (c) (and d) tendencies may be conceived of as the operators of the powers. Thus tendencies 'belong' to powers. (It is even stronger to say that, inherently powers are always tendential in character.) This may, more explicitly, be represented as:

$$P(i)[T] \to F(j) \qquad (f)$$

(where T implies the tendency is 'attached' to the power)

Operating 'through' the Effect in a Result (on which more than one power operate – as in representation (e) – all or some of which we may not know), we have

$$P(i)[T] \to F(j) \to R(j) \qquad (g)$$

This is what I call the *power notion of tendency*, or sometimes the *tendency as power* notion. It seems almost inevitable that this notion involves an ontological claim of a real existence of a tendency. (Or of a power being inherently tendential in character.)[8] The Result in this case may, of course, diverge from the Effect if we had more powers operating on the result.

A second notion of tendency, *tendency as expression*, or *tendency as outcome*, allots tendency to the Result. This may be represented as:

$P(i) \to F(j) \to R(j)[T^*]$ (h)
(where T^* implies tendential outcome)

Although this may involve an ontological claim about the existence of the Effect (F), this need not be the case. The Effect may indeed be a theoretical device (as Ruben, we have seen, interprets Marx).

Finally, with respect to Marx there is at least one further difficulty, related to the fact that *Capital* describes a multiple conceptual structure. When Marx uses the term 'expression' this is often the expression of a force (power) *at that* conceptual moment in his presentation, perhaps at a still abstract level. Thus we may in fact have a 'strain' of forces and expressions. Apparently 'expression' would then be rather similar to Effect. However, expressions are often 'preceded' by an 'immediate' operation of the force/power, which is rather more similar to Effect. The term for a more final empirical 'result' is the term 'manifestation'. There is, of course, not much point in spelling this further out before we get to the textual analysis, but the easiest way to pre-empt this is to say that in an equivalent of representation (h) there may follow a string of Effects and Results, of which the final term is a 'manifestation' of a power or a string of powers.

2   The case of Marx's tendency law of profits

In *Capital III*, Marx sets out his famous "Law of the tendential fall in the rate of profit". The aim of this section is *not* to find out about the details of this theory of Marx, but to find out about the notion of tendency in this theory: is it a 'power notion of tendency' or rather a 'notion of tendency as outcome' (§1.3).[9]

---

8   In my own political-economic-cum-methodological work (Reuten and Williams 1989 and Reuten 1991), I have used the concept of force/power as inherently tendential. The philosophical basis for it, however, is onto-epistemological rather than ontological.

9   Reading the title above makes one wonder how much weight should be given to that already: 'law of the tendency' (the heading in Marx's manuscript reads: "Law of the tendential fall in

This tendency law is presented in Part Three of *Capital III* in three chapters: ch. 13, the law itself; ch. 14, counteracting factors; and ch. 15, development of the law's internal contradictions. (In Marx's manuscript, from which Engels edited the final text after Marx's death, these three chapters are one continuous text – one chapter – not separated by headings or even a blank line.) I have used the following editions:

- Marx 1894G =   *Das Kapital III*, German text, edited by Engels.
- Marx 1894U =   *Capital III*, English translation (of 1894G) by Untermann (1909), Lawrence & Wishart (the main English reference until 1981).
- Marx 1894F =   *Capital III*, English translation (of 1894G) by Fernbach (1981), Penguin Books.
- Marx 1894M =   'Das Kapital III', printed German manuscript (without Engels's editorial work), edited by Müller, Jungnickel, Lietz, Sander and Schnickmann, 1992 (this text was not available to Untermann or Fernbach).

In my quotations from these texts all *italics* have been added, whilst an original emphasis is underlined. In general I quote from the English Fernbach translation. All the English quotes below have been checked against the German (1894G), and wherever appropriate additions have been made from the German {in curly brackets}. The 1894G text, again, has been checked against the manuscript text, any additions from the latter appear ⟨in hooked brackets⟩. Occasional comments of mine within a quote are [in square brackets].

2.1   Chapter 13, The Law Itself

This chapter covers about twenty pages (1894F, pp. 318–38). It opens with a numerical example in which at a constant rate of surplus-value (e = s/v) and a rising composition of capital (c/v), the rate of profit (r = s/(c+v) or R/(c+v)) is shown to decline. Rewriting the expression in the usual way (Marx does not do this) we have:

$$r = s/(c+v) = (ev)/(c+v) = e/(c/v + 1) \qquad (1)$$

After a comment of about one page the concept of tendency turns up. As we will see, the German text seems ambiguous as to the exact meaning of the term

---

the general rate of profit with {im} the progression of capitalist production"). In the text this phrase does not turn up anymore. Fine and Harris (1979, ch. 4) prefer the phrase "the law of the tendency of the rate of profit to fall (TRPF)" (see also Fine 1982, ch. 8).

tendency. The Fernbach and the Untermann translations apparently take different positions here. Marx writes (Fernbach's translation of 1981):

> [*] The hypothetical series we constructed at the opening of this chapter therefore expresses the *actual tendency of* capitalist production {die wirkliche Tendenz}.[10] With the progressive decline in the variable capital in relation to the constant capital, *this tendency leads to* a rising organic composition of the total capital, and the *direct result* of this is that the rate of surplus-value, with the level of exploitation of labour remaining the same or even rising, is *expressed* in a steadily falling general rate of profit [**]. (We shall show later on (ch. 14) why this fall does not present itself in such an absolute form, but rather more in the tendency to a progressive fall.) The progressive tendency for the general rate of profit to fall is thus simply {nur} <u>the expression, peculiar to the capitalist mode of production</u>, of the progressive development of the social productivity of labour. This does not mean that the rate of profit may not fall temporarily for other reasons as well, but ... (Marx 1894F, pp. 318–19)

Thus we have a tendency (T) of the capitalist mode of production (CMP), which has an immediate effect (F) to an expression (E):

$$\text{CMP}[T] \rightarrow c/v\uparrow \rightarrow (F): eEr\downarrow \qquad (2)$$

The tendency seems to be the power or the operation of the power (see representations f and g in the previous subsection §1.3). The tendency [T] leads to a rising value composition of capital (c/v), the immediate effect (F) of which is that the rate of surplus-value (e) gets expressed (E) in a falling rate of profit (r).

In the translation from the German of the second sentence in the quotation above, there is an important difficulty of interpretation (see the passage from * to **) relating to one kernel of the concept of tendency (power versus expression). The German text reads:

> [*] Die ⟨Der⟩ im Eingang hypothetisch aufgestellte Reihe ⟨Fall⟩ drückt also die wirkliche Tendenz der kapitalistischen Produktion aus. *Diese* ⟨*Sie*⟩ *erzeugt* ['produces' – what is it that produces: the tendency, *or*

---

10 The phrase "expresses the *actual* tendency" apparently leaves room for a tendency that does not actualise itself. In Hegelian jargon the terms "wirklich" and "actual" have a quite heavy connotation. However, in the course of this and the following chapters, the connotation of this term is no longer played upon. So, this seems not very important.

capitalist production?] mit der fortschreitenden relativen Abnahme des variabelen Kapitals gegen das konstante eine steigend ⟨fortwährende⟩ höhere organische Zusammensetzung des Gesamtkapitals, deren *unmittelbare Folge* ist, daß die Rate des Mehrwerts bei gleichbleibendem und selbst bei steigendem Exploitationsgrad der Arbeit sich in einer beständig sinkenden allgemeinen Profitrate *ausdrückt*. [**] (Marx 1894G, pp. 222–3; 1894M, p. 287)

The German text (*diese erzeugt*) leaves room for another interpretation from Fernbach's, that is, the mode of production produces the rise in the organic composition of capital, and this is expressed in the (tendental) fall of the rate of profit. The 1909 translation by Untermann follows this interpretation:

[*] The hypothetical series drawn up at the beginning of this chapter expresses, therefore, the actual tendency of capitalist production. *This mode of production produces* a progressive relative decrease of the variable capital as compared to the constant capital, and consequently a continuously rising organic composition of the total capital. The *immediate result* of this is that the rate of surplus-value ... is represented by {expressed in} a continually falling general rate of profit [**]. (Marx 1894U, pp. 212–13)

In my opinion the Untermann translation is the superior one as it fits the remainder of the quotation from ** onwards (esp. the italicised bit – see the quote from the Fernbach translation (first quotation of §2.1) which from here on is rather similar to the Untermann translation). Thus we seem to have a 'tendency as an expression' notion. The capitalist mode of production (CMP) inherently produces an increasing social productivity of labour (prodtt) and this gets expressed in a tendental fall of the rate of profit (r).

$$[\text{CMP: prodtt}\uparrow] \to c/v\uparrow \to (\text{F}): e(E)r\downarrow[T^*] \qquad (3)$$

(Cf. representation h in §1.3). It remains to be seen if representation (3) is consistent with the further text of this and the next two chapters.

The larger part of the current chapter (ch. 13, the law as such) is devoted to the concomitance of a (tendential) decline in the rate of profit and a rise in the mass of profit. This concomitance is stressed over and again. We have a

double-edged law of a decline in the profit *rate* (r) coupled with a simultaneous increase in the absolute *mass* of profit (R), arising from the same reasons {causes}. (Marx 1894F, p. 326; 1894G, p. 230)

Apart from in the quote above the term *tendency* appears only twice in this chapter. One passage reads:

> Thus *the same* development in the social productivity of labour is *expressed*, with the advance of the capitalist mode of production, on the one hand *in a progressive tendency* for the rate of profit to fall and on the other in a constant [beständigem; i.e continuous] growth in the absolute mass of the surplus-value or profit appropriated; so that by and large [im ganzen], the relative decline in the variable capital and profit goes together with an absolute increase in both. (Marx 1894F, p. 329; Marx 1894G, p. 233)

Again: the tendency seems the *expression* (now coupled, though, with a second expression). This may be represented as:

$$[\text{CMP: prodtt} \uparrow] \ldots\ldots (e = s/v) \begin{cases} (E)r\downarrow[T^*] \\ \\ (E)R\uparrow \end{cases} \qquad (4)$$

This is consistent with representation (3), that is the Tendency as Expression interpretation.[11]

This concludes the kernel of 'the law as such' or, as Marx also calls it, "the general law" (e.g. 1894F, p. 339). For the next chapter (14) it is useful to somewhat further spell it out in terms of representations (3) and (4). In my reading this law is *not* merely about the falling rate of profit itself (its tendential fall). The general law of the CMP is the following (see the first three pages of ch. 13 from which I have quoted above):

α. The CMP brings about a (progressive) increase in the social productivity of labour (the production of absolute and relative surplus-value as expressed in the rate of surplus-value e).

β. A dominant way of realising this (α), is by increasing the rate of surplus-value *concomitantly* on increasing the organic composition of capital.

---

11 The other quotation seems again consistent with the Tendency as Expression interpretation: "We have seen how it is that *the same* reasons that produce a tendential fall in the general rate of profit also bring about an accelerated accumulation of capital and hence a growth in the absolute magnitude or total mass of the surplus labour (surplus-value, profit) appropriated by it. Just as everything is expressed upside down in competition, and hence in the consciousness of its agents, so is this law – I mean this inner and necessary connection between two apparently contradictory phenomena" (Marx 1894F, p. 331; 1894G, p. 235).

γ. Its (α and β) *immediate* effect {Folge} is in a twofold expression, that is in: (a) a fall of the general rate of profit and (b) a rise in the social mass of profit. This may be represented as:

$$[\text{CMP: prodtt}\uparrow \leftrightarrow e\uparrow] \rightarrow [e\uparrow \leftrightarrow c/v\uparrow] \rightarrow (F): e = s/v \quad \left\{ \begin{array}{l} (E)r\downarrow[T] \\ \\ (E)R\uparrow \end{array} \right. \quad (5)$$

However, the law does not just operate in an immediate manner. (This is about α and β and γ – not merely about the latter or about the latter two.) So the law has the character of only/merely/just {nur} a *tendency* (cf. Marx 1894F, p. 319; 1894G, p. 223).

While in the chapter at hand the term tendency has not been used more than the three times referred to, it is nevertheless more often implicitly referred to as in e.g.:

> Viewed abstractly, the rate of profit might remain the same ... (Marx 1894F, p. 336; 1894G, p. 239; 1894M, p. 319)

or:

> The rate of profit could even rise, if a rise in the rate of surplus-value was coupled with a significant reduction in the value of the elements of constant capital, and fixed capital in particular. *In practice*, however, [!] the rate of profit *will fall in the long run*, as we have already seen. (Marx 1894F, p. 337; 1894G, p. 240; cf. 1894M, p. 319)

This last statement "in practice ... already seen" is remarkable indeed. Is is a rather definite statement about the expression of the law – or even its empirical manifestation. (I have found it peculiar considering especially the status of this chapter, i.e., prior to the theory about the counteracting causes that affect on the rate of profit.) It is interesting then to find that *this particular sentence is not in Marx's manuscript*.[12]

---

12 At least not in this part of the manuscript. I have checked merely these three chapters. (With respect to the point at hand, it is of secondary interest that pages 1894F, pp. 332–8 (from the * on page 332 onwards) or 1894G, 236–41 (at the end of page 235 separated with a line) have been removed from the second part of the manuscript (1894M, pp. 316–21) to here.) The remarkable sentence at hand has apparently been added so as to link up two sub-paragraphs of the manuscript.

2.2 Chapter 14, Counteracting Factors

The chapter on the 'counteracting factors'{causes}, covers about ten pages (Marx 1894F, pp. 339–48). It opens with an empirical observation, which is followed by a passage that is crucial to the interpretation of what Marx means by a tendency.

> If we consider the enormous development in the productive powers of social labour over the last thirty years {i.e., 1835–65} alone, compared with all earlier periods, and if we consider the enormous mass of fixed capital involved in the overall process of social production quite apart from machinery proper, then instead of the problem that occupied previous economists, the problem of explaining the fall in the profit rate, we have the opposite problem of explaining why this fall is not greater or faster. *Counteracting influences* must be at work, checking and canceling {aufheben} ⟨durchkreuzen⟩ the effect {Wirkung} of *the general law* and *giving it*[13] simply {nur} *the character of a tendency*, which is why we have described *the fall* in the general rate of profit *as a tendential fall*. The most general of these factors {Ursachen} are as follows. (Marx 1894F, p. 339; 1894G, p. 242; 1894M, pp. 301–2)

This text sustains my interpretation of the general law as a tendency law (representation 5, as paricularly comprising all the elements α and β and γ).[14] So we have the general law (ch. 13), which appears to be a tendential one because counteracting influences operate (ch. 14).

The causes are next commented upon under separate headings:

1. More intense exploitation of labour. Concerning an increase in the rate of surplus-value (e), we may distinguish: either such an increase *concomitant* on a rise in the composition of capital (c/v), with c increasing and v decreasing; or, such an increase *independent* of an increase of c (with c/v rising merely as a result). This section is about the latter. With e.g. increasing intensification of labour (or prolongation of the working day) one labourer works up more means of production (c), therefore e rises and, for the same amount of capital,

---

[13] "It" refers to the law and not to the effect (Wirkung): "Es müssen gegenwirkende Einflüsse im Spiel sein, welche die Wirkung des allgemeinen *Gesetzes* durchkreuzen und aufheben und *ihm* nur den Charakter einer Tendenz geben, weshalb wir auch den Fall der allgemeinen Profitrate als einen tendenziellen Fall bezeichnet haben" (Marx 1894G, p. 242).

[14] An argument for this point is in the clause "which is why we have described the fall in the general rate of profit as a tendential fall"; this would simply be a tautology if the law were not to comprise the α and β elements.

the amount of labour decreases. Hence for a given capital less labour is being exploited more intensively. For a given capital, profit, or the mass of surplus-value, $s = ev$. Each of the two factors on the righthand side, if I am right, are called contrary tendencies *by themselves*. This point, as I will show, is important to the general interpretation of 'the law'.

> It has already been shown, moreover, and this forms the real secret of the tendential fall in the rate of profit, that the procedures for producing relative surplus-value are based, by and large, either on transforming as much as possible of a given amount of labour into surplus-value or on spending as little as possible labour in general in relation to the capital advanced; so that *the same* reasons {Gründe} that permit the level of exploitation of labour to increase make it impossible to exploit as much labour as before with the same total capital. ⟨The same number of labourers is being exploited more, but a decreased number of labourers is being exploited by the same capital.⟩ These are the counteracting {*widerstreitenden*} tendencies which, while they act to bring about a rise in the rate of surplus-value, simultaneously lead [act] to a fall in the mass of surplus-value produced by a given capital, hence a fall in the rate of profit. (Marx 1894F, p. 340; 1894G, p. 243 1894M, p. 302)

The last sentence is puzzling. First, 'counteracting' seems rather: tendencies that counteract each other (rather than tendencies that act counter to an original tendency). Second, the bit after the comma is perhaps confusing: the fall in r is not the conclusion of the sentence. Rather the 'widerstreitenden' tendencies operate on the rate of profit in a non-uniform way.[15]

So it seems now that we have two influences (of the same offspring) that counteract *the law*; and this gives the law a tendential character.

Apart from this we see here introduced a theme that we will meet throughout this chapter, which is that tendency and counteractions (or again counteractions by themselves) are discussed in terms of one and the *same* offspring.

Thus we had in the previous chapter, for the total social capital, a fall in the rate of profit, together with an increase in the mass of profit (due to accumulation of capital and a social rise in variable capital). Now, looking

---

15   "Dies sind die widerstreitenden ⟨widerstrebenden⟩ Tendenzen, die, während sie auf eine Steigerung in der Rate des Mehrwerts, gleichzeitig auf einen Fall der von einem gegebnen Kapital erzeugten Masse des Mehrwerts und daher der Rate des Profits hinwirken" (Marx 1894G, p. 243; 1894M, p. 302).

at a *given* capital amount we see *e* rising and *s* falling (with *v* going down). For a conclusion we have:

> It does not annul {aufheben} the general law. But it has the effect {er macht} that this law *operates* {*wirkt*} *more as a tendency*, i.e., as a law whose absolute realisation is held up, delayed and weakened by counteracting factors {gegenwirkende Umstände}. ... the same factors tend {streben} both to reduce the rate of profit and to slow down the movement in this direction. (Marx 1894F, pp. 341–2; 1894G, pp. 244–5)

This quotation, in combination with the first one provided from ch. 14 (Marx 1894F, p. 339), reveals either an inconsistency or a subtle differentiation. In the earlier quotation counteracting influences were said to cancel {aufheben} the law's *operation*, hence its tendency character. Now the 'widerstreitenden' influences do not annul {aufheben}, but merely weaken the *general* law, hence the latter's operation as a tendency.

I now turn to the remaining 'counteracting factors' on which, in the context of this essay, I can be briefer.

2. *Reduction of wages below their value* (1894F, p. 342). This is a section of two sentences only.

> We simply make an *empirical reference* to this point here, as ... it has nothing to do with the general analysis of capital ... It is none the less one of the most important factors in stemming [aufhalten] the tendency for the rate of profit to fall. (Marx 1894F, p. 342)

This is a contingent element, i.e., one exogenous to this law. It is characteristic for Marx to make such an empirical reference.

3. *Cheapening of the elements of constant capital* (1894F, pp. 342–3). This very important factor is about the price effect of productivity increase on the *value* of constant capital, whence the change in the 'technical' composition of capital is not translated in an 'aliquot' change in the value composition. (On the general theoretical discussion of this issue, see Moseley 1992, ch. 1.) This issue is related to

> ... the devaluation of *existing* capital. This too is a factor that steadily operates to stay {aufhalten} the fall in the rate of profit ... We see here once again how the same factors {Ursachen} that produce the tendency for the rate of profit to fall also moderate the realisation of this tendency. (Marx 1894F, pp. 342–3)

4. *The relative surplus population* (1894F, pp. 343–4). This section is about the retardation of the rise in c/v, brought about by a rise in unemployment caused by any previous rise in c/v.

> The creation of such a surplus population is inseparable from the development of labour productivity and is accelerated by it, the same development as is expressed in the decline in the rate of profit. ... here again the same reasons that produce the tendential fall in the rate of profit also produce a counterweight to this tendency, *which paralyses* its effect {Wirkung, operation} to a greater or lesser extent. (Marx 1894F, pp. 343–4)

5. *Foreign trade* (1894F, pp. 344–7). The cheapening of prices by foreign trade may affect the rise in the organic composition not being translated (to the same extent) in the value composition (c/v).

2.3 Conclusions to the chapter on the counteracting factors

Marx's conclusion is:[16]

> We have shown in general, therefore, how *the same causes* that bring about a fall in the general rate of profit provoke counter-effects {Gegenwirkungen hervorrufen, i.e. *call forth counteractions*} that inhibit this fall, delay it and in part even paralyse it. *These do not annul {aufheben} the law*, but *they weaken its* effect {wirkung, operation}.[17] ... The law operates therefore simply as a tendency, whose effect {Wirkung} is decisive only under certain particular circumstances and over long periods. {*So wirkt das Gesetz nur als Tendenz, dessen Wirkung nur unter bestimmten*

---

[16] The last one and a half pages of section 5 of this chapter seem clearly concluding to this and the previous sections. There follows nevertheless a 'supplemented' section 6 (The increase in share capital – some eight sentences) in which it is stated that the rate of profit for share capital, which is lower than the average, does not enter the general rate of profit. If it did so, then the latter would even be lower than the prevailing general rate. It seems that this section 6 has rather the character of a footnote.

Apart from the concluding statement to be quoted in the main text, there is the following: "The tendential fall in the rate of profit is linked with a tendential rise in the rate of surplus-value, i.e., in the level of exploitation of labour. ... The profit rate does not fall because labour becomes less productive but rather because it becomes more productive" (Marx 1894F, p. 347). The first part of this quote, however, is awkward because so far nothing has been presented that counters a rise in the rate of exploitation. (This is also the first and last time that a "tendential rise in the rate of surplus value" is being alluded to.)

[17] Note again the same inconsistency about the annulment {aufhebung} of the law.

Umständen und im Verlauf langer Perioden schlagend hervortritt.}⟨dessen Wirkung nur unter bestimmten Umständen und auf lange perioden ausgedehnt schlagend hervortritt.⟩ (Marx 1894F, p. 346; 1894G, p. 249; 1894M, p. 308)

By now the possibility for another interpretation of Marx's notion of tendency is gradually being revealed. We have seen here and before that in the German text the term 'Wirkung' (operation, action) is used consistently to describe the law. (In the English text this is almost consistently translated by 'effect'.) It would perhaps go too far to reverse back to the 'power notion of tendency', nevertheless something like 'operators of powers' (see the comment just before and after representation (f) in §1.3) or at least operation of powers (causes) seems at stake.

After all there seem two tendential elements in the operation law. The first is that for various reasons internal to the law (endogenous reasons) an increase in the rate of surplus-value (e) (either that independent of c/v, or that concomitant on c/v) dominates over the effect of c/v on the rate of profit. Hence r↓[T*]. The second is that for various reasons – again internal ones – the value composition of capital (c/v) may in fact not rise. It may seem attractive then to represent the tendential character of the general law as follows:

$$[\text{CMP: prodtt}\uparrow \leftrightarrow e\uparrow] \to [e\uparrow \leftrightarrow c/v\uparrow][T] \to (F): e \begin{cases} (E)r\downarrow[T^*] \\ (E)R\uparrow \end{cases} \quad (6)$$

However, for the operation of the tendential element [e↑ ↔ c/v↑][T] these have explicitly been called *counteracting tendencies* in the case of $s = ev$ (section 1 of ch. 14) *only*; but even here not in a clear cut way. The term 'widerstreitenden' tendencies may in fact refer to merely these *themselves* only (i.e., e and v). In the other sections Marx writes rather in terms such as counteractions, not in terms of counteracting tendencies. From this one might infer that representation (6) is wrong. We are stuck, however, with an ambivalence as to the meaning of 'Wirkung' (operation, action).

Finally there is the issue of the empirical manifestation: "The law operates therefore simply as a tendency; it is only under certain particular circumstances – stretched over long periods – that its operation comes to the fore in an articulate way." (This is what I make, in translation, of Marx 1894M, p. 308.) Does this mean that this 'tendency law' in the long run results in a fall of the rate of profit? This is far from obvious from the quotation. It seems rather that: within a sufficiently long span of time there will always occur a constellation of circumstances for which the rate of profit will actually fall; at other constellations, however, the rate of profit might rise. (Nowhere in the text is there, to be sure, a statement about the average development in the rate of profit). For the time being, therefore, r~[T] in representation (5) seems not operational.

2.4   *Chapter 15, Development of the Law's Internal Contradictions*

This very perceptive chapter comprises about 25 pages (1894F, pp. 349–75). Again, I merely pick out the explicit references to the concept of tendency: there are only few here. Apparently, as we will see, this chapter is not very telling about the notion of tendency. Apparently, then, my current §2.4 cannot add much to the earlier conclusions. However, as I will indicate in my general conclusions, the fact that the term tendency is used so scarcely in this chapter *is* telling. The chapter is in 4 sections:

1. *General considerations* (1894F, pp. 349–55). This is a general summary of the process of production in reference to *Capital 1*. It provides comments on Ricardo's treatment of the issue.

2. *The conflict between the extension of production and valorisation* (1894F, pp. 355–9). In summary the argument in this section runs as follows. First. "As the capitalist mode of production develops, so the rate of profit falls" (p. 356) – as argued for in chapter 13. This fall would be counteracted by a decrease in the value (cheapening) of the components of capital (either variable capital ↔ increase in relative surplus-value; or constant capital) (argued for in chapter 14). This cheapening gives rise to the devaluation of the existing capital. The latter conditions the fall in the rate of profit, and delays it. Second. The mass of labour that capital can command does not depend on its value but rather on the mass of raw and ancillary materials, of machinery and elements of fixed capital, and of means of subsistence, out of which it is composed, whatever their value may be.

These (the first and second point) are two moments of the accumulation process: "sie schliessen einen Widerspruch ein, der sich in widersprechenden Tendenzen und Erscheinungen ausdrückt. Die widerstreitenden Agentien wirken gleichzeitig gegeneinander." (Marx 1894G, p. 259; cf. 1894F, p. 357.) This may be translated as: 'they contain a contradiction that is *expressed in contradictory tendencies* and phenomena. The antagonistic agencies act simultaneously in opposition to one another'. (Note that this is consistent again with the 'tendency as expression' notion.) We have simultaneously: impulses to increase and decrease of the working population; decrease in the rate of profit and devaluation of capital which puts a stop to this fall; development of productivity and a higher composition of capital.

These factors may at one time assert themselves side by side in space, and at another assert themselves in time one after the other; periodically "the conflict of antagonistic agencies finds vent in crises. Crises are never more than momentary violent solutions for the existing contradictions, violent eruptions that re-establish the disturbed balance for the time being."[18]

In the next two sections the term 'tendency' does not turn up any more, apart from in a comment on prevailing economic theory (1894F, p. 366). Section 4 is entitled "Supplementary Remarks" (1894F, pp. 368–75). In the face of the empirical manifestation of the law, section 3 deserves consideration:

3. Surplus capital alongside surplus population (1894F, pp. 359–68). This section contains the presentation of the process of economic crisis in terms of e.g.: concentration, overaccumulation, and devaluation of capital; capital to lie idle or destroyed, breakdown of the credit system, stagnation {Stockung} in production, fall in wages. For our purposes the following quote is important:

> The stagnation in production that has intervened prepares the ground – within the capitalist limits – for a later expansion of production. *And so we go round the whole circle once again.* (Marx 1894F, pp. 363–4; 1894G, p. 265)

Thus it seems that the fall in the profit rate is a periodical matter rather than a trend-like phenomenon (as quite some commentators on Marx have interpreted him). Of course, the "missing sentence" in Marx's manuscript, referred to at the end of my §2.1, backs up my conclusion.

3 Marx's and Marxian theory: concluding remarks

3.1 *General conclusions to the case*

Chapter 15 of Marx's *Capital III* has presented the 'tendency law' in its cyclical expression, that is in economic crisis/stagnation. Especially the devaluation of capital and the destruction of capital in crises/stagnation is highlighted –

---

[18] The first sentence of this quote is from the Untermann translation (p. 249) and the second from the Fernbach translation (p. 357). Immediately after this quote the term tendency turns up once more: "To express this contradiction in the most general terms, it consists in the fact that the capitalist mode of production tends towards an absolute development of the productive forces ...". I pay no attention to this, as in the manuscript we find, instead of the term tendency, the phrase "ein streben mit sich führt" (Marx 1894M, p. 323).

the effect of which is a rise in the rate of profit: "And so we go round the whole circle once again."

Why is it that in this last chapter the term tendency has been so scarcely used by Marx? Here the previous two chapters come together. If Marx's were a 'power notion of tendency' then we might expect that term to have been used over and again in that chapter 15. For the 'expression notion' this may be different. In fact chapter 15 is about expressions throughout. However, these are the expressions of a complex. Here it is shown how the rate of profit does not fall continuously, but rather cyclically. Thus, we simply do not have the, say, unilateral profit fall of chapter 13. In chapters 14 and 15 we see *why* the rate of profit does not fall continuously, and why, therefore, chapter 13 must formulate a 'tendency law'.

This backs up my first conclusion: 'tendency' refers only to 'the general law' of chapter 13 – so it is used merely in reference to that general law. There are no 'countertendencies'. There are, however, counteracting causes. The latter have been traced, where relevant, to the same offspring of the forces behind the tendential fall in the rate of profit itself – thus the interconnection has been sought.

There are, nevertheless, two exceptions to this. One apparent and one inconsistent to my conclusion. The first has been dealt with in §2.3 (e and v as counteracting themselves). The second is the phrase '*contradictory tendencies*' (1894F, p. 357) referred to in §2.4 under 2.

A second conclusion relates to the ambivalence as to the meaning of 'Wirkung' (operation, action) of 'the law' – pointed at in §2.3. It seems after all that the term operation is linked to the expression of the law. This is not so surprising if indeed Marx's is *not* a 'power notion of tendency'. If we have a force (non-tendential in itself, or ontologically non-tendential) which is not expressed immediately, then indeed we might well conceive of its 'working' as tendential. Therefore, my second conclusion is that a 'tendency' in the case of Marx discussed here is not a power or force. Tendency refers to the resulting *expression* of force (the working/operation of forces being laid down in a law) to the extent that this expression does not work out univocally, but rather in a contradictory way.

A third and tentative concluding remark concerns the ontology-epistemology question referred to in §1.3. In the text studied I have found no evidence at all that Marx's concept of tendency is an ontological one. It would be rash to conclude from this that his must therefore be an epistemological one (cf. Ruben referred to in §1.3). On the other hand I have also no evidence from this case, that Marx's notion of tendency is not an epistemological one.

3.2 Marxian theory and empirical research: some further and tentative concluding remarks

How might one do empirical research on the basis of tendency laws? Having considered the case above, one is bound to be left with this query. This issue deserves a full separate paper, nevertheless I will make a few tentative remarks. In order to make sense of empirical research in the light of tendency laws, I believe one is almost enforced to take a position similar to Lawson's (1989; 1992) reworking of Kaldor's notion of 'stylised facts'. Although Lawson adopts philosophically a realist position to the extent that powers and tendencies have ontologically a real existence, this position is not essential to the problem of empirical research that I am considering.

A tendency for Lawson is "a power that may be exercised and yet unrealised in manifest phenomena". Powers themselves exist "by virtue of certain enduring structures" (1989, p. 62). Laws then are defined similar as with Bhaskar and Mill (§1.2 above). Although the effects of tendencies, he writes,

> will frequently be modified or hidden by the operation of irregular countervailing mechanisms and so forth, their persistency coupled with the irregular operation of the countervailing influences may allow their effects to 'shine through'. And to the extent that any manifest phenomenon appears to reveal some degree of uniformity, generality or persistency ... it would seem to provide a *prima facie* case for supposing that some enduring generative mechanisms are at work. ... And conceptualisations of such partial regularities, of course, are the obvious candidates for representation as 'stylized facts'. ... stylized facts can provide an access to enduring things as indications of possible manifestations of the effects of (possibly a combination of) causal tendencies. (Lawson 1989, pp. 65–6)

I believe that a similar procedure is currently the best we have, that is, if we take serious the notion of tendency law without refraining from serious empirical work on their basis. Indeed, as Lawson indicates, Kaldor (after 1966) was concerned about the increasingly formalistic and sterile non-empirical economics of his days – times have not changed in this respect (see e.g. Rosenberg 1992).

I guess that anyone studying chapters 13–15 of Marx's *Capital III* (the case of §2 above) cannot be but impressed by the conscientious and thorough exhibition of that theory up to minutest detail (given its methodological level of abstraction). It may also appear a very realistic theory, even for those who would not want to share its value theoretical notions. (Schumpeter, e.g., it seems, owes much to Marx's approach – see Schumpeter 1943).

Nevertheless, that theory is insufficient and must be developed further. Marx's *Capital* is indeed an unfinished project: (a) from the point of view of his own aims (Reuten 1996); (b) in terms of the unclarity of the extent of its theoretical break from classical economics (Reuten 1993); (c) in terms of the unclarity of its methodological break from either 'analysis' in Ricardian vein, or dialectics in Hegel's traces (Murray 1988; Smith 1990, 1993; Arthur 1993a, 1993b). One problem, and challenge, is that the latter two aspects hang together.

Such theoretical development cannot be carried out in the absence of thorough empirical research. Indeed (restricting myself to the theory of the case of §2) I believe that the kind of empirical research as carried out by Weisskopf (1979), Wolff (1986), Moseley (1991), and Duménil and Lévy (1993; 1996) must be undertaken. Especially if these are combined with inter-comparisons and discussion as in Moseley (1991).

Of course, one can have many theoretical objections to such empirical research. Not merely because of their particular operationalisation of the theory and the many ad hoc decisions that one is bound to make in the face of poor statistics. One may foremost object to the empirical application of an incomplete theory (as indicated above). I believe that one must have reservations here. However, at the same time I am convinced that such empirical research must be carried out and cannot await theory development.

One argument for this is in the concern for the reclaiming of a 'real-world political economy', which comprises the explanation of stylised facts. Of course, *what* these latter are is not independent of a (theoretic) discourse. However, their communication and explanation affect the social discourse.

The, related, other argument is in the cross fertilisation of methodological, theoretical and empirical research. I firmly believe that methodological, theoretical and empirical research must be carried out alongside each other, short of the ideal of a really integrated triple approach.

References

Note. The last mentioned edition is the one quoted from.

Arthur, Christopher J. 1986, *Dialectics of labour: Marx and his relation to Hegel*, Oxford: Basil Blackwell.
Arthur, Christopher J. 1993a, 'Hegel's Logic and Marx's Capital', in Moseley (ed.) 1993, pp. 63–88.
Arthur, Christopher J. 1993b, 'Negation of the negation in Marx's *Capital*', *Rethinking Marxism* 6(4): 49–65.

Bhaskar, Roy 1975, *A realist theory of science*, Brighton: Harvester.

Bhaskar, Roy 1979, *The possibility of naturalism: a philosophical critique of the contemporary human sciences*, Brighton: Harvester.

Blaug, Mark 1980, *The methodology of economics, or how economists explain*, Cambridge: Cambridge University Press.

Blaug, Mark 1992, *The methodology of economics, or how economists explain*, second edition, Cambridge: Cambridge University Press.

Cartwright, Nancy 1989, *Nature's capacities and their measurement*, Oxford: Clarendon Press.

Duménil Gérard, and Dominique Lévy 1993, *The economics of the profit rate: competition, crises and historical tendencies in capitalism*, Aldershot: Edward Elgar.

Duménil Gérard, and Dominique Lévy 1996, 'The three dynamics of the third volume of Marx's Capital', paper presented at 'Marxian economics: a centenary appraisal', International conference on Karl Marx's third volume of *Capital*: 1894–1994, University of Bergamo, 15–17 December 1994. (Appreared in: *Marxian economics: a reappraisal*, volume 2, edited by Riccardo Bellofiore, London: Macmillan, 1998, pp. 209–24.)

Fine, Ben 1992, *Theories of the capitalist economy*, London: Edward Arnold.

Fine, Ben, and Laurence Harris 1979, *Rereading Capital*, London: Macmillan.

Hausman, Daniel M. 1992, *The inexact and separate science of economics*, Cambridge: Cambridge University Press.

Klant, Joop J. 1972, *Spelregels voor economen; de logische structuur van economische theorieën*, second edition 1978, Leiden: Stenfert Kroese.

Klant, Joop J. 1984, *The rules of the game: the logical structure of economic theories*, Cambridge: Cambridge University Press.

Lawson, Tony 1989, 'Abstraction, tendencies and stylised facts: a realist approach to economic analysis', *Cambridge Journal of Economics* 13: 59–78.

Lawson, Tony 1992, 'Abstraction, tendencies and stylised facts', in *Real-life economics: understanding wealth creation*, edited by P. Ekins and M. Max-Neef, London: Routledge, pp. 21–37.

Marshall, Alfred 1972 [1890], *Principles of economics*, 8th edition, London: Macmillan.

Marx, Karl 1894G, ed. F. Engels, *Das Kapital, Kritik der Politischen Okonomie, Band III, Der Gesamtprozesz der kapitalistischen Produktion*, MEW 25, Berlin: Dietz Verlag, 1972.

Marx, Karl 1894U, ed. F. Engels, *Capital, a critique of political economy, volume III, the process of capitalist production as a whole*; trans. of 1894G by Ernest Untermann (1909), London: Lawrence & Wishart, 1974.

Marx, Karl 1894F, ed. F. Engels, *Capital, a critique of political economy, volume III*; trans. of 1894G by David Fernbach, Harmondsworth: Penguin Books, 1981.

Marx, Karl 1894M, 'Gesetz des tendenziellen Falls der allgemeinen Profitrate im Fortschritt der kapitalistischen Produktion', in M. Müller, J. Jungnickel, B. Lietz, C. Sander und A. Schnickmann (eds), *Karl Marx, Ökonomische Manuskripte 1863–1867*, Text Teil 2, *Karl Marx, Friedrich Engels Gesamtausgabe (MEGA)*, Zweite Abteilung, Band 4, Teil 2: 285–340, Berlin: Dietz Verlag, 1992.

Mill, John Stuart 1836, 'On the definition of political economy; and on the method of investigation proper to it', *London and Westminster Review*, October, repr. in J.S. Mill, *Essays on some unsettled questions of political economy* (1844^1, 1877^3); text of 1844 repr. in J.M. Robson (ed.), *Collected works of John Stuart Mill*, volume IV (1967), pp. 309–39, Toronto: University of Toronto Press, 1975.

Murray, Patrick 1988, *Marx's theory of scientific knowledge*, Atlantic Highlands, NJ: Humanities Press.

Moseley, Fred 1991, *The falling rate of profit in the postwar United States economy*, London: Macmillan.

Moseley, Fred (ed.) 1993, *Marx's method in Capital: a re-examination*, Atlantic Highlands, NJ: Humanities Press.

Moseley, Fred 1994, 'Marx's economic theory: true or false? A Marxian response to Blaug's appraisal', in *Heterodox economic theories: true or false*, edited by Fred Moseley, Brookfield, VT: Edward Elgar.

Popper, Karl 1976 [1957], *The poverty of historicism*, London: Routledge & Kegan Paul.

Reuten, Geert 1991, 'Accumulation of capital and the foundation of the tendency of the rate of profit to fall', *Cambridge Journal of Economics* 15(1): 79–93. [Chapter 18 of the current book.]

Reuten, Geert 1993, 'The difficult labour of a theory of social value: metaphors and systematic dialectics at the beginning of Marx's *Capital*', in Moseley (ed.) 1993, pp. 89–113. [Chapter 6 of the current book.]

Reuten, Geert 1995, 'A revision of the neoclassical economics methodology: appraising Hausman's Mill-twist, Robbins-gist, and Popper-whist', *Journal of Economic Methodology* 3(1): 39–67.

Reuten, Geert 1996, 'Destructive creativity: institutional arrangements of banking and the logic of capitalist technical change in the perspective of Marx's 1894 law of profit', paper presented at 'Marxian economics: a centenary appraisal', International conference on Karl Marx's third volume of *Capital*: 1894–1994, University of Bergamo, 15–17 December 1994. (Appreared as revised in: *Marxian economics: a reappraisal*, volume 2, edited by Riccardo Bellofiore, London: Macmillan, 1998, pp. 177–93). [Chapter 20 of the current book.]

Reuten, Geert, and Michael Williams 1988, *The value-form determination of economic policy: a dialectical theory of economy, society and state in the capitalist epoch*, Amsterdam: Grüner.

Reuten, Geert, and Michael Williams 1989, *Value-form and the state; the tendencies of accumulation and the determination of economic policy in capitalist society*, London: Routledge.

Rosenberg, Alexander 1992, *Economics: mathematical politics or science of diminishing returns?* Chicago: University of Chicago Press.

Ruben, David-Hillel 1982, 'Marx, necessity and science', in *Marx and Marxisms*, edited by G.H.R. Parkinson, Cambridge: Cambridge University Press, pp. 39–56.

Schumpeter, Joseph A. 1966 [1943], *Capitalism, socialism and democracy*, London: Unwin University Books.

Smith, Tony 1990, *The logic of Marx's Capital: replies to Hegelian criticisms*, Albany: State University of New York Press.

Smith, Tony 1993, 'Marx's *Capital* and Hegelian dialectical logic', in Moseley (ed.) 1993, pp. 15–36.

Weisskopf, Thomas E. 1979, 'Marxian crisis theory and the rate of profit in the postwar US economy', *Cambridge Journal of Economics* 3: 341–78.

Wolff, Edward N. 1986, 'The productivity slow down and the fall in the rate of profit in the US economy 1947–76', *Review of Radical Political Economics* 18: 87–109.

CHAPTER 17

'Zirkel vicieux' or trend fall? – the course of the profit rate in Marx's *Capital III*

2004 article, originally published in *History of Political Economy* 36(1): 163–86. (For its abstract see the Abstracts of all chapters p. 9.)

Contents

Introduction   365
1   Two interpretations: trend fall versus cycle   367
   1.1   The standard view: trend fall   367
   1.2   The rival view: cyclical development   370
   1.3   Qualifications   371
   1.4   Conclusions   372
2   Marx's 1864–65 manuscript: the *Zirkel vicieux*   372
Summary and conclusions   378
Appendix 1: Comparison of some key texts in *Capital III*, Part Three, with its manuscript   378
Appendix 2: The tendency of the rate of profit to fall in Marx's manuscripts: a speculative history   381
   Preliminary remarks   381
   The first manuscript: the 'Grundrisse' (1857–58)   381
   The second manuscript (1861–63)   383
   A speculative history: in conclusion   386
References   387

Introduction[1]

Karl Marx's theory of 'the tendency of the rate of profit to fall' is one of the most controversial parts of his scientific oeuvre. The theory was published in

---

1   I thank Riccardo Bellofiore, Mark Blaug, Ben Fine, Paul Mattick Jr., Mary Morgan, Tony Smith, Michael Williams and two anonymous referees for very helpful comments on an earlier version of this article.

1894 as Part Three of Volume III of *Das Kapital*. There are two conflicting interpretations of this theory. The first says that the profit rate will vary (cyclically) around a *falling trend*; the second, that the profit rate will vary *cyclically* but not necessarily around a falling trend. Both interpretations may be combined with methodological qualifications as set out in the present article.

The two interpretations are relevant since at issue is Marx's general outlook on the dynamics of the capitalist system. It makes quite a difference whether the capitalist system is regarded as self-dissolving – which is the implication of the trend fall in the rate of profit – or as, in principle, a reproductive system, which the cyclical view implies.[2]

For several reasons the first interpretation was dominant until the last quarters of the twentieth century.[3] It is not surprising, therefore, that this is the view presented in many textbooks on the history of economic thought. The advantage of this reading is that it 'merely' requires emphasising certain parts of the text and deemphasising others.

Although it has its advantages, the first interpretation leaves us with a number of puzzles; but even greater difficulties arise with the second interpretation, since some passages of the text (that is, of any given edition of *Capital III*, excluding the manuscript) are blatantly inconsistent with it. Therefore, even if one has good grounds for the second interpretation (see §1 below), some textual counterevidence remains.

From this perspective it is of interest to compare especially these textual inconsistencies in published versions of *Capital III* with Marx's manuscript text. *Capital III* appeared eleven years after Marx's death. Friedrich Engels edited the book from Marx's manuscripts dating from 1864–65, that is, from some time before the 1867 publication of Volume I. For the textual comparison, which is set out in §2, we can make use of the German transcription of Marx's manuscript that was published in 1992.

The historian of thought usually has a position vis-à-vis the subject matter, and the present author is no exception. Whereas I consider the current Marxian paradigm to be fruitful for the analysis of capitalist economies, there is not much point in seeking consistency between Marx and the current Marxian

---

2 This – the system's being reproductive – concerns the 'pure economic' moment of the system. There might be other reasons (e.g. political ones) why the system might be self-dissolving. As to the first view: a stationary state is excluded, given Marx's view of the systemic necessity of the accumulation of capital.

3 In fact the theory itself did not occupy a prominent place in the debates of the *first* quarter of the century (these were largely framed in terms of Marx's reproduction schemes). However, this article is not about the general history of this theory but merely about one exegetical aspect of it.

paradigm.[4] Many of Marx's writings are ambiguous and often also inconsistent; they are also methodologically complex, contributing to an at least apparent ambiguity.[5] First, there is the normal inconsistency between the writings, and at times ambiguity within the writings, of someone who develops thoughts throughout his or her life. Second, Marx – as a confirmed critic of classical political economy – adopted the method of 'internal critique' to develop his own thought (a method largely taken over from Hegel).[6] This also applies to the case at hand: the 'law of the falling rate of profit' was, of course, a major theorem of classical political economy. All interpreters agree that Marx disputes the classical reasoning *behind* the law (i.e., Ricardo's); but did he accept the law *itself*?

A note: In what follows, unless otherwise indicated, whenever I refer to the 'text' of *Capital III*, I mean the published versions of *Capital III*, excluding the published version of the manuscript. When I refer to the 'manuscript' I refer to Marx's manuscript.

1   Two interpretations: trend fall versus cycle

In order to appreciate the comparison of the text of *Capital III* with Marx's manuscript in relation to the two rival readings (see §2), I will, as a reminder and without much textual ado, briefly set out in this section a stylised presentation of the two interpretations.

1.1   *The standard view: trend fall*
Part Three of *Capital III*, as edited by Engels, comprises chapters 13–15. In chapter 13, "The law as such", Marx sets out how the compulsion to achieve higher profits gives rise to the accumulation of capital in the shape of *productivity-raising* techniques of production along with a relative decline in the employment of labour. We have a tendential rise in the organic composition of capital: the ratio of the value of the means of production (K) to the value of labour-power $(wL$, where w is the wage rate and L the amount of labour). Thus:

---

[4] Throughout this article I distinguish between 'Marx's theory' and 'Marxian theory', the latter referring to the theory of authors working in the Marxian *paradigm*, which may be as homogenous or heterogenous as any other paradigm.

[5] In light of this, Tony Smith (2002) argues that it is rather problematic to speak of "interpretations" of Marx: they are bound to be "reconstructions".

[6] There are other methodological complexities that I neglect for the purposes of this essay (see Reuten 2003 [chapter 1 of the current book]).

$$(K/wL)\, \dagger \tag{1}$$

where † is the sign for the tendential rise.

If we restrict the outlay of total capital to the means of production and labour-power, denote the rate of depreciation by δ, and represent total surplus-value or total profits by the sign R and gross production by Y, we have[7]

$$\delta K + wL + R = Y \tag{2}$$

and for the rate of profit (r)

$$r = R/(K + wL) \tag{3}$$

Marx does not use this notation, although his own notation gives rise to it.[8]

From equations (1) and (3) it follows that at any given prevailing distribution between capital and labour (R/wL) – or, put more succinctly, if we keep that ratio of distribution 'momentarily' constant, that is,

$$R/wL = \text{constant}, \tag{4a}$$

then the rate of profit must tendentially decline. Or, if we consider the rate of surplus-value to be tendentially rising $(R/wL\, \dagger)$ and if

$$(R/wL)\dagger < (K/wL)\dagger \tag{4b}$$

then the rate of profit must tendentially decline, which can be seen from dividing the right-hand side of equation (3) by wL.

This, then, is a grand 'contradiction' of capital accumulation: the compulsion to make more profits gives rise to a tendential decrease in the rate of profit.[9]

---

[7] At this level of abstraction (prior to the differentiation of capital into industrial, commercial, and money capital as well as landed capital, set out in the remaining parts of *Capital III*), total surplus-value and total profits are the same.

[8] I use this notation rather than Marx's in order to keep this section concise. The term wL in equation (3) would require a turnover coefficient. Alternatively, and assuming that wages are paid at the end of the production period, we might write: $r = R/K = (R/wL)/(K/wL)$; in this last expression any consistent measure for wL will do (e.g. the wage bill for a year).

[9] Quite another controversy from the one dealt with in this article relates to the adequacy of the relations set out so far. Inequality (4b) need not hold if an at least parallel increase in R/wL goes along with an increase in K/wL (i.e., a parallel increase instead of a 'counteracting tendency'). Or, in general, why would capitalists introduce new techniques that in effect decrease

Chapter 14 of *Capital III* discusses the counteracting tendencies, most importantly the cheapening of the material elements of capital (the prices of wage goods whence w may decline, or those of the means of production whence the rise in K may be tempered or nullified), which, of course, affects inequality (4b).

In this standard interpretation, the following chapter, chapter 15 – which is somewhat mysteriously titled "Development of the law's internal contradictions" – does not substantially add to what has been said in the previous chapters. True, there are some interesting qualifications – such as allusions to the course of the business cycle, to the devaluation of capital, and to the concentration and centralisation of capital – but none of this can lessen the status of the previous two chapters. Key to the important status of chapters 13 and 14 is a statement made toward the end of chapter 13:

> Viewed abstractly, the rate of profit might remain the same. ... The rate of profit could even rise, if .... In practice, however, the rate of profit will fall in the long run, as we have already seen. (Marx 1894F, pp. 336–7)

Stated thus, chapter 13 may be taken as setting out the *dominant* tendency; the *counteracting* tendencies of chapter 14 merely slow down the process.

Within this interpretation in general, one strand has stressed the cyclical 'aspects' of the theory, nevertheless against the background of the "long-run" dominant tendency.[10]

---

the general rate of profit? This is a main point of Okishio 1961, although there are precursors of this criticism (see Groll and Orzech 1989). In an earlier paper (Reuten 1991; cf. Reuten and Williams 1989, ch. 4) I indicate how this criticism is based on an equilibrium notion, and that once we take account of heterogenous plants in a branch – stratified according to the technical composition of capital and different rates of profit – it is not difficult to provide sufficient support for Marx's theory. Whether Marx saw that is a different question we can leave to one side here. [For Reuten 1991 see ch. 18 of the current book.]

10   Economic crises restore the rate of profit and thus *slow down* the general process. This strand originates with Henryk Grossmann ([1929] 1967). Note that I said cyclical 'aspects'. Grossmann does not claim that this theory of Marx (or his own amplification of it) is a full theory of the business cycle (p. 138). Although the major part of Grossmann's work (pp. 287–579) covers a discussion of the 'counteracting tendencies', the title of the book indeed indicates the general idea of a *dominating* tendency: *Das Akkumulations- und Zusammenbruchsgesetz* [Law of breakdown] *des kapitalistischen Systems*. Nevertheless, Grossmann is careful enough to say that Marx never used the phrase "law of breakdown", or "theory of breakdown" – he claims, however, that Marx provided the "elements" for such a theory (p. 78).

Note that, like Marx, I have consistently used the term *tendency*. Throughout most of the twentieth century – up to its last quarter – this term was chiefly identified with 'trend', rather than, say, 'operating force'. However, even with a more sophisticated view of tendency, the *dominant tendency* interpretation of chapter 13 may still hold; so in effect we should observe at least a secularly declining rate of profit – in accordance with the statement just quoted.

1.2   *The rival view: cyclical development*

The focus of the rival interpretation is chapter 15 and its status vis-à-vis the earlier two chapters. In fact, in the way I have presented the summary of chapters 13 and 14, there is no major disagreement over the content of these earlier chapters – although there is disagreement over how they rank in importance.[11] The crucial point within this interpretation is that chapters 13 and 14 are formulated at a higher level of abstraction than chapter 15, which is seen as a more concrete and synthetic development from these earlier chapters. This is the chapter where Marx develops the cyclical 'aspects' of the theory. Thus, in effect, the earlier two chapters are interpreted as being of equal importance; hence we have no dominating tendency and analogous trend.[12]

---

11   The rival view seems to have originated with Ben Fine and Laurence Harris (1976). See also chapter 4 of their *Rereading Capital* (1979) and Lebowitz 1976. In a way, the rival view was prepared by Joan Robinson ([1942] 1969) and Paul Sweezy ([1942] 1968), both of whom argued, in short, that there is no reason in principle why the initial tendency should be dominant over the counteracting ones. Note that, as I said, there is no major disagreement over the earlier chapters in the way I have, for brevity, presented them here. Fine and Harris initiate their argument by making a sophisticated differentiation between the "technical," the "organic," and the "value" compositions of capital. In the same context this difference was also stressed by Paul Mattick ([1969] 1974, pp. 59–60). (See also appendix A of Groll and Orzech 1987 with references to Moszkowska and earlier work of Groll.) The rival view on this particular matter does not stand alone. It is part of a general reassessment of Marx's work that gradually emerged from the 1970s (see Reuten 2003 [ch. 1 of the current book]).

12   Hence chapter 13 by itself is not an empirical prediction of a trend fall in the rate of profit. Interestingly, this shift in interpretation seems to involve a minor 'paradigmatic' shift. For example, Michael Howard and John King, in their *History of Marxian economics* (1992) – apparently steeped in the old view – seem to be blind to the idea that a different interpretation is possible at all. In a rather voluminous work, they devote only ten lines and a footnote to it. "For some Marxian economists", they write, "Marx's 'law of the tendency' was not meant to be an empirical prediction concerning the secular course of the profit rate. ... This implies that Marx's analysis can never be wrong, because it is empirically empty" (p. 318). Their position would, of course, preclude any 'non-trend' theory of cyclical development (of the profit rate). It is hard to see why, by whatever methodological standards, a theory of a *secular trend* fall in the rate of profit would have more empirical content than a theory of a *cyclical* development of that rate. Another historical account

In chapter 15, in brief, Marx indicates how the tendential decline of the rate of profit is expressed cyclically. Along with the accumulation of capital and the concomitant rise in the organic composition of capital, the rate of profit declines – that is, in the upturn phase of the cycle. This gives rise to an economic crisis, in the process of which the rate of profit is restored, most importantly because of the writing down of capital values ('devaluation of capital') and the scrapping of capital (cf. section 3 of chapter 15). Marx (1894F, pp. 363–4) then writes:

> The stagnation in production that has intervened prepares the ground for a later expansion of production – within the capitalist limits. And so we go round the whole circle once again.

Thus it seems that the fall in the profit rate is a discontinuous, periodic matter rather than a trend-like phenomenon.[13]

But if this reading of the text (also) makes sense, as I think it does, then one is faced with a number of inconsistent passages, an important example of which was quoted at the end of the previous subsection.[14]

1.3   *Qualifications*

Although the methodological background of Marx's theory is not the subject of this article, it should be indicated, even if briefly, that we find in both camps quite a number of authors emphasising that given the abstract level of the

---

(Cullenberg 1994) equally takes its vantage point from the old interpretation. I mention these to illustrate that as late as the early 1990s, some circles had not felt the full impact of the rival view (this, of course, is not to say that these authors should have agreed with the rival view; the point is that they provided no, or no proper, account of it).

13 Thus whereas in the first interpretation we have a trend fall – the profit rate declines in the long run (even if halted at times) – the second interpretation is inconclusive about a trend – it might go up, down, or move horizontally; the rate of profit 'merely' goes down and up cyclically.

14 Fine and Harris (1976, p. 160; 1979, p. 61), for example, are well aware of the inconsistencies and go for a reconstructive approach. Faced with the inconsistencies not only in *Capital III* but also in *Capital I*, Groll and Orzech (1987) propose the plausible hypothesis that between the writing of the manuscript for *Capital III* (i.e., 1864–65) and the 1867 publication of *Capital I*, Marx changed his views (see also the communication Fine 1990 and Groll and Orzech 1990). Nevertheless, Groll and Orzech (1987, pp. 599, 601) indicate that "already in his initial formulation" Marx is "sceptical" of the secular trend conclusion. Groll and Orzech's view was especially plausible in the face of the evidence they had at the time (i.e., without the current evidence – see §2). As indicated in appendix 2, it is quite conceivable that Marx rather started changing his views around 1862.

theory of Volume III of *Capital*, it does not reach the theoretical level appropriate for empirical prediction. Of course, as is well known, Marx completed only a 'modest' part of his theoretical project.[15] In the current context it is especially noteworthy that although many parts of *Capital* discuss *aspects* of the business cycle, the analysis of the business cycle itself was planned only for the last book ("Book Six") of the project (cf. e.g. Marx 1894U, p. 358; 1894F, p. 480). Relatedly, we also find in both camps various interpretations of Marx's notion of 'tendency'.[16] (All this is about Marx; later Marxian theories reaching the empirical are beyond the scope of this article.)

1.4 Conclusions

A careful reading of the *Capital III* text on the development of the profit rate allows for two interpretations. In the first, dominant weight is given to "the law as such" (chapter 13) over its counteractions (chapter 14); the chapter 15 text must then be de-emphasised or be seen to depict cyclical development around a secular falling 'trend' in the rate of profit (even if Marx does not use this terminology). For the second reading, the earlier two chapters are analytically on a par, and chapter 15 is interpreted as a synthesising and concluding text. Although both readings are countered by insoluble puzzles and textual inconsistencies, those associated with the second interpretation seem 'harder'.

2 Marx's 1864–65 manuscript: the *Zirkel vicieux*

As far as the text of *Capital III* as edited by Engels is concerned, I think that we should leave the issue here: the text is ambiguous and we can interpret it in two ways. However, to the extent that one is also interested in Marx's ideas, it is useful to turn to Marx's manuscript, upon which Engels did his editorial work and which was published as transcribed in German in 1992 (Marx 1894M, manuscripts 1863–67; those that comprise Part Three *Capital III* dating from 1864–65). That is what I will do in this section.[17] I will review especially the passages that seem to give rise to the aforementioned ambiguities. Anticipating my conclusion, it seems that Engels himself had ideas on the issue that resulted in

---

15   See, for example, Oakley 1983, esp. pp. 107–8.
16   See Reuten 1997 [ch. 16 of the current book]. The aim of that paper was to inquire into Marx's general notion of 'tendency'; it took the same chapters 13–15 as a case for that purpose.
17   For a general commentary on Engels's edition in relation to the manuscript, see Vollgraf and Jungnickel 1994 and Heinrich 1996.

a particular emphasis. I am not saying that Engels was unfaithful to the text, but that his own ideas guided his organisation of the material.

To understand Marx's 'entry point', we should remember that in his day a 'law of the tendency of the rate of profit to fall' was taken for granted among economists, on both empirical and theoretical grounds. William Stanley Jevons ([1871] 1970, pp. 243–4), for example, writes, "There are sufficient statistical facts, too, to confirm this conclusion historically. The only question that can arise is as to the actual cause of this tendency."[18]

From here on, I will use the following shorthand references:
M = Marx 1894M = German manuscript transcription of 1992;
E = Marx 1894E = German text of 1894 as edited by Engels;
U = Marx 1894U = German text of 1894 in the English Untermann translation of 1909;
F = Marx 1894F = German text of 1894 in the English Fernbach translation of 1981.

The current parts of *Capital III* were devised by Marx as chapters (thus the current Part Three corresponds to chapter 3 of the manuscript). But that is not important. What is important is that Marx's manuscript under discussion is not divided into three: there are no section breaks, or even blank lines between the current chapters. We have no so-called "law as such" – or at least there is no particular focus on it.

The first pages of the manuscript are similar to the current text of *Capital III* (M, pp. 287–301; U, pp. 211–25; F. pp. 317–32). My reading of these is as follows. Marx sets out a hypothetical example of a falling profit rate. Then he writes: (1) this as a tendency is what we perceive in reality (F, p. 318); (2) it is what the economists perceived and have tried to explain (F, p. 319). Note that in general – throughout the text – Marx's reference to "law" (thus also the title of his chapter/part) is rather ambiguous. At least some of the time his "law" seems to refer to an empirical regularity.

Next Marx shifts the emphasis to what he apparently sees as a kernel of capitalist development: first, the accumulation and concentration of capital along with a rise in the productivity of labour, and second, a fall in the *rate* of profit along with a rise in the *amount* of profits. He repeats this over and again (e.g. M, pp. 291, 298, 300). To him, *this* seems to be the law: the inverse relation of the amount of profit and the rate of profit (see also below).

---

18   It is ironic that all the evidence we have from later commentators (Kuznets, Kaldor, et al.) is that the rate of profit in advanced capitalist economies has been trendless for over a century, that is, since 1860. In other words, most great economists from Adam Smith to Böhm-Bawerk and even Keynes believed in an empirical law that does not exist today.

After this, Marx's manuscript immediately moves – without even one blank line – to the counteracting tendencies (the text of chapter 14). Engels, however, first interpolates some text from much later in the manuscript (F, pp. 332–8; roughly M, pp. 316–20). In E, U, and F this is marked by a line or an asterisk (e.g. F, p. 332). This interpolation gives more weight to "the law as such".

Apart from this, at a crucial point in this text Engels also makes an (unmarked) interpolation of his own. On F, pp. 336–7 (cf. M, p. 319), Marx writes, as we saw above:

> Viewed abstractly, the rate of profit might remain the same. ... The rate of profit could even rise, if ...

After this, Engels interpolates:

> Aber in Wirklichkeit wird die Profitrate, wie bereits gesehn, auf die Dauer fallen. (E, p. 240)

In Fernbach's translation, Engels's interpolation reads:

> In practice, however, the rate of profit will fall in the long run, as we have already seen. (F, p. 337; cf. U, p. 230)[19]

In fact, we have not seen any such thing. Marx did not talk in terms of the "long run". The problem is that, of all three chapters, this (Engels's) sentence is in fact the strongest statement giving the impression of a 'trend' fall. Furthermore, it is associated with (Engels's) "law as such"; if in practice the rate of profit will fall, the "law as such" might seem dominant.[20]

---

19 See row 1of the table in Appendix 1 for a full comparison of this text.
20 Apart from this change and the ones mentioned below, there are several more, slight changes in Engels's text, each one of which is perhaps too small to mention. Nevertheless, they contribute to the general emphasis. Michael Heinrich (1996, pp. 456, 459, 464) writes about all of the manuscript for *Capital III*: "There are modifications to the original text on practically each page that have not been indicated. Hardly one paragraph remained as Marx had written it. Engels's modifications are not confined to 'stylistical' matters. ... [T]he 1894 edition was an extensive adaptation of Marx's manuscript, and Engels did not inform the readers about the true extent of his adaptation. ... The interventions ... offer solutions for problems which the manuscript left open ... and in some passages they even change the argumentation of the original text, if this obstructs Engels' interpretations." See also the extensive comments by Carl-Erich Vollgraf and Jürgen Jungnickel (1994, p. 47) about Engels's mark on the text ("Engels left only few of Marx's sentences untouched"). Neither Vollgraf and Jungnickel nor Heinrich refers specifically to the changes I indicate in this

The second strongest statement (this time by Marx himself) comes at the end of the text/chapter on the counteractions. Note that when Marx sets out the counteracting forces/tendencies, he repeatedly indicates that these do "not annul the general law", but make it operate as a tendency (F, p. 341). He also says that the latter "to a greater or lesser degree paralyse" its operation (F, p. 344; M, pp. 304, 306). This is again repeated in a conclusion on page 308 of M (page 346 of F). The final part may readily give rise to the two rival interpretations of trend versus cycle. In the Fernbach translation we have:

> The law operates therefore simply as a tendency, whose effect is decisive only under certain particular circumstances and over long periods. (F, p. 346)

The Marx-Engels text reads:

> So wirkt das Gesetz nur als Tendenz, dessen Wirkung nur unter bestimmten Umständen und im Verlauf langer Perioden schlagend hervortritt. (E, p. 249)[21]

Untermann's translation is closer to the German (Fernbach's "decisive" is rather dubious):

> Thus, the law acts only as a tendency. And it is only under certain circumstances and only after long periods that its effects become strikingly pronounced. (U, p. 239)[22]

This can be read in two ways: (1) only in the long run can the rate of profit be perceived to fall; hence "the law as such" is dominant; (2) the rate of profit falls in particular circumstances, namely, when the forces set out in the tendency-law indeed dominate the countertendencies (my interpretation of the German text is this second one).

---

article. Of course, to be attentive to specific changes is a matter of interpretation itself – specific changes in line with one's own interpretation may be envisaged as stylistic or near to that.

21 The phrase "und im Verlauf langer Perioden" is Engels's modification of what actually appears in Marx's manuscript, "und auf lange Perioden ausgedehnt" (M, 308). This is not very important.

22 See row 2 of the table in appendix 1 for a full comparison of this text.

After this, Marx (M, pp. 309–40) goes into the issues that Engels has placed in chapter 15, although in a different order. Note again that the manuscript is continuous: there are no indications for chapter/section breaks.[23] I have selected a number of passages from it that seem important. Much emphasis is on an issue introduced at the very beginning of the text: that increases in the productivity of labour via an increase in the organic composition of capital result in a combined increase in profits and a decrease in the rate of profit. He calls this a law: "The law that a fall in the rate of profit due to the development of productiveness is accompanied by an increase in the mass of profit ..." (U, pp. 225–6).[24] At the same time, prices fall.

On page 322 of M the statement is repeated, this time leaning toward a possible interpretation of 'trend':

> [We have seen that] as the capitalist mode of production develops, so the rate of profit falls, while the mass of profit rises together with the increasing mass of capital applied. (F, p. 356)

Next, Marx amplifies the issue of the depreciation of capital. One page further, though, he puts this in a different light, first rephrasing the issue in terms of a contradiction, then developing it into periodical crises:

> Simultaneously with the fall in the profit rate, the mass of capital grows, and hand in hand with it goes a depreciation of the existing capital, which checks this fall and gives an accelerating impulse to the accumulation of capital-value. Simultaneously with the development of productivity, the composition of capital becomes higher[:] there is a relative decline in the variable portion as against the constant. These different influences may at one time operate predominantly side by side spatially, and at another succeed each other in time; periodically [*periodisch*] the conflict of antagonistic agencies finds vent in crises.[25] The crises are always but moment-

---

23 I am not saying that an editor should not try to make a text more readable by structuring it. Marx's text was not ready for publication and Engels did a great job by making it ready. I argue that from the point of view of the two interpretations, Marx's original text leans more toward the view of 'synthesis of par tendencies' in which cyclical development plays a prominent role, whereas Engels's editorial intervention gives more room to a theory explaining trend.

24 Engels (E, 236) replaces Marx's term *herbeigeführte* (M, 316) with *verursachte* [caused], which Untermann renders as "due" and Fernbach as "occasioned" (F, 332).

25 Marx uses the term *periodisch* (see row 3 of the table in appendix 1). I don't understand why both Untermann (translating into "from time to time") and Fernbach (translating into

ary violent solutions of the existing contradictions – violent eruptions – which restore the disturbed balance. (M, p. 323; E, p. 259; F, p. 357; U, p. 249 – the translation is a composite of the several versions)[26]

Overproduction, as well as the over-accumulation and devaluation of capital, is the theme of the next pages of Marx's text. An important sentence is:

> Under all circumstances, however, the balance will be restored by the *destruction of capital* to a greater or lesser extent. (M, p. 328; cf. E, p. 264; F, p. 362; U, p. 253).

The balance will be restored![27] Next Marx sets out how a crisis and its aftermath restore the rate of profit and writes: "*And so we go round the whole circle once again*" (M, p. 329; E, p. 265; F, p. 364; U, p. 255; my italics). This is, of course, strong enough to make the point that we have a cycle of decrease and increase in the rate of profit.

Two sentences further on, Marx makes the point in an even stronger manner by talking of a "*Zirkel vicieux*" (cf. the French: *cercle vicieux*), which Engels renders as "*fehlerhafte Kreislauf*" and the translators as "cycle of errors" (F) and "vicious circle" (U). Marx – in otherwise fully German texts – apparently feels constrained to make use of the French *vicieux*, since in French *cercle vicieux* has a double meaning, namely that of a faulty circle (the one Engels picks up in his German term) and that of an endless circle, of lasting recurrence.[28]

"at certain points") fail to pick up the "periodic" reference here, especially since one paragraph further on, in the context of depreciation/devaluation of capital, they do translate *periodisch* into "periodical." *Periodisch* has a connotation of repetition/recurrence.

26 The translations have "for a time restore" and "balance for the time being". Engels has inserted the phrase "für den Augenblick." In this long quotation I have most of the time mixed the two translations. It is just not the case that the one is generally superior to the other (and this applies not merely to these chapters). I am not complaining; translation is a most difficult task, more difficult than merely writing in a foreign language (which is difficult enough). See row 3 of the table in Appendix 1 for a textual comparison.

27 Note that Engels (thus the translators) takes away Marx's emphasis, although he adds "durch Brachlegung und selbst Vernichtung" ("by capital's lying idle or even by its destruction" [Fowkes translation, p. 362]). See row 4 of the table in Appendix 1 for a comparison.

28 Some English dictionaries, such as the *American Heritage Dictionary*, indicate a similar double meaning for "vicious circle." See row 5 of the table in Appendix 1 for a textual comparison.

Summary and conclusions

Currently there are two interpretations of Part Three of Marx's *Capital III*: secular trend fall in the rate of profit versus mere cyclical development of that rate. The text as edited by Engels allows for either, although both interpretations, especially the 'cyclical' one, are countered by a number of blatant inconsistencies in the *Capital III* text.

A study of Marx's 1864–65 manuscript for *Capital III*, however, changes matters. Whereas it does not exclude the trend fall interpretation, the manuscript does lean more toward the cyclical view. I reported on the different order of the texts, although it is difficult to derive hard conclusions from the different impression that makes. I also examined the phrases in the *Capital III* text that would most suggest the secular trend interpretation. Their comparison with the manuscript text allows at least for the conclusion that the manuscript text is not inconsistent with the cyclical interpretation.

It would seem, then, that Marx's name for the law – the "law of the tendency of the rate of profit to fall" (TRPF) – is rather misleading. A more appropriate name would be "theory of the rate of the profit cycle" (TRPC). However, Marx's allegiance to the TRPF wording may well have to do with his general method of 'internal critique', since indeed 'this' law (the law Marx calls the TRPF) was seen as a very important law of the classical political economy of his day. Marx reformulates it in terms of rate *and* amount of profit and shows the cyclical manifestation of 'the' law: The recurrent "revolutionising" of the organic composition of capital generates a parallel increase in the mass of profit and a decrease in the rate of profit (the upswing of the cycle); and along with a restructuring and devaluation of capital, the rate of profit gets restored (the downswing of the cycle). "And so we go round the whole circle once again." A *Zirkel vicieux*.

Appendix 1. Comparison of some key texts in *Capital III*, Part Three, with its manuscript

In *Table 1* below, all italics are original; all bold is emphasis added by me; all underlining is emphasis added by me, being roughly Engels's insertions or deletions (the latter denoted with curly brackets) or major amendments or changes in emphasis in the translation.

TABLE 1   *Capital III, Part Three: textual comparison of key divergences between Marx's manuscript, Engels's text and the Fernbach translation*

	Marx's 1864–65 manuscript (Marx 1894M)	Engels's edition of *Das Kapital* III (Marx 1894E)	Fernbach translation of *Capital III* (Marx 1894F)
1	Abstrakt betrachtet, kann bei dem Fall des *Preisses der einzelnen Waare* in Folge der Vermehrung der *Anzahl* dieser lower priced commodities die Profitrate *dieselbe* bleiben, z.B. wenn die Vermehrung der Productivkraft der Arbeit *gleichmässig* und *gleichzeitig* auf *alle* Bestandtheile der Waaren wirkte, so daß der *Gesammtpreiß* der Waare in demselben *Verhältniß* der verschiednen Preißbestandtheile der Waare *dasselbe* (constant) bliebe, *fallen*, wie in dem bisher Untersuchten, steigen wenn mit der Erhöhung der Rate des Mehrwerths eine bedeutende Depreciation der constanten Capitaltheile verbunden wäre. (Betrachtet man nur den *Preiß der einzelnen* Waaren für sich oder mißt man blos die Arbeit in respect to the quantity of commodity produced by it, so die Untersuchung stets schief. Es kommt alles darauf an, wie groß die Gesammtsumme des ausgelegten Capitals. ...) (M, p. 319)	Abstrakt betrachtet, kann beim Fall des Preises der einzelnen Ware infolge vermehrter Productivkraft {...}, und bei daher gleichzeitiger Vermehrung der Anzahl dieser wohlfeilernWaren, die Profitrate dieselbe bleiben, z.B. wenn die Vermehrung der Productivkraft {...} gleichmäßig und gleichzeitig auf alle Bestandteile derWaren wirkte, so daß der Gesammtpreis derWare in demselben Verhältnis fiele, wie sich die Produktivität der Arbeit vermehrte, und anderseits das gegenseitige Verhältnis der verschiednen Preisbestandteile der Ware dasselbe bliebe {...}. Steigen könnte die Profitrate sogar, wenn mit der Erhöhung der Rate des Mehrwerths eine bedeutende Wertverminderung der Elemente des konstanten und namentlich des fixen Kapital verbunden wäre. **Aber in Wirklichkeit wird die Profitrate, wie bereits gesehn, auf die Dauer fallen. {...} In keinem Fall erlaubt der Preisfall der einzelnen Ware allein einen Schluß auf die Profitrate.** Es kommt alles darauf an, wie groß die Gesammtsumme des ausgelegten Capitals. (E, p. 239–40) [chapter 13]	Viewed abstractly, the rate of profit might remain the same despite a fall in the price of the individual commodity as a result of increased productivity, and hence despite a simultaneous increase in the number of these cheaper commodities – for example if the increase in productivity affected all the ingredients of the commodity uniformly and simultaneously, so that their total price fell in the same proportion as the productivity of labour increased, while the ratio between the various ingredients of the commodity's price remained the same. The rate of profit could even rise, if a rise in the rate of surplus-value was coupled with a significant reduction in the value of the elements of constant capital, and fixed capital in particular. **In practice, however, the rate of profit will fall in the long run, as we have already seen. In no case does the fall in the price of the individual commodity, taken by itself, permit any conclusion as to the rate of profit.** It all depends on the size of the total capital involved in its production. (F, pp. 336–37; cf. U, p. 230)

TABLE 1   *Capital III*, Part Three: textual comparison of key divergences (cont.)

	Marx's 1864–65 manuscript (Marx 1894M)	Engels's edition of *Das Kapital III* (Marx 1894E)	Fernbach translation of *Capital III* (Marx 1894F)
2	So wirkt das Gesetz nur als Tendenz, dessen Wirkung nur unter bestimmten Umständen und auf lange Perioden ausgedehnt schlagend hervortritt. (M, p. 308)	So wirkt das Gesetz nur als Tendenz, dessen Wirkung nur unter bestimmten Umständen und im Verlauf langer Perioden schlagend hervortritt. (E, p. 249) [chapter 14]	The law operates therefore simply as a tendency, whose effect is **decisive** only under certain particular circumstances and over long periods. (F, p. 346) Thus, the law acts only as a tendency. And it is only under certain circumstances and only after long periods that its effects become strikingly pronounced. (Untermann translation, p. 239)
3	Diese verschiednen Einflüsse machen sich bald neben einander im Raum, bald nach einander in der Zeit geltend und **periodisch** macht sich der Conflict der streitigen Agentien in Crisen Luft. Die Crisen sind immer nur momentane gewaltsame Lösungen der vorhandnen Widersprüche und gewaltsame Eruptionen, um **das gestörte Gleichgewicht wieder herzustellen**. (M, p. 323)	Diese verschiednen Einflüsse machen sich bald mehr nebeneinander im Raum, bald **mehr** nacheinander in der Zeit geltend; {...} periodisch macht sich der Konflikt der widerstreitenden Agentien in Krisen Luft. Die Krisen sind immer nur momentane gewaltsame Lösungen der vorhandnen Widersprüche, gewaltsame Eruptionen, die das gestörte Gleichgewicht für den Augenblick wiederherstellen. (M, p. 323) [chapter 15]	These various influences <u>sometimes tend to exhibit</u> themselves side by side, spatially; at other times one after the other, temporally; <u>and at certain points</u> the conflict of contending agencies <u>breaks through</u> in crises. Crises are never more than momentary, violent solutions <u>for</u> the existing contradictions, violent eruptions that re-establish the disturbed balance **for the time being**. (F, p. 357; cf. U, p. 253)
4	**Unter allen Umständen aber würde sich das Gleichgewicht herstellen** durch *Vernichtung von Capital* in grösserem oder geringerem Umfang. (M, p. 328)	Unter allen Umständen aber würde sich das Gleichgewicht herstellen durch <u>Brachlegung und selbst</u> Vernichtung von Kapital in größrem oder geringrem Umfang. (E, p. 264) [chapter 15]	Under all circumstances, however, the balance will be restored by capital's lying idle or even by its destruction, to a greater or lesser extent. (F, p. 362)

TABLE 1 *Capital III, Part Three: textual comparison of key divergences (cont.)*

Marx's 1864–65 manuscript (Marx 1894M)	Engels's edition of *Das Kapital III* (Marx 1894E)	Fernbach translation of *Capital III* (Marx 1894F)
5 Und so würde der Zirkel von neuem durchlaufen. Ein Theil des Capitals das depriciirt war durch Stockung seiner Function, würde seinen alten Werth wieder gewinnen. Es würde übrigens mit erweiterten Productionsbedingungen, einem erweiterten Markt, und mit erhöhter Productivkraft derselbe Zirkel vicieux wieder durchlaufen werden. (M, p. 329)	Und so würde der Zirkel von neuem durchlaufen. Ein Teil des Kapitals das durch Funktionsstockung entwertet war, würde seinen alten Wert wiedergewinnen. Im übrigen würde mit erweiterten Produktionsbedingungen, mit einem erweiterten Markt und mit erhöhter Produktivkraft derselbe <u>fehlerhafte Kreislauf</u> wieder durchgemacht werden. (E, p. 265) [chapter 15]	And so we go round the whole circle once again. One part of the capital that was devalued by the cessation of its function now regains its old value. <u>And apart from that</u>, with expanded conditions of production, a wider market and increased <u>productivity</u>, the same cycle of errors is pursued once more. (F, p. 364; cf. U, p. 255)

Note: All of these citations have been commented upon in the main text. Some of these citations are also examples of how insertions or changes in emphasis by Engels get reinforced in a translation. For example, see the second part of citation 3: Marx has "Die Crisen sind ... momentane ... Lösungen ... um das gestörte Gleichgewicht wieder herzustellen"; Engels-Marx reads "Die Krisen sind ... momentane ... Lösungen ... *die das gestörte Gleichgewicht für den Augenblick wiederherstellen*"; Fernbach's translation reads "Crises are .. momentary ... solutions ... that re-establish the disturbed balance for the time being."

Appendix 2. The tendency of the rate of profit to fall in Marx's manuscripts: A speculative history

Preliminary Remarks

It is interesting to compare the interpretation presented in the main text with Marx's earlier writings on this issue. I will do this in the first two sections of this appendix. A quite different matter is to derive conclusions from such a comparison (see the concluding section of this appendix below). In the main part of this article, I could 'safely' just present textual evidence about only one text (allegedly one). Hence my conclusions could be free from any otherwise complicating matters.

When comparing texts from different periods, such freedom is no longer possible, because the comparison is then bound to be speculative. Why does an author change his or her mind? Why does an author develop a theory in this or that way? I gladly reserve this speculative history for an appendix. Even so, speculative history in general is an intriguing aspect of historiography.

We will see that important statements in an early manuscript of Marx on the profit rate do not appear in the later ones. From that and the change in the structure of his texts, I will conclude that Marx's views on the (tendency of the) rate of profit to fall developed from a law about the *historical destination* of the capitalist system to a theory about the *functioning* of the system.

The first manuscript: the 'Grundrisse' (1857–58)
The "fall of the rate of profit" was discussed by Marx in a manuscript now called the *Grundrisse*. It was first published in Moscow in a very limited edition (1939–41) and then reprinted in Berlin in 1953 (the publication date usually referred to). All page references in this appendix are to the 1973 English translation by Martin Nicolaus (Marx 1953N).

This manuscript was written to aid Marx's own understanding; it was not intended for publication. The 'fall of the rate of profit' is discussed in the third section of the manuscript's last notebook (Notebook 7, pp. 745–58), its second half being comments on especially Smith and Ricardo (pp. 751–8).

The problem set and theoretical framework that the text addresses, in connection with the profit rate, seem to be very much (1) Ricardo's insufficient distinction between rate of surplus-value and rate of profit and (2) the inverse relation between the amount of profit and the rate of profit (remember that this last reformulation of the law by Marx was also highlighted in the manuscript of *Capital III*). It is after having set out this inverse relation that Marx uses the term *law*:

> This is in every respect the most important law of modern political economy. ... It is a law which, despite its simplicity, has never before been grasped and, even less, consciously articulated. (Marx 1953N, p. 748)[29]

Marx then sets out how "the development of the productive forces" (or "powers of production") is accompanied by a relative "decline of the part of the capital ... exchanged for immediate labour" (cf. equation (1) above – the concept of the "organic composition of capital" is not explicitly stated in this text, but the gist of it is described in various wordings). This process,

> when it reaches a certain point, suspends the self-realisation of capital. ... Beyond a certain point, the development of the powers of production becomes a barrier for capital; hence the capital relation a barrier for the

---

29   A similar sentence appears in the later manuscripts.

development of the productive powers of labour. When it has reached this point, capital, i.e., wage labour, ... is necessarily stripped off as a fetter ... to give room to a higher state of social production. (pp. 749–50)

These wordings clearly remind one of the work Marx did in his youth with Engels, *The German Ideology* (1845–46), and of their 1848 political pamphlet, *The Communist Manifesto*. The 1857–58 manuscript is far removed from the manuscript of *Capital III* and my interpretation of it. Even though on the last page (up to the comments) Marx moves on to the key crisis theme of the later manuscript, its context is different. He writes:

> These contradictions [of development of the powers of production] lead to explosions, cataclysms, crises, in which by momentaneous suspension of labour and annihilation of a great portion of capital the latter is violently reduced *to the point where it can go on*. ... Yet, *these regularly recurring* catastrophes lead to their repetition on a higher scale, and finally to its [capital's] violent overthrow. (p. 750; my italics)

Especially the last sentence points at a trend-wise development. Immediately after the text just quoted, Marx writes, "there are moments in the developed movement of capital which delay this movement other than by crises", and he next discusses these in about half a page (in hindsight one might think of these as the 'antediluvian' counteracting forces).

We may conclude that in the *Grundrisse* Marx adopts the view of the 'trend fall' in the profit rate. Crises as well as a number of other factors *delay* this trend fall. Moreover, the trend fall in the rate of profit is connected with the "overthrow" of the capitalist mode of production.

It seems relevant to note that, unlike in the later two manuscripts (i.e., the one discussed hereafter and the one discussed in the main text), Marx's 'own' discussion in the earlier pages (pp. 745–51) is *not* cast in terms of a tendency (it does appear in the comments of the second part; it also appears in a later reference back to the law on page 763).

The second manuscript (1861–63)

We now move on to Marx's 1861–63 manuscripts (*MEGA II*, Band 3, Teile 1–6, Berlin, 1976–82). A second main text on the (tendency of the) rate of profit to fall can be found in section 7 of Marx's Notebook XVI, dated December 1861–January 1862. All citations in this appendix are from Ben Fowkes's 1991 English translation, which appears in volume 33 of Marx's *Collected works*, pages 104–45.

This text – even more so than the *Grundrisse* text – has much the character of notes intended to aid the author's understanding. The relevant statements concerning the rival interpretations of the *Capital III* text about the development of the rate of profit are to be found early on in the manuscript (pp. 104–12). First of all, the reference is again to classical political economy: "This law, and it is the most important law of political economy, is that the *rate of profit has a tendency to fall with the progress of capitalist production*" (p. 104). Note this is now immediately cast in terms of a "tendency". Then Marx asks himself, "So where does this tendency for the general rate of profit to fall come from?" (i.e., what is its explanation?). Next, after a few lines on "the Ricardian and Malthusian school", Marx immediately refers to a – or *the* (?) – cyclical empirical expression of the law:

> But apart from theory there is also the practice, the crises from *superabundance of capital or, what comes to the same, the mad adventures capital enters upon in consequence of the lowering of {the} rate of profit. Hence crises – see Fullarton – acknowledged as a necessary violent means for the cure of the plethora of capital, and the restoration of a sound rate of profit.* (p. 105)[30]

Restoration of a sound rate of profit. Note that both the "their repetition on a higher scale" and the "finally ... its violent overthrow" of the *Grundrisse* text have disappeared (from here and the rest of this text).

After analysing the factors that might cause the general rate of profit to fall, especially a fall in the absolute magnitude of surplus-value and a fall in the ratio of variable to constant capital, Marx states:

> But the law of development of capitalist production (see Cherbuliez, etc.) consists precisely in the continuous decline of variable capital ... in *relation* to the constant component of capital. (p. 106)

Next he indicates that "the development of the productive power of capital" is key to the law and that this "implies, at the same time, the concentration of capital in large amounts at a small number of places" (pp. 107–8). This is followed by an explicit statement about the two factors of the law that work against each other, that is, the rate of surplus-value and the composition of capital:

---

30   Passages between asterisks appear in English in the German manuscript. Passages in curly brackets are added by the editors; often they are reconstructions of illegible handwriting, as in some quotations to follow.

> Both movements not only go {hand in hand} but condition each other. They are only different forms and phenomena in which the same law is expressed. But they work in opposite directions, in so far as the rate of profit comes into consideration. (p. 109)

Subsequently, Marx indicates that "for the rate of profit to remain the same" these factors "would have to grow in the same ratio" and continues:

> This is only possible within certain limits, and that it is rather the reverse, the tendency towards a fall in profit – or a *relative* decline in the amount of surplus-value hand in hand with the growth in the rate of surplus-value – which must predominate [for the law to hold?], as is also confirmed by experience. (p. 110; insertion in square brackets is mine)

Further on we read:

> If one considers the development of productive power and the relatively not so pronounced fall in the rate of profit, the exploitation of labour must have increased very much, and what is remarkable is not the fall in the rate of profit but that it has not fallen to a greater degree. (p. 111)

In terms of the rival interpretations, these passages on pages 110–11 are the most puzzling. It is not obvious what is meant by "confirmed by experience": is it a reference to the experience of a trend fall, or the experience of a phase of the cycle (that is, the upturn phase) in which the law predominates? This last interpretation is plausible in light of the "restoration" text quoted above (from page 105). This seems to be confirmed two pages further on:

> This fall in the rate of profit leads to ... a rise in the level of concentration of the means of production. .... Once it has reached a certain level, this rising concentration in turn brings about a new fall in the rate of profit. (p. 112)

The general impression this manuscript gives is that Marx is wondering and searching for a conceptual framework. The remainder of the text (pp. 113–45) is an analysis of the connections between the relevant concepts at stake: rising labour productivity together with a rising organic composition of capital; rising rates of surplus-value; profit; and the rate of profit. Often the analysis is carried by way of (tedious) numerical examples. In general, the text is unsystematic; indeed it is comprised of notes.

A speculative history: in conclusion

Marx begins his study of this issue from the empirical "law of the falling rate of profit" of the political economy of his days. He is intrigued by it – especially, I presume, because from the works of his youth onward he sees the capitalist mode of production as a *historical* mode of production that may be overcome. When it comes to the explanation of the law, he is not satisfied with the arguments put forward by especially Smith and Ricardo. Hence he comes up with his own explanation for a fall in the rate of profit (i.e., a rise in productivity!) and reformulates that law as one of a combination of two things: a decrease in the rate of profit and an increase in the amount of profit (in the final version, this is the stuff of chapter 13 of *Capital III*). Already in the *Grundrisse*, Marx has found this explanation (beyond Smith and Ricardo) and reformulation; the later manuscripts merely improve on it.

Having found this explanation, Marx wonders (starting already with the *Grundrisse*): If this were all, then we should expect a much faster fall in the rate of profit empirically. Hence, there must be factors delaying the fall. Some of these are mentioned in the earlier two manuscripts, but they gain full prominence only in the *Capital III* manuscript (chapter 14). Consequently, for Marx the law is now a tendency law ("Thus, the law acts only as a tendency").

Then from the 1861–62 to the 1864–65 manuscript it seems that Marx gets more and more convinced that economic crises do not merely play a "delaying" role (as in the 1857–58 text), but are the heart of the matter. My hunch is that by that time he had come to deeply understand economic crises.[31] Hence, in the *Capital III* manuscript he reformulates the 'systematic' of the theory – the entry point of the theory, the interconnections and how they connect, the order of the presentation of the relevant issues within the theory. The concept of as well as the term *crisis* no longer appears in either the exposition of the tendency law (chapter 13) or that of the countertendencies (chapter 14).[32] They have been moved to the synthetic part of the text (chapter 15). Economic crises now are the "violent *solutions* of the existing contradictions" (cf. F, p. 357; U, p. 253; my italics).

Consequently, in the exposition of the law – or any other part of the text – any reference to an "overthrow" of the mode of production has disappeared (as it had already in the 1861–62 text). Instead, the confines of the capitalist mode of production are twofold: (1) a rise in productivity generates a decrease in the rate

---

31   Chapter 15 of *Capital III* – with its interconnected notions of the depreciation of capital, of the concentration and centralisation of capital, and of *"neue Kombinationen"* [new combinations] – in fact witnesses that insight.

32   With one exception (Marx 1894F, p. 331) in a different context.

of profit, and this decrease must be overcome again and again through crises; (2) production does not cease when the need for goods is satisfied, but when the realisation and production of profit require this – that is, capitalist production adheres to a mandate of its own, and that mandate has little or nothing to do with meeting the production needs of society (Marx 1894M, p. 332; cf. 1894E, p. 268; 1894U, p. 258; 1894F, p. 367).[33]

Thus we see in Marx's views a movement from a law about the *historical destination* of the capitalist system to a theory about the *functioning* of the system. Note that this is no accident: it is consistent with all of *Capital*, in which – contrary to what some textbooks say about it – one finds no references to an overthrow of the capitalist system, and of the 2,200 pages perhaps five refer in passing to some future society. I am not saying that the evolution to that future society was no concern of Marx: I suggest that he no longer had mechanistic-economistic views about it.

References

Cullenberg, Stephen 1994, *The falling rate of profit: recasting the Marxian debate*, London: Pluto Press.

Fine, Ben 1990, 'On the composition of capital: a comment on Groll and Orzech', *HOPE* 22(1): 149–55.

Fine, Ben, and Laurence Harris 1976, 'Controversial issues in Marxist economic theory', in *Socialist Register 1976*, edited by Ralph Miliband and John Saville, 141–78, London: Merlin Press.

Fine, Ben, and Laurence Harris 1979 *Rereading 'Capital'*, London: Macmillan.

Groll, Shalom, and Ze'ev B. Orzech 1987, 'Technical progress and values in Marx's theory of the decline in the rate of profit: an exegetical approach', *HOPE* 19(4): 591–613.

---

33   On (1) Marx writes: "Die Schranke der kapitalistischen Produktionsweise tritt hervor: 1. Darin, daß die Entwicklung der Produktivkraft der Arbeit im Fall der Profitrate ein Gesetz erzeugt, das ihrer eignen Entwicklung auf einen gewissen Punkt feindlich gegenübertritt und daher beständig durch Krisen überwunden werden muß" (E, p. 268; cf. M, p. 332). Note that the German *Schranke* [confines, barrier] also has a connotation of taking to court. I am not altogether happy with the standard English translations of this text; in perhaps more clumsy English I would suggest: "The confines of the capitalist mode of production come to the fore: 1. In that the development of the 'forces of production' of labour generates a law of falling rate of profit which at a certain point confronts this development itself antagonistically, and hence must be overcome continuously [again and again] through crises" (U, p. 258 and F, p. 367; translation amended).

Groll, Shalom, and Ze'ev B. Orzech 1989, 'From Marx to the Okishio theorem: a genealogy', *HOPE* 21(2): 253–72.

Groll, Shalom, and Ze'ev B. Orzech 1990, 'Capital-labour relations: consistency or complication? A reply to Ben Fine', *HOPE* 22(1): 155–65.

Grossmann, Henryk 1967 [1929], *Das Akkumulations- und Zusammenbruchsgesetz des kapitalistischen Systems*, Frankfurt: Verlag Neue Kritik.

Heinrich, Michael 1996, 'Engels' edition of the third volume of *Capital* and Marx's original manuscript', *Science & Society* 60(4): 452–66.

Howard, Michael C., and John E. King 1992, *A history of Marxian economics, volume 2, 1829–1990*, London: Macmillan.

Jevons, W. Stanley 1970 [1871], *The theory of political economy*, Harmondsworth: Penguin Books.

Lebowitz, Michael A. 1976, 'Marx's falling rate of profit: a dialectical view', *Canadian Journal of Economics* 9(2): 232–54.

Marx, Karl 1984E, *Das Kapital: Kritik der Politischen Ökonomie.* Vol. III, *Der Gesamtprozeß der kapitalistischen Produktion*. Edited by F. Engels. *Marx-Engels Werke* 25, Berlin: Dietz Verlag, 1972.

Marx, Karl 1984U, *Capital: a critique of political economy*, vol. III, *The process of capitalist production as a whole*, 1909 translation of 1894E by Ernest Untermann, London: Lawrence & Wishart, 1974.

Marx, Karl 1984F, *Capital: a critique of political economy*, vol. III. Translation of 1894E by David Fernbach, Harmondsworth: Penguin Books, 1981.

Marx, Karl 1984M, *Karl Marx: Ökonomische Manuskripte 1863–1867*. Text, part 2. Edited by Manfred Müller, Jürgen Jungnickel, Barbara Lietz, Christel Sander, and Artur Schnickmann. Volume 4 of division 2 (*Das Kapital* and *Vorarbeiten*) of *Karl Marx, Friedrich Engels Gesamtausgabe* (*MEGAII/4*), Berlin: Dietz Verlag, 1992.

Marx, Karl 1953 [1939–41], *Grundrisse der Kritik der Politischen Ökonomie (Rohentwurf)*. Edited by the Marx-Engels-Lenin Institute, Berlin: Dietz Verlag.

Marx, Karl 1953N, *Grundrisse: foundations of the critique of political economy (rough draft)*. Translation of Marx 1953 [1939–41] by Martin Nicolaus, Harmondsworth: Penguin Books, 1973.

Marx, Karl 1991, 'Economic manuscript of 1861–1863 (continuation)'. Translated by Ben Fowkes, Vol. 33 of *Collected works*, New York: International Publishers.

Mattick Sr., Paul 1974 [1969], *Marx and Keynes: the limits of the mixed economy*, London: Merlin Press.

Okishio, Nobio 1961, 'Technical changes and the rate of profit', *Kobe University Economic Review* 7: 85–99.

Oakley, Allen 1983, *The making of Marx's critical theory: a bibliographical analysis*, London: Routledge & Kegan Paul.

Reuten, Geert 1991, 'Accumulation of capital and the foundation of the tendency of the rate of profit to fall', *Cambridge Journal of Economics* 15(1): 79–93.

Reuten, Geert 1997, 'The notion of tendency in Marx's 1894 law of profit', in *New investigations of Marx's method*, edited by Fred Moseley and Martha Campbell, pp. 150–75, Atlantic Highlands, NJ: Humanities Press.

Reuten, Geert 2003, 'Karl Marx: his work and the major changes in its interpretation', in *Companion to the history of economic thought*, edited by W.J. Samuels, J.E. Biddle, and J.B. Davis, pp. 148–66, Oxford: Blackwell.

Reuten, Geert, and Michael Williams 1989, *Value-form and the state; the tendencies of accumulation and the determination of economic policy in capitalist society*, London: Routledge.

Robinson, Joan 1969 [1942], *An essay on Marxian economics*, London: Macmillan.

Smith, Tony 2002, 'Surplus profits from innovation: a missing level in *Capital III*?', in *The culmination of capital: essays on volume III of Marx's 'Capital'*, edited by Martha Campbell and Geert Reuten, London: Palgrave Macmillan.

Sweezy, Paul M. 1968 [1942], *The theory of capitalist development*, London: Modern Reader Paperbacks.

Vollgraf, Carl-Erich, and Jürgen Jungnickel 1994, 'Marx in Marx's Worten? – Zu Engels's Edition des Hauptmanuskripts zum dritten Buch des *Kapital*', MEGA *Studien* 2: 3–55.

CHAPTER 18

Accumulation of capital and the foundation of the tendency of the rate of profit to fall

1991 article, originally published in *Cambridge Journal of Economics* 15(1): 79–93.
 (For its abstract see the Abstracts of all chapters, p. 9.)

Contents

Introduction 391
1 Accumulation of capital 392
2 Tendencies of capital interaction and capital stratification 393
  2.1 Inter- and intra-branch interaction 393
  2.2 Stratification 393
  2.3 Tendencies versus trends 394
3 Stratification and the money expression of labour and abstract labour 394
4 Tendencies of accumulation of capital 396
  4.1 The tendency towards the over-accumulation of capital 396
  4.2 The tendency for the value composition of capital to rise and the tendency of the rate of profit to fall 397
5 The contradiction of the TRPF 399
6 The conditions of existence of the contradiction of the TRPF: stratification and devalorisation 400
7 The TRPF and devaluation of capital 403
8 The TRPF and the restructuring and centralisation of capital 405
Summary and conclusions 407
References 409

Annotation (of 2023). This article sets out a foundation of the theory of "the tendency of the rate of profit to fall" (TRPF) in the "stratification of capital". As remarked in the article's footnote 3, the upshot of the article is, first, that the tendency at hand not only interacts with other tendencies of accumulation (§4), but, secondly, that the expressions of this tendency are likely to be manifest in a cyclical manner (§7–§8). Furthermore, as remarked at the end of §6, capital stratification by itself does not prove the existence of the TRPF, rather, the stratification of capital is generally the typical form of existence of capital. See also the six conclusions of the article.

Introduction[1]

The rate of profit tends to fall. In 1871 W.S. Jevons comments on this thesis: "There are sufficient statistical facts, too, to confirm this conclusion historically. The only question that can arise is as to the actual cause of this tendency" (1871, p. 246). Indeed the theory of the tendency of the rate of profit to fall (TRPF) was a substantial part of mainstream economic theorising from Adam Smith until the end of the nineteenth century. In more recent times, however, theory of it has been confined almost entirely to marxist or marxist-inspired work, where the tendency is related to the increase in the composition of capital associated with labour-expelling technical change.[2] However, even here the issue remains controversial, due partly to the fact that there is little agreement as to the appropriate level of abstraction. Some authors interpret the tendency as an empirical trend of either short-run cyclical or long-run secular development. The view proposed in this article, on the other hand, is that a tendency is a concept belonging to a specific level of abstraction, and so is quite different from the concept of an empirical trend.[3]

Another important controversy relates to the question of how technical change could ever produce a fall in the rate of profit, when new techniques are presumably only introduced in order to secure increases in the rate of profit. Thus, it is argued, rate of profit decreasing technical change will just not come about: if the rate of profit is to decrease, it must be for reasons other than changes in the composition of capital brought about by technical change (such

---

1 I would like to thank Michael Williams and Jörg Glombowski for their helpful comments on earlier versions of this paper and Marilyn Gruschka for correcting my English. The paper has also benefitted from comments made by two anonymous referees and the editors of the *CJE*. Any remaining errors are, of course, mine. A more extended discussion of the issues raised in this article is in Reuten and Williams (1989), as specified at the appropriate places.
2 See, however, the references in Harris (1983, p. 311) and Duménil, Glick and Rangel (1987a, pp. 332–3).
3 Recent empirical investigations of the rate of profit and related variables include Duménil, Glick and Rangel (1987a, 1987b), Lipietz (1986), Reati (1986), Webber and Rigby (1986), and Wolff (1986). The upshot of the present article is, first, that the tendency at hand not only interacts with other tendencies of accumulation (§4), but, secondly, that the expressions of this tendency are likely to be manifest in a cyclical manner (§7–§8).

as wage rate increase). Therefore, many authors (drawing in this respect on the seminal article by Okishio 1961) regard the TRPF as being insufficiently grounded; it lacks (as Roemer 1979 expresses it) a microeconomic foundation. This question is the main issue of this article.

In §5 it is indicated that the TRPF is based on contradictory forces in the economy (indeed new techniques are, in general, only introduced if these secure a higher rate of profit). Nevertheless, contradictory forces may coexist; the question is how these are reconciled. It will be argued in §6 that, besides the fact that authors such as Okishio and Roemer cast their analysis in one-sided physical (use-value) terms, their analysis is inadequate in that it is comparative static. Once the theory is cast in dynamic terms, conditions of existence for the TRPF (or, appropriate "microeconomic foundations") can indeed be provided, and the analysis of the "Okishians" reduces to a special case. However, whilst these conditions of existence may resolve these contradictory forces, they do not dissolve them. Their expression then is in the devaluation (§7) and the restructuring and centralisation of capital (§8). Before this, §1 introduces the accumulation of capital, and §2–§3 provide the elementary dynamic framework of the interaction of capitals. In §4 the tendency for the composition of capital to rise, and the derived tendency of the rate of profit to fall, is presented as merely one form of existence of the accumulation of capital; the other form being the tendency to over-accumulation of capital, and the derived labour-shortage profit squeeze.

1 Accumulation of capital

The inherent logic of capitalist production is valorisation, the expansion of value; more specifically production is geared towards continual increase of profit. This is achieved firstly by an increase in control over the labour process by capital, and secondly by accumulation of capital. The inherent limits of these are overcome by technical change. (Value is conceived of as a category which finds concrete expression only in money; it should not be taken to be a pre-market concept such as "labour embodied" – see Reuten 1988a and Reuten and Williams 1989, ch. 1.)

Firstly, the fact that production is geared to the increase in profits implies that capital is continually driven to increase control, with the effect of decreasing costs per unit of physical output and increasing the rate of profit. There are clearly limits to such cost reduction. For a given length of the working day and technique of production, the intensity of labour cannot be increased indefinitely. Thus, secondly, capital is enlarged, to be reproduced on an extended scale, via investment of profit, thereby extending the valorisation of capital to the accumulation of capital.

As valorisation is limited by the possible increase in the intensity of labour, this also limits the extent of accumulation of capital. The investment of capital in new techniques of production overcomes these limits. A new technique may both itself reduce unit costs and create the possibility for new organisational techniques to increase the intensity of labour, and thus decrease unit costs even further. With its introduction not only (potential) profits but also the rate of (potential) profit on the newly accumulated capital tends to increase.

2 Tendencies of capital interaction and capital stratification

2.1 *Inter- and intra-branch interaction*

The interaction of capitals is first determined at the level of inter-branch interaction. Capitalist production is indifferent to the particular use-values produced. Valorisation, the driving force of capital, determines that capital valorised and validated in the one branch may flow – via the mediation of money capital – to be accumulated in another, in pursuit of a higher rate of profit. Inter-branch interaction and accumulation of capital thence establish a *tendency* of equalisation of average rates of profit between branches.

Secondly, the interaction of capitals is determined at the intra-branch level. This interaction in product markets is induced by the compulsion continuously to realise the output produced. In connection with the generally temporary character of sales and purchase contracts (in general contractual sales above the average market price in one period would have the effect of repelling buyers in the next), it establishes a *tendency* towards uniform prices in a market. This tendency also applies to labour-power – it is again predicated on the temporary character of sales and purchase contracts (for labour-power) – so that the competition among capitals for labour establishes a tendency for wages, and the intensity of similar labour, to become uniform across capitals. The articulation of these tendencies ensures that the profits of any one capital come to depend on the technique of production adopted. The interaction of capitals therefore reinforces and reproduces more concretely the compulsion to accumulate capital in new techniques of production (§1).

2.2 *Stratification*

Accumulation of capital in new and cost reducing techniques of production applies to inter- as well as intra-branch investment of capital. In both cases the initiating capital secures an extra profit. The consequent threat of price competition and the necessity for continuous valorisation compels competitors to follow suit. However, each capital is burdened with the fixed costs of its already accumulated capital and will thus only scrap old plants when a new technique offers net profits (taking into account the capital of the old plant foregone) greater than the profits on its existing plant. Since, therefore, plants embodying new technology will in general not be immediately adopted by all capitals, each branch of production tends to be composed of a *stratification* of capitals dated according to cost of production, and associated rate of profit differences.

2.3 Tendencies versus trends

The concept of a tendency should be distinguished from that of an empirical trend. Though tendencies cannot be taken to be empirical statements in the sense that their effects can be directly observed, they do affect the concrete. To what extent tendencies are actualised (for example, the extent to which rates of profit are indeed equalised, or to what extent the TRPF results in an actual fall of the rate of profit) can never be established at the level of abstraction at which they have been derived (see also Weeks 1981, p. 205; and Cutler, Hindess, Hirst and Hussain 1977, vol. 1, ch. 6.). But before the theory can be confronted with the empirical, the interconnection of tendencies (as well as their articulation with contingencies) has to be theorised.

3 Stratification and the money expression of labour and abstract labour

The interplay of valorisation, accumulation and the tendencies of capital interaction (together with the credit system – see Reuten 1988b) constitutes the value of labour, of commodities and of labour-power – quantitatively expressed as prices in terms of money.[4]

The capitalist production process is a two-fold process of production of use-value and value (valorisation). Market prices have to be anticipated, thus

---

[4] Thus the concept of *value* does not refer to labour-time (as it would in a 'labour-embodied' theory of value). Nevertheless, because the dimension of some unit of labour is time, the *value of labour* (a concept incompatible with a Marxist labour-embodied theory) refers to some labour-time. Its quantitative expression is always in terms of a standard of money (e.g. £x or $y). Thus, the value of (one hour of) labour (time) in some plant is, e.g., £12 or $18 (indicated below by the symbol m). The concept 'labour-power' is the conventional Marxist one, i.e., the ability to perform labour for a definite period of time. Again the quantitative expression of the 'value of labour-power' per unit of time is in terms of a standard of money, e.g., £7 (i.e., the wage rate).

the labour process is pre-commensurated in terms of the anticipated output price. Because of the articulation of the tendencies of stratification and uniform prices, the anticipated value, m, of the labour-time in each unit of capital (plant) i generally differs. If the anticipated value of the *average* labour used up in some branch (k) is m_k then, in general, because of the stratification of capital, anticipated values will differ *within* each branch

$$m_i \neq m_j \tag{1}$$

(where m_i is the anticipated money expression of labour in plant i, measured in terms of some standard of money per unit of labour-time). *Across* branches, anticipated values will in general also differ

$$m_k \neq m_l \tag{2}$$

Thus these anticipated values are pre-market entities. It is only in the market that the commodity is actualised as an entity of double form (use-value and money). *Actual prices* are first determined, not by the labour used up in some particular plant according to the technique adopted in that plant, but as a recursive process by the labour used up in that plant in comparison to that required by the socially necessary technique (conceived for the present as the average technique). In this particular sense the price of a commodity is determined by socially necessary labour. The anticipated value m_i may thus diverge from the actual validation ("realisation")

$$m_i \gtrless m'_i \, ; \, m_k \gtrless m'_k \tag{3}$$

where m'_i and m'_k are the realised money expressions of labour. Then $m'_i l_i$ is the expression for abstract labour of plant i. Summing the labour realised in each plant (or branch), abstract labour is

$$\Sigma m'_i l_i \equiv m' l \equiv Y' \, ; \, ml \gtrless m' l \tag{4}$$

(where l_i and l are, respectively, the private and social aggregate labour expended, and Y' is the social aggregate value-added).[5]

---

5 This concept 'money expression of labour' (m' and m'_i), differs from Aglietta's "monetary expression of the working hour" (1976, p. 43; see also De Brunhoff 1976, p. 39) which we denote by m^*. The latter is used by Aglietta only at the macroeconomic level and it is predicated upon what he calls "the monetary constraint" that realisation is equal to production. Thus Aglietta's

4 Tendencies of accumulation of capital

4.1 The tendency towards the over-accumulation of capital

With increasing control over the labour-process and the intensity of labour, via the introduction of new techniques of production, the rate of surplus-value tends to rise. This is reflected in a tendency for the rate of accumulation to increase, an ultimate condition of which is a relatively abundant labour-force. Labour abundance may prevent increasing labour intensity being reflected in wage increases and facilitates the reflection in wage decreases of price decreases resulting from any decrease in unit costs. Ultimately, however, the accumulation of an increasing mass of surplus-value must deplete the reserve of labour, which, via an upward pressure on wages, counteracts the increase in the rate of surplus-value, eventually causing it to decrease, leading to a decrease in the rate of accumulation of capital.[6] Thus accumulation tends to take the form of *over-accumulation of capital*: it is extended up to the point where capital becomes abundant relative to labour, because of excessive valorisation.

One expression of this tendency towards the over-accumulation of capital is its effect on labour costs and production, thus it takes on the form of a labour-shortage profit squeeze.[7] The resulting interactions may give rise to a cyclical pattern of profits, accumulation and unemployment. (Note that the term cycle is used in the sense of fluctuation in general, without any specification as to duration.)[8]

$m^* = Y/l$ is the monetary condition that $Y = Y'$. My concept 'money expression of labour' is the reciprocal of Foley's (1986, p. 15) "monetary expression of labour".

6 The reserve of labour-power is determined by accumulation, demographic and social-demographic factors. Formally one can, of course, not exclude the possibility of a rate of surplus-value such that the rate of capital accumulation will be reduced to the growth rate of labour supply; for a Marxist account of this state see Glombowski (1983, pp. 378–81).

7 The other expression of over-accumulation of capital is in underconsumption (see Reuten and Williams 1989, ch. 3).

8 The theorisation of these or similar effects of labour shortage is part and parcel of almost every strand in economic theory, though there are important theoretical differences concerning the reactions to wage increases. Within the Marxist tradition (not excluding more Ricardian oriented authors) this theory has been developed at various levels of abstraction and from various methodological perspectives into what is labelled the 'theory of the profit squeeze'. In general, the focus in this theory is on class struggle over the distribution of income and its effect on accumulation and employment. The (initially) more empirically-oriented work derives from Glyn and Sutcliffe (1971, 1972) and Boddy and Crotty (1975). Model-analytic work derives in particular from Goodwin (1967) (for a short taxonomy and additional references, see Glombowski 1984, pp. 74–5; see also Goldstein 1985).

4.2 The tendency for the value composition of capital to rise and the tendency of the rate of profit to fall

The accumulation of capital in new techniques of production overcomes the constraint to increasing valorisation of capital imposed by the inherent limits to increasing labour intensity. The compulsion to introduce new techniques of production – reproduced by the interaction of capitals – is expressed in the continual change of the process of production, typically in the form of increase in labour productivity (§1–§2). This implies that in use-value terms, a unit of labour tends to work up an increasing mass of means of production (raw materials and depreciating fixed means of production), so that the technical composition of capital (TCC) tends to increase. It also implies, that at the *point in time* when a TCC-increasing technique is introduced, the composition of capital in terms of the prices at that point in time increases (that is the instantaneous value composition of capital (VCC) – the ratio of the value of the means of production to the value of labour-power – increases).[9] Therefore, an increasing share of any unit of profit accumulated tends to be invested in means of production, and a decreasing share in the wage fund. There is thus a tendency towards relative expulsion of labour.

The tendency for the TCC to increase thus counteracts the tendency towards the over-accumulation of capital; it retards, or even prevents, the eventual scarcity of labour and the associated upward pressure on wages. However, both labour-using accumulation and its negation in relative labour-expelling accumulation derive independently from the accumulation of capital and are therefore to be theorised first independently.[10]

The rate of profit r is the ratio of profit (value-added, $m'l$, minus wages wl) to capital laid out $(K+wl)$:

$$r = [(m' - w)l] / [K + wl] = [(m' - w)/w] / [K/(wl) + 1] \qquad (5)$$

(where K is capital invested in fixed and circulating means of production; w is the average money wage rate; m' is the money expression of social labour; and l is labour (measured in time); $K/(wl)$ is then the value composition of

---

9   As for the conceptual differences between the TCC, OCC (organic composition of capital) and VCC see Orzech and Groll (1989) and Reuten and Williams (1989, pp. 119–21). I refrain from using the term OCC because it is often associated with a 'labour-embodied' concept of value.

10 Thus whilst these tendencies interact, the one tendency is not merely a reaction to the other. Both these tendencies are continually operating forces. See also Hunt (1983, pp. 137–9).

capital). (Note that the components of capital are measured in disequilibrium rather than in equilibrium prices.)

The tendency for the VCC to rise, generates the tendency of the rate of profit to fall (TRPF), leading to a tendency for the rate of accumulation of capital to decrease. Formally a tendential fall in the rate of profit may be offset by a sufficient rise in the rate of surplus-value $(m'\text{-}w)/w$. However, m' and w are macroeconomic categories and their determination does not directly derive from changes in the composition of capital. Firstly, as for w, in the absence of inflation, an increase in the VCC and the social use-value productivity of labour tends (in the absence of quantity rationing – see §6 below) to be accompanied by decreasing commodity prices. But this does not immediately lead to changes in the wage rate, though the purchasing power of the wage is affected by it.[11] Changes in the wage rate are determined rather by the articulation of changes in the intensity and organisation of the labour process, and unemployment (§4.1).

Secondly, concerning m', because there is a tendency for the effect of increases in labour productivity on m' to be offset by concomitant price falls (that is in the absence of inflation), an increase in the *social average use value productivity* of labour need have no effect on social income $m'l$.[12] However, when m' is constant, value-added ($m'l \equiv \Sigma m'_i l_i$) may change if l changes. Furthermore, the micro counterpart of m', m'_i, may not be constant since it is a function of the deviation of the micro value productivity of labour from the branch average, m'_k, and the social average value productivity of labour m'. Similarly, to the extent that unit costs decrease, an increase in the average use-value productivity of labour in some branch k, tends to be expressed in a price decrease; however, m'_k also depends on the relative productivity increases between sectors. And again value-added in a branch, $m'_k l_k$, depends also on the size of the branch as measured by l_k.

Thus because the TRPF does not by itself immediately affect the macroeconomic categories m' and w, at this level of abstraction, the rate of surplus-value may be kept constant.[13] It does however immediately affect the micro and branch-level categories m'_i and m'_k, and the concomitant rates of surplus-value (see §6).

---

11 However, such price decreases do affect the composition of capital through its means of production component (see section 7).

12 Thus in the absence of inflation the effect of the increased number of use-values will tend to be offset by a decrease in the general price level (cf. Aglietta 1976, ch. 6).

13 See Reuten and Williams (1989, ch. 5), for the articulation of the TRPF and changes in the rate of surplus-value, as well as with the tendency to over-accumulation in general. See also Lipietz (1986, pp. 15–16).

5 The contradiction of the TRPF

The TRPF contradicts the logic of accumulation of capital as being geared towards *increase* in profit and the rate of profit (§1). This has led authors such as Okishio (1961), Himmelweit (1974) and Roemer (1979) to reject the TRPF.[14] The critique of these authors is usually considered to be the most telling, and their critique is relevant to the conceptualisation in this article so far. They would agree that: (1) the empirical discussion of whether the composition of capital is rising and the rate of profit falling does not bear upon the theoretical argument ("The empirical investigations, then, are certainly necessary, but they cannot provide refutation of a theory." – Roemer, 1979, p. 380); (2) an eventual refutation of the theory does not depend on a change in the rate of surplus-value (consequently the part of their argument relevant to this is couched in terms of the maximum rate of profit, with wages approaching zero).

Basicly their critique is that the TRPF lacks a microeconomic foundation. As capitals are impelled to increase profits and the rate of profit, they will only introduce new techniques that are cost-reducing, so, the argument goes, the average rate of profit cannot decrease. Typically, the average rate of profit will increase in terms of both old and new equilibrium prices.[15] As it stands all this is quite correct.[16] The crucial question is, however, to what extent their comparative static equilibrium account in Sraffian terms adequately deals with the

---

14   Various authors have generalised and/or tried to improve on the Okishio theorem (besides Roemer, e.g., Alberro and Persky 1979; Van Parijs 1980, 1983; Bowles 1981; Harris 1983; Coram 1986; and Bidard 1988), resulting in a more or less qualified rejection of the TRPF. Others, on the other hand, have shown that a combination of relaxation and restriction of the Okishian assumptions (in particular when the rate of surplus-value is held constant, or when fixed capital is introduced, or when competition is not neoclassical-perfect) leaves open the possibility of a fall in the rate of profit when the TCC increases (see Shaikh 1978, 1980; Salvadori 1981; Weeks 1981 (ch. 8), 1982; Fine 1982 (ch. 8); Laibman 1982; Hunt 1983; Negishi 1985 (ch. 4); Foley 1986 (ch. 8); Lipietz 1986; Schutz 1987; Moseley 1991, ch. 1–2). In general, the latter contributions have either reduced the TRPF to a special case, or left the 'microeconomic foundations' somewhat in the open.

15   When the constant real wage is conceived of as a commodity input (Roemer 1979, pp. 381–2) then the rate of profit always increases if the input-output matrix is indecomposable; if it is decomposable the rate of profit might remain the same.

16   Shaikh's (1978) critique of Okishio and Himmelweit – to which Roemer (1979) also replied – is that capitalists are forced (microeconomically) to reduce cost-prices whereby, indeed, according to the Okishio theorem, the profit margin on costs increases; at the same time, however, the profit rate might decrease. This is unconvincing, because it seems to imply that some fixed capital costs are not part of cost-prices. What is more, good arguments can be provided for the thesis that the profit rate is the first criterion from which the other two follow. See also the comments on Shaikh by Steedman (1980), Nakatani (1980),

dynamic problematic of the TRPF (cf. also Fine 1982, pp. 112–15, and Weeks 1982). Within the "Okishian" model, all new least-cost techniques are adopted by *all* capitals. Whilst this "procedure" may seem intuitively adequate when all capital is conceived of as circulating capital (as with Okishio and Himmelweit), it is not when fixed capital is taken into account (as with Roemer, challenged to do so by Shaikh 1978). Capitals will not in general adopt a new technique when its expected increase in revenue and the rate of profit does not compensate for the early obsolescence of the fixed capital of the old technique (see Section 6). But Roemer evades the dynamic problematic of the TRPF because of his odd conceptualisation of fixed capital. In one of his models, he assumes that all fixed capital lasts forever, and proposes that "if the rate of profit can be shown to rise as a consequence of technical innovation in a model when fixed capital lasts forever, *a fortiori* it should rise when fixed capital wears out, ..." (1979, p. 385). The static conception is shown here very clearly: the fixed capital does not need to be replaced. All capitals within a sector of production are homogeneous, so the problem of eventual devaluation of fixed capital (when prices decrease) which hits different capitals unevenly according to their state of amortisation, is defined away.[17] The same goes for his Von Neumann type model where he assumes that only those processes are operating "which produce a maximum profit rate".

However, this critique of the "Okishians" does not preclude the possibility that they are correct in arguing that the "micro-foundations" of the TRPF are indeed inadequate, or even lacking altogether.

6 The conditions of existence of the contradiction of the TRPF: stratification and devalorisation

The contradiction of the tendency of the overall rate of profit to fall and the tendential increase in profit and the rate of profit along with the accumulation of capital in new plants is resolved in the concretisation of the concept of capital stratification. It was argued above (§2.2) that capital tends to be stratified because, whilst valorisation is a continuous process, the accumulation of cap-

---

Bleaney (1980), Fine (1982, pp. 125–7) and Van Parijs (1983), as well as the reply to the first three by Shaikh (1980).

17 This is all the more remarkable because Roemer (rightly) accuses Shaikh (1978) of neglecting amortisation of fixed capital. It may be noted that this problem would remain even if technical changes could be perfectly foreseen (pp. 387–8), unless, of course, capitalists were, because of foreseen technical changes, to decide not to invest at all.

ital in means of production is a discrete "lumpy" process, as is entry to a new branch of production. Therefore the capital embodied in plants is dated differently. But as techniques and labour-productivity change continually over time, dated stratification is characterised according to these factors. And, as there is a tendency towards uniform prices in a market, this dated stratification is also a stratification of different rates of profit. (Thus the state of the economy conceptualised is not one of equilibrium, nor of perfect competition.)[18]

The prevalence of this stratification is derived from the compulsion towards valorisation, accumulation and preservation of capital. Therefore, when new techniques of production are available (with higher calculated plant rates of profit) the preservation of capital already accumulated may prevent immediate moves towards investment in new-technique and maximum rate of profit plants. Scrapping of plants is only enforced when prices no longer cover prime costs. Before that, the scrapping of plants in favour of investment in new ones is determined, firstly, by the difference in rates of profit on the investment in an already existing plant, and on that in a new plant (inclusive of the capital foregone because of scrapping) and, secondly, by the availability of means of finance (out of amortisation and/or out of additional credit). (This implies that a maximum rate of profit can only be gained by fully amortised capitals. Note that this conceptualisation here and in the remainder of this section differs from neo-classical vintage models.)[19]

Thus capital invested in a new plant and added to the stratification operates with up-to-date techniques of production – those with the highest VCC, maximal productivity of labour and minimal unit costs of production. Prior to the scrapping of plants, this investment increases the branch (or economy) production capacity, which induces one, or a combination of two, effects. The first is that plants in the branch operate at over-capacity as compared with the previous period; the second is that prices are driven downwards. In either case plants at the bottom of the stratification that no longer cover prime costs will have to be scrapped.[20] Thus when plant $(n+1)$ is added to the stratifica-

---

[18] In the case of perfect competition, capital would always immediately move to the new-technique plant (Salter 1960). An earlier presentation of the stratification framework set out here is in Reuten (1978, pp. 19–26). For a similar conceptualisation in this respect see Weeks (1981, pp. 204–8).

[19] In the neo-classical concept, obsolescence of plants is determined by the real wage (wage costs exceeding the average labour-productivity on a plant), rather than by the addition of plants to the stratification, introducing new cost-reducing techniques of production and by (as explained below) the resulting price decrease and/or over-capacity.

[20] The new plant capital may initiate this price decrease because it operates at minimal costs. It then functions as price leader. Subsequent scrapping is the typical process. Of course,

tion $(1,...,n)$, and when h plants are scrapped, the previous stratification $(1,...,n)$ becomes $(1+h,...,n, n+1)$. We shall pursue the alternative of price decreases (the over-capacity alternative has the same result in terms of the current argument; is has however different effects with respect to the employment of labour and effective demand). Because of a price decrease, the revenue of the remaining part of the previous stratification $(1+h,...,n)$ decreases, whereas the revenue of the new stratification $(1+h,...,n,n+1)$ typically increases with the average rate of growth.[21] The decreased revenue of the capitals in the previous stratification reflects their *devalorisation*, which is thus due to the labour productivity of any one capital in a particular period, relative to the average, lagging behind that in the previous period.[22]

Therefore, because investments and costs are unaffected whilst revenue decreases, the rate of profit of the capital accumulated in the *remaining part of the previous stratification* $(1+h,...,n)$ *decreases*. That of the capital invested in the *new plant* $(n+1)$ tends, at the new price to *increase* as compared with the average rate of profit $(1,...,n)$ at the previous price, or with the rate of profit of the plant just below it in the stratification, n, at the previous price.[23] Since the new

---

plants at the bottom of the stratification may be scrapped pre-emptively. The expected price decrease, or alternatively the expected over-capacity will be taken into account by the capital considering the new plant prior to the investment. In general, the initiation of a price decrease by this capital, in order to induce scrapping of plants at the bottom of the stratification so that the new plant can operate at near to full capacity, may be advantageous to it. Although I think that it is important to conceptualise the processes of adaptation (price decrease and scrapping) the argument here does not rely on it. In principle the argument (price decrease in particular) could also be cast in terms of a Sraffian equilibrium model with joint production. Whilst the reference here is to a branch, the argument typically holds for the economy as a whole. A formal but fairly simple model of the argument is presented in Reuten and Williams (1989, appendix to ch. 4).

21 Of course in the case of (macroeconomic or branch) stagnation revenue may remain constant or decrease. On the other hand, one branch may, of course, grow above average. This does not, however, affect the general argument.

22 Devalorisation of capital goes beyond any normal wear and tear. (Note the difference between the devalorisation of capital as introduced here, and the devaluation of capital as introduced in the next section.) It might be argued that to the extent devalorisation is foreseen at the point of investment, it is incorporated in calculating the 'marginal efficiency of capital'. But even if there were perfect foresight in this, the argument is unaffected. It cannot prevent devalorisation, and even with devalorisation net profits over the lifetime of the asset may still be positive and optimal.

23 Within the 'Okishian' argument it is sufficient that the $(n+1)$ composition of capital and rate of profit at the *old* prices is just above that of (n) at the old prices. So if the $(n+1)$ rate of profit is only just above that of (n), and if the $(1+h,...,n)$ rate of profit decreases at the new prices or capacity utilisation, then the Okishian argument is falsified for all plausible cases (those in which there is indeed accumulation of capital).

plant ($n+1$) operates at lower production costs than the previous plant (n), then in any case the rate of profit of the new plant capital at the new price is above both that of the nth and the average rate of profit. (This is in fact sufficient for the argument.) Because with the additional plant the *average* VCC tends to increase, the *average* rate of profit tends to decrease.[24] But it is because of the relatively greater labour productivity of the capital added to the stratification ($n+1$) that its comparative profitability increases, since the value productivity of labour in the ($1+h,...,n$) plants thereby decreases (typically by a decrease in output prices). Therefore, not only is the money expression of labour, m_i, stratified increasingly from ($1,...,i,...,n$), but it also tends to decrease (devalorisation) for all i when the stratification is extended.[25]

Thus, whilst the rate of profit on any one capital – previously invested in another branch or previously invested lower in the stratification – tends to *increase*, the average rate of profit in a branch or in the economy as a whole, tends to *decrease*. The contradiction of the tendency of the aggregate rate of profit to fall, and the increase in the rate of profit along with the accumulation of capitals in new plants, is thus resolved in the stratification of capitals.

This conceptualisation of capital stratification is, of course, not restricted to the tendency for the VCC to increase. Rather, it is the typical form of existence of capital, and therefore it constitutes also the conditions for the reproduction of the tendency of the rate of profit to fall. However, its effect on the average rate of profit will increase along with the increase of the relative share of fixed capital. To be sure, capital stratification by itself does not prove the existence of the TRPF (this would require a more encompassing study), but the account of stratification shows that the TRPF may consistently be reproduced by compatible "microeconomic behaviour".

7   The TRPF and devaluation of capital

It was shown in the previous section how the stratification of capital provides adequate conditions for the existence of the TRPF, thus resolving its contradic-

---

24   Price decreases, of course, affect capital outlay on circulating constant capital (raw materials etc.). It does not, however, affect previous capital outlay on fixed constant capital. The effect of the related devaluation of fixed capital is taken up in the next section.

25   The notion of the extra profits gained by the capitals at the top of the stratification is closely related to Schumpeter's notion of temporary monopoly profits accruing to the first capital to innovate, which are gradually eroded as the innovation diffuses through the industry and even the economy (see, e.g., Schumpeter 1943).

tion. But in this resolution the contradictions of the TRPF find further expression. One expression is the tendential negation of capital stratification (see §8). The other is that the price decrease typically associated with this form of accumulation, since it also affects input prices, may prevent the increasing technical composition of capital (TCC) being translated into an increasing value composition of capital (VCC).[26]

However, this price decrease affects the fixed capital outlay only of *new* plants, thereby decreasing the VCC when the top of the stratification TCC is replicated. Thus, as far as fixed capital outlay is concerned, this counteracting tendential price decrease does not affect the fall in the rate of profit of the prevailing capital, which is the effect of *devalorisation of capital* i.e., a relative decrease in valorisation of the previous stratification of capitals (§6). Input price decreases affect rather the *value* of the capital outlay of the previous stratification, and this *devaluation of capital* tends to be carried into effect by *output* price decreases. That is, when input prices decrease – affecting new plant investments – and when this is translated into output prices, it again decreases the revenue of the previous stratification of capital. Therefore there are two ways (depending on the accounting practice – historical or current cost accounting) in which devaluation of capital may be manifest. One is in a further decrease in the rate of profit, the other is in the immediate writing-off of capital when prices of the means of production decrease. In both cases the sum of depreciation allowances and surplus-value (i.e., the cash-flow) decreases.

From a one-sided physicalist (use-value) approach it might seem that such devaluation of capital does not affect its reproduction – in particular when (in case of current cost accounting) capital is devalued immediately so that the level of the profit rate is restored to that just prior to devaluation. Indeed physical reproduction (that is, the number of units of output of a plant) need not be affected by the input price decrease because new means of production can be bought at the lower price. But this does not take away the fact that because of devaluation the valorisation potential has decreased. This becomes obvious when a plant is wholly financed by credit: then the amortisation fund may be sufficient to buy a new plant, but not to cancel the credit.

Thus one expression of increasing labour productivity, TCC and instantaneous VCC is the devaluation of existing capital. Macroeconomically the de-

---

26 This effect depends upon the argument that price changes do not directly affect the money wage rate, and that the latter is determined rather in relation to the rate of unemployment. Therefore input-price decrease affects the value composition of capital (even if the price decrease were to be similar in all branches of the economy) rather than the rate of profit.

valuation of capital is the counterpart of the price decrease that counteracts the translation of the increase in the TCC into an increase in the VCC.[27]

8   The TRPF and the restructuring and centralisation of capital

The more rapid and sustained the productivity increase, the more it has the effect of wiping out the mass of profit of unamortised capitals, as expressed in both the decrease in the rate of profit along with the devalorisation and scrapping of plants (§6), and the devaluation of capital (§7). The speed of this productivity increase is contingent. Should it accelerate, then the rate of liquidation of the least efficient plants will also accelerate. Prices established in the market then approach the level of prices implied by the most efficient plants, which further devalues capital. With an accelerating rate of liquidation the forces giving rise to the TRPF tend to be expressed in the *restructuring* of capital, one form of which is the bankruptcy of capitals and the possible repurchase of liquidated assets by other capitals at near-to scrap value. Another form, which may prevent such bankruptcy is that of mergers, take overs and participations, that is, the *centralisation of capital*. Restructuring and centralisation *reduce* the *range* of the stratification of capital. Because stratification is a condition for existence of the TRPF, range reduction is a further expression of the contradiction of the TRPF.

Centralisation of capital counteracts the tendency for the TCC (and VCC) to rise; it tends to retard technical change, the implementation of which would require the building of new plants. Stratification proceeds by the temporary creation of over-capacity, and price reduction such that the least efficient plants are expelled from the stratification. This is only feasible (without a considerable reduction in profit and the rate of profit for the initiating capital) with a sufficiently large difference in productivity of labour and unit costs of production between the top and the bottom plant. With the reduction in the range of the stratification because of centralisation, it is exactly

---

27   It could be argued that within the conceptualisation of capital stratification presented in section 6, devaluation of capital also occurs, though only latently, when new techniques are introduced (prior to any input price decrease). Then, depending on the accounting practice, *devalorisation* may be manifest either in a decreasing money expression of labour (m_i), *or* in a reduction of the value of capital. In the first case valorisation decreases in comparison with the anticipated valorisation; in the second case previous valorisation is partly annihilated. As the cash-flow is not affected the net effect is, of course, the same. For expositional purposes I have referred only to the first manifestation.

this *difference* in costs which is reduced. Price decreases may then not lead to scrapping of plants, so that additional plants then tend to increase overcapacity.

However, innovation in new techniques and their implementation in additional plants may still be profitable if they create a sufficient cost difference. This may require technological and technical knowledge to build up, so that technical change would then tend to come in *waves*. During such a build-up, the scrapping of plants will stagnate, but once sufficient technical knowledge has accumulated, the stratification will be extended again etc., ultimately giving rise to renewed devaluation and centralisation.

Thus the contingent expression of the forces generating the TRPF, in centralisation of capital, counteracts the existence of the TRPF in capital stratification. So the rise of the VCC itself is counteracted. Because this has a wave-like character the TRPF is manifest in the form of cycles of centralisation. (Note again that the term cycle is used in the sense of fluctuation in general, without any specification as to duration or regularity.)

This concept of the process of "restructuring of capital" does not, in general, diverge from the mainstream marxist tradition. Fine and Harris in particular (1979, pp. 83–7) link the process of restructuring to the TRPF. An excellent treatment in this respect is given by Weeks (1981, pp. 208–13). The notion of "centralisation of capital" on the other hand does differ from that of the mainstream, in particular in the way the wave-like expression of the TRPF is theorised. The notion that technical change comes in waves is akin to Schumpeter's concept (see e.g. his 1943), but he offers no account as to why it is that inventions are produced during the slump and implemented at the beginning of and in the upturn. Within the framework presented here the argument is that inventions are produced throughout, but that their implementation in the slump would not pay, not just because there is a slump (since, as presumably over-capacity has been cured via restructuring, slack demand cannot be the problem), but because the centralisation of capital produces a decrease in the range of stratification, thus in fact competition between capitals remains only latent.

After a wave of centralisation of capital within a branch of production, new capitals may well enter the branch. At a high level of abstraction such flows of capital are induced by the tendency towards equalisation of average rates of profit (§2). More concretely, and in line with the presentation above, the technological and technical knowledge adopted in one branch, may profitably be applied in another – thus establishing new gaps in, and extending the range of, the stratification.

Summary and conclusions[28]

The TRPF contradicts the tendential increase in profit and the rate of profit associated with the accumulation of capital in new plants. This contradiction, however, has usually been conceived as an inconsistency, and so authors such as Okishio and Roemer have rejected the TRPF because of its lack of "microeconomic foundations". It has been shown that the TRPF may be adequately grounded if the comparative static analysis of these authors is replaced by a dynamic conceptualisation, incorporating fixed capital.

The contradiction is transcended in the existence of stratification of capital. It was argued that when new VCC increasing techniques of production are available (with higher productivity of labour and lower unit costs of production), preservation of capital already accumulated prevents immediate moves towards investment in plants embodying such techniques, and so capital tends to be stratified in a range of different compositions of capital, money expressions of labour and associated rates of profit. When additional capital is accumulated in new plants, the resulting capacity increase produces either a price decrease or over-capacity. Because of the resulting revenue decrease, submarginal plants at the bottom of the stratification will have to be scrapped. Therefore, because of the higher productivity of new plant capital relative to the previous stratification, its comparative profitability increases, along with a comparative profitability decrease (devalorisation) of the rest of the stratification. Therefore, whilst the rate of profit of newly accumulated capital may increase relative to the capital just below it in the stratification, even if its value composition is higher, the average rate of profit of the stratification decreases because of the average increase in the value composition of capital. Thus whilst the average rate of profit decreases, profit is "redistributed" from the bottom to the top of the stratification.

The price decrease associated with TRPF was shown to counteract the VCC increase of newly accumulated capital, but at the same time the price decrease of the means of production produces a devaluation of the capital previously accumulated in fixed means of production. This reduces the reproduction of accumulation. (General over-capacity instead of price decreases produces a similar result, although the VCC increase is then not counteracted.) A further, but contingent, expression of the TRPF lies in the restructuring and centralisation of capital. The more rapid and sustained the productivity increase, the

---

28 [2023 note] The following abbreviations are used. TRPF: theory of the tendency of the rate of profit to fall (Introduction and §4.2); VCC: value composition of capital (§4.2); TCC: technical composition of capital (§4.2).

more it has the effect that plants will have to be scrapped before the capital invested has been amortised. With accelerating liquidation of the least efficient plants, the forces giving rise to the TRPF are expressed in the restructuring of capital, one form of which is the centralisation of capital. The range of the stratification of capital is thereby reduced, counteracting the *gradual* increase in the VCC. Technical knowledge then tends to be implemented in waves, and therefore in this expression the TRPF is manifest cyclically.

The tendency towards over-accumulation of capital (§4) and the TRPF are tendencies at the same level of abstraction. If we blend out their systematic interrelation then they would both give rise to a tendential decline in the rate of accumulation and generate counteracting forces. Both also reveal, in their different ways, the contradictory nature of capitalism. The forces of valorisation and accumulation of capital are expressed in forms which appear to contradict their existence. Valorisation of capital tendentially gives rise to over-accumulation and therefore decrease of valorisation (expressed in labour-shortage profit squeeze but also underconsumption). Similarly the drive to increase the profit rate of the individual capitals tendentially gives rise to a decrease in the rate of profit of capital as a whole (expressed in devaluation, restructuring and centralisation of capital).

What are the conclusions that can be drawn?

(1) Adequate "microeconomic foundations" for the TRPF may be provided, independently of a change in the rate of surplus-value (§6). The generality of the Okishian theorem has thus been refuted, and that theorem is thus confined to a special case (i.e., neoclassical-perfect competition in the absence of fixed capital). The tendential increase in the VCC and the derived TRPF thus stands as an important economic force in explaining concrete economic development.

(2) Does this imply that the rate of profit must fall (i.e., must there by implication be an empirically observable *trend* fall in the rate of profit)? No, for the following reasons (3)–(6).

(3) The devaluation of capital associated with the TRPF is concretely (and empirically) expressed *either* in the writing off of capital (affecting the VCC) *or* in a fall of the rate of profit; which one of the two depends on the contingent accounting practice (§7).

(4) A further concrete expression of the TRPF is in the restructuring and centralisation of capital, whence the TRPF is manifest cyclically (§8).

(5) The TRPF interacts with the *tendency* towards over-accumulation of capital; one expression of this tendency is a (cyclical) change of the rate of surplus-value, as derived from *inter alia* the reserve of labour (§4).

(6) The issue is complicated even more due to the interconnectedness of all this with the credit system and e.g. processes of inflation (and the latter cannot

be simply levelled out by indexing). But further, this amalgam is modified by the outcome of economic policy. (See Reuten and Williams 1989, respectively chs. 5 and 9.)

I do not agree with Roemer that "empirical investigations ... cannot provide refutation of a theory" (see §5). Simple theories could simply be refuted. But I also do not agree with Reati (1986, p. 56) when he says that because "theoretical debate [concerning the TRPF] has not really settled the matter ... only empirical tests can lead to further progress". Empirical investigation is surely in need. But it makes no sense to test a theory that has not been fully constructed. And a full construction would need to encompass points (3)–(6) above.

References

Aglietta, Michel 1976, *Régulation et crises du capitalisme*, Calmann-Lévi, English translation by D. Fernbach, *A theory of capitalist regulation: the US experience*, London: NLB, 1979.

Alberro, Jose, and Joseph Persky 1979, 'The simple analytics of falling profit rates, Okishio's theorem and fixed capital', *Review of Radical Political Economics* 11, Fall.

Bidard, Christian 1988, 'The falling rate of profit and joint production', *Cambridge Journal of Economics* 12(4): 355–60.

Bleaney, Michael 1980, 'Maurice Dobb's theory of crisis: a comment', *Cambridge Journal of Economics* 4(1): 71–3.

Boddy, Radford, and James Crotty 1975, 'Class conflict and macro-policy: the political business cycle', *Review of Radical Political Economics* 7, Spring: 1–19.

Bowles, Samuel 1981, 'Technical change and the profit rate: a simple proof of the Okishio theorem', *Cambridge Journal of Economics* 5(2): 183–6.

de Brunhoff, Suzanne 1976, *État et capital*, Presses Universitaires de Grenoble & Maspero; English translation by M. Sonenscher, *The State, Capital and Economic Policy*, London: Pluto Press, 1978.

Coram, Bruce T. 1986, 'Marx, Roemer and the theory of the falling rate of profit', *Australian Economic Papers* 25, December: 265–71.

Cutler, Antony, Barry Hindess, Paul Hirst, and Athar Hussain 1977, *Marx's Capital and capitalism today*, Vol. I, London: Routledge & Kegan Paul.

Duménil, Gerard, Mark Glick, and Jose Rangel 1987a, 'The rate of profit in the United States', *Cambridge Journal of Economics* 11: 331–59.

Duménil, Gerard, Mark Glick, and Jose Rangel 1987b, 'Theories of the Great Depression: why did profitability matter?', *Review of Radical Political Economics* 19(2): 16–42.

Fine, Ben 1982, *Theories of the capitalist economy*, London: Edward Arnold.

Fine, Ben, and Laurence Harris 1979, *Rereading Capital*, London: Macmillan.

Foley, Duncan 1986, *Understanding capital: Marx's economic theory*, Cambridge, MA: Harvard University Press.

Glombowski, Jörg 1983, 'A Marxian model of long run capitalist development', *Zeitschrift für Nationalökonomie/Journal of Economics* 43(4): 363–82.

Glombowski, Jörg 1984, 'Kritische Kommentare zur Akkumulationstheorie', *Mehrwert* 25: 67–80.

Glyn, Andrew, and Bob Sutcliffe 1971, 'The critical condition of British capital', *New Left Review* 66.

Glyn, Andrew, and Bob Sutcliffe 1972, *British capitalism, workers and the profit squeeze*, Harmondsworth: Penguin Books.

Goldstein, Jonathan P. 1985, 'The cyclical profit squeeze: a Marxian microfoundation', *Review of Radical Political Economics* 17(1 and 2): 103–28.

Goodwin, Richard M. 1967, 'A growth cycle', in *Capitalism and economic growth*, edited by C.H. Feinstein, Cambridge: Cambridge University Press, pp. 54–8; revised and enlarged in E.K. Hunt and J.G. Schwartz (eds), *A critique of economic theory*, Harmondsworth: Penguin Books, 1972, pp. 442–9.

Harris, Donald J. 1983, 'Accumulation of capital and the rate of profit in Marxian theory', *Cambridge Journal of Economics* 7(4): 311–30.

Himmelweit, Susan 1974, 'The continuing saga of the falling rate of profit: a reply to Mario Cogoy', *Bulletin of the Conference of Socialist Economists* 9: 1–6.

Hunt, Ian 1983, 'An obituary or a new life for the tendency of the rate of profit to fall?', *Review of Radical Political Economics* 15(1): 131–48.

Jevons, W. Stanley 1871, *The theory of political economy*, reprinted 1970, Harmondsworth: Penguin Books.

Laibman, David 1982, 'Technical change, the real wage and the rate of exploitation: the falling rate of profit reconsidered', *Review of Radical Political Economics* 14(2): 95–105.

Lipietz, Alain 1986, 'Behind the crisis: the exhaustion of a regime of accumulation: a "Regulation School" perspective on some French empirical works', *Review of Radical Political Economics* 18(1 and 2): 13–32.

Moseley, Fred 1985, 'The rate of surplus-value in the post-war US economy: a critique of Weisskopf's estimates', *Cambridge Journal of Economics* 9(2).

Moseley, Fred 1991, *The falling rate of profit in the post-war US economy*, London: Macmillan.

Nakatani, Takeshi 1980, 'The law of falling rate of profit and the competitive battle: comment on Shaikh', *Cambridge Journal of Economics* 4(1): 65–68.

Negishi, Takashi 1985, *Economic theories in a non-Walrasian tradition*, Cambridge: Cambridge University Press.

Okishio, Nobio 1961, 'Technical changes and the rate of profit', *Kobe University Economic Review* 7: 85–99.

Orzech, Ze'ev B., and Shalom Groll 1989, 'Stages in the development of a Marxian concept: the composition of capital', *History of Political Economy* 21(1): 57–76.

van Parijs, Philippe 1980, 'The falling rate of profit theory of crisis: a rational reconstruction by way of obituary', *Review of Radical Political Economics* 12(1): 1–16.

van Parijs, Philippe 1983, 'Why Marxist economics needs microfoundations: postscript to an obituary', *Review of Radical Political Economics* 15(2): 111–24.

Reati, Angelo 1986, 'The rate of profit and the organic composition of capital in West German industry from 1960 to 1981', *Review of Radical Political Economics* 18(1 and 2): 56–86.

Reuten, Geert 1978, 'A concretization of the operation of the general rate of profit (on the problem of the alleged transformation of values into prices of production)', *Research Memorandum* no. 7801, Faculty of Economics, University of Amsterdam.

Reuten, Geert 1988a, 'Value as social form', in *Value, social form and the state*, edited by Michael Williams, London: Macmillan, pp. 42–61.

Reuten, Geert 1988b, 'The money expression of value and the credit system: a value-form theoretic outline', *Capital & Class* 35: 121–41.

Reuten, Geert, and Michael Williams 1989, *Value-form and the state; the tendencies of accumulation and the determination of economic policy in capitalist society*, London: Routledge.

Roemer, John E. 1979, 'Continuing controversy on the falling rate of profit: fixed capital and other issues', *Cambridge Journal of Economics* 3(4): 379–98.

Salter, Wilfred E.G. 1960, *Productivity and technical change*, Cambridge: Cambridge University Press.

Salvadori, Neri 1981, 'Falling rate of profit with a constant real wage: an example', *Cambridge Journal of Economics* 5(1): 59–66.

Schutz, Eric 1987, 'Non-produced inputs, differential profit rates and the Okishio theorem', *Review of Radical Political Economics* 19(2): 43–60.

Schumpeter, Joseph A. 1966 [1943], *Capitalism, socialism and democracy*, London: Unwin University Books.

Shaikh, Anwar 1978, 'Political economy and capitalism: notes on Dobb's theory of crisis', *Cambridge Journal of Economics* 2(3): 233–51.

Shaikh, Anwar 1980, 'Marxian competition versus perfect competition: further comments on the so-called choice of technique', *Cambridge Journal of Economics* 4(1): 75–83.

Shaikh, Anwar 1987, 'The falling rate of profit and the economic crisis in the US', in *The imperiled economy, book I: macroeconomics from a left perspective*, edited by Robert Cherry et al., New York: URPE.

Steedman, Ian 1980, 'A note on the 'choice of technique" under capitalism', *Cambridge Journal of Economics* 4(1): 61–4.

Webber, Michael J., and David L. Rigby 1986, 'The rate of profit in Canadian manufacturing, 1950–1981', *Review of Radical Political Economics* 18(1 and 2): 33–55.

Weeks, John 1981, *Capital and exploitation*, London: Edward Arnold.

Weeks, John 1982, 'Equilibrium, uneven development and the tendency of the rate of profit to fall', *Capital & Class* 16: 62–77.

Wolff, Edward N. 1986, 'The productivity slowdown and the fall in the US rate of profit, 1947–76', *Review of Radical Political Economics* 18(1 and 2): 87–109.

CHAPTER 19

From the 'fall of the rate of profit' in the *Grundrisse* to the cyclical development of the profit rate in *Capital*

(*with Peter Thomas*)

2011 article, originally published in *Science & Society* 75(1): 74–90.
(For its abstract see the Abstracts of all chapters on p. 9.)

Contents

Introduction   413
1   The 'law' of the rate of profit to fall in the *Grundrisse*   415
2   The *Grundrisse*'s 'crisis', 'law' and 'immanent critique': critical remarks   417
3   1861–63 Manuscript   420
4   1864–65 Manuscript (manuscript of *Capital III*)   422
5   Theoretical and political reasons for the reformulation of the 'law'   425
Themes for future research: conclusions   427
References   429

Introduction

Written at the onset of a major world crisis of the capitalist mode of production, the incomplete yet internally systematic 1857–58 notebooks subsequently published as the *Grundrisse* provide us with a unique window onto Marx's theoretical laboratory. This text brings together in an uneasy *modus vivendi* themes from Marx's earlier work in the 1840s, while anticipating elements that will only reach full fruition throughout the successive drafts of *Capital*. Marx disturbs this *modus vivendi* via two approaches, which dialectically interact throughout his analysis: on the one hand, the method of immanent critique leads Marx to reformulate concepts derived from his previous study of political economy, a reformulation that sometimes amounts to fundamental conceptual transformation alongside the maintenance of the older terminology; on the other hand, Marx's growing awareness of the potential durability and strength of the capitalist mode of production leads him to seek for more systematic conceptual determinations and explanations. In this perspective, the significance of the *Grundrisse* is that it constitutes a *Kampfplatz* upon which we can observe the struggle between different elements of Marx's project. This struggle is perhaps nowhere more evident than in the treatment in this text of the 'tendency of the rate of profit to fall', which has long constituted one of the most controversial elements of Marx's theory.

Marx's views on the 'law' or 'tendency' of the rate of profit to fall developed throughout his life from a law about the historical destination of the capitalist system as tending towards breakdown, into a theory about the functioning of the capitalist mode of production as a (potentially) reproductive system. The first view is compatible with a 'naturalistic' and teleological philosophy of history; it presupposes a unilinear conception of time and implicitly posits a diachronic 'exhaustion' of an originary rate of profit. The second view opens the way towards a type of 'conjunctural analysis', founded upon a cyclical notion of time as a synchronic intensification of contradictory articulations in a synchronically given system. Both views compete on the *Kampfplatz* of the *Grundrisse*; while the former seems to maintain its dominance, Marx nevertheless also initiates in this text lines of reasoning that will lead to the increasing theoretical hegemony of the latter in subsequent texts. In its turn, this will permit Marx to elaborate a notion of the capitalist mode of production that breaks with both the teleological historicism of the young Hegelian movement in which his political thought was formed as well as the 'naturalism' of classical political economy.

This thesis will be demonstrated by means of an analysis of three texts from different stages of Marx's intellectual development, beginning with the 1857–58 *Grundrisse* (§1–§2), passing by way of the 1861–63 manuscripts (§3), and concluding with Marx's manuscript from 1864–65 (§4) which was later edited by Engels as Part Three of *Capital* III (1894). We will argue that the *Grundrisse*'s discussion of this theme shares presuppositions with Marx's (and Engels's) earlier political positions in the 1840s. Furthermore, we will see that important statements in the *Grundrisse* on the profit rate issue do not appear in later texts. Nevertheless, we will also see that the *Grundrisse*'s immanent critique introduces important new perspectives that can be regarded – obviously, only in the *futur anterior* – as the conditions of possibility for the different statements on the rate of profit in the later texts. We will essay various possible political and theoretical reasons for this development and, in conclusion, suggest themes for future research that are raised by this analysis (§5).

1   The 'law' of the rate of profit to fall in the *Grundrisse*

Marx discusses the 'fall of the rate of profit' in the *Grundrisse* in the third section of the manuscript's last notebook (Notebook VII, pp. 745–58), written in the early months of 1858. The text addresses (a) Ricardo's insufficient distinction between rate of surplus-value and rate of profit, and (b) the inverse relation between sum of profit and rate of profit. Marx presents these arguments in synthetic form in the first part of the section; its second half consists of comments on and textual analysis of Smith and Ricardo in particular (but also of Malthus, Carey and Bastiat) (pp. 751–8). In the first half, Marx argues:

> Presupposing the same surplus-value, *the same surplus labour in proportion to necessary labour,* then, the *rate of profit* depends on the relation between the part of capital exchanged for living labour and the part existing in the form of raw material and means of production. Hence, the smaller the portion exchanged for living labour becomes, the smaller becomes the rate of profit. Thus, in the same proportion as capital takes up a larger place as capital in the production process relative to immediate labour, *i.e.,* the more the relative surplus-value grows – the value-creating power of capital – the more *does the rate of profit fall.*

It is only after having set out this inverse relation that Marx uses the term 'law' in relation to the profit rate:

> This is in every respect the most important law of modern political economy, and the most essential for understanding the most difficult relations. It is the most important law from the historical standpoint. It is a law which, despite its simplicity, has never before been grasped and, even less, consciously articulated. (p. 748)

Marx then sets out how "the development of the productive forces" is accompanied by a relative "decline of the part of the capital ... exchanged for immediate labour" (the concept of 'organic composition of capital' is not explicit in this text, though it is implicit in Marx's discussion of the inverse relation between relative surplus-value growth and profit rate fall). This process, i.e.,

> the development of the productive forces brought about by the historical development of capital itself, when it reaches a certain point, suspends the self-realisation of capital, instead of positing it. Beyond a certain point, the development of the powers of production becomes a barrier

for capital; hence the capital relation [becomes] a barrier for the development of the productive powers of labour. When it has reached this point, capital, *i.e.*, wage labour, enters into the same relation towards the development of social wealth and of the forces of production as the guild system, serfdom, slavery, and is necessarily stripped off as a fetter. The last form of servitude assumed by human activity, that of wage labour on one side, capital on the other, is thereby cast off like a skin, and this casting-off itself is the result of the mode of production corresponding to capital; the material and mental conditions of the negation of wage labour and of capital, themselves already the negation of earlier forms of unfree social production, are themselves results of its production process. (p. 749)

Immediately following, Marx explicitly inscribes his reflections under the banner of 'crisis'.

> The growing incompatibility between the productive development of society and its hitherto existing relations of production expresses itself in bitter contradictions, crises, spasms. The violent destruction of capital *not by relations external to it*, but rather as *a condition of its self-preservation*, is the most striking form in which advice is given it to be gone and to give room to a higher state of social production. (pp. 749–50; emphasis added)

A few lines later, he returns to this theme. The invitation to capital to leave politely has now taken on the tone of a menacing inevitability.

> These contradictions [of development of the powers of production] lead to explosions, cataclysms, crises, in which by momentaneous suspension of labour and annihilation of a great portion of capital the latter is violently *reduced to the point where it can go on*. ... Yet, these *regularly recurring catastrophes* lead to their repetition on a higher scale, and finally to its violent overthrow. (p. 750; emphasis added)

The last sentence in particular would seem to point to a trend-wise development of the fall of the profit rate, the accumulation of "regularly recurring catastrophes" finally descending into "violent overthrow".

Marx does indeed seem to lessen the impact of this crisis rhetoric somewhat when he speaks in the immediately following lines of "moments" that may "delay" the fall in the rate of profit. Among these he includes the devaluation of existing capital, transformation of capital into fixed capital not directly involved in production, unproductive waste of capital, lowering of taxes, reduction of ground rent and the creation of new branches of production. However, these factors only *delay* this trend fall; they do not negate it. It remains a "law" that leads, *via* repetition, to the "overthrow" of the capitalist mode of production.

We may conclude from this discussion that in the *Grundrisse* Marx adopts the view of a 'trend fall' in the profit rate.[1] Its presuppositions are the unfolding throughout time of the immanent contradictions of production founded upon capital, which progressively reduce the rate of profit. The momentary 'delay' of the diminution of the originary quantity of the rate of profit does not prevent its ultimate 'exhaustion'. When it is finally depleted, the capitalist mode of production comes to an end – violently.

2   The *Grundrisse*'s 'crisis', 'law' and 'immanent critique': critical remarks

Several elements of Marx's analysis of the fall of the rate of profit in the *Grundrisse* should here be noted.

(i) As we have seen, Marx regularly deploys metaphors and terms throughout this text that can be characterised as a 'rhetoric of crisis'. This 'apocalyptic' vision bears decisive similarities to the general young Hegelian atmosphere in which Marx passed his student years in Berlin, particularly as articulated in Bruno Bauer's early political theory (a strong influence on Marx in his formative years).[2] However, there is an important difference between these different uses of the theme of crisis, in terms of both their political context and their theoretical field of reference.

Marx and the young Hegelians more generally elaborated a theory of *political* crisis in the years leading up to 1848. This theory attempted to identify a political agent capable of resolving the crisis in a positive form, i.e., the supersession of what the *German Ideology* refers to as "all the old shit" (*den ganzen alten Dreck*) (*MECW* vol. 5, p. 70). Already in the closing pages of the text now known as *Towards the critique of Hegel's philosophy of right. Introduction*, Marx had identified this agent as the 'proletariat'. With the failure of the revolutions that coincided with the publication of the *Communist Manifesto*, the defeated

---

1   On the difference between 'trend' and 'tendency', see Reuten 1997 and 2004 [chapters 16 and 17 of the current book].
2   On Bauer's political theory and his influence on Marx, see Tomba 2002.

'48ers' tried to keep their hopes alive for a revival of this 'world-historical' subject. Fidelity to (the memory of) the theme of crisis, in the midst of widespread abandonment of revolutionary politics by their contemporaries, constituted one of their most potent psychological supports.[3]

The *Grundrisse*'s deployment of similar motifs in the discussion of the fall of the profit rate, on the other hand, explicitly does *not* invoke a directly political agent. Marx confines his analysis to the internal determinations of capital as such. The 'violent overthrow' occurs as a result of the working out of the inner laws of capital, conceived as a (self-destructive) subject. It is not an agent acting against the destructive *effects* of the capitalist mode of production's recurring crises that overthrow it, but capital itself as *causa sui* that prepares its own downfall. Arguably, Marx has here committed the error of too rapidly 'translating' terminology from one field to another (i.e., from political to economic theory), without attending to their substantially different contexts. While such haste may be unexceptional in notes written for personal use, their (re-)introduction into Marxian discussions of crisis theory following the publication of the *Grundrisse* provided support for an interpretation of *Capital III* in particular that neglected its *systematic* analysis of the capitalist mode of production.

(ii) It is sometimes not remembered that the "law" of the fall of the profit rate was not a theoretical novelty introduced by Marx.[4] On the contrary, Marx inherited it from the problematic of classical political economy, where it plays a decisive role in the thought of Smith and Ricardo in particular. As Marx notes in the *Grundrisse*: "A. Smith explained the fall of the rate of profit, as capital grows, by the competition among capitals" (p. 751).[5] Ricardo had found Smith's explanation of the law inadequate, but rather than abandoning it, he proposed his own explanation: "The falling rate of profit hence corresponds, with him [i.e., Ricardo], to the nominal growth of wages and real growth of ground rent" (p. 752).[6] In both Smith and Ricardo, the rate of profit is conceived as an ori-

---

3 Cf. Kouvelakis 2005 for an analysis of the legacy of 1848 in Marx's later political career.
4 Heinrich (2007) provides a valuable historical perspective on contemporary discussions.
5 Marx responds to Smith thus: "Competition can permanently depress the rate of profit in all branches of industry, i.e., the average rate of profit, only if and in so far as a general and permanent fall of the rate of profit, having the force of a law, is conceivable prior to competition and regardless of competition. Competition executes the inner laws of capital; makes them into compulsory laws towards the individual capital, but it does not invent them. It realizes them. To try to explain them simply as results of competition therefore means to concede that one does not understand them" (p. 752).
6 Marx describes this as Ricardo's "one-sided mode of conceiving it [i.e., the falling rate of profit], which seizes on only one single case, just as the rate of profit can fall because wages

ginary quantity, which is subsequently corrupted and depleted by the development of capitalist production. Just as the fertility of soil is conceived as a natural 'given' quantity, so the "fructiferous" nature of capital (revealingly, Marx's title for this section) can be exhausted by the decline of the profit rate to an absolute minimum.

Marx was, of course, well acquainted with these versions of the "law", as his extensive comments on Smith's and Ricardo's explanations testify. Marx subjects these views to immanent critique in the *Grundrisse*; at this stage, however, his thought remains indebted in many key respects to their general problematic. This is perhaps most noticeable in Marx's maintenance of the term "law" of the fall of the profit rate, and his linking of this law to the notion of an 'exhaustion' of the capitalist mode of production by the repetition of debilitating crises. The problem remains, as a subject for future research.

(iii) Despite its lingering crisis rhetoric and indebtedness to the problematic of classical political economy, the *Grundrisse* nevertheless also demonstrates Marx's first tentative departure from this 'naturalist' paradigm. He is not satisfied by Smith's and Ricardo's explanations of this "most important law of modern political economy" because they do not grasp the fall in the rate of profit as an inner and necessary determination of capital. Hence he comes up with his own explanation for a fall in the rate of profit: namely, a rise in productivity. He thus reformulates that "law" as one of a combined decrease of the rate of profit and increase of the mass of profit. This perspective will remain central to all the other manuscripts, albeit in increasingly clarified formulations.

Even more importantly, as a consequence of this 'reformulation' of the "law" in terms of an inverse relation between profit rate and amount, Marx also sketches out in the *Grundrisse* another element that will be further developed in later manuscripts, namely, the notion of factors that "delay" the fall of the rate of profit. As we will see, it is the redefinition of these "delays" in terms of 'tendency' (conceived as 'operative power' rather than empirical trend) that will open the way to Marx's linking of an increase in productivity, (potential) growth of the exploitation of labour and a notion of crises as "restorative" or *aufhebende* (sublating, rather than merely destructive) mechanisms.

---

momentarily rise etc., and which elevates a historical relation holding for a period of 50 years and reversed in the following 50 years to the level of a general law, and rests generally on the historical disproportion between the developments of industry and agriculture" (p. 752). He later adds sarcastically that as far as the law of the falling rate of profit is concerned, Ricardo "flees from economics to seek refuge in organic chemistry" (p. 754).

3   1861–63 Manuscript

We can now move on to Marx's 1861–63 manuscripts (*MEGA* II, Bd 3, Teile 1–6, 1976–82).[7] A second main text on the (tendency of the) rate of profit to fall can be found in Section 7 of Marx's Notebook XVI, dated December 1861–January 1862. This text – even more so than the *Grundrisse* – has much the character of notes intended to aid the author's understanding.

Marx once again refers to the "law" as "the most important law of political economy" (*MECW* 33, p. 104). However, his definition immediately qualifies this law as "a *tendency* [of the rate of profit] *to fall with the progress of capitalist production*" (*MECW* 33, p. 104). Then, Marx inquires into the reasons for this tendency of the general rate of profit to fall. He notes that the "whole of the Ricardian and Malthusian school is a cry of woe over the day of judgment this process would inevitably bring about", before arguing that

> apart from theory there is also the practice, the crises from *super abundance of capital or, what comes to the same, the mad adventures capital enters upon in consequence of the lowering of {the} rate of profit. Hence crises – see Fullarton – acknowledged as a *necessary violent means for the cure* of the plethora of capital, and the *restoration* of a sound rate of profit.* (*MECW* 33, p. 105; emphasis added).[8]

"Necessary violent means for the cure of the plethora of capital"; "restoration of a sound rate of profit". The crises are no longer repeated "on a higher scale", leading finally to the capitalist mode of production's 'violent overthrow', as in the *Grundrisse*. Rather, 'in practice', crises function as a corrective measure, which restore a "sound rate of profit" and thus presumably permit capital accumulation to begin once again (in a cyclical theory of upswing and downswing).

After analysing factors that might cause the general rate of profit to fall, especially (1) "if the absolute magnitude of surplus-value falls" and (2) "because the ratio of variable to constant capital falls", Marx states: "But the law of development of capitalist production (see Cherbuliez, etc.) consists precisely in the

---

[7] All citations are taken from the English translation by Ben Fowkes, *MECW* 33 (1991), pp. 104–45.
[8] Passages between asterisks appear in English in the German manuscript. Passages in curly brackets are added by the MEGA editors; often they are reconstructions of illegible handwriting.

continuous decline of variable capital ... *in relation* to the constant component of capital. ..." (*MECW* 33, p. 106). Clearly, this reformulates in more developed terms a perspective already present in the *Grundrisse*. Marx then continues to argue that: "The tendency towards a fall in the general rate of profit therefore = the development of the productive power of capital, i.e., the rise in the ratio in which objectified labour is exchanged for living labour." The "tendency towards a fall in the general rate of profit" is now no longer seen, as in the *Grundrisse*, as the gravedigger of the capitalist mode of production. On the contrary, it is now equivalent to "the development of the productive power of capital". Marx argues that this development "implies, at the same time, the concentration of capital in large amounts at a small number of places" (pp. 107–8). This is followed by an explicit statement about two factors that work against each other, that is, the rate of surplus-value and the composition of capital:

> Both movements not only go {hand in hand} but condition each other. They are only different forms and phenomena in which the same law is expressed. But they work in opposite directions, in so far as the rate of profit comes into consideration. (*MECW* 33, p. 109)

Subsequently, Marx indicates that "for the rate of profit to remain the same", these factors "would have to grow in the same ratio", and continues: "This is only possible within certain limits, and that it is rather the reverse, the tendency towards a fall in profit – or a *relative* decline in the amount of surplus-value hand in hand with the growth in the rate of surplus-value – which must predominate, as is also confirmed by experience" (*MECW* 33, p. 110).

Further on, we read that an increase in the exploitation of labour can in a certain sense 'delay' the fall of the rate of profit, to use the terminology of the *Grundrisse*; expressed in other terms, it 'absorbs' some of the tendency to fall of the profit rate.

> If one considers the development of productive power and the relatively not-so-pronounced fall in the rate of profit, the exploitation of labour must have increased very much, and what is remarkable is not the fall in the rate of profit but that it has not fallen to a greater degree. (*MECW* 33, p. 111)

Finally, Marx combines the *Grundrisse*'s distinction between the amount and the rate of profit with this focus upon an increase in the exploitation of labour. He concludes this most systematic part of his presentation with the following summary:

> The decline in the average rate of profit expresses an increase in the productive power of labour or of capital, and, following from that, on the one hand a heightened exploitation of the living labour employed, and [on the other hand] a *relatively reduced amount of living labour* employed at the heightened rate of exploitation, calculated on a particular amount of capital. (*MECW* 33, p. 111)

> It does not now follow automatically from this law that the *accumulation* of capital declines or that the absolute *amount* of *profit* falls (hence also the *absolute*, not *relative*, *amount* of surplus-value, which is expressed in the profit). (*MECW* 33, p. 111)

The remainder of the text (pp. 113–45) is an analysis of the connections between the relevant concepts: rising labour productivity together with a rising organic composition of capital; and rising rate of surplus-value, profit and the rate of profit. In general the text is unsystematic, petering into a series of undeveloped notes and jottings. The general impression this manuscript gives is that Marx is searching for a new conceptual framework. What is remarkable is that the "breakdown" perspective so central to the *Grundrisse*'s analysis is entirely absent from this text.

4   1864–65 Manuscript (manuscript of *Capital III*)

Finally, we can turn to the parts of Marx's manuscripts from 1863–67 that deal with the rate of profit, dating from 1864–65 (they were later edited by Engels for publication as *Capital* III in 1894). These manuscripts were only published in German in the *MEGA* in 1992. The first pages of the manuscript are similar to the published text of *Capital III*; for convenience's sake we will cite the 1894 text and refer to the 1864–65 manuscript in order to indicate significant variations.[9]

Marx begins by setting out a hypothetical example of a falling profit rate. Then he writes: (1) this as a tendency is what we perceive in reality (F, 318); (2) it is what the economists perceived and have tried to explain (F, 319). Next, Marx shifts the emphasis to what he apparently sees as a kernel of capitalist development: first, accumulation and concentration of capital along with

---

9 We adopt the following shorthand references in this section: M = Marx 1894M = German manuscript transcription of 1992; E = Marx 1894E = German text of 1894 as edited by Engels; U = Marx 1894U = German text of 1894 in the English Untermann translation of 1909; F = Marx 1894F = German text of 1894 in the English Fernbach translation of 1981.

rising productivity of labour, and second, a fall in the *rate* of profit along with a rise in the *amount* of profits (M, 291, 298, 300). To him, *this* seems to be the law: the inverse relation of mass and rate of profit (recall that since the *Grundrisse*, he has indicated this as the sphinx's riddle that classical political economy could not resolve).

After this, Marx immediately moves to the counteracting tendencies (the text of Chapter 14 in the published version of *Capital III*). In F, 336–7 (cf. M, 319) Marx writes: "Viewed abstractly, the rate of profit might remain the same. ... The rate of profit could even rise, if ..." (F, 336–7; cf. M, 319).

Directly following this formulation, Engels added: "In practice, however, the rate of profit will fall in the long run, as we have already seen" (F, 337; cf. U, 230), a phrase that seems inconsistent with Marx's general line of argument in the manuscript text.[10]

When Marx sets out the counteracting forces/tendencies at the end of this chapter, he repeatedly indicates that these do "not annul the general law", but make it operate as a tendency (F, 341). He also says that the latter "to a greater or lesser degree paralyze" its operation (F, 344; M, 304, 306). This is again repeated in a conclusion on page 308 in M (F, 346). Finally, he argues that: "The law operates [*wirkt*] therefore simply as a tendency, whose effect [*Wirkung*] becomes strikingly pronounced only under particular circumstances and when extended out over long periods [*auf lange Perioden ausgedehnt*]" (F, 346, trans. modified; cf. E, 249; U, 239; M, 308).

After this, Marx's manuscript (M, 309–40) returns to 'his' formulation of the law: namely, the proposition that increases in productivity of labour *via* an increase in the organic composition of capital result in a combined increase of the amount of profits and a decrease of the rate of profit. "The law that a fall in the rate of profit precipitated [*herbeigeführte*] by the development of productiveness is accompanied by an increase in the mass of profit. ..." (M, 316; cf. U, 225–6; cf. F, 332; E, 236). The *Grundrisse*'s inverse relation of profit rate and amount is here continued (cf. M, 322; F, 356). However, it is now the development of productivity that precipitates a fall in the rate of profit.

Next, Marx amplifies the issue of the depreciation of capital. One page further, though, he puts this in a different light, first rephrasing the issue in terms of a contradiction, then developing it into periodical crises. Significantly, these crises are conceived, as in the 1861–63 manuscript, in terms of restoration, rather than the 'overthrow' of the *Grundrisse*:

---

10   For an analysis of this and similar modifications of the text made by Engels and the support this gives to a trend fall interpretation, cf. Reuten 2004, p. 172 et seq. [Chapter 17 of the current book.]

> Simultaneously with the fall in the profit rate, the mass of capital grows, and hand in hand with it goes a depreciation of the existing capital, which checks this fall and gives an accelerating impulse to the accumulation of capital-value. Simultaneously with the development of productivity, the composition of capital becomes higher, there is a relative decline in the variable portion as against the constant. These different influences may at one time operate predominantly side by side spatially, and at another succeed each other in time; periodically [*periodisch*] the conflict of antagonistic agencies finds vent in crises. The crises are always but momentary violent solutions of the existing contradictions – violent eruptions – which restore the disturbed balance. (M, 323; E, 259; F, 357; U, 249; trans. modified)

The theme of restoration is emphasised in the next pages of Marx's manuscript on overproduction, over-accumulation and devaluation of capital. He writes: "Under all circumstances, however, the balance will be restored by the *destruction of capital* to a greater or lesser extent." (M, 328; cf. E, 264; F, 362; U, 253)

As if to underscore the point, Marx finally sets out how crisis and its aftermath restores the rate of profit.

> And so we go round the whole circle once again. One part of the capital that was devalued by the cessation of its function now regains its old value. But, with expanded conditions of production, a wider market and *increased productivity*, it will once again go through the same vicious circle [Zirkel vicieux]. (M, 329; emphasis added; cf. E, 265; F, 364; U, 255)

As in the 1861–63 manuscript, the law of the fall of the profit rate and its crisis do not issue in the overthrow of the capitalist mode of production; on the contrary, we have a cycle (or "vicious circle") of decrease and increase ('restoration') of the rate of profit that, insofar as the productivity of labour is thereby increased, may even be a ruse by means of which the capitalist mode of production strengthens its future potential capacity for the exploitation of labour.

By the time of the *Capital* III manuscript, therefore, the naturalistic and unilinear paradigm of classical political economy has been decisively left behind. The profit rate is no longer viewed as an originary quantity doomed to progressive exhaustion as it passes through time, following a secular trend fall within and across conjunctures. Instead, its cyclical rise and fall within a given economic conjuncture is theorised as a qualitative intensification of the contradictory articulation within the capitalist mode of production of increases in productivity, the exploitation of labour and the growth of capital by means of the expropriation of surplus-value. Rather than the "law of the tendency of the rate of profit to fall" (TRPF), a more appropriate name for Marx's 'law/tendency' might therefore be the 'theory of the rate of profit cycle' (TRPC). In this perspective, economic crises don't signify the capitalist mode of production's automatic end, but rather, only one of the possible conjunctural resolutions of its recurring immanent contradictions, in which an increase in productivity can give rise to a decrease in the rate of profit. This constitutes the *economic* confines or limits (*Schranke*) of the capitalist mode of production (M, 332; cf. E, 268; U, 258; F, 367), but does not prescribe its potential political *Schranke*.

5   Theoretical and political reasons for the reformulation of the 'law'

Why did Marx undertake this reformulation of "the most important law of political economy"? Several hypotheses can be considered.

(i) Marx, having seen the durability of the capitalist mode of production and its ability to withstand the crisis of the late 1850s, slowly begins to see the need to rethink his central concepts. In the *Grundrisse*, he remains under the spell of the memory of 1848 and its expected world-transforming "deluge" (as he wrote to Engels in a famous letter on 8 December 1857). In the 1860s, on the other hand, he revises his crisis rhetoric and focuses much more on a systematic analysis of the capitalist mode of production. This hypothesis is fundamentally *political* in nature; i.e., it sees the cause of theoretical reformulation in the revision of political perspectives.

However, as we have seen, already in the *Grundrisse* Marx has laid the theoretical foundations that could lead – not inevitably, but possibly – to his reformulation in the later manuscripts. While he first strongly criticises the 'naturalist' presuppositions of classical political economy in his main arguments, his conclusion then problematically transfers a political theory of crisis onto the terrain of political economy. The two elements of his argument are based upon opposed presuppositions; their uneasy *modus vivendi* in the *Grundrisse* has the potential to grow into a contradiction with further study and reflection.

(ii) Marx was led to reformulate the law of the falling rate of profit more for *theoretical* than for political reasons. His method of immanent critique in the *Grundrisse* has already reformulated a key aspect of the 'traditional' law, distinguishing between amount and rate of profit, and between rate of profit and rate of surplus-value. As the *Grundrisse* is primarily a compilation of notes for private use, Marx does not yet reformulate the "law as such"; but he is on the verge of a decisive theoretical development.

While there may be some good textual reasons to support this second hypothesis, it underemphasises the extent to which Marx's reformulation of the law remains only a 'work in progress' in the *Grundrisse*. In particular, it neglects the fact that in 1857–58 Marx has not yet clearly distinguished between a quantitative trend fall and the fall of the rate of profit as a 'tendency' or 'operative power'. Furthermore, it does not take into account the importance of the 1861–63 and 1864–65 manuscripts' articulation of the falling profit rate with the increase in productivity and thus the potential for a higher rate of exploitation of labour. Marx cannot yet fully explain why and how the capitalist mode of production might use cyclical upswings and downswings, despite the temporary destruction of capital, as a 'ruse' for the quantitative growth of its hegemony over labour in succeeding conjunctures *via* increased potential productivity.

(iii) Marx sought to confront the political problem of how to respond to the crisis of the late 1850s by deepening his theoretical reflection. Inheriting this "most important law of modern political economy" and dissatisfied with the capacity of previous formulations to explain theoretically what occurs 'in practice', Marx abandons the naturalism of classical political economy and formulates the law in relational rather than quantitative terms (*via* the elaboration of the distinction between surplus-value and profit). At this stage, however, he can ultimately find no better solution than the invocation of a memory of a previous political conjuncture in order to explain the purpose of crises in the capitalist mode of production (its 'overthrow').

As his critique deepens in the manuscripts of the early 1860s, however, he attempts to grasp crises 'as such', i.e., in terms of their internal functioning. He reformulates the falling rate of profit as a tendency that is equivalent to the development of the productive power of capital and articulates this with an increase in the potential of capital to exploit labour. The tendency of the rate of profit to fall now figures as an operative power in the production of crises, which are conceived as but one possible moment in any given cycle of accumulation, a moment by means of which capital prepares itself to "go through the same vicious circle" once again. The result of Marx's reformulation of the "law" is therefore the abandonment of an eschatological theory of crisis and emphasis upon the concrete analysis of capital's increased potential to exploit labour in the course of any given conjuncture. This seems to us to be the most satisfying hypothesis, which takes into account the intertwining of both political and theoretical reasons in Marx's reformulation.

Themes for future research: conclusions

In conclusion, we would like to enumerate briefly some themes for future research that arise from this textual analysis.

(i) The first concerns the relative weight in Marx's intellectual development of his debt to classical political economy, on the one hand, and his debt to Hegel, on the other. According to a well-known narrative, Marx inherited from Hegel a 'philosophy of history' whose teleological dimensions constituted a profound impediment to the development of a scientific analysis of the capitalist mode of production, regardless of however much he may have benefited from Hegel in other respects. Of course, this view has been challenged by many in recent years, but its continuing purchase in the field of Marxian theory can be attested to by the favourable recent reception of a work such as Jacques Bidet's *Exploring Marx's "Capital"* (2007, p. 3 et seq.). Bidet argues that Marx found in Hegel an "epistemological support/obstacle", which he attempted progressively to overcome. Based upon this analysis of the treatment of the fall of the rate of profit in the *Grundrisse* and subsequent manuscripts, however, we might suggest that more attention could be directed towards the "epistemological supports/obstacles" that Marx found in the concepts of classical political economy. No less than Hegel's system, classical political economy was founded upon its own 'naturalistic' and sometimes teleological presuppositions, albeit culturally and conceptually distinct from those of post-Hegelian philosophies of history. Future research could examine more closely the intertwining of Marx's attempts to liberate himself from the deleterious philosophical/historiosophical dimensions of both paradigms.

(ii) A second theme for future research might be the importance of the rate of profit for an analysis of the relationship between politics and economics in Marx's mature critique of political economy. The "law" was often interpreted in the twentieth century in an 'economistic' fashion as implying the automatic production of political effects (overthrow of the capitalist mode of production) from economic causes (crises produced by trend decline in rate of profit). As we have seen, certain elements in the *Grundrisse*'s discussion of the theme certainly seem to support this perspective, while the later manuscripts directly contradict it. They are limited to an analysis of the economic confines or limits (*Schranke*) of the capitalist mode of production. An explicit analysis of political responses to this situation lies beyond the scope of Marx's mature critique of political economy, as 'unfinished business' for future Marxian research.

Nevertheless, Marx's articulation of the fall in the profit rate with increases in productivity and the exploitation of labour takes us to the verge of properly political analysis. By focusing on the concrete analysis of each individual conjuncture, it provides us with knowledge of the limits within which capital and therefore *a fortiori* labour are forced to operate in the capitalist mode of production. Future research could attempt to take up this unfinished business by analysing further the already political nature of the economic limits of capital. This fundamentally concerns the juridical guarantees of profits in the capitalist mode of production and therefore private property of the means of production as its foundation.

(iii) Finally, a third theme for future research concerns the implications of this analysis for contemporary debates regarding the tendency of the rate of profit to fall and the nature of the contemporary conjuncture. The 'second Brenner debate' had already focused many theorists' attention on the question of the fall in the profit rate as a possible explanation for recent economic trends; the financial crisis that began in 2008 has witnessed a deepening and diffusion of this tendency.[11] While not taking up a position on these debates in this article, we suggest that the analysis of Marx's different texts discussing the fall in the profit rate provides a powerful critical perspective from which to consider both these debates and the contemporary conjuncture more generally. In particular, the findings in this article might alert us to the possibility that the current crisis may be merely another of capital's ruses, as it prepares the way for a restoration of a sound rate of profit in a future "vicious circle"; indeed, the various crisis 'management' programmes deployed by different governments over the last years would seem to indicate that some political forces, at least, are aiming at precisely such a 'pacific' resolution to the contemporary forms of the deep systemic conflicts that have continually been generated by the capitalist mode of production throughout its history. In this context, more attention needs to be devoted to the analysis of the extent to which and ways in which the current crisis may become functional to capital's increase in its hegemony over labour *via* increases in potential productivity. Such an analysis is the necessary prelude both to a critique of the explicitly *political limits* that enable the renewal of such a "vicious circle," and to the exploration of the political forms and practices that

---

11   Brenner 2002 and 2006 have stimulated wide-ranging debates in which the fall in the profit rate has figured as a central point of contention. Harman 2007 focuses in particular on this concept for an analysis of the current world economy.

would be necessary to overcome not merely those limits but the capitalist mode of production in its totality.

References

Bidet, Jacques 2007 [1985], *Exploring Marx's "Capital": philosophical, economic and political dimensions*, Leiden: Brill.

Brenner, Robert 2002, *The boom and the bubble*, London: Verso.

Brenner, Robert 2006 [1998], *The economics of global turbulence*, London: Verso.

Harman, Chris 2007, 'The rate of profit and the world today', *International Socialism* 115 (Summer).

Heinrich, Michael 2007, 'Begründungsprobleme. Zur Debatte über das Marxsche "Gesetz vom tendenziellen Fall der Profitrate"', in *Marx–Engels Jahrbuch 2006*, Berlin: Akademie Verlag, pp. 47–80.

Kouvelakis, Stathis 2005, 'Marx e la critica della politica', in *Sulle tracce di un fantasma. L'opera di Karl Marx tra filologia e filosofia*, edited by Marcello Musto, Rome: Manifestolibri.

Marx, Karl 1973 {written 1857–58}, *Grundrisse: foundations of the critique of political economy (rough draft)*, translated by Martin Nicolaus, Harmondsworth: Penguin.

Marx, Karl 1991, *Economic manuscript of 1861–1863 (continuation)*, translated by Ben Fowkes, in *Marx–Engels collected works* (MECW), Vol. 33, London: Lawrence and Wishart.

Marx, Karl 1894E, *Das Kapital: Kritik der Politischen Ökonomie*. Vol. III: *Der Gesamtprozeß der kapitalistischen Produktion*, edited by Friedrich Engels. *Marx Engels Werke* 25, Berlin: Dietz Verlag, 1972.

Marx, Karl 1894F, *Capital: a critique of political economy*, vol. III, translation of 1894E by David Fernbach, Harmondsworth: Penguin Books, 1981.

Marx, Karl 1894U, *Capital: a critique of political economy*, vol. III: *the process of capitalist production as a whole*, 1909 translation of 1894E by Ernest Untermann, London: Lawrence & Wishart, 1974.

Marx, Karl 1894M, *Karl Marx: Ökonomische Manuskripte 1863–1867*. Text, part 2, edited by Manfred Müller, Jürgen Jungnickel, Barbara Lietz, Christel Sander, and Artur Schnickmann, Volume 4 of Division 2 (*Das Kapital und Vorarbeiten*) of *Karl Marx, Friedrich Engels Gesamtausgabe* (MEGA 2/4), Berlin/Amsterdam: Dietz Verlag/Internationales Institut für Sozialgeschichte Amsterdam, 1992.

Marx, Karl, and Friedrich Engels {written 1846}, *The German ideology*, in *Marx–Engels collected works* (MECW), vol. 5, London: Lawrence and Wishart, 1976.

Marx–Engels collected works (MECW), London: Lawrence and Wishart.

MEGA, *Karl Marx, Friedrich Engels Gesamtausgabe*, Berlin/Amsterdam: Dietz Verlag/ Internationales Institut für Sozialgeschichte Amsterdam.

Reuten, Geert 1997, 'The notion of tendency in Marx's 1894 law of profit', in *New investigations of Marx's method*, edited by Fred Moseley and Martha Campbell, Atlantic Highlands, NJ: Humanities Press.

Reuten, Geert 2004, '*Zirkel vicieux* or trend fall? The course of the profit rate in Marx's *Capital III*', *History of Political Economy* 36(1).

Tomba, Massimiliano 2002, *Crisi e critica in Bruno Bauer. Il principio di esclusione come fondamento del politico*, Naples: Bibliopolis.

CHAPTER 20

Destructive creativity; institutional arrangements of banking and the logic of capitalist technical change

1998 article, originally published in *Marxian economics: a reappraisal*, vol. 2, edited by Riccardo Bellofiore, London: Macmillan, pp. 177–93.
   (For its abstract see the Abstracts of all chapters, p. 10.)

Contents

Introduction   431
1   Valorisation, accumulation and credit money   433
2   The law of the tendential fall in the rate of profit   436
3   Competition: the dynamic disequilibrium of capital stratification   437
4   Devalorisation and devaluation of capital: accounting practices   439
5   Industrial and finance capital: fragmented banking and economic crises   440
   5.1   Economic crisis and general restructuring of capital   440
   5.2   Cyclical devalorisation   441
6   Industrial and finance capital: integrated banking and continual inflation   441
   6.1   Continual inflation and restructuring   442
   6.2   Inflation and the conflict between industrial and finance capital and bank creditors   442
Summary and conclusions   444
References   445

Introduction[1]

The theory on 'the law of the tendential fall in the rate of profit' (TFRP) is very much the centrepiece of volume III of Marx's *Capital*. It is presented in Part

---

[1]   I am grateful to the discussants at the 1994 University of Bergamo conference on "Karl Marx's third volume of *Capital*: 1894–1994", as well as to Mary Morgan, an anonymous referee and the editor of this volume, Riccardo Bellofiore.

Three of that volume, prior to the theory on the differentiation of capital into several functional forms – the division of surplus-value into profit, interest and ground rent (parts 4–6). This indicates that there is a long way to go from the methodologically abstract level of that law to its actual concrete application. This indication is confirmed by Marx's plans for the contents of the respective volumes of *Capital*, as laid down in several notes and letters.[2]

Quite a number of authors have interpreted the TFRP as a macroeconomic law and have applied it at that level empirically (for example Gillman 1958; Weisskopf 1979; Wolff 1986; Moseley 1991). Whilst such an interpretation and application is defensible, Marx's method also points at a different line of research.[3] The latter – which I shall follow in this essay – conceives of the presentation in *Capital* as moving gradually from the abstract to the concrete, a presentation that is, however, incomplete (see also Bellofiore and Finelli 1998). Note that in the course of completion of the presentation, the *expression* of that law may be modified.

In this essay I will take the theory in *Capital* as the starting point.[4] From there on my aims are very restricted: I will merely initiate the theory of the TFRP at a more concrete level of presentation, taking into account sectors or branches of production (cf. Part Two of Volume III) as well as finance capital (cf. Part Five of Volume III).

In so doing my object is to gain a further understanding of the development of capitalism, especially in its recent manifestations. Such an object is surely akin to the aims that Marx set himself. Certain 'stylised facts', in the back of the mind of the theoretician, play an important role in such an aim. In the present context, three stylised facts seem to have played a role at the time of writing of Volume III: fairly regular cycles, increasing mechanisation, and falling rates of profit over time. The latter was not only an issue fitting the long run 'visions' of classical economists such as Smith, Ricardo and Mill (capitalism develop-

---

[2] See for example Wygodski 1965; Rosdolsky 1968; Zelený 1968; Mandel 1976; Oakley 1983.

[3] The immediate macroeconomic application seems to be in line with the statement that "the law in its generality is independent of that division" (of surplus-value into profit, interest and so on) (Marx 1894, p. 320; cf. Marx 1861–63, CW vol. 33, p. 104). The literature on Marx's method in *Capital* is extensive. See the references in note 2 and for example the papers in Schmidt 1969; Eberle 1973; Moseley 1993; Moseley and Campbell 1997; Arthur and Reuten 1998.

[4] I take it for granted that a tendency is quite different from an empirical trend – especially for nineteenth-century economics there can hardly be any doubt about this. ("Counteracting influences must be at work, checking and cancelling the effect [*Wirkung*] of the general law and giving it simply [*nur*] the character of a tendency, which is why we have described the fall in the general rate of profit as a tendential fall" – Marx 1894, p. 339). On the methodological status of Marx's TFRP in comparison with Mill's views on tendencies, see Reuten 1997. [Ch. 16 of the current book.]

ing into a stationary state), it indeed was an empirical phenomenon requiring explanation. ("There are sufficient statistical facts, too, to confirm this conclusion [of a tendentially falling rate of profit] historically. The only question that can arise is as to the actual cause of this tendency" writes Jevons 1871, pp. 245–6). These three stylised facts fit wonderfully well in Marx's theory of the TFRP.

However, the current stylised facts for OECD-type economies are somewhat different: compared with the nineteenth century, cycles in the twentieth century have not been that regular; mechanisation and the expulsion of labour was not *an issue* between 1945 and the 1970s, but reappeared high on the agenda afterwards; a falling rate of profit is not considered to be a general *phenomenon* requiring explanation; sectors/branches of production develop unevenly; enduring high rates of inflation in the second half of the century, especially in the 1970s, together with the 1979 policy turn followed by high rates of unemployment and an ever-more unequal distribution of income.[5]

In what follows I will indicate the lines along which the theory of the TRFP might be developed further so as to take account of both sets of stylised facts.

1 Valorisation, accumulation and credit money

Before setting out the indicated theoretical development from the TFRP, I shall briefly set out its underlying 'abstract-labour theory of the value-form'[6] as well as the institutional interconnection of capital accumulation and the credit system.

The inherent logic of capitalist production is valorisation (the expansion of value), more specifically, production is geared towards a continual increase in profits. Whilst the exploitation of labour (as well as the exploitation of nature) is the basis of any physical surplus, the surplus (profit and so on) is calculated in terms of money – the one and only capitalist measure of achievement. All elements that matter economically take on a bifurcated form: they have a heterogeneous physical form, but at the same time they are constituted as having a homogeneous money form (value). In being both heterogeneous and homogeneous, they are contradictory. The capitalist system does not transcend this contradiction – it is dealt with merely by reductionism, that is, by reducing the

---

5 On the plane of the interconnection of capital accumulation, employment and financial groupings and institutions, not only the year 1979, marking the turn to moderate inflation, but also 1973 as the *formal* end of the gold standard era, is of importance – it may be said to mark the maturity of capitalism.

6 It is akin to a monetary labour theory of value (Bellofiore 1989).

opposition to one of its poles: the money form. At the same time the other pole continues to exert pressure. On the surface of capitalism, dehumanisation is shown in that human labour takes on this bifurcated form, and the fetishism of money in that this is not usually conceived of as dehumanisation (cf. Marx 1867, ch. 1, section 4).

Consequently, in this chapter all the input and output entities of production are primarily measured in terms of money. This applies prominently to labour and labour productivity. Not only is heterogeneous labour-power, as an input, accounted for in terms of money (the wage), heterogeneous labour in actual capitalist production is also measured in terms of money, that is, it is ideally pre-commensurated in terms of the money value of its *output*.[7]

Valorisation and profit increase is engendered by the accumulation of capital, and in particular the investment of capital in labour-productivity-increasing production techniques. One important condition for the existence of accumulation is the expansion in some way of money or/and the circulation of money. Were this not the case then continual price decrease due to productivity increase would have the effect of continual devaluation of capital. In a limited way this expansion may be accomplished by private credit relations between firms. These limits are overcome by finance capital and financial intermediaries. The particular characteristic of banks as financial intermediaries is that they issue credit money, which is accepted as a medium of circulation.[8]

Credit money is either issued by substitution, or it is issued against loans, that is, created *ex nihilo*. Whereas the former is merely an act of money dealing that substitutes credit money for money that has validated previous production, *ex-nihilo-created* credit money is an *anticipation* of production and realisation in the future. So the bank that advances this credit money on the basis of

---

7 This is the kernel of a reading of Marx's value theory as an 'abstract-labour theory of the value-form' – expanded upon in Reuten 1988a, 1993; Reuten and Williams 1989, ch. 1; Williams 1992. For a critique, see Likitkijsomboon 1995. Reuten 1995 is a reply to the latter and includes a summary statement of the theory.

8 Throughout this essay a distinction is made between 'industrial capital' (enterprises engaged in production) and 'finance capital' (lenders of means of finance, including intermediaries such as banks). This is a theoretical differentiation. Thus, for example, enterprises engaged in production may at times act as lender of capital and as intermediary. Below, the term 'credit money' always refers to the 'money' (cheques, accounts and so on) issued by a financial intermediary such as a commercial bank. For the sake of brevity, all intermediaries issuing credit money and thus adopting a banking function are called 'banks', even if they are not a bank in a formal legal sense. A corollary of this is that no sensible borderline can be drawn between money and money capital (or finance capital). (See Reuten 1988b; Reuten and Williams 1989, pp. 88–9.)

a loan performs a *pre-validation* of production, which is socially validated when the anticipated production is realised (de Brunhoff 1976, p. 46; see also Aglietta 1976, pp. 332–5). Because pre-validation is not based on a compensatory withdrawal of money from circulation, its circuit is not closed (cf. de Brunhoff 1973, p. 94; and de Vroey 1984, p. 385). Therefore it can act as a lever to accumulation, that is, the expansion of valorisation.

This can only be effected if the pre-validation of the production of a capital, anticipating expansion, is confirmed at some stage by the actual expansion of *other* capitals. Expansion indeed can only be validated by expansion. Other capitals must accumulate, say, the value equivalent to the credit money they received from the pre-validated capital in payment, for example, for means of production, or indirectly for consumer goods out of wages. Thus they must generate extra effective demand.

If the borrowing capital is not successful, the bank suffers a loss in that it forgoes the principal as well as the interest agreed upon, which affects its solvency. There are then three possibilities. First, though the borrowing capital fails, other capitals nevertheless accumulate and expand, and the credit money that these other capitals received from the borrowing capital keeps on circulating in an *expansionary* manner. In this situation the bank's liquidity position is not affected. The second possibility is that the credit money keeps on circulating, but in an *inflationary* manner. Then the expansion of other capitals (and of the capital circuit as a whole) is 'fictitious'. The equivalent of the bank's loss (the principal) is then socialised in that it affects all holders of money (as well as creditors and debtors). Again, the bank's liquidity is not affected.

The third possibility is that other capitals do *not* expand in a compensatory way but withdraw from circulation the credit money received (directly or indirectly) in payment from the borrowing capital. That money then must act as store of value (unless concurrently other capitals cancel their own credit with their own bank), which would mean that credit money has to be a permanent and not merely a temporary store of value.[9] This is accomplished in an 'integrated banking system' where banks operate under the umbrella of a central bank (as distinct from a fragmented banking system). Following a massive withdrawal of credit money from circulation, it is for the central bank to decide whether to attempt to prevent bank crises or not. It may do so by covering

---

9 This implies that it is considered a sound deposit, whence it is 'full money'. Full money is measure of value, medium of circulation and a fiduciary store of value. These three 'functions' are interconnected (see Reuten 1988b). Any non-full money acting as a medium of circulation is predicated upon it being a temporary store of value.

the bank's loss through the provision of a loan to the bank. The additional money so issued by the central bank socially validates the pre-validation, but because it does not operate as a realisation of production in the market, it is only a *pseudo-social validation* (de Brunhoff and Cartelier 1974; de Brunhoff 1976, pp. 46–7; Aglietta 1976, p. 350). This then reinforces credit money as a fiduciary general equivalent on a par with central bank money. To the extent that the central bank guarantees that credit money is redeemable in central bank money (whence credit money develops into a full store of value), the banking system is then a fully integrated banking system. (Note that this guarantee may only apply to those banks that conform to the rules set by the central bank.) With this guarantee of redeemability, however, the central bank shifts the frictions inherent in pre-validation by banks to the social aggregate sphere. Consequently, the conditions for the existence of money (that it is a measure of value, a medium of circulation *and* a store of value) risk being eroded.

2 The law of the tendential fall in the rate of profit

Part Three of *Capital* Volume III comprises chapters 13–15. In chapter 13 Marx emphasised that capitalist investment in new techniques tends to go along with a relative expulsion of labour. Therefore accumulation is expressed as a tendency for the composition of capital to rise, and for any given distribution of income as a concomitant tendency for the rate of profit to fall (TFRP). Chapter 14 discusses the factors counteracting this fall, and chapter 15 presents in a synthetic view 'the law's internal contradictions'.

In the introduction I briefly pointed out the methodical status of the law. Put succinctly, the chapter 13 theory states that for a given distribution of income between capital and labour (R/wl; where R is profit, w is the wage rate and l is labour employed), and given the tendency for a rising composition of capital (K/wl; where K is capital invested in fixed and circulating means of production), there will be a tendency for the rate of profit to fall. This can be seen from the rearranged definition of the rate of profit, $r = R/(K + wl) = (R/wl) / (K/wl + 1)$, neglecting turnover coefficients. This presentation glosses over several facets of the matter, one issue being that Marx derived the concept of profit (Parts One and Two of Volume III) prior to the division of surplus-value into its functional forms. Thus 'profit' in chapters 13–15 is in fact a composite category.

In the remainder of this article, I will not only treat profit as decomposed, I will also apply profit and the law of profit to *branches* of industrial production in connection with finance capital.

3   Competition: the dynamic disequilibrium of capital stratification

An influential critique levied against the theory of the TFRP is that it lacks a microeconomic foundation: why should new techniques that decrease the rate of profit ever be introduced?[10] From the point of view of the methodical structure of *Capital* this critique is beside the point since the theory derives its interest from the macroeconomic level at which it is formulated:[11] "we once again stand on firm ground, where, without entering into the competition of the many capitals, we can derive the general law directly from the general nature of capital as so far developed" (Marx 1861–63, CW vol. 33, p. 104). Nonetheless the Okishian critique can be refuted *at a different level of abstraction*, that is, that of competition between capitals/firms. The Okishian type of argument not only places micro foundations at the macro level, it also relies on an implausible comparative static equilibrium account of technical change: firms (plants) within a sector of production are homogeneous, so new least-cost techniques are immediately adopted by *all* firms.

The reality of capitalist competition, however, is rather to be grasped by a dynamic disequilibrium account of industry. Capital tends to be embodied in stratified heterogeneous rather than homogeneous plants, because, whilst valorisation is a continuous process, the investment of capital in means of production is a discrete, 'lumpy' process. Therefore plants are dated differently.[12] Because techniques and labour productivity change over time, dated stratification is characterised according to these factors. And as there is a tendency for uniform prices in a market, this dated stratification is also a stratification of different rates of profit.

When new techniques of production are available (with higher calculated plant rates of profit), the preservation of capital already accumulated may prevent immediate moves towards investment in new-technique plants. Even provided firms can command sufficient means of finance (from amortisation and/or additional credit), they will usually only adopt a new technique when

---

10 The discussion of this problem was initiated by Okishio 1961; Shaikh 1978 reopened the discussion (for further references see Moseley 1991, ch. 1, and Reuten 1991).

11 Over the past decades within neoclassical economics, a similar misunderstanding of macroeconomics has developed. The supposed requirement for providing micro foundations to macroeconomics is just giving up macroeconomics. I am sorry that in my 1991 critique of the Okishian argument I did not take this into account.

12 The reference is to plants as a unit of management. A firm may comprise several plants, each dated differently. In addition to what is explained below, this may give rise to strategic market considerations to close down or open up plants.

the increase in the rate of profit that is expected as a result of its introduction compensates for the early obsolescence of the fixed capital of the old technique. The scrapping of plants is only enforced when prices no longer cover prime costs.

Capital added to the stratification generally operates with up-to-date techniques of production – those with the highest technical composition of capital, maximum productivity of labour and minimal unit costs of production. This investment increases the sector's production capacity, *inducing price competition or/and production at overcapacity*. In either case the revenue and profit rate of the previous stratification is reduced.[13] The 'top capital' may in fact use the strategy of price competition so as to enforce the scrapping of plants at the bottom of the stratification, the optimal price being that which just prevents 'bottom plants' from re-entering.

This stylised model of competition provides a sufficient base for the TFRP.[14] It is however not restricted to it, as it is not necessarily based on an increasing value composition of capital.

In sum, whilst the rate of profit of the newly invested capital tends to *increase compared with that rate of the capital just below in the stratification*, the average rate of profit of the branch as a whole tends to *decrease compared with the previous period*, even allowing for the expulsion of least-profitable plants. The extent of the rate of profit increase for the newly invested capital compared with the previous stratification depends on the productivity *difference* that can be achieved. The larger this difference the more overcapacity and/or price decrease that can be borne *and* the more it enforces the scrapping of capitals at the bottom of the stratification. As a result the achievement of productivity difference is the crucial course by which capital stratification proceeds.

Apart from this intra-branch effect of investment in new techniques, there is also an inter-branch effect. Because any new plant can buy its fixed means of production more cheaply (that is, cheaper than was the case for all the plants lower in the stratification) it can decrease its price. The capitals lower in the stratification must follow suit and see their revenue and rate of profit falling.[15]

---

13 For simplicity we may assume the overcapacity to be distributed proportionally over the stratification.

14 A more rigorous statement is in Reuten 1991, and a fairly simple formalisation in Reuten and Williams 1989, pp. 135–8.

15 Marx subsumed 'the cheapening of the elements of constant capital' under the *countertendencies* (Marx 1894, pp. 342–3). At a lower level of abstraction, however, much depends on the course of the competitive process.

4   Devalorisation and devaluation of capital: accounting practices

Capital presents, in my view, the conflict-ridden unfolding of the contradiction of the bifurcated form of commodities (see §1 above). In this perspective the theory of the TFRP is very much the apotheosis of all of *Capital*. From the perspective of a non-dialectical reading of *Capital* a great deal of that theory can be understood in terms of conflicts too, especially that between labour and capital. Even those who would prefer to see capitalism as harmonious, can see at least some point in a theory of conflict because it is part of the everyday phenomena of capitalism. With the theory of the TFRP, however, this is different: it can be understood in terms of contradiction only. It is not surprising therefore that this theory has met so much resistance, or neglect. It seems indeed rather paradoxical: capitalists strive for valorisation and profit rate increase; in the course of this, however, their deal is devalorisation and profit decrease; and accumulation of capital, as we will see below, is likely to result in devaluation of capital. But this is irrational! Moreover, it is both irrational and rational at the same time.

We saw in the previous section how the accumulation of capital (plant addition) may result in decreased revenue for capitals lower in the stratification. This reflects the *devalorisation* of capital, which is due to the labour productivity for anyone capital in some period lagging behind that in the previous period (in effect $R\downarrow$).[16] Thus valorisation results in devalorisation (note that this is independent of the rate of surplus-value). The rate of profit on capital is merely the expression of (de)valorisation (cf. Volume III, Part One: the transformation of s/v in r). We have also seen that this process results in the scrapping of plants: at the base of the 'normal' process of capitalist production is an ongoing destruction.

Profit rate decrease, however, is not the only expression of investment in new techniques and devalorisation. The other expression is *devaluation* of capital. The 'ultimate' devaluation is, of course, when unamortised capitals are forced to be scrapped (lower in the stratification). Devaluation, however, may also apply to the capitals remaining in the stratification. If the revenue for anyone capital falls (devalorisation) entrepreneurs have the choice either to account for this by the profit rate ($r\downarrow$) or to devalue the capital ($K\downarrow$); in the latter case previous accumulation is partly nullified. Thus depending on the particular accounting practice (historical or current cost accounting), *devalorisation* may

---

16 This is the value productivity. At the same time, in subsequent periods the relative physical productivity for any individual capital decreases compared with the branch average.

be manifested either in $r↓$ or in $K↓$. As cash flow is not affected by either practice, the net effect is, of course, the same.[17]

5 Industrial and finance capital: fragmented banking and economic crises

This section applies foremost to capitalism operating under the institutional make-up of a *fragmented* banking system, as experienced by OECD countries prior to the Bretton Woods Treaty of 1944.

5.1 *Economic crisis and general restructuring of capital*

The more rapid the technical change, the more it has the effect of wiping out the profit of unamortised capitals (as expressed in $r↓$ or $K↓$, eventually resulting in the scrapping of plants – see §3). Should amortisation fall short of the financial needs of renewed investment, then capitals merely fail and are extinguished. This becomes acute when bank credit has been used to pre-validate production (§1). The losses of bankrupt industrial capital are then transmitted to banks, and unless compensated for by the interest on other debts (or with the assistance of the central bank – see §6), credit expansion is hampered on a social scale. Local breaks in the circuit of capital may then multiply into the disruption of the social circuit, generating economic crisis. This process gives rise to a *general* restructuring of capital (bankruptcies, mergers, takeovers, or 'internal' reorganisations) curing and over-curing overcapacity, as well as to wage decrease due to crisis-generated unemployment. In all cases sub-marginal plants are extinguished so that restructuring *reduces* the *range of the stratification* of capital.

Therefore restructuring tends to retard investment and technical change. This is so because stratification proceeds by the temporary creation of (extra) overcapacity such that the least efficient plants are expelled from the stratification, which is only feasible with a sufficiently large productivity difference

---

[17] This makes empirical research on the TFRP a tricky enterprise. For various reasons, and starting gradually from the 1920s onwards, managers prefer current to historical cost accounting – thus devalorisation is accounted for in devaluation. At the same time the 'capital' (K) estimates of the national statistical bureaus, whilst taking into account price changes of capital goods as inputs, are based on fixed lifetimes of investments – so all the dynamics of devalorisation are exempted from the figures. Reliably working up from the balance sheets of individual companies is not merely a monk's work – it requires monks to be master accountants.

between the top and the bottom plant. With the reduction in the range of the stratification due to restructuring, this difference is reduced. The addition of new plants would then result in all plants taking the full burden of overcapacity.

5.2 Cyclical devalorisation

Innovation in new techniques may again be profitable if it creates a sufficiently large cost difference, which requires that technological knowledge be built up: a 'hoarding' of inventions. Technical change then tends to come in waves (cf. Schumpeter 1937, 1943). During such a build-up, there will be a stagnation in accumulation of capital as well as in price decrease, devalorisation and scrapping of plants (at the same time the solvency of the remaining capital will increase). But once sufficient technical knowledge has been gathered, the stratification will be extended again, and so on, repeating the process. Thus whilst inventions occur throughout the cycle, their implementation (innovation) is determined by the range of stratification. With short ranges, competition between capitals remains only latent.

With a fragmented banking system, therefore, the TFRP (devalorisation) is manifested by cycles/waves of restructuring that counteract the rise in the composition of capital.[18]

6 Industrial and finance capital: integrated banking and continual inflation

An important characteristic of the institutional make-up of the banking system in the second half of the twentieth century is that banks, rather than operating in fragmentary way, have been more fully integrated under the umbrella of central banks.[19] This has important implications for the course of the accumulation process.

---

[18] The term cycle is used to indicate fluctuations in general, without any specification as to their duration or regularity. The link between restructuring of capital and the TFRP derives from Marx 1894, ch. 15; it was re-emphasised by Fine and Harris (1979, pp. 83–7) and Weeks (1981, pp. 208–13). The notion of technical change coming in waves derives from Schumpeter 1937; 1943 – see also Bellofiore 1993, pp. 56–64.

[19] Within the confines of this chapter, I cannot go into apparent inverse movements such as the emergence of the Eurodollar market.

6.1 Continual inflation and restructuring

With the amortisation of pre-validated capitals falling short, pre-validation by banks has in fact proven to be inflationary rather than expansionary. Economic crisis and restructuring as described in the previous section, 'correct' and 'over-correct', so to say, the pseudo accumulation after the event. Within a fragmented banking system, banks are in fact forced to let this correction happen – and in the process they themselves risk being extinguished. Within an integrated banking system this is different: economic crises can be bypassed.

Banks that have granted credits to devalorised capitals within a branch of production are confronted with the problem of whether to accept the loss, or to provide those capitals with *new credits* so as to recover (part of) it in the future. The extension of such renewed credit is predicated upon an integrated banking system (see §1). Renewed pre-validation engenders continued monetary expansion, which may turn either into a physical expansion or into the continuation of inflation.[20]

Credit renewal for firms in problems will however be conditional on a *local* restructuring of capital. Renewed pre-validation will nonetheless give rise to a decrease in the range of the stratification of capitals, since more capital will tend to be concentrated within the advanced layer of the stratification. Banks can in fact facilitate capitals to move from the bottom part of the stratification, where they can no longer survive, to the top part, which is also the top technology – thus there occurs in fact a horizontal widening of the top of the stratification. Whilst this *process* of range reduction itself produces a local boom (a multiplication of the production of means of production for this branch), the subsequent *effect* of the range reduction once again produces a stagnation of investment, 'hoarding' of technology and better solvency positions (cf. §5.2).

6.2 Inflation and the conflict between industrial and finance capital and bank creditors

Along with the process described above, another one develops. The general and continual price increase ensuing from protracted pre-validation has the effect of *revaluating capital*, which may compensate for devalorisation.[21] (It should be

---

20 Any 'extra money' (de Vroey 1984, pp. 384–9) does not necessarily generate inflation; it is merely a monetary condition for inflation. Inflation requires in addition an upward movement of prices. The factors behind this are amplified upon in Reuten and Williams 1989, pp. 147–51; see also Aglietta 1976, pp. 313–15, 365–70. Throughout I use the term 'continual'/'continued' inflation to emphasise that upturns in the fragmented institutional setting were already (in part) inflationary.

21 The revaluation of capital, that is, the revaluation of the capital outlay in fixed means of

emphasised that this revaluation is the expression of *price* increase only. Along with it the devalorisation due to *technical* change goes on, and this may still be accounted for in a net devaluation of capital.) At the same time, in order for accumulation to continue, industrial capital must increase its indebtedness (because of the credit renewal required due to obsolescence as well as the ongoing price increase). This increasing indebtedness is the counterpart of the revaluation of capital. The decrease in the rate of profit implied by the TFRP is now (in part) *imposed on finance capital*, including banks, as its purchasing power is continuously reduced.[22] Thus the industrial capital gain is the equivalent of the finance capital loss, so that inflation reveals a potential conflict between them. Nevertheless the position of banks is different from non-bank finance capital. To the extent that banks maintain an adequate fit between short-term and long-term borrowing and lending (maturity matching), it is the banks' creditors that pay for the industrial capital revaluation.

Once inflation becomes self-perpetuating (cf. the second half of the 1960s and the 1970s for OECD countries) the conflict between industrial and finance capital is gradually played out in the following effects, which all result in an increasing share of interest in surplus-value, thus in a decrease of profit. First, in order to be able to recontract credits at higher interest rates, banks increasingly substitute short-term for long-term lending. Second, when contracts expire, non-bank finance capital tends to withdraw fixed interest assets (bonds) from industrial investment. Industrial capital then has to rely even more on short-term credit provided by banks.[23] Third, the decline of the share of non-bank finance capital in industrial investment, increases the risk for banks. In the absence of sufficient security, they will then require an extra risk premium on top of normal interest.

Thus the devalorisation of capital associated with the TFRP tends to be counteracted by continued inflation – whence industrial capital is being revalued. With the substitution of short-term bank credit for long-term finance, devalorisation is then re-imposed on industrial capital.

---

production due to their price increase, is most transparent when the latter have been purchased by means of external finance.

22   This will not be immediately and simply reflected in the interest rate, so as to keep the so-called 'real interest rate' constant (see Reuten 1988b; Reuten and Williams 1989, pp. 88–9). Empirically this is shown in Leeftink 1995, ch. 5.

23   Note that the finance capital invested in any alternative (such as in existing shares, real estate or art – driving up their prices) is ultimately deposited *with banks* or takes the form of near-banking call money. Much of finance capital has been floating in speculative spheres, contributing to the financial instability of the 1980s and 1990s.

In sum, the important similarity between the fragmented setting (§5) and the integrated financial setting is the dynamics of the change in the range of capital stratification, and the related acceleration and deceleration in the introduction of new techniques. The most important difference is that devalorisation and obsolescence, instead of being revealed in crisis, are made manifest in the increasing indebtedness of capitals and relatedly in continued inflation. The losses of capitals are in fact socialised. The crisis course goes along with *general* restructuring (including the restructuring of credit) and stagnation. With the continued inflationary reproduction, restructuring is (repeatedly) branch-local. The ensuing decrease in employment of labour due to labour expelling technical change now shows as 'structural' rather than crisis-cyclical. A permanently unemployed layer of labour (rather than a *reserve* army) serves to exert a drain on wages.

Summary and conclusions

Valorisation, accumulation, devalorisation – quite a Sisyphean process.

Any social law is predicated on an historical-institutional setting. Definite social systems vary over time in the evolving settings of their subsystems. Marx's 1894 'law of the tendency of the rate of profit to fall' is the apotheosis of his exposition of the internal logic of the capitalist system. It has been shown that a dynamic disequilibrium account of the stratification of capital in industry provides the ground for a concretisation of the law of profit. This is an 1894 rather than a 1994 achievement. The kernel of the law is the valorisation-devalorisation contradiction (ultimately deriving from the bifurcated form of capitalist entities). More concretely, an important expression of devalorisation, alternative to the rate of profit fall, is the devaluation of capital. The two important manifestations of these are the destruction of means of production and the unemployment of labour. One may call this, alternatively, the irrationality of rationality or the rationality of irrationality. The dynamics of devalorisation in the course of development is determined by the degree of technical change, together with the related fluctuating range of the stratification of capital.

The actual exhibition, via economic crises or continued inflationary reproduction, is determined by the institutional make-up of the banking system. In both cases the above-mentioned manifestations appear – abruptly in the first case and gradually in the second. On the individual plane, however, being laid off is always a misery. It must, moreover, be bitter to have been exploited for the purpose of a plant, destined for the scrapheap.

The concretisation of the law of the TFRP in this essay has been restricted. Concerning the relationship between industrial and finance capital, no attention has been paid to recent financial innovations, although it seems that these might fruitfully be incorporated in the present framework. Further, the confines of this essay did not allow for the incorporation of the factors affecting changes in the distribution of income and effective demand, as well as state intervention.

References

Aglietta, Michel 1976, *Régulation et crises du capitalisme* (Calmann-Lévi), English trans. D. Fernbach, *A theory of capitalist regulation: the US experience*, London: NLB, 1979.

Arthur, Christopher, and Geert Reuten (eds) 1997, *The circulation of capital: essays on volume II of Marx's 'Capital'*, London: Macmillan.

Bellofiore, Riccardo 1989, 'A monetary labor theory of value', *Review of Radical Political Economics* 21(1–2): 1–25.

Bellofiore, Riccardo 1993, 'Monetary macroeconomics before the *general theory*: the circuit theory of money in Wicksell, Schumpeter and Keynes', *Social Concept* 6(2): 47–89.

Bellofiore, Riccardo, and Roberto Finelli 1998, 'Capital, labour and time: the Marxian monetary labour theory of value as a theory of exploitation', in *Marxian economics: a reappraisal*, vol. 1, edited by Riccardo Bellofiore, London: Macmillan, pp. 48–74.

de Brunhoff, Susanne 1973, *La Monnaie chez Marx*, Paris: Editions Sociales, English trans. M.J. Goldbloom, *Marx on money*, New York: Urizen Books, 1976.

de Brunhoff, Susanne 1976, *État et Capital*, Presses Universitaires de Grenoble and Maspero, English trans. M. Sonenscher, *The state, capital and economic policy*, London: Pluto Press, 1978.

de Brunhoff, Susanne, and Jean Cartelier 1974, 'Une analyse marxiste de l'inflation', *Cronique Sociale de France* 4.

Eberle, Friedrich (ed.) 1973, *Aspekte der Marschen Theorie I; Zur methodischen Bedeutung des 3. Bandes des 'Kapital'*, Frankfurt a/M: Suhrkamp.

Fine, Ben, and Laurence Harris 1979, *Rereading Capital*, London: Macmillan.

Gillman, Joseph 1958, *The falling rate of profit*, New York: Carmen Associates.

Jevons, W. Stanley 1871, 1879, *The theory of political economy*, Harmondsworth: Penguin, 1970.

Leeftink, Bertholt 1995, *The desirability of currency unification*, PhD thesis, University of Amsterdam.

Likitkijsomboon, Pichit 1995, 'Marxian theories of value-form', *Review of Radical Political Economics* 27(2): 73–105.

Mandel, Ernest 1976, 'Introduction', in Marx 1867/1890, *Capital*, vol. I, Harmondsworth: Penguin, pp. 11–86.

Marx, Karl 1861–63, *Collected works*, vol. 33, New York: International Publishers, 1991.

Marx, Karl 1867, 1890, *Das Kapital, Kritik der politischen Ökonomie, Band I, Der Produktionsprozess der Kapitals*, English transl. Ben Fowkes, *Capital: a critique of political economy, volume I*, Harmondsworth: Penguin, 1976.

Marx, Karl 1894, ed. F. Engels, *Das Kapital, Kritik der Politischen Ökonomie, Band III, Der Gesamprozesz der kapitalistischen Produktion*, Berlin: Dietz Verlag, 1972, English trans. David Fernbach, *Capital: a critique of political economy, vol. III*, Harmondsworth: Penguin, 1981.

Moseley, Fred 1991, *The falling rate of profit in the post-war United States economy*, London: Macmillan.

Moseley, Fred (ed.) 1993, *Marx's method in Capital: a re-examination*, Atlantic Highlands, NJ: Humanities Press.

Oakley, Allen 1983, *The making of Marx's critical theory: a bibliographical analysis*, London: Routledge.

Okishio, Nobio 1961, 'Technical changes and the rate of profit', *Kobe University Economic Review* 7: 85–99.

Reuten, Geert 1988a, 'Value as social form', in *Value, social form and the state*, edited by Michael Williams, London: Macmillan, pp. 42–61.

Reuten, Geert 1988b, 'The money expression of value and the credit system: a value-form theoretic outline', *Capital & Class* 35: 121–41.

Reuten, Geert 1991, 'Accumulation of capital and the foundation of the tendency of the rate of profit to fall', *Cambridge Journal of Economics* 15(1): 79–93.

Reuten, Geert 1993, 'The difficult labour of a theory of social value: metaphors and systematic dialectics at the beginning of Marx's *Capital*', in Moseley (ed.) 1993, pp. 89–113.

Reuten, Geert 1995, 'Conceptual collapses: a note on value-form theory', *Review of Radical Political Economics* 27(3): 104–10.

Reuten, Geert 1997, 'The notion of tendency in Marx's 1894 law of profit', in *Investigations in Marx's method*, edited by Fred Moseley and Martha Campbell, Atlantic Highlands, NJ: Humanities Press, pp. 150–75.

Reuten, Geert, and Michael Williams 1989, *Value-form and the state; the tendencies of accumulation and the determination of economic policy in capitalist society*, London: Routledge.

Rosdolsky, Roman 1968, *Entstehungsgeschichte des Marxschen 'Kapital'*, Frankfurt a/M: Europäische Verlagsanstalt, English trans. Pete Burgess, *The making of Marx's 'Capital'*, London: Pluto Press, 1977.

Schmidt, Alfred (ed.) 1969, *Beiträge zur Marxistischen Erkenntnistheorie*, Frankfurt a/M: Suhrkamp.

Schumpeter, Joseph A. 1937, 1939, *Business cycles*, New York: McGraw-Hill.
Schumpeter, Joseph A. 1943, 1954, *Capitalism, socialism and democracy*, London: Unwin University Books, 1966.
Shaikh, Anwar 1978, 'Political economy and capitalism: notes on Dobb's theory of crisis', *Cambridge Journal of Economics* 2: 233–51.
Vroey, Michel de 1984, 'Inflation: a non-monetarist monetary interpretation', *Cambridge Journal of Economics* 8: 244–61.
Weeks, John 1981, *Capital and exploitation*, London: Edward Arnold.
Weisskopf, Thomas E. 1979, 'Marxian crisis theory and the rate of profit in the post-war US economy', *Cambridge Journal of Economics* 3: 341–78.
Williams, Michael 1992, 'Marxists on money, value and labour-power: a response to Cartelier', *Cambridge Journal of Economics* 16: 439–45.
Wolff, Edward N. 1986, 'The productivity slow down and the fall in the rate of profit in the US economy 1947–76', *Review of Radical Political Economics* 18 (Spring-Summer): 87–109.
Wygodski, Witali 1965, *Die Geschichte einer grossen Entdeckung; Ueber die Entstehung des Werkes 'Das Kapital' von Karl Marx*, Berlin: Verlag Die Wirtschaft, 1967 (Russian original, Moscow: Mysl, 1965).
Zelený, Jindrich 1968, *Die Wissenschaftslogik bei Marx und das Kapital*, Berlin: Akademie Verlag, English trans. Terrell Carver, *The logic of Marx*, Oxford: Basil Blackwell, 1980.

CHAPTER 21

The rate of profit cycle and the opposition between Managerial and Finance Capital; a discussion of *Capital III* Parts Three to Five

2002 article, originally published in *The culmination of capital: essays on volume III of Marx's 'Capital'*, edited by Martha Campbell and Geert Reuten, London/New York: Palgrave Macmillan, pp. 174–211.
(For its abstract see the Abstracts of all chapters, p. 10.)

Note: Readers who have read sections 1 and 2 of Chapter 17 above ('Zirkel vicieux' or trend fall?) can skip section 1 of the current chapter.

Contents

Introduction   449
1   **Marx's theory of the rate of profit cycle**   450
   1.1   General outline   450
   1.2   Marx's manuscript and Engels's emphasis   452
   1.3   Conclusions   457
2   **From capital in general to Finance Capital versus Managerial Capital**   458
   2.1   Introduction and overview: capital's falling apart   458
   2.2   From industrial capital (IC) to: IC and Money-dealing capital (MDC)   460
   2.3   From money to: Interest-bearing capital (IBC); and from industrial capital to: functioning capital in the shape of the enterprise   461
   2.4   Interest and profit of enterprise: fluctuation over the cycle of production   465
   2.5   From IBC and the enterprise to: IBC and Joint stock capital (JSC) in the form of IBC and the management of functioning capital   466
   2.6   Ideas of profit   467
   2.7   Money capital and finance capital (FC)   468
   2.8   Finance capital and Managerial capital (MC)   469
   2.9   Summary and Conclusions: Finance capital and Managerial capital – unity or opposition?   471
3   **Outline of a concretisation of the TRPC in light of capital's internal opposition-in-unity**   473

3.1 The concretisation of MCC and CC considered as capital in general 473
3.2 Finance Capital versus Managerial Capital in context of the TRPC 476
   (A) Managerial versus Finance Capital in a deflationary monetary regime 477
   (B) Managerial versus Finance Capital in an inflationary monetary regime 480
   (C) Balance of power: moderate inflation 482
Conclusions: FC's and MC's shifting opposition-in-unity in face of the rate of profit cycle 483
Abbreviations 484
References 485

Introduction[1]

The third volume of Karl Marx's *Das Kapital* (1894) was edited by Friedrich Engels from Marx's manuscripts dating from 1863–67. In Part Three of the book Marx sets out his views on 'The law of the tendency of the rate of profit to fall'. In Marx's day it was taken for granted amongst economists that there is such a law, both on empirical and theoretical grounds. Jevons, for example, writes: "There are sufficient statistical facts, too, to confirm this conclusion historically. The only question that can arise is as to the actual cause of this tendency" (1871, pp. 243–4). In Marx's hands, however, the law gets reshaped into what is more properly a 'theory of the rate of profit *cycle*' (TRPC). In §1 of this article it is argued – based on Marx's manuscripts – that to speak of Marx's 'law of the tendency of the rate of profit to fall' is misleading, and it is shown why this interpretation more likely expresses Engels's view on the matter.

Marx's theory, just referred to, is formulated at the level of 'capital in general', so prior to the differentiation of capital into Industrial Capital, Commercial Capital and Finance Capital (the latter treated under different names, mostly Money Capital) which he sets out in Parts Four and Five of the book. In §2 and §3 of the article I discuss Marx's firmly held view that his theory of the development of the profit rate is 'independent' of that differentiation (cf. Marx 1894F, p. 320); I conclude that this cannot, in general be sustained.

---

[1] An earlier version was presented at the 10th *International Symposium on Marxian Theory*, Amsterdam 2000. I am grateful to Chris Arthur, Riccardo Bellofiore, Martha Campbell, Paul Mattick, Fred Moseley, Patrick Murray, and Tony Smith for their comments on an earlier version of this essay.

In §2, I discuss, in apparent independence of this question, the upshot of Marx's analysis in Parts Four and Five of *Capital III*; namely that he sees capital dominated by Finance Capital.[2] Finance Capital is capital Capital and, as such, unity vis-à-vis labour. I argue that capital is rather to be seen as an internal opposition-in-unity of Finance Capital and Managerial Capital, where the latter is a concretised shape of production capital, as including Industrial Capital. Of course, this is a reconstruction, not an interpretation. It might be added that (especially) Part Five must be reconstructed anyway. As Engels remarks in his Preface to *Capital III*: "It was Part Five that presented the major difficulty [for his editorial work], and this was also the most important subject of the entire book. … we did not have a finished draft, or even an outline plan to be filled in, but simply the beginning of an elaboration which petered out more than once in a disordered jumble of notes …" (1894F, pp. 94–5). Engels reports that he himself made "at least three attempts" at reconstruction but finally gave up. In printed version, many of the 16 chapters of this Part have indeed remained a 'disordered jumble'.

In §3, I outline elements for a concretisation of the Part Three theory in light of the differentiation of capital generally (§3.1) and the opposition between Finance and Managerial Capital specifically (§3.2). I indicate how the relative dominance of one of these factions of capital depends on the particular 'monetary regime' and how this affects the devaluation of capital which is an intimate aspect of the Part Three 'theory of the rate of profit cycle'.

1   Marx's theory of the rate of profit cycle

1.1   *General outline*

Part Three of *Capital III* sets out Marx's theory of the 'law of the tendency for the rate of profit to fall' (TRPF). This is what Marx names it, and what it is called in much of Marxian theory. Although there is nothing wrong with that terminology – so long as a tendency is conceived of as a force, not a trend – the term has connotations de-emphasising what is crucial in Marx's presentation, namely the cyclical movement of the rate of profit and the dynamics that go along with it. A more accurate label would be the Theory of the Rate of Profit Cycle (TRPC), which is the one I adopt henceforth. In further explaining my terminology and the theory itself I proceed in two stages. In the remainder of this subsection I provide an outline of the theory, leaving to the next subsection a more detailed discussion of Marx's text.

---

[2]   Not in the specific meaning of Hilferding (1910).

Part Three, as edited by Engels, comprises the chapters 13–15. In chapter 13 Marx sets out how the compulsion towards profit increase gives rise to the accumulation of capital in the shape of productivity raising techniques of production along with a relative expulsion of labour. We have a tendential rise in the organic composition of capital: the ratio of the value of means of production (K) to the value of labour-power (wL, where w is the wage rate and L the amount of labour). Thus:

$$(K/wL)\dagger \tag{1}$$

where † is the sign for tendential rise. Again, a 'tendency' is not a trend in Marx's view, but a force which may get counteracted by other forces.[3]

If we restrict the outlay of total capital to means of production and labour-power, denote the rate of depreciation by δ, represent total surplus-value or total profit by the sign R and gross production by Y, we have:[4]

$$\delta K + wL + R = Y \tag{2}$$

and for the rate of profit (r):

$$r = R / (K + wL) \tag{3}$$

Marx does not use this notation, though his own notation gives rise to this. Similar ways of presenting capital outlay and the rate of profit have become usual in Marxian theory, though they are not altogether correct (see §3.1).

From equations (1) and (3) it follows that at any given prevailing distribution between capital and labour (R/wL) – put more succinctly if we keep that ratio of distribution 'momentarily' constant, that is

$$R/wL = \text{constant} \tag{4a}$$

the rate of profit must tendentially decline. Or more generally, if we consider a force for the rate of surplus-value to be tendentially rising (R/wL†) and if

$$(R/wL)\dagger < (K/wL)\dagger \tag{4b}$$

---

[3] Note that, for example, J.S. Mill adopted a similar view of 'tendency' (cf. Reuten 1996 and 1997). On the concept of tendency see also Lawson (1998).
[4] At this level of abstraction (prior to the differentiation of capital into industrial, commercial and money capital as well as landed capital) total surplus-value and total profit are the same.

then the rate of profit must tendentially decline, which can be seen from dividing through the right-hand side of representation (3) by wL.

This then is a paramount contradiction of capital accumulation; i.e., that the compulsion for profit increase gives rise to a tendential decrease in the rate of profit.[5]

Chapter 14 of *Capital III* discusses the counteracting tendencies, most importantly the cheapening of the material elements of capital (the prices of wage goods whence w may decline, or those of means of production whence the rise of K may be tempered or nullified) which, of course, affects representation (4b) as a condition.

Chapter 15 discusses the synthesis of the previous two. Crucially, in my view, Marx indicates in this chapter how the tendential drain on the rate of profit is expressed in a cyclical way. Along with the accumulation of capital and the concomitant rise in organic composition of capital, the rate of profit declines. This gives rise to economic crisis in the process of which the rate of profit gets restored, most importantly because of devaluation and destruction (i.e., scrapping) of capital (cf. section 3 of ch. 15). Marx then writes:

> The stagnation in production that has intervened prepares the ground for a later expansion of production – within the capitalist limits. And so we go round the whole circle once again. (Marx 1894F, pp. 363–4)

Thus it seems that the fall in the profit rate is a periodical matter rather than a trend-like phenomenon, contrary to many interpretations.

1.2 Marx's manuscript and Engels's emphasis[6]

My interpretation of Marx's theory is much akin to that of Fine and Harris (1976 and 1978, ch. 4). They rightly say that "a more accurate name for Marx's theory is 'the law of the tendency of the rate of profit to fall *and* of the counteracting influences to operate'" (1976, pp. 162–3). Certainly, Marx formulates both the tendential fall (ch. 13) and the counter tendencies (ch. 14) at the same level of abstraction. But, if this interpretation is correct, then one should at least wonder why Marx called his theory 'tendency of the rate of profit to *fall*', and why

---

5 A well-known criticism of this part of Marx's theory is that by Okishio (1961). Reuten and Williams (1989, ch. 4) and Reuten (1991) indicate how this criticism is based on an equilibrium notion, and that once we take account of heterogenous units of production in branches of the economy – stratified according to technical composition of capital and rates of profit – instead of homogenous units, it is not difficult to provide the mediations of Marx's theory.

6 Much of this subsection is similar to section 2 of my 2004 [chapter 17 of the current book].

so many have read Marx's text as different from the interpretation proposed here. The point is that a careful reading of the text does indeed allow for two interpretations. In the first, dominant weight is given to 'the law as such' (ch. 13), over its counteractions; chapter 14 then depicts a 'trend' fall in the rate of profit, even if stretched over a long time. The second reading emphasises chapter 15 as a synthesising and concluding text. Contributing to these different readings are very different notions of 'tendency'. Although I think the 'trend' notion of tendency (the first reading) does not fit Marx's, I will not stress this aspect in what follows.[7]

As far as the text of *Capital III* as edited by Engels is concerned, I think that we should leave the issue here, giving all room for reconstruction and further development of the theory in either way. However, to the extent that one is also interested in Marx's ideas it is useful to turn to Marx's manuscript text from which Engels did his editorial work, and which was published as transcription in German in 1992 (Marx 1894M, manuscripts 1863–67). That is what I will do in the remainder of this section. I will use the following shorthand references (as further specified in the bibliography):

M = Marx 1894M = German manuscript [= ms.] transcription of 1992;
G = Marx 1894G = German text of 1894 as edited by Engels;
U = Marx 1894U = idem in the English Untermann translation of 1909;
F = Marx 1894F = idem in the English Fernbach translation of 1981.

To begin with my conclusion: it seems that Engels himself had ideas on the issue at hand, which at least resulted in a particular emphasis. (I am not saying that Engels was unfaithful to the text, I am saying that his own ideas made him organise the material in the way he did.)

The current parts of *Capital III* were devised by Marx as chapters (so current Part Three corresponds to Chapter 3 of the ms.). That is not important. What is important is that Marx's text is not divided into three; there are no section separations; it runs on without even blank lines between the current chapters. That already makes a different impression: there is no so-called 'law as such', or at least there is no particular focus on it.

The first pages are similar to the current text (M, pp. 287–301; U, pp. 211–25; F, pp. 317–32). My reading of these is as follows. Marx sets out a hypothetical example of a falling profit rate. Then he writes: (1) this as a tendency is what we perceive in reality (F, p. 318); (2) it is what the economists perceived and have

---

[7] See Reuten 1997 for an elaboration of this. The aim of that paper was to inquire into Marx's general notion of 'tendency' – it took the same chapters 13–15 as a case for that. [See ch. 16 of the current book.]

tried to explain (F, p. 319). Note that in general – throughout the text – Marx's reference to 'law' (thus also the title of his Chapter/Part) is rather ambiguous. At least some of the time his 'law' seems to refer to an empirical regularity.

Next Marx moves the emphasis to what he apparently sees as kernel to capitalist development, first, accumulation and concentration of capital go along with rising productivity of labour, and second, a fall in the rate of profit goes along with a rise in the amount of profits. He repeats this over and again (e.g. M, pp. 291, 298, 300). This may seem the law to him: the inverse relation of mass and rate of profit (see also below).

After this Marx – even without one blank line – immediately moves to the counteracting tendencies (the text of ch. 14). Engels, however, first interpolates a text from much later in the manuscript (F, pp. 332–8; roughly M, pp. 316–20). In G, U and F this is marked by a line or an asterisk (e.g. F, p. 332). This interpolation gives more weight to 'the law as such'. Apart from this, at a crucial point in this text Engels also makes an (unmarked) interpolation of his own. On F, pp. 336–7 (M, p. 319) Marx writes:

> Viewed abstractly, the rate of profit might remain the same ... The rate of profit could even rise, if ...

After this Engels interpolates:

> Aber in Wirklichkeit wird die Profitrate, wie bereits gesehn, auf die Dauer fallen. (G, p. 240).
> In practice, however, the rate of profit will fall in the long run, as we have already seen. (F, p. 337; cf. U, p. 230)

In fact we never saw this. Marx did not talk in terms of 'long run'. The problem is that, of all three chapters, this (Engels's) sentence is in fact the strongest statement giving the impression of a 'trend' fall. Moreover, it is indeed associated with (Engels's) 'law as such'; if in practice the rate of profit will fall, the 'law as such' might seem dominant.[8]

The second strongest statement (this time by Marx himself) is at the end of the text/chapter on the counteractions. Note that when Marx sets out the counteracting forces/tendencies he repeatedly indicates that these do "not annul the general law", but make it operate as a tendency (F, p. 341). He also says that the latter "to a greater or lesser degree paralyse" its operation (F, p. 344; M, pp. 304,

---

[8] There are several more slight changes in Engels's text, each one of which is perhaps too small to mention. Nevertheless, they contribute to the general emphasis.

306). This is again repeated in a conclusion on page M, p. 308 (F, p. 346). The final part may readily give rise to the two rival interpretations of trend versus cycle. In the Fernbach translation we have:

> The law operates therefore simply as a tendency, whose effect is decisive only under certain particular circumstances and over long periods. (F, p. 346)

The Marx-Engels text reads:

> So wirkt das Gesetz nur als Tendenz, dessen Wirkung nur unter bestimmten Umständen ⟨und im Verlauf langer Perioden⟩ schlagend hervortritt. (G, p. 249)[9]

Untermann renders (closer to the German; Fernbach's "decisive" is rather dubious):

> Thus, the law acts only as a tendency. And it is only under certain circumstances and only after long periods that its effects become strikingly pronounced. (U, p. 239)

This can be read in two ways: (1) only in the long run can the rate of profit be perceived to fall; hence 'the law as such' is dominant; (2) the rate of profit falls in particular circumstances; that is, when the forces set out in the tendency-law indeed dominate over the counter-tendencies (my take on the German text is this second one).

After this Marx (M, pp. 309–40) goes into the issues that Engels has placed into chapter 15, though in different order. Note again that the text is continuous – there are no indications for chapter/section breaks.[10] I select a number of passages from it that seem important. Much emphasis is on an issue introduced at the very beginning of the text; namely that increases in productivity of labour via increase in the organic composition of capital result in a combined

---

9 Were the phrase in angle brackets has been replaced for Marx's: "und auf lange Perioden ausgedehnt" (M, p. 308). This is not too important.
10 I am not saying that an editor should not try to make a text more readable by structuring it. Marx's text was not ready for publication and Engels did a great job by making it ready. I argue that from the point of view of the two interpretations Marx's original text leans more towards a theory of cyclical development, Engels's gives more room to a theory explaining trend.

profit increase and rate of profit decrease. He calls this a law: "The law that a fall in the rate of profit due to the development of productiveness is accompanied by an increase in the mass of profit ..." (U, pp. 225–6).[11] Along this, prices fall.

In M, p. 322 this is repeated, this time leaning to a possible interpretation of trend: '[We have seen that] as the capitalist mode of production develops, so the rate of profit falls, while the mass of profit rises together with the increasing mass of capital applied' (F, p. 356). Next Marx amplifies on the depreciation of capital. One page further on, though, he puts this in a different light, first rephrasing the issue in terms of a contradiction, then developing it into periodical crises:

> Simultaneously with the fall in the profit rate, the mass of capital grows, and hand in hand with it goes a depreciation of the existing capital, which checks this fall and gives an accelerating impulse to the accumulation of capital-value. Simultaneously with the development of productivity, the composition of capital becomes higher, there is a relative decline in the variable portion as against the constant. These different influences may at one time operate predominantly side by side spatially, and at other succeed each other in time; periodically [*periodisch*] the conflict of antagonistic agencies finds vent in crises.[12] The crises are always but momentary violent solutions of the existing contradictions – violent eruptions – which restore the disturbed balance.[13] (M, p. 323; G, p. 259; F, p. 357; U, p. 249 – translation amended)

Over-production, over-accumulation and devaluation of capital is the theme of the next pages of Marx's text. An important sentence is:

---

11 Engels (G, p. 236) replaces Marx's term "herbeigeführte" (M, p. 316) with "verursachte" (i.e., caused) which Untermann renders as "due" and Fernbach as "occasioned" (F, p. 332).

12 I do not understand why both Untermann ("from time to time") and Fernbach ("at certain points") do not pick up the periodical here, all the more since one paragraph further on in the context of depreciation/devaluation of capital, they do translate the German *periodisch* into "periodical". *Periodisch* has a connotation of repetition/recurrence.

13 The translations have "for a time restore" and "balance for the time being". Engels has inserted the phrase "für den Augenblick". In this long citation I have most of the time mixed the two translations. It is just not the case that one is generally superior to the other (and this applies not merely to these chapters). I am not complaining; translation is a most difficult task, more difficult than merely writing in a foreign language (which is difficult enough).

Under all circumstances, however, the balance will be restored by the *destruction of capital* to a greater or lesser extent. (M, p. 328; cf. G, p. 264, F, p. 362, U, p. 253).

The balance will be restored! Note that Engels (thus the translators) takes away Marx's emphasis, though adds: "durch Brachlegung und selbst Vernichtung" – by capital's laying idle or even by its destruction. (Of course, laying idle implies postponement of a fall in the rate of profit. The "even" emphasises the former.)

Next Marx sets out how crisis and its aftermath restores the rate of profit and writes: "*And so we go round the whole circle once again*" (M, p. 329; G, p. 265; F, p. 364; U, p. 255 – my italics). This is, of course, strong enough to make the point that we have a cycle of decrease and increase of the rate of profit – along with increase and decrease of the mass of profit et cetera. Two sentences further on Marx makes the point even stronger by talking of a "*Zirkel vicieux*" (cf. the French: "cercle vicieux") which Engels renders as "fehlerhafte Kreislauf" and the translators as "cycle of errors" (F) and "vicious circle" (U). Marx – in otherwise fully German texts – apparently feels constrained to make use of the French "vicieux", since in French "cercle vicieux" has a double meaning, namely that of the English "vicious" (also the one Engels picks up in his German term) and that of an "endless circle", of lasting recurrence.

Again, one page further on (F, p. 365), Marx, back to discussing fall in the profit rate, sets out how it is "accompanied by a temporary rise in wages and a further fall in the profit rate, deriving from this". Clearly this must be a reference to the boom phase of the cycle and the labour-shortage accompanying it.

1.3   *Conclusions*
In current Marxian theory there are two interpretations of Part Three of *Capital III*: secular trend fall in the rate of profit, versus cyclical development of that rate. The text as edited by Engels allows for either one. I have indicated that the text of Marx's manuscript is much less ambiguous and that it leans more to the cyclical view. I have shown this in particular for some of the phrases in the text that suggest the secular trend interpretation. Therefore, Marx's name 'law of the tendency of the rate of profit to fall' is very misleading. However, his allegiance to that title may well have to do with his general method of 'immanent critique', since indeed 'this' law (not 'his'?) was seen to be a very important empirical law of the Classical Political Economy of his day. Anyway, Marx's text can be consistently read as a theory of parallel increase in the mass and decrease in the rate of profit (upswing of the cycle); turning into a restoring decrease in the mass and increase in the rate (downswing of the cycle); brought about by recurrent 'revolutionising' of the composition of capital, resulting in increased valorisa-

tion along with devalorisation and in accumulation along with devaluation of capital. A *Zirkel vicieux*.

2   From capital in general to Finance Capital versus Managerial Capital

2.1   *Introduction and overview: capital's falling apart*

Up to Part Three of *Capital III*, capital was presented as an organic unity in opposition to labour. Even if capitals compete for the highest profit and rate of profit, even if forced to expel competitors from the race, all capital is indifferent or identical in that respect. All capital is (potentially) valorising capital by subsuming and exploiting labour.[14]

In Part Four and Five of *Capital III* the organic unity of capital falls apart, apparently without restoration.[15] First, Marx conceptually demarcates 'commercial capital' as an 'independent' offshoot from capital, the latter now termed 'industrial capital'. Commercial capital specialises in the metamorphosis C′–M′ (and M–C), and so accomplishes a centralisation of the sales process. Second, 'money-capital' is identified as an 'independent' offshoot from industrial capital. Or, as Arthur (2002) highlights, Marx shows how from the point of view of 'capital in general' capital *externalises* in industrial, commercial and money capital.

Banks (or bank-like institutions) specialise in money-dealing activities (related to the circulation of money) and the bringing together of money-capital (M) for either commercial or industrial capital.[16] Their activity and that of money capital generally, is that of M–M (plus interest). Herein lies the great difference between the first and the second offshoots of industrial capital: whereas the first (commercial capital) engages in a particular *metamorphosis* within the circuit of industrial capital, the second does not. Money capital merely engages in a uniform transfer, turning money into money – or, as we will see later, money into money-capital.

Thus we see, at one and the same time, a falling apart of the general *individual* circuit of capital (Volume II, Part One) and a particular social synthesis in the shape of a recomposition of constituent parts of capital. In Part Four, Marx merely posits this recomposition (as 'functional', but also 'conceptual' in

---

14   On the concept of subsumption in Capital, see Murray (1998) and (2001).
15   Not quite so for Marx, as we will see in §2.5 and §2.8.
16   Fine (1985) argues that money-dealing is an aspect of commercial capital. Nevertheless, it becomes subsumed under Banking Capital.

the sense of particularisation) without explicitly showing the conflicts to which this might give rise. For example he explicitly states that both commercial and industrial capital normally share *equally* in the general rate of profit as per their respective capital investment (U, p. 395). For money-capital, this is less obvious; indeed, while industrial capital and commercial capital are organically unified by the, tendential, 'one for all, and all for one' general rate of profit, money capital seems to *separate* itself off in this respect. In this sense, capital seems to fall apart. Or is this a mere appearance, and can capital hope for restoration of unity (as Marx seems to suggest)? If capital does fall apart, it is no longer clear what capital is, or perhaps what strives to be Capital (i.e., capital Capital).

Whereas commercial capital is not returned to in Volume III, money capital and its relation to industrial capital receives thorough (though I think incomplete) treatment in the sixteen chapters of Part Five. Besides, Marx shows how the relation of separation between these two capital constituents, as based on the fact that they do *not* each specialise in a phase of metamorphosis of the circuit – as is the case of commercial capital – impacts on crises and cycles of production.

The object of this section is to extract out of Part Five of *Capital III* how Marx posits the interconnection of industrial capital and money capital. Is this interconnection one of inherent unity, one of separation-in-unity (as Hilferding conceived it), or one of opposition-in-unity and so conflict? Or can we perhaps lay bare epochal conditions for unity or conflict; that is, conditions implied by, or grounding, a particular regime of accumulation? (cf. §3.2) My aim will be a further articulation of the connection between these two constituents of capital as set out by Marx.

Especially the text of Part Five – as edited by Engels from Marx's notebooks – is in the shape of a phenomenal analysis rather than that of a systematic-dialectical presentation.[17] Even bare elements of the latter are missing. I will not endeavour any reconstruction of the dialectic, but rather bring out the conceptual analysis that Marx seems to develop. I will not go into Marx's analysis of credit and credit money, as set out in the same Part Five (on this see Campbell 2002).

Marx's analysis of 'money capital' may be seen to be developed in three phases – as summarised and commented upon in §2.2–§2.6 below: (1) the development of industrial capital's money-dealing into an autonomous *money-dealing capital* (§2.2); (2) the development of *interest-bearing capital* as a sep-

---

17   Some chapters do not even reach a phenomenal analysis, as they are rather comments on, especially, parliamentary investigations, e.g. on England's Bank Act of 1844.

arate entity which has 'functioning capital' in the shape of the enterprise as its counterpart (§2.3); (3) the development of interest-bearing capital into interest-bearing capital and *joint stock capital*, hence the development of enterprise into the management of 'functioning capital' (§2.5). At this stage we will see capital completely sublimated as M–M′.

In §2.8 I will indicate that Marx's analysis of joint stock capital is deficient and come up with elements for a reconstruction, which initiates oppositions within capital, particularly between Finance Capital (interest-bearing capital and joint stock capital) and Managerial Capital as set out in the concluding §2.9.

2.2   *From industrial capital (IC) to: IC and* **Money-Dealing Capital** *(MDC)*

Given the turnover time of capital (developed in *Capital II*, Part Two) a part of capital must always exist as a hoard, repeatedly dissolved into means of circulation and means of payment. This is what Marx calls "money capital in the process of [its] *technical functions*", that is the functions of money arising from monetary circulation associated with commodity circulation. It "acquires autonomy as the function of a special capital", that is, "*money-dealing capital*" (III-Four-19, F: 431–32, 438).[18] Note that Marx (F, p. 435) casts this 'intermediary function' of money-dealing capital (MDC) in terms of an institutional separation indicating, in my view, not a *necessary* separation (i.e., doubling or bifurcation), but 'merely' functional separating out of money capital from industrial and commercial capital. (In fact big industrial and commercial companies may adopt money-dealing roles themselves during the course of development of capitalism.)

It should also be noted that Marx considers money-dealing in what he calls its "pure form", that is, separate from the credit system (and particularly from credit money).[19] Further, at this stage MDC is treated in abstraction from the functions of lending and borrowing money-capital (to be treated in Part Five). Thus MDC 'pure' bears only on the technical functions mentioned. This by itself, Marx writes, "distinguishes money-dealing quite fundamentally from dealing

---

18   III-Four-19, F, pp. 431–2 refers to *Capital III*, Part Four, chapter 19 in the Fernbach translation, pp. 431–2. (Alternatively reference to the Untermann translation is indicated as U, p. xxx; reference to the German original as G, p. xxx.) From now on, I will use this short-hand reference, using only page references when Volume and Part are clear from the context.

19   Marx's proceeding in this respect, as initiated in Volume II, has been set out in careful detail by Martha Campbell (1998 and 2002). I thank her for pointing this out – in earlier work I neglected this.

in commodities, which mediates a metamorphosis" within the circuit of capital, i.e., M–C–M'–C' et cetera. However, with money-dealing too we have:

> the general form of capital M–M'. The advance of M means that the person advancing it receives M + ΔM. But the mediation between M and M' involves only the technical aspects of the metamorphosis, and not its material [*sachlichen*] aspects. ... It is equally clear that their profit is simply a deduction from surplus-value, since they are dealing only with values already realized ... (III-Four-19, F, pp. 437–8; G, pp. 333–4).

Contrary to commercial capital in this respect (III-Four-17, F, p. 395), Marx does not say that money-dealing capital must yield the average rate of profit, though both of these capital factions share in surplus-value.

2.3 *From money to: **Interest-Bearing Capital** (IBC); and from industrial capital to: functioning capital in the shape of the enterprise*

In chapter 21 (Part Five) Marx introduces 'Interest-bearing Capital' (IBC). It is not developed from money-dealing capital but rather from the general commodity form and the conversion of money into capital, whence money's 'use-value' consists in

> the profit it produces when converted into capital. In this capacity of potential capital, as means of producing profit, it becomes a commodity, but a commodity *sui generis*. Or, what amounts to the same, capital as capital becomes a commodity. (III-Five-21, U, pp. 338–9)

Because of this apparent capacity for potentially producing profit, a 'price' is offered for commanding it, that is, extra money above its value, or an interest.[20]

---

[20] Marx indicates that the term 'price' for this is irrational (ch. 21, U, p. 353 ff.); on this see also Schefold (1998, pp. 135–6). In their 1999 book, Itoh and Lapavitsas comment on interest and the "capacity of potential capital, as means of producing profit" and complain that this classical approach is problematic since "seen broadly, interest is not only a portion of the surplus value generated in accumulation, but also part of the money income accruing to borrowers across society" (p. 61). They seem to confuse money and money capital. Lending out money (including putting money in the bank or lending it to a friend) is *not* the same as lending *money capital* (which the bank might do by lending that money to a company; or an individual directly so). Surely not all interest is paid out of surplus-value (when workers amongst themselves, or mediated by a bank, lend and borrow money against interest no surplus-value comes in). But it is a fallacy to turn this around so as to conclude: "Interest ... simply reflects the general possibility of augmenting a sum of money through lending"

> (B)eing loaned out as capital, money is loaned as just the sum of money which preserves and expands itself ... This relation to itself, in which capital presents itself when the capitalist production process is viewed as a whole and as a single unity, and in which capital appears as money that begets money, is here imparted to it as its character, its designation, without any intermediary movement. And it is relinquished with this designation when loaned out as money-capital. (III-Five-21, U, p. 345)

This then is the ultimate sublimation of capital in the form of money-capital: to acquire the character of begetting money as an external thing, without the requirement of any intermediary movement.

> The characteristic movement of capital in general, the return of money to the capitalist, ... assumes in the case of interest-bearing capital a wholly external appearance, separated from the actual movement of which it is a form. (III-Five-21, U, p. 348)

Whereas from the point of view of IBC, capital may have the character of "money that begets money", to the "functioning capitalist" or the entrepreneur (industrialist or merchant) the interest on loan capital represents nevertheless a share in the gross profit of their enterprise, leaving for them what Marx calls the (net) *"profit of enterprise"* (III-Five-23, U, p. 373)

> It is indeed only the separation of capitalists into money-capitalists and industrial capitalists that transforms a portion of the profit into interest, [and] that generally creates the category of interest; and it is only the competition between these two kinds of capitalists which creates the rate of interest. (III-Five-23, U, p. 370)[21]

(Itoh and Lapavitsas 1999, p. 65) which is rather tautologous, and not explanatory. Fine (1985, p. 398) is to the point here: "it is not the payment of interest as such which characterises IBC, but the use to which the loan is put." 'Worker' in my example above is a character mask appropriate to the current level of abstraction (but the issue cannot be treated at this level). Generally, and more concretely, individuals as consumers may want to save for future *consumption* (e.g. at old age). That might involve a positive interest rate, but, depending on intertemporal preferences, might equally well involve a negative rate: I want to be able to consume at age 70 even if I have to pay a 'price' for that. But again this cannot be turned around (in the fashion of Marshall or Böhm-Bawerk): saving is not by definition 'waiting'. Robinson (1953, pp. 54–5) is superb on this.

21 If this creation of the category is read as a historical treatment, instead of a (nascent) systematic, this would, of course, be wrong, as Marx was well aware. Still, one might wonder

Here we see indeed the introduction of *two* competing points of view of capital; in the one money capital and interest is the starting point, in the other entrepreneurial capital and profit.[22]

From all of Part Five (recall that for Marx the material was largely in notebook form) one gets the impression that whereas Marx struggles with the question of what point of view should be given priority in his analysis of Capital, he decides for the priority of IBC. This is most clear for the determination of the rate of interest. Whereas in the first chapter 21 of the Part he states that there is no law of interest, "no law of division except that enforced by competition" (21, U, p. 356), the next chapters are in many respects a qualification of that view.[23] Early on in chapter 23, for example, he firmly states that given the processes related to the general rate of profit (i.e., the gross profit of enterprise as set out in Parts One to Three of *Capital III*), "the size of the [net] profit of enterprise is determined exclusively by the rate of interest" (23, U, p. 373). Here IBC is clearly given the dominant weight in the balance of competitive power.

The quantitative aspect of the rate of interest in connection to the business cycle will be briefly expanded upon in the next subsection. In the rest of the current subsection I will be concerned with the qualitative separation between interest and profit of enterprise. Given the theme of this article, it is important that the existence of interest *in the eye of the entrepreneur* is not merely the consequence of the brute power of one faction of capital (the moneyed) over other; but is rather seen as both the legal and due reward for a function of capital (cf. §2.8–§2.9).

> The interest he [the entrepreneur] pays to the latter [the owner of money-capital] thus appears as that portion of gross profit which is due to the ownership of capital as such. As distinct from this, that portion of profit which falls to the active capitalist appears now as profit of enterprise, deriving solely from the operations, or functions, which he performs with the capital in the process of reproduction, hence particularly those functions which he performs as entrepreneur in industry or commerce. In relation to him interest appears therefore as the mere fruit of owning cap-

---

why Marx for such a crucial category did not differentiate a general and a determinate concept (on the latter terms see Murray 1988).

22   We see these also represented in the orthodox economics literature from Böhm-Bawerk till today: in one view, interest reigns supreme (with any remaining net profit being just a disequilibrium residue); in the other view, it is rather profit that matters – interest can be done away with (in extremo, Keynes's 1936 view).

23   See also Schefold (1998, pp. 136–7) on the order of presentation of these chapters.

ital, of capital as such abstracted from the reproduction process of capital (...) as though they originated from two essentially different sources. (III-Five-23 U, pp. 374–5)

(Marx points out that whereas an individual money-capitalist may have the choice of lending out capital or using it as productive capital himself, this cannot be applied to "the total capital of society". It would be absurd, he writes, "to presume that capital would yield interest on the basis of capitalist production without performing any productive function, i.e., without creating surplus-value" (U, pp. 377–8).)

The separation of capital into IBC and functioning capital indeed shapes the sublimation of capital referred to. Interest-bearing capital as mere ownership of capital, which begets money, does not even confront labour:

> [the] antithesis to wage-labour is obliterated in the form of interest, because interest-bearing capital as such has not wage-labour, but productive capital for its opposite. (III-Five-23, U, p. 379)

The entrepreneur, the functioning capitalist, on the other hand steps down to perform a labouring function himself, so mediating between Capital and labour:

> his profit of enterprise appears to him as distinct from interest, as independent of the ownership of capital, but rather as the result of his function as a non-proprietor – a *labourer*.
>
> He necessarily conceives the idea for this reason that his profit of enterprise, far from being counterposed to wage-labour and far from being the unpaid labour of others, is itself a *wage* or wages of superintendence of labour, higher than a common labourer's ... because the work is far more complicated ... (III-Five-23, U, p. 380)[24]

This view represents till today one important strand for the explanation of profits within the neoclassical economics literature (see the analysis of current textbooks on this issue by Naples and Aslanbeigui 1996).

---

24   Marx comments: "So that the labour of exploiting and the exploited labour both appear identical as labour" (U, p. 383).

2.4 Interest and profit of enterprise: fluctuation over the cycle of production

In chapter 21, as I indicated in §2.3, Marx states that there is no law of interest. Again in chapter 22 he writes that the "circuit described by the rate of interests during the industrial cycle" falls outside the scope of his inquiry, since that "requires for its presentation the analysis of the cycle itself ... which cannot be given here" (22, U, p. 358). Chapter 30 (Part Five) nevertheless describes at least elements of the fluctuation of the interest rate during the cycle, though indeed in the absence of an analysis of the cycle itself. At least it is not a complete analysis, but rather one from only one aspect, that is the general expansion of Industrial Capital (again revealing the notebook character of the text: industrial capital instead of enterprise is a conceptual retreat; the same goes for 'money capital'). Table 1 provides a schematic excerpt of Marx's findings (cf. 30, U, pp. 488–90). He lets the cycle start at the end of the crisis period.

TABLE 1   *The cycle of the interest rate over the industrial cycle (Marx)*

Phase of cycle of industrial capital (IC)	Interest rate (inverse of relative abundance of loan capital)
End of crisis	
1. *Slack*	At minimum
Contraction of IC	
2. *Improvement in prosperity*	Between minimum and average
'The middle period': expansion of IC	
3. *Over-exertion*	At average
Expansion of IC: over-production (inflation of prices)	
4. *Crisis*	At maximum
Superabundance of idle IC	

In chapter 31 (Part Five), Marx indicates that in the prosperity phase "the industrial and commercial capitalists now prescribe terms to the money-capitalist" (U, p. 495). That is, the relative abundance of loan capital (which, of course, also existed in the slack, but without effect) provides a power base to IC. The expansion of accumulation in this phase, writes Marx, "is promoted by the fact that the low interest – which coincides ... with low ... and ... slowly rising prices – increases that portion of the profit which is transformed into profit of enterprise" (U, p. 495). That is, the low interest functions as leverage to the profit of enterprise. In contrast, during over-exertion and especially crisis, "the rate of interest may rise so high that it temporarily consumes the whole profit of some lines of business" (U, p. 502).[25]

These passages bring out the conflict of 'interest' within factions of capital. This will be the theme for the remainder of this article.

2.5 From IBC and the enterprise to: IBC and Joint Stock Capital in the form of IBC and the management of functioning capital

Capital's division between IBC and the enterprise is highlighted in the institutional existence of the joint stock company and joint stock capital (JSC). Marx initiates this movement at the end of chapter 23 (U, p. 387 ff.) and further expands on it in chapter 27.[26] With astonishing foresight Marx does not view the JSC as essentially different from IBC, but rather as a *developed form* of it. This is key to the rest of the current article. Joint stock companies entail the

> transformation of the actually functioning capitalist into a mere manager, administrator of other people's capital, and of the owner of capital into a mere owner, a mere money-capitalist. Even if the dividends which they receive include the interest and the profit of enterprise, i.e., the total profit (for the salary of the manager is, or should be, simply the wage of a specific type of skilled labour, whose price is regulated in the labour-market like that of any other labour), this total profit is henceforth received only in *the form of interest*, i.e., as mere compensation for owning capital that is now entirely divorced from the function in the actual process of reproduction, just as this function in the person of the manager is divorced from ownership of capital. *Profit thus appears [stellt sich so dar] … as a mere appropriation of the surplus-labour of others*, arising from the conversion of means of production into capital … (III-Five-27, U, pp. 436–7, emphases added)

This quotation brings out two important issues. First, dividends take the *form* of interest, and share capital takes the form of interest-bearing capital (external capital). (Note that this is much the way joint stock capital has further de-

---

25 See also U, pp. 361–2, 365, 366, 499 on the long-term development of the rate of interest.
26 Although Marx does not say this in exactly these words, the JSC is in fact the abolition of the entrepreneur. We have no longer the risk-taking individual, but merely the manager/management of joint stock who risk not their own capital, but the capital of others and hence, like labourers, risk "no more" ultimately than the loss of their jobs. Accordingly, 'entrepreneur' becomes a rather empty term; the conceptual stretching to 'institutionalised innovation' does not do this away.

veloped in the twentieth century: for the investor shares are just a portfolio alternative to bonds and other fixed interest-bearing investments; they differ merely on a scale of risk – as is also the case for varieties of IBC proper.)[27]

Second, and related, we seem to have a complete separation of ownership of capital and the management of the process of reproduction of capital. All distributed profits (interest plus dividends) take the form of interest and are lapsed into one category. (We see this reflected in twentieth-century neoclassical economic equilibrium theory in which interest and profit are treated as identical.)

Here then we see the *complete* sublimation of capital: all capital takes the form of interest-bearing capital $(M) \to (M + \Delta M)$.

Along with this complete sublimation, we see capital in one of its roles, the entrepreneurial, stepping down to adopt a labouring role, so seemingly forming an alliance with labour, in opposition to interest-bearing money capital.

It is tempting, following one of Hegel's favourite metaphors, to cast this in terms of the Trinity. God the Son steps down to mediate between God the Father and human beings, apparently becoming one of them. The perennial question being of course: is he human or God? Or perhaps both? The entrepreneurial mediator between Capital and labour, where does s/he stand? We return to this question in §2.8.

2.6   Ideas of profit

In the differentiation of capital shown by Marx, we discern the following succession in ideas of profit:

- *First*, from the standpoint of *naive capital* (manufacturing capital), profit is produced by labour through surplus-labour but it 'naturally' accrues as a just reward to the owners of means of production (functioning capitalists). (This is also the point of departure of Classical Political Economy, for which profit is at once produced by labour and a 'just reward' of ownership in work.)[28]
- *Second*, from the standpoint of (sophisticated) *undifferentiated industrial capital*, profit is seen as springing from capital – i.e., the undifferentiated owner-

---

27   For a portfolio holder investment in shares is decided upon in comparison with the going interest rate (and expectations about that rate). At any state of expectations about future dividends and future changes in share prices, the current price of shares varies inversely with the current rate of interest. (See also Itoh and Lapavitsas 1999, pp. 111–14, who, after bringing this out, bluntly state that the rate of interest is determined in the market: p. 113. Yes, but that is no explanation. Of course, for the individual portfolio investor, the rate of interest can be treated as a given.)

28   See Reuten (1999, pp. 96–7) for quotations from Smith's *Wealth of Nations*.

ship of capital together with capital in process. (This is the focus of twentieth-century mainstream Neoclassical Economics, though with 'interest' substituted for profit.)

- *Third*, from the standpoint of capital *differentiated into IC and IBC* (i.e., industrial capital, or enterprise, and interest-bearing capital), profit is differentiated into profit of enterprise as springing from the labour of the functioning capitalist (the entrepreneur) and into interest as springing from the ownership of money-capital. (This is the point of view of Institutional as well as Management Economics.)

- *Fourth*, from the standpoint of capital *completely differentiated* into ownership and management, profit=interest springs from 'the surplus-labour of others' but accrues as sublimated to the ownership of money-capital. Thus we have the developed state of the point of departure.

2.7 Money capital and **Finance Capital** (FC)

Marx, we have seen, calls the guises of capital in its circuit (M–C ...P... C'–M') production capital, commodity capital and money capital. For the capital externalisation (Arthur) he has the names industrial capital, commercial capital and – again – money capital (sometimes also loan capital and credit capital, with somewhat different connotations and meanings). Although for the first two we have different names for different aspects, this is (mostly) not the case for money capital.

So far in this section I have followed Marx's terminology current in his day, but in what follows I will generally adopt the term *finance capital* for the meaning of externalisation (that is, *finance* capital for financing proper, and *financial* capital for financing including money-dealing).[29] The term finance capital also has the advantage of connecting to contemporary everyday usage of the term.

In terms of the previous discussion, we thus have Finance Capital (FC) which consists of two factions, IBC and JSC. These differ, first, in degree of risk bearing and consequent degree of reward. Second, JSC has at least the formal ownership of the company. FC is alike in that it is an interest-bearing capital (in the case of IBC) or takes the *form* of interest-bearing capital (in the case of JSC).

Institutionally financial capital includes: (1) banks; (2) insurance companies; (3) pension funds; (4) investment companies; (5) individual investors. They all

---

29 Note that the term 'finance capital' is used in a general sense and not in the particular sense of Hilferding's (1910) *Finance Capital*, that is, a particular connection of banks and industry under the hegemony of the former.

make portfolio decisions concerning their investments and cannot be categorised institutionally into either IBC or JSC. They all invest money as capital. The first four, each for different purposes, also collect money from companies and individuals (including labour) so as to invest this either as *capital* or as *money* (see footnote 21).[30] In this particular sense they are money-dealers or rather financial intermediaries. The role of money-dealing in the technical sense of §2.2, however, is predominantly the domain of banks (though, as mentioned, other companies can also adopt this role). The crucial *differentia specifica* of banks is that they are legally granted to create credit money (that is, under authority and the umbrella of a central bank). This vests in them a financial power beyond the mere money collecting activity of the rest of FC.

2.8 Finance Capital and *Managerial Capital* (MC)

Marx does not develop the issue of ownership of capital versus management (§2.5) any further. With JSC, apparently, interest-bearing capital is the standpoint of Capital. The category of capital management is underdeveloped within Marx's analysis. In this subsection I briefly set out a further conceptualisation as relevant for the theme of this article.

In view of the separation between ownership and management that he outlines, Marx consistently amplifies on the JSC from the point of view of the capitalist mode of production generally, in particular the potential consequences of joint stock companies for social transition. He sees, with rare over-optimism, the JSC as a prefiguration of associated production:

> This result [the complete divorce of ownership of means of production and labour] of the ultimate development of capitalist production is a necessarily transitional phase towards the reconversion of capital into the property of producers ... of associated producers, as outright social property. (III-Five-27, U, p. 437)

Indeed this is one way a system contradiction can get resolved. The other is a system internal transcendence. What Marx could not see, at a time when the joint stock company was still in its infancy, was the emergence and development of *managerial capital* as a separate category of capital.

---

30   Evidently *non olet*: financial institutions may not care whether money collected is invested as capital or as money (e.g. mortgage loans). The point is the different use: investment or consumption. In the books of these institutions, this difference is generally crystal clear (though individuals might use mortgage loans for portfolio investment and, in the short run, firms might use business loans for consumption purposes).

Remarkably, managerial capital stems precisely from joint stock capital as a highlighted *form* of interest-bearing capital – that is, just the point so accurately emphasised by Marx. But whereas shareholders, as against loaners of capital, are the *legal* (juridical) owners of the company's capital, they are not necessarily the *economic* owners. The management not only commands share capital and loan capital (together, in the current finance jargon, 'external capital') but notably also the capital grown out of *retained profits*. This latter category may usefully be called *managerial capital*.[31] (In the current finance jargon it is called 'internal capital'.)

As long as the management satisfies the shareholders with an as-if-interest dividend, the growth of managerial capital may continue (to the extent that it drives up the price of their shares so that shareholders perceive it as being in their own interest). Although managers, as Marx emphasises, indeed view their work as the result of labour, this managerial capital grants managers an actual stake in capital. As long as they serve the company, they are the holders of this capital, and they may acquire a legal ownership in it through (combinations of): bonuses and share options; buying up shares and balance sheet reorganisations, so manipulating share prices and the exhibited rate of profit. On top, to the extent that the managerial capital is relatively large, there is no need for new share capital. Thus there is (at least) a potential conflict of interest between shareholders (JSC) and these holders of management capital, not because they are labourers – though they conceive of what they do as work – but because they *are* functioning capitalists, rather than 'mere manager, administrator of other people's capital' (cf. the indented quote in §2.5).[32]

Thus the mature JSC involves the movement of a separation between legal and economic ownership, whence the management of functioning capital develops into the separate category of 'functioning managerial capital'.

This obviously complicates the picture of capital. JSC seems indeed, as Marx emphasises, the most developed form of capital. Legally we indeed have a complete separation between capital ownership and capital in process – labour in process of production of surplus-value. Indeed as the mere ownership of money-capital can be shown to breed no extra money, surplus-value must flow

---

31 In practice, it has grown from both a mere reserve to secure dividends in bad times, and a vehicle for extended investment.

32 For an opposite view see Pinto (1998, pp. 224, 228) who downplays a potential conflict between financial capital and management. For him financial capitalists are 'the' capitalists. Note that in my view *capital* does not escape capitalist control (as Pinto suggests, referring to Berle and his followers, p. 224); it is in the firm control of managerial capitalists.

from capital in process, that is, the labour of management and the labour of the workers. Thus for Marx the JSC, as we have seen, seems to lance the ideology of the productivity of (money-)capital.[33]

As indicated, however, there is no complete economic separation between ownership and process. If for managers, managerial capital is the heart of the matter – and finance capital just an external bother of nuisance – we seem to have landed in a reworked *third* stage of the idea of profit, described in §2.6: in ideology part of gross profit springs from capital in process. Hence the term 'economic profits' in some of the neoclassical textbooks (see Naples and Aslanbeigui 1996). With it the ideology of the productivity of capital seems in part restored, to be effective both in theory and practice.

In this perspective we have a complex multitude of oppositions and alliances within and between capital and labour.

2.9 *Summary and Conclusions: Finance Capital and Managerial Capital – unity or opposition?*

In Marx's incomplete drafts for Part Five of *Capital III*, discussed in this section, an opposition between money-capital (loan and credit capital) and industrial capital is mainly addressed in his treatment of the industrial cycle (cf. §2.4), when the interest rate, and consequently the remaining net profit rate, rises and falls according to the shortage or abundance of money-capital *vis-à-vis* the needs of industrial capital.[34]

In Marx's presentation (or rather mere analysis) this is an opposition between the entrepreneurial industrial capital on the one hand, versus the interest-bearing capital (IBC) on the other. However, that opposition gets (or should get) superseded when Joint Stock Capital (JSC) enters and when therefore (in Marx's view) we have a complete legal and *economic* separation between ownership and management; that is, when all capital is furnished by IBC and JSC. In this constellation all gross profit goes to the financiers anyway – thus there is no conflict over the cycle. (From Marx's own point of view, therefore, chapter 27 on JSC is probably ill placed by Engels – or another new chapter should have followed.)

---

33 Hence, presumably, Marx's euphoria about the emergence of JSC – see the previous citation.

34 With respect to IBC particularly, Marx brings out in a discussion of parliamentary reports concerning England's Bank Act of 1844 how this act was aimed at safeguarding 'the value of money' as against the value of commodities, and how raising the rate of interest is used as an instrument for that (Part Five. ch. 32, U, pp. 514–16). We see here continuity in the policy of central banks till today.

In Marx's view of complete separation there is no conflict within capital over the division of the general rate of profit. The only conflict is that between labour and '*Capital = finance capital*', since the management of capital in process is the work of labour. The interesting upshot of this is that the initial externalisations of capital get, so to say, re-internalised into capital in general.

For finance capital (in the absence of managerial capital), we indeed have the complete sublimation of capital as M–M' on the one hand and the transparency of 'interest=profit' being the product of labour. In this perspective Marx's euphoria about the transitional potentiality of JSC is understandable.

Indeed this completely sublimated fourth stage of the idea of profit (§2.6) seems ideologically untenable, in as much as the first was.

From this point of view (Marx's) there is not much reason to reconsider the TRPC (Part Three) in the light of any oppositions within capital: with a fully developed JSC there is no conflict over the division of the profit governed by the, one for all, general rate of profit.

However, with the opposition between Finance capital and Managerial capital as set out in the previous subsection, there is ample room for such conflict within capital, which also complicates the capital–labour relation generally. Capital, the amalgamate of Finance capital (FC) and Managerial capital (MC), is first of all a unity-in-opposition to labour, representing the (economic) ownership of the means of production in the form of capital. It is an indirect opposition for FC and a direct one for MC (as emphasised by Marx in the context of the entrepreneur and profit of enterprise).

Second, not only is capital a unity-in-opposition to labour, it also is an internal opposition-in-unity which goes beyond and deeper than any normal conflict among capitals. With 'competition in general' all capital is in principle *alike* – even if relative power positions are in movement all the time (cf. capital's stratification). With the separations set out, however, capital is rather internally in opposition since capital factions are *not alike*: i.e., finance capital versus managerial capital. Whereas 'capital in general' is *indifferent* to branches of production – and can in principle flow from the one to the other and back – and whereas, within finance capital, it can flow to become either IBC (in strict sense) or JSC and back, with FC versus MC this is distinct. Although the management of enterprises can strategically manage the proportions between MC and FC (and within the latter IBC and JSC), MC *cannot* flow to become FC unless it abolishes itself. FC equally *cannot* flow to become MC, or it would equally abolish itself.[35]

---

35 This applies to categories (individuals could flow). Space does not allow us to go into the

The conflict between FC and MC comes to the fore first of all in the context of the cycle of production generally – Marx's analysis in this respect (§2.4) so regains relevance.[36] Second, and more important, amongst capital there is also a triangulated complex opposition-in-unity concerning the general monetary state of the economy: between MC and FC, within the latter between JSC and IBC, and again between IBC and MC.

In this light Marx's TRPC will briefly be reconsidered in the remaining part of this article.

3 Outline of a concretisation of the TRPC in light of capital's internal opposition-in-unity

In this section I set out elements for a concretisation of Marx's Theory of the Rate of Profit Cycle [TRPC] (*Capital III*, Part Three). I proceed in two steps. First the TRPC is reconsidered in light of the externalisations set out in Part Four, focusing on the components of capital (§3.1). Next I connect with the TRPC the conflicts between capital factions alluded to in the conclusions of the previous section (cf. Part Five), focusing on the finance of capital (§3.2).

3.1 *The concretisation of MDC and CC considered as capital in general*

In *Capital III*, Part Four, we have seen, Marx introduces Money-dealing capital (MDC) and Commercial capital (CC) as offshoots from what he then calls Industrial Capital. Here he also makes *explicit* that part of 'capital in general' is accumulated in money-dealing and commodity dealing. In discussions of the TRPC this is usually neglected.[37]

In the first section of this article we saw that, at the level of capital in general, the capital accumulated is usually presented as $(K + wL)$ in this or a similar notation (e.g. Marx's $C + V$; cf. equations 2 and 3 in §2). However, once capital's dealing in money and commodities has been made explicit, this is no longer adequate, since part of capital is accumulated in those dealings. In

---

further complication that within the institutions of financial capital, there is a similar opposition between management and their financiers. This, though, is less relevant for what follows.

36 A rising interest rate during the later phases of the cycle (over-exertion and crisis) will normally not so much affect JSC's dividend, but rather the managerial profit (or retained profits).

37 I have myself made this mistake (or grandiose simplification) even in writings where I explicitly considered the TRPC and finance capital at a more concrete level.

addition to accumulation in means of production (K) we have the following three capital items.

First, part of capital is accumulated in a hoard of currency money (M_{ch}).[38]

Second, part of capital is accumulated in commodities. Although commodities as raw materials and commodities in process may be considered to have been included in K, this is not at all obvious for commodities as ready product (C). Anyway, the latter have a different status from K especially when we consider technical change.

Third, money-dealing involves credit – even if this function is not adopted by a special category of capital.[39] At the level of capital in general the credit between capitals may be considered to cancel out. However, this is not so for the credit between capital and labour.[40]

On the other hand, even if the presentation of capital as $(K + wL)$ or as $(C + V)$ has the obvious advantage of bringing out labour's organic part in the production of capital, capital is in fact never invested or accumulated in a wage fund (though the amalgamate of money hoarded serves *for* that). Labour is always a service in flow; in the balance sheets its production result can only appear in commodity form or money form.

Total (active) capital accumulated ($\check{C}$), therefore is to be represented as:

$$\check{C} = K + C + M_{ch} + O \tag{5}$$

where:
$\check{C}$ = total capital
K = value of stock of means of production
C = value of stock of commodities
M_{ch} = money: currency hoard (of banks)

---

38   Campbell (1998) stresses this, at the level of *Capital II*.
39   Note that in *Capital* (III-Four-19) Marx considers 'money-dealing capital' in what he calls its 'pure form', that is 'separate from the credit system', and only later, in Part Five, 'fully develops' it: that is, including the credit system (U, pp. 436–8).
40   At the finance side of capital, even at the level of capital in general, part of capital is brought together by way of (as Marx indicates) the conversion of money into capital. In a developed monetary system, this involves the conversion of bank money of account into capital. At the macroeconomic level, the money of account of capitalists themselves may be considered to cancel out against their current accounts with banks. But not so for labour. In a developed monetary system, money in circulation chiefly takes the form of accounting money. Both the current accounts of and the deposits by labour are converted into either capital or consumer loans. O in equation 5 below must then taken to be net loans (positive or negative).

O = *net* credit between capital and labour (at the active side: consumer loans (to labour), including long term loans on mortgage basis; at the passive side: current accounts of and the deposits (by labour) converted into either capital or consumer loans).

For the rate of profit on 'capital in general' (with these modifications preferably called the macroeconomic rate of profit) we have:

$$r = R / [K + C + M_{ch} + O] \tag{6}$$

Dividing this expression through by wL we have:[41]

$$r = [R/wL] / [K/wL + C/wL - M_{ch}/wL + O/wL] \tag{7}$$

In the light of §1 the components R/wL and K/wL need no further comment. Suffice it to say that, as before, K/wL is a measure for the technique in use, or a measure for the relative expulsion of labour, and that it develops roughly in line with the cycle of the rate of growth of production, i.e., pro-cyclical. For the newly added components I restrict to the following notes, each time taking the cycle of production as reference point.

First C/wL. Generally, the ratio of commodity stock to wages moves counter-cyclically (though with changes in commodity stocks ahead of changes in wages). Thus the C-ratio has always exerted some counteraction to the K-ratio. Apart from that there is always *structural* pressure for a relative decline of commodity stocks (C) which is not particularly affected by the cyclical development. This is highlighted in 'just-in-time-production' (Smith 2000). With just-in-time-production we seem to have reached a limit for a *structural* decline of C/wL. Along with it goes a dampening of the cyclical counteraction of the C-ratio to the K-ratio.

Second M_{ch}/wL. Similarly the ratio of currency hoards to wages moves counter-cyclically, so exerting some counteraction to the K-ratio. Along with it there is a *structural* pressure for decline of the M_{ch}-ratio (which gained new momentum with the cutting loose from precious metal standards).[42] Its limit will, of

---

41 In earlier work I considered that this wL ought to be prefixed by some turn-over coefficient. This is redundant as long as wL is consistently measured. As the rate of profit is usually measured on a year base, one might *for example* take the wage bill for the year.
42 First by cutting loose money circulation from gold reserves. In the fourth quarter of the twentieth century even existing precious metal hoards have increasingly been sold on the market.

course, be reached when all 'world money' has become money of account. So here too the cyclical counteraction dampens.

Third O/wL. In the numerator we have *net* credit between capital and labour. Cyclically this credit to wages ratio seems approximately constant. (So we can neglect any structural trends – that is, in reference to the K/wL ratio; generally these loans (O) will contribute to the rate of profit.)

Two conclusions can be drawn from this short discussion. First, capital's dealing in commodities and money has exerted important influences on the development of the general rate of profit. The three factors discussed cannot be neglected in historical or contemporary empirical studies. Second, we have also seen that in a developed capitalist system the counteracting effects of these factors on that of the K/wL ratio gradually fade away. This might seem to underline the force of Marx's abstraction in his presentation of the cyclical development of the general profit rate.

3.2   *Finance Capital versus Managerial Capital in context of the TRPC*
The theory of the rate of profit cycle (TRPC), we have seen in §1, is formulated at the level of capital in general. In §2, I discussed Marx's view of the concretisation of capital-in-general into, on the one hand, the ownership of finance capital, as interest-bearing capital (IBC) or in its form (JSC), and on the other the labour of management of functioning capital. If this view is correct, a further development of the TRPC, at the more concrete level of the externalisation of capital (beyond §3.1), is not very pressing: forces acting on the profit rate are, before and after the externalisation, at the fore of the sharp opposition between capital and labour. Marx's capital differentiations do not affect this, which was indeed Marx's view (III-Three-12, F, p. 320).

However, in §2.8 and §2.9 when setting out the category of managerial *capital* (MC), we have seen that capital is an internal opposition-in-unity. How is the TRPC concretised in this perspective?

Let us start with recapitulating the abstract determinants that are not modified by the internal separation of capital. First, we have the requirement for production of surplus-value, hence the capital to labour opposition generally.[43] Second, the forces giving rise to pro-cyclical change in the organic composition of capital are not affected. Third, we have the contradiction that the drive for a higher rate of profit generates a pro-cyclical decline of that rate; it is restored

---

43   The moments of concretisation, though, may affect the *process* of production of surplus-value, to the extent that the dynamics of production undergo change. This applies both qualitatively and quantitatively.

through the cyclical restructuring of capital whence part of capital gets destroyed, and *'we go round the whole circle once again'* (Marx, as quoted in §1.2).

For Marx an intimate part of the cyclical development of the profit rate is the devaluation/depreciation of capital that goes along with (a) the cost decrease related to the rise in the composition of capital, and (b) the restructuring of capital. At the same time, however, processes of general price change – say price deflation and inflation – are bracketed by Marx. He can do this due to the fact that in his hands the labour theory of value operates – at least also – as an *analytical* measuring device.[44] The point is that bracketing processes of price change is a useful abstraction *both* when considering capital in general *and* when the externalisation of capital is played out in the way Marx sets it out (as indicated in the first paragraph of this subsection). However, if capital operates as an internal opposition-in-unity with Finance Capital and Managerial Capital as poles, this bracketing will not suffice. In the remainder of this section we will see how the playing out of this opposition depends on the *monetary regime* in operation. I will broadly distinguish two such regimes, a deflationary and an inflationary monetary regime, though without going into their institutional determinants (subsections A and B below).

Before setting these out let us first recall the profit rate decrease captured by the TRPC. The upturn processes associated with the TRPC result in the *newly* accumulated capitals – i.e., those with relatively high K/wL ratio and low unit costs – to realise relatively more profit in comparison with previously accumulated capital – i.e., those with relatively low K/wL ratio and high unit costs. For the latter the actual labour productivity of profit decreases, and they are confronted with an intertemporal *devalorisation*: they realise less value-added than before since prices have been driven down. Thus we have a 'redistribution' of value-added from old to newly accumulated capital (at an, on average, higher K/wL ratio).

(A) Managerial versus Finance Capital in a deflationary monetary regime

Along with this, however, we have a process affecting the *capital* accumulated rather than the production and distribution of *(surplus-)value*. Next to the

---

44 This is not the place to expand on this. Suffice to say that a labour theory of value can be adopted in three different ways: (1) because labour is considered the source of value; (2) because labour is seen to be an actual (less or more complicated) determinant of price; (3) because labour can (to some degree) function as an *analytical* measure. In my view Marx adopts (1) and (3), stressing that the monetary value-form is the *actual* measure. (Abstract-)labour-embodied theoreticians usually adopt all three. (For amplification see Reuten 1999.)

devalorisation, we 'normally' also have a *devaluation of capital*. Since generally more efficient production results in general price decrease, this also affects the value of the capital previously accumulated in means of production and commodity stocks (active capital). The point is that 'today's' price decrease of means of production, affects 'today's' new investments in means of production. Therefore, and *quite apart* from any new productivity rise (and along with it new price decrease) of today's investment, today's means of production can be bought cheaper.

This affects all capitals previously accumulated (yesterday's stratification of capital). There are now two possibilities. One is that they see their profit rate (further) falling (in case of historical cost accounting). Another is that they devalue their capital according to the price decrease of means of production (in case of current cost accounting).[45] Note that this is a pure balance sheet operation, which has the effect that (from this part) any decline in the rate of profit is no longer visible, i.e., after this operation.[46]

What we would 'normally' see, therefore, is that along with the upturn process associated with the TRPC, i.e., productivity increase and *devalorisation*, we see prices decline, or price 'deflation', resulting in *devaluation of capital*.[47]

So far we have, like Marx, only been looking at the 'active side' of capital (assets), and not at how it is being financed, i.e., its 'passive side' (liabilities). Clearly, at the level of capital in general 'finance' for any one capital is simply and merely the reinvestment of the surplus-value produced for that capital.[48] Also, we have thus far not differentiated between financial capital and what I shall call *business capital*, that is all capital of the non-financial sector. From now on I adopt both of these differentiations.

Business capital is most vulnerable for the devaluation of capital along with general price decline to the extent that it is financed by loan capital (LC). This can readily be seen if we compare the active side of business capital ($BÇ^b$), the

---

45   For the devalorisation they might have done the same.
46   Note that with the restructuring of capital in a later phase of the cycle, we see the same *and*, of course, also a devaluation of capital due to *material* destruction of capital which we see equally reflected in the value of capital on the balance sheet.
47   I put price 'deflation' in inverted commas since price deflation (as opposed to general price decrease) is *also* the result of a particular monetary regime. Its proper presentation falls outside the scope of this paper.
48   If we consider the passive side at the level of capital in general, then we see what happens at the active side directly translated at the passive side. Any devaluation of active capital is also a devaluation of passive capital. That looks ugly (and may be psychologically deceptive) but a general price decrease implies also that the purchasing power of the devalued passive capital has increased in parallel.

left-hand side in equations (8) below, with the passive side, i.e., the way business capital is financed, the right-hand sight of (8):

$$K^b + C^b + M_a^b = B\check{C}^b = (SC^b + LC^b) + MC^b \quad (8a)$$
$$K^b + C^b + M_a^b = B\check{C}^b = (FC) + MC^b \quad (8b)$$

where all superscripts b refer to business capital;
K^b = the investment in means of production (plant);
C^b = the investment in commodities; note that C^b is equal to the macro C in equations 5–7;
M_a^b = the accounting money of business held with banks;
$B\check{C}^b$ = business capital of (non-financial) companies
SC^b = share capital: invested in business companies by the financial sector
LC^b = loan capital: loaned to business companies by the financial sector, both long term (bonds etc) and short term (call money etc.)
MC^b = managerial capital of the business sector (non-financial companies)
FC = finance capital, i.e $FC = SC^b + LC^b$

Equations (8) represents, in fact, a short-hand balance sheet of business companies. In comparison with the macro equation (5) we have on the active side instead of the hoards of currency money (M_{ch}) and consumer loans (O) – taken on by financial companies – the accounting money of business held with banks (M_a^b).

Of course, not only means of production (K^b) but also the stock of commodities (C^b) are affected by devaluation of capital. Whereas these two components get devalued, the borrowed capital on the right-hand side (LC^b) remains the nominal sum of its initial value. The same applies to the share capital as quoted in nominal value.[49] Thus to the extent that the active capital is financed with loan capital, devaluation of capital is more than a nominal burden. It will outrun reserves built up as Managerial Capital, and in its absence the burden falls on share capital's now shrinking value. (The counterpart is that financiers having lent Loan Capital equally profit from the devaluation, as the purchasing power of their loan capital, when matured, has increased.)

'Normally' then, the enforced productivity increase captured by the TRPC, and the price decrease associated with it, not only operates on the production of surplus-value or business profit (devalorisation) but also on the value of the

---

49 To polish up the balance sheet, share capital may get devalued along with the active capital side. The alternative is to keep on showing the loss on the balance sheet (negative reserves).

stock of capital (devaluation). Loan capital operates 'normally' as a burden on the net results of business. From their perspective financiers will be eager to provide Loan rather than Share Capital. Together this puts finance capital in a relative power position. As long as the process keeps going, even sitting on their money breeds extra purchasing power.[50] Nevertheless when the long-run average rate of profit is (expected to be) larger than the long-run average price, decrease financiers will invest capital (in mixtures of LC and SC).

The depression effects that usually go along with price 'deflation', of course, also affect employment and should affect the wage rate. But as the great theoretician of deflation, Keynes (1936), indicates, nominal wage rate decreases are usually difficult to exert. The 'normal' situation of productivity increase and tantamount price decrease, then, is highly problematical for capital.

It may well be the case that Marx when composing his TRPC had a similar 'regime' in mind. What is more, his presentation of complete legal and *economic* separation between ownership and management, where the only conflict is that between labour and 'Capital = finance capital' is consistent with this. Whence the so-called Managerial Capital, if a category at all, is negligible. Marx's abstract presentation of the TRPC seems appropriate. Nevertheless, an opposition between capital factions seems implicit when taking into account the devaluation of capital.

(B)   Managerial versus Finance Capital in an inflationary monetary regime

We now turn to the 'abnormal' situation of productivity increase together with generalised price increase. In the context of this article, I cannot go into the processes producing inflation. I merely indicate that any price inflation (in fact prices increasing beyond the decrease implied by productivity increase) is the outcome of a particular monetary regime.[51] (Note that the term 'normal' merely serves as a reference point: the 'abnormal' was the 'normal' situation of at least the second half of the twentieth century.)

Along with the *devalorisation* captured by the TRPC (the Engels–Marx 'law as such') we see then, instead of devaluation of capital, a continuous *revaluation of capital*. From the point of view of business companies, this revaluation may compensate or overcompensate the devalorisation. An overcompensating revaluation of capital (active side/assets) is, of course, equally shown on the

---

50 In this perspective Keynes could make explicit that, at the supply side of loaning, interest is "the price for parting with liquidity", whereas he could on the other hand hold on to the view that labour is "the sole factor of production" (1936, pp. 213–14).

51 See Reuten and Williams (1989, pp. 147–57).

passive side (liabilities). Since both loan capital and share capital are stated in nominal value, this will be shown in business company reserves – what was called Managerial Capital in §2. Thus beyond any customary retention of *profits* as reserves, *capital* revaluation boosts Managerial Capital.

This makes explicit the tripartite opposition-in-unity of capital. Let us first take Share and Managerial Capital together (assuming no conflict between them) and counterpose these to Loan Capital. With revaluation of capital, the more loan capital business uses for its finance the more it gains in this respect. Thus both in a deflationary and in an inflationary monetary regime we see the conflict revealed though with reversed power positions.

It could be argued that in such an inflationary situation loan capital requires an inflation premium on top of the normal interest rate. However, in an inflationary situation we also have a complete shift in the power relations between loan capital and managerial (cum share) capital. Whereas in a deflationary situation loan capital can afford to 'sit' on its money (price decrease increases the purchasing power automatically), inflation compels lending out money capital at any price (loan capital is forced to 'part with liquidity' – a negative 'real' interest rate is better than none).[52] Inflation then puts managerial (cum share) capital in a power position.[53]

Second, a relative defeat of Loan Capital also affects the power structure between Managerial Capital (MC) and Share Capital (SC). To the extent that company reserves have grown, MC gains a relative independence from SC: there will usually be no need for new additional share capital, and the old share capital is stuck 'forever' in the company (even if its holders may change). Managerial Capital can then actually treat SC as a flexible interest-bearing-capital (cf. Marx). What is more, to the extent that Loan Capital due to the monetary regime is on the defensive – with relatively low real rates of interest – 'rates of dividend' can decrease. The working out of this potential conflict is highly dependent on regional business and fiscal law, as well as on the structure of financial institutions (banks, pension and insurance funds – including the latter's Managerial Capital). Their description is beyond the scope of this article.

---

52   The empirical figures of the second half of the twentieth century confirm this (see Reuten and Went 1999).

53   Note that this applies to some lesser extent to the banking section of finance capital, depending on the size of their own managerial finance capital – to the extent that their managerial finance capital is invested in business loans they do suffer. Note also, it is not just loan capital that suffers but also labour, to the extent that their money reserves are put on accounts with banks to be converted into capital.

If the monetary regime is crucial to the relative power structure of capital's opposition-in-unity, the question is, of course, if especially an inflationary monetary regime can last in capitalism. Three factors are of importance here.

First, such a regime boosts managerial business profits, hence general economic growth. A first limit approaches when full employment is reached; therefore, labour can seek higher wages, putting a drain on business profits.

Second, continuing inflation is constrained by the very functions of money (especially money as a store of value) and so the monetary system generally. Loan capital will increasingly take flight into investment in commodities (including precious metals and real estate). Ultimately this will have the effect that loan capital is converted into money of account, and so ends up with banks.[54] Increasingly then the conflict is not between managerial capital and finance capital generally, but between managerial capital and *banks* especially.

In the context of the current article, however, a third factor is of primary interest: the contradiction of the opposition between finance and managerial capital. To the extent that managerial capital increasingly extends the reach of its power over finance capital, business managerial profits increase and *hence* business managerial capital (MC^b). However, when managerial capital outgrows finance capital (see equation 8) or, in the limit, gets rid of finance capital – for share capital by buying up shares – the full burden of the cyclical *devalorisation* as captured by the TRPC falls on managerial capital. This is so since revaluation of capital can no longer provide compensation for the devalorisation of capital (we merely have an inflation of both sides of the business balance sheet).[55]

Interestingly this limit case would take us back again to Marx's presentation of the TRPC for capital in general.

(C)   Balance of power: moderate inflation

The fact that managerial capital in the limiting case of an inflationary regime bears the full burden of TRPC's devalorisation, does not mean that MC has an interest in deflation; indeed we saw in subsection (A) that with continuous deflation MC vanishes. Only with inflation, MC enters the arena. The contradiction is rather that MC is in opposition to FC over the distribution of profit, but ultimately loses when it ultimately wins.[56] The joint interest of MC and FC is

---

54 That is, if financiers *net* invest in commodities, it must end up as money of account.
55 That is of K^b and C^b on the left-hand side of equation 8, and of MC^b on the right-hand side.
56 In this context it is interesting to note that, in the still moderately inflationary circumstances of 1999, a large multinational company such as Unilever paid its shareholders an amount of *cash* above normal dividend of $8 billion instead of cancelling loan capital.

to maintain a regime of moderate inflation, so pressing down 'real' wages automatically; that is, a regime under which MC and FC can coexist in moderate harmony.[57]

Summing up. Marx in his exposition of the TRPC brackets general price change – hence generalised devaluation or revaluation of capital. Deflation and devaluation of capital seem to fit his view of the dominance of finance capital. Only with inflation and revaluation of capital does it become explicit that capital is an opposition-in-unity. Moderate inflation, thus also moderate revaluation of capital – along with the devalorisation and restructuring of capital as captured by the TRPC – seems to provide a modus vivendi for both factions of capital.

Conclusions: FC's and MC's shifting opposition-in-unity in face of the rate of profit cycle

In §1, we saw that the *Capital III* theory of the development of a general rate of profit has a misleading name: Tendency of the Rate of Profit to Fall (TRPF). An alternative reading of the theory as one of cyclical development of the rate of profit (TRPC) is supported by Marx's manuscript text for Part Three. Marx seems to posit the contradiction that forces generating an increase of profits also result in a decrease in the rate of profit (upswing of the cycle) which – along with restructuring of capital – generates a decrease of profits and an increase in the rate of profit (downswing of the cycle). "And so we go round the whole circle once again." It is a silly cycle of valorisation and construction then devalorisation and destruction, as based on the rationality of money. It is not a mighty God's punishment, as in the case of Sisyphus perpetually rolling his stone uphill never arriving at the top, but the fetish of Money that engenders the *Zirkel vicieux*.

In §2, when discussing Parts Four and Five of *Capital III*, we have seen how Marx aptly conceives of joint stock capital or share capital (JSC) as a *form* of interest-bearing capital. He also envisioned the appearance of JSCs as pointing to a complete separation of capital ownership and capital in process, or between capital ownership and labour as including managerial labour. Finally then, for Marx, Finance Capital shining as Capital, operates as a *unity* vis-à-vis labour (§2.1–§2.6).

---

57 Consider also that central banks, especially the European Central Bank, now regard a price inflation of 2% as the 'price stability' target.

I have argued that this view neglects the difference between legal ownership and economic ownership. In fact, managers of JSCs command their company's capital and have economic ownership of what I have called *managerial capital*, as grown out of retained profits (and especially – as we saw later – out of revaluation of capital). So, management has, at least potentially, a firm stake in capital generally. In this way I posited the developed form of capital, contrary to Marx, as an 'internal opposition-in-unity', where factions of capital are in conflict over the distribution of profit (§2.7–§2.9).

In §3 we saw how this opposition is played out in the context of the TRPC, especially relating to the devaluation of capital. This opposition does not do away with devaluation – paradoxically, not even when we have an inflationary revaluation of capital! The conflict is over what faction of capital bears it, which depends on the monetary regime. First, in a deflationary regime Finance Capital will exert hegemony (similar to Marx's view), though, because of the depressive effects that go along with it, such a regime means a Pyrrhic victory for Finance Capital. Second, a full inflationary regime means a self-defeating hegemony for Managerial Capital – on the one hand because it bears the full burden of the effects implied by the TRPC, including capital 'devaluation'; on the other hand because such a regime undermines the pragmatic functions of money. Third, a regime of moderate inflation (what Central Banks nowadays call 'price stability') provides a *modus vivendi* for both of the capital factions, operating in relative harmony in opposition to labour – without, though, doing away the *Zirkel vicieux*.

Abbreviations

CC	Commercial capital
FC	Finance capital
IBC	Interest-bearing capital
IC	Industrial capital
JSC	Joint stock capital
MC	Managerial capital
MDC	Money-dealing capital
SC	Share capital
TRPC	Theory of the rate of profit cycle
TRPF	Law of the tendency for the rate of profit to fall

References

Note: All years in brackets are the original dates of publication as referred to in the text; editions quoted from may differ and are provided where appropriate.

Arthur, Christopher J. 2002, 'Capital in general and Marx's *Capital*', in Campbell and Reuten (eds) 2002.
Arthur, Christopher, and Geert Reuten (eds) 1998, *The circulation of capital: essays on volume II of Marx's 'Capital'*, London: Macmillan.
Bellofiore, Riccardo (ed.) 1998, *Marxian economics: a reappraisal (volumes 1 & 2)*, London/New York: Macmillan/St. Martin's.
Campbell, Martha 1998, 'Money in the circulation of capital', in Arthur and Reuten (eds) 1998, pp. 129–58.
Campbell, Martha 2002, 'The credit system', in Campbell and Reuten (eds) 2002, pp. 212–27.
Campbell, Martha, and Geert Reuten (eds) 2002, *The culmination of capital: essays on volume three of Marx's 'Capital'*, London: Palgrave Macmillan.
Fine, Ben 1985, 'Banking capital and the theory of interest', *Science & Society* 49(4): 387–413.
Fine, Ben, and Laurence Harris 1976, 'Controversial issues in Marxist economic theory', in *Socialist register 1976*, edited by R. Miliband and J. Saville, London: Merlin Press.
Fine, Ben, and Laurence Harris 1979, *Rereading Capital*, London: Macmillan.
Hilferding, Rudolf 1910, *Finance capital: a study of the latest phase of capitalist development*, London: Routledge & Kegan Paul, 1981.
Itoh, Makoto, and Costas Lapavitsas 1999, *Political economy of money and finance*, London: Macmillan.
Jevons, W. Stanley 1871^1, 1879^2, *The theory of political economy*, Harmondsworth: Penguin Books, 1970.
Keynes, John Maynard 1936, *The general theory of employment, interest and money*, London: Macmillan.
Lawson, Tony 1998, 'Tendencies', in *The handbook of economic methodology*, edited by J. Davis, W. Hands, and U. Mäki, Cheltenham: Edward Elgar, pp. 493–8.
Marx, Karl 1894G, ed. F. Engels, *Das Kapital, Kritik der Politischen Ökonomie, Band III, Der Gesamtprozesz der kapitalistischen Produktion*, MEW 25, Berlin: Dietz Verlag, 1972.
Marx, Karl 1894U, *Capital: a critique of political economy, volume III, The process of capitalist production as a whole*, trans. of 1894G by Ernest Untermann (1909), London: Lawrence & Wishart, 1974.
Marx, Karl 1894F, *Capital: a critique of political economy, volume III*, trans. of 1894G by David Fernbach (1981), Harmondsworth: Penguin Books, 1981.

Marx, Karl 1894M, eds. M. Müller, J. Jungnickel, B. Lietz, C. Sander, und A. Schnickmann, Karl Marx, Ökonomische Manuskripte 1863–1867, Text Teil 2, *Karl Marx, Friedrich Engels Gesamtausgabe (MEGA)*, Zweite Abteilung, Band 4, Teil 2, pp. 285–340, Berlin/Amsterdam: Dietz Verlag/Internationales Institut für Sozialgeschichte Amsterdam, 1992.

Marx, Karl CW 33, 'Economic manuscript of 1861–1863 (continuation)', in *Collected works*, vol. 33, New York: International Publishers, 1991.

Murray, Patrick 1988, *Marx's theory of scientific knowledge*, Atlantic Highlands, NJ: Humanities Press.

Murray, Patrick 1998, 'Beyond the "commerce and industry" picture of capital', in Arthur and Reuten (eds) 1998, pp. 33–66.

Murray, Patrick 2000, 'Marx's "truly social" labour theory of value: abstract labour in Marxian value theory, part II', *Historical Materialism* 6 (Summer).

Naples, Michele, and Nahid Aslanbeigui 1996, 'What *does* determine the profit rate? The neoclassical theories presented in introductory textbooks', *Cambridge Journal of Economics* 20: 53–71.

Okishio, Nobio 1961, 'Technical changes and the rate of profit', *Kobe University Economic Review* 7: 85–99.

Pinto, Nelson 1998, 'Finance capital revisited', in Bellofiore (ed.) 1998, vol. 1, pp. 216–32.

Reuten, Geert 1991, 'Accumulation of capital and the foundation of the tendency of the rate of profit to fall', *Cambridge Journal of Economics* 15(1): 79–93.

Reuten, Geert 1996, 'A revision of the neoclassical economics methodology: appraising Hausman's Mill-twist, Robbins-gist, and Popper-whist', *Journal of Economic Methodology* 3(1): 39–67.

Reuten, Geert 1997, 'The notion of tendency in Marx's 1894 law of profit', in Moseley and Campbell (eds) 1998, pp. 150–75.

Reuten, Geert 1998, 'Destructive creativity: institutional arrangements of banking and the logic of capitalist technical change', in Bellofiore (ed.) 1998, vol. 2, pp. 177–93.

Reuten, Geert 1999, 'The source versus measure obstacle in value theory', *Rivista di Politica Economica* 89(4–5): 87–115.

Reuten, Geert, and Robert Went 1999, 'Monetarismus als politische Doktrin; Kritik des institutionalisierten Monetarismus der Europäischen Wirtschafts- und Währungsunion', Supplement der *Zeitschrift Sozialismus* 3(99): 12–38.

Reuten, Geert, and Michael Williams 1989, *Value-form and the state; the tendencies of accumulation and the determination of economic policy in capitalist society*, London: Routledge.

Robinson, Joan 1953, 'The production function and the theory of capital', *Review of Economic Studies* 21: 81–106; reprinted in G. Harcourt and L. Laing, *Capital and growth*.

Schefold, Bertram 1998, 'The relationship between the rate of profit and the rate of interest: a reassessment after the publication of Marx's manuscript of the third volume of *Das Kapital*', in Bellofiore (ed.) 1998, vol. 1, pp. 127–44.

Smith, Tony 2000, *Technology and capital in the age of lean production*, Albany: State University of New York Press.

APPENDIX A

List of the author's academic publications on Marx's *Capital*

(Publications included in the current book are marked with an asterisk *. Those not collected here and marked † can be found at http://reuten.eu: in its search box insert the year of publication. Most often these are the pre-publication author's version.)

2019*   'Marx's conceptualisation of value in *Capital*', in *The Oxford handbook of Karl Marx*, edited by Matthew Vidal, Tony Smith, Tomás Rotta and Paul Prew, Oxford: Oxford University Press, pp. 129–50 (online publication 2018, print publication 2019).

2018†   'The redundant transformation to prices of production: a Marx-immanent critique and reconstruction', in *Marx's 'Capital': An unfinished and unfinishable project?*, edited by Marcel van der Linden and Gerald Hubmann, Leiden/Boston/Köln: Brill Academic Publishers, pp. 157–94.

2017*   'The productive powers of labour and the redundant transformation to prices of production: a Marx-immanent critique and reconstruction', *Historical Materialism* 25(3), pp. 3–35.

2015†   'How money constitutes value: from "abstract labour" to money', in *Returns of Marxism: Marxist theory in a time of crisis*, edited by Sara Farris, Amsterdam: IIRE, pp. 87–100; and Chicago: Haymarket Books, 2016. [Revised and shortened version of 'Money as constituent of value' (2005).]

2014†   'Marx's macro-economie *avant la lettre*', *Tijdschrift voor Politieke Economie* (TPE-digitaal), 8(3), pp. 97–114.

2014†   'An outline of the systematic-dialectical method: scientific and political significance', in *Marx's Capital and Hegel's Logic*, edited by Fred Moseley and Tony Smith, Leiden/Boston/Köln: Brill Academic Publishers, pp. 243–68 (paperback: Chicago, Haymarket Books, 2015).

2013†   'Crisis and the rate of profit in Marx's laboratory' (with Peter Thomas), in *Marx's laboratory: critical interpretations of the Grundrisse*, edited by Riccardo Bellofiore, Guido Starosta and Peter Thomas, Leiden: Brill Academic Publishers, pp. 311–28 (paperback: Chicago, Haymarket Books, 2014).

2011* 'From the "fall of the rate of profit" in the *Grundrisse* to the cyclical development of the profit rate in *Capital*' (with Peter Thomas), *Science & Society* 75(1), pp. 74–90.

2009* 'Marx's rate of profit transformation: methodological, theoretical and philological obstacles – an appraisal based on the text of *Capital III* and manuscripts of 1864–65, 1875 and 1878', in *Re-reading Marx: new perspectives after the critical edition*, edited by Riccardo Bellofiore and Roberto Fineschi, London/New York: Palgrave Macmillan, pp. 211–30.

2006 'The interconnection of systematic dialectics and historical materialism', in *Recent developments in economic methodology, vol. II*, edited by John Davis, Cheltenham: Edward Elgar [adapted version of 2000 article in *Historical Materialism*].

2006† 'On the quantitative homology between circulating capital and capital value – the problem of Marx's and the Marxian notion of "variable capital"'; paper presented at ismt-15 and at the Historical Materialism Annual Conference.

2005* 'Money as constituent of value: the ideal introversive substance and the ideal extroversive form of value in Marx's *Capital*', in *Marx's theory of money: modern appraisals*, edited by Fred Moseley, London/New York: Palgrave Macmillan, pp. 78–92.

2004* 'Productive force and the degree of intensity of labour: Marx's concepts and formalizations in the middle part of *Capital I*', in *The constitution of capital: essays on volume I of Marx's 'Capital'*, edited by Riccardo Bellofiore and Nicola Taylor, London/New York: Palgrave Macmillan, pp. 117–45.

2004* 'The inner mechanism of the accumulation of capital: the acceleration triple; a methodological appraisal of "Part Seven" of Marx's *Capital I*', in *The constitution of capital: essays on volume I of Marx's 'Capital'*, edited by Riccardo Bellofiore and Nicola Taylor, London/New York: Palgrave Macmillan, pp. 274–98.

2004* '"Zirkel vicieux" or trend fall? The course of the profit rate in Marx's "Capital III"', *History of Political Economy* 36(1), pp. 163–86.

2003* 'Karl Marx: his work and the major changes in its interpretation', in *A companion to the history of economic thought*, edited by Warren Samuels, Jeff Biddle and John Davis, Oxford: Blackwell, pp. 148–66.

2002* 'Marx's Capital III, the culmination of capital; Introduction', in *The culmination of capital: essays on volume III of Marx's 'Capital'*, edited by Martha Campbell and Geert Reuten, London/New York: Palgrave Macmillan, pp. 1–15.

2002* 'The rate of profit cycle and the opposition between Managerial and Finance Capital: a discussion of "Capital III" Parts Three to Five', in

The culmination of capital: essays on volume III of Marx's 'Capital', edited by Martha Campbell and Geert Reuten, London/New York: Palgrave Macmillan, pp. 174–211.

2000* 'The interconnection of systematic dialectics and historical materialism', *Historical Materialism* 7, pp. 137–65.

1999 'Knife-edge caricature modelling: the case of Marx's reproduction schema', in *Models as mediators: perspectives on natural and social science*, edited by Mary Morgan and Margaret Morrison, Cambridge: Cambridge University Press, pp. 196–240.

1999† 'The source versus measure obstacle in value theory', *Rivista di Politica Economica* 89(4–5), pp. 87–115.

1998* 'Marx's Capital II, the circulation of capital – general introduction' (with Christopher Arthur), in *The circulation of capital: essays on volume II of Marx's 'Capital'*, edited by Christopher Arthur and Geert Reuten, London/New York: Palgrave Macmillan, pp. 1–16.

1998* 'The status of Marx's reproduction schemes: conventional or dialectical logic?' in *The circulation of capital: essays on volume II of Marx's 'Capital'*, edited by Christopher Arthur and Geert Reuten, London/New York: Macmillan, pp. 187–229.

1998* 'Dialectical method', in *The handbook of economic methodology*, edited by John Davis, Wade Hands and Uskali Mäki, Cheltenham: Edward Elgar, pp. 103–7.

1998* 'Marx's method', in *The handbook of economic methodology*, edited by John Davis, Wade Hands and Uskali Mäki, Cheltenham: Edward Elgar, pp. 283–7.

1998* 'Destructive creativity: institutional arrangements of banking and the logic of capitalist technical change', in *Marxian economics: a reappraisal*, vol. 2, edited by Riccardo Bellofiore, London/New York: Macmillan, pp. 177–93.

1997* 'The notion of tendency in Marx's 1894 law of profit', in *New investigations of Marx's method*, edited by Fred Moseley and Martha Campbell, Atlantic Highlands, NJ: Humanities Press, pp. 150–75.

1993* 'The difficult labour of a theory of social value: metaphors and systematic dialectics at the beginning of Marx's "Capital"', in *Marx's method in Capital: a re-examination*, edited by Fred Moseley, Atlantic Highlands, NJ: Humanities Press, pp. 89–113.

1991* 'Accumulation of capital and the foundation of the tendency of the rate of profit to fall', *Cambridge Journal of Economics* 15(1), pp. 79–93.

APPENDIX B

List of the author's academic publications on, or within, the post-Marx Marxian paradigm

(Publications marked † can be found at http://reuten.eu: in its search box insert the year of publication. Most often these are the pre-publication author's version.)

2023   'On the distribution of wealth and capital ownership; an empirical application to OECD countries around 2019', *Historical Materialism*, vol 31(4), pp. 90–114. Open access at https://brill.com/view/journals/hima/31/4/article-p90_3.xml

2019   *The unity of the capitalist economy and state – a systematic-dialectical exposition of the capitalist system*, Leiden: Brill (725pp). Open access at: https://brill.com/view/title/38778. Part One of this book (pp. 1–291) is on the Capitalist Economy. Much of it is a development from and a synthesis of the essays presented in the current book.

2011†   'Economic stagnation postponed: background of the 2008 financial-economic crisis in the EU and the USA', *International Journal of Political Economy* 40(3): 50–8.

2003†   'On "becoming necessary" in an organic systematic dialectic: the case of creeping inflation', in *New dialectics and political economy*, edited by Robert Albritton and John Simoulides, London/New York: Palgrave Macmillan, pp. 42–59.

2002†   'Marxian macroeconomics: an overview', in *Encyclopedia of macroeconomics*, edited by Brian Snowdon and Howard Vane, Aldershot: Edward Elgar, pp. 464–69.

2002†   'Marxian macroeconomics: some key relationships', in *Encyclopedia of macroeconomics*, edited by Brian Snowdon and Howard Vane, Aldershot: Edward Elgar, pp. 469–80.

2002†   'Business cycles: Marxian approach', in *Encyclopedia of macroeconomics*, edited by Brian Snowdon and Howard Vane, Aldershot: Edward Elgar, pp. 73–80.

2001†   'The logic of accumulation', in *Encyclopedia of international political economy*, edited by R.J. Barry Jones, London/New York: Routledge, pp. 3–5.

2001†   'Disproportionality', in *Encyclopedia of international political economy*, edited by R.J. Barry Jones, London/New York: Routledge, pp. 358–9.

1999† 'Monetarismus als politische Doktrin: Kritik des institutionalisierten Monetarismus der Europäischen Wirtschafts- und Währungsunion [Monetarism as political doctrine: a critique of the institutionalised monetarism of the European economic and monetary union' (with Robert Went), *Supplement der Zeitschrift Sozialismus* 99(3): 12–38.

1998† 'Het kapitalisme in de jaren 1970: retrospectief op een perspectief [Capitalism in the 1970s]', in *Het Kapitalisme sinds de jaren '70*, edited by Bart van Riel, Leo van Eerden, Sjef Stoop, and Clemens van Diek, Tilburg: Tilburg University Press, pp. 21–35.

1997† 'The contradictory imperatives of welfare and economic policy in the mixed economy' (with Michael Williams), *Review of Political Economy* 9(4): 411–31.

1995† 'Conceptual collapses: a note on value-form theory', *Review of Radical Political Economics* 27(3): 104–10.

1994† 'The political economy of welfare and economic policy' (with Michael Williams), *European Journal of Political Economy* 10(2): 253–78.

1993† 'After the rectifying revolution: the contradictions of the mixed economy' (with Michael Williams), *Capital & Class* 49: 77–112.

1993† 'The necessity of welfare: the systemic conflicts of the capitalist mixed economy' (with Michael Williams), *Science & Society* 57(4): 420–40.

1991† 'Staats-theoretische stromingen in de politieke economie [Strands of theories of the state in political economy]' (with Marco Wilke), in *Tussen Scylla en Charybdis: de veranderende gedaantes van de politieke economie*, edited by Leo Golbach and Wim Jansen, Tilburg: Tilburg University Press, pp. 17–27.

1991† 'Over de verwevenheid van welvaarts- macro-economische- en microeconomische politiek [On the interconnection of welfare- macro- and microeconomic policy]', in *Tussen Scylla en Charybdis: de veranderende gedaantes van de politieke economie*, edited by Leo Golbach and Wim Jansen, Tilburg: Tilburg University Press, pp. 29–41.

1989 *Value-form and the state: the tendencies of accumulation and the determination of economic policy in capitalist society* (with Michael Williams), London/New York: Routledge (339pp). [excerpts †]

1988† 'Value as social form', in *Value, social form and the state*, edited by Michael Williams, London: Macmillan, pp. 42–61.

1988 *The value-form determination of economic policy: a dialectical theory of economy, society and state in the capitalist epoch* [dissertation] (with Michael Williams), Amsterdam: Grüner Publishing Company (512pp).

1988† 'The money expression of value and the credit system: a value-form theoretic outline', *Capital & Class* 35: 121–41.

1979† 'Politieke ekonomie: stellingname of onderzoekproject? [Political economy: stand or research programme?]', *Tijdschrift voor Politieke Ekonomie* 3(2): 7–28.
1979† 'Meerwaarde en winst; over gedachtenconstructies en theorie [Surplus-value and profit; on mind constructs and theory]', *Tijdschrift voor Politieke Ekonomie* 2(4): 108–15.
1978† 'Over meerwaarde en winst: een kritiek [On surplus-value and profit: a critique]', *Tijdschrift voor Politieke Ekonomie* 2(1): 151–64.

APPENDIX C

Authored and edited books

Authored books (academic)

2023 *Design of a worker cooperatives society: an alternative beyond capitalism and socialism, and the transition towards it,* Leiden: Brill (476 pages). Open access at https://brill.com/display/title/63765

2019 *The unity of the capitalist economy and state – a systematic-dialectical exposition of the capitalist system,* Leiden: Brill (725 pages). Open access at https://brill.com/display/title/38778. Part One of this book (pp. 1–291) is on the Capitalist Economy. Much of it is a development from and a synthesis of the essays presented in the current book.

1989 *Value-form and the state: the tendencies of accumulation and the determination of economic policy in capitalist society* (with Michael Williams), London/New York: Routledge (339 pages).

1988 *The value-form determination of economic policy: a dialectical theory of economy, society and state in the capitalist epoch* [dissertation] (with Michael Williams), Amsterdam: Grüner Publishing Company (512 pages).

Authored book (professional)

2017 *De kleine Marx* [Marx in a nutshell: summary of the three volumes of Capital with focus on the parts most relevant for current capitalism], Amsterdam: Atlas Contact (80 pages). Third unaltered edition 2023. [Abstract and contents]: https://reuten.eu/2017-de-kleine-marx/]

Edited Books (academic)

2002 *The culmination of capital: essays on volume III of Marx's 'Capital'* (editor, with Martha Campbell), London/New York: Palgrave Macmillan (280 pages).

1998 *The circulation of capital: essays on volume II of Marx's 'Capital'* (editor, with Christopher Arthur), London/New York: Macmillan (240 pages).

1998   *De Prijs van de euro; de gevaren van de Europese monetaire unie* [The price of the euro: the dangers of the European monetary union], (editor, with Kees Vendrik and Robert Went), Amsterdam: Van Gennep (206 pages).

1981   *Rekenen op kernenergie* [Counting on nuclear energy], (editor, with Wim Hafkamp), Leiden: Stenfert Kroese (177 pages).

1980   *Investeren en werkloosheid, visies op besluitvorming en planning* [Investment planning as an instrument of economic policy], (editor, with Wim Hafkamp), Alphen a.d. Rijn/Brussels: Samsom (165 pages).

1980   *Ekonomisch beleid uit de klem; analyse, kritiek en aanbevelingen* [On reflationary economic policy in the Netherlands], (editor, with Casper van Ewijk, Rob de Klerk, and Boe Thio), Amsterdam: SUA (215 pages).

Index of names

Page numbers followed by 'n' mean that this regards a footnote on that page.
Page numbers followed by A mean that this regards an acknowledgement.

Aftalion, Albert 264
Aglietta, Michel 395n; 398n; 409; 435–36; 442n; 445
Alberro, Jose 399n; 409
Albritton, Robert 32
Allisson, François 264
Altena, Alexander van xn-A; 109n-A; 127n-A
Althusser, Louis 72; 73; 112
Aristotle 21
Arthur, Christopher J. xn-A; 15n-A; 21; 23-27; 33; 71-74; 77n-A; 77n; 80n; 82n; 84n; 86n; 88n; 89n; 91n; 97; 97n; 100-01; 108n-A; 109; 125n; 126; 132; 136n-A; 139n; 15n-A; 151; 153n-A; 158; 179; 207; 210; 215-16; 220n-A; 221n; 222n-A; 254n; 255-57; 268n-A; 271n; 272n; 273n; 274n; 275n; 278-79; 283n-A; 285; 299n; 302; 306n-A; 331n; 337-n-A; 340n; 344; 361; 432n; 445; 449n-A; 458; 468; 485
Aslanbeigui, Nahid 464; 471; 486
Aveling, Edward[1] 44n; 45n; 50n; 105; 163n; 172n; 202n; 279n; 315; 317n

Backhaus, Hans-Georg 21-22; 27; 33; 73; 74; 125n; 221n; 257; 311n; 333
Bacon, Francis 108n
Banaji, Jairus 23; 33; 97; 98n; 101
Bang, Willi 302; 314n; 334
Bastiat, Frédéric 415
Bauer, Bruno 430
Bauer, Otto 264
Bellofiore, Riccardo xn-A; 26-27; 51; 33-48; 60; 73-74; 125; 132; 136n-A; 136n; 151-52; 153n-A; 159n; 179; 184n; 191n; 204; 269n; 273n; 274; 279; 283n-A; 302; 311n; 334; 365n-A; 431n-A; 432; 433n; 441n; 445; 449n-A; 485
Bendien, Jurriaan xn-A; 306n-A; 312n
Benhabib, Seyla 20; 33; 70; 74

Berle, Adolph 470n
Bernstein, Eduard 112
Bhaskar, Roy 8; 338; 340; 341n
Bidard, Christian 399n; 409
Bidet, Jacques 427; 429
Blaug, Mark xn-A; 15n-A; 153n-A; 338; 341; 362; 365n-A
Bleany, Michael 400n; 409
Boddy, Radford 396n; 409
Böhm-Bawerk, Eugen von 299; 299n; 300; 373n; 462n; 463n
Bonefeld, Werner 73; 74
Boumans, Marcel xn-A; 220n-A; 252n; 257; 264
Bowles, Samuel 399n; 409
Brenner, Robert 428; 428n; 429
Brown, Andrew xn-A; 77n-A
Brunhof, Suzanne de xn-A; 136n-A; 395n; 409; 435; 436; 445
Budgen, Sebastian xn-A; 77n-A
Burke, Rebecca 77n-A
Burns, Tony 23; 33

Campbell, Martha xn-A; 21; 26; 27; 33-34; 48; 60; 71; 73; 101-02; 108n-A; 136; 136n; 148; 151; 153n-A; 211; 216; 220n-A; 233; 235n; 240; 258; 269n-A; 277n; 279; 303; 311n; 334; 337n-A; 432n; 449n-A; 459; 460n; 474n; 485
Carchedi, Guglielmo xn-A; 108n-A; 220n-A
Carey, Henry Charles 415
Cartelier, Jean 436; 445
Cartwright, Nancy 338n; 362
Carver, Terrell 73; 74
Cassel, Gustav 264
Cherbuliez, Antoine-Elisée 284; 420
Clarke, Simon 201; 204
Colander, David 262n; 265
Conrad, Joachim 302; 314n; 334
Coram, Bruce T. 389n; 409

---

[1] When about his translation.

Crotty, James   396n; 409
Cullenberg, Stephen   371n; 387
Cutler, Antony   394; 409

Davis, John   xn-A; 16n; 101
De Vroey, Michel   125; 132; 435; 442n; 447
Desai, Meghnad   216n; 217; 246n; 258
Domar, Evsey D.   216n; 217; 236
Duménil, Gérard   32; 34; 361; 260; 391n; 409

Eberle, Friedrich   274n; 279; 432n; 445
Echeverria, Rafael   109; 132
Edgworth, Francis Y.   77
Eldred, Michael   21; 34; 115; 125; 125n; 132; 221n; 258
Elson, Diane   29; 34; 48n; 60; 139n; 151; 157n; 179; 310n; 334
Engels, Friedrich[2]   16; 52; 69; 71; 72; 183; 203; 272-71; 274n; 284-85; 285n; 293-94; 299; 300; 302; 312n; 313; 325n; 333n; 334; 372; 374; 376n; 377; 379-81; 423; 453; 454-55; 456n; 457; 471

Fernbach, David[3]   214; 215n; 272n; 324n; 348-49; 375; 376n; 377n; 379-81; 455; 456n
Feuerbach, Ludwig   88
Feyerabend, Paul   131
Fine, Ben   xn-A; 31; 34; 124n; 133; 194n; 204; 347n; 362; 365n-A; 370n; 371n; 387; 399n; 400; 401n; 406; 409; 441n; 445; 452; 458n; 462n; 485
Finelli, Roberto   xn-A; 27; 33; 273n; 279; 283n-A; 432; 445
Foley, Duncan K.   xn-A; 31; 34; 136n-A; 246n; 258; 396n; 399n; 410
Forster, Michael   67; 68
Fowkes, Ben[4]   50; 52n; 56n; 138; 145n; 146n; 154; 156n; 162n; 166; 166n; 167n; 171n; 172n; 173n; 174n; 175n; 185; 315; 315n; 317n; 322n; 324n
Fraser, Ian   23; 33
Freeman, Christopher   326n

Freiligrath   79n
Freud, Sigmund   339
Friedman, Milton   262n
Frisch, Ragnar   260; 264

Galbraith, John Kenneth   262n
Gehrke, Christian   222n; 258
Germer, Claus   xn-A; 136n-A
Gerstein, Ira   124n; 133
Gillman, Joseph   432; 445
Gleicher, David   125; 133
Glick, Mark   391n; 409
Glombowski, Jörg   xn-A; 391n-A; 396n; 410
Glyn, Andrew   396n; 410
Goldstein, Jonathan P.   396n; 410
Goodwin, Richard M.   396n; 410
Gramsci, Antonio   112
Groll, Shalom   31; 34; 369n; 370n; 371n; 387-88; 397n; 411
Grossman, Henryk   264; 369n
Gruschka, Marilyn   391n-A
Gunn, Richard   74

Hanemann, Liesel   302
Hanlon, Marnie   21; 34; 125n; 258
Harcourt, Geoffrey C.   216n; 217
Harman, Chris   428n; 429
Harris, Donald J.   246n; 258; 391n; 399n; 410
Harris, Laurence   31; 34; 125n; 133; 194n; 204; 347n; 362; 370n; 371n; 387; 406; 409; 441n; 445; 452; 485
Harrod, Roy F.   216n; 236
Hartmann, Klaus   296n; 302
Hausman, Daniel M.   338; 362
Hayward, Danny   xn-A
Hegel, Georg W. F.   21; 23; 40; 63-67; 68; 73-73; 79; 85; 87n; 88n; 101; 108-10; 111; 113-14; 132; 133; 138n; 145; 183; 211; 258; 273; 274n; 367; 427
Heinrich, Michael   xn-A; 272n; 279; 283n-A; 284; 284n; 302; 372n; 374n; 388; 418n; 429
Hilferding, Rudolf   216; 450n; 459; 485

---

2   When regarding his own writings, or when about his way of editing *Capital*.
3   When about his translation.
4   When about his translation.

Himmelweit, Susan   124n; 125; 133; 399; 400; 410
Hindess, Barry   394; 409
Hirst, Paul   394; 409
Horowitz, David   216n; 217; 258; 264
Howard, Michael C.   32; 34; 216n; 216n; 217; 313; 334; 370n; 388
Hubmann, Gerald   41; 60; 306n; 335
Hunt, Ian   397n; 399n; 410
Hussain, Athar   394; 409

Iljenkow   73
Inwood, Michael   173n; 179; 320n; 334
Itoh, Makoto   xn-A; 32; 136n-A; 201n; 204; 461n; 462n; 467n; 485

Jasny, Naum   216n; 217
Jevons, W. Stanley   77; 373; 388; 391; 410; 433; 445; 449; 485
Jungnickel, Jürgen   57; 60; 62; 272n; 280; 281; 284; 285n; 303; 304; 335; 347; 362; 372n; 374n; 388; 389; 429; 486

Kaldor, Nicolas   233; 233n; 258; 360; 373n
Kalecki, Michał   216; 216n; 217; 233; 252n; 258; 264
Kant, Immanuel   20; 63
Kautsky, Karl   17; 214
Kemp, Tom   207
Keynes, J. Maynard   18; 26; 46n; 117; 216n; 223; 233; 463n
King, Jesse E.   32; 34; 216n; 216n; 217; 313; 334; 370n; 388
Klant, Joop J.   341; 362
Klapperstück, Edgar   302; 314n; 334
Kleiber, Lucia   21; 34; 125n; 258
Klein, Lawrence R.   224; 258; 260; 264; 265
Kopf, Eike   284n; 299n; 302; 314n; 335
Korsch, Karl   112
Koshimura, Shinzaburo   246n; 258
Kouvelakis, Stathis   418n; 429
Kuhn, Thomas S.   40; 176
Kurz, Heinz D.   216n; 217; 222n; 258
Kuznets, Simon   373n

Laibman, David   31; 34; 399n; 410
Lakatos, Imre   124; 133
Landreth, Harry   262n; 265
Lange, Oscar   216n; 217; 264n
Lapavitsas, Costas   xn-A; 136n-A; 461n; 462n; 467n; 485
Lawson, Tony   164n; 338; 360; 362; 451n; 485
Lebowitz, Michael A.   31; 34; 370n; 388
Leeftink, Bertholt   443n; 445
Leontief, Wassily   216; 224; 229n; 258; 264; 264n
Lévy, Dominique   32; 34; 259; 362
Levy, Gerald   xn-A; 15n-A
Likitkijsomboon, Pichit   xn-A; 74; 136n-A; 434n; 445
Lipietz, Alain   391n; 398n; 399n; 410
Louçã, Francisco   xn-A; 220n-A
Lukács, György   112
Luxemburg, Rosa   216; 264

Machiavelli, Niccolò   108n
Malthus, Thomas Robert   192; 199; 200; 384; 415; 420
Mandel, Ernest   207; 216n; 217; 246n; 258; 432n; 446
Marshall, Alfred   77; 338; 362; 462n
Marx, Karl   passim
Maslow, Abraham H   339
Mattick Jr., Paul   xn-A; 15n-A; 21; 23; 31; 35; 73; 74; 81n; 108n-A; 108n; 133; 210; 213; 218; 220n-A; 269n; 274n; 280; 337n-A; 365n-A; 449n-A
Mattick Sr., Paul   370n; 388
Mehring, Franz   79n; 102
Mepham, John   73; 74
Mészáros, István   80n; 102; 271n; 280
Mill, John Stuart   21; 96; 102; 342; 343; 343n; 344; 345; 360; 363; 432; 432n; 451n
Mirowski, Philip   108; 124; 126; 126n; 133
Mitchell, Wesly Clair   264
Moggridge, Donald E.   215n; 218
Mohun, Simon   31; 35; 124n; 125; 133;
Moore, Samuel[5]   44n; 45n; 50n; 105; 166n; 172n; 202n; 279n; 315; 317n

---

5   When about his translation.

Morgan, Mary   x*n*-A; 220*n*-A; 337*n*-A; 365*n*-A; 431*n*-A
Morishima, Michio   246*n*; 259
Morrison, Margaret   x*n*-A; 220*n*-A
Moseley, Fred   x*n*-A; 25; 31; 32; 35; 71; 73; 74; 102; 108*n*-A; 136*n*-A; 151-52; 153*n*-A; 180; 208*n*; 112*n*; 218; 220*n*-A; 222*n*; 259; 269*n*; 274*n*; 280; 283*n*-A; 290; 291; 303; 306*n*-A; 307*n*; 335; 337*n*-A; 354; 361; 363; 410; 432; 432*n*; 437*n*; 446; 449*n*-A
Moszkowska, Natalie   370
Murray, Patrick   x*n*-A; 16*n*-A; 21; 22; 23; 31; 35-36; 70; 72-73; 76; ch.5 (pp. 77-103) passim; 108*n*-A; 109; 113; 114; 114*n*; 115; 116; 126; 131; 133; 136*n*-A; 139*n*; 147; 152; 153*n*-A; 158; 172*n*; 180; 184*n*; 190*n*; 204; 209; 210; 212*n*; 218; 220*n*-A; 228*n*; 259; 269*n*; 271*n*; 274*n*; 277*n*; 280; 283*n*-A; 337*n*-A; 340*n*; 361; 363; 449*n*-A; 458*n*; 463*n*; 486
Musgrave, Alan   118*n*; 123; 133
Mussell, Simon   x*n*-A

Nakatani, Takeshi   399*n*; 410
Naples, Michele   464; 471; 486
Negishi, Takashi   399*n*; 410
Nelson, Anitra   x*n*-A; 136*n*-A
Nijsten, Bart   x*n*-A
Norman, Richard   67; 68; 71; 74; 77*n*; 102

Oakley, Allen   19; 36; 100*n*; 102; 214*n*; 215*n*; 218; 222; 259; 270*n*; 272*n*; 280; 372*n*; 388; 432*n*; 446
Okishio, Nobio   369*n*; 388; 392; 399; 399*n*; 400; 402*n*; 407; 408; 410; 437; 437*n*; 446; 452*n*; 486
Ollman, Bertil   65; 67; 68
Orzech, Ze'ev B.   31; 34; 369*n*; 370*n*; 371*n*; 387-88; 397*n*; 411

Paolucci, Henri   108*n*; 134
Parijs, Philippe van, see Van Parijs
Peirce, Charles   164*n*
Persky, Joseph   399*n*; 409
Pinto, Nelson   470*n*; 486
Popper, Karl   63; 109; 338; 339; 363
Proudhon, Pierre-Joseph   121
Psychopedis, Kosmas   74

Quesnay, François   222; 222*n*; 224; 227; 233; 233*n*
Quételet, L. Adolphe J.   42; 314*n*

Rangel, Jose   391*n*; 409
Realfonzo, Riccardo   136*n*; 151; 152
Reati, Angelo   391*n*; 409; 411
Reijnders, Jan   264; 265
Ricardo, David   22; 26; 70; 78; 92; 96; 102; 120; 123; 137*n*; 171*n*; 201; 224; 233*n*; 262*n*; 271; 288; 310; 311; 357; 361; 382; 386; 415; 418; 418*n*; 419; 419*n*; 432
Rigby, David L.   391*n*; 411
Robinson, Joan   216*n*; 218; 224; 228*n*; 259; 370*n*; 389; 462*n*; 486
Rodenburg, Peter   197*n*; 204; 262*n*; 265
Roemer, John E.   392; 399; 399*n*; 400; 400*n*; 407; 409; 411
Rosdolsky, Roman   432*n*; 446
Rosenberg, Alexander   339; 360; 364
Roth, Mike   21; 34; 115; 125*n*; 132; 258
Roth, Regina   x*n*-A; 41; 57; 60; 62; 283*n*-A; 284; 284*n*; 296*n*; 300; 303; 304; 335
Ruben, David-Hillel   73; 74; 242; 345; 346; 359; 364
Rubin, Isaak Illich   21; 36; 92; 98; 203

Salter, Wilfred E.G.   401*n*; 411
Salvadori, Neri   399*n*; 411
Samuels, Warren   x*n*-A; 16*n*-A
Samuelson, Paul M.   264; 265
Sawyer, Malcolm C.   216*n*; 218
Sayers, Sean   71; 74; 77*n*; 102
Schefold, Bertram   48*n*; 61; 306*n*; 311*n*; 312*n*; 336; 461*n*; 463*n*; 487
Schmidt, Alfred   73; 75; 109; 134; 432*n*; 446
Schumpeter, Joseph A.   262; 262*n*; 263; 264; 265; 326*n*; 360; 364; 403*n*; 406; 411; 441; 441*n*; 447
Schutz, Eric   399*n*; 411
Shaikh, Anwar   497*n*; 400; 400*n*; 411; 437*n*; 447
Simoulidis, John   32
Skinner, Andrew   126; 134
Smith, Adam   22; 26; 46*n*; 70; 126; 192; 200; 222; 262*n*; 265; 288; 373*n*; 382; 391; 418; 418*n*; 419; 432; 467*n*

Smith, Tony   xn-A; 16n-A; 23; 27; 36; 38n-A; 56n; 61; 68; 71; 73; 75; 77n-A; 77n; 83n; 84n; 85n; 88n; 91n; 99n; 103; 108n-A; 109; 113; 114; 114n; 115; 116; 122; 131; 134; 136n-A; 153n-A; 158; 171n; 180; 184n 190n; 204; 213; 220n-A; 220n; 260; 269n; 271; 274n; 281; 283n-A; 296n; 304; 309n; 335; 337n-A; 340n; 344; 361; 364; 365n-A; 367n; 389; 449n-A; 475; 487
Spiethoff, Arhur   264
Steedman, Ian   124n; 134; 399n; 411
Stiebeling, George C.   325n; 336
Stone, Giovanna   216n; 218
Stone, Richard   216n; 218
Sutcliffe, Bob   396n; 410
Sweezy, Paul A.   24; 36; 40; 54; 61; 71; 75; 96; 103; 370n; 389

Taussig, Frank W.   96; 103
Taylor, Nicola   xn-A; 16n-A; 26; 33; 94n; 97n; 103; 151; 153n-A; 158; 159n; 160n; 179; 180; 204; 302; 314n;
Thio, K. Boe T.   xn-A; 306n-A; 318
Thompson, William   230; 230n
Tinbergen, Jan   264
Tomba, Massimiliano   xn-A; 181n-A; 417n; 430
Tugan-Baranovsky, Mikhail   216; 264; 265

Van Parijs, Philippe   399n; 400n; 411

Vollgraf, Carl-Erich   41; 42; 57; 60; 61-62; 272n; 281; 284; 284n; 285n; 286n; 300; 303; 304; 308; 308n; 314; 319n; 335; 336; 372n; 374n; 389
Vroey, Michel de   125; 132; 435; 442n; 447
Vygodskij, Vitalij   273n; 281

Walras, Léon   77
Webber, Michael J.   391n; 412
Weeks, John   394; 399n; 400; 401n; 406; 412; 441n; 447
Weisskopf, Thomas E.   361; 364; 432; 447
Williams, Michael   IX; xn-A; 27; 36; 48; 62; 103; 109n-A; 136n; 152; 221n; 260; 311n; 336; 365n-A; 391n-A; 434n; 447
Williams, Michael (with Reuten)   23; 67; 73; 80n; 81n; 82n; 84n; 91n; 94n; 110n; 114; 114n; 125n; 127n; 128; 128n; 129; 136n; 158; 159n; 160n; 185n; 212n; 221n; 254; 256; 274n; 326n; 341n; 344; 346n; 369n; 391n; 392; 396n; 397n; 398n; 402n; 409; 434n; 438n; 442n; 443n; 452n; 480n
Wit, Debbie de   xn-A
Wolf, Julius   325n; 336
Wolff, Edward N.   32; 36; 361; 364; 391n; 412; 432; 447
Wygodski, Witali   432n; 447

Zelený, Jindrich   73; 432; 447

Index of subjects

- References to the three volumes of *Capital* are abbreviated as *C-I*, *C-II* and *C-III*; 'Part' is abbreviated as 'Pt'.
- This index is not exhaustive for each one (main) term, it rather focuses on references where a main term/concept is explained.
- Many references are to sections of a chapter; in this case, for example, 2§5 stands for chapter 2, section 5; in case of a subsection, for example, 2§5.2.
- In case the reference is to a full (sub)section, it is followed by its page numbers in brackets; for example 2§5.2 (44-45).
- Reference to a single page, or some pages, are as, for example, 2§5.2: 44, or also ch.2: 44, 49.
- In case of many references for a lemma, page and/or section numbers in bold indicate the main one(s) as to explanation of a term/item.
- The lemmas are most often subdivided into sub-lemmas.
- Many lemmas have a cross-reference (see: ... see also: ...). In case this reference is to a sub-lemma this is indicated as, for example, see: 'surplus-value' sub 'relative surplus-value'.

abstract labour
    (duality of) concrete and abstract labour   2§2.1: 42
    'time' of abstract labour: no real existence   ch.7-concl: 150
    abstract labour as concrete abstraction in practice   6§4.3 (125-26)
    abstract labour cannot be measured   7§2.2: 142
    disappearance of the term after *C-I*, Pt One   7§2.1: 141
    reconstruction of   6§5 (127-30)
    simplified constituent of value   7§2.1: 141
    see also: 'ambiguity Marx's abstract labour'
    see also: 'labour embodied'
abstraction
    abstraction in practice   6§4.3 (125-26)
    levels of abstraction   1§3.5: 23-25; ch.3: 64-65; ch.4: 71; 6§1: 112; 13§2.1 (273-74); 14§2 (285)
    levels of abstraction: claims to general truth   15§1: 247
    quantification between levels of abstraction, error of   6§4.1: 122
    types of (reductive, simplifying)   6§3.2: 116-17; 6§5: 128
accumulation of capital
    assumptions (Marx) for his exposition of   9§1.3 (183-86)
    brief general delineation   18§1 (392-93)
    changes of the composition of capital   9§3.2 (193-96)
    changes of the productive forces   9§2.2: 188-90; 9§3.2: 188-90
    changes of wages induced by growth of capital   9§3.1 (190-93)
    conversion of surplus-value into capital   1§4: 29; 9§2.1: 186
    cursory survey *C-III*, Pt Seven   9§1.2 (183)
    cyclical course of accumulation   9§3.3: 199
    cyclical course of accumulation commented on by Schumpeter   12§1: 263
    cyclical course of accumulation, see also: 'labour shortage: cyclical'
    decennial cycle   9§3.3: 199; 9§3.3: 200; 12§1: 263
    dynamics of accumulation: formalisation   9§2.2 (186-90); 9§3: 190-97
    Faustian conflict: accumulation versus enjoyment   9§2.1: 186; 11§2.1: 225
    general law of capitalist accumulation: defined   9§3.1: 190

INDEX OF SUBJECTS 503

    general law of capitalist accumulation: expanded on   9§3 (190-202)
    increase rate of exploitation generates wage increase   9§3.1: 192-93
    law of capitalist production (accumulation induced wage Δ)   9§3.1: 192
    Marx's accumulation acceleration triple   9§3.2: (193-96)
    Marx's introduction of concept of 'acceleration'   9§2.2: 190; 16§2.2: 350n and 355; 17§2: 376; 21§1.2: 456
    total (average) social capital in C-I, Pt Seven   9§3.2: 194; 9§3.3: 198
    see also: 'capital composition: rising'
    see also: 'over-accumulation of capital' sub 'tendency towards'
    see also: 'profit rate – tendential manifestation' sub 'cyclical development'; see also: the other profit rate lemmas
ambiguity Marx's abstract labour
    expounded in comments on Patrick Murray's views   5§3 (91-98)
assumptions: types of
    all types below (as well as reductive assumption)   ch.6 passim
    approximation   14§3.1: 286
    heuristic   ch.9: 186, 191
    negligibility/neglectable   ch.11: 225-26, 229;
    simplifying (serves tractability)   14§3.1: 286
    stage simplification (serves tractability; dropped later)   14§3.1: 286
    see also: 'abstraction' sub 'types of (reductive, simplifying)'

banking system
    fragmentary versus integrated   20§1 435; 20§5: 440-39; 20§6: 442, 444
banks
    banks issue credit money, created *ex-nihilo*   20§1: 434-33
    losses of banks   20§1: 435
    losses of banks and CB-engendered pseudo-social validation   20§1: 434-35
    see also: 'credit money'
break
    see: 'paradigmatic break (Marx)'
breakdown / overthrow of capitalism
    absent from Marx's *Capital*   19§4: 423-24
    evolution of Marx's views on the issue   19§5 (425-26)
    Grossman on   17§1.1: 369n
    in Marx's *Grundrisse* manuscript   19§1: 416-17; 19§2: 418

capital
    see: 'circuit of individual capital'
    see: 'circulation of total capital'
    see: 'fixed capital'
    see 'functional forms of capital'
capital composition: general
    organic composition   ch.9: 193-94
    technical composition   ch.9: 193
    value composition   ch.9 193-94
capital composition: rising
    affects rate of accumulation and rate of profit   18§4.2 (397-98)
    see also: 'accumulation of capital' sub 'Marx's accumulation acceleration triple'; see also: 'profit rate, tendency: micro foundation'

Capital editions (German; English)
    Capital-I: editions (note)   intro Part B: 105
    Capital-II: editions   10§3: (214-15)
    Capital-III: editions   13§1: 269-70, 270 n2
    see also: 'Marx's *Capital* (general)' sub 'internet links'
Capital: coverage in this book
    C-I, Pt One: commodities and money   chs. 6 and 7
    C-I: Pts Three to Five: production absolute and relative sv   ch.8
    C-I: Pt Seven: the process of accumulation of capital   ch.9
    C-I and *C-III:* Marx's conceptualisation of value   ch.2
    C-II: Pt Three: reproduction & circulation total social capital   ch.11
    C-III: Pt Two: transformation of profit into average profit   chs. 14 and 15
    C-III: Pt Three: law of the tendential fall in the rate of profit   chs. 16 to 19
    C-III: Pts Two, Three, Five (on, or developments from)   ch.20
    C-III: Pts Three, Four Five: profit rate cycle and functional forms of capital   ch.21
    see also 'Marx's *Capital* (general)'
Capital-II: influence
    general   10§4 (215-16)
    of repro. schemes on mainstream business cycle theory   12§2: (263-64)
centralisation of capital   ch.9: 196, 203; 18§8 (405-06)
circuit of individual capital
    in *Capital-I*   8§1.1: 158-59
    in *Capital-II* (prior to its Pt. Three)   ch.1: 29-30; ch.10: 213
circulation of total capital
    general notions: *C-II*, Pt Three   ch.10: 213; ch.11-intro (220-23)
    social (macro) circulation: see: 'reproduction schemes *C-II*'
class (social)
    term (in non-statistical sense) hardly ever used in *Capital*   ch.1: 20
commensuration (by money)
    commensuration (homogenisation): ideal commensuration   7§2.2: 143, Table 1, row 5; 7§3.1 (144-45)
    ideal pre-commensuration   8§1.1: 159; 20§1: 434
    ideal pre-commensuration: differs across and within branches   18§3 (394-95)
    see also: 'profit rate, tendency: micro foundation'
commodity money   7§3.3 (147-48); 7§4 (148-49)
    see also: 'credit money' and 'money'
competition
    general account (Marx citation)   ch.9: 186
    see also: 'interaction of capitals'
    see also: 'stratification of capital'
composition of capital
    see: 'capital composition'
credit money
    issued by banks and created *ex nihilo*   20§1: 434-35
    see also: 'money'
critique versus criticism   1§3.2 (20); ch.4: 70

departments of production defined   ch.10: 213; ch.11: 227
determinants [a]: two categories

INDEX OF SUBJECTS 505

    immanent (introversive) vs. extroversive: jargon *C-I*, Pt One   7§1.3: 138 and 138 n.7
    inner vs. outer: jargon *C-I*, Pt Seven   7§1.3: 138 n.7
    two 'moments' that inseparably belong together   7§1.3: 138
    see also: 'determinants [b] ...'; 'determinants [c] ...'
determinants [b]: jargon *C-I*, Pt One
    extroversion outlined: in its ch. 3   7§2.2 (137-38)
    immanent and extroversive moments of value: in its chs. 1 and 3   7§1.3 (138-39)
determinants [c]: jargon *C-I*, Pt Seven
    inner moment of capital accumulation: its 'pure' analysis   ch.9: 185
    Part Seven (must be) restricted to this inner moment   ch.9: 182, 202
devalorisation of capital
    defined   20§4 (439-40)
    devalorisation of capital: cyclical   20§5.2 (441); 21§1.3: 458; 21§3.2: 477-78
    see also: 'valorisation'
    see also: 'devaluation of capital'
    see also: 'revaluation of capital'
    see also: 'stratification of capital'
devaluation of capital
    as affecting the profit rate: general   16§2.2: 354; 16§2.4: 357
    devaluation of capital: cyclical   16§2.4 358
    devaluation of capital: extended accounts of   20§1: 434; 20§4 (439-40); ch.21-intro: 450; 21§1.1: 452; 21§1.2: 456-57; 21§1.3: 458; 21§3.2: 477-78, 483; ch.21-concl 484
    see also: 'devalorisation of capital'
    see also: 'revaluation of capital'
    see also: 'stratification of capital'
dialectic
    general overview   ch.3: 63
    Hegel's: general overview   ch.3: 63-67
    Marx's: general overview   ch.4: 69-73
    see also: 'systematic dialectics'
dimensions in *Capital*
    in *C-I* to *C-III* treated in increasing complexity/concretion   8§1.1: 157
    main dimensions: labour-time and monetary value   2§2.3 (48)
    see also: 'monetary dimension'

economic crisis
    and accumulation of capital   9§3.3-E (199)
    and general restructuring of capital   21§5.1 (440-39)
    and reduction range of the stratification of capital   20§5.1 (440-41)
    in a fragmented versus an integrated banking system   20§6.1 (442)
    in reproduction schemes context   11§2.1: 224; 11§2.7: 234; 11§3.1: 236-37
    see also: 'banking system'
    see also: 'stratification of capital'
economic growth
    see: 'accumulation of capital'
    see also: 'profit rate – tendential manifestation'
Engels's mark on *C-II* and *C-III*
    regarding *C-II* (Engels's selection from Marx's notebooks)   10§3: 215
    regarding *C-III* (general)   13§1: 272-73

fictitious capital expansion   20§1: 435
finance capital (in Hilferding sense)   21§2.7: 468 n29
finance capital (non-Hilferding sense)
    see: 'industrial and finance capital'
    see also: 'functional forms of capital' sub '[h] finance capital and managerial capital'
fixed capital   ch.8: 163n; ch.9: 187; ch.11: 222; 228; 230; 234; 235; 248
formalisations in/of *Capital*
    in *C-I*, Pt Seven (derived from text)   9§2.2 (186-90); 9§3,2 (193-96); 9§3.3-A (197)
    in *C-I*, Pts Three to Six (Marx)   8§2.1 (161-66)
    in *C-I*, Pts Three to Six (reconstructions)   8§2.3 (168-72); 8§2.5 (176-78)
    in *C-II*, Pt Three (Marx)   passim in 11§2.4 (229-31), 11§2.5 (231-33), 11§3.2 (237-48) and 11§3.3 (248-51)
    in *C-II*, Pt Three: numerical schemes (Marx)   idem previous sub-lemma
    in *C-II*, Pt Three: numerical schemes formally reconstructed   idem previous sub-lemma
    see also: 'reproduction schemes *C-II*'
    numerical schemes as tool in economics until 1935   ch.11: 252 n32
    of results versus processes (*C-I*, Pts Three to Six)   ch.8-intro: 154
functional forms of capital[1]
    [a] capital unity in opposition to labour: up to *C-III*, Pt. Three   21§2.1: 458
    [a] falling apart of unity: *C-III*, Pts Four to Five   21§2.1: 458
    [a] overview of *C-III*, Pts Four to Five   21§2.1 (458-60)
    [a] overview, 'capital' renamed as *'industrial capital'* [IC]   21§2.1: 458
    [a] overview, 'commercial capital' offshoot from IC   21§2.1: 458
    [a] overview, *'money capital'* [MC] offshoot from IC   21§2.1: 458-59
    [a] overview, *'money-dealing capital'* [MDC]: form of MC   21§2.1: 460
    [b] overview, *'interest-bearing capital'* [IBC]: form of MC   21§2.1: 459-60
    [b] overview, *'joint stock capital'* [JSC]: form of MC   21§2.1: 460
    [c] overview, *'functioning capital'* [FGC]: counterpart of IBC and JSC   21§2.1: 460
    [c] overview, restauration of unity? (cf. [a] second line)   21§2.1: 459
    [d] from IC to IC and 'money-dealing capital' [MDC]   21§2.2 (460-61)
    [d] from IC to IC and MDC: functional separation   21§2.2: 460
    [d] MDC considered as 'pure form'   21§2.2: 460
    [d] MDC shares in surplus-value (average profit rate unsure)   21§2.2: 461
    [e] from money to 'interest-bearing capital' [IBC]; counterpart: from industrial [IC] to functioning capital [FGC]   21§2.3 (461-64)
    [e] IBC: money begetting money: sublimation of capital   21§2.3: 462
    [e] IBC: share in *surplus-value* [SV]   21§2.3: 462
    [e] IBC: share in SV, leaving for FGC 'profit of enterprise'   21§2.3: 462
    [e] relation IBC versus FGC: IBC dominant weight?   21§2.3: 463
    [e] profit of enterprise: conceived as entrepreneurial labour   21§2.3: 464
    [f] fluctuation of interest rate over the cycle of production   21§2.4: 465-66
    [g] Joint stock capital (JSC) and management of enterprise   21§2.5 (466-67)
    [g] joint stock capital [JSC] as developed form of IBC   21§2.5: 466
    [g] JSC: transforms functioning capitalist into mere manager   21§2.5: 466
    [g] JSC: transposition: complete sublimation of capital   21§2.5: 467

---

1   The insertions [a] to [l] serve a logical order of this lemma.

INDEX OF SUBJECTS 507

　　[g] profit: ideas of profit along with differentiation of capital   21§2.6 (467-68)
　　[h] JSC and transition: Marx's rare over-optimism   21§2.8: 469
　　[i] money capital [MC] and finance capital [FC] (*reconstruction*)   21§2.7 (468-69)
　　[i] factions of FC: IBC and JSC   21§2.7: 468
　　[i] banks: legally granted to create credit money   21§2.7: 469
　　[i] 'finance capital' and 'managerial capital' (*reconstruction*)   21§2.8 (469-71)
　　[i] 'managerial capital' delineated: economic ownership   21§2.8: 469-70
　　[i] legal versus economic ownership of shareholders   21§2.8: 470
　　[i] managers as functioning capitalists   21§2.8: 470
　　[i] shareholders' concern: share price   21§2.8: 470
　　[k] summary and (reconstructive) conclusions   21§2.9 (471-73)
　　[l] conclusion (1): capital's unity-in-opposition to labour   21§2.9: 472
　　[l] conclusion (2): capital factions internally opposed   21§2.9: 472-73
　　see also: 'profit rate tendency: concretisation'
future society in *Capital*
　　of 2,200 pages 5 refer in passing to some future society   ch.1: 16; ch.17, Appendix 2: 387
　　term 'communism' mentioned in five footnotes   ch.1: 16

growth of capital
　　see: 'accumulation of capital'
　　see also: 'profit rate, tendential manifestation' sub 'cyclical development'

historical materialism
　　delineated   1§3.1 (19-20); ch.4: 69-70
　　historical materialism and systematic-dialectics   5§2.6 (90-91)
　　see also: 'systematic-dialectics'

immanent critique
　　see: 'critique versus criticism'
industrial and finance capital
　　conflict between industrial (IC) and finance capital (FC)   20§6.2 (442-44)
　　conflict in times of inflation as (partly) imposed on FC   20§6.2: 442
　　conflict in times of inflation different for banks and other FC   20§6.2: 442
　　conflict in times of inflation: banks' substitution of short for long lending   20§6.2: 442
　　conflict in times of inflation: other FC declines bonds finance   20§6.2: 442
　　non-bank FC bonds decline affects banks' risk   20§6.2: 442
　　see also: 'inflation, price inflation'
inflation: price inflation
　　in face of failure of enterprises (industrial capitals)   20§1: 435
　　pseudo-social validation   20§1: 436
　　reversed (possibly) into physical expansion   20§6.1 (442)
　　see also: 'industrial and finance capital'
interaction of capitals
　　inter-branch interaction   18§2.1 (393)
　　intra-branch interaction   18§2.1 (393)
　　intra-branch interaction, resulting in stratification of capitals   18§2.2 (393-94)
　　see also: 'stratification of capital'
interpretation of *Capital*
　　main kinds of: exegetic, historiographic, heuristic   6§2.1 (112)

method-related interpretations of Marx's *Capital*   1§3 (19-25)
   see also: 'reconstruction'
investment of capital
   see: 'accumulation of capital'

labour
   complex (empowered) and simple labour [in *C-I*, Pt One]   2§2.1-d (45-46); 15§3.5 (321-22)
   complex to simple labour reduction never operationalised   2§2.1-d: 46
   empowered labour (identical to potentiated) [in *C-I*, Pt Four]   2§3.1-b (49-51); 15§3.2 (316-19)
   intensity of labour [*C-I*, Pt Four]   2§3.1-a (48-49); 15§3.3 (319-20)
   labour creates value (it is not itself value)   2§2.1-e: (46-47); 6§2.1: 119; 15§1: 310
   potentiated labour (identical to empowered labour; see above)
   productive power(s) of labour [*C-I*, Pt One]   2§2.1-c (44)
   socially necessary labour-time [*C-I*, Pt One]   2§2.1-b (43-44)
   see also: 'abstract labour'
   see also: 'labour embodied'
labour embodied
   abstract-labour-embodied (in *C-I*, ch.1)   6§3.2-B and 6§3.3 (118-20)
   abstract-labour-embodied (problems of)   6§4.2 (123-25)
   concrete-labour-embodied   6§4.2-A (123)
   substance of value in labour-embodied theories   6§4.2-C (124-25)
   see also: 'abstract labour'
labour shortage: cyclical
   not posited by Marx as an explanation of cycles   ch.9: 200
labour theory of value
   phrase never used in *Capital*   ch.2-intro: 38
labour value(s)
   phrase never used in *Capital*   2§2.3 (48)

macroeconomic foundations of micro   ch.10: 212
macroeconomics, Marx's
   macroeconomics 'avant la lettre' (*C-I*, Pt Seven; *C-II*, Pt Three)   ch.12 (260-63)
   Marx's averages account in most of *C-I*: no macroeconomics   2§1.6 (41-42)
   Marx's macro account at the *C-III* Pt, Three level   20§3: 437
   see also: 'reproduction schemes *C-II*' sub '[a] construction of a macroeconomics'
manifestation (title *C-III*)
   title *C-III*: in Marx's ms. versus Engels's version   2§4-intro: 52
Marx
   brief sketch of his life   1§1 (16-17)
   Marx as continuous critic of Marx   2§1.5 (41)
Marx's *Capital* (general)
   aim of   2§1.1 (39-40)
   cursory survey of *Capital* (systematic structure *C-I* to *C-III*)   1§4 (25-31)
   cursory survey of *C-II*   10§2 (213-14)
   cursory survey of *C-III*   13§2.3 (275-78)
   historical order of writings of and for   2§1.4 (40-41)
   historical order of publications affects interpretation   1§2: (17-19)
   interconnection of *C-I* and *C-II*   10§1 (208-12)

INDEX OF SUBJECTS

    interconnection of *C-I*, *C-II* and *C-III*   13§2.2 (274-75)
    internet links (MECW; MEGA; MEW; MIA)   ch.2: 59
    paradigmatic break; see: 'paradigmatic break (Marx)'
    research draft status of manuscripts for *C-II* and *C-III*   ch.1: 22; 11§1: 221; 13§1 (269-73)
    see also: Marx's method in *Capital*
Marx's method in *Capital*
    averages account [in most of *C-I*]   2§1.6: (41-42); 15§3.1: 314-15; 15§3.2: 319
    averages: deviation from averages in *C-I*, Pt Four   2§3.1 (48-51)
    finding of endogenous dimensional reference points   8§1.1: 157
    method-related interpretations of *Capital*   1§3 (19-25)
    see also: 'abstraction' sub 'levels of abstraction'
    see also: 'dialectic' sub 'Marx's: general overview'
    see also: 'formalisations in *Capital*'
    see also: 'moment (expositional)'
    see also: 'systematic-dialectics'
    see also (regarding (non-)averages in *C-I*): 'transformation of *C-III*, Pt Two', the entries [c] starting with *C-I* account
metamorphoses
    of forms of capital (prior to functional forms *C-III*)   ch.10: 211, 213
    in face of functional forms of capital (*C-III*, Pts Four to Five)   21§2.1: 458-59; 21§2.2: 461
    see also: 'functional forms of capital'
metaphors
    as borrowed from natural sciences   ch.6-intro: 108; ch.6: 119
    at the beginning of Marx's *Capital*   6§3.3: 119
    of embodiment and substance   6§3 3: 119; 6§4.2-C (124-25)
microeconomic foundations
    see: 'profit rate, tendency: micro foundation'
moment (expositional)
    defined   ch.5: 82 **n.16**; ch.6: 111; ch.9: 185
    interconnection of moments   ch.5: 81-82, 99
monetary dimension   2§2.3 (48); 7§1.3: 139 (and 139 n.8)
    see also: 'money'
money
    actual measure of value   2§2.2 (47-48)
    form of money (*C-I* ch.1); systemic existence (*C-I* ch.3)   7§1.1 (137)
    hypostasisation of money (price-form void of value)   7§3.4 (148)
    ideal (or imaginary) money   7§3.3 (147-48)
    imaginary measurement by imaginary money   7§3.4 (148)
    inverse quantity theory of money   7§3.4: 147 n.20
    money measure compared with non-economic measures   7§2.1 (140-42)
    money of account, imaginary money   7§3.3 (147-48)
    money's measure versus standards of price   7§3.2: 145-46
    value: no existence without money   7§1.3 (138-39)
    see also: 'commodity money'
    see also: 'credit money'

naturalism
    naturalism versus scientism   16§1.2: 342
    naturalistic as against socio-historical concepts   1§3.3 (21)

naturalistic labour-embodied theory of value   ch.5: 92, 97
naturalistic view of history in Marx's *Grundrisse* (apparently)   ch.19-intro: 414
naturalistic view of history left behind in *Capital*   ch.19-intro: 414; 19§4: 424
see also: 'paradigmatic break (Marx)'

over-accumulation of capital
    tendency towards   18§4.1 (396)
    see also: 'capital composition: rising' sub 'tendency to rising capital composition'
OCC
    abbreviation for: organic composition of capital   ch.9: 193-94

paradigmatic break (Marx)
    inevitable inconsistency of   ch.5: 98; 13§1: 271
    language problems of   2§1.2 (40); ch.5: 98; 13§1: 271
    path-breaking publication and change of views: lag between   ch.1: 18-19
pre-commensuration
    see: 'commensuration'
pre-validation of production
    by banks' issue of *ex-nihilo-created* credit money   20§1: 434-35
    lever to capital accumulation   20§1: 435
    requires expansion of *other* capitals   20§1: 435
    see also: 'validation'
prices of production
    in 1864–65 manuscript for *C-III*   2§4.1 (52-54)
    reconstruction in face of the later written final version *C-I*   2§5.2 (54-56)
    reconstruction: philological puzzles of   2§5.3 (56-58)
    see also (extended): 'transformation of *C-III*, Pt Two'
production in *Capital*
    production of *capital* rather than commodity production   ch.10: 209-10
production of capital
    dimensions of   8§1.1: 155-57
    how capital 'produces'; how labour produces capital   8§1.2: 160
    unity of labour process and valorisation process   8§1.1: 156
    value-form of production   8§1.1: 156-57
    see also: 'valorisation'
production process (capitalist)
    see: 'production of capital'
productive power of labour
    see: 'labour' sub 'productive power(s) of labour'
    see: 'surplus-value' sub 'relative surplus-value'
profit rate
    connecting monetary dimension and time dimension   8§1.1: 157
    rate of profit: *the* measure of capital   8§1.1: 157
    see also: 'profit rate – tendency law of'
    see also: 'profit rate – tendential manifestation'
    see also: 'profit rate tend.: Marx's manuscripts'
profit rate – fall
    in 19th cent. mainstream economics   ch.18-intro: 316-17
    in Smith and Ricardo   19§1: 415; 19§2: 418-19

INDEX OF SUBJECTS 511

profit rate – tendency law of
    C-III, Pt Three: 'law of the tendential fall in the rate of profit'   (see below)
    delineation: focus on the notion of 'tendency' in the text   16§2 (346-58); 16§3.1 (358-59)
    delineation: focus on trend versus cycle interpretation C-III   17§1 (367-72); 21§1.1 (450-52)
    delineation: focus on trend versus cycle interpretation of *ms.*   17§2 (372-78); 21§1.2 (450-52)
    interpretation: 'trend' dominant until last quarters 20th cent.   ch.17-intro: 366
    interpretation: methodological and other problems for   ch.17-intro: 366-67
    microeconomic foundation of the law, see: 'profit rate, tendency: micro foundation'
    relevant 'stylised facts' around 1865 (relevant for the law)   ch.20-intro: 432-33
    relevant stylised facts in 2nd half 20th century   ch.20-intro: 433
    interpretation: received view in text books: trend fall   17§1.1 (367-70)
    interpretation: rival view: cyclical development   17§1.2 (370-71)
    interpretational perspective of ms. (1864–65) for C-III (outline ms.)   17§2 (372-77)
    see also: 'capital composition: rising'
    see also: 'over-accumulation of capital sub 'tendency towards'
    see also: 'profit rate – tendential manifestation'
    see also: 'profit rate tend.: Marx's manuscripts'
    see also: 'profit rate tendency: concretisation'
    see also: 'profit rate, tendency: micro foundation'
    see also: 'tendency'
profit rate – tendential manifestation
    cyclical development   16§2.4: 357-58; 16§3.1 (358-59)
    see also: 'profit rate, tendency: micro foundation sub 'waves ...''
profit rate tend.: Marx's manuscripts
    C-III, Pt Three ms. (1864–65) compared with Engels's 1894   ch.17 Annex 1 (378-81)
    C-III, Pt Three ms. (1864–65) compared with 1857–58 ms.   ch.17 Annex 2: 381-83
    C-III, Pt Three ms. (1864–65) compared with 1861–63 ms.   ch.17 Annex 2: 383-86
    evolution of Marx's views from 1857 to 1865   ch.17 Annex 2: 386-87; 19§5 (425-26)
    in manuscript of 1857–58 (Grundrisse)   19§1-§2 (415-19)
    in manuscript of 1861–63   19§3 (420-22)
    in the manuscript for C-III, Pt Three (1864–65)   19§4 (422-25)
    see also: 'breakdown / overthrow of capitalism'
    see also: 'profit rate – tendency law of'
profit rate tendency: concretisation
    concretisation in light of 'functional forms of capital' (C-III): *reconstruction*   21§3 (473-83)
    concretisation of C-III Pt Four: commercial capital   21§3.1 (473-76)
    concretisation of C-III Pt Four: money-dealing capital   21§3.1 (473-76)
    concretisation of C-III Pt Five in context of TRPF   21§3.2 (476-80)
    internal separation of capital: finance and managerial capital   21§3.2: 476
    Marx brackets price deflation and inflation   21§3.2: 477
    monetary regime (1): deflationary   21§3.2-A (477-80)
    monetary regime (1): deflationary; devalorisation and devaluation of capital   21§3.2-A: 477-78
    monetary regime (1): deflationary; power capital factions   21§3.2-A: 480
    monetary regime (2): inflationary   21§3.2-B (480-82)
    monetary regime (2): inflationary; capital revaluation   21§3.2-B: 480-81
    monetary regime (2): inflationary; power capital factions   21§3.2-B: 481-82
    monetary regime (3): moderate inflation; balance of power   21§3.2-C (482-83)
    monetary regime (3): moderate inflation; real wages pressure   21§3.2-C: 482-83

summary and conclusions   ch.21: 483-84
see also: 'functional forms of capital'
see also: 'profit rate – tendency law of'
profit rate, tendency: micro foundation
    alleged lack of microeconomic foundations (Okishio & co.)   18§5 (399-400); 20§3 (437-39)
    existing foundations, introduction   ch.18-intro: 392; 20§3 (437-39)
    foundation in stratification and *devalorisation* of capital   18§6 (400-03); 20§4 (439-40)
    foundation in stratification and *devaluation* of capital   18§7 (403-05); 20§4 (439-40)
    foundations of devalorisation/devaluation: accounting   18§7: 404; 20§4: 439-40
    possibly resulting in restructuring and centralisation of capital   18§8 (405-06)
    waves/cycles of centralisation of capital   18§8: 406
    see also: 'stratification of capital'
pseudo-social validation   20§1: 436
    see also: 'validation'

rate of profit
    see: 'profit rate'
real abstraction
    see: 'abstraction' sub 'abstraction in practice'
reconstruction
    facing paradigmatic break problems   2§1.2 (40)
    facing Marx being a continuous critic of Marx   2§1.5 (41)
    reconstruction delivered as an interpretation   ch.5: 94-96, 98
    immanent reconstruction   ch.8-intro: 154
    reconstruction versus interpretation summarised   13§1: 271-72
    see also: 'interpretation of *Capital*'
    see also: 'paradigmatic break (Marx)'
references: general to Marx's works
    weblinks to MECW, MEGA, MEW and MIA   ch.2: 59
reproduction schemes *C-II*[2]
    [a] assumptions for all reproduction models/schemes   2§2.1-2§2.2: 225-27
    [a] construction of a macroeconomics   11§2.1 (223-27); 11§4.1 (252-53)
    [a] construction of a two-sector macroeconomic model   11§2.2–§2.3 (223-29)
    [a] cursory outline of *C-II*, Pt Three   11§1 (221-23)
    [a] money circulation within and between departments   11§2.6 (233-34)
    [a] money circulation: Marx's 'widow's cruse' argument   11§2.6 (233-34)
    [a] numerical versus generalised schemes/models (numerical common tool in economics until 1935)   ch.11: 252 n.32
    [a] systematic-dialectics and M's schemes: compatibility   11§4.2 (253-56)
    [a] terms scheme and model for *C-II*, Pt Three   11§1: 223
    [a] terms scheme and model in mainstream economics   12§2: 264
    [a] see also: 'macroeconomics, Marx's'
    [b] assumptions for simple reproduction (next to those of the 1st sub-lemma)   11§2.3 (228-29)
    [b] simple (stationary) reproduction: scheme   11§2.4 (229-31)

---

2   The insertions [a] to [c] serve a logical order of this lemma.

INDEX OF SUBJECTS 513

    [b] simple (stationary) reproduction: value-added   11§2.5 (231-33)
    [b] simple reproduction and fixed capital   11§2.7 (234)
    [c] assumptions for expanding reproduction (growth)   11§3.1 (235-37); 11§3.2: 237
    [c] expanding reproduction: accidental balance   11§3.1: 236-37
    [c] expanding reproduction: formal recapitulation   11§3.3 (248-51)
    [c] expanding reproduction: reconstructive method of steady state transitions   11§3.2: 237-240
    [c] expanding reproduction: schemata   11§3.2: 240-48
    [c] expanding reproduction: scheme B: increased growth   11§3.2: 240-47
    [c] expanding reproduction: scheme C: decreased growth   11§3.2: 247-48
restructuring of capital
    general account   ch.17: 377-78; 18§8 (405-06); 20§5.1 (440-41); 21§3.2: 477
    local restructuring, condition for credit renewal by banks   20§6.1 (442)
    restructuring in face of continual inflation   20§6.2: 444
    see also (for second entry): 'pre-validation of production'
revaluation of capital   20§6.2 (442-44); 21§3.2: 480-81
    see also: 'devalorisation of capital'
    see also: 'devaluation of capital'

schemes of reproduction C-II
    see: 'reproduction schemes C-II'
stratification of capital
    defined   18§2.2 (393-94); 20§3: 437-38
    expressed in differing money expressions of labour   18§3 (394-95)
    expressed in differing rates of profit   18§6 (400-03)
    range of stratification   18§8 (405-06); 20§5.2 (441)
    range of stratification and banks facilitation to move to top   20§6.1 (442)
    see also: 'profit rate, tendency: micro foundation'
surplus-value
    absolute and relative surplus-value: explanatory factors   8§1.2: 161
    absolute and relative surplus-value: overview   8§1.2: 161
    absolute surplus-value: determinants of   8§2.1 (161-66)
    rate of surplus-value   8§2.1 (161-66)
    rate of surplus-value: reconstruction technological trajectories   8§2.3 (168-72)
    relative surplus-value: determinants of   8§2.2 (166-68); 8§2.4 (172-76)
    see also: 'transformation of C-III, Pt Two' sub '[c] C-I account of inter-sector diverging rates of surplus-value'
systematic-dialectics
    general account   1§3.5 (23-25); 5§2.2-2.6 (81-91); 6§1 (109-12)
    research stages and their starting points   5§2.4 (84-86)
    systematic starting point of *Capital* (its exposition)   6§3.1 (115-16)
    see also (brief): 'dialectic'
    see also: 'abstraction' sub 'levels of abstraction'
    see also: 'abstraction' sub 'levels of abstraction: claims to general truth'
    see also: 'historical materialism' sub 'historical materialism and systematic-dialectics'
    see also: 'moment (expositional)'

TCC
    abbreviation for: technical composition of capital   ch.9: 193

technical change
    see: 'capital composition: general'
    see: 'capital composition: rising'
    see: 'labour' sub 'productive power(s) of labour [C-I, Pt One]'
technical change, labour expelling
    at continual inflation 'structural' rather than crisis-cyclical   20§6.2: 444
technology and technique
    the product of labour and labour only   15§4.2: 326; 15§4.3: 327
tendency
    20th cent. disappearance of concept in economics' mainstream   ch.16-intro: 338
    delineation tendential powers, effects and phenomenal results   16§1.3 (342-46)
    Marx's concept of: case of the law of profits (C-III, Pt Three)   16§2 (346-58)
    tendency laws and empirical research   16§3.2 (360-61)
    tendency versus trend   16§1.1: 338; 18§2.3 (394)
    see also: 'profit rate – tendency law of'
    see also: 'profit rate – tendential manifestation'
    see also: 'over-accumulation of capital, tendency towards'
tendency: other authors on
    Bhaskar 1975, 1979: laws are always tendential   16§1.2 (340-42)
    Cartwright 1989: merit 'tendency' for explanation generally   ch.16-intro: 338n
    Lawson 1989, 1992: tendencies-based empirical research   16§3.2: 360
    Marshall 1890: nearly all laws of science are tendential   ch.16-intro: 338
    Mill (J.S.) 1836: common reference for writings on tendency   16§1.3: 342
    Popper 1957, mixing up tendency and trend   16§1.1: 339
transformation of C-III, Pt Two[3]
    [a] *general matters*
    [a] Engels's edition from M's research manuscript 1864–65   14§1 (284); 14§4.4: 300
    [a] overview and appraisal of the C-III Pt Two manuscript   14§4.1 (294-96)
    [a] Marxian transformation problem   ch.15-intro: 306-07
    [b] *methodological account*
    [b] appraisal hinges on view of method adopted by Marx   ch.14-intro: 283
    [b] formalisation of alternative interpretations of method   14§3 (285-94)
    [b] main concepts and definitions   14§3.1 (285-87)
    [b] method of concretion at C-I level   14§3.2 (287-88)
    [b] method of concretion at C-III level   14§3.3 (288-90)
    [b] method of completion at C-I level   14§3.4 (290-91)
    [b] method of completion at C-III level   14§3.5 (291-93)
    [b] methods of concretion and completion: conclusions   14§3.6 (293-94)
    [b] method of concretion: better interpretation of C-I (1867)   14§3.6: 293
    [b] method of completion: better interpretation of C-III ms. (1864–65)   14§3.6: 293
    [b] most post-Marx solutions methodologically inconsistent   14§3.6: 294
    [c] *historiographic account*
    [c] introduction   ch.15-intro (306-09)
    [c] introduction: Marx's method and value dimensions   15§1 (309-11)
    [c] introduction: stages account, claims to general truth   15§1: 309
    [c] introduction: standard critique of Marx's transformation   15§2: 312-13

---

3   The insertions [a] to [d] serve a logical order of this lemma.

INDEX OF SUBJECTS 515

    [c] *C-I* account: changes in intra-sector productive powers   15§3.1 (point 4) 314-15
    [c] *C-I* account: degree of value-generating labour density   15§3.3 (319-20)
    [c] *C-I* account: degree of value-generating labour-potency (empowerment)   15§3.2 (316-19)
    [c] *C-I* account of inter-sector diverging rates of surplus-value   15§3.2 (316-19)
    [c] *C-I* 's diverging rates of surplus-value: conclusions   15§3.6 (322-25)
    [c] potentiated (empowered) labour in *C-I*, ch.1   15§3.5 (321-22)
    [c] return to the matter in a 1878 ms.: diverging rates of surplus-value   2§5.3: 57-58; 14§5 (300-01)
    [c] see also (brief account): 'prices of production'
    [c] see also: 'labour'
    [d] *Marx-immanent reconstruction*
    [d] introduction   ch.15-intro: 307; 15§4.1 (324-25)
    [d] main elements of reconstruction   15§4.2 (325-26)
    [d] reconstruction: core analytics of   ch.15 Appendix (329-33)
    [d] reconstruction: implications   15§4.3 (326-27)
    [d] see also (brief account): 'prices of production'
transubstantiation   ch.6: 116, 124; 7§3: 146
TRPF (also TFRP)
    abbreviation of 'theory of the tendency of the rate of profit to fall'; see: 'profit rate – tendency law of'
TRPC
    abbreviation of 'theory of the rate of profit cycle'   19§4: 425; 21§1.1: 450

underconsumption: cyclical
    not posited by Marx as an explanation of cycles   ch.9-intro: 182
unemployment
    condition necessary for continuous accumulation of capital   ch.9: 183
    in context of accumulation of capital   18§4.1: 396
    in various other contexts (most often cyclical)   16§2.2 (point 4): 355; 20§5.1: 440; 20§6.2: 444
    term not existing in Marx's days, hence not used by Marx   ch.9: 197; ch.12: 262

validation
    similar to sale of output (realisation)   18§2.1: 393; 18§3: 395
    see also: 'pre-validation of production'
valorisation   8§1.1: 156, 156n5, 158-59; 8§1.2: 159-60; 8§2.1: 162-63; 18§1: 392-93
    see also 'devalorisation of capital'
value
    creation of value by labour (labour is not itself value)   2§2.1-e (46-47); ch.6: 119; 15§1 (point 3): 310
    dimension of value, see 'monetary dimension'
    entity existing prior to exchange?   ch.6: 118-19
    entity existing prior to exchange? see also 'commensuration'
    explanation of monetary value by labour-time   2§2.1-e (46-47); 2§2.3 (48); 8§1.1: 156-57
    inner and outer moments: inseparable   7§1.2 (137-38)
    introversive substance and extroversive form   7§1.3 (138-39)
    Marx's conceptualisation of value   ch.2: passim
    no dual account systems of value (reconstruction)   ch.15-intro: 307; 15§4.3: 327
    static and dynamic conceptualisation of value in *Capital-I*   2§2.1 (42-47); 2§3.1 (48-51)
    substance of value, in labour-embodied theories   6§4.2-C (124-25); 6§4.4: 127

value no existence without money   7§1.2 (137-38); 7§1.3 (138-39)
   see also: 'dimensions in *Capital*'
   see also: 'monetary dimension'
   see also: 'money'
   see also: 'transformation of *C-III*, Pt Two' sub '[c] *historiographic account*'
   see also: 'valorisation'
value-form
   in *C-I*, ch.1   6§3.4 (120-22)
   term only sporadically used by Marx after *C-I*, ch.1   7§1.3: 139
value-form theory
   regarding the individual circuit of capital   1§3.4 (21-22); 8§1.1: 156
VCC
   abbreviation for: value composition of capital   ch.9: 193; 18§4.2: 397-98
   see also: 'capital composition: general'

www.ingramcontent.com/pod-product-compliance
Lightning Source LLC
Chambersburg PA
CBHW062112040426
42337CB00043B/3693